国家出版基金项目
NATIONAL PUBLICATION FOUNDATION

国际海事组织海员行为示范

MODEL COURSE 1.02

油船特殊培训

SPECIALIZED TRAINING FOR OIL TANKERS (2006)

中华人民共和国海事局 译

中英对照

大连海事大学出版社
DALIAN MARITIME UNIVERSITY PRESS

国际海事组织 1999 年第一次出版
4 Albert Embankment, London SE1 7SR

图书在版编目(CIP)数据

油船特殊培训 : 汉英对照 / 国际海事组织著 ; 中华人民共和国海事局译. — 大连 : 大连海事大学出版社, 2016.1
(国际海事组织海员行为示范)
书名原文: SPECIALIZED TRAINING FOR OIL TANKERS
ISBN 978-7-5632-3282-6

Ⅰ. ①油… Ⅱ. ①国… ②中… Ⅲ. ①油船—技术培训—教材—汉、英 Ⅳ. ①U674.13

中国版本图书馆 CIP 数据核字(2016)第 024519 号

大连海事大学出版社出版
地址:大连市凌海路 1 号　邮编:116026　电话:0411-84728394　传真:0411-84727996
http://www.dmupress.com E-mail:cbs@dmupress.com
大连住友彩色印刷有限公司印装　　大连海事大学出版社发行

2016 年 1 月第 1 版　　2016 年 1 月第 1 次印刷
幅面尺寸:210 mm × 297 mm　　印数:1~3000 册
印张:35.25　　字数: 1089 千

出 版 人:徐华东　　策　　划:徐华东
责任编辑:苏炳魁　刘若实　　责任校对:张　冰　张　慧
封面设计:解瑶瑶　　版式设计:孟　冀　解瑶瑶

ISBN 978-7-5632-3282-6　　定价:88.00 元

国际海事组织海员行为示范
编审委员会

《油船特殊培训》

翻　译： 党　坤　　吴桂涛

审　校： 胡甚平　　林叶锦

CONTENTS

***Note:**
The part on the use of simulator is included as a guideline where a simulator is used as a tool for training under this model course.

目　录

* 注释:

在本示范课程中模拟器使用部分包括模拟器作为培训工具使用的指导原则。

Foreword

Since its inception the International Maritime Organization (IMO) has recognized the importance of human resources to the development of the maritime industry and has given the highest priority to assisting developing countries in enhancing their maritime training capabilities through the provision or improvement of maritime training facilities at national and regional levels. IMO has also responded to the needs of developing countries for postgraduate training for senior personnel in administrations, ports, shipping companies and maritime training institutes by establishing the World Maritime University in Malmö, Sweden, in 1983.

Following the adoption of the International Convention on Standards of Training, Certification and Watchkeeping for Seafarers, 1978 (STCW), a number of IMO Member Governments had suggested that IMO should develop model training courses to assist in the implementation of the Convention and in achieving a more rapid transfer of information and skills regarding new developments in maritime technology. IMO training advisers and consultants also subsequently determined from their visits to training establishments in developing countries that the provision of model courses could help instructors improve the quality of their existing courses and enhance their implementation of the associated Conference and IMO Assembly resolutions.

In addition, it was appreciated that a comprehensive set of short model courses in various fields of maritime training would supplement the instruction provided by maritime academies and allow administrators and technical specialists already employed in maritime administrations, ports and shipping companies to improve their knowledge and skills in certain specialized fields. With the generous assistance of the Government of Norway, IMO developed model courses in response to these generally identified needs and now keeps them updated through a regular revision process taking into account any amendments to the requirements prescribed in IMO instruments and any technological developments in the field.

These model courses may be used by any training institution and, when the requisite financing is available, the Organization is prepared to assist developing countries in implementing any course.

E. E. MITROPOULOS

Secretary-General

前 言

国际海事组织(IMO)自成立伊始就认识到人力资源在海运业发展中的重要性,并最优先考虑通过在国家和地区层面上提供或改善培训设备来帮助发展中国家增强其海事培训能力。为应对发展中国家主管机关、港口、航运公司及海事培训机构高层人员对研究生培训的需求,IMO于1983年在瑞典的马尔默成立了世界海事大学。

在《1978年海员培训、发证和值班标准国际公约》(STCW)通过的初期,一些IMO成员国政府就建议IMO应制定示范课程,以帮助对该公约的实施以及对航海技术新发展方面信息和技能的迅速转化。IMO培训顾问和咨询专家在对发展中国家的培训机构进行访问后确定,提供示范课程有助于教员改进现有课程的质量,也有助于提升对相关会议和IMO大会决议的实施。

此外,令人欣慰的是,海事培训领域中一套综合性简短课程将对海事院校提供的授课加以补充,并使得已在海事行政机关、港口和航运公司工作的行政管理人员和技术专家能够提高其在某些专业领域中的知识和技能。为此,在挪威政府的慷慨帮助下,IMO编写了示范课程以应对那些普遍发现的需求,同时考虑到对IMO文件中规定要求的任何修正及该领域内的任何技术发展,通过定期修订程序对示范课程进行更新。

任何培训机构可以使用这些示范课程,在筹措到必需的资金时本组织也准备帮助发展中国家实施任何课程。

E. E. 米乔普勒斯

秘书长

1.02 MODEL COURSE

Introduction

■ Purpose of the model course

The purpose of the IMO model courses is to assist maritime training institutes and their teaching staff in organizing and introducing new training courses, or in enhancing, updating or supplementing existing training material where the quality and effectiveness of the training courses may thereby be improved. The purpose is also to enhance the capabilities of shipboard personnel who sail on specialized carriers such as an oil tanker. It is not the intention of the course to compartmentalize the trainee's way of thinking in terms of tanker operation. The idea is to make him/her aware of the specialization of operations specific to a tanker and, sensitize him/her towards the responsibilities that s/he will face on such a vessel.

It is not the intention of the model course programme to present instructors with a rigid "teaching package" which they are expected to "follow blindly". Nor is it the intention to substitute audio-visual or "programmed" material for the instructor's presence. As in all training endeavours, the knowledge, skills and dedication of the instructors are the key components in the transfer of knowledge and skills to those being trained through IMO model course material.

Because educational systems and the cultural backgrounds of trainees in maritime subjects vary considerably from country to country, the model course material has been designed to identify the basic entry requirements and trainee target group for each course in universally applicable terms, and to specify clearly the technical content and levels of knowledge and skills necessary to meet the technical intent of IMO conventions and related recommendations.

This course is for Masters, officers and others on board oil tankers who have immediate responsibilities for the cargo handling in port and care in transit. By successfully doing this course, the aforementioned shipboard personnel will fulfil the mandatory minimum requirements of regulation V/1 of STCW 1978, as amended in 1995. The coverage of the model course is wide in scope and includes oil tanker safety, fire safety measures and systems, prevention and control of pollution, operational practice and obligations under applicable laws and regulations, thereby covering all training necessary to apply the provisions of Annex I of MARPOL 73/78. In addition, the course covers the managerial aspects on board by including a section on risk assessment and management, as well as contingency planning that is in line with the ISM Code and the SMS on board.

In order to keep the training programme up to date in future, it is essential that users provide feedback. New information will provide better training in safety at sea and protection of the marine environment. Information, comments and suggestions should be sent to the Head of the STCW and Human Element Section at IMO, London.

■ Use of the model course

Use of the model course: the instructor should review the course plan and detailed syllabus, taking into account the information provided under the entry standards specified in the course framework. The actual level of knowledge and skills and the prior technical education of the trainees should be kept in mind during the review, and any areas within the detailed syllabus which may cause difficulties because of differences between the actual trainee entry level and

介 绍

■ 示范课程的目的

IMO示范课程的目的是帮助海事培训机构及其教学人员组织和引入新的培训课程，或者在于提高、更新或补充现有的培训材料，这些材料使培训课程的质量和培训效果可能会得到提高。该课程的目的也是可以提高特种运输船舶(比如油船)上人员的工作能力。该课程没有打算使学员关于油船操作的思维方式与(其他船操作的思维方式)相隔绝。意图使其意识到液货船特殊操作的特性，使其敏感地意识到在这样的船上将面临的责任。

本示范课程计划的意图并不是向教员呈交一个可以使他们“盲目跟从”的“教学包”，其意图也不是替代教员已有的视听材料或“程序化的”材料。像所有的培训一样，通过IMO示范课程材料把知识和技术传授给培训对象，知识、技巧和教员的奉献精神是关键的组成部分。

由于接受海事培训的培训对象所在国家的教育体制和文化背景存在着巨大差异，因此示范课程的目的是使培训对象认识一些基本的要求和掌握一些常用的术语，同时也详细地说明了IMO公约和相关决议案所要求必须满足的技术要点、知识水平。

IMO示范课程针对的是在油船上工作的船长、高级船员以及其他人员，他们对港口货物操作以及航行中货物的维护负有直接责任。通过成功开设该课程，上述船员将能够满足STCW78/95 V/1部分的法定最低要求。该课程的覆盖面比较广，包括油船安全、消防安全措施和体系、污染防控、操作实践以及适用法规下的责任，因此，覆盖了MARPOL73/78附则Ⅰ要求的所有培训内容。另外，该课程通过引入风险评估和管理以及符合ISM规则和船上SMS体系应急反应计划而包含了管理学方面的知识。

为了保证培训项目未来能及时更新，使用者提供的反馈信息非常重要，这些反馈信息将对海上安全和海洋环境保护方面的培训提供更好的帮助。信息、意见和建议应该送到STCW公约总部和在伦敦的国际海事组织人力资源部。

■ 示范课程的使用

示范课程的使用：教员应该认真研究课程计划和教学大纲细则，充分考虑在课程框架里所规定的入学标准的信息。在研究教学大纲过程中，教员应对学员的知识和技术水平、学员的技术教育背景有所掌握。由于实际的学员和设计课程所假定的学员之间的入门水平存在差异，教员也应该注意到教学大纲里的每一块内容的开展都有可能遇到困难。

that assumed by the course designers should be identified. To compensate for such differences, the instructor is expected to delete from the course, or to reduce the emphasis on, items dealing with knowledge or skills already attained by the trainees. S/he should also identify any academic knowledge, skills or technical training which they may not have acquired.

The instructor, using his/her professional judgement, can analyse the detailed syllabus and the academic knowledge required to allow training in the technical area to proceed. The instructor can then design the appropriate pre-entry course or, alternatively, insert the elements of academic knowledge required to support the technical training elements concerned at appropriate points within the technical course.

Adjustment of the course objective, scope and content may also be necessary if in a country's maritime industry the trainees completing the course are to undertake duties which differ from the course objective specified in the model course.

Within the course plan the course designers have indicated assessment of the time that should be allotted to each area of learning. However, it must be appreciated that these allocations are arbitrary and assume that the trainees have fully met all entry requirements of the course. The instructor should therefore review these assessments and may need to reallocate the time required to achieve each specific learning objective or training outcome.

■ Lesson plans

After adjusting the course content, if so required, to suit the trainee intake and any revision of the course objectives, the instructor can then draw up lesson plans based on the detailed syllabus. The detailed syllabus contains speci.c references to the textbooks or teaching material proposed to be used in the course. Where no adjustment has been found necessary in the acquisition of knowledge and proficiency of the detailed syllabus, the lesson plans may simply consist of the detailed syllabus with keywords or other reminders added to assist the instructor in making his/her presentation of the material.

■ Presentation

The presentation of concepts and methodologies must be repeated in various ways until testing and evaluating the trainee's performance and achievements satisfy the instructor, that the trainee has attained the required proficiency under each specific learning objective or training objective. The syllabus is laid out in the form of acquiring knowledge, understanding and proficiency format and each objective specifies what the trainee must be able to do as the learning or training outcome. Taken as a whole, these objectives aim to meet the knowledge, understanding and proficiency specified in the appropriate tables of the STCW Code.

■ Implementation

For the course to run smoothly and to be effective, considerable attention must be paid to the availability and use of:

- Properly qualified instructors
- Support staff

为了弥补这些差异,教员可根据学员已经掌握的知识和技能删除一些课程或者降低难度。教员也应该明确所有对学员不做要求的学术知识技能或技术培训。

利用其专业判断力,教员能够分析具体的教学大纲细则及其要求的学术知识,从而推动技术领域的培训活动。接下来,教员能设计出一个合适的预科课程,或者有选择地在技术课程中适当的插入一些技术培训所需要的理论知识。

如果在某个国家的海远界中,完成该课程的学员所承担的职责与示范课程所要求的目标不一致,那么对课程的目标、范围和内容进行调整也是必要的。

在课程计划中,课程设计者对每个知识点的时间分配做出了估计。然而,只有学员完全符合课程的入门要求,这些时间分配才是合理的。因此,教员应该对这些评估进行研究,并根据学习目标和要达到的训练结果对这些时间分配进行改正或重新进行分配。

■ 教案

如果为了适应学员的接受能力和修正课程目的而调整了课程内容,教员应基于大纲细则拟订教案。教学大纲的细则包含了具体参阅书目或在课程中推荐使用的教学材料。对于大纲中的必需学习项目没有必要调整的部分,教案仅仅包含一些带有要点的大纲细则或者能够帮助教员讲课的注释。

■ 学员展示

概念和方法的介绍必须要用不同的方式反复进行,直至教员对学员的动手能力和成绩进行测试和评估后,认为学员在每项教学目标和训练目标下均获得所要求的技能为止。教学大纲以获取的知识、理解能力以及熟练程度而展开,并且每一项目标都具体规定了必须达到的学习或培训效果。总之,主要目的是满足STCW规则所要求的知识、理解能力以及熟练程度。

■ 实施

为了课程能顺利、有效地进行,下列有益因素值得重视:

- 完全合格的教员
- 辅助人员

- Rooms and other spaces
- Equipment
- Textbooks, technical papers, and
- Other reference material

Thorough preparation on part of the instructor is the key to successful implementation of the course. IMO has produced a booklet entitled "Guidance on the Implementation of IMO Model Courses", which deals with this aspect in greater detail and which is appended to this model course.

In certain cases, the requirements for some or all of the training in a subject are covered by another IMO model course. In these cases, the specific part of the STCW Code which applies is given and the user is referred to the other model course.

■ Guidance to course developers and instructors

This specialized oil tanker training course comprises two main parts. These are oil tanker safety and cargo operations.

The frst, oil tanker safety, covers the hazards involved in cargo operations and the systems, equipment and constructional features of oil tankers that exist to control the hazards.

Cargo operations cover loading and ballasting, including the use of the inert gas system and, where appropriate, crude oil washing.

These two aspects are necessarily interlinked. One approach to achieving the standard of competence is through properly supervised on-board training. Where this is the case, and suitable records are kept, then the extent of the training delivered in the specialized oil tanker course may reflect this.

Instructors should emphasize in their teaching the hazards involved in the operations on board oil tankers. They should explain, in as much detail as is necessary to ensure these operations are undertaken safely, the systems, equipment and constructional features that exist to control those hazards.

The lessons delivered during the course should be tailored to the needs of the trainees. Officers with extensive experience on board oil tankers and those who have received guided instruction on board may need less classroom teaching than those with simply the minimum sea experience on oil tankers generally.

Instructors should keep in mind that some of the topics in this model course are also introduced in the model course for the Officer in Charge of a Watch in the function controlling the Operation of the Ship and Care for the Persons on Board. These topics may therefore be treated as a revision of earlier learning.

Physical properties of oils and vapours are covered in the Oil Tanker Familiarization model course and can also be found in the basic physics of the Officer in Charge of a Watch model course (for both navigation and marine engineering functions); therefore the basic physics in

- 教室或其他场所
- 设备
- 教材、技术论文
- 其他参考材料

教员认真备课是成功实施本课程的关键。IMO已经出版了一本叫“IMO示范课程实施指南”的小册子,它在这方面进行了更详细的说明并附在这个课程后面。

在一些情况下,一门课程或全部培训要求包含在其他IMO示范课程中。在这些情况下,会给出STCW规则适用部分的内容,用户就可以参考其他的示范课程。

■ 课程开发者和教员指南

该专业油船培训课程包含两个主要部分,即油船安全和货物操作。

第一部分,油船安全,包括了在货物操作中的危害和油船用来控制危害的系统、设备和结构特征。

第二部分,货物操作包括了装卸和压载,以及在这过程中惰性气体的使用以及适当的原油洗舱。

这两个部分有着必然的联系。达到适任标准的一个方法是通过受到适当监督的在船培训。在这种情况下,应该有适当的记录,可通过专业油船培训课程的内容来反映。

教员应该在教学中强调在油船操作中的危害。他们应该尽可能详细地解释这些系统、设备和结构特征对控制危害的作用,以确保这些操作在安全的条件下进行。

课程应为学员的需求量身定做。一般来说,那些在油船上有着丰富经验的高级船员和已经在船上获得指导的学员可能需要的理论教学要少于那些工作经验较少的学员。

教员们也应该牢记,在示范课中有些主题是为值班驾驶员或值班轮机员所设置的,他们负责船舶操纵和船员安全,因此,这些材料可以被用作早期的学习资料。

油和水蒸气的物理性质包含在油船熟悉示范课程中,也有一些能在船员值班示范课中找到(如航海和轮机的功能),因此,该示范课程2.1节中的基本原理是对培训的修订和扩展。同样,学员应

Section 2.1 of this model course is a revision and extension of that training. Similarly, entrants should have completed an approved shore-based fire-fighting course (STCW regulation V/1, paragraph 1), and hence fire-fighting principles in Section 3.5 are a very brief revision of this topic.

Ship construction (Sections 1.1, 4.1 and 5.1) and regulatory matters (Sections 1.2 and 4.3) are also covered in the model course for the Officer in Charge of a Watch in the function controlling the Operation of the Ship and Care for the Persons on Board. These topics may similarly be treated as a revision of earlier learning.

A new section each on risk management and contingency planning on tankers has been included. This Section will include the following:

- Management of Risk on an oil Tanker
- Background
- Definitions
- Risk on an oil Tanker
- Risk Assessment Process
- Risk Management in Practice

The idea is to help the trainees develop a proactive attitude on how to anticipate emergency and act accordingly.

The part on contingency planning is to make the trainee aware regarding the treatment of contingencies on board a tanker as a project so that subsequent project management ensures a professional way of dealing with emergencies right from the strategy, planning to action stages.

■ Training and STCW 1995 Convention

The standards of competence that have to be met by seafarers are de.ned in Part A of the STCW Code in the standards of Training, Certification and Watchkeeping for Seafarers Convention, as amended in 1995. This IMO model course has been revised and updated to cover the competences in STCW 1995. It sets out the education and training to achieve those standards.

Special training requirements for masters, chief engineer officers, chief mates, second engineer officers and any person with immediate responsibility for loading, discharging and care in transit or handling of cargo on oil tankers are detailed in section A-V/1 of the STCW Code. This model course aims to provide a specialized training programme referred to in paragraph 2.2 of regulation V/1, appropriate to these duties.

For ease of reference, the course is divided into separate sections.

Part A provides the framework for the course with its aims and objectives and notes on the suggested teaching facilities and equipment. A list of useful teaching aids, IMO references and textbooks is also included.

该完成一个被认可的岸基消防课程(STCW公约中的V/1,第1节),因此,在3.5节中的消防原理是这个主题的一个摘要。

船舶建造(1.1,4.1及5.1节)和相关法规(1.2及4.3节)也包含在负责船舶操纵和船员安全的值班驾驶员和值班轮机员的示范课程中,同样这些主题也应作为对早期学习的资料。

本课程中包含了关于油船风险管理和应急计划的新章节,具体包含以下内容:

- 油船风险管理
- 背景
- 定义
- 油船风险
- 风险评估过程
- 风险管理实践

其目的是帮助学员在如何参与应急响应并采取相应行动措施方面建立一种积极的态度。

关于应急计划的这部分是要让学员意识到油船应急处理是一个整体项目，这样以确保在后续应急处理项目中的策略、筹划以及行动阶段采取的专业方式。

■ 培训和STCW95公约

船员必须满足的适任能力标准定义在《STCW95公约》的A部分中。为了满足《STCW95公约》的要求,示范课程也做了相应的修订和更新,其目的在于:通过教学和培训使学员达到该公约的标准。

对船长、轮机长、大副、大管轮和其他油船装卸、货物转运或过驳、货物操作直接责任人的具体培训要求在《STCW公约》A-Ⅴ/1中有详细的说明。该示范课程的目的是参照公约Ⅴ/1部分2.2节的内容提供一项专业培训计划。

为便于参考,该课程分为若干独立章节。

A部分为该课程的目标、目的及教学设施设备注释提供了一个框架,也包括了有用的教具、IMO参考书目以及教材清单。

Part B provides an outline of lectures, demonstrations and exercises for the course, together with a suggested sequence and timetable. From the teaching and learning point of view, it is more important that the trainee achieves the minimum standard of competence defined in the STCW Code than that a strict timetable for each topic is followed. Depending on their experience and ability, some students will naturally take longer to become proficient in some topics than in others.

Part C gives the Detailed Teaching Syllabus. This is based on the theoretical and practical knowledge specified in the STCW Code. It is presented in a logical sequence, starting with basic knowledge and information on petroleum and its hazards, safety and pollution prevention, and concluding with inert gas systems and crude oil washing operations. Each subject area is covered by a series of *required performances*, in other words what the trainee is expected to be able to do as a result of the teaching and training. In this way the overall required performance of knowledge, understanding and proficiency is met. IMO references, textbook references and suggested teaching aids are included to assist the teacher in designing lessons.

Part D contains an Instructor Manual. Against each heading in the detailed teaching syllabus the teaching guidelines have been divided into:

- Key concepts to be delivered
- Lecture suggestions
- Sample questions

It is envisaged that such micro level division of each heading in the teaching syllabus will give the instructor, with varied backgrounds around the world, ample guidelines on developing his/her work plan, as well as the flexibility to adapt keeping in mind the level of the trainees. Furthermore, additional notes, as well as simulator exercises for instructors who may have access to a liquid-cargo-handling simulator, have also been provided.

The Convention defines the minimum standards to be maintained in Part A of the STCW Code. Mandatory provisions concerning Training and Assessment are given in section A-1/6 of the STCW Code. These provisions cover: qualification of instructors; supervisors as assessors; in-service training; assessment of competence; and training and assessment within an institution. A corresponding Part B of the STCW Code contains non-mandatory guidance on training and assessment.

A separate IMO model course addresses Examination and Assessment of Competence. This course explains the use of various methods of demonstrating competence and criteria for evaluating competence as tabulated in the STCW Code and may be helpful in developing any necessary assessments that can include a form of a written examination. As a further aid to the instructor therefore, suggestions have been made on how to set a very specific objective-type question paper for this course. In case a simulator is being used for training pertaining to this model course, then it is suggested that this form of assessment be independent of the assessment done on the simulator.

B部分为该课程的教学、演示以及练习大纲，还有教学顺序和时间表的建议。从教与学的观点来看，学员能满足《STCW公约》所要求的最低标准，比严格按照每一个主题的时间表进行教学要重要得多。依靠经验和能力，一些学员会比其他学员花费更多的时间来熟悉主题。

C部分是基于《STCW公约》中理论和实践知识的具体教学大纲。其以一定的逻辑顺序呈现：从原油的基本知识和信息开始，然后是有关原油的危害、安全和防止油污染，最后以惰气系统和原油洗舱操作结束。每一个方面都有一系列的要求指标，换句话说，学员都要达到教学和培训的效果。通过这种方式，能够满足在知识、理解、熟练方面所要求的指标。IMO参考书目、教材参考书目以及教学建议有助于教员设计课程。

D部分包含教员手册。相对于详细教学大纲中的标题，将教学指南划分为：

- 表达的关键概念
- 教学建议
- 范例问题

对教学大纲中每个标题进行详细划分会给予世界各地背景不同的教员以详细的指导，以使其制订工作计划可以适应不同水平的学员。另外还向教员提供了附加注释和能进行液货操作模拟训练的模拟器练习。

公约定义了《STCW公约》A部分的最低标准。关于培训和评估的法定条款包含在《STCW公约》A部分1/6条款中。这些规定包括：教员资质，作为评估员的监管人员，工作中培训，适任评估，在培训机构中的培训和评估。《STCW公约》B部分是培训和评估的非强制性指南。

有一门独立的IMO示范课程被称为“适任考试和评估”。该课程阐述了在《STCW公约》框架下，验证适任的各种不同方法的使用以及评估适任的标准，这些方法和标准或许会有助于制定包含书面考试的评估规则。因此，为了进一步帮助教员，在如何为该课程设计一份非常具体的试卷方面提出建议。如果在该课程中使用模拟器，则建议该形式的评估应独立于使用模拟器培训的评估。

■ Responsibilities of Administration

Administrations should make sure that training courses delivered by colleges and academies are such as to ensure officers completing training do meet the standards of competence required by STCW regulation V/1 paragraph 2.2.

■ Validation

The Sub-Committee on Standards of Training and Watchkeeping has validated the information contained in this document for use by technical advisors, consultants and experts for the training and certification of seafarers so that the minimum standards implemented may be as uniform as possible. "Validation", in the context of this document, means that the Sub-Committee has found no grounds to object its content. The Sub-Committee has not granted its approval to the document, as it considers that this work must **not** be regarded as an official interpretation of the Convention.

In reaching a decision in this regard, the Sub-Committee was guided by the advice of a validation group comprised of representatives designated by ILO and IMO.

■ 管理部门的责任

管理部门应该确保院校的培训课程能够使完成培训的高级船员满足《STCW公约》V/1部分第2.2节的要求。

■ 生效

培训和值班标准分委会已验证本文件中的信息已被海员培训和发证的技术指导、顾问以及专家所应用,这样最低标准的运用就有可能统一。该文件中的“生效”意味着该分委会已没有理由对其内容进行修改。由于分委会认为该项工作不能视为公约的官方解读,所以其并没有授权批准该文件。

在针对此工作做出决议过程中,由ILO和IMO指派的代表所组成的工作组提出的建议将指导该分委会的工作。

Part A: Course Framework

■ Aims

This course provides training for masters, chief engineers, officers and any person with immediate responsibility for the loading, discharging and care in transit or handling of cargo. It comprises a specialized training programme appropriate to their duties, including oil tanker safety, fire safety measures and systems, pollution prevention, operational practice and obligations under applicable law and regulations. The course takes full account of section A-V/1 of the STCW Code adopted by the International Convention on Standards of Training, Certification and Watchkeeping for Seafarers, 1978, as amended 1995.

Any of this training may be given on board or ashore. It should be supplemented by practical instruction on board and, where appropriate, in a suitable shore-based installation.

■ Objective

Provided they hold an appropriate certificate and are otherwise qualified in accordance with regulation V/1-2.2 of the International Convention on Standards of Training, Certification and Watchkeeping for Seafarers, 1978, as amended in 1995, those successfully completing the course should therefore be able to take immediate responsibility for loading, discharging and care in transit or handling of cargo on oil tankers. They will make a safer and more effective contribution to the operation and control of the cargo on a tanker, which will improve the ship safety and provide greater protection to the environment. In particular, during the course, there will be:

- Familiarization with the equipment, instrumentation and controls used for cargo handling on a tanker
- A greater awareness of the need of proper planning, the use of checklists and the time scales involved in the various cargo handling operations
- An enhanced awareness to apply proper and safe procedures at all times when carrying out the various operations on board an oil tanker
- An acquisition of experience in identifying operational problems and solving them
- An improvement in the ability to make decisions which promote safety and protect the marine environment
- An increased ability to plan and co-ordinate actions during emergencies

■ Entry standards

The course is open to seafarers who have completed a shore-based fire-fighting training course[1] approved by the Administration, and who have relevant experience appropriate to their duties on oil tankers, as stipulated in STCW regulation V/1 paragraph 2.1, and sub-paragraphs 1.1 or 1.2. The following then is the minimum entry requirement:

---

[1] Refer to section A-VI/3 of the STCW Code.

A部分:课程框架

■ 目的

本课程的目的是对船长、轮机长、高级船员以及对货物装卸、转运或过驳、货物操作负有直接责任的其他人员提供培训。包含与职责相适应的专门培训项目,即油船安全、消防安全措施及系统、防污染、操作实践及适用法规下的义务。本课程充分考虑了从《STCW 78/95公约》所采纳的《STCW公约》A-Ⅴ/1部分中的相关条款。

这些培训可能在船上或岸上进行。应以船上实践指导的方式进行培训,如果合适,也可以在岸基设施中进行。

■ 目标

如果他们持有适任证书或者能满足《STCW 78/95公约》Ⅴ/1-2.2中的要求,那些成功完成培训的学员应该能够胜任油船上货物装卸、转运或过驳、货物操作的工作。他们应该能够在油船上更安全有效的进行操作和货物管理,从而提高船舶的安全性并能更好的保护环境。特别地,通过课程培训应达到如下目标:

- 熟悉油船上货物装卸的设备、仪器和控制装置
- 在各种货油操作中对需要正确的计划、对使用检查对照表和时间进度表要有强烈的意识
- 进一步的意识到当在油船上进行各种操作时应遵守适当和安全的程序
- 获得发现操作中的问题并解决问题的经验
- 提升决策能力以提高安全以及保护海洋环境
- 提高在紧急事件中制订计划并协调行动的能力

■ 入学标准

本课程的开放对象为已经完成由主管机关批准的岸基消防培训课程[1]的船员,以及在油船上有相关工作经验的船员,就像《STCW公约》V/1、2.1及其1.1和1.2节所规定的那样。以下是最低入学标准:

[1] 参考 STCW 规则中的 A-VI/3 部分

- Relevant experience on board a tanker as stipulated by STCW 78 (Regulation V/1, paragraph 2.1)
- An approved advanced fire-fighting course

■ Course certificate

The specialized oil tanker training programme must be approved by the Administration. Masters and officers who are qualified in accordance with regulation V/1 paragraphs 1 or 2, as appropriate (that, they have experience appropriate to their duties on tankers, and complete this training programme), shall be issued with an appropriate certificate.

An existing certificate may be suitably endorsed by the issuing Administration.

■ Course intake limitations

The number of trainees will not exceed 20 and practical training (including the simulation exercise, if a simulator is provided) should be taken in small groups not exceeding four per group.

■ Staff requirements

The instructor shall have appropriate training in instructional techniques and training methods (STCW Code section A-I/6, paragraph 7). It is recommended that qualified personnel who are experienced in the handling and characteristics of oil tanker cargoes give all training and instruction and the safety procedures involved. Staff may be recruited from deck and the engine departments who have served on board a tanker in a senior capacity and have the necessary practical experience.

- 《STCW 78公约》(第V/1部分2.1节)规定的相关油船资历
- 通过了高级消防课程

■ 课程证书

专业油船培训项目须经主管机关批准。应该向那些满足公约V/1部分1或2节要求的船长和高级船员(他们有油船任职资历并完成了培训项目)签发相应的证书。

对现有证书须由签发机关背书。

■ 课程人数限制

学员的数量不应超过20人,实操(如果提供模拟器,包括模拟训练)时每一小组的人员不应超过4人。

■ 教员要求

教员在教学技术和培训方法方面应该受过相应的培训(《STCW公约》第A-1/6部分第7节)。建议安排那些对货油的特性和操作有经验的人员教授所有的培训、指导以及其中的安全作业程序。招募的教员应该是曾在油船甲板部和轮机部任职能力较强的人员,并且具备必要的实践经验。

STCW 95 training scheme for personnel on oil tankers

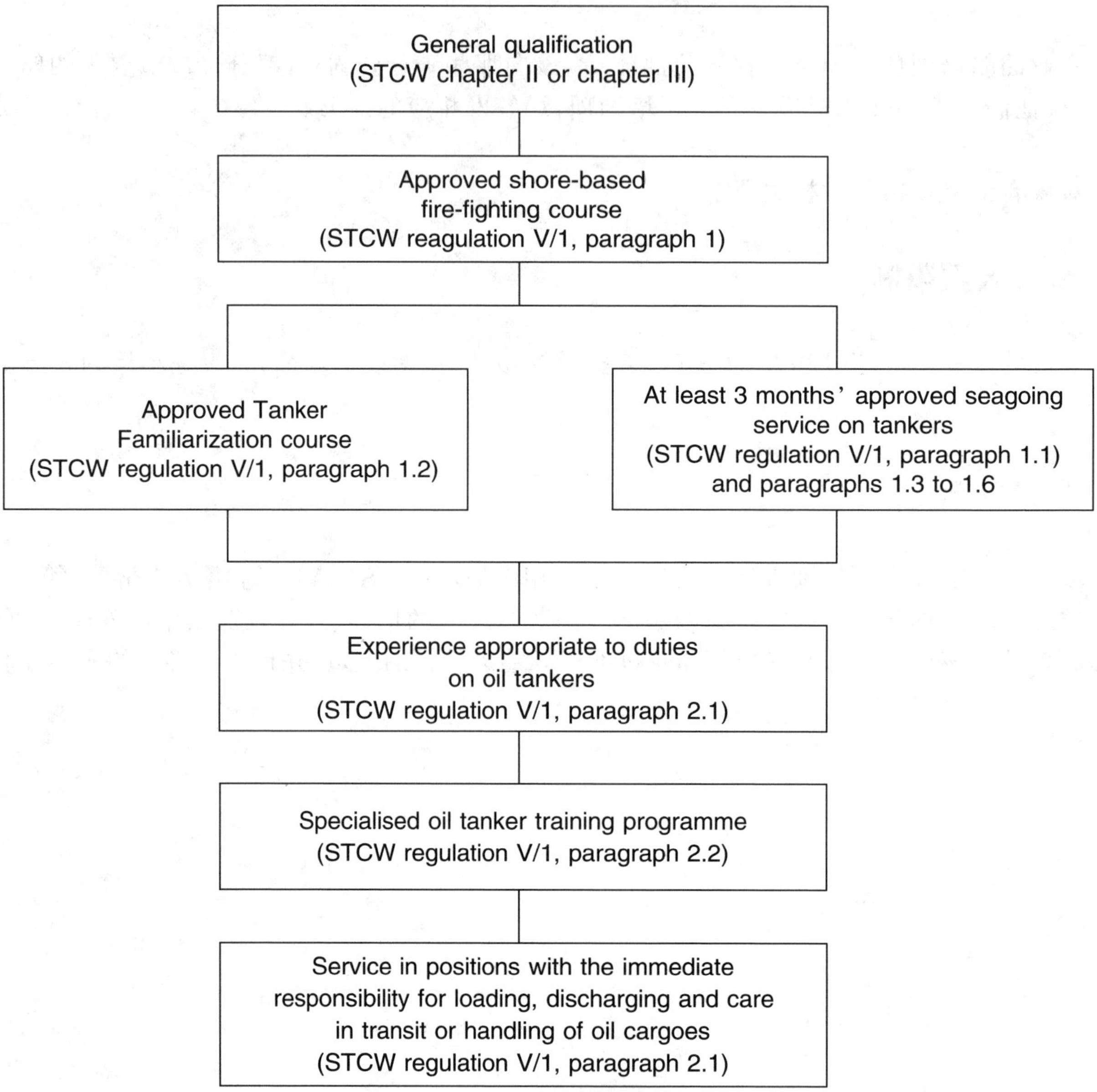

Note:

Administrations may require additional training at sea or ashore to meet national requirements.

《STCW95》关于油船船员的培训计划

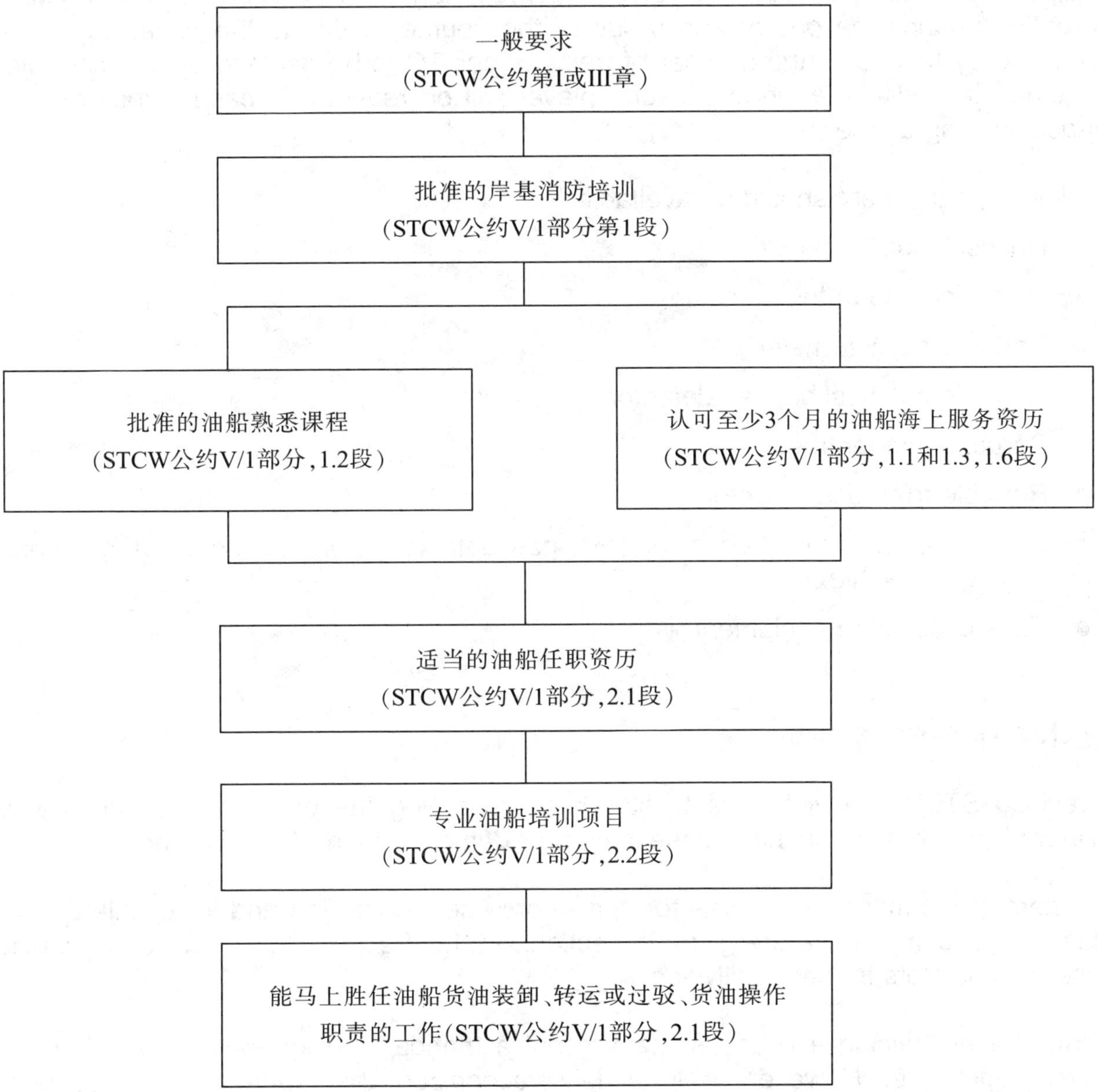

注释：

主管机关可以要求附加海上或陆上训练来满足国内培训要求。

Training facilities and equipment

Proper classroom facilities with an overhead projector (OHP) are sufficient for most of the course. However, dedicated Computer Based Training (CBT) modules to be run on an ordinary PC, as well as exercises on an operational, hands-on liquid-cargo-handling simulator will greatly enhance the quality and result of the course. If this is the case, then sufficient PCs for use by trainees (the number of trainees per PC to be decided by the instructor) will be required. In addition, a video cassette player will be required in case videos are used in the teaching programme.

The following equipment should be available:

- Resuscitator
- Breathing apparatus
- Portable oxygen meter
- Portable combustible-gas detector
- Portable interferometer
- Portable toxic-gas detector
- Chemical absorption tubes for toxic-gas detector (for benzene, carbon monoxide, hydrogen sulphide)
- Tank evacuation equipment

Use of simulators

The revised STCW Convention sets standards regarding the performance and the use of simulators for mandatory training, assessment or demonstration of competence.

The general performance standards for simulators used in training and for simulators used in assessment of competence are given in section A-1/12. Section B-I/12 provides guidance on the use of simulators in these activities.

Simulator-based training and assessment is not a mandatory requirement for this oil tanker training programme. However, it is widely recognized that well-designed lessons and exercises can improve the effectiveness of training and shorten training times compared to traditional methods.

If using a simulator-based training, instructors should ensure that the aims and objectives of these lessons are defined within the overall training programme and that tasks are selected so as to relate as closely as possible to shipboard tasks and practices. Instructors should refer to reference R8, section A-I/12, part 2.

■ 教学设施和设备

带有投影仪的教室设施能够满足大多数课程的需求。然而，在普通电脑上运行的专用培训(CBT)模块以及手动可操作的液货操作模拟器将会在很大程度上强化培训课程的效果和质量。如果是这样的话,要有足够的电脑供学员使用(多少名学员共用一台电脑由教员决定)。此外,如果教学项目中要用视频,那么需要一台视频/录音机播放器。

还应该有以下设备：

- 人工呼吸器
- 呼吸装置
- 便携式氧气探量仪
- 便携式可燃气体检测器
- 便携式干涉仪
- 便携式有毒气体检测仪
- 对有毒气体进行检测的化学吸收管(用来测量苯、一氧化碳、硫化氢)
- 油舱逃生设备

■ 模拟器的使用

修订后的STCW公约对用于适任强制培训、评估和演示的模拟器的性能和使用设置了标准。

在STCW公约A部分1/12节中,对用于培训和适任评估模拟器的通用标准进行了阐述。在该公约B部分1/12节中提供了在这两方面使用模拟器的一些指南。

基于模拟器的培训和评估并不是该油船培训项目的强制要求。然而,普遍认为与传统方法相比,经过良好设计的教学内容和训练可以提高培训效果和缩短培训时间。

如果使用模拟器为基础培训,教员应该确保课程的目的和目标贯穿于整个培训项目中,培训的内容要尽可能地接近船上实际情况。教员应该参阅参考书R8中A-I/12部分的2节。

■ Teaching aids

A1 Instructor's manual (Part D of the course)

A2 Videos/CDs pertaining to the relevant subject can prove to be a good tool to augment the delivery of the modular course.

A3 Videos

"Operation and Maintenance of Inert Gas Systems" (Catalogue Code No. 708)
"Crude Oil Washing" (Catalogue Code No. 707)
"Don't Go Down the.... (Catalogue Code No. 15)
"Over and Under Pressurisation of Tanks" (Catalogue Code No. 533)
"Prevention and Reaction to Marine Oil Spills: Under MARPOL"
(Catalogue Code No. 792)
"Permit to Work" (Catalogue Code No. 621)
"The International Safety Management Code" (Catalogue Code No. 524)

Video:
"Feeding the Powerhouse of Growth"

A4 CBT Modules
"Tanker Operations I and II"
"Inert Gas Generator"
"Flue Gas Generator"
"SOPEP" (Shipboard Oil Pollution Emergency Plans)

A5 PC-Tank

■ Bibliography (B)

B1 ICS/OCIMF/IAPH, *International Safety Guide for Oil Tankers and Terminals.* 4th edn. [London, Witherby and Co. Ltd (32/36 Aylesbury Street, London EC1R 0ET, U.K.), 1996] (ISBN 1-85609-081-7)

B2 C. Baptist (Captain), *Tanker Handbook for Deck Officers.* 7th edn. [Glasgow, Brown, Son & Ferguson Ltd (4-10 Darnley Street, Glasgow, G41 2SD, U.K.), 1991] (ISBN 0-85174-587-3)

B3 ICS/OCIMF, *Ship-to-Ship Transfer Guide (Petroleum).* 3rd edn. (London, Witherby & Co. Ltd, 1997) (ISBN 1-85609-097-3)

B4 ICS/OCIMF, *Clean Seas Guide for Oil Tankers.* 4th edn. (London, Witherby & Co Ltd, 1994) (ISBN 1-85609-2)

B5 ICS, *Safety in Oil Tankers* [London, International Chamber of Shipping (Carthusian Court, 12 Carthusian Street, London, EC1M 6EB, U.K.)]

B6 ICS, *Guide to Helicopter/Ship Operations.* 3rd edn. (London, Witherby & Co. Ltd, 1989) (ISBN 0-948691-44-1)

B7 L. G. Taylor (Captain), *Cargowork.* 12th edn. [Glasgow, Brown, Son & Ferguson Ltd (4–10 Darnley Street, Glasgow, G41 2SD, U.K.), 1992] (ISBN 0-85174-605–5)

■ 教具

A1 教员手册(课程的D部分)

A2 与相关课程有关的录像/CDs是课程模块教学的良好工具。

A3 视频

"惰性气体系统的操作与维护"(目录编码 No.708)
"原油洗舱"(目录编码 NO.707)
"不要进入……"(目录编码 NO.15)
"油舱超压及压力不足"(目录编码 NO.533)
"MARPOL公约海上溢油事故的预防和反应:"(目录编码 NO.792)
"作业许可"(目录编码 NO.621)
"国际安全管理规则"(目录编码NO.524)

视频:
发展的动力来源

A4 CBT 模块
"油船操作I和II"
"惰性气体发生器"
"烟道气发生器"
"船舶油污应急计划"

A5 PC—舱

■ 参考文献(B)

B1 ICS/OCIMF/IAPH,国际油船和油码头安全指南.第4版[London, Witherby and Co. Ltd (32/36 Aylesbury Street, London EC1R 0ET, U.K.), 1996] (ISBN 1-85609-081-7)

B2 C.Baptist(船长). 甲板部高级船员油船手册.第4版Ferguson Ltd (4-10 Darnley Street, Glasgow, G41 2SD, U.K.), 1991] (ISBN 0-85174-587-3)

B3 ICS/OCIMF,船对船过驳指南.第3版(London, Witherby & Co. Ltd, 1997) (ISBN 1-85609-097-3)

B4 ICS/OCIMF,油船海洋清洁指南.第4版(London, Witherby & Co Ltd, 1994) (ISBN 1-85609-2)

B5 ICS,油船安全[London, International Chamber of Shipping (Carthusian Court, 12 Carthusian Street, London, EC1M 6EB, U.K.)]

B6 ICS,直升机/船舶操作指南.第3版[Glasgow, Brown, Son & Ferguson Ltd (4-10 Darnley Street, Glasgow, G41 2SD, U.K.), 1992] (ISBN 0-85174-605-5)

B7 L.G.Taylor (船长). 货物操作. 第12版 [Glasgow, Brown, Son & Ferguson Ltd (4-10 Darnley Street, Glasgow, G41 2SD, U.K.), 1992] (ISBN 0-85174-605-5)

B8 INTERTANKO, *Intact Stability in Double Hull Tankers*, 1996
B9 INTERTANKO, *Measures to Prevent Accidental Pollution*, 1990
B10 INTERTANKO, *Effective Crude Oil Washing*
B11 *Draeger -Tube Handbook*, 11th edition (Drager Sicherheitstechnik GmbH, Revalstrasse 1, D-23560, Lubeck, Germany, 1998) (ISBN 3-926762-06-3)

■ IMO Reference (R)

R1 SOLAS, 1974, Consolidated Edition 1997 (IMO – 110 E)
R2 IMO 2 – International Convention for Prevention of Pollution from Ships, 1973, and Protocol of 1978 relating to the International Convention for the Prevention of Pollution from Ships, 1973 (MARPOL 73/78), including the consolidated edition of latest amendments
R2.1 Annex I of MARPOL 73/78: Regulations for the Prevention of Pollution by Oil
R2.2 Unified Interpretations of the Provisions of Annex I
R3 MARPOL – How to do it?
R4 Inert Gas Systems (IMO – 860 E)
R5 Crude Oil Washing Systems (IMO – 617 E)
R6 International Convention on Civil Liability for Oil Pollution Damage (IMO – 410 E)
R7 Provisions concerning the Reporting of Incidents involving Harmful Substances under MARPOL 73/78 (IMO – 516 E)
R8 International Convention on Standards of Training, Certification and Watchkeeping for Seafarers, 1978/1995
R9 Dedicated Clean Ballast Tanks (IMO – 619 E)
R10 Oily-water Separators and Monitoring Equipment (IMO – 608 E)
R11 International Safety Management Code (ISM Code) (IMO – 186 E)

Details of distributors of IMO publications that maintain a permanent stock of all IMO publications may be found on the IMO web site at http://www.imo.org.

■ Textbooks (T)

T1 J. Hoisaether, *Workbook 2 – Safety Training for Officers and Crew on Tankers and Combination Carriers.* (Trondheim, The Ship Research Institute of Norway, 1981) (ISBN 82-7174-170-5)

B8　国际独立油船东协会,双壳油船的完整稳性,1996。

B9　国际独立油船东协会,防止事故性污染的措施,1900。

B10　国际独立油船东协会,有效的原油洗舱

B11　德尔格检测管使用手册,第11版

■ IMO参考书目(R)

R1　1974年海上人命安全公约,1997年综合文本(IMO-110E)

R2　IMO2-MARPOL73/78公约和议定书,包括最新修改的综合文本

R2.1　MARPOL73/78附录I:防止油类污染规则

R2.2　附录I条款的统一解释

R3　MARPOL—如何做?

R4　惰性气体系统(IMO—860E)

R5　原油洗舱系统(IMO—617E)

R6　国际油污损害民事责任公约(IMO—410E)

R7　MARPOL73/78公约中的有关有害物质造成事故的报告条款(IMO—516E)

R8　STCW 78/95公约

R9　专用清洁压载舱(IMO-619E)

R10　油水分离器及监控设备(IMO-608E)

R11　国际安全管理规则(ISM规则)(IMO-186E)

储存IMO所有出版物永久信息的IMO出版物分布信息可以在其网站上查找，如http://www.imo.org

■ 教科书(T)

T1　J.Hoisaether，工作手册2——油船、混装船船员安全培训手册。(Trondheim, The Ship Research Institute of Norway, 1981) (ISBN 82-7174-170-5)

Part B: Course Outline and Timetable

Minimum requirements for the training of masters and officers on oil tankers (STCW chapter V, regulation V/1 paragraph 2)

Note:

It is suggested that a relevant liquid cargo-handling simulator(oil) can serve as an efficient teaching tool. Should such a system be available, then the class/lecture hours should be adapted to incorporate such without raising the overall duration of the course. Areas that may be suitable for such a training are indicated with an*.

S. No	**Course outline**	**Approximate time (hours)**
		Lectures, demonstrations and practical work
	Knowledge, understanding and proficiency	
1	**Introduction**	
	(STCW Code, Section A-V/1 paragraph 9)	
1.1	Oil tankers	1.0
1.2	International and national regulations concerning oil tankers	1.0
		2.0
2	**Basic properties of petroleum and its hazards**	
	(STCW Code, Section A-V/1, paragraph 11)	
2.1	Basic physics-revision	0.5
2.2	Properties of petroleum	0.5
2.3	Hazards associated with the handling and carriage of petroleum	
	– Toxicity in general	0.5
	– Toxicity of petroleum	0.5
	– Toxicity of inert gas	0.5
	– Oxygen deficiency	0.5
	– Flammability and explosiveness	1.0
	– Electrostatic hazard	1.0
	– Hazard to the marine environment	1.0
		6.0
3	**Safety**	
	(STCW Code, Section A-V/1, paragraph 12/13)	0.5
3.1	General precautions	1.5
3.2	Entry into enclosed spaces	0.5
3.3	Precautions against electrostatic hazard	1.5
3.4	Gas indicators	1.0
3.5	Fire-fighting principles-revision	1.0
3.6	Protective equipment	
		6.0

B部分:课程概要和时间表

油船船长和高级船员的最低培训要求(STCW公约V章,V/1部分第2段)

注释:

有关液货(油)装卸模拟器可以作为一种有效的教学工具,如果这种教学体系被采用,那么会节约很多课程时间,这套教学体系适用于带*号的培训领域。

序号	课程概要	大致学时(小时) 讲课、示范和实操
	知识、理解和熟练	
1	**介绍** (STCW 公约 A-V/1 部分 9 段)	
1.1	油船	1.0
1.2	与油船有关的国内外法规	1.0
		2.0
2	**原油的基本性质和危害** (STCW 公约 A-V/1 部分 11 段)	
2.1	基本物理性质–复习	0.5
2.2	原油的特性	0.5
2.3	关于原油运输和操作的危害	
	– 一般毒性	0.5
	– 原油的毒性	0.5
	– 惰性气体的毒性	0.5
	– 氧气不足	0.5
	– 易燃性和爆炸性	1.0
	– 静电的危害	1.0
	– 海洋环境的危害	1.0
		6.0
3	**安全** (STCW 公约 A-V/1 部分 12/13 段)	
3.1	一般预防措施	0.5
3.2	进入封闭空间	1.5
3.3	防止静电危害的措施	0.5
3.4	气体监测仪	1.5
3.5	防火原理–复习	1.0
3.6	保护装置	1.0
		6.0

S. No	Course outline	Approximate time (hours)
		Lectures, demonstrations and practical work
	Knowledge, understanding and proficiency	
4	**Pollution prevention**	
	(STCW Code, Section A-V/1 paragraphs 9, 14)	
4.1	Ship and equipment	0.5
4.2	Operational pollution	1.0
4.3	Oil Record Book (ORB)	1.0
4.4	Action in case of oil spills	1.0
4.5	Air pollution	0.5
		4.0
5	**Oil tanker design and equipment**	
	(STCW Code, Section A-V/1, paragraph 10)	
5.1	Construction	0.5
5.2	Pumping, piping and discharge arrangements	1.5
5.3	Cargo heating systems	0.5
5.4	Venting arrangements	1.0
5.5	Level gauges	0.5
5.6	Environment protection equipment and slop-tank operations*	4.0
		8.0
6	**Oil tanker operations**	
	(STCW Code, Section A-V/1, paragraphs 10, 12)	
6.1	General precautions	1.0
6.2	Loading and discharging operations*	3.0
6.3	Ballasting and de-ballasting*	1.0
6.4	Tank cleaning	1.0
6.5	Slop-tank operations	1.0
6.6	Purging and gas-freeing*	1.0
6.7	Ship/shore liaison	1.0
		9.0
7	**Cargo and ballast pumps**	
	(STCW Code, Section A-V/1, paragraph 10)	
7.1	Pump theory and characteristics	1.0
7.2	Pressure surge	1.0
		2.0
8	**Emergency procedures**	
	(STCW Code, Section A-V/1, paragraph 10)	
8.1	Emergency plan	0.5
8.2	Emergency alarms	0.5
8.3	Emergency organization	0.5
8.4	Action on discovering an emergency	0.5
		2.0

序号	课程概要	大致学时(小时) 讲课、示范和实操
	知识、理解和熟练	
4	**防治污染** (STCW 公约 A-V/1 部分 9,14 段)	
4.1	船舶和设备	0.5
4.2	操作性污染	1.0
4.3	油类记录簿(ORB)	1.0
4.4	溢油反应	1.0
4.5	空气污染	0.5
		4.0
5	**油船的设计和设备** (STCW 公约 A-V/1 部分 10 段)	
5.1	结构	0.5
5.2	泵浦、管路和排放布置	1.5
5.3	货油加热系统	0.5
5.4	通风布局	1.0
5.5	液位计	0.5
5.6	环境保护装置及污液舱操作 *	4.0
		8.0
6	**油船操作** (STCW 公约 A-V/1 部分 10,12 段)	
6.1	一般预防	1.0
6.2	装卸作业 *	3.0
6.3	加装、排放压载水 *	1.0
6.4	洗舱	1.0
6.5	污液舱的操作	1.0
6.6	驱气和除气 *	1.0
6.7	岸 / 船的联系	1.0
		9.0
7	**货油泵和压载泵** (STCW 公约 A-V/1 部分 10 段)	
7.1	泵的原理和特性	1.0
7.2	压力波动	1.0
		2.0
8	**应急程序** (STCW 公约 A-V/1 部分 10 段)	
8.1	应急计划	0.5
8.2	应急警报	0.5
8.3	应急组织	0.5
8.4	发现应急情况的行动	0.5
		2.0

S. No	Course outline	Approximate time (hours)
		Lectures, demonstrations and practical work
	Knowledge, understanding and proficiency	
9	**Inert Gas Systems (IGS)** (STCW Code, Section A-V/1, paragraphs 10, 12)	
9.1	General	0.5
9.2	The inert gas system	0.5
9.3	Inert gas plant	0.5
9.4	Scrubber, inert gas blowers, inert gas pressure-regulating valves	1.0
9.5	Non-return devices	0.5
9.6	Inert gas distribution and venting	1.0
9.7	Gas-analysing, recording and indicating equipment	0.5
9.8	Operations*	2.0
9.9	Meters, indicators and alarms	0.5
9.10	Emergency procedures	0.5
9.11	Maintenance and testing	0.5
		8.0
10	**Crude oil washing (COW)*** (STCW Code, Section A-V/1, paragraphs 10, 12)	
10.1	Introduction	0.5
10.2	Design of COW systems	1.0
10.3	COW piping	0.5
10.4	Tank washing machines	0.5
10.5	Pumps	0.5
10.6	Stripping systems	0.5
10.7	Operations	1.5
		5.0
11	**Management of risk on oil tanker**	
11.1	Background	0.5
11.2	Definitions	0.5
11.3	Risk on oil tankers	1.0
11.4	Risk assessment process	1.0
11.5	Risk management in practice	1.0
		4.0
12	**Contingency Planning**	
12.1	General	0.5
12.2	Management	0.5
12.3	Preparation of the contingency plan	1.0
		2.0

序号	课程概要	大致学时(小时) 讲课、示范和实操
	知识、理解和熟练	
9	**惰性气体系统** (STCW 公约 A-V/1 部分 10,12 段)	
9.1	概述	0.5
9.2	惰性气体系统	0.5
9.3	惰性气体装置	0.5
9.4	洗涤塔、惰性气体鼓风机和压力调节阀	1.0
9.5	止回设备	0.5
9.6	惰性气体的分配和通风	1.0
9.7	气体的分析、记录和指示装置	0.5
9.8	操作 *	2.0
9.9	仪表、指示器和报警	0.5
9.10	应急程序	0.5
9.11	保养与测试	0.5
		8.0
10	**原油洗舱 *** (STCW 公约 A-V/1 部分 10,12 段)	
10.1	简介	0.5
10.2	原油洗舱系统设计	1.0
10.3	原油洗舱管系	0.5
10.4	洗舱机	0.5
10.5	泵	0.5
10.6	扫舱系统	0.5
10.7	操作	1.5
		5.0
11	**油船的风险管理**	
11.1	背景	0.5
11.2	定义	0.5
11.3	油船存在的风险	1.0
11.4	风险评估程序	1.0
11.5	风险管理实践	1.0
		4.0
12	**应急计划**	
12.1	概述	0.5
12.2	管理	0.5
12.3	应急计划的准备	1.0
		2.0

S. No	Course outline	Approximate time (hours)
		Lectures, demonstrations and practical work
	Knowledge, understanding and proficiency	
13 13.1 13.2	**Assessment and Discussion** **Discussion** **Examination**	 1.0 1.0
		2.0
	TOTAL	**60**
	Total number of days @ 6 hours per day from 0900 to 1600 with 1 hour lunch break	**10 days**

序号	课程概要	大致学时（小时）
		讲课、示范和实操
	知识、理解和熟练	
13	**评估和讨论**	
13.1	**讨论**	1.0
13.2	**考试**	1.0
		2.0
	总计	**60**
	总计天数（每天 6 小时 9:00–16:00，中午休息一小时）	**10 天**

Part B: Course Timetable – example

Teaching staff should note that timetables are suggestions only as regards sequence and length of time allocated to each objective. These factors may be adapted by lecturers to suit individual groups of trainees depending on their experience and ability and on the equipment and staff available for training.

	1st Period (1.5 hours) **(0900 – 1030 hrs)**	**2nd Period** (1.5 hours) **(1030 – 1200 hrs)**		**3rd Period** (1.5 hours) **(1300 – 1430 hrs)**	**4th Period** (1.5 hours) **(1430 – 1600 hrs)**
Day 1	1.1 Oil tankers (1.0 hour) 1.2 Int. & national regulations regarding oil tankers (0.5 hour)	1.2 Int. & national regulations regarding oil tankers (0.5 hour) 2.1 Basic physics – revision (0.5 hour) 2.2 Properties of petroleum (0.5 hour)	**MEAL BREAK (1200 – 1300 hrs)**	2.3 Toxicity in general (0.5 hour) 2.3 Toxicity of petroleum, toxicity of inert gas (1.0 hour)	2.3 Oxygen deficiency (0.5 hour) 2.3 Flammability and explosiveness (1 hour)
Day 2	2.3 Electrostatic hazard (1.0 hour) 2.3 Hazard to the marine environment (0.5 hour)	2.3 Hazard to the marine environment (0.5 hour) 3.1 General precautions (0.5 hour) 3.2 Entry into enclosed spaces (0.5 hour)		3.2 Entry into enclosed spaces (1.0 hour) 3.3 Precautions against electrostatic hazard (0.5 hour)	3.4 Gas indicators (1.5 hours)

B部分：课程时间表—实例

教员应该注意到时间表仅仅是按时间的长度和顺序来分布的。教员可以根据实际情况制订不同的课程时间表，这主要取决于学员的经验和能力，以及培训设备。

	第 1 时段 (1.5 学时) **(09:00 – 10:30)**	**第 2 时段** (1.5 学时) **(10:30 – 12:00)**		**第 3 时段** (1.5 学时) **(13:00 – 14:30)**	**第 4 时段** (1.5 学时) **(14:30 – 16:00)**
第 1 天	1.1 油船 (1.0 学时) 1.2 有关油船的国内外法规 (0.5 学时)	1.2 有关油船的国内外法规 (0.5 学时) 2.1 基本物理性质——复习 (0.5 学时) 2.2 原油的特性 (0.5 学时)	**中午休息 (12:00 – 13:00)**	2.3 一般毒性 (0.5 学时) 2.3 原油的毒性、惰性气体的毒性 (1.0 学时)	2.3 氧气不足 (0.5 学时) 2.3 易燃性和易爆性 (1 学时)
第 2 天	2.3 静电危害 (1.0 学时) 2.3 对海洋环境的危害 (0.5 学时)	2.3 对海洋环境的危害 (0.5 学时) 3.1 一般预防措施 (0.5 学时) 3.2 进入封闭空间 (0.5 学时)		3.2 进入封闭空间 (1.0 学时) 3.3 防止静电危害的措施 (0.5 学时)	3.4 气体监测仪 (1.5 学时)

	1st Period (1.5 hours) **(0900 – 1030 hrs)**	**2nd Period** (1.5 hours) **(1030 – 1200 hrs)**		**3rd Period** (1.5 hours) **(1300 – 1430 hrs)**	**4th Period** (1.5 hours) **(1430 – 1600 hrs)**
Day 3	3.5 Fire-fighting principles – revision (1 hour) 3.6 Protective equipment (0.5 hour)	3.6 Protective equipment (0.5 hour) 4.1 Ship & equipment (0.5 hour) 4.2 Operational pollution (0.5 hour)	**MEAL BREAK (1200 – 1300 hrs)**	4.2 Operational pollution (0.5 hour) 4.3 Oil Record Book (1.0 hour)	4.4 Action in case of oil spills (1 hour) 4.5 Air pollution (0.5 hour)
Day 4	5.1 Construction (0.5 hour) 5.2 Pumping, piping & discharge arrangements (1 hour)	5.2 Pumping, piping & discharge arrangements (0.5 hour) 5.3 Cargo heating systems (0.5 hour) 5.4 Venting arrangements (0.5 hour)		5.4 Venting arrangements (0.5 hour) 5.5 Level gauges (0.5 hour) 5.6 Environment protection equipment and slop-tank operations (0.5 hour)	5.6 Environment protection equipment and slop-tank operations (1.5 hours)

	第 1 时段 (1.5 学时) **(09:00 – 10:30)**	**第 2 时段** (1.5 学时) **(10:30 – 12:00)**		**第 3 时段** (1.5 学时) **(13:00 – 14:30)**	**第 4 时段** (1.5 学时) **(14:30 – 16:00)**
第 3 天	3.5 防火原理——复习 (1 学时) 3.6 保护装置 (0.5 学时)	3.6 保护装置 (0.5 学时) 4.1 船舶和设备 (0.5 学时) 4.2 操作性污染 (0.5 学时)	**中午休息 (12:00 – 13:00)**	4.2 操作性污染 (0.5 学时) 4.3 油类记录簿 (1.0 学时)	4.4 溢油反应 (1 学时) 4.5 空气污染 (0.5 学时)
第 4 天	5.1 结构 (0.5 学时) 5.2 泵浦、管路和排放布置 (1 学时)	5.2 泵浦、管路和排放布置 (0.5 学时) 5.3 货油加热系统 (0.5 学时) 5.4 通风布置 (0.5 学时)		5.4 通风布置 (0.5 学时) 5.5 液位计 (0.5 学时) 5.6 防污染设备及污液舱操作 (0.5 学时)	5.6 防污染设备及污液舱操作 (1.5 学时)

	1st Period (1.5 hours) **(0900 – 1030 hrs)**	**2nd Period** (1.5 hours) **(1030 – 1200 hrs)**		**3rd Period** (1.5 hours) **(1300 – 1430 hrs)**	**4th Period** (1.5 hours) **(1430 – 1600 hrs)**
Day 5	5.6 Environment protection equipment and slop-tank operations (1.5 hours)	5.6 Environment protection equipment and sloptank operations (0.5 hour) 6.1 General precautions (1.0 hour)	**MEAL BREAK (1200 – 1300 hrs)**	6.2 Loading & discharging operations (1.5 hours)	6.2 Loading & discharging operations (1.5 hours)
Day 6	6.3 Ballasting & deballasting (1.0 hour)	6.4 Tank cleaning (0.5 hour) 6.5 Slop-tank operations (1 hour)		6.6 Purging and gas freeing (1.0 hour) 6.7 Ship/shore liaison (0.5 hour)	6.7 Ship/shore liaison (0.5 hour) 7.1 Pump theory & characteristics (1 hour)

	第 1 时段 (1.5 学时) **(09:00 – 10:30)**	**第 2 时段** (1.5 学时) **(10:30 – 12:00)**		**第 3 时段** (1.5 学时) **(13:00 – 14:30)**	**第 4 时段** (1.5 学时) **(14:30 – 16:00)**
第 5 天	5.6 防污染设备及污液舱操作 (1.5 学时)	5.6 防污染设备及污液舱操作 (0.5 学时) 6.1 一般预防 (1.0 学时)	**中午休息 (12:00 – 13:00)**	6.2 装卸操作 (1.5 学时)	6.2 装卸操作 (1.5 学时)
第 6 天	6.3 加装、排放压载水 (1.0 学时)	64 洗舱 (0.5 学时) 6.5 污液舱操作 (1 学时)		6.6 驱气和除气 (1.0 学时) 6.7 岸 / 船间的联系 (0.5 学时)	6.7 岸 / 船的联系 (0.5 学时) 7.1 泵浦的原理和特性 (1 学时)

	1st Period (1.5 hours) **(0900 – 1030 hrs)**	**2nd Period** (1.5 hours) **(1030 – 1200 hrs)**		**3rd Period** (1.5 hours) **(1300 – 1430 hrs)**	**4th Period** (1.5 hours) **(1430 – 1600 hrs)**
Day 7	7.2 Pressure surge (1.0 hour) 8.1 Emergency plan (0.5 hour)	8.2 Emergency alarms (0.5 hour) 8.3 Emergency organization (0.5 hour) 8.4 Action on discovering an emergency (0.5 hour)	**MEAL BREAK (1200 – 1300 hrs)**	9.1 General (0.5 hour) 9.2 The inert gas system (0.5 hour) 9.3 Inert gas plant (0.5 hour)	9.4 Scrubber, inert gas blowers and gas pressure regulating valves (1.0 hour) 9.5 Non-return devices (0.5 hour)
Day 8	9.6 Inert gas distribution & venting (1 hour) 9.7 Gas-analysing, recording and indicating equipment (0.5 hour)	9.8 Operations (1.5 hours)		9.8 Operations (0.5 hour) 9.9 Meters, indicators & alarms (0.5 hour) 9.10 Emergency procedures (0.5 hour)	9.11 Maintenance and testing (0.5 hour) 10.1 Introduction (0.5 hour) 10.2 Design of COW systems (0.5 hour)

	第 1 时段 (1.5 学时) **(09:00 – 10:30)**	**第 2 时段** (1.5 学时) **(10:30 – 12:00)**		**第 3 时段** (1.5 学时) **(13:00 – 14:30)**	**第 4 时段** (1.5 学时) **(14:30 – 16:00)**
第 7 天	7.2 压力波动 (1.0 学时) 8.1 应急计划 (0.5 学时)	8.2 应急警报 (0.5 学时) 8.3 应急组织 (0.5 学时) 8.4 发现应急情况的行动 (0.5 学时)	**中午休息 (12:00 – 13:00)**	9.1 概述 (0.5 学时) 9.2 惰性气体系统 (0.5 学时) 9.3 惰性气体装置 (0.5 学时)	9.4 洗涤塔、惰性气体鼓风机和压力调节阀 (1.0 学时) 9.5 止回设备 (0.5 学时)
第 8 天	9.6 惰性气体的分配和通风 (1 学时) 9.7 气体的分析、记录和指示装置 (0.5 学时)	9.8 操作 (1.5 学时)		9.8 操作 (0.5 学时) 9.9 仪表、指示器和报警 (0.5 学时) 9.10 应急程序 (0.5 学时)	9.11 保养与测试 (0.5 学时) 10.1 简介 (0.5 学时) 10.2 COW 系统设计 (0.5 学时)

	1st Period (1.5 hours) **(0900 – 1030 hrs)**	**2nd Period** (1.5 hours) **(1030 – 1200 hrs)**		**3rd Period** (1.5 hours) **(1300 – 1430 hrs)**	**4th Period** (1.5 hours) **(1430 – 1600 hrs)**
Day 9	10.2 Design of COW systems (0.5 hour) 10.3 COW piping (0.5 hour) 10.4 Tank washing machines (0.5 hour)	10.5 Pumps (0.5 hour) 10.6 Stripping systems (0.5 hour) 10.7 Operations (0.5 hour)	**MEAL BREAK (1200 – 1300 hrs)**	10.7 Operations (1 hour) 11.1 Background (0.5 hour)	11.2 Definitions (0.5 hour) 11.3 Risk on oil tankers (1.0 hour)
Day 10	11.4 Risk assessment process (1 hour) 11.5 Risk management in practice (0.5 hour)	11.5 Risk management in practice (0.5 hour) 12.1 General (0.5 hour) 12.2 Management (0.5 hour)		12.3 Preparation of the contingency plan (0.5 hour) 12.3 Preparation of the contingency plan (0.5 hour) 13.1 Discussion (0.5 hour)	13.1 Discussion (0.5 hour) 13.2 EXAMINATION (1 hour)

	第 1 时段 (1.5 学时) **(09:00 – 10:30)**	**第 2 时段** (1.5 学时) **(10:30 – 12:00)**		**第 3 时段** (1.5 学时) **(13:00 – 14:30)**	**第 4 时段** (1.5 学时) **(14:30 – 16:00)**
第 9 天	10.2 原油洗舱系统设计 (0.5 学时) 10.3 原油洗舱管系 (0.5 学时) 10.4 洗舱机 (0.5 学时)	10.5 泵 (0.5 学时) 10.6 扫舱系统 (0.5 学时) 10.7 操作 (0.5 学时)	**中午休息 (12:00 – 13:00)**	10.7 操作 (1 学时) 11.1 背景 (0.5 学时)	11.2 定义 (0.5 学时) 11.3 油船存在的风险 (1.0 学时)
第 10 天	11.4 风险评估程序 (1 学时) 11.5 风险管理实践 (0.5 学时)	11.5 风险管理实践 (0.5 学时) 12.1 概述 (0.5 学时) 12.2 管理 (0.5 学时)		12.3 应急计划的准备 (0.5 学时) 12.3 应急计划的准备 (0.5 学时) 13.1 讨论 (0.5 学时)	13.1 讨论 (0.5 学时) 13.2 考试 (1 学时)

Part C: Detailed Teaching Syllabus

■ Specialized Training for Oil Tankers – Introduction

The detailed teaching syllabus is presented as a series of knowledge, understanding and proficiency to be acquired. The objective, therefore, describes what the trainee must do to demonstrate that the specified knowledge or skill has been transferred and competence achieved.

Thus each training objective is supported by a number of related performance elements in which the trainee is expected to be proficient. The teaching syllabus shows the required performance expected of the trainee in the tables that follow.

In order to assist the instructor, references are shown to indicate IMO references and publications, textbooks and teaching aids that instructors may wish to use in preparing and presenting their lessons.

The material listed in the course framework has been used to structure the detailed teaching syllabus; in particular,

- Teaching Aids (indicated by **A**)
- Bibliography (indicated by **B**)
- IMO references (indicated by **R**), and
- Textbooks (indicated by **T**)

Will provide valuable information to instructors. The abbreviations used are:

- App. Appendix
- Art. Article
- Pa. Paragraph
- Reg. Regulation
- Sec. Section

The following are examples of the use of references:

"A1" refers to the Instructor Manual in Part D of this model course

"R2" refers to MARPOL 73/78 Consolidated Edition

"T1" refers to *Workbook 2 – Safety Training for Officers and Crew on Tankers and Combination Carriers*

Note:

Throughout the course, safe working practices are to be clearly defined and emphasized with reference to current international requirements and regulations.

It is expected that the national institution implementing the course will introduce references to national requirements and regulations as necessary.

C部分:教学大纲细则

■ 油船专业培训——介绍

该教学大纲细则描述了学员必须了解、理解或精通的知识和技术。因此,教学目标是学员必须能够展示他们所学的和能胜任的专门知识和技能。

因此,每项培训目标都由大量相关指标来衡量,学员应该精通这些指标。教学大纲在下面的表格中列出了对学员的要求。

为了帮助教员,参考书包括:IMO参考书和发行物、教材及教员们在备课和讲课时所需要的技术资料和教具。

课程框架中所列资料已用于搭建教学大纲细则;尤其是:

- 教具(用**A**表示)
- 参考书目(用**B**表示)
- IMO参考书目(用**R**表示)
- 教科书 (用**T**表示)

将为教员提供有价值的信息。所用到的缩写是:

- App. 附录
- Art. 条款
- Pa. 段
- Reg. 规则
- Sec. 节

下面举例说明:

"A1"指的是在该示范课中D部分的教员守则

"R2"指的是《MARPOL73/78公约》的97年综合文本

"T1"指的是工作手册2,即油船、混装船的船员安全培训手册

注释:

根据现行国际规则和要求,在整个课程中,应该明确和强调安全操作规程。

执行该课程的培训机构应尽可能的介绍国家和/或地区的规则和要求。

Knowledge, understanding and proficiency		IMO Reference	Textbooks, Bibliography	Teaching Aid
Required performance				
1	**Introduction** (1.5 hours)	STCW Code Sec. A-V/1, pa. 9		A2
1.1	**Oil tankers** (1 hour)			
.1	defines: – oil tanker – crude oil tanker – product carrier – combination carrier	R2.1 Reg. 1 (4) Reg. 1 (29) Reg. 1 (30) Reg. 1 (5)		A1
.2	describes combination carriers as oil/bulk/ore (OBO) or oil/ore (O/O) carriers		B1	A1
.3	identifies and describes an OBO and an O/O carrier from cross-sectional diagrams		B1	A1
.4	explains the purpose of and differences between OBO and O/O carriers		B1	A1
.5	describes the LOT procedures		B1	A1
.6	describes the features of a double-hull tanker		B1	A1
.7	describes the features of a mid-deck design tanker		B1	A1
.8	explains the principle of hydrostatic balance loading		B1	A1
1.2	**International and national regulations concerning oil tankers** (1 hour)	R8-STCW Code Sec. A-V/1		
.1	states that shipping activities are of international nature and that the international forum for maritime and therefore for shipping matters is IMO	R1; R2.1		A1
.2	states that the IMO has drawn up conventions which affect ships	R1; R2.1		A1
.3	states that the conventions directly affecting ships and shipping activities are the conventions SOLAS 1974 as amended, MARPOL 73/78 as amended and STCW 78 as amended in 1995; and states their full title	R1; R2 R2.1		A1
.4	states that the countries that are party to the above conventions have the provisions of those Conventions incorporated into their national laws	R2.1		A1
.5	states that oil tankers are affected by the above conventions either through the laws of the Flag State or the Port State	R1		A1
.6	states that compliance with the structural requirements of SOLAS is certified by means of Cargo Ship Safety Construction Certificate with the oil tanker Supplement	R1, R8		A1
.7	states that compliance with the equipment requirements of SOLAS is certified by means of Cargo Ship Safety Equipment Certificate with the oil tanker Supplement	R8		A1
.8	states that a Safety Management System in compliance with the ISM Code must be in place on board all tankers of 500 GT and upwards	R8, R11		A1, A3

知识、理解和熟练	IMO 参考书目	教科书，参考文献	教具
技能要求			
介绍（1.5 学时）	STCW 公约 A-V/1 节 9 段		A2
1.1 油船（1 学时）			
.1 定义：	R2.1		A1
– 油船	Reg. 1 (4)		
– 原油油船	Reg. 1 (29)		
– 成品油船	Reg. 1 (30)		
– 混装船	Reg. 1 (5)		
.2 描述油 / 散装 / 矿石混装船（OBO）和油 / 矿石混装船（O/O）		B1	A1
.3 通过截面图介绍和认识 OBO 船和 O/O 船		B1	A1
.4 说明 OBO 船和 O/O 船的用途及它们之间的差别		B1	A1
.5 描述 LOT 程序		B1	A1
.6 描述双层底舱的特性		B1	A1
.7 描述中层甲板的特性		B1	A1
.8 说明装货静态平衡原理		B1	A1
1.2 与油船有关的国内外法规（1 学时）	参考书目 8 STCW 公约 A-V/1 节		
.1 阐述航运活动是关系全球的，声明国际海事组织是解决海事争端、研讨海事事务的组织	R1; R2.1		A1
.2 阐述国际海事组织已经制定的有关船舶的公约	R1;		A1
.3 阐述直接影响船舶及海运活动的公约有 SOLAS 1974 及其修正案 MARPOL73/78 及其修正案和 STCW78/95 公约并阐述它们的全称	R2.1 R1; R2		A1
.4 阐述以上公约的缔约国都已将公约中的相应条款纳入本国相应的法律和规则中	R2.1 R2.1		A1
.5 阐述上述公约通过船旗国法规或港口国法规来影响油船	R1		A1
.6 阐述通过油船增设的货船安全结构证书来保证油船满足 SOLAS 1974 公约对于结构的要求	R1, R8		A1
.7 阐述通过油船增设的货船安全设备证书来保证船舶满足 SOLAS 1974 公约对于设备的要求	R8		A1
.8 阐述在所有 500 总吨及以上油船的适当位置必须有符合 ISM 规则的安全管理系统	R8, R11		A1, A3

Knowledge, understanding and proficiency		IMO Reference	Textbooks, Bibliography	Teaching Aid
Required performance				
.9	states that construction and equipment requirements under MARPOL 73/78 is certified by means of International Oil Pollution Prevention Certificate with Supplement B	R1, R11		A1
.10	states that Flag States are responsible for the issuance of the certificates but may appoint another agency on their behalf	R2.1		A1
.11	states that, in many ports, oil tanker operations are governed by local regulations	R1, R2.2		A1
.12	states that the Port State authorities may verify compliance with the aforementioned Conventions, including ILO Conventions (ILO 147)			A1
.13	states that oil tankers have the potential to cause marine and/or coastal pollution	R1		A1
.14	states that the owner of the ship is liable for clean-up costs and other damages	R2.1		A1
.15	states that a number of maritime countries, party to the CLC and Fund Conventions (69/92; 71/92) require a ship owner to be insured against such damages	R6		A1
.16	states that the proof of insurance is the Certificate of Insurance or other Financial Security in respect of Civil Liability or other Financial Security in respect of Civil Liability for Oil Pollution Damage, which is issued by Flag State under the provisions of the Convention	R6		A1
.17	states that the Convention limits the ship owners liability for oil pollution damage in accordance with the tonnage of the ship	R6		A1
.18	states that an owner cannot limit his/her liability if an oil pollution incident occurred as a result of his/her fault	R6		A1
2	**Basic properties of petroleum and its hazards** (5.5 hours)			
2.1	**Basic physics** (0.5 hour)			
.1	describes the three states of matter			A1
.2	defines melting, sublimation, evaporation, melting point and boiling point			A1
.3	describes surface tension, adhesion, cohesion, hydrostatic pressure, miscibility, solubility and diffusion as these terms apply to liquids			A1
.4	defines the viscosity and saturated vapour pressure of liquids			A1
.5	describes diffusion, pressure and miscibility as applied to gases/vapour			A1
.6	defines the critical pressure and temperature of gases			A1
.7	describes the structure of atoms and molecules.			A1
.8	states that a negatively charged body has an excess of electrons			A1
.9	states that a positively charged body has a shortage of electrons			A1

知识、理解和熟练	IMO 参考书目	教科书,参考文献	教具
技能要求			
.9 阐述通过颁发国际防油污证书(附录 B)来保证满足 MARPOL 73/78 公约对于船舶结构和设备的要求	R1, R11		A1
.10 阐述船旗国负责签发证书,但也可以指定其他授权代理机构代发	R2.1		A1
.11 阐述在许多港口,油船操作要遵从当地的有关法规	R1, R2.2		A1
.12 阐述港口当局应确认油船符合上述公约规定,包括国际劳工组织公约 (ILO 147)			A1
.13 阐述油船有对海洋或海岸造成污染的隐患	R1		A1
.14 阐述船东有义务承担清除污染的费用和其他破坏的责任	R2.1		A1
.15 阐述关于国际油污损害民事责任国际公约 (1969 年 /1992 年;1971 年 /1992 年)的许多缔约国要求船东针对此类损害投保	R6		A1
.16 阐述保险的证明是在公约的规定下由船旗国签发的关于油污染损害民事责任的保险证书或其他金融安全证书	R6		A1
.17 阐述公约根据船舶吨位限定了船东对于油污染破坏应承担的责任	R6		A1
.18 阐述如果由于船东的失误或默许而造成的油污染事故,船东不能限定其自身的责任	R6		A1
2 原油的基本性质和危害 (5.5 学时)			
2.1 基本物理性质 (0.5 学时)			
.1 阐述物质的三种状态			A1
.2 定义融化、升华、蒸发、溶点和沸点			A1
.3 阐述适用液体的表面张力、附着力、凝聚力、液体静压力、可混合性、溶解性和扩散性			A1
.4 定义液体的黏度和饱和蒸气压力			A1
.5 阐述适用气体或蒸汽的扩散性、压力和可混合性			A1
.6 定义气体的临界压力和临界温度			A1
.7 阐述原子和分子的结构			A1
.8 阐述带负电物体是电子过剩			A1
.9 阐述带正电物体是缺少电子			A1

Knowledge, understanding and proficiency		IMO Reference	Textbooks, Bibliography	Teaching Aid
Required performance				
.10	states that similarly charged bodies repel each other and oppositely charged bodies attract each other			A1
.11	describes induction and how the induction of an electrode may cause it to become charged			A1
.12	describes how a charged electrode may be discharged			A1
.13	states that a discharge releases energy which may cause a spark			A1
2.2	**Properties of petroleum** (0.5 hour)			
.1	states that crude petroleum as discharged at the well head is a mixture of a large number of different hydrocarbon molecules		B7	A1
.2	states that the molecules are termed 'light' or 'heavy' according to the number of carbon atoms in the molecule		B7	A1
.3	states that the boiling point of the constituent compounds range from −162℃ (methane) to a value in excess of 140℃		B7	A1
.4	states that the composition of petroleum depends on the source		B7	A1
.5	states that crude oil is a mixture of hydrocarbons ranging from those which are partly gaseous under normal atmospheric conditions to those which are liquid and solid		B7	A1
.6	states that crude oil is split into fractions in an oil refinery process termed as 'distillation'		B7	A1
.7	states that heavy fractions (containing a large number of carbon atoms) can be split into lighter fractions (containing a smaller number of carbon atoms) by means of an oil refinery process termed as 'cracking'		B7	A1
.8	states that each petroleum fraction has a range of physical properties specific to itself		B7	A1
.9	defines the volatility of petroleum as the tendency of crude oil or an oil product to produce gas		B7	A1
.10	states that volatility is characterised by the vapour pressure		B7	A1
.11	states that the true vapour pressure (TVP) of a petroleum mixture is difficult to measure, but that a correlation exists between TVP and Reid vapour pressure (RVP), which is relatively easy to measure		B7	A1
.12	states that the carriage of petroleum and petroleum products in bulk poses health and environmental hazards		B7	A1
2.3	**Hazards associated with the handling and carriage of petroleum** (5 hours) **Toxicity in general** (0.5 hour)			
.1	states that poisoning may occur orally, through inhalation or by skin contact		B1	A1
.2	states that poisoning may be acute or chronic		B1	A1
.3	states that the toxicity of a substance is difficult to measure and that it is therefore rated on the basis of studies performed on animals and extrapolated from the human body		B1	A1

知识、理解和熟练	IMO 参考书目	教科书，参考文献	教具
技能要求			
.10　阐述电荷同性相斥、异性相吸			A1
.11　阐述感应现象及电极的感应现象如何使它带电			A1
.12　阐述电极如何放电			A1
.13　阐述放电释放的能量可以产生火花			A1
2.2　石油的特性 (0.5 学时)			
.1　阐述从油井抽出的原油是由大量的碳氢化合物组成的混合物		B7	A1
.2　阐述根据分子中所含碳原子的数量将分子分为“轻分子”或“重分子”		B7	A1
.3　阐述化合物成分的沸点范围从-162℃(甲烷)到 140℃		B7	A1
.4　阐述原油成分取决于其产地		B7	A1
.5　阐述原油是在大气压下呈气态、液态或固态的碳氢化合物的混合物		B7	A1
.6　阐述原油在精炼过程中裂化成一系列馏分，这个过程被称作蒸馏		B7	A1
.7　阐述重馏分(包含大量的碳原子)通过被称作“裂解”的精炼过程被分裂成一些轻馏分(包含较少的碳原子)		B7	A1
.8　阐述每种原油馏分都有一些自身特有的物理特性		B7	A1
.9　将原油的挥发性定义为原油或原油产品产生气体的倾向		B7	A1
10　阐述原油的挥发性表现为原油蒸气压力		B7	A1
.11　阐述原油混合物蒸汽的绝对压力(TVP)是很难测量的，但是 TVP 和雷德蒸气压力(RVP)之间存在的相互关系很容易确定		B7	A1
.12　阐述原油及原油产品的散装运输对健康和环境的危害		B7	A1
2.3　关于原油运输和操作的危害(5 学时) **通常的毒性**(0.5 学时)			
.1　阐述通过吸入或皮肤接触可以发生中毒		B1	A1
.2　阐述中毒可能是急性的或慢性的		B1	A1
.3　阐述对于很难测定物质的毒性，一般都是通过在动物身上做一些基础试验研究来推断该毒性对人体的危害		B1	A1

Knowledge, understanding and proficiency	IMO Reference	Textbooks, Bibliography	Teaching Aid
Required performance			
.4 lists and describes the criteria by which toxicity is measured and expressed		B1	A1
Toxicity of petroleum (0.5 hour)			
.5 describes the effects of ingesting petroleum		B1	
.6 describes the effects of petroleum on the skin and in the eyes		B1	
.7 states that the main effects of petroleum gas on persons and the complications it may cause		B1	A1
.8 describes the symptoms of narcosis		B1	A1
.9 states that the toxicity of petroleum gas varies widely, depending on its main hydrocarbon constituents		B1	A1
.10 lists typical toxic constituents of petroleum gas		B1	A1
.11 describes the threshold limit value (TLV) that is generally accepted for petroleum gas		B1	A1
.12 states that this TLV must NOT be taken as applicable to gas mixtures containing benzene or hydrogen sulphide		B1	A1
.13 states that the human body can tolerate a concentration above TLV for short periods		B1	A1
.14 explains why: – the absence of a smell of gas is insufficient guarantee of its absence – a combustible gas indicator cannot be expected to measure TLV accurately		B1	A1
.15 states that leaded gasoline is considerably more toxic than unleaded gasoline if ingested or absorbed through the skin but there is little difference between toxicity of vapours of leaded and unleaded petroleum		B1	A1
Toxicity of inert gas (0.5 hour)			
.16 states that the main hazard associated with inert gas is its low oxygen content, but that it may also contain toxic gases		B1	A1
.17 lists the main toxic constituents of inert gas		B1	A1
.18 describes the fate of the nitrogen oxides in fresh flue gas		B1	A1
.19 states that nitrogen dioxide is more toxic than nitric oxide		B1	A1
.20 states that: – the sulphur dioxide content depends on the sulphur content of the fuel oil and on the efficiency of the scrubber – the carbon monoxide content depends on combustion conditions		B1	A1
.21 states that NO_X and SO_X are now regulated by Annex VI of MARPOL 73/78		B1	A1
Oxygen deficiency (0.5 hour)			
.22 states that oxygen content of air is 21% by volume but may be lower in enclosed spaces		B1	A1
.23 explains the reasons for a lower oxygen content		B1	A1
.24 explains why reliance should not be placed on symptoms for indicating an oxygen-deficient atmosphere		B1	A1

知识、理解和熟练		IMO 参考书目	教科书,参考文献	教具
技能要求				
4	列举和描述用来测定和表示物质毒性的标准		B1	A1
	原油的毒性(0.5 学时)			
.5	描述吸入原油的后果		B1	
.6	描述原油对皮肤和眼睛的影响		B1	
.7	阐述原油气体对人体的主要影响和可能引起的并发症		B1	A1
.8	描述昏迷的症状		B1	A1
.9	阐述由于原油主要烃类组成不同而致使其气体毒性也有很大差别		B1	A1
.10	列举原油气中主要的有毒成分		B1	A1
.11	阐述原油气的中毒阈限值(TLV)		B1	A1
.12	阐述这个中毒阈限值绝对不适用于含有苯和硫化氢的混合气体		B1	A1
.13	阐述人体能在短时内忍受超出中毒阈限值的环境		B1	A1
.14	解释为什么: – 没有气体的味道不能充分保证该气体不存在 – 可燃气体指示器不能准确地测量到 TLV		B1	A1
.15	阐述如果进入消化系统或被皮肤吸收,含铅汽油通常比不含铅汽油的毒性大得多,但是对于含铅和不含铅的石油蒸汽其毒性差别很小		B1	A1
	惰性气体的毒性(0.5 学时)			
.16	阐述惰性气体的主要危害是其中氧气含量低,但是它也可能含有有毒气体		B1	A1
.17	列举惰性气体的主要有害成分		B1	A1
.18	阐述新鲜烟气中氮氧化物的变化过程		B1	A1
.19	阐述二氧化氮比一氧化氮毒性更大		B1	A1
.20	阐述: – 二氧化硫的含量取决于燃油中硫的含量和洗涤塔的效率 – 一氧化碳的含量取决于燃烧状况		B1	A1
.21	阐述目前氮氧化物和硫氧化物的排放要根据 MARPOL 公约附则 6 的要求进行控制		B1	A1
	缺氧(0.5 学时)			
.22	阐述空气中氧气的体积含量为 21%,但在封闭的空间中含量可能要低一些		B1	A1
.23	解释氧气含量低的原因		B1	A1
.24	解释为什么不应依赖于氧气不足的征兆来判断氧气是否充足		B1	A1

Knowledge, understanding and proficiency	IMO Reference	Textbooks, Bibliography	Teaching Aid
Required performance			
.25 states that persons have varying susceptibility to oxygen deficiency but that all will suffer if the oxygen content drops below 16% by volume		B1	A1
.26 states that if oxygen is less than 21 % atmosphere may be extremely dangerous unless it is known which gas has replaced the oxygen		B1	A1
.27 describes the symptoms that appear when the oxygen content decreases		B1	A1
Flammability and explosiveness (1 hour)			
.28 states that liquids cannot burn unless flammable vapours are emitted		B1	A1
.29 defines flashpoint		B1	A1
.30 describes the combustion process for hydrocarbons		B1	A1
.31 describes flammable range, lower flammable limit (LFL) and upper flammable limit (UFL)		B1	A1
.32 explains the fire tetrahedron		B1	A1
.33 states that hydrocarbon gas may not be evenly distributed within a space		B1	A1
.34 describes the determination of flashpoint		B1	A1
.35 explains why the flashpoint determined by the open-cup (o.c.) test is somewhat higher that that determined by the closed-cup (c.c.) test		B1	A1
.36 states that for many safety related rules, a division has been made between hydrocarbon liquids with a flashpoint of 60℃ and above and those with a flashpoint below that temperature		B1	A1
.37 identifies a flammability composition diagram and with the aid of the diagram describes the effects of: – gas-freeing – purging – purging and gas-freeing of cargo tanks		B1	A1
.38 lists as source of ignition: – open fires – naked lights – sparks from accidents, work or tools – electrostatic discharges		B1	A1
.39 describes the process of gas evolution in a tank		B1	A1
.40 lists causes for this gas to be expelled from a tank		B1	A1
.41 explains the dangers of gas dispersion for the ship's accommodation and terminal jetties		B1	A1
.42 states that the dispersion of air/vapour mixtures to be below Lflis speeded up by strong winds		B1	A1
Electrostatic hazards (1 hour)			
.43 explains what charge separation is and when it occurs		B1	A1
.44 explains that no hazard exists if the different materials remain in contact and immobile relative to one another		B1	A1
.45 states that a large voltage differential develops after charge separation		B1	A1

知识、理解和熟练	IMO 参考书目	教科书，参考文献	教具
技能要求			
.25 阐述缺氧敏感性因人而异，当氧气的体积含量降到 16%以下时人将受到危害		B1	A1
.26 阐述如果空气中氧气体积含量低于 21%将会非常危险，除非知道哪种气体代替了氧气		B1	A1
.27 阐述当氧气含量降低时出现的征兆		B1	A1
易燃性和易爆性(1 学时)			
.28 阐述只有易燃蒸气散发出来液体才能燃烧		B1	A1
.29 定义闪点		B1	A1
.30 阐述烃类的燃烧过程		B1	A1
.31 阐述易燃范围，可燃下限(LFL)和可燃上限(UFL)		B1	A1
.32 解释着火三要素		B1	A1
.33 阐述烃类气体在一个空间内的分布可能不均匀		B1	A1
.34 阐述闪点的测定		B1	A1
.35 解释在敞口容器实验中测定的闪点高于在封闭容器实验中测定的闪点的原因		B1	A1
.36 阐述在很多相关的安全规则中已经把闪点在 60 ℃及以上的烃类和闪点在 60 ℃以下的烃类做了划分		B1	A1
.37 确定易燃成分图表和根据图表描述以下操作效果 – 除气操作 – 驱气 – 油舱气体的释放和排除		B1	A1
.38 列举火源 – 明火 – 裸灯 – 事故、工作中或工具产生的火星 – 静电放电		B1	A1
.39 阐述油舱中油气产生的过程		B1	A1
.40 列举油舱驱气的原因		B1	A1
.41 解释油气扩散对船舶居住区和码头的危险		B1	A1
.42 阐述在强风作用下可使低于易燃下限的空气 / 油气混合物加速扩散混合		B1	A1
静电危害(1 学时)			
.43 解释什么是电荷分离以及什么时候发生		B1	A1
.44 解释不同材料保持接触并无相对运动的情况下不存在危害		B1	A1
.45 阐述电荷分离后产生较大的电压差		B1	A1

Knowledge, understanding and proficiency	IMO Reference	Textbooks, Bibliography	Teaching Aid
Required performance			
.46 explains the creation of an electric field		B1	A1
.47 describes the charge separation within a conductor in an electrostatic field		B1	A1
.48 describes the process of charge relaxation and factors relevant to relaxation		B1	A1
.49 states that highly conductive materials can retain their charge if insulated by a poor conductor		B1	A1
.50 states that an electrical breakdown between two points, giving rise to a discharge, depends on the strength of the electrostatic field between the points		B1	A1
.51 states that a field strength of 3000 kV per meter is sufficient to cause the breakdown of air or petroleum gases		B1	A1
.52 states that field strength near protrusions is greater than the overall field strength, and that a discharge may occur between a protrusion and the space around it or between a protrusion and another object nearby		B1	A1
.53 states that single-electrode discharges are unlikely to lead to explosions on tankers		B1	A1
.54 gives examples of two-electrode discharges and describes when these discharges may cause ignition		B1	A1
.55 describes the instantaneous release of energy with respect to: – conductors – liquid non-conductors – solid non-conductors – intermediate liquid & solid non-conductors		B1	A1
.56 explains when liquids are considered to be non-conductors		B1	A1
.57 defines and lists static accumulator oils		B1	A1
.58 explains the function of anti-static additives		B1	A1
.59 explains why all distillates must be treated as static accumulator oils unless they contain anti-static additives		B1	A1
.60 lists the processes giving rise to charges within distillates		B1	A1
.61 explains the electrostatic hazards of equipment permanently mounted in the upper part of a tank, and the measures to minimize the hazards		B1	A1
.62 explains how operations can cause a charged mist to develop within a tank		B1	A1
.63 explains the dangers of introducing steam, inert gas or carbon dioxide into a charged atmosphere		B1	A1
Hazards to the marine environment (1 hour)			
.64 explains the damage the oil causes to the marine environment as a result of blanketing, ingestion by sea organisms and the deterioration of amenities			A1
.65 explains the meaning of toxic load			A1
.66 explains that it is when the toxic load, of an area, is exceeded after an incident that causes harm to the marine environment			A1

知识、理解和熟练	IMO 参考书目	教科书，参考文献	教具
技能要求			
.46 解释电场的产生		B1	A1
.47 阐述在静电场中导体内的电荷分离		B1	A1
.48 阐述电荷的放电过程和影响放电的因素		B1	A1
.49 阐述强导电材料在被绝缘体绝缘情况下能保留其电荷		B1	A1
.50 阐述能够引起放电的两点间电击穿取决于两点间静电场的强度		B1	A1
.51 阐述一个 3000 kV/m 强度的电场足够造成空气或油气被击穿		B1	A1
.52 阐述电场突起附近的电场强度要比电场其他部分的强度大，这样在突起和它附近的某空间之间或在突起与它附近的另一物体之间将有可能发生放电现象		B1	A1
.53 阐述在油船上单电极放电不会引起爆炸		B1	A1
.54 举例说明双电极放电并阐述在何时这种放电将可能导致燃烧		B1	A1
.55 阐述与下述材料有关的能量的瞬间释放 – 导体 – 绝缘液体 – 绝缘固体 – 中间液体和固体绝缘体		B1	A1
.56 解释液体在什么情况下可以被认为是绝缘体		B1	A1
.57 定义并列举静电储集性油类		B1	A1
.58 解释防静电添加剂的作用		B1	A1
.59 解释为什么原油所有的馏分都必须作为静电储集性油对待，除非油中添加了防静电添加剂		B1	A1
.60 列举原油蒸馏产生电荷的过程		B1	A1
.61 解释油舱上部所安装设备的静电危害和使危害降到最低的措施		B1	A1
.62 解释在油舱内什么样的操作能产生带电油雾		B1	A1
.63 解释将蒸气、惰性气体或二氧化碳引入带电空气中的危害		B1	A1
对海洋环境的危害(1 学时)			
.64 解释油对海洋环境所造成的破坏，比如油膜大片覆盖海面、被海洋生物摄取、海滨环境退化等			A1
.65 解释什么是毒性负荷			A1
.66 解释当损害海洋环境的事故发生后，何时区域内的毒性负荷会超标			A1

Knowledge, understanding and proficiency	IMO Reference	Textbooks, Bibliography	Teaching Aid
Required performance			
.67 explains that oil can interfere with other legitimate uses of the sea (water inlets, fish farming, fishing industry and coastal tourism)			A1
.68 explains that oil tankers can introduce oil into the sea: – in port, as a result of: – leaking hoses or loading arms – overflow from tanks – equipment failure – improperly set sea valves – at sea, as a result of: – stranding or collision – lightering operations – tank washing and line flushing – de-ballasting – thermal expansion of oil in tanks or piping			A1
.69 states that pollution as a result of stranding and collision constitutes a minor parl, and operational pollution the major part, of marine pollution by oil			A1
.70 describes the causes of air pollution			A1
.71 states that air pollution is now covered under Annex VI of MARPOL 73/78			A1
.72 states that the Baltic Sea Area is now a special area under Annex VI			A1
3 Safety (6 hours)	STCW Code Sec. A-V/1 Pa. 12, 13		
3.1 General precautions (0.5 hour)			
.1 explains the desirability of eliminating both flammable atmospheres and sources of ignition, but that this is not always possible	R8	B1, B5	A1
.2 lists pump-room and tank deck as possibly having flammable atmospheres and the accommodation as possibly having ignition sources	R8	B1, B5	A1
.3 explains that the accommodation should therefore be kept free of flammable gases	R8	B1, B5	A1
.4 explains that the pump-room, cargo deck, deck stores, forecastle, centre castle, dry cargo holds etc. should be kept free ignition sources	R8	B1, B5	A1
.5 states that inert gas increases the safety from fire and explosion but does not obviate the need for precautions	R8	B1, B5	A1
.6 describes the danger of mixing bunkers with volatile cargo	R8	B1, B5	A1
.7 states that smoking may only be permitted at times and in places specified by the Master and that additional restrictions may apply in port	R8	B1, B5	A1
.8 states that matches and lighters may only be used in designated smoking areas and may not be carried in places where hydrocarbon vapours may be encountered	R8	B1, B5	A1

知识、理解和熟练	IMO 参考书目	教科书，参考文献	教具
技能要求			
.67 解释油污染能影响合法利用海洋的其他方面(入海口、水产养殖、捕鱼业以及近海旅游)			A1
.68 解释油船能造成油进入海洋中的原因： – 在港口,有以下原因： – 泄漏孔或装卸吊臂 – 油舱溢油 – 设备故障 – 海水阀设置错误 – 在海上,有以下原因： – 搁浅或碰撞 – 减载操作 – 洗舱和管路冲洗 – 排放压载水 – 油舱或油管中油的热膨胀			A1
.69 阐述在油对海洋的污染中,由于搁浅和碰撞所造成的污染只占少部分,操作性污染才是主要部分			A1
.70 阐述空气污染的原因			A1
.71 阐述空气污染被添加到 MARPOL 公约附则Ⅵ中			A1
.72 阐述波罗的海被附则Ⅵ归为特殊限制区域			A1
3 安全 (6 学时)	STCW 公约 A-V/1 节 12, 13 段		
3.1 一般预防措施 (0.5 学时)			
.1 解释尽可能消除可燃气体或着火源,但总不尽人意	R8	B1, B5	A1
.2 列举可能含有可燃气体的泵舱和油舱甲板,以及可能含有着火源的住舱	R8	B1, B5	A1
.3 解释住舱因此没有可燃气体			
.4 解释泵舱、装卸货甲板、甲板储藏室、前甲板、中甲板、干货舱等处应没有着火源	R8 R8	B1, B5 B1, B5	A1 A1
.5 阐述虽然惰性气体增加了防火和防爆的安全性,但不能不采取预防措施	R8	B1, B5	A1
.6 阐述挥发性货物和燃料混合的危险性	R8	B1, B5	A1
.7 阐述只能在船长指定的时间和地点吸烟并且在港口可能要适用附加限制	R8	B1, B5	A1
.8 阐述火柴和打火机只可以在指定的吸烟区使用,不能带入可能含有原油油气的区域	R8	B1, B5	A1

Knowledge, understanding and proficiency	IMO Reference	Textbooks, Bibliography	Teaching Aid
Required performance			
.9 states that naked lights and open flame are prohibited in places where hydrocarbon vapours may be encountered	R8	B1, B5	A1
.10 explains that care should be taken to ensure the integrity of pump-room lighting, and describes the precautions to be taken if additional lighting is required	R8	B1, B5	A1
.11 states that portable and permanent notices prohibiting smoking and naked lights should be conspicuously exhibited	R8	B1, B5	A1
.12 describes the special precautions for galleys and galley personnel	R8	B1, B5	A1
.13 lists electrical and electronic equipment which should not be permitted on tank decks or other areas where flammable gas may be encountered	R8	B1, B5	A1
.14 explains precautions to be taken before hammering, sand-blasting or using power tools	R8	B1, B5	A1
.15 explains the dangers of non-inerted tanks	R8	B1, B5	A1
.16 lists the precautions to be taken when hot work is to be undertaken in a cargo tank	R8	B1	A1
.17 states that periodic gas tests should be carried out during the work	R8	B1	A1
.18 lists the precautions for hot work on pipes	R8	B1	A1
.19 describes the permits required for work alongside a jetty involving hot work or electrical equipment	R8	B1	A1
.20 states that no maintenance, dismantling or modification should take place at a tanker berth without written permission from the terminal manager	R8	B1	A1
3.2 Entry into enclosed spaces (1.5 hours)			
Pump-rooms			
.1 explains that the ship's SMS requires special procedures to be followed if entering an enclosed space		B1	A1
.2 explains why pump-room constitutes a special hazard		B1	A1
.3 lists the sources of leakage of hydrocarbon vapour as pump-seals, valve glands, drain cocks and mud boxes		B1	A1
.4 explains measures to minimize pump-room hazards		B1	A1
.5 explains why outlet ducts should permit the removal of hydrocarbon vapours from the bottom of the pump-room		B1	A1
.6 lists the precautions for entering pump-rooms		B1	A1
.7 states that the pump-room lifeline and harness should be rigged ready for immediate use, and that approved breathing apparatus and resuscitation equipment should be available in an accessible location		B1	A1
Cargo tanks			
.8 states that no one should enter a cargo tank unless their entry is sanctioned by a responsible officer		B1	A1
.9 lists the precautions to be taken for entering a cargo tank		B1	A1

知识、理解和熟练		IMO 参考书目	教科书，参考文献	教具
技能要求				
.9	阐述在可能含有原油油气的区域,禁用裸灯和明火	R8	B1, B5	A1
.10	解释要注意确保泵舱照明的完整性,并且阐述如果需要附加照明所要采取的预防措施	R8	B1, B5	A1
.11	阐述要在显眼的位置上张贴禁止吸烟和明火的永久公告牌	R8	B1, B5	A1
.12	阐述厨房和厨房人员所需的特殊预防措施	R8	B1, B5	A1
.13	列举不允许在油舱甲板或其他可能含有可燃气体的区域使用的电气和电子设备	R8	B1, B5	A1
.14	解释在敲锈、喷砂或使用动力工具之前应采取的预防措施	R8	B1, B5	A1
.15	解释无惰性气体油舱的危险性	R8	B1, B5	A1
.16	列举当在货油舱进行明火作业时所应采取的措施	R8	B1	A1
.17	阐述在工作中应定期进行气体测试	R8	B1	A1
.18	列举对油管进行明火作业的预防措施	R8	B1	A1
.19	阐述在靠码头进行作业(包括明火作业和电气设备工作)时要得到的许可	R8	B1	A1
.20	阐述没有港口管理者的书面许可，油船在泊位上不能进行改造结构、维修保养、拆卸等作业	R8	B1	A1
3.2 进入封闭空间(1.5 学时)				
泵舱				
.1	解释根据船舶 SMS 的要求进入封闭空间时的特殊程序		B1	A1
.2	解释泵舱有特殊危险的原因		B1	A1
.3	列举烃类蒸气的漏泄源,诸如泵密封、阀盖密封、放残考克和渣油箱		B1	A1
.4	解释使泵舱危险降到最低的措施		B1	A1
.5	解释为什么允许出口管排除泵舱底部产生的烃类蒸气		B1	A1
.6	列举进入泵舱的预防措施		B1	A1
.7	阐述泵舱应配备救生绳索及索具以备急用,以及在容易拿到的地方应配备可用的呼吸器和抢救设备		B1	A1
货油舱				
.8	阐述在没有得到主管驾驶员同意情况下任何人不得进入货油舱		B1	A1
.9	列举进入货油舱所采取的预防措施		B1	A1

Knowledge, understanding and proficiency	IMO Reference	Textbooks, Bibliography	Teaching Aid
Required performance			
Cofferdam, double bottom or other enclosed space			
.10 state that the same precautions apply as for entering cargo tanks		B1	A1
.11 states that toxic gas must be suspected to be present in spaces into which volatile petroleum may have leaked		B1	A1
3.3 Precautions against electrostatic hazard (0.5 hour)			
.1 lists precautions for using equipment in a flammable atmosphere where electrostatic hazard exists	IMO 1	B1	A1
.2 states that non-conductive equipment may be used, provided natural fibre ropes are used	IMO 1	B1	A1
.3 states that no special precautions are necessary within metal pipes	IMO 1	B1	A1
.4 states that no special precautions are necessary in an inert atmosphere	IMO 1	B1	A1
.5 states that high electrostatic potentials are present in an inert atmosphere because of particulates in suspension	IMO 1	B1	A1
.6 states that if there is reason to doubt that the atmosphere is inert the above precautions also apply	IMO 1	B1	A1
.7 states that metal floats do not present a hazard, provided they are earthed by means of conductive guide wires	IMO 1	B1	A1
.8 lists the precautions to be taken when loading and discharging static accumulator oils in non-inerted tank atmospheres	IMO 1	B1	A1
3.4 Gas indicators (1.5 hours)			
.1 describes the operating principle of: – a catalytic-filament combustible-gas indicator – a non-catalytic heated-filament gas indicator – a refractive index meter – chemical indicator tubes – an oxygen meter with paramagnetic sensors – an oxygen analyser with electrolytic sensor – an oxygen analyser with selective chemical absorption liquid		B1, B11	A1
.2 correctly carries out instrument-check procedures and gas measurements, using the above gas indicators		B1, B11	A1
.3 explains why a catalytic-filament combustible-gas indicator is unsuitable for measuring hydrocarbon vapours in an inert atmosphere		B1, B11	A1
3.5 Fire-fighting principles – revision (1 hour)			
.1 lists the methods of controlling a fire as: – removal of oxygen (smothering) – cooling – inhibition of burning process		B1	A1

知识、理解和熟练	IMO 参考书目	教科书,参考文献	教具
技能要求			
隔舱、双层底或其他封闭空间			
.10 阐述进入这些空间的预防措施要与进入货油舱的相同		B1	A1
.11 阐述在这些封闭空间中可能已漏入挥发性的原油而存在有毒气体		B1	A1
3.3 防止静电危害的措施(0.5 学时)			
.1 列举在可燃气体中由于存在静电危害,在使用设备时应采取的预防措施	IMO 1	B1	A1
.2 阐述使用非导电设备和天然纤维绳索	IMO 1	B1	A1
.3 阐述在金属管中不需要特殊的预防措施	IMO 1	B1	A1
.4 阐述在惰性气体中不需要特殊的预防措施	IMO 1	B1	A1
.5 阐述在惰性气体内由于悬浮微粒使其存在高电势	IMO 1	B1	A1
.6 阐述如果有理由怀疑空气中含有惰性气体,也应该采取上述预防措施	IMO 1	B1	A1
.7 阐述只要金属浮体通过导线接地就不存在危险	IMO 1	B1	A1
.8 列举在不充惰油舱中装卸静电储集性油时所采取的预防措施	IMO 1	B1	A1
3.4 气体监测仪(1.5 学时)			
.1 阐述下述仪表的工作原理: – 催化灯丝可燃气体检测仪 – 非催化炽热灯丝气体检测仪 – 折射率测定仪 – 化学显示剂玻璃管 – 顺磁传感元件型测氧仪 – 电解质传感元件型测氧仪 – 选择性化学吸收液型测氧仪		B1, B11	A1
.2 正确运用上述仪表执行仪器检查程序并对气体进行检测		B1, B11	A1
.3 解释催化灯丝可燃气体检测仪不适用于检测惰性气体中烃类气体的原因		B1, B11	A1
3.5 防火原理——修订(1 学时)			
.1 列举防火的方法 – 切断氧气(窒息) – 冷却 – 抑制燃烧过程		B1	A1

Knowledge, understanding and proficiency	IMO Reference	Textbooks, Bibliography	Teaching Aid
Required performance			
.2 states that: – removal of oxygen can be achieved by foam or inert gas – cooling is best effected by water (spray or fog) – inhibition of the burning process is effected by chemical dry powder		B1	A1
.3 describes water as fire-extinguishing agent and states that: – it is readily available – it has an effective cooling action – it should not be used on oil fires as a jet, but as a spray or fog – it should not be directed towards electrical equipment		B1	A1
.4 describes foam as a fire-fighting agent and states that: – there are high-, medium-and low-expansion foams – it has a limited cooling effect – it should not come into contact with electrical equipment – various foam concentrates are incompatible with each other – foam concentrates deteriorate with time		B1	A1
.5 describes carbon dioxide as a fire-fighting agent and states that: – it is an excellent smothering agent – it must be used in conditions where it is not diffused, i.e. in enclosed spaces – it may generate static electricity and should not be injected into explosive atmospheres – personnel should have left the space into which carbon dioxide is to be injected		B1	A1
.6 states that when HALON was used as a fire extinguishing agent, there were two types: – Halon 1211 – used in portable extinguishers – Halon 1301 – used in fixed extinguishers		B1	A1
.7 states that HALON as a fire-fighting agent has been de-commissioned under the Montreal Protocol		B1	A1
.8 states that under IMO guidelines, as of 01.1.1994 HALON has been prohibited on new ships built after this date		B1	A1
.9 states that for existing installations IMO has not set a deadline as all Halon use on board will eventually be de-commissioned based on the de-commissioning of Halon ashore		B1	A1
.10 states that there are regulations for the protection of cargo tanks, the cargo tank deck area and pump-rooms		B1	A1
.11 states that: – the protection of cargo tank deck area shall be achieved by a fixed deck foam system – the protection of cargo tanks shall be achieved by a fixed inert gas system		B1	A1

知识、理解和熟练	IMO 参考书目	教科书，参考文献	教具
技能要求			
.2 阐述 – 通过泡沫或惰性气体可切断氧气 – 用水(束状或雾状)是最好的冷却介质 – 抑制燃烧过程可以用化学干粉灭火剂		B1	A1
.3 阐述水是一种灭火介质并阐述： – 它随时可用 – 它有有效的冷却作用 – 在扑灭燃油失火时，应采用水雾方式而不应用喷射方式 – 它不应直接用于电器设备灭火		B1	A1
.4 阐述泡沫是一种灭火介质并阐述： – 有高、中和低膨胀泡沫 – 它有一定的冷却效果 – 它不应接触电气设备 – 各种泡沫灭火剂彼此不相容 – 泡沫浓缩物时间长了会变质		B1	A1
.5 阐述二氧化碳是一种灭火介质并阐述： – 它是一种极其有效的使火窒息的介质 – 它必须在无法扩散的条件下使用，例如封闭空间 – 它可能产生静电，不应释放到可能发生爆炸的空间 – 人员应撤离要释放二氧化碳的空间		B1	A1
.6 阐述 HALON(卤代烃哈龙)是一种灭火介质，包括两种类型： – HALON1211 用作手提灭火器 – HALON1301 用作固定灭火装置		B1	A1
.7 阐述根据 Montreal 议定书，HALON已经被淘汰		B1	A1
.8 阐述根据 IMO 指南，从 1994 年 1 月 1 日起，禁止新造船装设 HALON 灭火设备		B1	A1
.9 阐述对于已经在船上安装的 HALON灭火设备，IMO 没有对其规定最后的淘汰期限，在船上使用的 HALON将会随着陆地 HALON的淘汰而淘汰。		B1	A1
.10 阐述货油舱、货油舱甲板区域和泵舱的一些消防法规		B1	A1
.11 阐述： – 通过安装甲板泡沫系统保护货油舱甲板区域 – 通过安装惰性气体系统保护货油舱		B1	A1

Knowledge, understanding and proficiency	IMO Reference	Textbooks, Bibliography	Teaching Aid
Required performance			
.12 states that protection of the pump-room shall be achieved by: – a CO_2 system, – a high-expansion foam system, or – a fixed pressure water-spraying system		B1	A1
.13 states that pump-room protection systems must be operated from a position outside the pump-room		B1	A1
.14 states that some tankers may be exempted from the inert gas requirements owing to the size or age		B1	A1
.15 states that an inert gas system is required on all new tankers and most existing tankers of 20,000 dwt and above		B1	A1
3.6 Protective equipment (1 hour)			
.1 acts as a member of a team and takes charge of team exercises with: – tank evacuation equipment – resuscitation equipment – SCBA			A1
4 Pollution prevention (4 hours)	STCW Code Sec. A-V/1 Pa. 9		
4.1 Ship and equipment (0.5 hour)			
.1 states that an oil tanker must comply with constructional requirements with respect to: – segregated ballast capacity – slop–tank capacity – limitation of tank size – survival capability in case of damage – overboard piping arrangements – emergency towing arrangements	R1, R2.2, R7	B7, B9	A1
.2 states that an oil tanker must have approved equipment for: – monitoring and controlling discharges of oil and oil/water mixtures into the sea – establishing the oil/water interface in slop-tanks	R1, R2.2, R7	B7, B9	A1
.3 states that the ship and its equipment shall be maintained in satisfactory condition	R1, R2.2, R7	B7, B9	A1
.4 states that different requirements may apply to certain oil tankers such as: – oil tankers engaged in specific trades – oil tankers having special ballast arrangements – oil tankers carrying asphalt or similar cargoes – oil tankers trading within special areas or within 50 miles of the nearest land – vessels engaged in alternate crude oil/product transport	R1, R2.2, R7	B7, B9	A1
.5 states that such different requirements are reflected in the IOPP Certificate	R1, R2.2, R7	B7, B9	A1

知识、理解和熟练	IMO 参考书目	教科书，参考文献	教具
技能要求			
.12 阐述泵舱的保护将采取以下措施来实现：		B1	A1
– CO_2 系统			
– 高膨胀率泡沫系统			
– 固定式压力喷水系统			
.13 阐述泵舱消防系统必须在泵舱之外操作		B1	A1
.14 阐述一些油船根据它的尺寸或船龄可以不装设惰性气体系统		B1	A1
.15 阐述在所有的新造船和目前存在的两万吨及以上的船舶上必须装设惰性气体系统		B1	A1
3.6 保护设备(1 学时)			
.1 小组中的一员或一组应接受下列设备操作的培训			A1
– 油舱逃生设备			
– 抢救设备			
– 自给式呼吸器			
4 污染的预防(4 学时)	STCW 公约 A-V/1 节 9 段		
4.1 船舶和设备(0.5 学时)			
.1 阐述油船在结构上必须满足下列相关要求：	R1, R2.2, R7	B7, B9	A1
– 隔离压载舱的容量			
– 渣油舱容量			
– 油舱尺寸的限制			
– 破坏性事故中的逃生能力			
– 舷外管路设备			
– 应急拖曳设备			
.2 阐述油船必须有批准的设备以用于：	R1, R2.2, R7	B7, B9	A1
– 监控油或油水混合物的入海排放			
– 在溢油舱中建立油水界面			
.3 阐述船舶及其设备应保持在良好的状态	R1, R2.2, R7	B7, B9	A1
.4 阐述不同的要求适用于不同的油船，比如：	R1, R2.2, R7	B7, B9	A1
– 特种油船			
– 压载舱布置特殊的油船			
– 运输沥青或相似货物的油船			
– 在特殊区域或据最近陆地不超过 50 海里的油船			
– 原油 / 成品油油船			
.5 阐述这些不同要求体现在国际防油污证书(IOPP)中	R1, R2.2, R7	B7, B9	A1

Knowledge, understanding and proficiency	IMO Reference	Textbooks, Bibliography	Teaching Aid
Required performance			
4.2 Operational pollution (1 hour)			
At sea			
.1 states that load-on-top (LOT) procedures are normally allowed on oil tankers	R7		A1
.2 states that the discharge provisions applicable to oil must be complied with	R7		A1
.3 states that, when discharge into the sea in compliance with the discharge provisions is not possible, oil and oily mixtures should be discharged to shore reception facilities	R7		A1
.4 states that reception facilities require notice, including information on produce and quantity	R7		A1
.5 states that the Masters must send a report to the Flag State in case of any inadequacies observed regarding reception facilities	R7		A1
.6 states that sea surface and discharge outlets must be observed when discharging ballast or decanting slop-tanks	R7		A1
.7 states that the surface of clean or segregated ballast must be observed prior to discharge	R7		A1
.8 states that the pumps must be running before opening sea inlets to prevent pipeline contents polluting the sea	R7		A1
In port			
.9 states that: – moorings must be kept adjusted when a ship is alongside to prevent the ship from ranging – oil/water levels must be watched in cargo and slop-tanks when handling ballast or cargo – over side discharge scuppers must be plugged when handling cargo or ballast, or when bunkering – sea valves must be closed and secured during cargo work – a watch must be kept both at the manifold and when patrolling the deck			A1
– hoses and loading arms must be drained before disconnecting – after tank and pipe stripping, the residues should be discharged by means of the small-diameter line (if fitted)			A1
4.3 Oil Record Book (ORB) (1 hour)			
.1 states that the ship is provided with an ORB	R2.2, R7		A1
.2 states that the format of ORB is uniform and that all operations involving oil and oily mixtures should be recorded, where possible in coded entries	R2.2, R7		A1
.3 states that, where the use of coded entries is not possible, entries should be recorded in English or French in addition to the national language (Flag State)	R2.2, R7		A1
.4 explains that coded entries and the use of English or French are to facilitate inspection by foreign authorities	R2.2, R7		A1

知识、理解和熟练	IMO 参考书目	教科书，参考文献	教具
技能要求			
4.2 操作性污染(1 学时)			
在海上			
.1 阐述原油船通常允许采用 LOT 程序	R7		A1
.2 阐述必须按照关于油的一些排放规则进行操作	R7		A1
.3 阐述当不能按照排放规则进行排放时，油和油水混合物应排放到陆地上的接收设备中	R7		A1
.4 阐述接收设备所要求的注意事项，包括产品和数量	R7		A1
.5 阐述船长在注意到接收设备接收能力不足时必须向船旗国报告	R7		A1
.6 阐述在排放压载水或清空溢流舱时一定要注意观察海面和排出口	R7		A1
.7 阐述在排放之前一定要察看专用或清洁压载水的表面是否有油	R7		A1
.8 阐述为防止管路中的液体对海洋造成污染，在打开泵的海水进口阀前，泵应先起动	R7		A1
在港口			
.9 阐述：			A1
– 当船舶靠泊时必须要注意调整其系泊防止移位			
– 在处理压载水或装卸货时必须要察看油舱和溢油舱中的油 / 水位			
– 装卸货油、处理压载水或加油时应将排水孔堵上			
– 在进行货油操作时海水阀应可靠的关闭			
– 在甲板巡班时必须细心、必须察看货油总管			
– 必须在软管和装卸臂在拆开连接之前把油放掉			A1
– 油舱和管系冲洗后，残留物应通过小管径管子(如果安装了)排放			
4.3 油类记录簿(1 学时)			
.1 阐述船上配备有油类记录簿	R2.2, R7		A1
.2 阐述油类记录簿格式统一，并且根据指定的语言记录所有油类及含油混合物的操作	R2.2, R7		A1
.3 如果指定的语言不可用，记载内容除用本国语言(船旗国)外还应用英语或法语作记录	R2.2, R7		A1
.4 解释指定的语言和使用英语或法语是为了方便外国主管机关检查	R2.2, R7		A1

Knowledge, understanding and proficiency	IMO Reference	Textbooks, Bibliography	Teaching Aid
Required performance			
.5 states that foreign authorities may ask to inspect the book and have copies of entries certified as true entries by the master, and that the ship is required to co-operate in these matters	R2.2, R7		A1
.6 states that ORB must be kept on board in a readily available location and must be preserved for a period of three years following the date of last entry	R2.2, R7		A1
4.4 Action in case of oil spills (1 hour)			
At sea			
.1 states that all oil spills must be reported	R6, R7		A1
.2 states that the initial report must be sent to the nearest coastal State as soon as possible and by the fastest telecommunication means available	R6, R7		A1
.3 lists the contents of initial report as: – name of ship – frequency or radio channel guarded – name, address and contact details of owner and representative – type of ship – date and time (UTC) of the incident – description of the incident, including damage sustained – ship's position, course, speed, as appropriate at time of incident – type of oil involved – other cargo carried	R6, R7		A1
.4 states that a follow-up report should be sent as further details become available	R6, R7		A1
In port			
.5 lists the following actions to be taken: – duty officer to shut down pumping and close valves from which oil is escaping – duty officer to call master and chief officer – duty officer to alert engine room and if necessary have them pressurise the fire main – chief officer to prepare fire-fighting gear if necessary – Master to inform terminal – if the spill is on deck, chief officer to organize treatment with absorbent material	IMO 1, IMO 8		A1
4.5 Air pollution (0.5 hour)			
.1 explains that air pollution may be caused by inert gas or hydrocarbon gas finding their way into the atmosphere because of: – breathing or venting of loaded tanks – purging or gas-freeing operations – loading or ballasting cargo tanks		B1	A1

知识、理解和熟练	IMO 参考书目	教科书，参考文献	教具
技能要求			
5 阐述国外主管机关可能要求检查油类记录簿并可能将任何记录制成副本并要求船长证明该副本是该项纪录的正确副本,这些工作要求船方要给予配合	R2.2, R7		A1
.6 阐述油类记录簿应存放于船上可随时取来检查的地方并且根据最后一页的日期在船上保留三年	R2.2, R7		A1
4.4 溢油处置措施(1 学时)			
在海上			
.1 阐述所有的溢油事故都必须报告	R6, R7		A1
.2 阐述最初报告应通过最快的通信方式尽快发给最近的沿岸国	R6, R7		A1
.3 最初报告的内容包括: – 船名 – 监听电台频率或无线电频道 – 船东或船东代表的姓名、地址及联系信息 – 船舶类型 – 发生事故的日期和时间 – 事故简况,包括遭受的破坏 – 发生事故时船舶位置、航线、航速 – 溢油的种类 – 装载的其他货物	R6, R7		A1
.4 阐述当更多的信息可用时发送跟踪报告	R6, R7		A1
在港口			
.5 列举以下所采取的措施: – 发生油泄漏时,值班驾驶员应停掉泵,关闭阀门 – 值班驾驶员告知船长和大副 – 值班驾驶员通知机舱,如有必要使其启动主消防设备 – 如有必要,大副准备灭火用具 – 船长通知码头 – 如果发生甲板溢油,大副组织人员用吸油材料处理	IMO 1, IMO 8		A1
4.5 空气污染(0.5 学时)			
.1 解释因为以下原因使得惰性气体和油气会进入空气而对大气造成污染: – 油舱的吸排气 – 驱气操作 – 向货油舱中装货或加压载水		B1	A1

Knowledge, understanding and proficiency	IMO Reference	Textbooks, Bibliography	Teaching Aid
Required performance			
.2 states that now air pollution is covered under Annex VI of MARPOL 73/78		B1	A1
.3 states that Baltic Sea Area is a special area under Annex VI of MARPOL 73/78		B1	A1
.4 states that some ports have specific regulations (other than stated above) prohibiting or limiting air pollution		B1	A1
.5 states that air pollution prevention measures may take the form of: – on board ship procedures to contain vapour and inert gas – the use of vapour return lines		B1	A1
.6 describes containment procedures as being the displacement of vapour and gas from tanks being filled (i.e. ballasted) to tanks being emptied (i.e. discharged), using common vent piping as the gas-transfer line		B1	A1
.7 explains that the tank atmosphere pressure must be watched since the rate of ballasting is unlikely to equal the rate of discharging		B1	A1
.8 recognizes special procedures apply when loading or discharging using vapour emission control systems		B1	A1
5 Oil tanker design and equipment (8 hours)	STCW Code Sec. A-V//1 Pa. 10		
5.1 Construction (0.5 hour)			
Safety considerations			
.1 states that an oil tanker can be divided into fore part, tank area and after part, and the tank area is separated, from fore and after parts, by means of cofferdams	R1, R7	B7, B8	A1
.2 states that accommodation spaces, main cargo control stations and service spaces must be positioned aft of the tank area, but that some exceptions to this rule are possible	R1, R7	B7, B8	A1
.3 states that the navigation bridge may be fitted above the tank area where necessary, but that there must be an open space between the navigation bridge and the cargo tank deck	R1, R7	B7, B8	A1
.4 states that means must be provided to keep deck spills away from the accommodation	R1, R7	B7, B8	A1
.5 states that entrances, air inlets and openings to accommodation, service spaces and control stations shall not face the cargo area	R1, R7	B7, B8	A1
.6 states that windows and side scuttles facing the cargo area and for some distance away from the cargo area on each side must be of non-opening type	R1, R7	B7, B8	A1
.7 states that special requirements have been laid down for the fire integrity of bulkheads and decks of oil tankers	R1, R7	B7, B8	A1
.8 states that oil tanker design will change in future as double-hull phasing in has commenced	R1, R7	B7, B8	A1
.9 states that double-hull phase in is being effected under IMO regulations as well as OPA 90	R1, R7	B7, B8	A1

知识、理解和熟练	IMO 参考书目	教科书,参考文献	教具
技能要求			
.2 阐述现在空气污染已纳入 MARPOL 公约附则Ⅵ中		B1	A1
.3 阐述在附则Ⅵ中将波罗的海规定为特殊限制区域		B1	A1
.4 阐述有些港口有禁止或限制大气污染的特殊规定		B1	A1
.5 阐述防止大气污染的措施可采取以下形式: – 在船上采取措施容纳油气和惰性气体 – 使用油气回收管		B1	A1
.6 阐述用通用透气管作为气体输送管,将油类蒸汽和气体从满载油舱(例如装有压载水)排放到空油舱中(例如已完成排放)作为控制气体排放的措施		B1	A1
.7 解释因为压载速率和排放速率不一定相等所以必须监视油舱压力		B1	A1
.8 当使用蒸汽排放控制系统装卸货时,应采用适用的特殊操作规程		B1	A1
5 油船设计和设备(8 学时)	STCW 公约 A-V/1 节 10 段		
5.1 结构(0.5 学时)			
安全考虑			
.1 阐述油船分成前部、油舱区和后部,油舱区通过隔舱与船的前、后部分开	R1, R7	B7, B8	A1
.2 阐述生活区、货油控制站和服务空间必须位于油舱区的后部,但也可能有例外	R1, R7	B7, B8	A1
.3 如果必要的话阐述驾驶台可以安装在油舱区域的上部,但在驾驶台和货油舱甲板之间要有开放的空间	R1, R7	B7, B8	A1
.4 阐述使甲板溢油远离生活区所必须采取的措施	R1, R7	B7, B8	A1
.5 阐述生活区、服务区和控制站的入口、空气进出口都不应朝向油舱区	R1, R7	B7, B8	A1
.6 阐述面向货油区的窗户和舷窗和两舷距货油舱有一定距离的舷窗必须是封闭式的	R1, R7	B7, B8	A1
.7 阐述针对油船舱壁和甲板的防火整体性,有特殊要求	R1, R7	B7, B8	A1
.8 阐述未来油船的设计会发生改变,因为已进入双层底时代	R1, R7	B7, B8	A1
.9 阐述油船双层底结构设计受 IMO 规则和美国 90 油污法案影响	R1, R7	B7, B8	A1

Knowledge, understanding and proficiency	IMO Reference	Textbooks, Bibliography	Teaching Aid
Required performance			
.10 states that double-hull phase in is dependent on the year of build of the ship and that by 2015 all tankers will be double-hulled	R1, R7	B7, B8	A1
.11 states that under IMO rules the alternative mid-deck design is also acceptable	R1, R7	B6	A1
.12 explains the merits and demerits of double hull and mid deck tanker designs	R1, R7	B6	A1
.13 draws the cross section of: – double hull tanker – mid-deck tanker	R1, R7	B6	A1
.14 states that as per revised Annex I of MARPOL 73/78, from 2007 the pump-room will have a double bottom protection	R1, R7	B6	A1
Environmental considerations			
.15 defines segregated ballast tank (SBT)	R2.2	B6	A1
.16 describes which oil tankers must be provided with SBT	R2.2	B6	A1
.17 describes that the capacity and distribution of SBT must be such that: – ballast is sufficient for all but severe weather conditions – at all stages of the voyage, the ship is trimmed by stern with the propeller submerged	R2.2	B6	A1
.18 states that product tankers of 40,000 tonnes DWT and above built before 1980 may, in lieu of SBT, operate with dedicated clean ballast tanks (CBT)	R2.2	B6	A1
.19 states that crude oil tankers of 40,000 tonnes DWT and above built before 1980 may, in lieu of SBT, be equipped and operated with a crude oil washing (COW) system	R2.2	B6	A1
.20 defines CBT	R2.2	B6	A1
.21 states that capacity requirements of CBT are similar to those of SBT	R2.2	B6	A1
.22 explains how SBT and CBT contribute towards the protection of the marine environment	R2.2	B6	A1
.23 lists the advantages of SBT over CBT	R2.2	B6	A1
.24 explains how COW contributes towards the protection of the marine environment	R2.2	B6	A1
.25 states that crude oil tankers of 20,000 tonnes DWT and above built after 1979 must be provided with and operate a COW system in addition to SBT	R2.2	B6	A1
.26 states that oil tankers may have been provided with SBT even if not required to do so, but the capacity need not necessarily comply with the international requirements	R2.2	B6	A1
.27 states that, on tankers built after 1979, the location of SBT offers protection to some extent against oil spills caused by stranding or collision	R2.2	B6	A1
.28 states that subdivision and stability requirements for oil tankers are intended to provide survival capability in case of stranding or collision damage	R2.2	B6	A1
.29 states that there are requirements with respect to the number and minimum capacity of slop-tanks	R2.2	B6	A1

知识、理解和熟练	IMO 参考书目	教科书,参考文献	教具
技能要求			
.10 阐述双层底结构与油船建造的年份有关并且规定在 2015 年后所有的油船都要有双层底结构	R1, R7	B7,B8	A1
.11 阐述根据 IMO 规则可替换的中间甲板结构也是允许的	R1, R7	B6	A1
.12 解释双层底和中间甲板结构各自的优缺点	R1, R7	B6	A1
.13 画出截面图: – 双层底结构 – 中间甲板结构	R1, R7	B6	A1
.14 阐述根据修订的 MARPOL 附则 Ⅰ,从 2007 年开始,泵间也要求为双层底结构	R1, R7	B6	A1
环境考虑			
.15 定义专用压载舱	R2.2	B6	A1
.16 阐述哪种油船必须设有专用压载舱(SBT)	R2.2	B6	A1
.17 解释专用压载舱的容积和分布必须满足如下要求: – 压载量在各种航行条件下都应满足要求,除了恶劣海况 – 在所有航行状况下,船舶的尾吃水应满足尾部螺旋桨浸没在水中的要求	R2.2	B6	A1
.18 阐述 1980 年前建造的 40000 吨及以上的成品油船,可以采用清洁压载舱(CBT) 替代专用压载舱	R2.2	B6	A1
.19 阐述 1980 年前建造的 40000 吨及以上的原油油船,可装设原油洗舱(COW)系统以替代专用压载舱	R2.2	B6	A1
.20 定义 CBT	R2.2	B6	A1
.21 阐述 CBT 的容积要求与 SBT 的相近	R2.2	B6	A1
.22 解释 CBT 和 SBT 如何保护海洋环境	R2.2	B6	A1
.23 列举与 CBT 相比 SBT 的优点	R2.2	B6	A1
.24 解释 COW 如何实现对海洋环境的保护	R2.2	B6	A1
.25 阐述 1979 年后建造的 20000 吨及以上的原油船除设有 SBT 外还必须设有 COW 系统	R2.2	B6	A1
.26 阐述即使不做要求的油船也可装设 SBT,但其容积可不满足国际规则的要求	R2.2	B6	A1
.27 阐述 1979 年以后建造的油船,专用压载舱的位置可在一定程度上防止因搁浅或碰撞而造成溢油事故	R2.2	B6	A1
.28 阐述对油船更细的要求和稳性的要求是在发生搁浅和碰撞破坏时提供逃生的能力	R2.2	B6	A1
.29 阐述对于溢流舱数量和最小舱容有相关要求	R2.2	B6	A1

Knowledge, understanding and proficiency	IMO Reference	Textbooks, Bibliography	Teaching Aid
Required performance			
.30 states that the applicability of some IMO requirements depends on the age or size of the oil tanker	R2.2	B6	A1
.31 states that all of the above requirements apply equally to combination carriers	R2.2	B6	A1
.32 states that there are additional requirements for combination carriers concerning slop-tanks and cargo lines in wing tanks	R2.2	B6	A1
.33 states that tankers aged 5 years and over are subject to an enhanced survey programme	R2.2	B6	A1
5.2 Pumping, piping and discharge arrangements (1.5 hours)			
.1 describes an oil tanker's cargo system	R2.2	B2	A1
.2 explains the difference between a free-flow tanker and a pipeline tanker	R2.2	B2	A1
.3 explains the advantages and limitations of the free-flow system	R2.2	B2	A1
.4 states that: – pipeline systems on board tankers differ in their degree of sophistication, depending on employment of the tanker – ULCC and VLCC have relatively simple pipeline system – some product (parcel) tankers may have very sophisticated pumping and piping system	R2.2	B2	A1
.5 states that all oil tankers require a high overboard line, enabling discharge above the waterline	R2.2	B2	A1
.6 describes the 'stripping system'	R2.2	B2	A1
.7 states that stripping is essential to reduce cargo residues in tanks and pipelines	R2.2	B2	A1
.8 states that stripping system is important to handle tank draining when tank washing	R2.2	B2	A1
.9 states that not all tankers have separate stripping systems	R2.2	B2	A1
.10 states that large crude oil tankers need to have a means of emptying pump lines and discharging the residues via a special small-diameter pipeline	R2.2	B2	A1
.11 describes: – a gate or sluice valve – a butterfly valve – a non-return valve – an angle stop valve	R2.2	B2	A1
.12 explains that a pressure-relief valve is needed only for positive displacement pumps and in the discharge of the pump	R2.2	B2	A1
.13 explains that the pressure-relief valve re-circulates the oil into the suction side of the pump	R2.2	B2	A1
.14 explains that a non-return valve is fitted on the discharge side of the pump to prevent oil flowing back when the pump stops	R2.2	B2	A1

知识、理解和熟练	IMO 参考书目	教科书,参考文献	教具
技能要求			
.30 阐述 IMO 相关要求的适用性取决于油船的船龄和尺寸	R2.2	B6	A1
.31 阐述以上所有要求同样适用于混装船	R2.2	B6	A1
.32 阐述对于混装船,针对其污液舱和边舱的货油管路有附加要求	R2.2	B6	A1
.33 阐述 5 年及以上的油船要增加检查程序	R2.2	B6	A1
5.2 泵浦、管路和排放设备(1.5 学时)			
.1 阐述油船货油系统	R2.2	B2	A1
.2 解释自流油船和管装油船的差别	R2.2	B2	A1
.3 解释自流系统的优缺点	R2.2	B2	A1
.4 阐述: – 根据油船的用途,管路系统的复杂程度也不一样 – ULCC 和 VLCC 的管系相对简单 – 某些成品油船(多个小型隔舱)可能有非常复杂的泵和管系	R2.2	B2	A1
.5 阐述所有油船要求有高的舷外管,以使在水线以上进行排放	R2.2	B2	A1
.6 阐述“扫舱系统”	R2.2	B2	A1
.7 阐述扫舱能有效地减少油舱和管系中的残油	R2.2	B2	A1
.8 阐述在洗舱时扫舱系统对处理油舱残渣非常重要	R2.2	B2	A1
.9 阐述不是所有油舱都有独立扫舱系统	R2.2	B2	A1
.10 阐述大型油船需有能力排空泵管系以及通过小口径管系排放残留物	R2.2	B2	A1
.11 描述: – 闸阀 – 蝶阀 – 止回阀 – 角形截止阀	R2.2	B2	A1
.12 解释仅需在容积式泵的排放端设减压阀	R2.2	B2	A1
.13 解释油通过减压阀后又流回泵吸入端	R2.2	B2	A1
.14 解释止回阀装在泵的排出端以防止停泵时油的回流	R2.2	B2	A1

Knowledge, understanding and proficiency	IMO Reference	Textbooks, Bibliography	Teaching Aid
Required performance			
.15 explains why many deep-well pumps do not have non-return valves	R2.2	B2	A1
.16 describes an eductor with the aid of a drawing	R2.2	B2	A1
.17 explains that an eductor is frequently used for discharging ballast and stripping tank-washing slops	R2.2	B2	A1
5.3 Cargo heating systems (0.5 hour)			
.1 lists oils which may require heating as: – bitumen – heavy lubricating oils – high pour-point gas oils – heavy fuel oils – some crude oils		B2	A1
.2 states that steam heating coils are generally used for heating cargo tanks		B2	A1
.3 states that steel heating coils suffer serious corrosion attack from crude oil cargoes but may be used for cargoes of lubricating oil		B2	A1
.4 explains why wing tanks generally require more steam than cargo tanks		B2	A1
.5 states that bitumen requires far more heat than other oils and may therefore only be carried in special ships		B2	A1
.6 states that slop-tanks are heated to facilitate the separation of water and oil		B2	A1
5.4 Venting arrangements (1 hour)			
.1 states that petroleum gas is expelled from cargo tank vents during many cargo handling and associated operations	R1	B1	A1
.2 states the importance of such gases being sufficiently dispersed to prevent the creation of flammable gas mixtures	R1	B1	A1
.3 states that there can be flammable gas concentrations external to cargo tanks in the case of volatile cargoes with a high vapour pressure	R1	B1	A1
.4 lists a few examples of such cargoes and situations which lead to gas evolution	R1	B1	A1
.5 explains gas evolution and venting during loading	R1	B1	A1
.6 lists other operations leading to venting of gas	R1	B1	A1
.7 explains gas dispersion and variables affecting gas dispersion	R1	B1	A1
.8 states that wind can assist in gas dispersion	R1	B1	A1
.9 states that the venting system of cargo tanks is entirely distinct from such systems in other compartments of the ship	R1	B1	A1
.10 states that venting arrangements may be independent for each cargo tank or combined with those for other tanks	R1	B1	A1
.11 states that, in the latter case, means are provided to isolate each cargo tank	R1	B1	A1

知识、理解和熟练	IMO 参考书目	教科书,参考文献	教具
技能要求			
.15 解释许多深井泵没有止回阀的原因	R2.2	B2	A1
.16 描述有引射流体的喷射泵	R2.2	B2	A1
.17 解释喷射泵经常用来排放压载水和洗舱	R2.2	B2	A1
5.3 货油加热系统(0.5 学时)			
.1 列举需要加热的油: – 沥青 – 重滑油 – 高倾点轻油 – 重燃料油 – 某些原油		B2	A1
.2 阐述蒸气加热盘管常用于油舱加热		B2	A1
.3 阐述钢质加热盘管将遭受来自原油货物的严重腐蚀侵害,但可用于滑油		B2	A1
.4 解释边舱对蒸气的需求通常比中间舱大的原因		B2	A1
.5 阐述沥青对于蒸气的需求要远远大于其他油类,因此它只能用特殊的船来运输		B2	A1
.6 阐述污液舱应加热有利于油水分离		B2	A1
5.4 通风布置(1 学时)			
.1 阐述在进行多项货物操作时原油气体通过油舱透气口排出	R1	B1	A1
.2 阐述有效地驱散这种油气可防止产生可燃混合气体的重要性	R1	B1	A1
.3 阐述在挥发性货油舱上部空间油气压力较高时,在油舱外部也能形成一定浓度的可燃混合气	R1	B1	A1
.4 举例说明何种货油及在何种情况下能形成可燃混合气体	R1	B1	A1
.5 解释在装货期间油气的形成及透气	R1	B1	A1
.6 列举排除油气的其他操作	R1	B1	A1
.7 解释油气的扩散和影响油气扩散的因素	R1	B1	A1
.8 阐述风有助于油气扩散	R1	B1	A1
.9 阐述油舱的透气系统与船上其他舱室的通风系统完全不同	R1	B1	A1
.10 阐述每个舱可有各自独立的透气系统,也可以是几个舱共用透气系统	R1	B1	A1
.11 阐述共用透气系统时,应有油舱相互隔离的方法	R1	B1	A1

Knowledge, understanding and proficiency	IMO Reference	Textbooks, Bibliography	Teaching Aid
Required performance			
.12 states that venting system must be provided with devices to prevent the passage of flame into the cargo tanks	R1	B1	A1
.13 states that provisions must be made to guard against liquid rising in the venting system to a height which would exceed the design head of the cargo tanks	R1	B1	A1
.14 states that such provision shall include high-level alarms or overflow control systems, together with gauging devices and tank-filling control procedures	R1	B1	A1
.15 states that the height of vent openings must be not less than 2 meters above the deck	R1	B1	A1
.16 states that distances above deck and away from openings are dependent on the fitting of high-velocity vents	R1	B1	A1
.17 states that PV valves must be fitted	R1	B1	A1
.18 explains the reason for, and the functioning of PV valves	R1	B1	A1
.19 explains, with the aid of a drawing, the functioning of purge pipes	R1	B1	A1
.20 states that as per SOLAS amendments, tankers carrying petroleum products require secondary means of venting	R1	B1	A1
.21 states that the above amendment is applicable to tankers that carry petroleum products with a flashpoint less than 60°C or crude oil	R1	B1	A1
.22 explains the secondary means of venting	R1	B1	A1
.23 explains vapour recovery line construction arrangements as per MARPOL Annex VI	R1	B1	A1
5.5 Level gauges (0.5 hour)			
.1 describes, with aid of drawing, the operating principle of: – mechanically operated float gauges – electrically powered servo-operated gauges – electrical capacitance gauges – bubbler gauges – pneumatic or hydraulic level gauges using a closed cell – other differential-pressure-type gauges – ultrasonic and sonic gauges – radioactive gauges – surface-sensing-type-gauges			A1
.2 describes the terms 'accuracy' and 'repeatability' and the factors influencing both			A1
5.6 Environmental protection equipment (4 hours) *In case a simulator is provided, training for Sec. 5.6 can be done on a simulator (suggested Ex.6, 7)*			
.1 states that compliance with discharge provisions is further ensured by an oil discharge monitoring and control system	R2.1, R10	B4	A1
.2 describes what the system must be able to do	R2.1, R10	B4	A1
.3 describes the meaning of starting interlock	R2.1, R10	B4	A1
.4 describes the effects of malfunctioning of the system	R2.1, R10	B4	A1

知识、理解和熟练	IMO 参考书目	教科书,参考文献	教具
技能要求			
.12 阐述透气系统必须设有防止火焰进入油舱的装置	R1	B1	A1
.13 阐述在油舱顶部必须设计超过油舱一定高度的透气系统防止液体从此溢出	R1	B1	A1
.14 阐述这种设备应包括高位报警和溢油控制系统,还要加上测量装置和货油加载控制程序	R1	B1	A1
.15 阐述透气口的高度至少应高出甲板 2 米	R1	B1	A1
.16 高出甲板及远离舱口的距离取决于所安装的高速透气口设备	R1	B1	A1
.17 阐述必须安装 PV 阀	R1	B1	A1
.18 解释安装 PV 阀的原因和作用	R1	B1	A1
.19 借助图纸解释扫气管的作用	R1	B1	A1
.20 阐述根据 SOLAS 公约要求,装载成品油的货舱需要二次透气	R1	B1	A1
.21 阐述上述公约要求适用于装载闪点低于 60℃的成品油以及原油的船舶	R1	B1	A1
.22 解释透气的第二种方式	R1	B1	A1
.23 解释 MARPOL 公约附则Ⅵ中要求的蒸气回收系统	R1	B1	A1
5.5 液位计(0.5 学时)			
.1 借助图纸解释下列设备的工作原理 – 机械浮子式测量装置 – 电动伺服测量装置 – 电容量测量装置 – 吹气式测量装置 – 使用闭式单元的气动或液压液位测量装置 – 其他压差型测量装置 – 超声波测量装置 – 放射性测量装置 – 表面敏感型测量装置			A1
.2 阐述术语“精确性”和“再现性”及其影响因素			A1
5.6 环境保护设备(4 学时)			
如果有模拟器,则第 5.6 节的培训可在模拟器上进行			
.1 阐述通过排油监控系统进一步确保油的排放符合规定	R2.1, R10	B4	A1
.2 描述这种监控系统的功能	R2.1, R10	B4	A1
.3 说明起动连锁含义	R2.1, R10	B4	A1
.4 说明系统故障的影响	R2.1, R10	B4	A1

Knowledge, understanding and proficiency	IMO Reference	Textbooks, Bibliography	Teaching Aid
Required performance			
.5 states that the malfunctioning equipment should be repaired before the next ballast voyage	R2.1, R10	B4	A1
.6 states how long records must be maintained	R2.1, R10	B4	A1
.7 states that any failure or malfunctioning of the equipment must be recorded in the oil record book	R2.1, R10	B4	A1
.8 lists the different principles involved in measuring oil content as ultraviolet fluorescence, turbidity measurement, light absorption, gas measurement and infra-red absorption	R2.1, R10	B4	A1
.9 lists the advantages and disadvantages of the principles involved	R2.1, R10	B4	A1
.10 states that effective LOT procedures depend on determination of the oil/water interface in slop-tanks and other factors	R2.1, R10	B4	A1
.11 explains, with the aid of drawing, the operating principle of a portable oil/water interface detector	R2.1, R10	B4	A1
6 Oil tanker operations (9 hours)	STCW Code Sec. A-V/1 Pa. 10, 12		
6.1 General precautions (1 hour)			
Superstructure			
.1 lists operations during which openings in the superstructure should be closed		B1	A1
.2 describes measures to prevent flammable gas entering the ventilation system		B1	A1
.3 describes measures taken to adjust the air-conditioning system		B1	A1
.4 explains that precautions are also necessary when tankers conduct cargo-and ballast-handling, purging, gas-freeing or tank-cleaning operations in adjacent berths		B1	A1
.5 states that the number of crafts coming alongside should be kept to a minimum		B1	A1
.6 states that all cargo tank lids should be closed and secured during the operations referred to under objective 6.1.1		B1	A1
.7 describes what must be done with respect to sighting and ullage ports, cargo vent outlets and high-velocity vents		B1	A1
.8 states that covers of tank-washing openings should only be removed from those tanks in which tank-cleaning or gas-freeing operations are taking place		B1	A1
.9 states that the lids of SBT should be kept closed when cargo or ballast is handled, to prevent the drawing in of flammable gas		B1	A1
Pump-rooms		B1	
.10 states that tanks or lines containing petroleum should not be drained into the pump-room bilges		B1	A1
.11 states that the pump-room ventilation system must be in operation throughout cargo handling		B1	A1

知识、理解和熟练	IMO 参考书目	教科书,参考文献	教具
技能要求			
.5 阐述下一空载航行前故障设备必须修理好	R2.1, R10	B4	A1
.6 阐述记录的保存期限	R2.1, R10	B4	A1
.7 阐述设备的任何故障在油类记录簿中都必须有记录	R2.1, R10	B4	A1
.8 列举测定燃油成分时使用的工作原理:紫外线荧光、浊度测量、光吸收、气体测量和红外吸收法	R2.1, R10	B4	A1
.9 列举这些工作原理的优缺点	R2.1, R10	B4	A1
.10 阐述有效的 LOT 程序取决于溢流舱中油 / 水界面的测定或其他因素	R2.1, R10	B4	A1
.11 借助图纸解释便携式油 / 水界面探测器的工作原理	R2.1, R10	B4	A1
6 油船操作(9 学时)	STCW 公约 A-V/1 节 10, 12 段		
6.1 一般预防(1 学时)			
上部结构			
.1 列举在某些操作过程中哪些居住区的开口应该关闭		B1	A1
.2 阐述防止可燃气体进入通风系统的方法		B1	A1
.3 阐述所采取的调整空调系统的方法		B1	A1
.4 解释当在码头上油船进行货油操作和压载水操作、清洗、气体释放或油舱清洗操作时,有必要采取适当的预防措施		B1	A1
.5 阐述同时靠港船舶的数量应保持最小		B1	A1
.6 阐述当进行 6.1.1 所示的操作时所有货舱舱盖应被关闭和固定		B1	A1
.7 描述针对观察口、货物透气口及高速透气口的必做工作		B1	A1
.8 阐述洗舱机盖在进行油舱清洗或气体释放时才应移开		B1	A1
.9 阐述专用压载舱盖在装货油或压载水操作时应保持关闭,以防止可燃性气体的吸入		B1	A1
泵舱		B1	
.10 阐述含油油舱或管路不应放残至泵舱舱底。		B1	A1
.11 阐述泵舱通风系统在整个货油操作过程中必须持续工作		B1	A1

Knowledge, understanding and proficiency	IMO Reference	Textbooks, Bibliography	Teaching Aid
Required performance			
Cargo hoses			
.12 states that: – the provision of hoses is the responsibility of the terminal, but the master may reject a hose that appears to be defective – lifting bridles and saddles should be provided to support all hoses, and excessive weight on the ship's manifold is to be avoided		B1	A1
.13 states that an insulating flange (or an insulating length of hose) should be fitted		B1	A1
.14 explains that: – metal on the seaward side of the insulation should be electrically continuous to the ship – metal on the landward side of the insulation should be electrically continuous to the shore		B1	A1
6.2 Loading and discharging operations (3 hours) *In case a simulator is provided, training for Sec. 6.2 can be done on a simulator (suggested Ex.3)*			
.1 explains how volume of oil on board can be determined by means of soundings or ullage measurements and calibration tables		B8	A1
.2 explains that, in order to calculate the cargo lifted, the oil volume must be converted to weight by multiplication by its specific gravity (density at 15°C in vacuum)		B8	A1
.3 defines specific gravity (density at 15°C in vacuum)		B8	A1
.4 explains that relative density depends on temperature		B8	A1
.5 states that information on relative density used by the terminal is based on the standard temperature of 60°F		B8	A1
.6 states that an alternative scale of the weight/volume ratio that is used in the oil industry is the API scale		B8	A1
.7 defines the API scale		B8	A1

.8 lists units commonly used in the oil industry:
– for volume as:
  – cubic feet
  – cubic meters
  – barrels (of 42 US gallons)
– for weight as:
  – tonnes of 1000 Kg
  – tonnes of 2000 lbs
  – tonnes of 2240 lbs
		B8	A1

.9 states that tables are available for converting the different units in order to calculate weights		B8	A1

知识、理解和熟练	IMO 参考书目	教科书,参考文献	教具
技能要求			
货油软管			
.12 阐述:		B1	A1
– 提供软管是码头方的责任,但是船长可以拒绝接受看似有缺陷的软管			
– 应提供以支撑全部软管供起吊绳索和护套,避免船舶主管承受过大重量			
.13 阐述应安装一个绝缘法兰(或一段绝缘软管)		B1	A1
.14 解释:		B1	A1
– 海水侧绝缘体上的金属应以导电的方式连续地连接到船上			
– 陆地侧绝缘体上的金属应以导电的方式连续地连接到岸上			
6.2 装卸操作(3 学时)			
如有模拟器,则第 6.2 节的培训可在模拟器上进行(练习 3)			
.1 解释船上存油量如何通过测深或损耗量和舱容表来决定		B1	A1
.2 解释为了计算货油装卸量,必须将油的体积通过乘以其比重(15 ℃时的密度)转换为重量		B1	A1
.3 确定比重(15 ℃时的密度)		B8	A1
.4 解释相对密度取决于温度		B8	A1
.5 阐述码头所使用的相对密度的信息是基于标准的 60 °F 温度		B8	A1
.6 阐述在石油工业中使用的重量 / 体积比的替代比例是美国石油协会(API)标度		B8	A1
.7 定义 API 标度		B8	A1
.8 列出石油工业中常用单位:		B8	A1
– 体积单位,如:		B8	A1
– 立方英尺			
– 立方米			
– 桶(42 美加仑)			
– 重量单位,如:			
– 吨,1000 千克			
– 吨,2000 磅			
– 吨,2240 磅			
.9 阐述可用单位换算表计算重量		B8	A1

Knowledge, understanding and proficiency	IMO Reference	Textbooks, Bibliography	Teaching Aid
Required performance			
.10 calculates: – the mass of full cargo to be lifted, given deadweight scales, loading and discharge port, length of voyage, ballast fuel, stores and consumption – the volume of cargo that can be lifted, given the relative density or API at 60°F and the cargo temperature – whether bending, hogging, and sheering stresses are within acceptable limits, given the load distribution and appropriate graphs		B8	A1
.11 states that the loading and discharging plan must take into account the ship's stability		B8	A1
.12 states that an emergency shutdown procedure must be agreed upon between ship and terminal		B8	A1
.13 explains that loading should initially be by gravity		B8	A1
.14 explains the checks to be carried out after pumps have been started		B8	A1
.15 states that, when discharging is about to begin, the shore valves to receiving tanks must be opened before the tanker's manifold valves are opened		B8	A1
.16 explains that special measures are necessary when pressure might exist in the shore line and no check valves are fitted		B6	A1
.17 explains the danger of line blowing and the precautions to be taken		B6	A1
.18 states that special procedures apply for ship-to-ship transfers		B6	A1
6.3 Ballasting and de-ballasting (1 hour) *In case a simulator is provided, training for Sec. 6.3 can be done on a simulator (suggested Ex.3)*			
.1 states that ballast quantity is at the discretion of the master	R2.1	B1, B8	A1, A5
.2 describes considerations affecting ballast quantity and the tanks to be used	R2.1	B1, B8	A1, A5
.3 states that due account should be taken of stress forces when choosing ballast tanks and while ballasting or de-ballasting is in progress	R2.1	B1, B8	A1, A5
.4 lists additional considerations influencing ballast quantity as lightening operations, passing under bridges, berth constraints and draught requirements for fairway/channels	R2.1	B1, B8	A1, A5
.5 states that ballasting and de-ballasting often take place in stages, such as: – at the discharge terminal – during sea passage – when heavy weather is expected – prior to arrival in loading port – at the loading terminal	R2.1	B1, B8	A1, A5
.6 explains that ballasting operations whilst alongside should be discussed with the terminal prior to commencement	R2.1	B1, B8	A1, A5
.7 states that, in earlier times, ballast was always taken into cargo tanks	R2.1	B1, B8	A1, A5

知识、理解和熟练	IMO 参考书目	教科书，参考文献	教具
技能要求			
.10 计算： – 装载货物总质量，应考虑载重吨、装卸货港、航线长度、燃油存量、物料及消耗情况 – 装载货物的总体积，应考虑相对密度或 60°F 时的 API 值以及货油温度 – 根据给定负荷分配和正确的曲线图来判断弯曲应力、剪切应力是否在可接受范围内		B8	A1
.11 阐述装卸计划必须考虑船舶稳性		B8	A1
.12 阐述船方和码头必须统一应急停止程序		B8	A1
.13 解释刚开始时必须通过重力装货		B8	A1
.14 解释起动泵后需要进行的检查		B8	A1
.15 阐述当卸油准备开始时，接收货油的岸阀必须要在开启船上总阀之前打开		B8	A1
.16 解释当岸上的管路里可能存有压力并且未安装止回阀时，有必要采取特殊措施		B6	A1
.17 解释管路泄漏的危险和应该采取的预防措施		B6	A1
.18 阐述适用船—船过驳的特殊程序		B6	A1
6.3 装载、排放压载水(1 学时) 如有模拟器，则第 6.3 节的培训可在模拟器上进行(推荐练习 3)			
.1 阐述压载水数量取决于船长的判断力	R2.1	B1, B8	A1, A5
.2 描述影响压载水数量和压载舱使用的因素	R2.1	B1, B8	A1, A5
.3 阐述在吸、排压载水过程中选择压载舱时，在考虑应力的情况下确定压载水的数量	R2.1	B1, B8	A1, A5
.4 列出由于航道 / 运河要求、经过桥梁、泊位限制及吃水限制影响时对压载水数量的额外考虑因素而进行减载操作	R2.1	B1, B8	A1, A5
.5 阐述装载和排放压载水经常分期进行，如： – 卸货码头 – 航行期间 – 当遇上恶劣天气时 – 在抵达装油港口之前 – 在装油港口	R2.1	B1, B8	A1, A5
.6 解释靠岸时在压载操作开始之前应该与港方协商	R2.1	B1, B8	A1, A5
.7 阐述在以前压载水总是装到油舱里	R2.1	B1, B8	A1, A5

Knowledge, understanding and proficiency	IMO Reference	Textbooks, Bibliography	Teaching Aid
Required performance			
.8 states that, at a later period, tankers were provided with segregated ballast capacity for coming alongside and leaving the jetty	R2.1	B1, B8	A1, A5
.9 explains that, on oil tanker provided with SBT or operating with CBT, there may be reasons for taking additional ballast in cargo tanks	R2.1	B1, B8	A1, A5
.10 describes CBT operations during a normal tanker voyage in general terms	R2.1	B1, B8	A1, A5
.11 states that CBT operations appropriate to a ship are contained in an approved Dedicated Clean Ballast Tank Operation Manual	R2.1	B1, B8	A1, A5
.12 states that, if no SBT or CBT capacity has been provided, or if additional ballast is required, ballast must be taken into dirty cargo tanks	R2.1	B1, B8	A1, A5
.13 states that this will constitute dirty ballast	R2.1	B1, B8	A1, A5
.14 states that the discharge of dirty ballast is subject to discharge provisions	R2.1	B1, B8	A1, A5
.15 lists the discharge provisions for oil and oily mixtures from the cargo-tank area of all oil tankers	R2.1	B1, B8	A1, A5
.16 states that the discharge provisions do not apply to clean ballast or to segregated ballast	R2.1	B1, B8	A1, A5
.17 defines clean ballast	R2.1	B1, B8	A1, A5
.18 describes the change of ballast at sea in compliance with the discharge requirements	R2.1	B1, B8	A1, A5
.19 states that the ballast change is necessary to arrive in the loading port with clean ballast	R2.1	B1, B8	A1, A5
.20 states that LOT procedures result in oily water collecting in the slop-tanks	R2.1	B1, B8	A1, A5
.21 states that more stringent discharge provisions apply in certain sea areas, called special areas	R2.1	B1, B8	A1, A5
.22 lists the special areas under Annex I of MARPOL 73/78 as: – Antarctic Area – Baltic Sea Area – Mediterranean Sea – Black Sea – Gulf Area – Gulf of Aden Area – Red Sea – North-West European Waters	R2.1	B1, B8	A1, A5
.23 states that under the revised Annex I of MARPOL 73/78, likely to be in force from 1st January 2007, Oman Sea Area will also be declared as a special area	R2.1	B1, B8	A1, A5
.24 states that more areas can be declared as special areas in the future	R2.1	B1, B8	A1, A5
.25 states that only clean and segregated ballast may be discharged within special areas	R2.1	B1, B8	A1, A5
.26 states that, on ships equipped with COW system, ballast should not be put into cargo tanks unless these have been crude oil washed	R2.1	B1, B8	A1, A5

知识、理解和熟练	IMO 参考书目	教科书, 参考文献	教具
技能要求			
.8 阐述一段时间后装有专用压载舱油船具有靠泊和离开码头的能力	R2.1	B1, B8	A1, A5
.9 解释设有 SBT 或用 CBT 操作的油船，也存在用货油舱装压载水的原因	R2.1	B1, B8	A1, A5
.10 描述一般意义上的油船正常航行期间的 CBT 操作	R2.1	B1, B8	A1, A5
.11 阐述适合于船舶的 CBT 操作规程包含在批准的专用清洁压载舱操作手册中	R2.1	B1, B8	A1, A5
.12 阐述如果没有 SBT 或 CBT,或者需要额外的压载水,压载水必须打入油污货舱	R2.1	B1, B8	A1, A5
.13 阐述这将形成了脏的压载水	R2.1	B1, B8	A1, A5
.14 阐述脏污压载水的排放受排放规则的制约	R2.1	B1, B8	A1, A5
.15 列举从货油舱中排放油和油类混合物的排放规则	R2.1	B1, B8	A1, A5
.16 阐述排放规则不适用于清洁压载或专用压载	R2.1	B1, B8	A1, A5
.17 定义清洁压载	R2.1	B1, B8	A1, A5
.18 描述根据排放要求在海上更换压载水	R2.1	B1, B8	A1, A5
.19 阐述对于使用清洁压载的船舶抵达装油港前必需更换压载水	R2.1	B1, B8	A1, A5
.20 阐述装于上部法导致含油污水积存在污油水舱	R2.1	B1, B8	A1, A5
.21 阐述更加严格的条款用于特定海域区域,这些区域称为特殊区域	R2.1	B1, B8	A1, A5
.22 根据 MARPOL 公约附则 I 中的特殊区域有： – 南极地区 – 波罗的海地区 – 地中海地区 – 黑海地区 – 海湾地区 – 亚丁湾地区 – 红海地区 – 欧洲西北水域	R2.1	B1, B8	A1, A5
.23 阐述根据修订后并在 2007 年 1 月 1 日生效的 MARPOL 公约附则 I,阿曼海域也将被定为特殊区域	R2.1	B1, B8	A1A5
.24 阐述将来会有更多的特殊区域	R2.1	B1, B8	A1A5
.25 阐述只有清洁压载水和专用压载水可以在特殊区域排放	R2.1	B1, B8	A1A5
.26 阐述在装有 COW 系统的船上,除非货油舱已用原油洗舱,压载水不能压入货油舱	R2.1	B1, B8	A1A5

Knowledge, understanding and proficiency	IMO Reference	Textbooks, Bibliography	Teaching Aid
Required performance			
.27 describes COW operations	R2.1	B1, B8	A1, A5
.28 states that, in view of explosion hazards, COW must take place in an inerted tank atmosphere	R2.1	B1, B8	A1, A5
.29 lists as explosion hazards: – the use of high capacity washing machines – the uncontrolled evolution of gas	R2.1	B1, B8	A1, A5
.30 states that some crude oils are unsuitable for COW	R2.1	B1, B8	A1, A5
.31 states that tanks which have been crude oil washed require additional water washing before taking in clean ballast	R2.1	B1, B8	A1, A5
.32 states that a description of the COW system on board and of the correct operation of the system are contained in an approved COW Operations and Equipment Manual	R2.1	B1, B8	A1, A5
.33 states that all ballast – segregated, clean and dirty – should be discharged above the waterline	R2.1	B1, B8	A1, A5
.34 lists the conditions in which discharge is permitted below the waterline	R2.1	B1, B8	A1, A5
.35 states that particular care must be taken when ballasting some double hull tankers due to possible loss of stability	R2.1	B1, B8	A1, A5
6.4 Tank cleaning (1 hour)			
.1 lists the reason for tank washing as cleaning cargo tanks for the next cargo, cleaning cargo tanks for clean ballast, sludge control, tank entry for repairs, or dry-docking			A1
.2 describes tank cleaning with: – cold water – hot water – chemicals			A1
.3 states that tank cleaning produces large quantities of oil-contaminated water			A1
.4 states that the volume of water may be reduced if tanks have first been crude oil washed			A1
.5 describes tank washing with portable and fixed machines			A1
.6 describes movements of single-and multiple-nozzle machines			A1
.7 states that tank washing stirs up oily residues within a tank, thereby generating hydrocarbon gas			A1
.8 states that tank washing also causes electrostatic hazards as a result of water mist, water slugs and introduction into the tanks of portable tank-washing machines			A1

知识、理解和熟练	IMO 参考书目	教科书,参考文献	教具
技能要求			
.27 描述 COW 操作	R2.1	B1, B8	A1, A5
.28 考虑到爆炸危险,阐述 COW 必须在惰化的舱内进行	R2.1	B1, B8	A1, A5
.29 列举爆炸危险: – 大容量洗舱机的使用 – 不可控制的气体散发	R2.1	B1, B8	A1, A5
.30 阐述部分原油不适于 COW	R2.1	B1, B8	A1, A5
.31 阐述已用原油清洗的舱在装入清洁压载水之前需要附加的水洗	R2.1	B1, B8	A1, A5
.32 阐述船上的 COW 系统及正确操作包含在认可的 COW 设备和操作手册中	R2.1	B1, B8	A1, A5
.33 阐述所有压载水—专用的、清洁的和脏污的—应该在水线以上排放	R2.1	B1, B8	A1, A5
.34 列举允许在水线以下排放的情况	R2.1	B1, B8	A1, A5
.35 阐述必须特别注意双层底油船的压载,因为船舶有可能失去稳性	R2.1	B1, B8	A1, A5
6.4 洗舱(1 学时)			
.1 列举洗舱原因:为下批货油准备清洁油舱、为清洁压载准备清洁油舱、控制油渣量、进舱维修、进入坞修			A1
.2 描述用下列物质洗舱: – 冷水 – 热水 – 化学物质			A1
.3 阐述洗舱会产生大量含油污水			A1
.4 阐述如果先用原油清洗的油舱,可以减少用水量			A1
.5 描述使用便携式和固定式洗舱机洗舱			A1
.6 描述单喷嘴和多喷嘴洗舱机的动作过程			A1
.7 阐述洗舱在舱内搅起油渣,因此产生烃类气体			A1
.8 阐述洗舱因为水雾、水片和便携式洗舱机进入舱内也能引起静电危险			A1

Knowledge, understanding and proficiency	IMO Reference	Textbooks, Bibliography	Teaching Aid
Required performance			
.9 states that, because of the factors described in objectives 6.4.7 and 6.4.8, the tank atmosphere should be made safe against explosions and that: – this could be done by washing tanks in a too-lean, a too-rich or an inert atmosphere – it is difficult to maintain a too-rich atmosphere – if the ship is so equipped, tank washing should be done in an inert atmosphere – an inert atmosphere is imperative if using high-capacity washing machines, crude oil washing, or washing in the re-circulation mode			A1
.10 states that tank washing water should be transferred to the slop-tank			A1
.11 describes tank washing with the open-cycle and closed-cycle (re-circulation) modes			A1
.12 lists the precautions to be taken when tanks must be washed in an uncontrolled atmosphere			A1
6.5 Slop-tank operations (1 hour)			
.1 describes why slop-tanks are essential for effective LOT procedures	R2.1	B2, B4	A1
.2 states that oil tankers require one or two slop-tanks, depending on the size of the vessel	R2.1	B2, B4	A1
.3 states that, during changing of ballast, the slop-tanks receive the oily part of the dirty ballast	R2.1	B2, B4	A1
.4 with the aid of a drawing, explains slop-tank operations with one or two slop-tanks during tank washing and decanting	R2.1	B2, B4	A1
.5 states that slop-tank fills rapidly during open-cycle tank washing, but that during closed-cycle tank washing the level of the slop-tank also rises	R2.1	B2, B4	A1
.6 explains this rise in level	R2.1	B2, B4	A1
.7 states that slop-tanks can be heated for better separation of oil and water	R2.1	B2, B4	A1
.8 states that decanting operations come under the discharge requirements	R2.1	B2, B4	A1
.9 explains why, if LOT procedures have been properly executed, the slop-tank should contain oil, emulsion and water upon arrival in the loading port	R2.1	B2, B4	A1
.10 states that a cargo of crude oil may be loaded on top of the contents of the slop-tank	R2.1	B2, B4	A1
.11 describes what is decanting	R2.1	B2, B4	A1
6.6 Purging and gas-freeing (1 hour) *In case a simulator is provided, training for Sec. 6.6 can be done on a simulator (suggested Ex.4)*			
.1 lists the reasons for gas-freeing as tank washing, tank entry or repairs		B1	A1
.2 defines gas-freeing as the replacement of hydrocarbon vapour or inert gas by air		B1	A1

知识、理解和熟练	IMO 参考书目	教科书,参考文献	教具
技能要求			
.9 阐述因为在 6.4.7 和 6.4.8 中所描述的因素,舱内气体应确保安全,防止爆炸,以及: – 在油气稀少、油气过浓或充惰状态下实现洗舱 – 维持高浓的气体非常困难 – 如果船舶设有充惰设备,洗舱应在充惰状态下进行 – 如果使用大容量洗舱机、原油洗舱或以循环方式洗舱,惰性气体必不可少			A1
.10 阐述洗舱水应该排放到污油水舱			A1
.11 描述开式循环和闭式循环方式洗舱			A1
.12 列举必须在不可控制气体中洗舱时需要采取的预防措施			A1
6.5 污液舱的操作(1 学时)			
.1 描述为何污液舱对有效的装于上部法必不可少	R2.1	B2, B4	A1
.2 阐述油船需要一或二个污液舱,取决于船的大小	R2.1	B2, B4	A1
.3 阐述在置换压载水期间,污液舱接收含油的脏污压载水	R2.1	B2, B4	A1
.4 借助于图表解释洗舱和移驳期间,一个或两个污液舱情况下的污液舱操作	R2.1	B2, B4	A1
.5 阐述在开式循环洗舱时污液舱快速上升,但闭式循环洗舱时污液舱的水位也上升	R2.1	B2, B4	A1
.6 解释液位上升的原因	R2.1	B2, B4	A1
.7 阐述可以加热污液舱以获得更好的油水分离效果	R2.1	B2, B4	A1
.8 阐述移驳操作根据排放要求而定	R2.1	B2, B4	A1
.9 解释如果正确使用装于上部法,在卸油港污液舱将含油、乳化液和水的原因	R2.1	B2, B4	A1
.10 阐述原油可以装于污液舱内液体的上方	R2.1	B2, B4	A1
.11 描述什么是移驳	R2.1	B2, B4	A1
6.6 驱气和除气(1 学时)			
如有模拟器,则第 6.6 节的培训可在模拟器上进行(推荐练习 4)			
.1 列举除气的原因:洗舱、进入舱内或维修		B1	A1
.2 定义除气是用空气替换烃类气体或惰性气体		B1	A1

Knowledge, understanding and proficiency	IMO Reference	Textbooks, Bibliography	Teaching Aid
Required performance			
.3 explains that accommodation openings should be closed when purging or gas-freeing		B1	A1
.4 explains that hydrocarbon gas remains inside a tank after cargo discharge		B1	A1
.5 explains that such vapours may be mixed with inert gas in IGS-fitted ships or with air in ships not fitted with an IGS		B1	A1
.6 states that there is no explosive atmosphere in an inerted tank		B1	A1
.7 explains why atmosphere should never be allowed to come within the flammable range when gas-freeing an inerted tank		B1	A1
.8 defines purging with inert gas as replacing the hydrocarbon vapours with inert gas		B1	A1
.9 explains, with the aid of a flammability composition diagram, how purging will prevent a flammable atmosphere developing within a tank		B1	A1
.10 explains how gas-freeing a non-inerted tank will result in the tank atmosphere being in the explosive range for some time		B1	A1
.11 states that gas-freeing is done by portable fans or fixed ventilating systems		B1	A1
.12 states that the IGS is used for purging and may also be used for gas-freeing		B1	A1
.13 states that gas-freeing may take place through displacement or mixing		B1	A1
.14 describes both methods in general terms		B1	A1
.15 defines a gas-free tank		B1	A1
.16 explains why a tank atmosphere may become dangerous again if ventilation is discontinued		B1	A1
.17 states that the inert gas supply must be blanked off or the valve closed in the branch piping to a gas-free tank		B1	A1
.18 lists the general safety precautions applicable when gas-freeing		B1	A1
6.7 Ship/shore liaison (1 hour)			
.1 lists the information to be provided by the terminal for loading and for discharging		B1	A1
.2 lists the information to be provided by the tanker for loading and for discharging		B1	A1
.3 states that an operational agreement should be made in writing before loading or discharging		B1	A1
.4 lists and explains the subjects to be covered by the loading and discharging plan		B1	A1
.5 describes pre-loading tank inspection, and the limitations when surveyors cannot enter a tank		B1	A1
.6 states that: – reliable ship/shore communications are essential – both parties should therefore establish, agree in writing and maintain reliable primary and stand-by communications system		B1	A1

知识、理解和熟练	IMO 参考书目	教科书,参考文献	教具
技能要求			
.3 解释当驱气或除气时生活区开口应该关闭		B1	A1
.4 解释卸油后残存在油舱内的烃类气体		B1	A1
.5 解释这些气体在装有 IGS 的船上可能和惰性气体混合,或者在未装有 IGS 的船上与空气混合		B1	A1
.6 阐述在已惰化的舱内没有爆炸气体		B1	A1
.7 解释对惰化舱进行除气时空气决不允许达到着火范围		B1	A1
.8 定义用惰性气体驱气是用惰性气体置换烃类气体		B1	A1
.9 借助于燃烧三要素解释驱气能防止可燃气体在舱内积聚		B1	A1
.10 解释非惰性舱的除气有时可能导致舱内气体出现在爆炸范围内		B1	A1
.11 阐述除气通过便携式风机或固定式通风系统完成		B1	A1
.12 阐述惰性气体系统(IGS)用于驱气,也可用于除气		B1	A1
.13 阐述除气可以通过置换或混合进行		B1	A1
.14 描述上述两种方法		B1	A1
.15 定义不含油气的舱		B1	A1
.16 解释如果通风中断,舱内气体将重新变危险的原因		B1	A1
.17 阐述惰气到不含油气货舱的供给管路应被封死或关闭支管阀		B1	A1
.18 列举除气时一般的安全预防措施		B1	A1
6.7 船/岸联络(1 学时)			
.1 列举应由岸方提供的用于装卸油的信息		B1	A1
.2 列举应由船方提供的用于装卸油的信息		B1	A1
.3 阐述装卸货油前应制定一个可操作的书面协议		B1	A1
.4 列举并解释装卸油计划中应包含的项目		B1	A1
.5 描述当验船师无法进入预装油舱的检查和限制		B1	A1
.6 阐述: – 可靠的船/岸通信至关重要 – 因此双方应该建立、书面同意并保持可靠的主用和备用通信系统		B1	A1

Knowledge, understanding and proficiency	IMO Reference	Textbooks, Bibliography	Teaching Aid
Required performance			
.7 states that, when different grades of oil are handled, their names and description should be clearly understood by both parties		B1	A1
.8 states that ship/shore safety checklist should be completed jointly by ship and shore staff		B1	A1
.9 generally describes the checklist and explains the reason and relevance of the check items		B1	A1
7 Cargo and ballast pumps (2 hours)	STCW Code Sec. A-V/1 Pa. 10		
7.1 Pump theory and characteristics (1 hour)			
.1 states that the suction action of a pump is really atmospheric pressure pushing the liquid into the inlet side of the pump			A1
.2 explains that for that reason a pump could in theory draw up liquid to a height which equals atmospheric pressure, i.e. approximately 10 meters			A1
.3 states that, in practice, the situation is less favourable and that the height of 10 meters is decreased by the combined effects of: – net positive suction head (NPSH) of the pump – line resistance – true vapour pressure – vertical distance between pump and suction			A1
.4 states that these combined effects may nullify atmospheric pressure			A1
.5 explains that, if the combined effects exceed 10 meters, the liquid being pumped will boil			A1
.6 explains how low vapour pressure of the liquid being pumped will improve suction			A1
.7 explains how positive trim of the ship will improve suction			A1
.8 explains how a full tank increases suction			A1
.9 states that decreasing the pumping rate will decrease NPSH and the line resistance, thereby increasing suction			A1
.10 explains that the discharge pressure will fluctuate when the liquid boils			A1
.11 states that the phenomenon causes cavitation within the pump			A1
.12 states that starting a centrifugal could cause a rush of liquid through the discharge piping, leading to excessive line resistance			A1
.13 explains that for that reason a centrifugal pump must be started against a closed discharge valve, and for electrically-driven pumps the starting current will be too high resulting in an automatic shut down			A1
.14 identifies a graph showing the characteristics of a centrifugal pump			A1
.15 explains the meaning of head			A1

知识、理解和熟练	IMO 参考书目	教科书,参考文献	教具
技能要求			
.7 阐述处理不同种类的油时,双方应彻底理解它们的名称和说明		B1	A1
.8 阐述船 / 岸安全检查表应该由船岸人员共同完成		B1	A1
.9 简单描述检查表并解释原因及相关检查项目		B1	A1
7 货油泵(2 学时)	STCW 公约 A-V/1 节 10 段		
7.1 泵的原理和特性(1 学时)			
.1 阐述泵的吸入实际上是大气压推动液体进入泵吸口			A1
.2 解释泵理论上能够吸入的液体高度等于大气压的原因,即大约 10 米水柱			A1
.3 阐述实际上,应小于理想状况,因此 10 米水柱的高度因为下列原因的综合作用而降低: – 泵的净吸入能头(NPSH) – 管路阻力 – 实际气化压力 – 泵和吸入口之间的垂直高度			A1
.4 阐述这些综合作用可以使大气压无效			A1
.5 解释如果综合作用超过 10 米,所泵送的液体将汽化			A1
.6 解释所泵送液体的低汽化压力如何改善吸入			A1
.7 解释船体正吃水将如何改善吸入			A1
.8 解释满载货舱如何改善吸入			A1
.9 阐述降低泵的流量将降低 NPSH 和管路阻力,因此增加吸入			A1
.10 解释当液体汽化时排压将波动			A1
.11 描述泵内穴蚀现象			A1
.12 阐述起动离心泵时能引起液体在排出管路冲击,导致管路阻力异常增加			A1
.13 解释由于上述原因,离心泵必须封闭起动,对于电动泵起动电流将导致自动跳闸			A1
.14 认识离心泵性能曲线图			A1
.15 解释“压头”的含义			A1

Knowledge, understanding and proficiency	IMO Reference	Textbooks, Bibliography	Teaching Aid
Required performance			
.16 explains the different curves on the graph and their mutual relationship			A1
.17 explains the meaning of NPSH			A1
.18 explains the meaning of 'design point'			A1
.19 explains that the actual discharge rate also depends on static and dynamic backpressure of the shore installation			A1
.20 draws a typical Q-H curve and a shore installation curve			A1
.21 explains that long shore piping of small dimensions would mean a steep shore installation curve			A1
.22 shows how a Q-H curve can be drawn for two pumps running in parallel			A1
.23 shows how the discharge rate of such pumps is affected by steep and near-horizontal shore installation curves			A1
.24 explains that with steep shore installation curves there may be little if any advantage in letting more than one pump discharge into the shore system			A1
.25 explains the danger of running two or more pumps in parallel if their characteristics are not exactly the same or if the pumps are running at different speeds			A1
.26 derives the discharge rate of the pump, using a Q-H curve and a shore installation curve			A1
Practical aspects			
.27 explains why a stripping pump must be self-priming			A1
.28 lists the main types of cargo pumps and explains the advantages of deep-well pumps			A1
.29 describes the working of a centrifugal pump			A1
.30 describes the difference between a simplex pump and a duplex pump			A1
.31 states that reciprocating pumps are fitted with three gauges, and describes the function of each gauge			A1
.32 states that reciprocating pumps are self-priming			A1
.33 explains why such pumps are not of high capacity			A1
.34 describes the working of centrifugal pump			A1
.35 states that centrifugal pumps: – are generally used as cargo pumps – are not self-priming – may be driven by steam turbine, by electricity or by direct drive diesel motor			A1
.36 states that: – the speed of turbine driven pumps can be varied by adjusting the steam supply to the turbine – a turbine driven pump has a tachometer in addition to the three gauges – electrically driven pumps may be designed to run at constant speed – an electrically driven pump has a volt and ampere meter to indicate power and load in addition to the three gauges			A1

知识、理解和熟练	IMO 参考书目	教科书,参考文献	教具
技能要求			
.16 解释图中不同曲线及其相互关系			A1
.17 解释 NPSH 的含义			A1
.18 解释“设计工况”的含义			A1
.19 解释实际排量也取决于岸上管路的静压和背压			A1
.20 绘制典型的 *Q-H* 曲线和岸上管路特性曲线			A1
.21 解释较长的小口径岸方管路意味着岸上管路特性曲线较陡			A1
.22 演示如何画出两台并联运行的泵的 *Q-H* 曲线			A1
.23 阐述泵的排量如何受到陡峭的和几乎水平的岸上管路特性曲线的影响			A1
.24 解释如果允许多台泵向岸方卸货,将会降低岸方设备的陡峭曲线的影响			A1
.25 解释如果泵的特性不十分相似或者泵在不同的转速下运行时,并联运行两个以上泵的危险性			A1
.26 根据 *Q-H* 曲线和岸上管路特性曲线给出泵的排量			A1
实践方面			
.27 解释扫舱泵必须具有自吸能力的原因			A1
.28 列举货油泵的主要类型及解释深井泵的优势			A1
.29 描述离心泵的工作过程			A1
.30 描述单级离心泵和多级离心泵的不同			A1
.31 阐述往复泵具有三块仪表并描述每块仪表的功能			A1
.32 阐述往复泵的自吸能力			A1
.33 解释该泵排量不宜过大的原因			A1
.34 描述离心泵的工作过程			A1
.35 阐述离心泵: – 通常用作货油泵 – 没有自吸能力 – 可能由蒸气透平、电力、柴油机驱动			A1
.36 阐述: – 驱动泵的透平转速可通过调整透平供气压力进行调节 – 除了上述三块表之外,透平驱动泵还有一个转速表 – 电动泵可能被设计成定速运行 – 电动泵除了上述三块表之外,还有一个电压表和电流表以显示功率和负载			A1

Knowledge, understanding and proficiency	IMO Reference	Textbooks, Bibliography	Teaching Aid
Required performance			
.37 states that centrifugal pumps are capable of being driven at high speed, that the cargo cools the pump and that loss of suction entails the danger of overheating and fire			A1
.38 describes the working of a rotary positive displacement pump, explaining that such pumps are self priming			A1
.39 explains why such pumps are not in general use on board oil tankers			A1
.40 describes the working of a screw pump, explaining that such pumps are self-priming			A1
.41 states that screw pumps are capable of being driven at high speed	IMO 2.1		A1
.42 explains why few oil tankers are equipped with screw pumps	IMO 2.1		A1
.43 explains the products for which screw pumps are suitable	IMO 2.1		A1
7.2 Pressure surge (1 hour)			
.1 explains how a pressure surge occurs		B1	A1
.2 describes what may be the result of a pressure surge leading to excessive pressure stresses		B1	A1
.3 lists the three pressure components in liquid being pumped		B1	A1
.4 explains how the rapid closure of a valve can superimpose an additional pressure on the liquid		B1	A1
.5 describes the effects closing the valve will have: – downstream – upstream – at the pump		B1	A1
.6 describes the pressures to which the pump is subjected		B1	A1
.7 states that $2L/a$ is known as the pipeline period		B1	A1
.8 defines L as the length of piping and a as the speed of sound in the liquid		B1	A1
.9 states that the system is liable to serious pressure surges if valve closure time is equal to or less than the pipeline period		B1	A1
.10 explains why long pipelines are more liable to pressure surges and that valve closure times must be adjusted accordingly		B1	A1
.11 states that offshore moorings are liable to have long pipelines		B1	A1
.12 lists measures to prevent pressure surges as: – a reduction in the linear flow rate – an increase in the effective valve closure time		B1	A1
8 Emergency procedures (2 hours)	STCW Code Sec. A-V/1 Pa. 14		
8.1 Emergency plan (0.5 hour)			
.1 states that every oil tanker greater than 150 tonnes must have an oil pollution emergency plan	R2.1	B1, B6	A1

知识、理解和熟练		IMO 参考书目	教科书，参考文献	教具
技能要求				
.37	阐述离心泵能够达到较高转速；货物能冷却该泵；失吸可能会引起过热和火灾			A1
.38	描述旋转容积式泵的工作过程，并解释自吸原理			A1
.39	解释上述泵一般不用于油船的原因			A1
.40	描述螺杆泵的工作过程，并解释自吸原理			A1
.41	阐述螺杆泵能够达到较高的转速	IMO 2.1		A1
.42	解释为何油船很少会装设螺杆泵	IMO 2.1		A1
.43	解释螺杆泵适用的介质	IMO 2.1		A1
7.2	**压力波动**(1 学时)			
.1	解释压力冲击的发生原因		B1	A1
.2	描述压力过高导致压力冲击的结果		B1	A1
.3	列举泵送液体的三种压力构成		B1	A1
.4	解释阀的快速关闭将对液体施加一个额外压力		B1	A1
.5	描述关闭阀产生的影响 – 阀后 – 阀前 – 泵		B1	A1
.6	描述泵所承受的压力		B1	A1
.7	阐述 $2L/a$ 被称作管路周期		B1	A1
.8	定义 L 为管路的长度，a 为液体内的音速		B1	A1
.9	阐述如果阀的关闭时间等于或小于管路周期，系统容易受到严重的压力冲击		B1 B1	A1 A1
.10	解释长管路更容易受到压力冲击，并且阀的关闭时间必须作相应的调整		B1 B1	A1 A1
.11	阐述海上系泊应该有较长的管路			
.12	列举防止压力冲击的措施： – 线性流速的降低 – 延长有效阀关闭时间			
8	**应急程序**(2 学时)	STCW 公约 A-V/1 节 14 段		
8.1	**应急计划**(0.5 学时)			
.1	阐述 150 总吨以上的油船必须有油污应急计划	R2.1	B1, B6	A1

Knowledge, understanding and proficiency	IMO Reference	Textbooks, Bibliography	Teaching Aid
Required performance			
.2 states that planning and preparation are essential for dealing successfully with emergencies arising from oil spillages, fires, explosions, personnel affected by petroleum and other calamities, and lists the information which should be readily available as: – type of cargo and its disposition – location of other hazardous substances – general arrangement plan of the ship – stability information – location of fire-fighting equipment	R2.1	B1, B6	A1
.3 explains how towing hawsers must be rigged when the ship is alongside	R2.1	B1, B6	A1
8.2 Emergency alarms (0.5 hour)			
.1 describes the different alarms used in cases of emergencies such as: – general emergency – fire alarm – CO_2 alarm			A1
.2 states that other important alarms are: – inert gas alarm – high-level alarm – engine room alarms – bridge alarms – accommodation alarms – galley alarms			A1
8.3 Emergency organization (0.5 hour)			
.1 states the need for an emergency organization and lists the main components of the organization as: – a command centre located in a normally safe position on the vessel, with communication equipment readily available – an alternative emergency position to be identified if the normal command centre cannot be occupied – a senior officer identified as being in control during the emergency, with another senior officer being identified as his/her deputy – an emergency team formed under the control of crew members to take action as directed from the command centre – a second emergency team formed to assist the emergency team as necessary – an engineering team formed under the control of a senior engineer		B1, B6	A1
.2 states the need for realistic drills to be undertaken periodically		B1, B6	A1

知识、理解和熟练	IMO 参考书目	教科书,参考文献	教具
技能要求			
.2 阐述对于成功地处理因为溢油、火灾、爆炸、受原油伤害的人和其他灾难而言,应急计划和准备工作至关重要,并列举方便可用的信息如: – 货油种类及其特点 – 其他有害物质的位置 – 船舶整体布置图 – 稳性信息 – 消防设备的位置	R2.1	B1, B6	A1
.3 解释船靠岸时拖缆如何被锁紧	R2.1	B1, B6	A1
8.2 应急警报(0.5 学时)			
.1 描述发生下列紧急情况时使用的警报: – 一般紧急状况 – 消防警报 – CO_2 警报			A1
.2 阐述其他重要警报: – 惰性气体警报 – 高位警报 – 机舱警报 – 驾驶台警报 – 生活区警报 – 厨房警报			A1
8.3 应急组织(0.5 学时)			
.1 阐述应急组织的必要性,并列出该组织的主要构成: – 指挥中心通常位于船上的安全位置,设有随时可用的通讯设备 – 如果正常指挥中心不可用,指定一个替代应急位置 – 指定一名高级驾驶员作为应急时的指挥,另一名高级驾驶员作为其代表 – 在船员中形成一个应急小组,按照指挥中心的命令采取行动 – 形成第二个应急小组在必要时对第一个应急小组提供帮助 – 形成一名由高级轮机员指挥的机舱应急小组		B1, B6	A1
.2 阐述要定期执行实际演习的必要性		B1, B6	A1

Knowledge, understanding and proficiency	IMO Reference	Textbooks, Bibliography	Teaching Aid
Required performance			
8.4 Action on discovering an emergency (0.5 hour)			
.1 states that if an emergency occurs the immediate action must be to: – raise the alarm – provide information to the command centre as to the location and nature of the emergency – shut down all cargo operations and close valves – remove all craft from alongside		B1	A1
9 Inert Gas Systems (IGS) (8 hours)			
9.1 General (0.5 hour)			
.1 describes which oil tankers must be provided with an IGS	R1, R2.1, R4		A1, A3, A4, A5
.2 lists exceptions to this requirement	R1, R2.1, R4		A1, A3, A4, A5
.3 states that oil tankers with COW must always be provided with an IGS	R1, R2.1, R4		A1, A3, A4, A5
.4 defines inert gas	R1, R2.1, R4		A1, A3, A4, A5
.5 describes the effect of inert gas with the aid of a flammability composition diagram	R1, R2.1, R4		A1, A3, A4, A5
.6 states that cargo tanks of oil tankers fitted with an IGS should be in a non-flammable condition at all times	R1, R2.1, R4		A1, A3, A4, A5
.7 states that, in order to maintain the cargo tanks in a nonflammable condition, the system is required to: – inert empty cargo tanks – be operative during cargo and ballast handling – purge tanks prior to gas-freeing – top up pressure in cargo tanks when necessary	R1, R2.1, R4		A1, A3, A4, A5
.8 states that some refined products, such as certain aviation fuels, release oxygen into ullage space of an inerted tank	R1, R2.1, R4		A1, A3, A4, A5
9.2 The inert gas system (0.5 hour)			
.1 describes the inert gas system as consisting of three distinct parts, which: – produce the inert gas – cool and clean the gas – distribute the gas	R4		A1, A3, A4, A5
.2 describes good quality inert gas from the generating plant as containing: – nitrogen (77% by volume) – carbon dioxide (13% by volume) – oxygen (4% by volume) – water (5% by volume) and small quantities of undesirable by-products such as nitrogen oxides, sulphur dioxide, carbon monoxide and soot particles	R4		A1, A3, A4, A5

知识、理解和熟练	IMO 参考书目	教科书,参考文献	教具
技能要求			
8.4 发现紧急情况时的行动(0.5 学时)			
.1 阐述如果紧急情况发生,必须立即采取的行动: – 发出警报 – 向指挥中心提供紧急情况的位置和状态 – 停止所有的货油操作并关闭阀门 – 移走附近的船只		B1	A1
9 惰性气体系统(IGS)(8 学时)			
9.1 概述(0.5 学时)			
.1 描述哪类油船必须设置惰性气体系统	R1, R2.1, R4		A1, A3, A4, A5
.2 列举该要求的例外情况	R1, R2.1, R4		A1, A3, A4, A5
.3 阐述带有原油洗舱的油船必须提供惰性气体系统	R1, R2.1, R4		A1, A3, A4, A5
.4 定义惰性气体	R1, R2.1, R4		A1, A3, A4, A5
.5 借助于燃烧构成图描述惰性气体的作用	R1, R2.1, R4		A1, A3, A4, A5
.6 阐述装有惰性气体系统的油船货舱始终处于不可燃状态	R1, R2.1, R4		A1, A3, A4, A5
.7 阐述,为了维持货舱的不可燃状态,要求系统: – 惰化空货舱 – 货油和压载水操作期间保持可操作状态 – 除气前对货舱进行驱气 – 必要时对货舱加压	R1, R2.1, R4		A1, A3, A4, A5
.8 阐述对精练的成品油如航空用油,释放氧气进入被惰化的舱的空挡量	R1, R2.1, R4		A1, A3, A4, A5
9.2 该惰性气体系统(0.5 学时)			
.1 描述惰性气体系统由三个不同部分构成: – 产生惰性气体 – 冷却和净化惰气 – 分配惰气	R4		A1, A3, A4, A5
.2 描述发生装置产生的高质量惰性气体包含: – 氮气(占体积的 77%) – 二氧化碳(占体积的 13%) – 氧气(占体积的 4%) – 水蒸气(占体积的 5%) 并有少量不希望产生的副产品如氮氧化物、二氧化硫、一氧化碳和烟灰颗粒	R4		A1, A3, A4, A5

Knowledge, understanding and proficiency	IMO Reference	Textbooks, Bibliography	Teaching Aid
Required performance			
.3 states that the gas is cooled and cleaned in the scrubber, where: – undesirable by-products and water are removed from it – its temperature is reduced to approximately 30 °C	R4		A1, A3, A4, A5
.4 states that the inert gas must be kept under positive pressure to prevent the ingress of air	R4		A1, A3, A4, A5
.5 states that the distribution system takes the inert gas to the cargo tanks	R4		A1, A3, A4, A5
.6 explains why precautions must be taken to prevent a backflow of gas from the cargo tanks to the generating plant	R4		A1, A3, A4, A5
.7 lists the main dangers of malfunctioning as: – a rise in the oxygen content of the gas – a drop in the supply pressure – insufficient cooling and cleaning in the scrubber – backflow of hydrocarbon gas to the generating plant	R4		A1, A3, A4, A5
9.3 Inert gas plant (0.5 hour)			
.1 lists the main sources of inert gas in an oil tanker as: – the main and auxiliary boilers (flue gas) – an independent inert gas generator – a gas turbine plant with an afterburner	R4		A1, A3, A4, A5
.2 states that the main purpose of the plant is to produce a good quality, inert gas with low oxygen content (i.e. 5% by volume or less)	R4		A1, A3, A4, A5
.3 states that: – in the case of flue gas, the quality of the inert gas depends on the boiler load – in port, the boiler load depends mainly on the number of cargo pumps in service – if the discharge rate has to be reduced, a way to increase the boiler load may have to be found – this may be achieved by circulating seawater through appropriate piping by means of the ballast pump – boiler load may in many ships also be increased by dumping steam directly to the condenser	R4		A1, A3, A4, A5
.4 states that inert gas is let into the system by means of the inert gas uptake valve or valves	R4		A1, A3, A4, A5
.5 explains considerations for selecting the location of the fluegas uptake point	R4		A1, A3, A4, A5
.6 explains considerations with respect to material and arrangements of the uptake valves	R4		A1, A3, A4, A5
.7 explains considerations with respect to material and arrangements of the piping	R4		A1, A3, A4, A5
9.4 Scrubber, IG blowers, IG pressure regulating valves (1 hour)			
.1 describes the working of the scrubber with the aid of a drawing	R1, R4		A1, A3, A4, A5

知识、理解和熟练	IMO 参考书目	教科书,参考文献	教具
技能要求			
.3 阐述在洗涤塔内冷却和净化气体,在洗涤塔内: – 去除不必要的副产品和水蒸气 – 温度降低到大约30 ℃	R4		A1, A3, A4, A5
.4 阐述惰性气体必须保持正压以防止空气进入	R4		A1, A3, A4, A5
.5 阐述分配系统把惰性气体导入货舱	R4		A1, A3, A4, A5
.6 解释要采取预防措施防止货舱内的气体倒流至惰气发生装置的原因	R4		A1, A3, A4, A5
.7 列举故障的主要危险: – 惰气中氧气浓度上升 – 供给压力降低 – 洗涤塔内冷却和净化不足 – 烃类气体倒流至发生装置内	R4		A1, A3, A4, A5
9.3 惰性气体装置(0.5学时)			
.1 列举油船上惰性气体的主要来源: – 主锅炉和辅锅炉(烟道气) – 独立的惰性气体发生器 – 带有后燃烧器的气体透平装置	R4		A1, A3, A4, A5
.2 阐述装置的主要目的是产生氧气含量低(所占体积不大于5%)的高质量惰性气体	R4		A1, A3, A4, A5
.3 阐述: – 在用烟道气情况下,惰性气体质量取决于锅炉负荷 – 在港内,锅炉负荷主要取决于工作货油泵的数量 – 若排量降低,必须找到增加锅炉负荷的方法 – 可由压载泵经恰当的管路打循环水的方法实现 – 在许多船上,锅炉负荷可以通过直接向冷凝器排放蒸气的方法实现	R4		A1, A3, A4, A5
.4 阐述惰性气体通过惰性气体吸入阀进入系统	R4		A1, A3, A4, A5
.5 解释选择烟道气吸入点位置需要考虑的因素	R4		A1, A3, A4, A5
.6 解释关于吸入阀材料和设置需要考虑的因素	R4		A1, A3, A4, A5
.7 解释关于管路材料和布置应考虑的因素	R4		A1, A3, A4, A5
9.4 洗涤塔、惰气鼓风机和压力调节阀(1学时)			
.1 借助图纸描述洗涤塔的工作过程	R1, R4		A1, A3, A4, A5

Knowledge, understanding and proficiency	IMO Reference	Textbooks, Bibliography	Teaching Aid
Required performance			
.2 states that the construction of the scrubber should allow for hot corrosive gases	R1, R4		A1, A3, A4, A5
.3 explains the corrosive properties of the scrubber equivalent	R1, R4		A1, A3, A4, A5
.4 states that the drainage of the effluent should not be impaired when the ship is fully loaded	R1, R4		A1, A3, A4, A5
.5 lists scrubber instrumentation and alarms	R1, R4		A1, A3, A4, A5
.6 states that at least two blowers are required to deliver the scrubbed inert gas to the cargo tanks	IMO 1, IMO 2.1, IMO 4, IMO 5		A1, A3, A4, A5
.7 states that in generator systems one blower may be permitted provided sufficient spares are carried	R1, R4		A1, A3, A4, A5
.8 states that each blower has an inlet valve and a discharge valve	R1, R4		A1, A3, A4, A5
.9 states blower capacity	R1, R4		A1, A3, A4, A5
.10 explains that blowers may also have an air inlet and may therefore also be used to gas-free cargo tanks	R1, R4		A1, A3, A4, A5
.11 explains that corrosion-resistant materials or coatings must be used in the construction of blowers and casings	R1, R4		A1, A3, A4, A5
.12 explains that fan casings should be fitted with drains	R1, R4		A1, A3, A4, A5
.13 states that sufficient openings should be provided to permit inspection	R1, R4		A1, A3, A4, A5
.14 states that failure of the blowers should be indicated by an alarm	R1, R4		A1, A3, A4, A5
.15 states that a means should be fitted for continuously indicating the temperature and pressure of the inert gas at the discharge side of the blowers	R1, R4		A1, A3, A4, A5
.16 states that the inert gas blowers should shut down automatically in the event of: – low water pressure or low flow rate in the scrubber – high water level in the scrubber – high gas temperature	R1, R4		A1, A3, A4, A5
.17 states that a minimum inert gas pressure of 200 mm water gauge should be maintained in any one cargo tank or combination of cargo tanks in the event of discharge at maximum discharge rate	R1, R4		A1, A3, A4, A5
.18 lists possible causes of loss of inert gas pressure between blower and cargo tanks	R1, R4		A1, A3, A4, A5
.19 describes the two functions of the gas pressure regulating valve	R1, R4		A1, A3, A4, A5
.20 states that the valve is automatically controlled by means of a pressure transmitter and pressure controller	R1, R4		A1, A3, A4, A5
.21 by means of sketches, shows different arrangements for controlling the inert gas pressure in the inert gas main, i.e.: – throttling the regulating valve – re-circulating the inert gas to the scrubber – leading the inert gas into the atmosphere	R1, R4		A1, A3, A4, A5
.22 states that the pressure in the inert gas main must be monitored and that an alarm must be given when the pressure exceeds a set limit	R1, R4		A1, A3, A4, A5

知识、理解和熟练	IMO 参考书目	教科书，参考文献	教具
技能要求			
.2 阐述洗涤塔的结构应允许高温腐蚀气体	R1, R4		A1, A3, A4, A5
.3 解释洗涤塔排放物的腐蚀性质	R1, R4		A1, A3, A4, A5
.4 阐述船舶满载时烟道放残不应受到影响	R1, R4		A1, A3, A4, A5
.5 列举洗涤塔上的仪表和报警	R1, R4		A1, A3, A4, A5
.6 阐述需要至少两台风机把洗涤塔惰性气体输送到货舱	IMO 1, IMO 2.1, IMO 4, IMO 5		A1, A3, A4, A5
.7 阐述如果备件充足,在发生器系统中可以允许只带一台风机	R1, R4		A1, A3, A4, A5
.8 阐述每台风机带有一个进口阀和一个出口阀	R1, R4		A1, A3, A4, A5
.9 阐述风机排量	R1, R4		A1, A3, A4, A5
.10 解释风机也可以有空气进口,因此可用于货舱除气	R1, R4		A1, A3, A4, A5
.11 解释在风机和壳体的构造中,必须使用耐腐蚀材料或涂料	R1, R4		A1, A3, A4, A5
.12 解释风机壳体应装放残装置	R1, R4		A1, A3, A4, A5
.13 阐述必须提供足够的检查口	R1, R4		A1, A3, A4, A5
.14 阐述风机故障应由报警指示	R1, R4		A1, A3, A4, A5
.15 阐述风机出口处应装有持续指示惰性气体温度和压力的仪表	R1, R4		A1, A3, A4, A5
.16 阐述惰性气体风机在下列情况下应自动关闭： – 洗涤塔内水压或流量低 – 洗涤塔内水位高 – 烟气温度高	R1, R4		A1, A3, A4, A5
.17 阐述以最大卸油速度工作时,任何货舱或货舱组合必须使惰性气体最小维持 200 mm 水柱的压力	R1, R4		A1, A3, A4, A5
.18 列举在风机和货舱之间惰性气体压力损失的原因	R1, R4		A1, A3, A4, A5
.19 描述气体压力调节阀的两个作用	R1, R4		A1, A3, A4, A5
.20 阐述该调节阀是通过压力传感器和压力控制器自动控制	R1, R4		A1, A3, A4, A5
.21 通过草图，指出在惰性气体总管中不同的惰性气体压力控制方法，即： – 调节阀节流 – 惰性气体回流到洗涤塔 – 惰性气体放入大气	R1, R4		A1, A3, A4, A5
.22 阐述必须检测惰性气体总管中的压力,并在压力超出设定值时发出报警	R1, R4		A1, A3, A4, A5

Knowledge, understanding and proficiency	IMO Reference	Textbooks, Bibliography	Teaching Aid
Required performance			
.23 states that an audible alarm should be given when the pressure of inert gas falls below 50 mm water gauge, or, alternatively, the main cargo pumps should shut down automatically	R1, R4		A1, A3, A4, A5
.24 describes when automatic shut down of the gas regulating valve is required	R1, R4		A1, A3, A4, A5
9.5 Non-return devices (0.5 hour)			
.1 explains the reasons for fitting non-return devices	R4		A1, A3, A4, A5
.2 states that non-return devices consist of a deck water seal and a deck mechanical non-return valve	R4		A1, A3, A4, A5
.3 describes the deck water seal as the principal barrier	R4		A1, A3, A4, A5
.4 describes, with the aid of a sketch, the functioning of: – a wet-type seal – a semi-dry-type seal – a dry-type seal	R4		A1, A3, A4, A5
.5 states that an alarm must be activated when the water level falls by a predetermined amount, but the seal should not be rendered ineffective when the alarm is given	R4		A1, A3, A4, A5
.6 states that heating arrangements should be provided to prevent freezing of the seal	R4		A1, A3, A4, A5
.7 states that sight glasses and inspection openings should be provided to allow inspection	R4		A1, A3, A4, A5
.8 explains the two functions of the deck mechanical non-return valves	R4		A1, A3, A4, A5
.9 states that the deck mechanical non–return valve should be located forward of the deck water seal and be fitted with a positive means of closure	R4		A1, A3, A4, A5
.10 states that, alternatively, a separate deck isolating valve must be fitted	R4		A1, A3, A4, A5
.11 explains the advantages of having a separate deck isolating valve	R4		A1, A3, A4, A5
9.6 Inert gas distribution and venting (1 hour)			
.1 states that the inert gas distribution system consists of: – the inert gas main, which runs from the deck isolating valve forward along the cargo tanks area – branch lines, which run from the inert gas main to the individual tanks	R4		A1, A3, A4, A5
.2 states that tanks may be isolated from the inert gas main by means of valves or blanks in the branch lines	R4		A1, A3, A4, A5
.3 states that the inert gas piping may also serve as vent piping	R4		A1, A3, A4, A5
.4 states that, in such cases, the inert gas main ends in the riser	R4		A1, A3, A4, A5
.5 states that other venting arrangements are possible	R4		A1, A3, A4, A5

知识、理解和熟练	IMO 参考书目	教科书， 参考文献	教具
技能要求			
.23 阐述当惰性气体压力低于 50 mm 水柱表压时，发出声音报警或主货油泵自动停车	R1, R4		A1, A3, A4, A5
.24 描述何时需要自动关闭气体调节阀	R1, R4		A1, A3, A4, A5
9.5 止回装置(0.5 学时)			
.1 解释安装止回装置的原因	R4		A1, A3, A4, A5
.2 阐述止回装置由一个甲板水封和一个甲板机械止回阀构成	R4		A1, A3, A4, A5
.3 描述甲板水封是主要的屏障	R4		A1, A3, A4, A5
.4 借助于草图描述下述形式的止回设备的功能： – 湿式密封 – 半干式密封 – 干式密封	R4		A1, A3, A4, A5
.5 阐述当水位低于预设水位时，应发出报警，但是发生报警时，水封不应该失效	R4		A1, A3, A4, A5
.6 阐述应提供加热装置以防止水封结冰	R4		A1, A3, A4, A5
.7 阐述应提供观察镜和检查口以允许检查	R4		A1, A3, A4, A5
.8 解释甲板机械止回阀的两个作用	R4		A1, A3, A4, A5
.9 阐述甲板机械止回阀应处于甲板水封之前并装有可靠的关闭装置	R4		A1, A3, A4, A5
.10 阐述必须选择性的安装一个独立甲板隔离阀	R4		A1, A3, A4, A5
.11 解释安装有独立甲板隔离阀的优点	R4		A1, A3, A4, A5
9.6 惰性气体分配和通风(1 学时)			
.1 阐述惰性气体分配系统包括： – 惰性气体总管，它从甲板隔离阀向前沿着货舱区域铺设 – 支管，从惰性气体总管向单独货舱铺设	R4		A1, A3, A4, A5
.2 阐述货舱可以通过支管上的阀或盲板与惰性气体总管隔离	R4		A1, A3, A4, A5
.3 阐述惰性气体管路也可充当透气管路	R4		A1, A3, A4, A5
.4 阐述用作透气管路时，惰性气体总管末端向上弯曲	R4		A1, A3, A4, A5
.5 阐述可能采用其他通风设施	R4		A1, A3, A4, A5

Knowledge, understanding and proficiency	IMO Reference	Textbooks, Bibliography	Teaching Aid
Required performance			
.6 states that the inert gas and venting system must allow for: – gas-freeing – purging – inerting – cargo and ballast handling – tank entry .7 states that for those purposes the following provisions must be made: – blanks or valves to isolate tanks – vent stacks or vent risers – p/v valves – liquid-filled p/v breakers .8 sketches a typical inert gas and vent piping arrangement, illustrating the location of the above provisions and describing the above operations .9 describes mixing and displacement methods for changing the atmosphere in tanks .10 describes, with the aid of sketches, the functioning of a liquid-filled p/v breaker .11 explains why the liquid level in the breaker and the specific gravity of the liquid are important .12 describes methods to prevent freezing of the liquid-filled p/v breaker **9.7 Gas-analysing, recording and indicating equipment** (0.5 hour) .1 lists the requirements for a fixed oxygen analyser .2 describes where a sampling point should be provided for use with portable instruments .3 states that portable instruments must be provided for measuring concentrations of oxygen and flammable vapour .4 explains the limitations of meters working on the catalyticfi lament principle .5 states that all metal parts of portable instruments and sampling tubes introduced into a tank should be earthed against the ship's structure **9.8 Operations** (2 hours) *In case a simulator is provided, training for Sec. 9.8 can be done on a simulator (suggested Ex.2)* .1 lists the procedures for starting the inert gas plant .2 lists shut-down procedures for the inert gas plant .3 lists safety checks to be carried out when the inert gas plant has been shut down			

知识、理解和熟练	IMO 参考书目	教科书,参考文献	教具
技能要求			
.6 阐述惰性气体和通风系统必须考虑到: – 除气 – 驱气 – 惰化 – 货油和压载水操作 – 进舱	R4		A1, A3, A4, A5
.7 阐述为了达到这些目的,必须提供下述设施: – 用于隔离货舱的盲板或阀 – 通风管束或上升管 – p/v 阀 – 充液式 p/v 破坏阀	R4		A1, A3, A4, A5
.8 草绘典型惰性气体和通风管路布置图,说明上述设施的位置并描述其操作	R4		A1, A3, A4, A5
.9 描述货舱内更换空气的混合和置换方法	R4		A1, A3, A4, A5
.10 借助于草图,描述充液 p/v 破坏阀的作用	R4		A1, A3, A4, A5
.11 解释破坏阀中的液位和液体比重很重要的原因	R4		A1, A3, A4, A5
.12 描述防止充液式 p/v 破坏阀结冰的方法	R4		A1, A3, A4, A5
9.7 气体分析、记录和指示装置(0.5 学时)			
.1 列举固定式氧气分析仪的要求	R4		A1, A3, A4, A5
.2 描述为便携式仪器提供的取样点位置	R4		A1, A3, A4, A5
.3 阐述便携式仪器必须能测量氧和可燃气体的浓度	R4		A1, A3, A4, A5
.4 解释以催化灯丝原理工作的仪表的局限性	R4		A1, A3, A4, A5
.5 阐述便携式仪器和伸入舱内的采样管的所有金属部件应通过船体接地	R4		A1, A3, A4, A5
9.8 操作(2 学时) 若有模拟器,9.8 节的培训可在模拟器上进行(练习 2)			
.1 列出起动惰性气体装置的程序	R4		A1, A3, A4, A5
.2 列出停止惰性气体装置的程序	R4		A1, A3, A4, A5
.3 列出惰性气体装置停止后应进行的安全检查项目	R4		A1, A3, A4, A5

Knowledge, understanding and proficiency		IMO Reference	Textbooks, Bibliography	Teaching Aid
Required performance				
.4	states that cleaned and gas–freed tanks should be inerted prior to loading, ensuring that: – purge pipes and vents are opened to the atmosphere – those openings are closed when the oxygen content has fallen below 8% by volume – tanks are pressurised in excess of 100 mm water gauge and kept in common with the inert gas main – states that re-inerting after a breakdown follows the same procedure	R4		A1, A3, A4, A5
.5	states that no sounding, ullaging or sampling equipment should be lowered into the tank while inerting	R4		A1, A3, A4, A5
.6	lists the conditions which must be checked before discharging ballast from cargo tanks	R4		A1, A3, A4, A5
.7	lists the measures to be taken when loading cargo	R4		A1, A3, A4, A5
.8	states that a positive inert gas pressure of at least 100 mm water gauge should be maintained during the loaded voyage	R4		A1, A3, A4, A5
.9	states that good quality inert gas (O_2 content < 5% by volume) must be used for topping up	R4		A1, A3, A4, A5
.10	explains why the inert gas pressure may have to be decreased initially before discharge commences	R4		A1, A3, A4, A5
.11	states that: – tanks should then be pressurised before discharge – discharge should not commence before all of the conditions are in order – oxygen content of the inert gas in the main should be continuously recorded	R4		A1, A3, A4, A5
.12	explains how inert gas containment can be practised by transferring inert gas from cargo tanks being loaded to those being de-ballasted	R4		A1, A3, A4, A5
.13	states that the measures to be taken before ballasting cargo tanks are the same as those before loading	R4		A1, A3, A4, A5
.14	states that simultaneous cargo and ballast handling requires careful monitoring of the quality and pressure of inert gas	R4		A1, A3, A4, A5
.15	states that, during the ballast voyage, all tanks other than those to be gas-freed should be kept inerted	R4		A1, A3, A4, A5
.16	states that, before inert gas is introduced into a cargo tank, it should be established that the oxygen content of the gas is not more than 5% by volume	R4		A1, A3, A4, A5
.17	states that cargo tanks should be washed in the inert condition and under positive pressure	R4		A1, A3, A4, A5
.18	lists the conditions for tank entry	R4		A1, A3, A4, A5
.19	explains why certain oils with high flashpoints need not be carried in inerted tanks	R4		A1, A3, A4, A5
.20	explains the conditions in which tanks containing such oils may have to be inerted	R4		A1, A3, A4, A5
.21	describes inerting procedures when product contamination may occur	R4		A1, A3, A4, A5
.22	explains the considerations which apply to combination carriers with an inert gas system	R4		A1, A3, A4, A5

知识、理解和熟练	IMO 参考书目	教科书，参考文献	教具
技能要求			
.4 阐述完成清洁和除气工作的货舱在装货前应惰化，并确保： – 驱气管路和放气口通大气 – 当氧气体积含量低至 8%时关闭这些通风口 – 货舱加压至 100 mm 水柱压力以上并保持与惰性气体总管压力相等 – 阐述在故障之后的再惰化并按照相同的程序	R4		A1, A3, A4, A5
.5 阐述惰化期间不应把测深、测空挡量或取样设备放到舱内	R4		A1, A3, A4, A5
.6 列举在从货舱排放压载水之前应检查的条件	R4		A1, A3, A4, A5
.7 列举装油时应采取的措施	R4		A1, A3, A4, A5
.8 阐述载货航行时，惰性气体应维持至少 100 mm 水柱压力	R4		A1, A3, A4, A5
.9 阐述必须使用良好质量的惰性气体(氧气体积含量不大于 5%)装货	R4		A1, A3, A4, A5
.10 解释在开始卸货前，惰性气体压力为何必须降低	R4		A1, A3, A4, A5
.11 阐述： – 卸油前货舱应该加压 – 所有条件就绪前不得开始卸货 – 连续记录惰气总管中惰性气体的含氧量	R4		A1, A3, A4, A5
.12 解释通过从装油货舱向排压载水货舱输送惰性气体时，惰性气体如何被污染	R4		A1, A3, A4, A5
.13 阐述在对货舱压载前要采取与装货前相同的措施	R4		A1, A3, A4, A5
.14 阐述同时进行货油和压载操作时需要认真监控惰性气体的质量和压力	R4		A1, A3, A4, A5
.15 阐述在压载航行时，除了必须除气的货舱外其余货舱必须保持惰化	R4		A1, A3, A4, A5
.16 阐述惰性气体中含氧量不应超过 5%体积比才能将其灌入货舱	R4		A1, A3, A4, A5
.17 阐述洗舱应在惰化和正压的条件下进行	R4		A1, A3, A4, A5
.18 列举进舱的条件	R4		A1, A3, A4, A5
.19 解释为何特定高闪点油不须在惰化舱内运输	R4		A1, A3, A4, A5
.20 解释装运这种油的货舱在什么条件下需要惰化	R4		A1, A3, A4, A5
.21 描述成品油可能发生污染时的惰化程序	R4		A1, A3, A4, A5
.22 解释装有惰性气体系统的混装船所需考虑的因素	R4		A1, A3, A4, A5

Knowledge, understanding and proficiency	IMO Reference	Textbooks, Bibliography	Teaching Aid
Required performance			
9.9 Meters, indicators and alarms (0.5 hour)			
.1 lists the following meters and indicators in the inert gas system: – means for continuously indicating the pressure and temperature of inert gas at the discharge side – means for continuously indicating and recording pressure of the inert gas forward of the non-return devices – means for continuously indicating the recording of the oxygen content at the discharge side of the gas blowers	R1		A1, A3, A4, A5
.2 lists meters/indicators/alarms required in the cargo control room or at a position accessible to the officer in charge of cargo operations	R1		A1, A3, A4, A5
.3 lists meters required on the navigating bridge	R1		A1, A3, A4, A5
.4 states that a meter is required in the machinery control room or in the machinery space to indicate the oxygen content of the inert gas being supplied	R1		A1, A3, A4, A5
.5 lists alarms required for the inert gas system	R1		A1, A3, A4, A5
.6 states that, on combination carriers, the alarm arrangements are such as to ensure that the gas pressure in the slop–tanks can be monitored at all times	R1		A1, A3, A4, A5
.7 states that an independent audible alarm shall be provided to operate on predetermined limits of low pressure in the inert gas mains	R1		A1, A3, A4, A5
.8 states that the alarms required in accordance with objectives 9.11.5 – 9.11.7 shall be fitted in the machinery space and the cargo control room	R1		A1, A3, A4, A5
.9 describes when automatic shutdowns are required on inert gas blowers and a gas regulating valve	R1		A1, A3, A4, A5
.10 lists the additional alarms required if gas is provided by an inert gas generator	R1		A1, A3, A4, A5
9.10 Emergency procedures (0.5 hour)			
.1 lists measures to prevent air being drawn into a tank should the inert gas system fail to deliver inert gas of good quality and adequate pressure	R4		A1, A3, A4, A5
.2 describes measures to maintain the inerted condition on crude oil and product tankers if the inert gas system cannot be repaired	R4		A1, A3, A4, A5
.3 describes alternative measures on product tankers when discharging or de-ballasting with the inert gas plant out of action	R4		A1, A3, A4, A5
.4 lists measures on product tankers when tank washing is necessary in a non-inerted condition	R4		A1, A3, A4, A5

知识、理解和熟练	IMO 参考书目	教科书, 参考文献	教具
技能要求			
9.9 仪表、指示器和报警(0.5 学时)			
.1 列举惰性气体系统中使用的仪表和指示器: – 用于连续指示惰气排出侧压力和温度的设备 – 用于连续指示和记录止回装置前惰性气体压力的设备 – 用于连续指示和记录风机排出侧含氧量的设备	R1		A1, A3, A4, A5
.2 列举在货油控制室或主管货油操作的驾驶员易到达的地点内所应设置的仪表 / 指示器 / 报警	R1		A1, A3, A4, A5
.3 列举驾驶台所需要的仪表	R1		A1, A3, A4, A5
.4 阐述在集控室或机舱内装设的用于指示供给惰性气体含氧量的仪表	R1		A1, A3, A4, A5
.5 列举惰性气体系统所需要的报警	R1		A1, A3, A4, A5
.6 阐述在混装船上,报警布置应确保随时监控污液舱内的气体压力	R1		A1, A3, A4, A5
.7 阐述应提供独立声音报警,在惰性气体总管压力降到预设低压极限时动作	R1		A1, A3, A4, A5
.8 阐述满足 9.11.5 和 9.11.7 的报警装置应装在机舱和货控室	R1		A1, A3, A4, A5
.9 描述在什么时候惰性气体风机和气体调节阀上需要装自动停止装置	R1		A1, A3, A4, A5
.10 列举如果气体由惰性气体发生器提供,需要的附加报警装置	R1		A1, A3, A4, A5
9.10 应急程序(0.5 学时)			
.1 列举系统不能输送良好质量和足够压力的惰性气体时为防止空气被吸入舱内应采取的措施	R4		A1, A3, A4, A5
.2 描述如果惰性气体系统故障不能修复,为维持已惰化的原油油船和成品油船应采取的措施	R4		A1, A3, A4, A5
.3 描述在成品油船上,惰性气体装置失效进行排放压载水或卸油时应采取的替代措施	R4		A1, A3, A4, A5
.4 列举成品油船在无惰化的条件下必须进行洗舱时应采取的措施	R4		A1, A3, A4, A5

Knowledge, understanding and proficiency	IMO Reference	Textbooks, Bibliography	Teaching Aid
Required performance			
9.11 Maintenance and testing (0.5 hour)			
.1 lists and describes inspections and checks to be made on: – inert gas scrubber – inert gas blowers – deck water seal – non–return valve – scrubber effluent line – alarms	R4		A1, A3, A4, A5
10 Crude oil washing (COW) (5 hours) STCW Code Sec. A-V/1 Pa. 10, 12 *In case a simulator is provided, training for Sec. 10 can be done on a simulator (suggested Ex.5)*			
10.1 Introduction (0.5 hour)			
.1 defines crude oil washing (COW)	R2.1, R5	B1, B10	A1 – App. 4
.2 lists advantages and disadvantages of COW over water washing of cargo tanks	R2.1, R5	B1, B10	A1 – App. 4
.3 states that COW is mandatory for many crude oil tankers under international pollution regulations	R2.1	B1, B10	A1 – App. 4
.4 states that the International Oil Pollution Prevention (IOPP) Certificate of the ship indicates if COW is mandatory	R2.1	B1, B10	A1 – App. 4
.5 explains that not effecting COW operations when so required is a contravention of international rules which may lead to fines and detention of the ship	R2.1	B1, B10	A1 – App. 4
10.2 Design of COW systems (1 hour)			
.1 states that the design of COW systems must comply with international specifications	R2.1	B1, B10	A1 – App. 4
.2 lists the following items as part of a COW system: – pump – piping – fixed washing machines – stripping system	R2.1	B1, B10	A1 – App. 4
.3 states that a ship effecting COW operations must have an operational inert gas system	R2.1	B1, B10	A1 – App. 4
.4 lists the factors influencing the effectiveness of COW	R2.1	B1, B10	A1 – App. 4
.5 states that the number and location of washing machines is governed by the international specifications (IMO Guidelines on COW – 1983 edition)	R2.1	B1, B10	A1 – App. 4
.6 states that the washing pressure and nozzle diameter govern jet length	R2.1	B1, B10	A1 – App. 4
.7 states that there is a relationship between the diameter of the COW piping, the number of washing machines served by the piping and the fluid velocity in the piping	R2.1	B1, B10	A1 – App. 4

知识、理解和熟练	IMO 参考书目	教科书,参考文献	教具
技能要求			
9.11 保养和测试(0.5 学时)			
.1 列举并描述对下列设备进行的检查和试验:	R4		A1, A3, A4, A5
– 惰性气体洗涤塔			
– 惰气鼓风机			
– 甲板水封			
– 止回阀			
– 洗涤塔烟气管			
– 报警装置			
10 原油洗舱(COW)(5 学时)			
STCW 公约第 A-V/1 节第 10,12 段			
如果有模拟器,则第 10 节的培训可在模拟器上进行(推荐练习 5)			
10.1 介绍(0.5 学时)			
.1 定义原油洗舱(COW)	R2.1, R5	B1, B10	A1 – App. 4
.2 列举 COW 和水洗货舱的优缺点	R2.1, R5	B1, B10	A1 – App. 4
.3 阐述按照国际防污染规则,强制要求许多原油油船采用 COW	R2.1	B1, B10	A1 – App. 4
.4 阐述在船舶国际防止油污(IOPP)证书中指出 COW 是否为强制性	R2.1	B1, B10	A1 – App. 4
.5 解释在该要求下,没有有效的 COW 将违背国际规则而导致船舶罚款和滞留	R2.1	B1, B10	A1 – App. 4
10.2 COW 系统设计(1 学时)			
.1 阐述 COW 系统设计必须符合国际规范	R2.1	B1, B10	A1 – App. 4
.2 列举下列 COW 系统的部件:	R2.1	B1, B10	A1 – App. 4
– 泵			
– 管路			
– 固定洗舱机			
– 扫舱系统			
.3 阐述船舶有效的 COW 操作必须有可操作的惰性气体系统	R2.1	B1, B10	A1 – App. 4
.4 列举影响 COW 效果的因素	R2.1	B1, B10	A1 – App. 4
.5 阐述洗舱机的数量和位置是由国际规范决定的(IMO COW 导则 1983 版)	R2.1	B1, B10	A1 – App. 4
.6 阐述洗舱压力和喷嘴直径决定喷射长度	R2.1	B1, B10	A1 – App. 4
.7 阐述 COW 管路直径、管路连接的洗舱机数量和管路中液体流速之间的关系	R2.1	B1, B10	A1 – App. 4

Knowledge, understanding and proficiency	IMO Reference	Textbooks, Bibliography	Teaching Aid
Required performance			
.8 explains how too many washing machines operating on a given pipeline may lead to low pressure at the washing machine, thereby decreasing its effectiveness	R2.1	B1, B10	A1 – App. 4
.9 states that the effectiveness of the COW system is verified under a given set of conditions and that COW operations should therefore be carried out under the same conditions as during the test procedures	R2.1	B1, B10	A1 – App. 4
10.3 COW piping (0.5 hour)			
.1 states that the COW system consists of permanent pipe work	R5	B1, B10	A1 – App. 4
	R5	B1, B10	A1 – App. 4
.2 explains that exceptions are allowed in the case of combination carriers where tank washing machines are located in the hatch covers	R5	B1, B10	A1 – App. 4
.3 states that provisions have been made to prevent over pressure	R5	B1, B10	A1 – App. 4
.4 states that the COW and water washing piping may be combined, but that hydrants in such combined systems must be blanked off during COW	R5	B1, B10	A1 – App. 4
.5 explains the need to anchor the COW piping to the ship structure	R5	B1, B10	A1 – App. 4
.6 states that to anchor the end of branch pipes tank cleaning machines can be used, but that special arrangements are necessary when removing such washing machines	R5	B1, B10	A1 – App. 4
.7 explains that, if common piping is used for COW, and water washing, such piping may pass through a heater, which should be effectively blanked off from the COW supply during COW	R5	B1, B10	A1 – App. 4
.8 states that the oil should be drained from the line before such piping is used for water washing			
10.4 Tank-washing machines (0.5 hour)			
.1 states that only fixed washing machines may be used		B1, B10	A1 – App. 4
.2 states that these machines may be deck mounted, or mounted inside a tank (in which case they are known as submerged machines)	R5	B1, B10	A1 – App. 4
.3 describes washing machines as either single- or multi-nozzle machines	R5	B1, B10	A1 – App. 4
.4 describes the operation and washing pattern of: – single-nozzle tank washing machine – multi-nozzle tank washing machine	R5	B1, B10	A1 – App. 4
.5 explains that single-nozzle machines may be programmable	R5	B1, B10	A1 – App. 4
.6 explains that single-nozzle machines are subject to reaction forces	R5	B1, B10	A1 – App. 4
.7 explains methods of driving washing machines	R5	B1, B10	A1 – App. 4
.8 describes how the movement of deck-mounted and submerged machines may be verified	R5	B1, B10	A1 – App. 4
.9 states that each machine can be isolated from its supply line by means of a stop valve	R5	B1, B10	A1 – App. 4

知识、理解和熟练	IMO 参考书目	教科书,参考文献	教具
技能要求			
.8　解释在既定的管路上工作太多的洗舱机如何导致洗舱机低压,因此降低其效果	R2.1	B1, B10	A1 – App. 4
.9　阐述 COW 系统效果是在给定条件下验证的,因此 COW 操作应在与试验程序相同的条件下进行	R2.1	B1, B10	A1 – App. 4
10.3 COW 管路(0.5 学时)			
.1　阐述 COW 系统由固定管系组成	R5	B1, B10	A1 – App. 4
.2　解释对于混装船,其洗舱机位于舱盖上,允许有例外	R5	B1, B10	A1 – App. 4
.3　阐述有防止超压的装置	R5	B1, B10	A1 – App. 4
.4　阐述 COW 和水洗管路可以组合,但是在这样的组合系统中在 COW 操作中消防栓必须盲封	R5	B1, B10	A1 – App. 4
.5　解释需要把 COW 管路固定到船舶结构上	R5	B1, B10	A1 – App. 4
.6　阐述洗舱机可以用于固定支管的端部,但是当移动这样的洗舱机时需要特殊的布局	R5	B1, B10	A1 – App. 4
.7　解释,如果用于 COW 和水洗的通用管路可能经过加热器,在 COW 操作时,水洗管路必须有效地从 COW 管路中封堵	R5	B1, B10	A1 – App. 4
.8　阐述在这样的管路用于水洗之前,管路必须放残	R5	B1, B10	A1 – App. 4
10.4 洗舱机(0.5 学时)			
.1　阐述仅能使用固定洗舱机	R5	B1, B10	A1 – App. 4
.2　阐述这些洗舱机可以安装于甲板或者安装于舱内(这种情况下称为埋入式洗舱机)	R5	B1, B10	A1 – App. 4
.3　描述洗舱机可以是单喷嘴,也可以是多喷嘴	R5	B1, B10	A1 – App. 4
.4　描述下列操作和洗舱模式: – 单喷嘴洗舱机 – 多喷嘴洗舱机	R5	B1, B10	A1 – App. 4
.5　解释单喷嘴洗舱机允许是编程的		B1, B10	A1 – App. 4
.6　解释单喷嘴洗舱机承受反作用力	R5	B1, B10	A1 – App. 4
.7　解释驱动洗舱机的方法	R5	B1, B10	A1 – App. 4
.8　描述如何判断安装于甲板和埋入式洗舱机的运动	R5	B1, B10	A1 – App. 4
.9　阐述每个洗舱机都可通过截止阀从供给管路上隔离	R5	B1, B10	A1 – App. 4

Knowledge, understanding and proficiency	IMO Reference	Textbooks, Bibliography	Teaching Aid
Required performance			
.10 states that, if a washing machine is removed: – the supply line must be blanked off – the tank washing opening must be closed	R5	B1, B10	A1 – App. 4
10.5 Pumps (0.5 hour)			
.1 states that the pumps used for COW may be cargo pumps or dedicated pumps	R5	B1, B10	A1 – App. 4
.2 states that, if cargo pumps are used, the COW supply may be either bled off the discharge piping or delivered by one pump	R5	B1, B10	A1 – App. 4
.3 describes how, in former case, to ensure sufficient pressure in the COW piping if the terminal presents too little back-pressure	R5	B1, B10	A1 – App. 4
10.6 Stripping systems (0.5 hour)			
.1 states that effective stripping is essential for good COW results	R5		A1 – App. 4
.2 states that a positive trim is important for good COW results	R5		A1 – App. 4
.3 states that the stripping system must be able to remove oil at a rate 1.25 times the total throughput of all washing machines	R5		A1 – App. 4
.4 states that remote readout facilities must be provided in the cargo control room for monitoring the efficiency of the stripping system	R5		A1 – App. 4
.5 states that means such as level gauges, hand dipping and stripping performance gauges are provided for checking that the tank bottoms are dry after COW	R5		A1 – App. 4
.6 states that stripping system can drain cargo lines and pumps after discharge and that a special small diameter line is provided to discharge those stripping ashore	R5		A1 – App. 4
10.7 Operations (1.5 hours)			
.1 states that a ship under obligation to use COW is provided with a COW Operations and Equipment Manual, which is of standard format	R2.1, R5		A1 – App. 4
.2 lists sections which must be included in the manual	R2.1, R5		A1 – App. 4
.3 states that tanks to be washed depend on whether cargo tanks are used for ballast or not	R2.1, R5		A1 – App. 4
.4 states that ballast should only be taken in cargo tanks which have been crude oil washed	R2.1, R5		A1 – App. 4
.5 lists the following cargo tanks to be crude oil washed: – cargo tanks required for ballast after departure – cargo tanks required for ballast prior to arrival – cargo tanks required for ballast during heavy weather (if anticipated)	R2.1, R5		A1 – App. 4
.6 states that, for sludge-control purposes, no tank need be washed more than once every four months	R2.1, R5		A1 – App. 4
.7 states that, before arrival in the discharging port, the COW system should be examined whilst under pressure	R2.1, R5		A1 – App. 4

知识、理解和熟练	IMO 参考书目	教科书,参考文献	教具
技能要求			
.10 阐述如果洗舱机被移动,那么: – 必须盲封供给管路 – 必须关闭洗舱开口	R5	B1, B10	A1 – App. 4
10.5 泵(0.5 学时)			
.1 阐述用于 COW 的泵可以是货油泵或专用泵	R5	B1, B10	A1 – App. 4
.2 阐述如果使用货油泵,COW 的供油或者从泵排出管路上引出或者由一台泵专门输送	R5	B1, B10	A1 – App. 4
.3 描述在前者的情况下,如果码头背压太低,如何在 COW 管路中保证足够的压力	R5	B1, B10	A1 – App. 4
10.6 扫舱系统(0.5 学时)			
.1 阐述有效的扫舱对 COW 非常重要	R5	B1, B10	A1 – App. 4
.2 阐述正吃水差对 COW 的效果很重要	R5	B1, B10	A1 – App. 4
.3 阐述扫舱系统必须能够以全部洗舱机总流量的 1.25 倍扫除残油	R5	B1, B10	A1 – App. 4
.4 阐述必须在货控室提供可读数遥测设施以监测扫舱系统的效率	R5	B1, B10	A1 – App. 4
.5 阐述应提供诸如液位计、手动测深设备和扫舱操作表等装备以检查 COW 操作后舱底是否干净	R5	B1, B10	A1 – App. 4
.6 阐述扫舱系统在卸油后能对货油管路和泵进行放残,并且提供一条小直径管路以便把扫舱物排到岸上	R5	B1, B10	A1 – App. 4
10.7 操作(1.5 学时)			
.1 阐述强制使用 COW 的船舶配备有标准格式的 COW 操作和设备手册	R2.1, R5		A1 – App. 4
.2 列举手册中必须包含的项目	R2.1, R5		A1 – App. 4
.3 阐述是否需要清洗取决于货舱是否用于压载	R2.1, R5		A1 – App. 4
.4 阐述仅能在经原油洗舱后的货舱进行压载	R2.1, R5		A1 – App. 4
.5 列举下列货舱应用原油清洗: – 开航后需要压载的货舱 – 抵港前需要压载的货舱 – 在恶劣天气(如果可预见)时需要压载的货舱	R2.1, R5		A1 – App. 4
.6 为了控制油渣,阐述货舱仅需要四个月清洗一次	R2.1, R5		A1 – App. 4
.7 在抵达卸油港之前,阐述应在有压力的情况下应检查 COW 系统	R2.1, R5		A1 – App. 4

Knowledge, understanding and proficiency	IMO Reference	Textbooks, Bibliography	Teaching Aid
Required performance			
.8 states that COW should be carried out in accordance with the parameters set out in the COW Operations and Equipment Manual for: – number of washing machines – pressure of washing fluid – duration of washing – program of washing machine – trim of ship – stripping requirements	R2.1, R5		A1 – App. 4
.9 states that washing fluid may be obtained from the discharge line or from the slop-tank	R2.1, R5		A1 – App. 4
.10 states that only dry crude may be used	R2.1, R5		A1 – App. 4
.11 defines dry crude	R2.1, R5		A1 – App. 4
.12 describes this use of dry crude as being a precaution against electrostatic generation	R2.1, R5		A1 – App. 4
.13 explains that, in order to ensure that dry crude is used for COW, discharge should start with de-bottoming the cargo tanks which supply the crude for COW	R2.1, R5		A1 – App. 4
.14 defines de-bottoming as drawing off at least 1 meter of liquid from the cargo tank	R2.1, R5		A1 – App. 4
.15 explains how to obtain dry crude when using slop-tanks	R2.1, R5		A1 – App. 4
.16 states that COW, using oil from the slop-tanks, may be effected by the re-circulating method	R2.1, R5		A1 – App. 4
.17 explains why the level in the slop-tank must be watched	R2.1, R5		A1 – App. 4
.18 states that COW and cargo operations must be halted if the oxygen content in the tanks rises above 8% by volume	R2.1, R5		A1 – App. 4
.19 states that, before crude oil washing a tank, the oxygen content in the tank should be measured: – 1 meter below deck – in the middle of the ullage space	R2.1, R5		A1 – App. 4
.20 given a COW Operations and Equipment Manual and a stowage plan, draws up a discharging and COW programme	R2.1, R5		A1 – App. 4
.21 demonstrates ability to programme and monitor tank washing machines	R2.1, R5		A1 – App. 4
.22 demonstrates ability to calibrate the oxygen meter and to measure the oxygen content of a cargo tank	R2.1, R5		A1 – App. 4
.23 using a pumping, piping and COW piping plan, lines up the valves for discharging and COW operations	R2.1, R5		A1 – App. 4
.24 explains the items of the: – pre-arrival checklist – checklist before crude – checklist during COW – checklist after COW	R2.1, R5		A1 – App. 4
.25 explains how the effectiveness of COW can be checked by measuring the amount of oil floating on top of the departure ballast	R2.1, R5		A1 – App. 4
.26 explains the measures taken to prevent marine pollution during ballasting and tank-washing operations	R2.1, R5		A1 – App. 4

知识、理解和熟练	IMO 参考书目	教科书,参考文献	教具
技能要求			
.8 阐述 COW 应根据 COW 操作和设备手册中设定的参数进行: – 洗舱设备的数量 – 清洗液体的压力 – 洗舱的持续时间 – 洗舱机的程序 – 船舶吃水差 – 扫舱要求	R2.1, R5		A1 – App. 4
.9 阐述洗舱液体可以从排放管路或污液舱中获得	R2.1, R5		A1 – App. 4
.10 阐述仅能使用干原油	R2.1, R5		A1 – App. 4
.11 定义干原油	R2.1, R5		A1 – App. 4
.12 描述干原油的使用是防止产生静电的预防措施	R2.1, R5		A1 – App. 4
.13 解释,为了确保干原油用于 COW,用于供给 COW 的货舱的排放应该从舱底开始	R2.1, R5		A1 – App. 4
.14 定义清除舱底是从货舱吸出至少 1 米的液体	R2.1, R5		A1 – App. 4
.15 解释使用污液舱时如何获得干原油	R2.1, R5		A1 – App. 4
.16 阐述使用污液舱内的油进行的原油洗舱,可能受到循环方法的影响	R2.1, R5		A1 – App. 4
.17 解释为什么要观测污液舱内的液位	R2.1, R5		A1 – App. 4
.18 阐述如果舱内的氧气体积含量超过 8%,必须停止 COW 和货油操作	R2.1, R5		A1 – App. 4
.19 阐述在原油洗舱前,必须测量舱内的含氧量: – 甲板下 1 米 – 空挡的中部并且不应超过 8%体积比	R2.1, R5		A1 – App. 4
.20 根据 COW 操作和设备手册及储存计划,制定卸货和 COW 程序	R2.1, R5		A1 – App. 4
.21 演示说明编制程序和监测洗舱机的能力	R2.1, R5		A1 – App. 4
.22 演示说明校准含氧量仪和测量货舱内含氧量的能力	R2.1, R5		A1 – App. 4
.23 使用泵、管路和 COW 管路图,排列卸油和 COW 操作阀的顺序	R2.1, R5		A1 – App. 4
.24 解释下列各项: – 抵港前检查单 – 原油洗舱前检查单 – 原油洗舱过程检查单 – 原油洗舱结束后检查单	R2.1, R5		A1 – App. 4
.25 解释如何通过测量漂浮在所加载的压载水水面上油的数量来检查 COW 的效果	R2.1, R5		A1 – App. 4
.26 解释在压载和洗舱操作时采取的防止海洋污染的措施	R2.1, R5		A1 – App. 4

Knowledge, understanding and proficiency	IMO Reference	Textbooks, Bibliography	Teaching Aid
Required performance			
.27 explains that all crude oil washing should be completed before the ship leaves its final port of discharge	R2.1, R5		A1 – App. 4
.28 explains why crude oil washing may have to be carried out at sea	R2.1, R5		A1 – App. 4
.29 explains that the tanks must be available for inspection at the next port	R2.1, R5		A1 – App. 4
.30 states that crude oil washing operations should be recorded in the Oil Record Book in accordance with the coded list of items	R2.1, R5		A1 – App. 4
.31 explains the importance of maintenance of the COW and inert gas systems: – states that failure of equipment may lead to COW not being effected – states that COW not being effected may lead to delays of the ship – states that the inert gas supply not functioning properly results in cargo operations being suspended	R2.1, R5		A1 – App. 4
.32 explains the meaning of crude oils not suitable for COW	R2.1, R5		A1 – App. 4
.33 explains where the information on unsuitable crude oils may be found	R2.1, R5		A1 – App. 4
.34 states that unsuitable crude oils may not be carried in a tanker under obligation to use COW, unless that tanker is provided with SBT of sufficient capacity	R2.1, R5		A1 – App. 4
.35 states that COW operations may come under Port State inspection	R2.1, R5		A1 – App. 4
11 Management of risk on oil tanker (4 hours)			A1
11.1 Background (0.5 hour)			A1
.1 states that no oil, whether naturally occurring or refined, is absolutely free from potential harmful effects			A1
.2 states that all people involved in the carriage should consider the available information on their potential hazards before making any decisions *Please note: The potential hazard is intrinsic to the oil and independent of how it is handled*			A1
.3 states that managerial decisions on board an oil tanker should aim to minimize risk associated with oil carriage (probability of spill) by handling appropriate to the hazardous properties			A1
11.2 Definitions (0.5 hour)			
.1 states that risk is a measure of the probability that a harmful event (death, injury or loss) arising from a spill may occur under specific conditions of carriage or handling			A1
.2 explains that, in general terms, acceptability of risk may differ for different people			A1
.3 states that for the carriage of oil by sea, the risk involved should be considered in absolute terms			A1

知识、理解和熟练	IMO 参考书目	教科书,参考文献	教具
技能要求			
.27 解释原油洗舱应在船舶离开最后卸油港之前完成	R2.1, R5		A1 – App. 4
.28 解释原油洗舱必须在航行中进行的原因	R2.1, R5		A1 – App. 4
.29 解释在下一港口货舱可以随时被检查	R2.1, R5		A1 – App. 4
.30 阐述原油洗舱操作必须记录在油类记录簿中,并与项目编号相一致	R2.1, R5		A1 – App. 4
.31 解释维护 COW 和惰性气体系统的重要性:	R2.1, R5		A1 – App. 4
– 阐述设备故障将导致 COW 失效			
– 阐述效果不佳的 COW 可能导致船舶延期			
– 阐述惰性气体的不能正常供给会导致中断货油操作			
.32 解释不适用于 COW 的原油	R2.1, R5		A1 – App. 4
.33 解释可以找到不适用原油洗舱的原油资料的地点	R2.1, R5		A1 – App. 4
.34 阐述不适用 COW 的原油不应由强制使用 COW 的油船运输,除非船舶装备有足够容量的 SBT	R2.1, R5		A1 – App. 4
.35 阐述 COW 操作可能要在港口国监督下进行	R2.1, R5		A1 – App. 4
11 油船的风险管理(4 学时)			A1
11.1 背景(0.5 学时)			A1
.1 阐述没有油(不管是原油还是经提炼过的油)是绝对没有潜在危害的			A1
.2 阐述油船上的所有人在做出任何决定之前都要考虑潜在危害的可用信息 注意:这种潜在危害是油所固有的,与操作方法无关			A1
.3 阐述油船上的管理决定应该通过恰当处理油的危险特性致力于减小风险(如溢油)			A1
11.2 定义(0.5 学时)			
.1 阐述风险是用来衡量在运输和操作等特殊条件下由溢油引起的有害事件(死亡、伤害或损失)的可能性			A1
.2 一般说来,解释对于不同的人可接受的风险不同			A1
.3 阐述海上石油运输涉及的风险应该考虑绝对数值			A1

Knowledge, understanding and proficiency	IMO Reference	Textbooks, Bibliography	Teaching Aid
Required performance			
.4 defines risk assessment on board an oil tanker as identification and quantification of risk resulting from a specific operation during its handling and transit			A1
.5 states that risk assessment is concerned with determining those factors which are especially dangerous and determining the likelihood of occurrence			A1
.6 states that risk should be assessed against defined limits of carriage and established on the basis of existing management system on board			A1
.7 defines risk management as a decision-making process to select the optimal steps for reducing a risk to an acceptable level			A1
.8 states that risk management involves considerations of type of vessel, competence, communication, safety awareness, training and engineering factors			A1
.9 states that in the context of carriage of oil in bulk by sea, risk management consists of 3 steps: risk assessment (evaluation), spill control, and risk monitoring			A1
.10 states that risk perception is the way in which we see risk and determine its importance			A1
.11 risk perception by society for carriage of oil by sea and therefore, by the regulatory authorities (IMO) reflects the culture of the society and changes with time as more information becomes available			A1
11.3 Risk on oil tankers (1 hour)			
.1 explains that at the loading level, consideration must be given to the siting of tanks, loading pressure, ensuring proper loading practices in order to reduce the exposure of crew to the hazards and the surrounding area to acceptable levels (this may involve taking into account local weather and prevailing winds, etc.)			A1
.2 understands that at the shipboard personnel level, the person often does not understand the potential risk of mishandling of oil			A1
.3 clear instructions for stowage and carriage must be designed and conveyed so that precautions to be taken by the ship staff are well understood			A1
.4 explains that handling of oil cargo must ensure safe practices and must take into account potential mishandling that the product may receive in the hands of uninformed people			A1
.5 states that ultimately, risk management is the responsibility of each individual on board an oil tanker and reflects their relevant training or lack of it			A1
11.4 Risk assessment process (1 hour)			
.1 states that the incidences where potentially toxic vapours (the hazard) may be present must be identified			A1

知识、理解和熟练	IMO 参考书目	教科书,参考文献	教具
技能要求			
.4 定义油船风险评估用来确定和量化在操作和运输中的特殊操作存在的风险			A1
.5 阐述风险评估与判定非常危险的因素和可能发生的事件有关			A1
.6 阐述风险评估应该以船上规定的界限为背景,以船上现存的管理体系为基础建立			A1
.7 定义风险管理作为决策方法,旨在选择最优的步骤来将风险降到可接受的水平			A1
.8 阐述风险管理应该考虑船舶类型、船员能力、通信、安全意识、培训和技术条件			A1
.9 阐述在海上散装油船环境条件下,风险管理包括三步:风险评估、溢油控制和风险监测			A1
.10 阐述风险感知是看到风险并确定其重要性的方法			A1
.11 海上石油运输的风险被社会所认知并通过权力机构(IMO)反映出来,并且这种社会风险认知因为有更多的可用信息而随着时间变化			A1
11.3 油船风险(1 学时)			
.1 解释装载能力必须考虑油舱的位置和装载压力,确保合理的装载从而使船员和周围区域受到危险的程度降低到可以接受的水平(这可能涉及考虑天气和恒风等影响)			A1
.2 理解全体船员的业务水平,有些人可能不知道错误操作过程中的潜在危险			A1
.3 必须准确设计和传达关于装载和运输的说明,从而让船员明白需要采取的预防措施			A1
.4 解释油类操作必须确保安全并且必须考虑那些不知情的人的错误操作所产生的潜在危害			A1
.5 最终阐述风险管理是每个油船船员的责任,其反映了每个人相关训练水平该这方面的不足			A1
11.4 风险评估过程(1 学时)			
.1 阐述必须能够识别潜在的有毒气体可能存在的危险			A1

Knowledge, understanding and proficiency	IMO Reference	Textbooks, Bibliography	Teaching Aid
Required performance			
.2 states that: – exposure to potentially toxic vapours usually involves mixed exposures – there may be more than one vapour in the process and there may be more than one adverse effect			A1
Dose and effect			
.3 states that the dose which will have a critical effect must be identified			A1
.4 states that: – the relationship between dose and effect is very different from one oil cargo to another – the frequency of dosing may alter the effect – in some cases a frequent, low dose exposure may provide a more severe effect than a less frequent but higher dose			A1
Exposure assessment			
.5 explains that an exposure assessment must be made from the identification of the potentially toxic vapours and knowledge of their properties			A1
.6 states that exposure falls into two main types – anticipatable and accidental			A1
.7 states the main difference between anticipatable and accidental exposure as that the first may be calculated and the other may only be estimated approximately at best			A1
.8 states that anticipatable exposure is that which is likely to occur because of the improper procedures being followed by the person while handling an oil cargo			A1
.9 states that anticipatable exposure should be obvious in that it must be an identifiable consequence of a defined method of mishandling			A1
.10 states the importance of proper handling with view to 8.4.8 and 8.4.9			A1
Accidental exposure			
.11 states that accidental exposure is that exposure: – which results from an accident during transport, or during cargo handling – when more commonly a spillage occurs due to a damaged pipe or other equipment, or a tanker running aground			A1
11.5 Risk management in practice (1 hour)			
.1 states that if the result of risk assessment indicates that the risk is too high, risk management must be undertaken with the aim of risk reduction			A1
.2 states that risk management is a complex issue taking into account many factors such as a wide range of scientific, technical and legal considerations			A1
.3 states that scientific considerations relate to the chemical and physical properties of the oil/petrochemical product that are carried			A1

知识、理解和熟练	IMO 参考书目	教科书,参考文献	教具
技能要求			
.2 阐述: – 潜在有毒气体辐射通常是多种方式的辐射 – 操作中可能存在多种气体,可能产生多种不利影响			A1
剂量和影响			
.3 阐述必须能够识别会产生临界效应的剂量			A1
.4 阐述: – 对于不同的油类货物,剂量和影响的关系不同 – 暴露的频率可以改变影响 – 在一些情况下,少量的辐射也许会比低频率而大量的辐射产生更严重的影响			A1
辐射评估			
.5 解释辐射评估必须基于辨别潜在有毒气体和了解其特性			A1
.6 阐述辐射分为两种类型:可预见型和事故型			A1
.7 阐述两种不同类型的区别:可预见型可以进行计算,而事故型只能大约估计			A1
.8 阐述可预见型的辐射是由于人员对货物的不当操作而导致可能发生的辐射			A1
.9 阐述可预见的辐射必须很明显,必须明确某种确定的错误操作会产生的结果			A1
.10 根据 8.4.8 和 8.4.9,阐述合理操作的重要性,			A1
意外辐射			
.11 阐述事故型辐射: – 由运输或货物操作过程中的事故引起 – 常见于由管系或其他设备损坏、船舶搁浅而导致的溢油			A1
11.5 风险管理实践(1 学时)			
.1 阐述如果风险评估的结果显示风险太高,那么风险管理的目标就是降低风险			A1
.2 阐述风险管理是一个复杂的问题,需要考虑各种因素,例如科学、技术和法律等广泛的领域			A1
.3 阐述科学方面需要注意的事项涉及到装载的石油、石化产品的理化性质			A1

Knowledge, understanding and proficiency	IMO Reference	Textbooks, Bibliography	Teaching Aid
Required performance			
.4 states that the technical aspects relate to the process of carriage, ship type and its equipment			A1
.5 states that the other inter-related factor includes the legal considerations as: – national (the Flag State) – local (the Port State)			A1
Risk management and law			
.6 states that risk management is often controlled by legislation which lays down allowable limits of spill (e.g. within or without a special area) and puts specific duties on management and workers such as MOU being undertaken with respect to PSC			A1
.7 states that on a global basis, the mantle rests with IMO			A1
.8 states that the oil industry plays a vital role in assisting the development of legislation at the international level, which is later incorporated into the legislation at the national level			A1
.9 states that law covers risk interactions that include workplace, product and the environment			A1
Acceptability of risk			
.10 explains that risk management team on board has to determine that in case of an incident what level of exposure is acceptable to people exposed			A1
.11 states that the acceptable and unacceptable levels are easy to ascertain			A1
.12 states that the ease/difficulty of risk management decision making is dependent as follows: – ↓ risk – ↑ safety = easy decision – ↑ risk – ↓ safety = easy decision – in between = difficult decision			A1
.13 states that it is usually a level of tolerable exposure lying between these that is difficult to decide			A1
.14 states that, for example, four risk zones can be: – death or permanent incapacity – disability – discomfort – detectability			A1
.15 further states that risk management on board should, at worst, ensure that exposure to a potentially harmful incident lies in the area between disability and discomfort (Risk Zones 3 and 4)			A1
.16 defines death or permanent incapacity as the most severe category with death or permanent incapacity occurring immediately or shortly after exposure. This includes severe effects such as, permanent (unless surgically corrected) blindness			A1
.17 defines disability as a condition where individuals who are markedly helped by external assistance; treatment results in full recovery			A1

知识、理解和熟练	IMO 参考书目	教科书,参考文献	教具
技能要求			
.4 表明技术方面涉及到运输过程、船型及其设备			A1
.5 表明其他相关因素包括法律因素: – 国家(船旗国) – 地方(港口国)			A1
风险管理和法律			
.6 表明风险管理通常由法律控制,该法律规定了溢油的容许限度并且规定了管理者和工作人员的具体职责,比如 PSC 执行 MOU(谅解备忘录)的规定			A1
.7 表明在全球范围内,其覆盖范围取决于 IMO			A1
.8 表明石油工业在促进国际立法方面,起至关重要的作用,然后该国际立法应国内化			A1
.9 表明法律覆盖了风险中的相互作用,包括工作地点、产品和环境			A1
可接受风险			
.10 说明船上风险管理小组必须决定,如果发生事故,可接受的人员辐射程度			A1
.11 表明可以接受的和不可接受的程度很容易确定			A1
.12 表明风险管理决策的难易程度取决于: – 风险下降,安全上升 = 容易确定 – 风险上升,安全下降 = 容易确定 – 介于两者之间 = 决策困难			A1
.13 表明对于介于两者之间决策困难的情况通常是可以容许的程度			A1
.14 表明四个危险区域等级是: – 死亡或永久失去能力 – 残疾 – 不适 – 可检测			A1
.15 进一步阐述船上风险管理应该最起码保证人员辐射在介于残疾和不适之间的危险区域(3、4)			A1
.16 定义“死亡或永久失去能力”为最严重的种类,其发生是立即或很短暂的。这包括严重的影响,例如永久失明(除非经外科手术治疗)			A1
.17 定义“残疾”为明显需要外界帮助的情况,治疗能够完全康复			A1

Knowledge, understanding and proficiency	IMO Reference	Textbooks, Bibliography	Teaching Aid
Required performance			
.18 defines discomfort as the category that includes those for whom a full recovery is probable without external assistance, although systematic relief may be possible and reassurance desirable			A1
12 Contingency Planning (2 hours)			
12.1 General (0.5 hour)			
.1 states that an oil spill can be a great risk to human health, the vessel, coastal communities and industry and the marine environment			A1 – App. 6
.2 states that an oil spill can also seriously damage the industry's and the owner/operator's reputation			A1 – App. 6
.3 states that an oil can enter the marine environment as a result of accidental or deliberate releases			A1 – App. 6
.4 states that accidental releases can occur as a result of natural disasters, human error or due to technical and mechanical faults in oil transfer			A1 – App. 6
.5 states that intentional releases could include dumping slop wastes, acts of war, terrorism or sabotage			A1 – App. 6
.6 further states that incidents involving vessel groundings, collisions, fire, explosion, cargo reaction etc. could also cause oil spills from vessels involved			A1 – App. 6
12.2 Management (0.5 hour)			
.1 states that there are three fundamental elements that make up effective management of a chemical spill			A1 – App. 6
.2 states the three elements as: – a response team – clear roles and responsibilities – effective communication			A1 – App. 6
.3 explains the response team as typically with functional responsibilities (headed by the Master) to address command, planning, operations and logistics arrangements			A1 – App. 6
.4 explains that the key aim of the response organization is to rapidly move from reactive to proactive management			A1 – App. 6
.5 further explains that the above may also be conceived as turning the oil spill emergency into a managed project			A1 – App. 6
.6 explains that clear roles and responsibilities amount to a 'job description' for each of the identified personnel on board the ship			A1 – App. 6
.7 explains that effective communications means information flow within the ship and to the outside world			A1 – App. 6
.8 states that effective communication is a serious challenge and requires both modern technology and disciplined personnel			A1 – App. 6
.9 states that staff with an identified role in a response plan are given effective training on a regular basis			A1 – App. 6

知识、理解和熟练	IMO 参考书目	教科书，参考文献	教具
技能要求			
.18 定义“不适”作为一种分类包括没有外界帮助能自行恢复的情况，虽然可能有系统的救助并且给予安慰也是可取的方式			A1
12 应急计划(2 学时)			
12.1 概述(0.5 学时)			
.1 阐述溢油对人的健康、船舶、沿岸区域及产业和海洋环境有很大的危害			A1 – App. 6
.2 阐述溢油也严重损害行业和船东 / 操作者的名誉			A1 – App. 6
.3 阐述油类会因为意外或故意排放进入海洋环境			A1 – App. 6
.4 阐述事故性溢油会因为自然灾害、人的过失和在运输过程中技术或机械故障而发生			A1 – App. 6
.5 阐述故意排放包括排放含油污水、战争行为、恐怖主义或蓄意破坏			A1 – App. 6
.6 进一步阐述船舶搁浅、碰撞、火灾、爆炸、货物反应等也可以引起船舶溢油事故			A1 – App. 6
12.2 管理(0.5 学时)			
.1 阐述形成对化学品泄漏的有效管理需要三个基本要素			A1 – App. 6
.2 阐述三个基本要素： – 一个反应小组 – 明确的角色和责任 – 有效地通讯			A1 – App. 6
.3 解释这个“反应小组”典型的作用和职责(由船长领导)，发出命令、制定计划、进行操作和逻辑安排			A1 – App. 6
.4 解释反应小组的关键目标是能够对危险迅速做出反应，进行可能的处理			A1 – App. 6
.5 进一步解释上面的内容可以设想为将溢油的紧急情况转变为一个处理方案			A1 – App. 6
.6 解释“明确的角色和责任”等同于对船上每个人的“工作描述”			A1 – App. 6
.7 解释“有效地通信”指信息在船上的流动以及和外界的交流			A1 – App. 6
.8 阐述“有效地通信”是一个严峻的挑战，同时需要现代科技和人员纪律			A1 – App. 6
.9 阐述在反应计划中有明确责任的船员应该定期给予有效的培训			A1 – App. 6

Knowledge, understanding and proficiency	IMO Reference	Textbooks, Bibliography	Teaching Aid
Required performance			
.10 states that the training on board will include the appropriate level of tuition in oil spill equipment deployment, depending on their role			A1 – App. 6
.11 states that familiarization with relevant contingency plans and procedures will also form part of the regular training package on board			A1 – App. 6
.12 states that spill drills are an excellent way to exercise and train personnel in their emergency roles and to test contingency plans and procedures			A1 – App. 6
.13 states that the planning process is not a one-off event and contingency plans require periodic review and maintenance			A1 – App. 6
12.3 Preparation of the Contingency Plan (1 hour)			
.1 states that an oil contingency plan should comprise three parts: – strategy section – action section – data section			A1 – App. 6
.2 explains that the strategy section describes the scope (perceived risks, roles/responsibilities of those charged with implementing the plan and the proposed response strategy)			A1 – App. 6
.3 explains that the action section sets out the emergency procedures that will allow rapid assessment of the spill and the mobilization of response (personnel and equipment)			A1 – App. 6
.4 explains that the data contains all data sheets, of the cargo being carried, required to support an oil spill response effort and conduct the response according to an agreed strategy – pre spill			A1 – App. 6
.5 states that data section also includes the details of prevailing condition – post spill			A1 – App. 6
Strategy section			
.6 states that strategy section is sub-divided into 6 subsections. Introductory sub-section 1 contains the following elements: a) introduction and scope b) authorities and responsibilities c) statutory requirements, relevant agreements			A1 – App. 6
.7 states that sub–section 2, oil spill risks, includes: a) Identification of activities and risks b) types of oils likely to be spilled c) probable fate of spilled oil d) development of oil spill scenarios e) special local considerations			A1 – App. 6
.8 states that sub-section 3, spill response strategy, includes: a) response objectives b) limiting and adverse conditions c) strategy for open sea d) strategy for coastal zones e) strategy for waste storage and disposal			A1 – App. 6

知识、理解和熟练	IMO 参考书目	教科书，参考文献	教具
技能要求			
.10 阐述船上的培训应该包括根据人员角色，讲解溢油设备的使用			
.11 阐述熟悉有关应急计划和程序也应作为定期培训计划的一部分			
.12 阐述溢油演习是一种很好的方式来练习和培训每个人的应急角色，并且检测应急计划和程序			
.13 阐述应急计划不是一经制定就不变，而是需要定期检查和维护			
12.3 应急计划的准备（1 学时）			
.1 阐述应急计划包括三部分： – 策略部分 – 行动部分 – 数据部分			A1 – App. 6
.2 解释"策略部分"描述了一个范围（感知的风险、计划中分配了任务的人员的角色 / 责任和提议的反应策略）			A1 – App. 6
.3 解释"行动部分"设定应急程序，迅速做出溢油等级评估并进行溢油反应动员（人员和设备）			A1 – App. 6
.4 解释"数据部分"包括装载货物的所有数据表，要求用来支持溢油反应，并根据溢油前做出的策略部署做出反应			A1 – App. 6
.5 阐述"数据部分"也包括溢油后处理的一般情况的详细资料			A1 – App. 6
策略部分			
.6 阐述"策略部分"又分成了 6 个小节，开头第 1 小节包含下面的内容： a) 简介和范围 b) 权限和责任 c) 法律要求和有关协议			A1 – App. 6
.7 阐述第 2 小节，溢油风险，包括： a) 活动和风险识别 b) 可能发生溢油的种类 c) 溢油可能的结果 d) 溢油情况的发展 e) 特殊地方的考虑			A1 – App. 6
.8 阐述第 3 小节，溢油反应策略，包括： a) 反应目标 b) 限制和不利条件 c) 开放海域策略 d) 沿海策略 e) 垃圾储存和处理策略			A1 – App. 6

Knowledge, understanding and proficiency	IMO Reference	Textbooks, Bibliography	Teaching Aid
Required performance			
.9 states that sub-section 4, equipment, supplies and services, includes: a) on board oil spill equipment b) inspection, maintenance and testing			A1 – App. 6
.10 states that sub-section 5, management, manpower and training, includes: a) emergency/safety officer b) incident organization chart c) manpower availability d) training/safety schedules and drill/exercise programme			A1 – App. 6
.11 states that sub-section 6, communication and control, includes: a) command centre on board b) communications equipment c) reports, manuals, and incident logs			A1 – App. 6
Actions			
.12 states that actions section is sub-divided into 3 subsections as: – initial procedures – control of operations – termination of operations			A1 – App. 6
.13 states that sub-section 1, initial procedures, includes: – raising alarm – assembling full response team – identifying immediate response priorities – mobilizing immediate response – establishing command centre – identifying resources immediately at risk, informing parties – deciding to escalate response by informing port/shore authorities			A1 – App. 6
.14 states that sub-section 2, control of operations includes: – updating information (sea/wind/weather forecasts) – reviewing and planning operations – obtaining additional equipment and supplies – preparing incident log and management of reports – briefing port officials, operators and local P & I			A1 – App. 6
.15 states that sub-section 3, termination of operations, includes: – deciding final and optimal levels of emergency operation – standing-down equipment, cleaning, maintaining, replacing – preparing formal detailed report – reviewing plans and procedures from lessons learnt			A1 – App. 6

知识、理解和熟练	IMO 参考书目	教科书，参考文献	教具
技能要求			
.9 阐述第 4 小节,设备、供给和服务,包括: a) 船上溢油设备 b) 检查、维护和测试			A1 – App. 6
.10 阐述第 5 小节,管理、人力和培训,包括: a) 紧急 / 安全员 b) 事故组织图 c) 人力可用性 d) 训练 / 安全时间表和演戏 / 练习计划			A1 – App. 6
.11 阐述第 6 小节,通讯和控制,包括: a) 船上指挥中心 b) 通讯设备 c) 报告、手册和事件日志			A1 – App. 6
行动			
.12 阐述“行动部分”被分成了 3 个小节,包括: – 初始程序 – 操作的控制 – 操作的结束			A1 – App. 6
.13 阐述第 1 小节“初始程序”包括: – 发出警报 – 聚集整个反应小组 – 确认应急反应优先次序 – 组织动员应急反应 – 建立指挥中心 – 识别即将面临风险的资源,并通知各方 – 决定通过通知港口 / 沿岸当局来逐步升级反应			A1 – App. 6
.14 阐述第 2 小节“操作的控制”包括: – 更新信息(海水、风、天气预报) – 修订和计划操作 – 获得额外的设备和供应 – 准备事件日志和管理报告 – 概述港口官员、操作者和当地的保险协会			A1 – App. 6
.15 阐述第 3 小节“操作的结束”包括: – 决定应急操作最后和最佳水平 – 停止设备并对其清洁、维护和更换 – 准备正式的详细报告 – 根据学到的教训来修订计划和程序			A1 – App. 6

Knowledge, understanding and proficiency	IMO Reference	Textbooks, Bibliography	Teaching Aid
Required performance			
.16 states that the data section contains: – coastal charts, currents, tidal information (ranges and streams), prevailing winds – risk locations and probable fate of oil – sea zones and response strategies – coastal zones and response strategies – clean-up waste on board, storage and subsequent disposal ports			A1 – App. 6
13 Assessment and discussion (2 hours)			
13.1 Discussion (1 hour)			A1
13.2 Examination (1 hour)			

知识、理解和熟练	IMO 参考书目	教科书，参考文献	教具
技能要求			
.16 阐述“数据部分”包括： – 沿岸海图、海流、潮汐信息(变化和流动)，盛行风 – 危险位置和溢油可能的结果 – 海上区域和反应策略 – 沿岸区域和反应策略 – 清理船上废物，储存并随后到港处理			A1 – App. 6
13 评估和讨论(2 学时)			
13.1 讨论(1 学时)			A1
13.2 考试(1 学时)			

Part D: Instructor Manual

■ Introduction

The instructor manual provides guidance on the material that is to be presented during the course. Under each Section, corresponding to the Section in the detailed syllabus, Key Concepts are noted that need to be delivered to the students. This is followed by a few lecture suggestions for the topic and finally sample questions that the students should be able to answer at the end of the study of each Section.

The modular course delineates the requirements of training of shipboard personnel engaged, and directly responsible, for the carriage of oil in bulk. The details set out in the course is based on the specification as set out in Section A-V/1 of the STCW Code of the International Convention on Standards of Training, Certification and Watchkeeping for Seafarers, 1978, as amended in 1995.

The course material is arranged as follows:

1. Introduction
2. Basic properties of petroleum and its hazards
3. Safety
4. Pollution prevention
5. Oil tanker design and equipment
6. Oil tanker operations
7. Cargo and ballast pumps
8. Emergency procedures
9. Inert Gas Systems (IGS)
10. Crude Oil Washing (COW)
11. Management of risk on oil tanker
12. Contingency planning
13. Assessment/Discussion (this can include a written exam)

IGS applies only to officers who are to have duties related to inert gas systems, and COW applies to those who are to have duties relating to COW operations on crude oil tankers.

The books used extensively as references throughout the course are:

B1 *International Safety Guide for Oil Tankers and Terminals*

B2 *Tanker Handbook for Deck Officers*, and

B7 *Cargo work*

The course outline, as well as the timetable provides the type of allocation that is required. However, the instructor (s) will of course use their professional judgement to make

D部分:教员手册

介 绍

教员手册对课程中出现的材料提供了指导。在各节中,对应于大纲细则部分,为学员提供了注释后的关键概念,接下来是一些主题教学建议,最后是一些学员在每节课程教学结束后能够回答的实例问题。

规范课程描述了与船上人员操作有关的培训要求,与散装油船运输直接相关的部分。课程详细设定是基于《STCW78/95公约》的A-V/1节的规定。

课程材料内容包括如下:

1 介绍

2 石油的基本性质及危险

3 安全

4 防污染

5 油船设计和设备

6 油船操作

7 货油泵和压载泵

8 应急程序

9 惰性气体系统(IGS)

10 原油洗舱(COW)

11 油船风险管理

12 应急计划

13 评估/讨论(这可能包括书面考试)

在原油船上,IGS仅适用于负责惰性气体系统的高级船员,COW适用于与COW操作有责任的人员。

在整个课程中本书所广泛使用的参考资料是:

B1 油船及码头国际安全指南

B2 驾驶员油船手册

B7 货油操作

课程概要和时间表提供要求的分配类型,然而,教员当然可以依靠他们的专业判断进行必要

adjustments as necessary so that the best is delivered to the students. It is important to note however, that the instructor (s) must study the detailed syllabus. It will be necessary to prepare material for use with an overhead projector (OHP), as one of the aids. As a rule of thumb, in order to give a one-hour lecture, the instructor should have a four-hour study of the topic.

The diagrams provided as part of Appendix I give examples of the back-up material that will be useful as overhead projector (OHP) slides and trainee handouts.

Examples of exercises of simulator-based training have been provided. They can be as a useful guide where a simulator is provided to enhance the training as part of the model course. The exercise illustrates a format that may be used when setting up exercises to supplement this course. Furthermore, this kind of description may be useful in the newly required quality standard systems, which will have to be introduced at training institutes according to STCW 95.

Finally, it is important the instructor stresses throughout the course that the rules and regulations on board need to be followed and delineates the larger picture of the outcome of successful following of the rules, as well as the outcome of not following them.

The following appendices form part of this manual:

Appendix 1: Notes on the Construction, Equipment and Operation of Oil Tankers

Appendix 2: *Evaluation and Prevention of Electrostatic Hazards Associated with Oil Tanker Operations*, By J B Mills and R C Oldham; published by the Institute of Marine Engineers, London UK

Appendix 3a: Inert Gas Plants – IGS: Theory, Requirements, by Per O Hatlen; published by the Ship Research Institute of Norway, Trondheim, Norway

Appendix 3b: Inert Gas Plants – IGS: Operation, by Per O Hatlen; published by the Ship Research Institute of Norway, Trondheim, Norway

Appendix 4: Crude Oil Washing: Implementation and Operating Procedures, by Captain W D J Barker and T W Allsop; published by the Institute of Marine Engineers, London UK

Appendix 5: Case studies

Appendix 6: Contingency planning

Appendix 7: Examples of simulator exercises

Appendix 8: Snap Shots of Liquid Cargo (Oil) Handling Simulator

Appendix 7 and 8 are provided to act as a guideline in case a simulator is provided as an additional training tool as part of this model course.

Each heading of the instructor s manual corresponds to a chapter in the syllabus for the model course under Part C.

Appendix 9: Definitions

的调整,把最好的内容教给学生。然而,最重要的,教员必须认真研究这个教学大纲细则。作为一种教学手段,有必要准备使用投影仪的教学材料。作为重要的原列,为了这一个小时的教学活动,教员应该用四个小时研究教学主题。

提供作为附录Ⅰ的图表给出了备份材料的范例,这有助于使用幻灯片和印发学员资料。

手册中提供了基于模拟器的训练实例。如果有模拟器,这些实例可以作为一种有用的指导,模拟器训练也作为课程的一部分加强了训练效果。实例推出了一个格式,这个格式可作为本课程训练的补充。此外,根据STCW95公约的要求,这种描述对需要引进最新质量标准体系的培训机构很有用。

最后,很重要的是教员要在整个课程中强调需要遵守的船上的规章条例,并描绘一下成功遵守这些规定和不遵守这些规定的效果。

以下附录是这本手册的一部分:

附录1:油船的结构、设备和操作注释。

附录2:油船作业静电危险的评估和预防。J.B.密而斯和R.C.奥儿德哈母著,英国伦敦海运工程学院出版。

附录3a:惰性气体系统(IGS)的原理及要求。珀奥哈特伦著,挪威特龙赫母挪威船舶研究所出版。

附录3b:惰性气体系统(IGS)的操作。珀奥哈特伦著,挪威特龙赫母挪威船舶研究所出版。

附录4:原油洗舱的实施和操作程序。W.D.J.巴可船长和T.W.奥儿少珀著,英国伦敦海运工程学院出版。

附录5:案例研究。

附录6:应急计划。

附录7:模拟器训练实例。

附录8:液货船(油船)模拟器操作的截屏图

如果有模拟器作为本示范课程的附加教学工具,则附录7和8为其提供指导。

该教员手册的每个标题均对应C部分本示范课程教学大纲中的章节。

附录9:定义

Guidance Notes

1 Introduction

1.1 Oil tankers 1 hour

This is a brief review of the way in which oil tankers have developed over the past 100 years and how they have evolved into crude oil and product tankers, combination carriers and even more specialized vessels. Since the trainees are familiar with oil tankers, little time need be spent on this subject. Differences between combination carriers and oil tankers must be highlighted, together with the additional hazards the former may pose. The material contained in the International Safety Guide for Oil Tankers and Terminals (B1) and chapter 1 of the Tanker Handbook for Deck Officers (B2) will provide an adequate basis for the lessons. This part of the course introduces the principle of pollution–free operations through load on top (LOT) procedures.

It is also useful to rehearse oil tanker terminology. When this has been done, all of the trainees will have the same understanding of the terms and expressions used throughout the course. Refer also to sections 1.1 to 1.5 of appendix 1, and appendix 6 to this manual.

Key Concepts

1. Types of tankers carrying petroleum products

Lecture Suggestions

- Describe the cross-sectional details about the types of vessels that carry oil and petroleum products
- Describe the types of trade routes where the use of various types of tankers can be expected
- Describe the changing over associated with oil/ore and oil/bulk/ore carriers
- Discuss the pressures faced by personnel to ensure an efficient changeover
- Describe the principles of hydrostatic balance loading

Sample Questions

- Which are the four types of tankers?
- Which are the various combination carriers?
- In which type of tanker design can the concept of hydrostatic balance loading be used?

1.2 International and national regulations concerning oil tankers 1 hour

The purpose of this lecture is not to introduce a law course, but to sketch the legislative background under which a tanker operates. The lecture should make trainees aware of these regulations and how they are enforced not only by their Administration, but also in the ports the ship frequents. The international conventions referred to as R1, R2 and R5 form the basis for the lecture, which need not be very detailed. The learning objectives provide guidance on the level of knowledge required.

指南注释

1 介绍

1.1 油船 1学时

在这里简单地回顾油船发展的一百多年历史,以及它们怎样演变成为原油和成品油船、混装船、甚至特种船的过程。由于学员都熟悉油船,在这一问题上不需要花很多时间。但必须强调混装船和一般油船之间的差别,以及前者的额外风险。这些内容包含在油船和油码头国际安全指南(B1)以及油船驾驶员手册(B2)第一章中,它会提供了足够的基础内容。本课程的这部分通过装于上部程序(LOT)介绍了防污染操作的原理。

这对详述油船术语也很有用。这么做,会使学员在整个课程中对油船术语和表达有相同的理解。这些可以参考这本手册附录1中的1.1到1.5节以及附录6。

关键概念

1.运输石油产品的油船种类

教学建议

- 描述关于运输石油和石油产品的各类船舶的横断面细节
- 描述希望不同种类的油船的航线类别
- 描述有关油/矿和油/散货/矿多用途船的转换
- 讨论人员在确保有效地转换时所面临的压力
- 描述流体静力平衡装载的原理

问题范例

- 油船可以分为哪四种类型?
- 多用途船分为哪几种?
- 哪种油船的设计可以用到流体静力平衡的概念?

1.2 与油船有关的国内外法规 1学时

这一讲的目的不是介绍法律课程,而是概括油船运营的法律背景。课程应使学员了解这些法规,以及法规不仅由其管理部门并且由船舶经常去的港口当局执行。国际公约R1、R2和R5形成了教学基础,不需要很详细的讲解。学习目标提供了知识掌握程度的指南。

Key Concepts

1. IMO as the primary rule making body
2. Tankers governed by SOLAS, MARPOL and STCW
3. International rules and national legislation of a country (Flag State rules)
4. Port State control
5. Tankers are a potential for pollution
6. Accidental and operational pollution
7. Certificates on a tanker
8. Ship owner's strict liability in case of oil pollution damage
9. CLC and Fund Conventions

Lecture Suggestions

- Describe the functions of IMO in brief mainly highlighting the rule making functions at the international level
- Give an outline of SOLAS, MARPOL and STCW – the areas these conventions govern the tanker operation
- Explain the issuance of certificates under the aforementioned conventions
- Describe that for a convention to come into force in a particular country, it has to be incorporated into its national legislation
- Describe the rules under which the Port State functions
- Describe that operational pollution is a bigger threat than accidental pollution
- Describe the concept of toxic load of an area

Sample Questions

- What is the purpose of IMO and how does it relate to the world of shipping?
- If a State is party to an IMO Convention, what does it have to do to ensure compliance within its territory?
- Under what authority can Port State Control inspect a vessel?
- Which part of SOLAS, MARPOL and STCW directly deals with tanker operations?
- Name the four main certificates carried on board a tanker.
- Who is responsible for issuing these certificates?
- Can the issuing authority delegate this responsibility? If yes, then to whom?
- Why is operational pollution considered a bigger threat?

关键概念

1. IMO作为主要规则的制定主体
2. 油船受到SOLAS、MARPOL和STCW公约的控制
3. 国际规则和国家法律(船旗国规则)
4. 港口国监督
5. 油船是一种潜在的污染源
6. 事故性和操作性污染
7. 油船的证书
8. 发生油污损害后船东的严格赔偿责任
9. 国际油污损害民事责任公约(CLC)和基金公约

教学建议

- 简要描述IMO的作用,并主要强调其在国际层面上的规则制定的作用
- 对SOLAS、MARPOL和STCW管理油船运营的部分做一个概述
- 解释上述公约提及证书的签发
- 描述一个国际公约要对一个特定的国家生效,必须与该国的法律相融合
- 描述有关港口国职能的规则
- 描述操作性污染相对于事故性污染而言是一个更大的威胁
- 描述区域毒性负荷的概念

问题范例

- IMO的用途是什么以及其怎样与国际航运界发生联系?
- 如果一个国家是IMO公约的成员国,其如何确保遵从地区的需求?
- 港口国监督(PSC)基于什么授权对船舶进行检查?
- SOLAS、MARPOL和STCW的哪部分直接涉及油船操作?
- 说出油船的四个主要证书。
- 谁负责签发这些证书?
- 证书签发机构可以授权这项责任吗?如果可以,授权给谁?
- 为什么认为操作性污染是一种更大的威胁?

- How does compliance with MARPOL ensure that operational pollution on board a vessel is kept to a minimum?

2 Basic properties of petroleum and its hazards

2.1 Basic physics 0.5 hour

The purpose of this subsection is to explain various elementary physical phenomena to allow a better understanding of the hazards posed by petroleum and petroleum products. Attention must be paid to explaining the nature of static electricity, including how it is generated, and how substances may become statically charged. No particular knowledge of oil tankers is required to explain these fundamentals. Appendix 2 provides information on the evaluation and prevention of electrostatic hazards.

Key Concepts

1. Explain the physical terms with which the student should be familiar in order to understand and practically use the knowledge in the carriage of oil cargoes.

Lecture Suggestions

- Explain in simple terms all the 13 physical properties mentioned in the learning objectives under the section
- Give practical examples of usage on a tanker of the 13 physical properties discussed
- Explain electrostatic discharge in detail

Sample Questions

- Random explanation of the 13 physical properties
- What are charge generation, charge accumulation and electrostatic discharge?
- What is the electrostatic hazard on crude oil carriers as well as, on product carriers?
- What kind of electrostatic hazard can be encountered during tank washing?

2.2 Properties of petroleum 0.5 hour

Things should be kept simple. The essential message is that petroleum is made up of a range of hydrocarbon molecules, with molecular weights ranging from light to heavy. The relationship between the number of carbon atoms in a molecule and the physical properties should be explained. Appendix 1, section 2.1, together with reference B1, provides the necessary information to supplement the syllabus.

Key Concepts

1. Composition of petroleum
2. The hydrocarbon molecule and refinery process

- 如何遵守MARPOL来确保船上的操作型污染降到最低水平?

2　原油的基本性质和危害

2.1　基本物理性质　0.5学时

这一节的目的是解释各种基本的物理现象,以便更好的理解石油和石油产品的危险。应该注意解释静电的特性,包括它怎样产生以及物质如何变成带静电的状态。不需要用油船的特殊知识来解释这些基本内容。附录2提供了关于静电危害的评估和预防的信息。

关键概念

1. 用学员熟悉的物理术语进行解释,以便学员理解并在油船货油运输中实际应用该知识

教学建议

- 用简单的措辞解释所有在本章学习目标中提到的13种物理特性
- 给出油船上应用这13种物理性质的实例
- 详细解释静电放电

问题范例

- 随机解释13种物理性质
- 什么是电荷产生、电荷积累和静电放电?
- 静电在原油船和成品油船上的危害有哪些?
- 在洗舱过程中会遇到哪些静电危害?

2.2　石油的特性　0.5学时

应做简单介绍。核心内容是石油是由一系列碳氢化合物的分子按重量由轻到重的方式组成的。应该解释清楚碳原子在分子中的数量和物理性质之间的关系。附录1的2.1节和参考资料B1中的内容给大纲提供了必要的补充。

关键概念

1. 石油的构成
2. 碳氢化合物分子和提炼过程

3. Volatility
4. Health and environmental hazard associated with petroleum products

Lecture Suggestions

- Describe the details of hydrocarbon molecule, including the light and heavy hydrocarbon molecules
- Explain the composition of petroleum
- Explanation of terms in the processes involved, in a refinery, for generation of petroleum products from crude oil
- Description of the concept of volatility of petroleum
- The details of health and environmental hazards involved in carriage and handling of petroleum

Sample Questions

- What is the composition of crude oil?
- What is a hydrocarbon molecule?
- What is the categorisation of a hydrocarbon molecule?
- What is the composition of petroleum dependent upon?
- What is meant by distillation?
- What are the refinery processes involved in splitting of hydrocarbon to produce petroleum products?
- What is volatility and why is its knowledge important in the carriage of petroleum?
- What is the characteristic of vapour pressure?
- What are the hazards involved in the carriage of petroleum?

2.3 Hazards involved with the handling and carriage of petroleum 5 hours

The syllabus divides the different hazards into a number of categories, i.e.:

- *Toxicity, both from petroleum and from constituents of inert gas*
- *Oxygen deficiency*
- *Flammability and explosiveness*
- *Electrostatic hazards; and*
- *Hazards to the marine environment*

Each of which should be dealt with in depth. It is only by understanding the different aspects of danger that measures to counteract these dangers will be fully appreciated. Reference B1 and appendix 1, sections 2.2 and 4.2 provide further guidance. Further information on electrostatic hazards may be found in appendix 2.

3. 挥发性
4. 与石油产品有关的健康和环境危害

教学建议

- 描述碳氢化合物分子的详细内容,包括轻分子和重分子
- 解释石油的构成
- 解释在原油提炼产品过程中涉及的术语
- 描述石油挥发性的概念
- 在石油运输和操作过程中对健康和环境危害的详细内容

问题范例

- 原油的组成包括什么?
- 什么是碳氢化合物分子?
- 碳氢化合物分子的类型有哪些?
- 石油的组成取决于什么?
- 蒸馏是指什么?
- 涉及裂解碳氢化合物来产生石油产品的提炼过程有哪些?
- 挥发性是指什么以及为什么这方面的知识对于石油运输很重要?
- 蒸汽压力的特性是什么?
- 石油运输过程中的危害有哪些?

2.3 关于原油运输和操作的危害　　5学时

教学大纲把不同的危险分成了很多种类,即:

- 毒性,既来自于石油也来自于惰性气体的成分
- 氧气不足
- 易燃性和爆炸性
- 静电危害
- 对海洋环境的危害

其中每一内容应该深入讲解。通过从不同角度理解危害,才能完全掌握应对这些危害的方法。参考资料B1和附录1中2.2和4.2节为进一步的学习提供了指导。更多关于静电危害的内容可以查阅附录2。

Toxicity in general and of petroleum

Key Concepts

1. Petroleum and poisoning
2. Measurement of toxicity of petroleum
3. Effect of petroleum on human health
4. Relationship of hydrocarbon constituents and toxicity
5. Threshold limit value (TLV)
6. Pitfalls in assumptions associated with toxicity

Lecture Suggestions

- Different ways poisoning can occur
- Different nature of poisoning
- Effects of ingesting petroleum, contact with skin and eyes
- Description of narcosis
- Explain the varying degrees of toxicity of petroleum
- Explain the cautions to be adhered to ascertain the presence of vapour of petroleum

Toxicity of inert gas and oxygen deficiency

Key Concepts

1. Constituents of inert gas and its hazards in handling
2. Description of nitrogen oxides and sulphur oxides
3. Oxygen content and enclosed spaces
4. Importance of ensuring oxygen content with reliable means

Lecture Suggestions

- Explain in some detail the hazards involved with the low oxygen content in an inert gas
- The behaviour of nitrogen and sulphur oxides
- Explain in detail the atmosphere in an enclosed space as well as, the reason for oxygen deficiency in such a space
- Describe the pitfalls in the undue reliability on only the symptoms of oxygen deficiency
- The dangers involved when the oxygen content in a space is $< 21\%$ by volume

通常的毒性和石油的毒性

关键概念

1. 石油和中毒
2. 石油毒性的测量
3. 石油对人的健康的影响
4. 碳氢化合物成分和毒性的关系
5. 阈限值(TLV)
6. 与毒性有关假设的隐患

教学建议

- 中毒可以通过不同的方式发生
- 不同性质的中毒
- 吞下石油及其接触眼睛和皮肤的危害
- 描述昏迷状态
- 解释石油毒性的变化程度
- 解释确认石油蒸汽存在后应采取的措施

惰性气体的毒性和氧气不足

关键概念

1. 惰性气体的成分和操作中的危害
2. 描述氮氧化物和硫氧化物
3. 氧气含量和封闭空间
4. 用可靠的方法保证氧气含量的重要性

教学建议

- 详细解释惰性气体中含有少量氧气的危害
- 氮氧化物和硫氧化物的表现形式
- 详细解释封闭空间的空气以及在这种环境中氧气不足的原因
- 描述过分依靠只是氧气不足现象的隐患
- 当某空间氧气体积含量低于21%时涉及的危险

Sample Questions

- Is it true that an inert gas is not only deficient in its oxygen content but also may contain toxic gases?
- Which are the toxic gases that an inert gas contains?
- What does the sulphur dioxide content in a flue gas depend upon?
- What does the carbon monoxide content in a flue gas depend upon?
- What are the dangers involved in an enclosed space on board a tanker?
- What are the symptoms when the oxygen content decreases?
- Can you rely solely on the symptoms to ascertain the deficiency of oxygen content in an enclosed space?

Flammability and explosiveness

Key Concepts

1. Burning of vapours of a petroleum product and the flashpoint
2. The fire tetrahedron
3. Open-cup and closed-cup test
4. Flammability composition diagram
5. Gas-freeing and purging
6. Sources of ignition on board a tanker

Lecture Suggestions

- Describe the burning process of a flammable liquid
- Explain the concept, and calculation, of flashpoint
- Explain the flammability diagram in all its details
- Describe open-cup and closed-cup method of determination of flashpoint
- Describe details of gas-freeing, purging of cargo tanks
- Delve into some detail about isolation of accommodation spaces where there is a potential of gas accumulation, such as during cargo handling

Sample Questions

- What burns when a flammable liquid catches fire?
- What is meant by the flashpoint of a liquid? Why is it important to calculate? How do you calculate the flashpoint of a liquid?
- Describe the two methods of determining the flashpoint.
- Can you determine the LFL and UFL of a liquid from its flammability diagram?
- Why is it important to gas free and purge a tank? How do you achieve this operation?

问题范例

- 惰性气体不仅是氧气不足而且含有有毒气体的说法对吗?
- 惰性气体中含有哪些有毒气体?
- 烟道气中硫氧化物的含量取决于什么?
- 烟道气中一氧化碳的含量取决于什么?
- 油船封闭空间存在哪些危险?
- 含氧量降低的征兆是什么?
- 你能仅仅依靠这些征兆来确定封闭空间的含氧量不足吗?

易燃性和易爆性

关键概念

1. 石油产品蒸气燃烧和闪点
2. 燃烧四面体
3. 开口杯和闭口杯测试
4. 可燃性组成图
5. 除气和驱气
6. 油船上的着火源

教学建议

- 描述可燃液体的燃烧过程
- 解释闪点的概念和计算
- 解释可燃性图表的所有细节
- 描述测定闪点的开口杯和闭口杯方法
- 描述油舱除气和驱气的细节
- 当存在油气聚集的潜在风险时,比如货物操作期间,深入研究生活区空间隔离的细节问题

问题范例

- 当可燃性液体着火时是什么在燃烧?
- 可燃液体的闪点指什么?为什么测定其闪点很重要?如何测定液体闪点?
- 描述测定闪点的两种方法。
- 你能根据可燃液体燃烧图确定其燃烧的上、下限吗?
- 为什么油舱的除气和驱气很重要?如何完成这项操作?

- What are the sources of ignition on board a tanker and what would you do to minimize these sources on board?
- What role does weather play in dispersion of vapour mixtures?

Electrostatic hazards

Key Concepts

1. Basic electrostatic phenomenon – charge generation, accumulation and discharge
2. Electrostatic hazard on crude oil tankers
3. Electrostatic hazard on product tankers
4. The electrostatic hazard during tank washing

Lecture Suggestions

- Explain the concept of electric field and the circumstances on board a tanker when it is created
- Describe the principle of charge separation and relaxation
- Discuss the types of conductors and the release of energy
- Explain the circumstance when breakdown of charge takes place
- Describe the field strength and its potency – the factors that influence the potency of the field strength
- Give a description of explosions on tanker due to electrostatic discharges
- Discuss the types of oils considered to be static accumulators and the usage of anti-static additives
- Explain the precautions with regard to electrostatic charge and portable as well as, non-portable equipment on board a tanker
- Explain the precautions to be taken while introducing steam, inert gas or CO_2 into an electrostatically charged atmosphere

Sample Questions

- What is an electric field and under what circumstance can it be created on board a tanker?
- What is charge separation and why does it occur on a tanker?
- What is a conductor? Give examples of conductors and non-conductors, both liquid and solid on board a tanker
- What is the relationship between electrical breakdown between two points and the subsequent discharge?
- On what factors is the field strength dependent upon?
- What is accumulator oil?

- 油船上的着火源是什么？如何减少这些火源？
- 在蒸气混合物的弥散过程中天气状况扮演了怎样一种角色？

静电危害

关键概念

1. 基本静电现象—电荷产生、积累和释放
2. 在原油船上的静电危害
3. 在成品油船上的静电危害
4. 洗舱过程中的静电危害

教学建议

- 解释电场的概念以及油船上产生电场的环境
- 描述电荷分离和释放的原理
- 讨论导体的种类和能量释放
- 解释发生电荷击穿的环境
- 描述电场强度及其效力以及影响电场强度效力的因素
- 描述油船因为静电放电而爆炸的案例
- 讨论会积累静电的油的种类以及防静电添加剂的用法
- 解释油船上对手提式和非手提式设备静电的预防
- 解释当把蒸气、惰气和二氧化碳引入到带静电的空气中时所需采取的预防措施

问题范例

- 什么是电场以及其在油船上的什么环境下会产生电场？
- 什么是电荷分离以及为什么会在油船上发生？
- 什么是导体？分别举出油船上液体和固体中分属于导体和绝缘体的例子。
- 两点间电荷击穿和随后的电荷释放之间的联系是什么？
- 电场强度取决于哪些因素？
- 什么是储集性油？

- How is accumulator oil made non-accumulator?
- What are electrostatic hazards in using portable and fixed equipment on board a tanker?
- What precautions are necessary prior to injecting steam, inert gas or CO_2 in a charged atmosphere?

Hazards to the marine environment

Key Concepts

1. Concept of toxic load
2. Behaviour of oil in water
3. Economic losses caused to coastal industries as a result of oil in water
4. Operational and accidental pollution from a tanker
5. Air pollution and tanker
6. Annex VI of MARPOL 73/78

Lecture Suggestions

- Explain the harmful effects of oil on the marine organisms
- Describe as to what is at stake – the coastal industries such as fishing, aquaculture and coastal tourism
- Describe the ways by which oil enters the water-accidental pollution as well as operational pollution
- Explain that operational pollution is a bigger threat to the marine environment than the accidental pollution
- Delineate the potential of air pollution from a tanker
- Introduce Annex VI of MARPOL that covers air pollution effective May 2005

Sample Questions

- What do you understand by the toxic load of a marine area?
- What happens to oil in water?
- Why is time of essence in undertaking a clean up operation after an oil spill?
- Which are the coastal industries that can be affected by the pollution of the marine environment?
- Under which international regulation is air pollution covered now?
- What are the sources of air pollution from a tanker?
- Which area is now designated as a ‘Special Area’ to cover air pollution?

- 如何把储集性油变成非储集性油?
- 在油船上使用手提式和固定式设备时有哪些静电危害?
- 在把蒸气、惰气和二氧化碳注入要充入的空气中前必须采取什么预防措施?

对海洋环境的危害

关键概念

1. 毒性负荷的概念
2. 油在水中的表现形式
3. 水中有油对沿岸产业造成的经济损失
4. 油船的操作型和事故型污染
5. 空气污染和油船
6. MARPOL 73/78公约附则Ⅵ

教学建议

- 解释油对海洋生物的有害影响
- 描述沿岸产业:渔业、养殖业和近海旅游业有什么风险
- 描述油进入水中的途径:事故型污染和操作型污染
- 解释操作型污染比事故型污染对海洋环境造成的威胁更大
- 描述来自油船的潜在大气污染
- 介绍在2005年5月生效的有关大气污染的MARPOL公约附则Ⅵ

问题范例

- 对海洋区域的毒性负荷你了解什么?
- 水中有油会发生什么情况?
- 为什么在溢油后的清洁操作中时间最关键?
- 哪些沿岸产业会受到海洋环境污染的影响?
- 目前哪些国际规则控制空气污染?
- 油船上空气污染的来源是什么?
- 现在哪些区域被指定为空气污染的“特殊区域”?

3 Safety

3.1 General precautions

0.5 hour

Safety precautions are closely related to the hazards associated with the handling and carriage of petroleum. Safety on board oil tankers is ensured through a combination of constructional and equipment features and safe working practices. If the hazards are understood, safety measures would seem obvious. Trainees should be made aware of the need for safety precautions where hazards may seem less obvious. Such situations arise when ballast tanks or void spaces are entered adjacent to spaces where toxic oxygendeficient gases are present. Such situations also arise when sections of pipeline, which may be in open connection to gas-dangerous spaces further down the line, are opened up for repairs. Particular reference should be made to hot work and preparations and essential precautions to be taken. Most of the information on safety aspects is given in reference B1. This is supplemented by information in appendix 1, section 3.1.

Key Concepts

1. Elimination of sources of ignition and flammable atmosphere not a possibility but taking precaution against them is a requirement
2. Places of flammable atmosphere on board a tanker
3. Use of inert gas and conscientious effort to take precautions
4. Importance of relevant notices in visible positions on board
5. Hot work on board a tanker

Lecture Suggestions

- Explain the inability of creating an ideal situation of elimination of sources of ignition and flammable atmosphere and the practical scenario of taking precautions
- Delineate the areas of flammable atmosphere inter alia, the main deck and the pump-room
- Explain the importance of isolating the accommodation area from the flammable atmosphere as one of the precautions
- Explain the areas that should be kept free of sources of ignition
- Describe how inert gas can increase the levels of safety but the personnel cannot overlook the need to take precautions
- Explain precautions to ensure eliminating sources of ignition such as, smoking in areas designated by the Master, prohibition on the usage of naked lights
- Explain where and how are the safety notices to be placed
- Explain how galley can be a source of fire
- Inform the students of precautions for using power tools on deck that have a potential to cause a spark
- Describe the importance and usage of hot work permits
- Safety precautions when along side and handling cargo

3 安全

3.1 一般预防措施

0.5学时

安全措施与石油装卸和运输中的危险紧密相连。油船上的安全是靠船舶结构和设备特点以及安全作业实践综合保障的。如果理解危险,相应的安全措施显而易见。如果风险不是很明显,则应该提高学员在安全预防方面需要的意识。这种情况经常发生在进入压载舱或封闭空间,其相邻舱室存在有毒气体且氧气不足时。这种情况也发生在当某段管路一端与危险的气体空间连接,而对另一端进行开放修理的时候。对于热工作业时,应特别提到需做必要的准备工作及采取基本的预防措施。安全方面的大部分信息可参阅资料B1。这是由附录1中的3.1节补充的。

关键概念

1. 消除着火源和可燃气体是不可能的,但是要求针对这些因素采取预防措施
2. 油船上可燃气体存在的区域
3. 使用惰性气体并且要认真努力的采取预防措施
4. 重要的是在船上明显的区域提供相关告示
5. 油船上的热工作业

教学建议

- 解释不可能存在完全消除着火源和可燃气体的理想环境,现实中只能是采取预防措施
- 描述区域内的可燃气体,尤其是主甲板和泵舱
- 解释将生活区与可燃气体隔离作为一种预防措施的重要性
- 解释需要防止出现着火源的区域
- 描述惰性气体怎样提高安全水平以及人员不能因此而忽略采取预防措施的需要
- 解释确保消除着火源的预防措施,如只能在船长指定的区域吸烟,禁止使用明火等
- 解释张贴安全告示的方式和地点
- 解释为何厨房会成为着火源
- 告诉学员在油船甲板上使用电动工具需要采取的防范措施,其可能产生火花
- 描述热工作业许可的重要性及其使用
- 在靠码头和货物装卸期间的安全预防措施

Sample Questions

- Why is it not possible to have an atmosphere free of flammable gases on board a tanker?
- What will you do to reduce the sources of ignition as well as the flammable atmosphere on a tanker?
- How will you isolate the accommodation from the flammable atmosphere?
- Does the usage of inert gas completely absolve the personnel from taking precautions? If not, why?
- What precautions will you take to prevent the usage of naked lights?
- What precautions are taken against smoking?
- Are you aware that flammable gases can accumulate in the pump-room?
- Describe the precautions you will take in the pump-room
- What points will you bear in mind prior to posting safety notices on board?
- Do you understand that galley can be a potential source of fire on a tanker?
- What precautions will you take for a safe operation within the galley?
- Which kind of power tools can you allow for usage on deck?
- Under what conditions is a hot work permitted on a tanker?
- What rules will you follow for conducting work over side in a port?

3.2 Entry into enclosed spaces 1.5 hours

Refer to B1 and to appendix 1, sections 3.2 and 3.3.

Pump-rooms, cargo tanks, cofferdams, DB tanks or other enclosed spaces

Key Concepts

1. SMS on board and entry into enclosed spaces
2. Special nature of pump-room vis-ὰ-vis flammable atmosphere
3. Emergency equipment in pump-room
4. Restriction of entry into enclosed spaces be it cargo tanks, other tanks or any enclosed space
5. Common precautions apply in the categories stated above

Lecture Suggestions

- Describe briefly what the SMS says about entry into enclosed spaces
- Explain the sources and reason of pump being a volatile area that entails special precautions

范例问题

- 为什么在油船上空气中不可能不含可燃性气体?
- 如何减少油船上的着火源以及可燃性性气体?
- 如何将生活区与可燃气体隔离?
- 惰性气体的使用能完全免除人员采取预防措施吗?如果不能,为什么?
- 采取什么措施来防止使用明火?
- 采取什么措施来防止吸烟?
- 你知道可燃气体会在泵舱积聚吗?
- 描述在泵舱采取的预防措施。
- 在船上张贴安全告示之前你会记住到哪些要点?
- 你能理解油船上厨房是潜在的着火源吗?
- 为了在厨房里安全操作你会采取哪些预防措施?
- 在甲板上你会允许使用哪些电动工具?
- 油船上允许热工作业的条件是什么?
- 在港口进行舷外作业应遵守什么规则?

3.2 进入封闭空间 1.5学时

参考B1和附录1中3.2和3.3节。

泵舱、货舱、隔离舱、双层底舱和其他封闭空间

关键问题

1. 在船上安全管理体系和进入封闭空间的内容
2. 相对于可燃气体,泵舱的特殊性
3. 泵舱的应急设备
4. 进入封闭空间的限制,包括货舱、其他舱和任何封闭空间
5. 适用于上述各项的通用预防措施

教学建议

- 简要描述SMS有关进入封闭空间的要求
- 解释泵成为不确定处需要特殊采取预防措施的起因和理由

- Describe the usage of emergency equipment in the pump-room in case of evacuation
- Give the students the details of precautions applicable in all cases of entry into enclosed spaces

Sample Questions

- Are you familiar about SMS on board?
- What does it say about entry into pump-rooms?
- Are you aware that the pump-room constitutes special hazards?
- What are these special hazards?
- How is the hazardous atmosphere in the pump-room created?
- What will you do to minimize the pump-room hazards?
- What questions will you ask yourself before entering a pump-room?
- What emergency equipment will you check before entering a pump-room?
- Can you list the precautions for entry into any kind of enclosed space?

3.3 Precautions against electrostatic hazard 0.5 hour

Refer to B1 and to appendix 2.

Key Concepts

1. Electrostatic hazard and inert as well as, non-inert atmosphere
2. Use of equipment in such atmosphere

Lecture Suggestions

- Discuss the precautions necessary while using equipment on deck in a charged atmosphere
- Describe the type and use of non-conductive equipment
- Explain the presence of particulates in suspension and the associated hazard in an inert atmosphere

Sample Questions

- What is the difference between inert and non-inert atmosphere?
- What kind of equipment will you use in the different types of atmosphere stated above?
- What precautions will you take?
- Is inerted atmosphere entirely safe from electrostatic hazard in order to use say, a measuring instrument?
- From where will you get the information whether the cargo to be loaded is static accumulator or not?

- 描述应急辙离时泵舱应急设备的使用
- 给学员提供在所有情况下进入泵舱都适用的详细预防措施

问题范例

- 你熟悉船上的SMS吗?
- SMS对于进入泵舱有什么要求?
- 你知道泵舱存在的特殊危害吗?
- 这些特殊危害是什么?
- 泵舱内的有害气体是怎样产生的?
- 你会怎样做来把泵舱的危害减至最小?
- 在进入泵舱前你会问你自己什么问题?
- 在进入泵舱前你会检查什么应急设备?
- 你能列举出进入任何封闭空间的预防措施吗?

3.3 防止静电危害的措施 0.5学时

参见B1和附录2。

关键概念

1. 静电危害和惰化及未惰化的气体
2. 在上述环境中使用设备

教学建议

- 讨论在充满电荷的甲板上使用设备时有必要采取的预防措施
- 描述绝缘性设备的种类和用法
- 解释在惰化的空气中悬浮颗粒的出现及其危险

问题范例

- 惰化和未惰化气体的区别是什么?
- 对于上述提到的不同种类空气中你会使用什么类型的设备?
- 你会采取哪些预防措施?
- 在完全惰化的气体中比如使用一个测量仪表,没有静电危险吗?
- 你可以从哪里得到有关待装货油是静电储集性或不是的信息?

- Are you aware of the precaution that you will have to take in case of loading static accumulator oil in a non-inerted tank?

3.4 Gas indicators 1.5 hours

Refer to B1. Trainees should be instructed in using and calibrating the instruments, which are provided for measuring the atmosphere of enclosed spaces.

Key Concepts

1. Operating principle of six indicators
2. Usage in different atmosphere

Lecture Suggestions

- As indicated in Key Concepts above

Sample Questions

- The instructor should ask the principles of operation of six types of gas indicators at random
- Can you state the type of atmosphere where you will use the six indicators?

3.5 Fire-fighting principles – revision 1 hour

This should take the form of a refresher lecture. Trainees should have completed a course on fire-fighting aspects applicable to tankers, so that a classroom lecture will be sufficient. Emphasis should be laid on cargo-associated fires. Statutory requirements for oil tanker should be explained, using the 1974 SOLAS Convention (R1) as a basis.

Key Concepts

1. Fire tetrahedron as the basic principle of fire-fighting
2. Principles of removing the sides of the fire tetrahedron singularly
3. Water, foam, carbon dioxide as a means of fire-fighting
4. Halon disrupts the chain of chemical reaction in a fire
5. Use of halon prohibited today
6. Rules governing fire-fighting, and the availability of the fire-fighting equipment as required by such rules

Lecture Suggestions

- Revise the principles involving the removal of the sides of the fire triangle singularly
- Explain the availability of material and equipment to be used in the aforementioned exercise
- Describe the properties of water, foam and CO_2

- 如果将静电储集性油装入未惰化的货舱中,你知道必须采取的预防措施吗?

3.4 气体监测仪 1.5学时

参考B1。应该指导学员使用和校正用来测量封闭空间气体的仪器。

关键概念

1. 六种监测仪的工作原理
2. 在不同空气中的用法

教学建议

- 如上述关键概念所示

问题范例

- 教员应随机提问六种监测仪的工作原理
- 你能分别说出使用这六种监测仪的大气类型吗?

3.5 防火原理—修订 1学时

该内容采取进修的讲课形式。学员应该已完成了油船消防课程,所以课堂讲授足够了。根据《SOLAS 74公约》,着重解释油船货物相关的法定要求。

关键概念

1. 燃烧四面体作为基本的防火原理
2. 移走燃烧四面体每个面的原理
3. 水、泡沫和二氧化碳作为灭火方式
4. Halon破坏燃烧化学反应链
5. Halon现在已经被禁止使用
6. 防火的规则以及这些规则下的防火设备的可用性

教学建议

- 涉及移走着火三要素的边进行灭火的原理的修订
- 解释在上述的练习中材料和设备的可用性
- 描述水、泡沫和二氧化碳的性质

- Explain briefly what halon did in fire-fighting and its present day ban due to it being a greenhouse gas contributing in the depletion of the Ozone layer
- Explain that prohibition on the use of halon is under Article 2B of the Montreal Protocol on substances that Deplete the Ozone Layer (the Montreal Protocol is part of the Vienna Convention on the Protection of the Ozone Layer)
- Briefly explain the SOLAS requirement for the fire-fighting equipment on board a tanker

Sample Questions

- Are you absolutely clear in the concept of the fire tetrahedron as the basis of firefighting?
- Which side of the said fire tetrahedron is the easiest to remove in order to extinguish the fire?
- What material will you use in different scenarios to extinguish a fire?
- Are you absolutely clear as to what material cannot be used in different types of fire?
- What do you understand by high-expansion foam?
- What is the shelf life of different categories of foam?
- What is halon?
- What did it do to extinguish a fire?
- Why is its use prohibited today and the prohibition comes under which international Protocol of which Convention?
- Where will you find the details of fire-fighting equipment that is to be carried on board a tanker?

3.6 Protective equipment 1 hour

Trainees should exercise with the equipment in use on oil tankers.

Key Concepts

1. An understanding of the basic requirements of the equipments and under what circumstance they are used

Lecture Suggestions and Practical demonstration/conduct an exercise

- Explain the functioning of all the parts of the equipments
- Discuss the maintenance of the equipments
- Emphasize the importance of keeping the equipments in a state of readiness at all times

Sample Questions

- Under what circumstances would you use the following equipment?

- 简要解释Halon的灭火方法以及现在其被禁用是因为它会产生消耗臭氧层的温室气体
- 解释Halon被禁用是基于蒙特利尔议定书中2B章节有关消耗臭氧层物质的内容(蒙特利尔议定书是维也纳关于保护臭氧层公约的一部分)
- 简要解释SOLAS公约关于油船防火设备的要求

问题范例

- 你完全清楚燃烧四面体作为防火的基本概念吗?
- 为了灭火,燃烧四面体的哪个面最容易移走?
- 灭火时不同的情况你会使用什么灭火材料?
- 你对于不同类型的火不能使用哪种材料完全清楚吗?
- 你怎么理解高膨胀率泡沫?
- 不同种类的泡沫的有效期限是多少?
- Halon是什么?
- 它怎样来灭火?
- Halon为什么今天会被禁用以及它的禁用是基于哪个公约的哪个议定书?
- 你会在哪儿找到油船上灭火设备的细节?

3.6 保护设备 1学时

学员应该使用油船上的设备进行练习。

关键概念

1. 理解设备的基本要求及其适用环境

教学建议和实际演示/指导练习

- 解释设备所有部分的作用
- 讨论设备的维护
- 强调使设备随时可用的重要性

问题范例

- 在什么情况下你会使用下面的设备?

- Tank evacuation equipment
- Resuscitation equipment
- SCBA

- Can you show the functioning of the aforementioned equipment (ask for a practical demonstration from a trainee)?
- What are the parameters you would check to ensure a proper maintenance of the equipment?
- How frequently would you check to ensure readiness at all times?
- Where would you record the maintenance done?
- Which authority can inspect the state of the said equipment?

4 Pollution prevention

The principles of the prevention of marine pollution by oil have been laid down in the International Convention for the Prevention of Pollution from Ships – Annex I (reference R2.2). The convention, commonly referred to as MARPOL 73/78, contains provisions for the construction, equipment and operations of oil tankers. In this respect the Convention is similar to SOLAS 1974, although in the case of MARPOL it is the protection of the marine environment, not safety considerations, which forms the basis of the provisions. It follows that in the course, chapters concerning the construction, equipment and operation of oil tanker reflect the provisions of both conventions. For trainees the source of the regulations is not of great relevance, but for a better understanding of the requirements they should be informed of the principles underlying the provisions of MARPOL 73/78. In addition to the convention (R2.1), section 4 of appendix 1 of this course contains much useful information on the aim of MARPOL 73/78 and the means provided to achieve these aims. The detailed teaching syllabus makes clear the depth to which the subject matter should be treated.

4.1 Ships and equipment — 0.5 hour

Through this section trainees should learn the means, which have been made available to them for the prevention of marine pollution. Reference R2.2 and sections 4.4 and 4.5 of appendix 1 of this course provide guidance on this issue.

Key Concepts

1. Constructional and equipment requirements of a tanker, including exemptions
2. Changes expected in future with respect to double hull and mid-deck design
3. Maintenance of equipment
4. IOPP Certificate

Lecture Suggestions

- Explain the constructional requirements with regard to carriage of ballast and piping arrangements

- 油舱辙离设备
- 抢救设备
- 自给式呼吸机

- 你能指出上述设备的功能吗(要求学员进行示范)?
- 为确保正确维护设备,你应该检查的参数有哪些?
- 怎样的检查频次才能确保一直处于准备就绪状态?
- 你会把维修结果记录在哪儿?
- 哪个主管机关可以检查上述设备的状态

4　污染的预防

防止海洋油污染的原则已经在《国际防止船舶造成污染公约》—附则Ⅰ(参见R2.2)中进行了陈述。公约,一般指的是MARPOL 73/78公约,包含油船结构、设备和操作的有关条款。在这方面,MARPOL公约与SOLAS 1974相似,尽管MARPOL是基于海洋环境保护,而不是出于安全考虑的公约。基于此,在该课程中有关油船的结构、设备和操作的章节,反映了两个公约的条款。对于学员来说,法规的出处不是最主要的,只是为了更好地理解法规的要求,应告知他们MARPOL 73/78条款中的基本原则。除了公约(R2.1),本课程附录1中的第4节中包含很多关于MARPOL 73/78公约的目的以及实现这些目的的措施。教学大纲细则明确了该主题应掌握的深度。

4.1 船舶和设备　　0.5学时

通过这一节,学员应该学会一些已经应用于海洋环境保护的方法。参考R2.2和本课程附录1中的4.4和4.5节在这一问题上提供的指导。

关键概念

1. 油船结构和设备要求,包括免除情况
2. 将来预期的改变,包括双壳和中甲板设计
3. 设备的维护
4. IOPP证书

教学建议

- 解释有关携带的压载水和管路布置的结构要求

- Explain in detail what are double hull and a mid-deck design tanker as these design requirements will become mandatory in the future
- Describe what are approved equipment and the areas where it is of extreme importance to be provided such as control of discharge
- Explain that all of above is a way to protect the marine environment, apart from contributing to increased safety on board
- Describe the contents of IOPP Certificate

Sample Questions

- Which are the six areas where constructional requirements are governed by law?
- What in your opinion does compliance with the constructional requirement achieve, that is other than safety?
- Can you describe the equipment that contributes towards the protection of the marine environment?
- Which types of oil tankers have different requirements for them?
- What information is contained in the IOPP Certificate?

4.2 Operational pollution 1 hour

Trainees should be made aware that most of the marine pollution from ships is caused by the day-to-day operations of ships. The sections on cargo, ballast and tank-washing operation go into this matter more deeply and at this stage the principles of the operational procedure must be dealt with.

At sea and in port

Key Concepts

1. Stipulations for discharge from an oil tanker
2. Shore reception facilities and Master's responsibility
3. Visual observations during discharge of dirty ballast
4. Pollution prevention precautions while in port

Lecture Suggestions

- Describe the objective and the various stages of LOT procedure
- Explain the importance of adhering to the discharge stipulations
- Explain that failure to abide by the discharge stipulations makes the vessel liable to fines
- Discuss the procedures to use the shore reception facility
- Explain that the Master should inform the Flag State in case not satisfied by the reception facilities

- 详细解释什么是双壳和中甲板设计,因为这些设计要求在未来会成为强制性要求
- 描述哪些是认可的设备和非常重要的区域,例如排放控制区域
- 解释上面所述除了有助于提高船舶安全性外主要是为了保护海洋环境
- 描述IOPP证书的内容

问题范例

- 法律规定在结构要求方面的6个区域是哪些?
- 在你看来符合结构要求除了安全性外还能有什么好处?
- 你能描述有助于海洋环境保护作用的设备吗?
- 哪种类型的油船对它们有不同的要求?
- IOPP证书里包含了什么信息?

4.2 操作性污染

1学时

学员应该知道大部分来自船舶的海洋污染都是由船舶日常操作引起。关于货物、压载和洗舱操作这一节要更深一步的详细阐述,而且必须在这个阶段讨论操作程序的原则。

在海上和港内

关键概念

1. 油船的排放规定
2. 岸上接收设施和船长的责任
3. 污染压载水排放期间的视觉观察
4. 港内的污染预防措施

教学建议

- 描述装于上部法的目标和各个阶段
- 解释遵守排放规定的重要性
- 解释违反排放规定会使船舶可能受到罚款处罚
- 讨论使用岸上接收设施的程序
- 解释万一本船与接收设施不匹配船长应该通知船旗国

- Explain that visual observations need to be made during the entire operation of discharge of dirty ballast
- Discuss the various precautions to be taken in port

Sample Questions

- What is the purpose of following LOT procedures?
- Can you describe the various stages of the LOT procedures?
- State the dirty ballast discharge stipulations
- Under what circumstances will you use a reception facility?
- Are you aware that the intention of using the reception facility requires prior notice as well as, preparation?
- In case dissatisfied by the reception facility, what should the Master do? Whom should she/he inform and why?
- Describe the seven precautions that you will take while in port

4.3 Oil Record Book (ORB) 1 hour

The Oil Record Book is a legal document and is subject to inspection by flag State and port State authorities. Trainees must be made aware of the importance of keeping the book up to date. Exercises should be devised to enable trainees to gain proficiency in recording operations.

Key Concepts

1. Entries in an Oil Record Book

Lecture Suggestions

- Discuss in detail the types of entries that are to be made in an ORB
- Explain the importance of making correct entries as the same is an evidence admissible in a court of law as well as, shore authorities authority to check the same at random
- Tell the students the validity period of ORB. Explain that this is because in case of an oil pollution incident, the claims can be made up to three years from the date of the incidence

Sample Questions

- What is the difference between an ORB aboard a tanker and a non-tanker?
- After which operations is an entry required in the ORB?
- In what format will you make an entry and the language(s) to be used?
- Are you aware that shore authorities, such as the Port State Control, can ask for the ORB to be inspected at random?

- 解释在整个排放污染压载水的过程中都需要进行视觉观察
- 讨论在港内需要采取的各种预防措施

问题范例

- 遵从装于上部法的目的是什么?
- 你能描述装于上部法的各个阶段吗?
- 阐述污染压载水排放规定。
- 在什么条件下可以使用接收设施?
- 你知道在使用接收设施之前应该提前通知和做好准备吗?
- 如果与接收设施不匹配,船长应该怎样做?他应该通知谁,为什么?
- 描述在港内是应该采取的七项预防措施。

4.3 油类记录簿 (ORB) 1学时

油类记录簿是法定文件,接受船旗国和港口国当局检查。学员必须知晓保持记录更新的重要性。应该设计一些练习,使学员能够精通记录操作。

关键概念

1. 油类记录簿的录入

教学建议

- 详细讨论油类记录簿中录入条目的种类
- 解释正确记录的重要性,既可以作为法庭上可接受的证据,也可以接受港口主管机关的随机检查
- 告诉学员油类记录簿的有效期。解释这是因为如果发生油污染事故,索赔有效期可以从事故发生日起三年有效

问题范例

- 油船和非油船的油类记录簿有什么区别?
- 哪些操作要求记录在油类记录簿里?
- 要用哪种格式及语言记录这些条目?
- 你知道港口当局,例如港口国监督(PSC),可以随机对油类记录簿进行检查吗?

- For how long will you maintain the ORB on board? Can you tell the reason behind the set time frame?

4.4 Action in case of oil spills — 1 hour

There is a distinct difference between treating oil spills in port and at sea. In port action will be initiated immediately to mitigate the effects of a spill. Spills at sea are frequently left alone to break up, disperse or evaporate. The decision is up to the State which is most directly affected, either the port State or the coastal State. Trainees should be made aware that reporting oil spills is a convention requirement and very probably a statutory requirement, and that no observance of this requirement may be subject to penalties. Reference R6 sets out the obligations and contains guidelines on how to comply with them.

At sea and in port

Key Concepts

1. Reporting of oil spills – preliminary as well as subsequent reports
2. Actions to be taken when in port

Lecture Suggestions

- Discuss in detail the reasons behind making reports a requirement by law and, to ensure a quick and an effective clean up operation thereby respecting the marine environment
- Describe the details of types and times of making reports
- Discuss the procedures to be followed in case of a spill when in port

Sample Questions

- Why is it imperative to make a report in case of an oil spill?
- To whom will you make the report?
- At what times will you make the report?
- State the items that you will include in the reports.
- State the six immediate actions you will take in case of a spill while in port.

4.5 Air pollution — 0.5 hour

This is a matter of growing international concern. Rules to control air pollution are included in a new Annex VI to MARPOL, which will enter into force 12 months after the date in which it has been accepted by not less than 15 states, the combined tonnage of which is not less than 50% of the world's fleet. Trainees should be made aware that there may be local or national rules, which must be complied with. Refer to section 4.6 of appendix 1 for further information.

Key Concepts

1. Causes and prevention of air pollution on board a tanker

- 你会把油类记录簿留船保存多久?你知道设定时间规定背后的原因吗?

4.4 万一发生溢油后的行动 1学时

在港口和在海上处理溢油有着明显的区别。在港口,必须立即采取行动来减轻溢油影响。在海上,通常让溢油自行分解、消散或蒸发。由受直接影响最严重的国家,一般是港口国或沿岸国做出决定。学员应该知晓报告溢油是公约的要求,并且很可能是强制要求,不遵守该要求可能面临处罚。参考书目R6 规定了该义务及如何遵守该义务的指南。

在海上和港内

关键概念

1. 报告溢油—初始报告及随后的报告
2. 在港内需要采取的行动

教学建议

- 详细讨论事故后根据法律要求做出报告并确保迅速有效地清理以保护海洋环境的原因
- 详细描述报告的种类和次数
- 讨论万一在港内发生溢油时需要遵循的程序

问题范例

- 万一发生溢油为什么进行报告很重要?
- 你会报告给谁?
- 你会做几次报告?
- 阐述报告中包含的项目。
- 阐述万一发生港内溢油,你会采取的6个紧急行动。

4.5 空气污染 0.5学时

这是一个逐渐受到国际社会关注的问题。控制大气污染的规则包含在新MARPOL公约的附则Ⅵ中,它将在不少于15个国家接受日期后的12月内生效,并且这些国家的商船总吨位应不少于世界商船总吨位的50%。学员应知道地区或国家法规要与之相符合。进一步的内容参考附录1中的4.6节。

关键概念

1. 油船引发大气污染的原因和预防

Lecture Suggestions

- Describe the reason for the importance of the issue of air pollution
- Discuss that shore industries are already tackling the issue of air pollution and that now it is the turn of the marine industry to put a check
- Discuss that Annex VI of MARPOL now covers air pollution. This Annex came into force on 19th May 2005. The Baltic Sea area is a special area under Annex VI
- Describe the areas where vapours can cause an air pollution and the containment procedures

Sample Questions

- What are the sources of air pollution on a tanker?
- What procedures are employed to contain air pollution from a tanker?
- Under what international regulation is air pollution covered now?
- Which sea area is a special area under the aforementioned regulation?

5 Oil tanker design and equipment

5.1 Construction

0.5 hour

As indicated earlier, construction requirements reflect both safety and environmental considerations. Both approaches are spelled out in the detailed teaching syllabus. Refer to both SOLAS 1974 (R1) and MARPOL 73/78 (R2.1). Section 4 of appendix 1 contains useful supplementary information insofar as part of it concerns environmental matters.

Safety considerations

Key Concepts

1. An idea of the placing of cargo spaces, accommodation and the navigation bridge
2. The principle governing such a placement

Lecture Suggestions

- Discuss the division of a tanker from safety point of view
- Discuss the importance of cofferdams as a means of separation
- Give a description of the maintenance of fire integrity on board a tanker

Sample Questions

- How is an oil tanker divided and what means are used for such a division?
- How is the accommodation protected?

教学建议

- 描述公布空气污染重要性的理由
- 讨论岸上产业已经着手应对空气污染，现在轮到海上产业进行自身反省
- 讨论现在已涵盖空气污染的《MARPOL公约》附则Ⅵ内容。该附则2005年5月19日生效，其中波罗的海被附则Ⅵ确定为特殊区域
- 讨论油船蒸气可以引起空气污染的区域和控制程序

问题范例

- 油船的空气污染源是什么？
- 可以用什么程序控制油船引起的空气污染？
- 现在空气污染受哪些国际公约控制？
- 根据上述规则哪个海域被定为特殊海域？

5　油船设计和设备

5.1 结构　　0.5学时

正如前面指出的，结构要求反映了安全和环境保护两方面的考虑。两方面的研究途径在教学大纲细则中做了细致说明。参考SOLAS 1974(R1)和MARPOL 73/78(R2.1)。附录1中的第4节包含了有关于环境保护方面的补充内容。

安全考虑

关键概念

1. 有关货物空间、生活区和驾驶台布置的理念
2. 做出如上安排的原则

教学建议

- 从安全的角度来讨论油船的分舱
- 讨论干隔舱作为一种分隔手段的重要性
- 对油船防火整体性的维护进行描述

问题范例

- 油船如何分区以及在划分中用到了什么方法？
- 如何保护生活区？

Environmental considerations

Key Concepts

1. Protection of the marine environment achieved through the positioning as well as, types of ballast tanks and COW
2. Rules governing existence of COW on a tanker
3. Enhanced inspection program

Lecture Suggestions

- Discuss in some detail the concept of SBT and CBT
- Ensure that the students are aware of the SBT, CBT and COW requirements as per MARPOL
- Touch briefly on how COW contributes to the protection of the marine environment (this is discussed in detail at a later stage)
- Discuss the enhanced inspection programme for oil tankers

Sample Questions

- What are SBT and CBT? Why are they so named?
- What is the basic difference between the two and state the advantages of SBT over CBT?
- What are the criteria used to determine the size of SBT and CBT?
- What is the MARPOL requirement governing SBT and CBT?
- What is COW and how does its operation contribute to the protection of the marine environment?
- What is the MARPOL requirement governing COW?
- What is an enhanced inspection programme for an oil tanker?

5.2 Pumping, piping and discharge requirements 1.5 hours

Pipeline configurations and cargo pumps are matters subject to commercial considerations. Trainees should be made familiar with the different options available and their advantages and disadvantages. MARPOL 73/78 lays down requirements with respect to the overboard line and the stripping of pumps and pipelines. Trainees must be made aware that the choice of the high or low overboard line is governed by that Convention.

Key Concepts

1. Types and sizes of tankers
2. Free-flow and pipeline tankers
3. Stripping system
4. Valve systems used on tankers

环境考虑

关键概念

1. 通过压载舱的定位和类型以及原油洗舱来实现海洋环境的保护
2. 现有油船原油洗舱的管理规则
3. 强化检查项目

教学建议

- 详细讨论专用压载舱和清洁压载舱的概念
- 确保学员明白MARPOL公约中专用压载舱、清洁压载舱以及原油洗舱的要求
- 简要提及原油洗舱如何保护海洋环境(后面会详细讨论)
- 讨论油船的强化检查项目

问题范例

- 什么是专用压载舱和清洁压载舱？为什么这样命名？
- 上述两者之间有什么基本不同？阐述专用压载舱相对清洁压载舱的优点。
- 用来决定专用压载舱和清洁压载舱舱容的标准是什么？
- 关于专用压载舱和清洁压载舱MARPOL公约有哪些要求？
- 什么是原油洗舱？它是怎样做到保护海洋环境的？
- 关于原油洗舱MARPOL公约有哪些要求？
- 什么是对油船的强化检查项目？

5.2 泵系、管系和排放设备 1.5学时

管线配置和货油泵是基于经济方面的考虑。学员应该熟悉不同的选择方案及其优缺点。MARPOL 73/78 制定了关于出海管和扫舱泵及管线的要求。学员必须知道选择高或低位出海管受公约制约。

关键概念

1. 油船的类型及大小
2. 油船的自由流动和管系
3. 扫舱系统
4. 油船的阀系统

Lecture Suggestions

- Give a brief description on the evolution of the tanker
- Give details of the six sizes of tankers in existence today: ULCC, VLCC, Suezmax, Aframax, Panamax and handysize
- Discuss the types of piping system that may be found on tankers
- Describe the details of stripping system and how does it contribute towards the protection of the marine environment
- Explain the functions of various types of valves used on a tanker

Sample Questions

- How many sizes of tankers exist today? Give details of their sizes.
- What are the two types of piping that can be found on a tanker?
- What factors govern the type of piping on board a tanker?
- Can you give details of the stripping system on a tanker with respect to its piping and operation?
- What type of pump is used for stripping system?
- Name the four types of valves that are used on a tanker. Give a brief explanation.
- What is an eductor and in what circumstances is it used?

5.3 Cargo heating systems 0.5 hour

Refer to B2.

Key Concepts

1. Circumstances under which it may be required to heat a cargo on a tanker
2. Means used for heating
3. Types of material used for heating coils
4. Slop-tanks and heating

Lecture Suggestions

- Discuss the process of heating cargo on a tanker
- Give details of methods of heating the cargo and the medium used
- Describe the precautions to be taken while using steam
- Explain the reason for heating the slop-tanks

Sample Questions

- Can you name the four types of oils that require heating?
- Which medium is used for heating?

教学建议

- 对油船的发展做一个简要地描述
- 对今天现存的六种类型的油船给出一些细节性描述：超大型油船、大型油船、苏伊士型、阿芙拉型、巴拿马型和灵便型油船
- 讨论油船上应用的管系类型
- 描述扫舱系统的细节并描述它如何有助于海洋环境的保护
- 解释油船上各种类型阀的作用

问题范例

- 目前存在几种尺寸的油船？对各种尺寸给出一些细节描述。
- 在油船上可以发现的两种管系是哪两种？
- 什么因素决定油船上管系的种类？
- 你能对油船扫舱系统的管系和操作给出详细描述吗？
- 扫舱系统用到了哪种泵？
- 说出油船上使用的四种阀并进行简要解释。
- 什么是喷射器以及其在什么条件下使用？

5.3 货油加热系统 0.5学时

参考B2。

关键概念

1. 油船需要加热货油的环境条件
2. 加热的方法
3. 加热盘管的材料类型
4. 污液舱和加热

教学建议

- 讨论油船加热货油的程序
- 给出货油加热方法及其使用媒介的细节
- 描述使用蒸汽加热时的预防措施
- 解释加热污液舱的原因

问题范例

- 你能说出四种需要加热的货油吗？
- 可以用来加热的介质有哪些？

- What wear and tear can be expected in the coils when using the aforementioned medium for heating the cargo?
- Why is heating required for slop–tanks?

5.4 Venting arrangements 1 hour

Venting arrangements are subject to SOLAS 1974, and the detailed teaching syllabus refers to the relevant regulations of that Convention.

Key Concepts

1. Instances when petroleum gases can be expelled from a cargo tank
2. Importance to ensure its dispersion
3. Means used to disperse the petroleum gases so generated

Lecture Suggestions

- Discuss the instances when petroleum gases can be released on board a tanker
- Explain the types of gases that can accumulate
- Describe to the students the means of venting to disperse the accumulated gases
- Inform them that as per the new SOLAS amendments a tanker now requires a secondary means of venting
- Explain that cargo tank venting is an exclusive operation
- Discuss that venting the cargo tanks can be independent for each tank or can be a combination arrangement for more than one tank
- Discuss the precautions to be undertaken to ensure to prevent the cargo from rising in the ventilation pipes
- Make the students understand the requirement for a p/v valve

Sample Questions

- When does petroleum gas have the potential to be accumulated on board?
- What do you think can be the hazard in the accumulation of such a gas?
- What will you do to disperse such petroleum gas?
- How many types of venting arrangement exist on board?
- What does the new SOLAS amendment say in this regard?
- What precautions will you take in using the venting system?
- What is the function of a p/v valve?

- 当使用上述介质加热货油时,盘管可能会发生哪些损坏和裂口?
- 为什么污液舱需要加热?

5.4 通风布置 1学时

通风布置是属于《SOLAS 74公约》的内容,教学大纲细则参考了公约的相关规则。

关键概念

1. 油气从货油舱排出的实例
2. 确保油气逸散的重要性
3. 用来驱散油气的方法

教学建议

- 讨论油船油气释放的实例
- 解释可以发生积聚的气体种类
- 向学员描述用来驱散油气的通风方法
- 告诉学员根据SOLAS新的修订案要求,油船需要有第二种通风方法
- 解释货舱通风是一项特定的操作
- 讨论货舱通风可以每个舱单独进行,也可以多舱联合进行
- 讨论为确保防止货油进入通风管道而采取的预防措施
- 使学员理解压力/真空阀的要求

问题范例

- 什么时候船上油气可能发生积聚?
- 你认为这些气体的积聚有哪些危害?
- 采取什么措施来驱散油气?
- 油船上有几种通风布置?
- 针对上述内容,新修订的《SOLAS公约》有哪些要求?
- 在使用通风系统时你会采取哪些预防措施?
- 压力/真空阀的功能是什么?

5.5 Level gauges 0.5 hour

Overflows of cargo tanks carry safety, as well as environmental, implications; level gauges constitute important equipment to prevent such overflows. In addition, accurate measurements are necessary to avoid disputes on cargoes carried. Section 5 of appendix 1 contains useful information on the different types of gauges commonly used on oil tankers.

Key Concepts and Lecture Suggestions

1. Discuss the nine type of gauges used on a tanker
2. Testing the accuracy of the gauges

Sample Questions

- Random explanation of the nine gauges by the students

5.6 Environmental protection equipment 4 hours

The detailed teaching syllabus indicates the knowledge, which should be acquired by trainees. The requirements for oil tankers have been set out in Annex I of MARPOL 73/78 (R2.2). Additional information on the working principles of the equipment is contained in appendix 1, section 4.5. Requirements with respect to equipment and test specifications of oil discharge monitoring and control equipment may be found in the IMO publication Oilywater Separators and Monitoring Equipment, referred to as R9.

Key Concepts

1. Equipment used to contribute towards the protection of the marine environment

Lecture Suggestions

- Describe the oil discharge monitor in detail
- Discuss the importance of proper functioning of the equipment and records maintained in the ORB
- Explain the various principles involved in measuring the oil content

Sample Questions

- What does the usage of oil discharge monitoring equipment achieve?
- What does the system tell you?
- What will you do in case the system malfunctions?
- What entries will you make regarding the functioning or malfunctioning of the system and where will you make the entries?
- What are the five principles of measuring the oil content?
- What does the LOT procedure depend upon?

5.5 液位计 0.5学时

油舱溢油会带来安全、环境问题;液位计是防止发生溢油问题的重要设备。另外,有必要实施精确测量以避免由于货差带来的争议。附录1中的第5节包含了油船广泛使用的不同类型液位计的有用信息。

关键概念和教学建议

1. 讨论油船上使用的九种液位计
2. 测试液位计的准确性

问题范例

让学员随机解释这九种液位计

5.6 环境保护设备 4学时

教学大纲细则指出了学员应掌握的知识。对油船的要求在《MARPOL公约》(R2.2)附则Ⅰ中已经有陈述。关于设备工作原理的补充内容包含在附录1中的4.5节。关于设备要求和排油监控设备试验的详细说明可以在IMO出版的油水分离器及监控设备中找到,参考R9。

关键概念

1. 用来保护海洋环境的设备

教学建议

- 详细描述排油监控器
- 讨论油类记录簿记录设备运行正常和维修记录内容的重要性
- 解释油分含量监测所涉及的各种原理

问题范例

- 使用排油监测设备的目的是什么?
- 这个系统告诉了你什么?
- 万一系统故障你会怎样做?
- 关于系统的运行和故障你会做哪些记录以及记录在哪儿?
- 检测油分含量的五个原理是什么?
- 装于上部法程序的依据是什么?

6 Oil tanker operations

Like oil tanker construction and equipment, oil tanker operations involve safety, environmental and commercial considerations. The detailed learning objectives indicate what the student should be able to do, but the instructor must fall back on his experience to teach the subject. The emphasis should be on safety, and accidents with oil tankers should be discussed to establish what went wrong. Reference B1 provides much of the safety-related information. Section 4 of Appendix 1 deals with operations aimed at pollution prevention. Reference B2 also deals extensively with operations. Additional information on cargo calculations may be found in section 6 of appendix 1. In particular, the section on Operations is very suitable for, application of a liquid cargo-handling simulator to practise the various procedures involved. Reference is made to the dedicated Model Course 2.06 Cargo and Ballast –handling Simulator.

An example of the exercise format and description, which can be applied, to set up such a simulator course is given in Appendix 5 to the Instructor Manual. Use of a simulator for training is not a mandatory requirement. See guidance on the use of simulators for training in reference R7, Section A-I/I 2.

6.1 General precautions 1 hour

Superstructure, pump-rooms, cargo hoses

Key Concepts

1. Securing the accommodation from flammable gases
2. Processes for securing ullage and tank-washing ports as a means to prevent the release of hydrocarbon gases
3. Precautions against drainage of cargo lines
4. Proper check and use of cargo hoses

Lecture Suggestions

- Discuss with the students the importance of isolating the accommodation at all times, by checking the accommodation space ventilation and adjusting the airconditioning system, to prevent any flammable gas entering
- Discuss the risk of unnecessary crafts coming along side in port
- Explain that only the relevant openings, during specific operations, be kept open and the others kept shut
- Describe that the drainage of lines into the pump-room bilges creates a risk of flammable gases in the pump-room
- Discuss in detail the checking of cargo hoses prior to its use
- Discuss the importance of insulating flange with the cargo hose

Sample Questions

- Why is it important to isolate the accommodation at all times?

6 油船操作

像油船结构和设备一样,油船操作也包括安全、环境以及商业方面的考虑。具体的学习目标已指明学员应该学会做什么,但教员应该根据自己的经验讲授这节课。必须强调安全,通过讨论油船事故来明确什么样的操作是错误的。参考书目B1提供了很多与安全有关的信息。附录1中的第4章涉及操作目的是防污染。参考书目B2更广泛地涉及操作。关于货油计算的补充信息可以在附录1中的第6章找到。特别地,关于操作这一章非常适合用液货船操纵模拟器来实践各种涉及的程序。参考书目是专用于示范课程 2.06的货油和压载操作模拟器。

教员手册附录5中有一个模拟器练习的格式和描述的例子, 可以用来建立这样的模拟课程。使用模拟器训练不是强制要求。参考书目R7,A-I/12部分提供了模拟器训练指南。

6.1 一般预防 1学时

上层结构、泵舱和货物软管

关键概念

1. 确保生活区免受可燃气体的危害
2. 堵住气隙和洗舱口过程是防止释放烃类气体的手段
3. 货物管系放残的预防措施
4. 正确检查和使用货油软管

教学建议

- 与学员讨论随时隔离生活区的重要性, 通过检查生活区通风系统以及调节空调系统防止可燃气体进入
- 讨论在港内不必要的船舶并靠风险
- 解释在特殊操作期间只有相关的开口打开,其他的关闭
- 描述管系放残至泵舱污水井内会造成泵舱内产生可燃气体的危险
- 详细讨论货油软管使用前的检查环节
- 讨论货油软管绝缘法兰的重要性

问题范例

- 为什么生活区一直要隔离很重要?

- What procedures will you undertake to achieve the above?
- What precautions will you take on deck with regard to various openings while carrying out specific operations on deck?
- Why is it dangerous to drain the cargo lines into the pump-room bilges?
- Although the provision of hoses is the responsibility of the terminal, what checks will you make prior to accepting them to handle cargo?
- What kind of insulation will you ensure while connecting the cargo hoses?

6.2 Loading and discharging operations 3 hours

Key Concepts

1. Relationship of specific gravity and temperature
2. Units of measurement
3. API Scale
4. Methods of calculation of the volume/weight of cargo
5. Loading and discharging precautions

Lecture Suggestions

- Revise the concept of specific gravity (SG) and that SG of oil changes with temperature
- Describe the principle behind the need to calculate the volume of oil at a standard temperature of 15°C
- Explain the alternative method of calculation, by the oil industry, using the API scale
- Make the students aware of the various units of measurements used for measuring weight and volume
- Show a practical calculation and give an exercise to the students to calculate volume and weight of cargo using tables
- Show a practical calculation for ROB/OBQ
- Discuss the precautions to take while loading and discharging. This should include inter alia the stability, bending moments and shear force on one hand and line checks on the other

Sample Questions

- What do you understand by SG and how does SG of oil vary with temperature?
- At what temperature of oil are all the calculations made? What is the temperature used by the shore terminals normally?
- What do you understand by the API Scale?
- Are you aware of the units that you will find being used by the oil industry for calculating the volume of oil? State the three units each of volume and weight

- 你会采取什么程序来达到上述目标?
- 当在甲板上进行特殊操作时,针对甲板上的各种开口,你会采取什么预防措施?
- 为什么货油管系放残至泵舱污水井内很危险?
- 尽管是码头责任提供软管,在接受并进行货油操作之前你会做什么检查?
- 在连接货油软管时你会确保哪种绝缘?

6.2 装卸操作

3学时

关键概念

1. 比重和温度之间的关系
2. 测量单位
3. 美国石油学会油量计算标准
4. 计算货油体积重量的方法
5. 货物装卸的预防措施

教学建议

- 复习比重及比重随温度变化的概念
- 描述需要在标准温度(15 ℃)下计算货油体积的原理
- 解释石油工业使用API标度进行计算的可替换方法
- 使学员知道用于测量重量和体积的各种测量单位
- 演示一个实际计算,并给学员一个练习题,让其利用表格计算货油的重量和体积
- 做一个计算船舶残油/底油的实例
- 讨论装卸货时的预防措施。其应该包含的内容一方面是稳性、弯曲力矩和剪应力,另一方面是水线检查

问题范例

- 你怎样理解比重及其如何随温度变化?
- 油的计算是在什么温度下进行的?岸上通常多少度?
- 你怎样理解API标度?
- 你知道石油业用于计算油体积的单位吗?分别说体积和重量的三个单位。

- What are the dangers involved in terms of stability and stresses while loading and discharging? What precautions will you take to overcome these dangers?

6.3 Ballasting and de-ballasting 1 hour

Key Concepts

1. The requirement for carrying ballast on a tanker and the principles of ballasting
2. The delicacy of handling dirty ballast and the discharge provisions
3. Clean and segregated ballast capacity and usage
4. Introduction to Crude Oil Washing (COW)
5. Load on Top (LOT) procedures

Lecture Suggestions

- Explain as to why ballasting and de-ballasting is a delicate operation on tankers and augurs high level of seriousness and professionalism
- Discuss the stages, and subsequent precautions to be taken while undertaking ballast/de-ballast operations
- Discuss the evolution of SBT and CBT and what is their purpose
- Also discuss the operations to be undertaken while handling segregated and clean ballast
- Describe the processes of handling dirty ballast such as LOT procedures
- Discuss the procedures, with respect to regulations, for the discharge of dirty ballast
- Discuss, only briefly (as the same is dealt with in detail later), the COW operations

Sample Questions

- Why, in your opinion, handling of ballasting operation is an important issue that leaves virtually very little room for error?
- At whose discretion is the quantity of ballast taken on board?
- What are the deciding factors that are taken into consideration while taking ballast?
- In which tanks is ballast taken?
- What type of ballast results in non-designated ballast tanks?
- How will you handle this dirty ballast?
- Can you explain the entire LOT procedure?
- How does LOT procedure help in protecting the marine environment?
- What do you understand by clean and segregated ballast?
- What is COW and what does it achieve? Who developed this concept of COW? (Answer: the oil industry in the 1970s)

- 在装卸货时涉及的稳性和应力的危险有哪些?你会采取哪些预防措施来应对这些危险?

6.3 加装、排放压载水

1学时

关键概念

1. 油船携带压载水的要求和压载原理
2. 污染压载水处理的敏感性和排放规定
3. 清洁和专用压载舱容及用途
4. 介绍原油洗舱
5. 装于上部法的程序

教学建议

- 讨论为什么油船压载水的加装和排放是一项细致的操作以及预示较高的严肃性和专业性
- 讨论加装、排放压载水操作期间各阶段和随后的预防措施
- 讨论专用压载舱和清洁压载舱的发展过程和他们的用途
- 还要讨论处理专用和清洁压载水的操作方法
- 描述处理污压载水的方法,如装于上部法
- 讨论根据规则要求污染压载水的排放程序
- 简要讨论(后续内容会详细描述)原油洗舱操作

问题范例

- 在你看来为什么处理压载水是一项很重要的工作,不容许出现一点失误?
- 由哪些指标决定船舶压载量?
- 压载时需要考虑的决定性因素是什么?
- 哪些舱需要压载?
- 哪种类型的压载导致非指定压载舱?
- 你如何处理污压载水?
- 你能解释完整的装于上部法吗?
- 装于上部法如何保护海洋环境?
- 你怎样理解清洁和专用的压载水?
- 什么是原油洗舱以及它是如何实现的? 谁提出了这个概念?
  (答案:上世纪70年代由石油工业提出)

6.4 Tank cleaning

1 hour

Key Concepts

1. Reasons for the tanks to be cleaned
2. Methods of handling the cleaning operation that is, using a closed or open cycle wash
3. Types of medium used for cleaning
4. The machines used for cleaning – fixed or portable
5. Generation of hydrocarbon gas during tank cleaning operation
6. Electrostatic hazard while tank cleaning

Lecture Suggestions

- Discuss with the students in bit of a detail as to the reasons for tank cleaning
- Describe the importance of the operation that tank cleaning requires efficient handling of the large amount of dirty ballast so generated
- Discuss the methods of dealing with the dirty ballast
- Describe the various mediums used in cleaning a cargo tank
- Explain the reasons of the presence of hydrocarbon gases while undertaking a tank cleaning operation
- Explain the presence of electrostatically charged atmosphere that can be present and the precautions to be taken

Sample Questions

- Why is tank cleaning a tedious operation and requires a high level of expertise?
- What does tank cleaning generate?
- How will you handle the large amount of dirty ballast so generated?
- What is a closed and open cycle wash?
- How will you choose which cycle to use?
- What are the types of machines used for tank cleaning?
- What are the three types of mediums used for tank cleaning?
- How is hydrocarbon gas generated during a tank cleaning operation?
- What causes the presence of an electrically charged atmosphere to be present in such an operation?
- What precautions will you take to handle the hydrocarbon gas as well as the electrically charged atmosphere?

6.4 洗舱

1学时

关键概念

1. 需要洗舱的原因
2. 洗舱操作的方法,使用闭式和开式循环
3. 洗舱介质的种类
4. 洗舱机—固定式和手提式
5. 在洗舱过程中烃类气体的产生
6. 洗舱过程中的静电危险

教学建议

- 与学员详细一点地讨论关于洗舱的原因
- 描述洗舱要求有效处理产生的大量污压载水的重要性
- 讨论处理污压载水的方法
- 描述在洗舱时用到的各种介质
- 解释在洗舱时产生烃类气体的原因
- 解释在洗舱时产生带静电空气的原因和需要采取的预防措施

问题范例

- 为什么洗舱是单调的工作并且需要高水平的专业技能?
- 洗舱会产生什么?
- 如何处理产生的大量污压载水?
- 什么是闭式和开式循环洗舱?
- 你如何选择使用哪种循环?
- 洗舱机有哪些种类?
- 洗舱的三种介质是什么?
- 洗舱时烃类气体是怎样产生的?
- 什么原因引起洗舱过程中静电空气的出现?
- 你会采取什么措施来处理洗舱中产生的烃类气体和带静电的空气?

6.5 Slop-tank operations 1 hour

Key Concepts

1. Slop-tanks and effective LOT procedures
2. Decanting and use of Oil Discharging Monitor (ODM)
3. Heating the slop-tanks
4. Regulations governing the discharge from slop-tanks

Lecture Suggestions

- Explain the relationship between LOT procedures and slop-tanks
- Discuss the regulations governing slop-tank operations
- Discuss the process of decanting and subsequent use of ODM
- Ensure that the students are well aware of discharge requirements
- Describe why heating is sometimes done in a slop-tank and what does it achieve

Sample Questions

- What is the relationship between tank cleaning, slop-tank and LOT procedure?
- Although we have discussed in the past, but can you detail the discharge stipulations required by the law?
- What is decanting?
- What parameters will you feed in the ODM prior to its operation?
- When you heat the slop-tank – what will you achieve in doing so?

6.6 Purging and gas freeing 1 hour

Key Concepts

1. Reasons for gas freeing a tank
2. Concept and methods to achieve gas freeing
3. Precautions for the accommodation while gas freeing operation is undertaken
4. Importance of constant monitoring of tank atmosphere despite gas freeing

Lecture Suggestions

- Discuss with students the need for gas freeing of tanks
- Explain the concept of gas freeing with the aid of the flammability diagram. Ensure that the concept of the diagram is absolutely clear to all the students
- Delineate the importance of ensuring that the accommodation is isolated during gas freeing operation and venting of gases is done by approved venting arrangements

6.5 污液舱的操作 1学时

关键概念

1. 污液舱和有效地装于上部法程序
2. 减载过驳及排油监控器(ODM)的使用
3. 污液舱加热
4. 管理污液舱排放的规则

教学建议

- 解释装于上部法和污液舱之间的关系
- 讨论管理污液舱操作的规则
- 讨论减载过驳过程和随后排油监控器的使用
- 确保学员熟知排放要求
- 描述为什么有时对污液舱加热及其要达到的目的

问题范例

- 洗舱、污液舱和装于上部法之间有哪些联系?
- 尽管我们已经在以前讨论过了,但是你能详述法律要求的排放规定吗?
- 什么是减载过驳?
- 在操作之前,你需要向排油监控器输入哪些参数?
- 什么时候加热污液舱? 这样做的目的是什么?

6.6 驱气和除气 1学时

关键概念

1. 油舱除气的原因
2. 完成除气的概念和方法
3. 在进行除气操作时对生活区的预防措施
4. 尽管进行了除气也要持续监测舱内空气成分的重要性

教学建议

- 与学员讨论油舱除气的需要
- 用可燃性图解释除气的概念。确保学员对该图的概念完全清楚。
- 描述在除气和使用认可的装置排气过程中将生活区隔离的重要性

- Stress that a constant monitoring of the atmosphere is imperative despite the gas freeing operation

Sample Questions

- Why is gas freeing of tanks necessary and what do you achieve? What is at stake?
- How is gas freeing achieved? Describe the two methods.
- Why is it important to isolate the accommodation while gas freeing?
- Why is it required that the tank atmosphere be constantly monitored even though gas freeing has been conducted?

6.7 Ship/shore liaison 1 hour

Key Concepts

1. Essential nature of communication between ship and shore
2. Free flow of information prior to commencing cargo work
3. Written confirmation from ship and shore
4. Comprehension of items on a checklist by both ship and shore personnel

Lecture Suggestion

- Explain that communication between the ship and the shore is a delicate affair and nothing should be taken for granted
- Explain that information sharing between the shore and the ship should flow smoothly and pre-decided. Any possible hiccups should be cleared at the first instance but in any case prior to starting cargo operation
- Stress the need for having it in written confirmation from both ends regarding the entire process of cargo handling
- Stress that the shore as well as, the ship checklist should be discussed and there should be a joint communiqué

Sample Questions

- Why is it necessary to establish proper communication between the shore and the ship personnel? What is endangered in the absence of a proper communication?
- What will you do to ensure a smooth flow of information both ways?
- Are you aware that it is required to have it in writing, and give it in writing, that all areas of cargo operation have been properly understood?
- Are you aware that the ship as well as the shore checklist should be properly discussed between both the parties?
- Will you commence cargo operation if you feel that there is a lacuna existing in the communication between the ship and shore?
- What will you do in such a scenario?

- 强调尽管进行了除气也必须要持续监测舱内空气成分

范例问题

- 为什么要进行除气以及要达到什么目的？有什么危险？
- 如何实现除气？描述两种方法。
- 为什么除气时隔离生活区很重要？
- 为什么尽管进行了除气也必须要持续监测舱内空气成分？

6.7 岸/船间的联系 1学时

关键概念

1. 船岸通信联系的本质特征
2. 开始货物操作之前的通信顺畅
3. 船岸之间的书面凭证
4. 船岸人员对检查表项目的理解

教学建议

- 解释船岸通信是一件很微妙的事情,没有任何事应该被视为理所当然
- 解释船岸之间的共享信息应该流通顺畅,并事先拟定。无论任何情况下都要在货物操作之前立即解决任何可能的小问题
- 关于整个货物操作过程中强调需要双方都要有书面凭证
- 强调岸方和船方的检查表应该经过讨论,并做出一个联合声明

问题范例

- 为什么必须在船岸人员之间建立正常的通信联系？缺乏正常的通信联系会有什么危险？
- 你会怎样确保双方通信顺畅？
- 你知道要求收到和发出一份书面材料,证明完全理解货物操作的各个方面吗？
- 你知道岸方和船方的检查表应该经过双方的讨论吗？
- 如果你感觉船岸双方之间的通信联系有点问题你会开始货物操作吗？
- 在这种情况下你会怎样做？

7 Cargo and ballast pumps

Under this heading, the trainee may be instructed on pump theory and the dangers of pressure surges. This instruction is valuable under–pinning knowledge. Appendix 1, section 7 contains notes on pump theory and characteristics. Reference B1 deals extensively with pressure surges, which are a safety hazard.

7.1 Pump theory and characteristics 1 hour

Key Concepts

1. Atmospheric pressure and pump suction
2. Ideal situation and actual situation with respect to pump suction
3. Factors influencing the suction of a pump
4. Effect of trim on pump suction
5. Quantity of liquid in a tank and its effects on pump suction
6. Cavitation of a pump
7. Different types of pumps, and their working, on board a tanker
8. Explanation of terms such as, head, NPSH and design point

Lecture Suggestions

- This is a section, which requires that the students understand the theory as well as, the practice of operating pumps. Therefore, it should include the various parameters that effect the functioning of a pump such as:
  - atmospheric pressure
  - the trim
  - quantity of liquid in a tank
  - other factors
- Describe what the ideal situation is with regard to the suction of a pump and the factors that prevent the ideal situation
- Describe the working principles of various pumps (deep well, centrifugal, reciprocating, simplex and duplex pumps)
- Explain the terms used in the functioning of a pump
- Discuss what is cavitation of a pump

Sample Questions

- What are the factors that affect the pump suction?
- What are the factors that reduce the efficiency of a pump?
- Give a description of the principle of four types of pump.
- What do you understand by the terms head, NPSH and design point?

7 货油泵和压载泵

根据这个标题,学员应学习关于泵的理论和压力波动的危险。这一内容结合原理知识讲授更有效。附录Ⅰ第7节中包含关于泵的理论和特性的注释。参考书目B1广泛论及压力波动概念,也是安全隐患。

7.1 泵的原理和特性 1学时

关键概念

1. 空气压力和泵吸入
2. 关于泵吸入的理想条件和实际条件
3. 影响泵吸入的因素
4. 纵倾对泵吸入的影响
5. 舱内液体的数量和对泵吸入的影响
6. 泵的气蚀
7. 油船上不同种类的泵及其工作过程
8. 解释这些术语,例如扬程、净吸入压头和设计工况

教学建议

- 在本章中要求学员理解泵操作的原理和实践,因此,包含影响泵运行的各种参数,例如:
  - 空气压力
  - 纵倾
  - 舱内液体数量
  - 其他因素
- 描述什么是泵吸入的理想条件以及哪些因素破坏了这些理想条件
- 描述各种泵的工作原理(深井泵、离心泵、往复泵、单级和多级泵)
- 解释在泵运行过程中用到的术语
- 讨论什么是泵的气蚀

问题范例

- 影响泵吸入的因素有哪些?
- 什么因素会降低泵的效率?
- 对四种泵的工作原理进行描述。
- 你怎样理解这些术语,如压头、净吸入压头和设计工况?

- What is meant by cavitation of a pump? What will you do in case cavitation occurs and what precautions would you take?

7.2 Pressure surge 1 hour

Key Concepts

1. Reasons for a pressure surge
2. Consequences of pressure surge
3. Valve operation and pressure surge
4. Prevention of pressure surge

Lecture Suggestions

- Delve into with some detail the reasons for a pressure surge and what should be done to prevent it as well as action when a surge is discovered

Sample Questions

- Explain the principle of pressure surge and what happens when pressure surge takes place.
- What will you do when you discover a pressure-surge taking place?
- Are you aware that valve operation has to be carried out carefully to prevent a pressure surge?

8 Emergency procedures 2 hours

These procedures are shown in reference B1. Appendix 1, section 8 describes the different emergency alarms and other important alarms on board oil tankers.

8.1 – 8.4

Emergency plan, emergency alarms and emergency organization, action on discovering an emergency 0.5 hour each

Key Concepts

1. Types of emergencies encountered on a tanker
2. Importance of emergency plans
3. Types of emergency plan
4. Information contained in various emergency plans
5. Types of alarms and their identification
6. Effectiveness of emergency planning is based on an effective emergency organization

- 什么是气蚀？万一泵发生气蚀时你会怎样做？你会采取什么预防措施？

7.2 压力波动 1学时

关键概念

1. 压力波动的原因
2. 压力波动的后果
3. 阀操作和压力波动
4. 压力波动的预防

教学建议

- 深入、细致地研究压力波动的原因以及发生压力波动时如何预防压力波动和采取哪些措施

问题范例

- 解释压力波动的原理以及在压力波动时会发生什么现象。
- 当你发现压力波动时你会采取什么措施？
- 你知道必须仔细执行阀的操作以防止压力波动吗？

8 应急程序 2学时

该程序详见参考书目B1。附录1 第8节中描述了油船上不同的应急警报和其他的重要警报。

8.1–8.4
应急计划、应急警报、应急组织以及发现应急情况后的行动 每项0.5学时

关键概念

1. 油船上遇到的紧急情况的种类
2. 应急计划的重要性
3. 应急计划的种类
4. 各种应急计划中包含的信息
5. 报警的种类及其辨别
6. 应急计划的有效性基于有效的应急组织

Lecture Suggestions

- Stress on the fact that no emergency can be tackled without the existence of an effective emergency organization, effective planning and continuous practice to execute the plan
- Delve on the various emergencies and subsequent plans and their contents
- Ensure that the students are certain about the various alarms on board
- Discuss the actions on discovering an emergency

Sample Questions

- Are you aware of the various emergencies that can occur on board a tanker, be it affecting human health, property and the marine environment?
- Why do you think it is imperative to have an emergency plan?
- What is achieved by the existence of an emergency plan?
- What does an emergency plan contain?
- What are the components of an emergency organization?
- Are you aware that without an emergency organization, an emergency plan cannot be effective?
- How will you judge the effectiveness of an emergency drill on board?
- Can you identify the various emergency alarms on board a tanker?
- What action will you take on discovering an emergency, while at sea or when in port?

9 Inert Gas Systems (IGS)

Refer to R3 and appendices 3a and 3b. This part of the course is not required for those persons who are to take charge of cargo and operations on tankers not fitted with IGS and whose certificates on completion of training are so endorsed.

9.1 General — 0.5 hour

Key Concepts

1. Legal requirements on tankers to be provided with IGS
2. Relationship of COW and IGS
3. Concept of IGS on tankers

Lecture Suggestions

- Explain which tankers are required to be fitted with IGS and what are the exceptions
- Describe in detail what is meant by inert gas and describe its functions in relation to the flammability diagram

教学建议

- 缺乏有效的应急组织、有效的计划和对计划持续训练的情况下谈不到应急处理,强调这是不争的事实
- 研究各种紧急情况以及后续的计划及其内容
- 确保学员明白船上的各种警报
- 讨论发现紧急情况后的行动

问题范例

- 你知道油船上发生的各种紧急情况及其对人的健康、财产和海洋环境的影响吗?
- 为什么你认为有一个应急计划很重要?
- 制订应急计划要实现的目标是什么?
- 应急计划中包含了哪些内容?
- 应急组织包括哪些部分?
- 你知道没有应急组织,那么应急计划也不会起作用吗?
- 你如何判断船上应急演习的有效性?
- 你能辨认油船上的各种警报吗?
- 当在海上和在港内发现紧急情况时你会分别采取什么行动?

9 惰性气体系统(IGS)

参考R3和附录3a、附录3b。这部分课程内容对在不装设IGS系统的油船上负责货物及其操作的人员不做要求,而且完成培训后他们的证书也是如此背书的。

9.1 概述 0.5学时

关键概念

1. 关于油船需要配备惰性气体系统的法律要求
2. 原油洗舱和惰性气体系统的联系
3. 油船惰性气体系统的概念

教学建议

- 解释哪些油船要求装设惰性气体系统以及哪些可以作为例外
- 详细解释什么是惰性气体及其关于燃烧图的作用

- Discuss what the inert gas is supposed to do

Sample Questions

- Which tankers should have an IGS on board?
- What are the exceptions as per international law with regard to IGS?
- What do you understand by IGS? Can you show on the flammability diagram how does the usage of inert gas reduce the flammable atmosphere in a tank?
- State the four functions of IGS.

9.2 The inert gas system 0.5 hour

Key Concepts

1. Main functions and quality of inert gas
2. Ingress of air and maintenance of positive pressure of inert gas and
3. Dangers associated with the malfunctioning of inert gas

Lecture Suggestions

- Describe the main features of an inert gas system
- Explain the meaning of a good quality of inert gas
- Discuss the relationship between the backflow of air into a tank and the maintenance of positive pressure of inert gas
- Discuss in some detail the consequences of a malfunction in the inert gas system

Sample Questions

- What should an inert gas system do?
- What are the constituents of a good quality of inert gas?
- Where is the gas cooled and scrubbed?
- What will happen if a positive pressure of inert gas is not maintained?
- What is a back flow of inert gas into the generating plant and what precautions will you take to prevent the same?
- What will happen if the inert gas system malfunctions?

9.3 Inert gas plant 0.5 hour

Key Concepts

1. Sources of inert gas on board
2. Purpose of an inert gas plant
3. Flue gas from boiler and inert gas

- 讨论惰性气体的用途

问题范例

- 哪些油船需要装设惰性气体系统?
- 根据有关惰性气体系统的国际法规,哪些船可以是例外?
- 你怎么理解惰性气体系统?你能不能在燃烧图表上演示惰气是怎样降低舱内可燃气体的含量的?
- 阐述惰性气体系统的4个作用。

9.2 惰性气体系统　　0.5学时

关键概念

1. 惰性气体的主要作用和质量
2. 空气的进入和保持惰性气体的正压
3. 关于惰性气体故障的危险

教学建议

- 描述惰性气体系统的主要特征
- 解释高质量惰性气体的含义
- 解释舱内空气回流和保持惰性气体正压的联系
- 较详细地讨论惰性气体系统故障的后果

问题范例

- 惰性气体系统能用来做什么?
- 高质量的惰性气体的组成什么?
- 惰气在哪里被冷却和清洗?
- 如果惰气无法保持正压,会发生什么情况?
- 什么是惰性气体回流进入惰气发生装置以及你会采取什么措施防止此类事故的发生?
- 如果惰性气体系统故障,会发生什么情况?

9.3 惰性气体装置　　0.5学时

关键概念

1. 船上惰性气体的来源
2. 惰性气体装置的用途
3. 锅炉烟道气和惰气

4. Inert gas uptake valve and its location
5. Specific materials used for inert gas piping and its valves

Lecture Suggestions

- Discuss in some detail the various sources of generation of inert gas on board
- Discuss the main purpose of an inert gas plant
- Describe in detail usage, and precautions, if the flue gas from the boiler is being used as inert gas
- Briefly discuss the function of an uptake valve and the importance of its location
- Briefly discuss the reason for specific materials used for the inert gas valves and piping

Sample Questions

- How is inert gas produced on board?
- What are the considerations, and precautions, to be taken while using flue gas from the boiler as inert gas?
- What is the function of an inert gas uptake valve and what is the importance of its location?
- Why only specific materials are used for the inert gas uptake valve and the piping?

9.4 Scrubber, Inert Gas Blowers, Inert Gas Pressure–regulating Valves 1 hour

Key Concepts

1. Functions, working and construction of a scrubber unit
2. Corrosion and the scrubber unit
3. Instrumentation and alarms of the scrubber
4. Number and capacity of inert gas blowers
5. Dual purpose of inert gas blowers
6. Reasons for corrosion of the blowers and the importance of timely inspections
7. Alarm systems and automatic shut down
8. Functions of the pressure-regulating valve
9. Control of the pressure-regulating valve and the subsequent control if inert gas flow into the tanks
10. Monitoring of inert gas pressure
11. Alarm system

Lecture Suggestions

- Discuss in detail, with the aid of sketches, the functions of a scrubber unit

4. 惰气烟气抽气阀及其位置

5. 惰气管路和阀使用的特殊材料

教学建议

- 详细讨论油船上惰性气体产生的来源
- 讨论惰性气体装置的主要用途
- 详细描述使用锅炉烟道气作为惰性气体的用法和预防措施
- 简要讨论烟气抽气阀的作用及其位置的重要性
- 简要讨论惰气管路和阀需要使用特殊材料的原因

问题范例

- 在船上惰性气体是怎样产生的?
- 使用锅炉烟道气作为惰气时有哪些注意事项和预防措施?
- 烟气抽气阀有什么作用及其位置有什么重要性?
- 为什么惰气管路和阀只能使用特殊材料?

9.4 洗涤塔、惰气鼓风机和惰气压力调节阀 1学时

关键概念

1. 洗涤塔的功能、运行和结构
2. 洗涤单元及其腐蚀
3. 洗涤塔的检测仪表和警报
4. 惰气鼓风机的数量和排量
5. 惰气鼓风机的双重用途
6. 惰气鼓风机腐蚀的原因和定时检查的重要性
7. 报警系统和自动关闭
8. 压力调节阀的作用
9. 如果惰气流入舱内的随后控制和压力调节阀的控制
10. 惰气压力的监测
11. 报警系统

教学建议

- 借助于示意图详细讨论洗涤塔的作用

- Discuss in detail the association of corrosion with the scrubber unit
- Ensure that the students are aware of the instrumentation and alarms associated with a scrubber unit
- Discuss the number of blowers that are required and the circumstances when this number can be reduced
- Explain the minimum capacity of the blowers and the importance of the stated capacity that has been set
- Describe the dual status of the inert gas blowers and the circumstances where it can be used otherwise
- Discuss the reasons as to why there is a potential for severe corrosion of the inert gas blowers
- Ensure that the students are aware of the alarm systems associated with the blowers and the conditions under which an automatic shut down will take place
- Discuss the two functions of the pressure-regulating valve
- Describe the details of various methods used for operation of the pressureregulating valve to regulate the inert gas pressure
- Explain the importance of monitoring the inert gas pressure
- Ensure that the students are well aware of the alarm system associated with the monitoring of the inert gas pressure

Sample Questions

- What is a scrubber?
- What kind of gas do you think would be sent to the tanks in the absence of a scrubber unit?
- Will such a gas be safe as inert gas for use?
- Why is corrosion associated with the scrubber unit?
- What is done to minimize the corrosion of the scrubber unit?
- Are you aware of the various alarms associated with the scrubber unit?
- How many inert gas blowers are to be on board?
- Under what conditions this number is reduced?
- The blowers have a minimum capacity. What is the reason for this? What does the minimum capacity of an inert gas blower accomplish?
- What is the reason of excessive corrosion of inert gas blowers? How will you inspect for this?
- Are you aware of the alarm system associated with inert gas blowers?
- Under what circumstances will the inert gas blower have an automatic shutdown?
- What in your opinion are the main functions of a pressure-regulating valve?

- 详细讨论腐蚀与洗涤单元的联系
- 确保学员知道洗涤塔的检测仪表和警报
- 讨论鼓风机要求的数量以及在什么情况下可以减少
- 解释风机的最小排量以及达到规定排量的重要性
- 描述惰气鼓风机的双重作用及其另作他用的情况
- 讨论惰气风机为什么会发生严重腐蚀的原因
- 确保学员明白与风机有关的报警系统以及在什么条件下会发生自动关闭
- 讨论压力调节阀的两个作用
- 详细描述操纵压力调节阀来调节惰气压力的各种方法
- 解释监测惰气压力的重要性
- 确保学员熟知与惰气压力监测有关的报警系统

问题范例

- 什么是洗涤塔?
- 在没有洗涤塔的情况下你认为哪种气体会被送至舱内?
- 作为使用的惰气,这种气体安全吗?
- 为什么腐蚀与洗涤单元有关?
- 采取什么措施可使洗涤单元的腐蚀减至最小?
- 你知道与洗涤单元有关的各种报警吗?
- 船上应该配有几台惰气鼓风机?
- 在什么条件下这个数量会减少?
- 惰气风机有一个最小排量。原因是什么?这个最小排量能实现什么目的?
- 惰气风机过度腐蚀的原因是什么?如何进行检查?
- 你知道与惰气风机有关的警报吗?
- 在什么条件下惰气风机会自动关闭?
- 在你看来压力调节阀的主要作用是什么?

- What are the various methods used in handling the pressure-regulating valve to control the pressure of the inert gas?
- Why is it important to monitor the inert gas pressure? What are the aspects that you would be keeping an eye on?

9.5 Non-return devices 0.5 hour

Key Concepts

1. Reasons for non-return devices
2. Types of non-return devices
3. Functions and functioning of different types of seals
4. Deck water seal
5. Heating of water seals
6. Location of seals on deck
7. Deck isolation valve
8. Associated alarm system

Lecture Suggestions

- Discuss in detail the reason for having non-return devices and the types of nonreturn devices that there are on tankers
- Discuss in some detail the functions of various types of seal
- Describe the water seal in detail and the functioning of the same in terms of heating and inspection
- Give an understanding to the students of the location of the seal
- Explain the deck isolation valve and its location on board
- Ensure that the students are well aware of the alarm system associated with the water level in the deck water seal

Sample Questions

- Why is there a need on tankers to have a non-return device?
- What are the various types of non-return devices? How do they function?
- What is the location on board of the non-return devices?
- What is a deck-water seal?
- Why is it required to provide heating to the water seal and under what circumstances is it done?
- Under what circumstances will the alarm sound with regard to the deck water seal?
- What is a deck isolation valve?

- 控制压力调节阀来调节惰气压力的方法有哪些?
- 为什么监测惰气压力很重要?你会关注哪个方面?

9.5 止回设备

0.5学时

关键概念

1. 设止回设备的原因
2. 止回设备的类型
3. 不同种类密封的功能和作用
4. 甲板水封
5. 水封的加热
6. 甲板水封的位置
7. 甲板隔离阀
8. 有关的报警系统

教学建议

- 详细讨论安装止回设备的原因和油船上止回设备的种类
- 详细讨论各种密封的功能
- 详细描述水封及对其加热和检查的作用
- 让学员理解水封的位置
- 解释甲板隔离阀及其在船上的位置
- 确保学员熟知与甲板水封水位相关的报警系统

问题范例

- 为什么油船上需要有止回设备?
- 止回设备有哪些种类?如何发挥作用?
- 油船上止回设备的位置在哪?
- 什么是甲板水封?
- 为什么需要对水封加热以及在什么情况下加热?
- 甲板水封在什么条件下会发出报警?
- 什么是甲板隔离阀?

9.6 Inert gas distribution and venting 1 hour

Key Concepts

1. Distribution system of inert gas
2. Venting systems
3. Piping arrangement for inert gas and venting
4. Function and provisions of inert gas distribution and venting systems
5. P/V breaker

Lecture Suggestions

- Discuss the main points of the inert gas distribution system for example, what does it contain
- Discuss the functions of isolating valves and the inert gas piping that can double as vent piping
- Describe in detail what the inert gas and the venting system must allow for
- Discuss what provisions are available to achieve the aforementioned allowance
- Explain the functions of a p/v breaker and the precautions associated with its function

Sample Questions

- What are the three main parts of the inert gas distribution system?
- How are the tanks isolated from the inert gas system?
- What is the other function of the inert gas piping?
- Which are the other venting systems available?
- What are the six operations that the inert gas and venting system must be able to accomplish?
- What are the four provisions available to achieve the aforementioned operations?
- What is a p/v breaker and what are its functions?

9.7 Gas-analysing, recording and indicating equipment 0.5 hour

Key Concepts

1. Oxygen analyser
2. Sampling points location
3. Catalytic-filament principle and its limitations
4. Use of portable instruments and earthing

Lecture Suggestions

- Explain the purpose of gas analysing instruments such as an oxygen analyser

9.6 惰性气体的分配和通风 1学时

关键概念

1. 惰性气体的分配系统
2. 通风系统
3. 惰性气体及通风的管系布置
4. 惰性气体的分配和通风系统的功能和规定
5. P/V断路器

教学建议

- 讨论惰性气体分配系统的要点,例如,包含了什么
- 讨论隔离阀的作用和可以兼做通风管路的惰性气体管路
- 详细描述惰性气体及其通风系统必须考虑到什么
- 讨论哪些规定可以实现上述的考虑
- 解释P/V断路器的作用和与其作用相关的预防措施

问题范例

- 惰气分配系统的三个主要部分是什么?
- 油舱是如何与惰气系统隔离的?
- 惰气管系的其他作用是什么?
- 还有哪些其他可用的通风系统?
- 惰性气体系统和通风系统必须实现的六种操作是什么?
- 实现上述操作的四项规定是哪些?
- 什么是P/V断路器以及它有什么功能?

9.7 气体的分析、记录、指示装置 0.5学时

关键概念

1. 含氧量分析仪
2. 取样点布置
3. 催化灯丝原理和其局限性
4. 便携式设备的使用和接地

教学建议

- 解释气体分析仪的用途,如含氧量分析仪

- Discuss the principle involved in the specific location of sampling points
- Ensure that the students are aware of the importance of earthing a portable instrument

Sample Questions

- What is an oxygen analyser?
- What precautions will you take prior to using a portable instrument and why?
- What are the limitations of instruments based on the catalytic-filament principle?

9.8 Operations 2 hours

Key Concepts

1. Starting and shutting down procedures of the inert gas plant and the subsequent precautions
2. Ballast operations involving cargo tanks and inerting
3. Padding and inert gas pressure
4. Discharge operations and inerting
5. Monitoring of inert gas pressure while simultaneous cargo and ballast operations
6. Checking quality of inert gas prior to its usage
7. Combination carriers and inert gas

Lecture Suggestions

- Discuss in complete details the starting and shutting down procedures of an inert gas plant. Please emphasize the importance of strict adherence of safe procedures while undertaking inerting operations
- Discuss the precautions to be taken during the entire inerting process whether it is during loading, discharging, ballasting or while sounding or sampling a tank
- Describe the process of inert gas containment between two tanks
- Emphasize the importance of constant monitoring of inert gas for quality as well as, pressure

Sample Questions

- Can you state in systematic detail the starting and shutting down procedure of an inert gas plant?
- Can you list the precautions to be adhered to while undertaking the aforementioned operation?
- What specific precautions will you take prior to ballasting a cargo tank with respect to inerting?
- What is padding the void space above the cargo and its relation with the inert gas pressure?

- 讨论关于特殊取样点位置的原则
- 确保学员知道便携式设备接地的重要性

问题范例

- 什么是含氧量分析仪?
- 在使用便携式含氧量分析仪前需要采取什么预防措施以及为什么?
- 基于催化灯丝原理的设备有哪些局限?

9.8 操作 2学时

关键概念

1. 惰气装置的起停程序和随后的预防措施
2. 涉及货舱和惰化的压载操作
3. 填充及惰性气体的压力
4. 卸货操作和惰化
5. 货物及压载操作的同时监测惰性气体的压力
6. 惰气使用前质量的检查
7. 混装船和惰气

教学建议

- 详细讨论惰气装置的起停程序。请强调在惰气操作时严格遵守安全程序的重要性
- 讨论整个惰化过程中需要采取的预防措施,不管是装载、卸放、压载还是油舱测深和取样
- 描述两个舱之间惰气的混合过程
- 强调持续监测惰气质量和压力的重要性

问题范例

- 你能详细、系统地阐述惰气装置的起动和关闭程序吗?
- 你能列出在进行上述操作时需要遵守的预防措施吗?
- 在压载之前关于舱的惰化你会采取什么特殊预防措施?
- 货物上部空间的填料是什么及其与惰气压力有什么联系?

- What will you do to monitor the inert gas pressure when simultaneous cargo and ballasting operations are underway?
- Why is it important as well as, imperative to check the quality of inert gas prior to its usage?
- What operational procedures are required for inerting on a combination carrier?

9.9 Meters, indicators and alarms 0.5 hour

Key Concepts

1. Types of meters
2. Various locations of meters
3. All the alarms for the inert gas system
4. Alarms on board the combination carriers with regard to inert gas system

Lecture Suggestions

- Ensure that the students are fully aware of various meters, with regard to the inert gas system, in different locations whether it is the navigating bridge, engine control room or the cargo control room
- Ensure that the students are fully aware of various alarms, with regard to the inert gas system, in different locations whether it is the navigating bridge, engine control room or the cargo control room
- Discuss briefly the special alarms with respect to the inert gas system on combination carriers

Sample Questions

- Which are the three main aspects of the inert gas system operation for which meters are required?
- Which are the main areas where you will find the aforementioned meters?
- What are the alarms specific to the inert gas operation that you will find in different locations?
- What special alarms are provided on combination carriers with regard to inert gas?

9.10 Emergency procedures 0.5 hour

Key Concepts

1. Emergency procedures in the event of non-availability of inert gas be it while loading, discharging, ballast operations or gas freeing

Lecture Suggestions and Sample Questions

- Give details of procedures and precautions that the students should follow in the event of non-availability of inert gas. Please take one issue at a time such as, lack of good quality inert gas, insufficient pressure or, complete failure of the inert gas

- 在同时进行货油和压载操作时你会怎样监测惰气压力?
- 为什么惰气使用前的质量检查是重要而且必要的?
- 混装船的惰化过程要求哪些操作程序?

9.9 仪表、指示器和报警 0.5学时

关键概念

1. 仪表的种类
2. 仪表的不同位置
3. 惰气系统的所有报警
4. 混装船惰气系统的报警

教学建议

- 确保学员完全熟知与惰气系统相关的不同位置的各种仪表,不管是在驾驶台、机舱还是货物控制室
- 确保学员完全熟知与惰气系统相关的不同位置的各种报警,不管是在驾驶台、机舱还是货物控制室
- 简要讨论与混装船上惰气系统有关的特殊报警

问题范例

- 惰气系统操作的三个主要方面是哪些?会用到哪些仪表?
- 上述仪表的主要应用范围是哪些?
- 在不同位置的惰气系统的特殊报警有哪些?
- 混装船上为惰气系统提供了哪些特殊的报警?

9.10 应急程序 0.5学时

关键概念

1. 装载、卸货、压载和除气时在惰性气体不可用的情况下的应急程序

教学建议和问题范例

- 向学员提供一些在惰性气体不可用时应该遵循的程序和预防措施的细节。请每次都讲一个问题,例如,高质量的惰气不足、压力不足或惰气系统完全故障。

system. The situation warrants a complete understanding, and therefore an increase in the level of confidence on part of students, to be able to handle such an emergency. The questions to be put to students should be on the same line.

9.11 Maintenance and testing 0.5 hour

Key Concepts and Lecture Suggestions

1. Inspections and checks to be maintained on the six areas of inert gas generation and distribution

Sample Questions

- Can you write down, in a systematic order, the list of checks that you will make on the following areas of inert gas operation?
  - inert gas scrubber
  - inert gas blowers
  - deck water seal
  - non-return valve
  - scrubber effluent line
  - alarms
- What, in your opinion, is the need for making periodic checks? What will you achieve?

10 Crude oil washing (COW)

Refer to R4, as well as appendix 1, section 4, and appendix 4. During practical exercises with tank-washing machines or in lectures, the opportunity should be taken to point out where failures usually occur and how to remedy them. Similarly, this part of the course is not required for those persons who are to take charge of cargo and operations on tankers not fitted with COW. Certificates issued on completion of training should be endorsed to this effect.

10.1 Introduction 0.5 hour

Key Concepts

1. Concept of COW
2. A requirement by international law for many crude oil tankers
3. Contravention of this requirement leads to fines
4. IOPP Certificate and COW

Lecture Suggestions

- Discuss the evolution of COW and its importance in the protection of the marine environment and its advantages over other means of washing cargo tanks

要确保学员完全理解,从而提高部分学员在处理此类紧急事件时的信心水平。这些问题应该以同样的方式向学员提出。

9.11 维护与测试

0.5小时

关键概念和教学建议

1. 对惰性气体生产和分配系统中的六个部分检查和核查

问题范例

- 你能依系统顺序写出关于惰气操作的如下各方面的检查表吗?
  - 惰气洗涤塔
  - 惰气鼓风机
  - 甲板水封
  - 止回阀
  - 洗涤塔流出管线
  - 警报
- 在你看来什么需要做定期检查?你能实现什么目的?

10 原油洗舱(COW)

参考R4,也可以参考附录1的第4章和附录4。在用洗舱机做实际训练或在讲课过程中,应该指出何处经常发生错误和怎样修复。同样地,这部分课程内容对在不装设COW系统的油船上负责货物及其操作的人员不做要求,且完成培训后他们的证书也是如此背书的。

10.1 介绍

0.5学时

关键概念

1. 原油洗舱的概念
2. 国际法律关于原油船的要求
3. 违反这些法律会受到罚款处罚
4. IOPP证书和原油洗舱

教学建议

- 讨论原油洗舱的发展历程以及在保护海洋环境方面的重要性及其相对于其他洗舱方式的优点

- Explain that COW is mandatory these days and that any contravention (not using COW when certified to use) of the law leads to fines on the tanker
- Ensure that the students are aware of the IOPP Certificate and COW

Sample Questions

- What do you understand by COW? Who developed this technique (oil industry in the 1970s)?
- How does a COW operation contribute in the protection of the marine environment?
- Where will you find the information that your vessel is certified to use COW?
- What will happen, if certified, and COW operation is not carried out?

10.2 Design of COW systems 1 hour

Key Concepts

1. Compliance of COW to international specifications
2. Main components of COW system
3. COW and inert gas system
4. Effectiveness of a COW operation

Lecture Suggestions

- Discuss briefly the specifications under which the COW system is governed
- Describe in detail the main components of the COW system
- Explain why inert gas is required to ensure a smooth COW operation
- Discuss the COW operation and its effectiveness

Sample Questions

- What are the specifications of a COW system and where will you find the international rule in this regard?
- What are the four main components of a COW system?
- W hy is it imperative to have an inert gas system in operation while affecting a COW?
- How will you judge the effectiveness of a COW?

10.3 COW piping 0.5 hour

Key Concepts

1. Permanent piping system for COW
2. Exceptions to this rule

- 解释原油洗舱现在已强制执行,任何违反法规(已注册使用原油洗舱而不用)的油船都会受到罚款处罚
- 确保学员知道IOPP证书和原油洗舱

问题范例

- 你怎么理解原油洗舱? 谁发明了这项技术(20世纪70年代的石油工业)?
- 原油洗舱在保护海洋环境方面是如何做出贡献的?
- 你能在什么地方找到关于你所在船舶注册使用原油洗舱的信息?
- 如果已经注册但不使用原油洗舱时将会发生什么?

10.2 COW系统设计 1学时

关键概念

1. 符合关于原油洗舱的国际规范
2. 原油洗舱系统的主要组成
3. 原油洗舱和惰气系统
4. 原油洗舱操作的有效性

教学建议

- 简要讨论管理原油洗舱系统的规范
- 详细描述原油洗舱系统的主要组成
- 解释为什么要用惰气来确保顺利的原油洗舱
- 讨论原油洗舱操作和其有效性

问题范例

- 原油洗舱系统的规范有哪些? 你能在哪里找到关于这些内容的国际规则?
- 原油洗舱系统的四个主要组成部分是什么?
- 为什么原油洗舱必须要有惰性气体系统?
- 如何判断原油洗舱的有效性?

10.3 COW管系 0.5学时

关键概念

1. 原油洗舱的固定管系
2. 该规则的例外情况

3. Piping arrangements for COW with respect to other washing arrangements on board

Lecture Suggestions

- Describe the piping arrangement for COW in detail and explaining that this is a permanent arrangement on board barring a few exceptional cases
- Describe the piping arrangement of the COW in relation to the piping of other fixed washing arrangements
- Discuss the precautions to be taken, by way of blanking off, when COW and washing piping is combined

Sample Questions

- Do you understand the basic principle of COW piping?
- In which circumstances is the COW piping arrangement may not be permanent?
- What precautions will you take when the COW piping is combined with other piping used for water washing?
- What precautions will you take when the aforementioned combined piping passes through a heater?

10.4 Tank-washing machines 0.5 hour

Key Concepts

1. Fixed washing machines
2. Mounting of these machines
3. Types of washing machines
4. Operation of washing machines
5. Precautions while using and dismantling the washing machines

Lecture Suggestions

- Delineate to the students the type of washing machines used on tankers
- Discuss the options regarding the mounting of these machines
- Describe the types of washing machines used and a description of their individual operation
- Discuss the methods of isolating the machines from its supply line
- Ensure that the students are aware of the precautions to be taken while using and dismantling the washing machines

Sample Questions

- What types of washing machines are used on tankers?
- In how many ways can a fixed washing machine be mounted? Name them

3. 原油洗舱系统管系布置以及船上其他洗舱布置

教学建议

- 详细描述原油洗舱的管系布置并解释这是一种固定的船上布置,但有些情况例外
- 描述原油洗舱管系布置与其他固定式洗舱管系布置的关系
- 讨论当COW通过封闭相关管路与其他水洗管系共用管路时,需要采取的预防措施

问题范例

- 你理解COW管系的基本原则吗?
- 在什么条件下COW管系可以不采用固定式布置?
- 当COW管系和其他水洗管系联合使用时,你会采取什么预防措施?
- 当上述的联合管系通过加热器时,需要采取什么预防措施?

10.4 洗舱机

0.5学时

关键概念

1. 固定式洗舱机
2. 机器的安装
3. 洗舱机的类型
4. 洗舱机的操作
5. 使用和拆卸洗舱机的注意事项

教学建议

- 向学员描绘油船上使用的洗舱机类型
- 讨论关于洗舱机安装的选择
- 描述洗舱机的类型并说明它们各自的操作方法
- 讨论将洗舱机与其补给管路相隔离的方法
- 确保学员知道使用和拆卸洗舱机时应采取的预防措施

问题范例

- 油船上使用了哪些类型的洗舱机?
- 固定式洗舱机可以用多少种方法进行安装?并说出这些方法

- How many types of washing machines are found on tankers? Name them
- What are the functions of the types of washing machines named above?
- How will you isolate the washing machine from its supply line?

10.5 Pumps 0.5 hour

Key Concepts and Lecture Suggestions

1. Types of pumps used for COW – cargo or dedicated pumps

Sample Questions

- When cargo pump is being used for COW, how will you ensure sufficient pressure for COW?

10.6 Stripping systems 0.5 hour

Key Concepts

1. Effective stripping and COW
2. Positive trim, COW and stripping
3. Capacity of the stripping system
4. Remote monitoring of the stripping system
5. Small diameter line and the stripping system

Lecture Suggestions

- Explain that there is a close relationship between effective stripping and a COW operation
- Discuss the importance of maintaining a positive trim for executing an effective stripping operation that in turn will effect the COW operation
- Describe the capacity of the stripping system as 1.25 times the total throughput of maximum number of all COW machines that can be used simultaneously
- Explain that a remote monitoring of stripping operation can be carried out from the cargo control room and that this should be kept under a close watch
- Describe the function of the small diameter line to drain the cargo line and the pumps

Sample Questions

- What is the function of the stripping system?
- How is it related to the COW operation?
- What affect has a positive trim on the stripping operation?
- What should be the capacity of the stripping system?

- 油船上有多少种洗舱机？说出它们的名称
- 上述各类洗舱机的功能是什么？
- 如何将洗舱机与其补给管路相隔离？

10.5 泵 0.5学时

关键概念和教学建议

1. 原油洗舱用到的泵的种类——货油泵和专用泵

问题范例

- 当货油泵用于原油洗舱时,如何保证原油洗舱系统的压力？

10.6 扫舱系统 0.5学时

关键问题

1. 有效扫舱和原油洗舱
2. 正吃水差、原油洗舱和扫舱
3. 扫舱系统的流量
4. 扫舱系统的远程监控
5. 小口径管路和扫舱系统

教学建议

- 解释在有效扫舱与原油洗舱操作之间有紧密的联系
- 讨论在执行有效的扫舱操作时保持正吃水差的重要性,反过来也会影响原油洗舱操作
- 描述扫舱系统的流量相当于全部洗舱机同时工作总流量的1.25倍
- 解释在货油控制室能对扫舱系统进行远程监控,并对其保持严密监视
- 描述小口径管路对货油管路和货油泵放残的作用

问题范例

- 扫舱系统的作用是什么？
- 扫舱系统如何与原油洗舱建立联系？
- 正吃水差对扫舱操作有什么影响？
- 扫舱系统的流量应该是多少？

- How will you monitor the stripping operation?
- What is the purpose of the small diameter line provided on tankers?

10.7 Operations 1.5 hours

Key Concepts

1. COW Manual and its usage
2. Factors affecting to conduct a COW operation
3. Taking ballast in cargo tanks and COW
4. Time frame for washing sludge tank
5. Fluid used for COW
6. Dry crude
7. De-bottoming and COW
8. COW and inert atmosphere in the tank
9. Tank atmosphere monitoring
10. Programming the washing machines for COW operation
11. Measuring effectiveness of COW
12. Time frame for completion of COW operation
13. COW and the subsequent entries in the Oil Record Book (ORB)
14. Unsuitable oils to conduct a COW operation
15. COW and Port State Control inspection

Lecture Suggestions

- Discuss the various parameters of COW Operations and Equipment manual
- Explain that the decision to undertake COW in a particular tank is dependent upon whether ballast is being taken in the tank or not
- Further explain that taking ballast in a cargo tank is directly dependent upon COW
- Discuss the tanks that are to have been cleaned using COW
- Discuss the time frame for cleaning a sludge tank
- Explain that it is only the dry crude that can be used for COW purposes and the reasons behind its usage
- Describe the process of de-bottoming to ensure that dry crude is used for COW
- Reiterate the importance of maintaining an inert atmosphere while conducting COW and how the failure of maintaining an inert atmosphere can jeopardize the COW operation
- Discuss the checklist for COW

- 如何监控扫舱操作?
- 油船上提供小口径管路的目的是什么?

10.7 操作 1.5学时

关键概念

1. 原油洗舱手册及其使用方法
2. 影响原油洗舱操作的因素
3. 货油舱压载和原油洗舱
4. 清洗油舱油渣的时间
5. 原油洗舱使用的液体
6. 干原油
7. 清除舱底和原油洗舱
8. 原油洗舱和舱内惰气
9. 舱内气体监测
10. 对洗舱机进行编程以用于原油洗舱
11. 原油洗舱有效性测定
12. 完成原油洗舱操作的时间期限
13. 原油洗舱和随后在油类记录簿中的记录
14. 不适用原油洗舱操作的油类
15. 原油洗舱和港口国检查

教学建议

- 讨论原油洗舱操作和设备手册的各项参数
- 解释决定是否对某个特定的货舱进行原油洗舱取决于该货舱是否压载
- 进一步解释货舱的压载直接取决于原油洗舱
- 讨论使用原油洗舱的货舱
- 讨论清理油渣舱的时间期限
- 解释只有干原油可以用于原油洗舱及其具有这种用途的原因
- 描述清除舱底操作过程以确保使用干原油进行原油洗舱
- 重申在原油洗舱操作中保持舱内为惰性气体的重要性以及无法保持舱内为惰性气体环境对原油洗舱操作的危害
- 讨论原油洗舱操作检查表

- Discuss the ways to measure the effectiveness of a COW operation
- Explain the timeframe for the completion of COW operation
- Describe the entries that have to be made in the ORB with respect to COW
- Discuss briefly the crude oils that are not suitable for a COW operation and the reasons behind it
- Ensure that the students are aware that the COW operation can be subjected to a Port State Control inspection

Sample Questions

- Are you aware of the COW Operations and Equipment Manual? What does it contain and how will you use it? What are the parameters you will find in the Manual in deciding an effective COW operation?
- What are the deciding factors to carry out a COW operation in a tank?
- Which are the tanks that are crude oil washed?
- From where is the fluid taken to carry out a COW operation?
- What type of crude oil is used for a COW operation?
- What is the reason behind using only dry crude for COW?
- What do you understand by the term 'de-bottoming' and where is it used?
- Why is it important to maintain an inert atmosphere in the tank where COW is being done? When will you stop the COW operation in relation to the inert atmosphere in the tank?
- Can you state the items, in a systematic way, of the COW checklist?
- How will you measure the effectiveness of a COW operation?
- By what time should a COW operation be complete?
- Where will you make entries of a COW operation?
- Which type of crude oil is not suitable for a COW operation? Where will you find this information?
- In a port, who can inspect a COW operation?

11 Management of risk on oil tanker

Risk, on an oil tanker, is closely associated with hazard identification, of ranking risks as intolerable, tolerable or negligible, and of risk reduction. Risk management has today become a key factor in a whole new approach to the culture of safety and environment protection on oil tanker that a shipboard person should strive to promote. What is stressed in this section is the importance of understanding instinctively what it means to develop and implement a safety culture on oil tanker, which by its very nature incorporates a "consideration of risk". "Risk" on oil tanker is one of those terms to which it is difficult to pin a formal definition. It may perhaps be easier to agree on a definition of what risk, and subsequently, risk management is not. Risk management is not of unthinking compliance. It is not simply about ensuring that the ship meets all the prescribed standards and all the necessary certificates

- 讨论原油洗舱操作有效性的测定方法
- 解释完成原油洗舱操作的时间期限
- 描述关于原油洗舱必须记入油类记录簿的项目
- 简要讨论不适用原油洗舱的原油及其原因
- 确保学员知道原油洗舱需要接受港口国监督检查

问题范例

- 你知道原油洗舱操作和设备手册吗?它有什么内容以及如何使用?在手册中你会找到哪些决定原油洗舱操作有效性的参数?
- 油船进行原油洗舱操作的决定性因素有哪些?
- 哪些舱需要用原油清洗?
- 进行原油洗舱的油液来自于何处?
- 什么原油适用于原油洗舱?
- 只能使用干原油的原因是什么?
- 你怎么理解“清除舱底”一词以及在哪里使用?
- 为什么在原油洗舱操作中保持舱内为惰性气体环境很重要?什么时候停止与舱内惰性气体环境有关的原油洗舱操作?
- 你能系统地阐述原油洗舱检查表的条目吗?
- 你如何测定原油洗舱操作的有效性?
- 什么时候应该完成原油洗舱操作?
- 你会把原油洗舱操作记录在哪里?
- 哪种原油不适合进行原油洗舱?你能在哪里找到这些信息?
- 在港口,谁可以检查原油洗舱操作?

11 油船风险管理

油船风险与危险识别密切相关,风险等级分为不能容忍的、可以接受的、可以忽略的,并且应降低风险。现今风险管理已经成为油船上安全和环境保护新方法的关键因素,油船上的人员应该努力提高风险管理水平。本节强调理解在油船上制定和执行安全文化的重要性,其与“风险考虑”自然结合。油船上的“风险”是一种很难给予明确定义的术语。可能很容易定义什么是风险,但是风险管理则不同。风险管理不是盲目的服从。它不是简单地确保油船达到了规定的标准以及所有

are up-to-date and in place. It is more than that. Compliance is, of course, a pre-requisite – a starting point. But, beyond mere compliance is a mindset in which oil tanker personnel need to plan and set their own performance standards – actively managing risk as a routine part of their everyday work rather than just responding to external events. This is the beginning of risk management on oil tanker. In a risk management process on board, every small action to minimize risk is part of a cumulative process that ends in a safe and efficient operation.

11.1 Background 0.5 hour

Trainees should be made aware that most of the risk on oil tanker is part of the day-to-day operations. The section explains the issue of risk management on oil tanker.

Key Concepts

1. Continuous presence of risk on oil tankers
2. Managerial decision to minimize risk on oil tankers

Lecture Suggestions

- Discuss the hazard and the intrinsic nature of oil
- Discuss the usage of management tool for minimization of risk

Sample Questions

- Is any oil or petrochemical product carried by a tanker free from risk?
- What is the relationship between the potential hazard and the way it is handled?
- What is the purpose of management tool for shipboard management in terms of minimization of risk?

11.2 Definitions 0.5 hour

Under this heading, the trainee may be instructed on the meaning of risk assessment on oil tanker.

Key Concepts

1. Risk on an oil tanker is a function of probability of a cargo spill and its consequences on human health and the marine environment
2. Potential harm to the marine environment
3. Definition of risk in absolute terms
4. Risk Management as a part of management system on board

Lecture Suggestions

- Explain the defined limits of exposure and assessment of risk
- Delineate the steps of risk management

必需证书能够及时更新和准确放置。事实并非如此。当然,服从是首要的,是起点。但是,比服从更重要的是船舶人员需要制订计划以及设定他们的绩效标准—积极地管理风险并作为日常工作的一部分而不是仅仅应对外部事件。这是油船风险管理的开端。在船舶风险管理过程中,每个降低风险的措施都是整个累积过程的一部分,并最终达到安全有效的操作。

11.1 背景　　0.5学时

学员应该知道油船上的大部分风险都是日常工作的一部分。本节解释了油船上的风险管理问题。

关键概念

1. 油船风险的持续出现
2. 减小油船风险的管理决定

教学建议

- 讨论油的危险和固有性质
- 讨论降低风险的船舶管理工具的使用

问题范例

- 油船运输的石油和石化产品中有不存在风险的吗?
- 潜在的风险及其处理方法之间有什么联系?
- 在降低风险方面,船舶管理工具的目的是什么?

11.2 定义　　0.5学时

在该标题下,指导学员学习油船风险管理的意义。

关键概念

1. 油船上的风险是可能发生的溢油及其给人体健康和海洋环境带来的影响
2. 对海洋环境的潜在危害
3. 风险绝对值的定义
4. 风险管理是船舶管理体系的一部分

教学建议

- 解释暴露极限和风险评估
- 描绘风险管理步骤

- Discuss the various parameters and risk management
- Inform the concept of perception of risk on board

Sample Questions

- What is risk assessment in terms of oil carriage by sea?
- Against what limits should the risk be assessed on board?
- What is the main function of risk management on board an oil tanker?
- What are the factors that are considered while managing a risk aboard an oil tanker?
- What are the three steps of risk management?
- What is risk perception and how does it relate to risk management?
- What does perception of risk indicate?

11.3 Risk assessment on oil tankers 1 hour

Things should be kept simple. The essential message is that risk on oil tanker is made up of a range of issues. The relationship between the probability and the intensity of a potential incidence happening should be explained.

Key Concepts

1. Lack of understanding by shipboard personnel of the existence of risk in a scientific manner
2. Management of risk on an oil tanker rests both with the individual as well as, with the team

Lecture Suggestions

- Discuss in detail the risk considerations at the time of loading and discharging
- Inform the students that there has to be a clear cut awareness of risk among ship's personnel
- Explain that clear instructions for cargo stowage goes a long way in minimizing the risk
- Make the students aware that risk management is ultimately a responsibility of each individual

Sample Questions

- What are the risk factors to be considered at the time of loading and discharging?
- What is the potential risk of mishandling an oil cargo?
- Ultimately, where does the "buck stop" in terms of risk management on board an oil tanker?

- 讨论各项参数和风险管理
- 阐述油船风险感知这一概念

问题范例

- 什么是在海上原油运输方面的风险评估?
- 油船应该依据什么限制进行风险评估?
- 油船风险管理的主要功能是什么?
- 在油船上进行风险管理时应考虑的主要因素有哪些?
- 风险管理的三个步骤是什么?
- 什么是风险感知及其与风险管理有什么关系?
- 风险感知预示什么?

11.3 油船风险评估　1学时

应该让事情尽量简单一点。关键信息是油船风险由一系列的问题组成。应该对潜在事故发生的可能性和强度之间的关系进行解释。

关键概念

1. 船上人员对风险的存在缺乏科学的理解
2. 油船上风险的管理依赖于个人和团队

教学建议

- 详细讨论在装卸货时须考虑的风险因素
- 告知学员在船舶人员中必须有一个鲜明的风险意识
- 解释清楚货物装载对减小风险有长远的影响
- 使学员意识到风险管理是每个人的责任

问题范例

- 在装卸货时需要考虑的风险因素有哪些?
- 对货油不正确操作有哪些潜在风险?
- 最终,油船风险管理的“追究人”在哪里?

11.4 Risk assessment process 1 hour

The section divides the different levels of risk into a number of categories, each of which should be dealt with in some detail. It is only by understanding the different aspects of risk that measures to manage the risk will be fully appreciated.

Key Concepts

1. Identification of hazard in relation to presence of toxic vapours
2. Number of hazards in relation to levels of toxicity of the cargo
3. Critical dose and the time component
4. Knowledge of properties of oil/petrochemical and subsequent assessment
5. Anticipatable and accidental exposure
6. Spill and exposure control and monitoring
7. Managing risk in terms of potential and the acceptable level
8. Continuous monitoring of risk

Lecture Suggestions

- Describe how to prepare a hazard profile vis–ɑ̀–vis toxicity of an oil cargo
- Describe the different hazards that exist on an oil tanker
- Explain what is a critical dose
- Explain how do you identify the critical dose of an oil cargo
- Discuss what role does the time component play with regard to exposure
- Discuss the exposure assessment based on oil properties
- Describe what are different categories of exposure
- Also delineate the limitations of calculation in types of exposure on board
- Explain that the sole purpose of all of the above discussions is to sensitize the student, in a scientific manner, regarding the levels of risk that exists on board a tanker and that how important it is to ensure the minimization of risk at every level

Sample Questions

- On what factors is the hazard dependent on an oil tanker?
- What is meant by critical dose in relation to an oil cargo?
- Where does the time factor come in relation to the critical dose?
- How do you assess the exposure limit? Where will you find this information?
- What are the two types of exposures?
- What is the difference?

11.4 风险评估过程 1学时

该节内容将不同等级的风险划分成了不同种类,应该对每一类风险进行详细处理。只有通过理解风险的不同方面,管理风险的措施才能充分发挥作用。

关键概念

1. 与有毒蒸气有关的危险识别
2. 与货物毒性等级相关的危险数量
3. 临界剂量和时间组成
4. 石油/石化产品特性的知识和后续的评估
5. 可预见性辐射和事故性辐射
6. 溢油和辐射的控制和监控
7. 潜在和可接受水平的风险管理
8. 持续的风险监控

教学建议

- 描述如何准备与货油毒性相对应的危害特性
- 描述油船上存在的不同危险
- 解释什么是临界剂量
- 解释如何确定货油的临界剂量
- 讨论时间组成就辐射而言扮演了一个什么样的角色
- 基于原油的性质讨论辐射评估
- 描述辐射有哪些不同的种类
- 描绘船上辐射类型计算的局限性
- 解释上面所有讨论内容的唯一用途是让学员变得敏感,用一种科学的态度,认识油船上存在的风险的等级以及在每个等级下确保降低风险的重要性

问题范例

- 在油船上的危险取决于哪些因素?
- 关于货油临界剂量指什么?
- 关于临界剂量,时间因素有什么影响?
- 如何评定辐射极限?从哪里找到这些资料?
- 两种辐射是哪两种?
- 它们有什么区别?

11.5 Risk management in practice 1 hour

Trainees should be made aware that most of the risk on oil tankers is caused during the day-to-day operations. For instance, there is a distinct difference between risks in port and at sea on oil tanker. At this stage, the awareness for trainees is most important that the aim is towards risk reduction. The prioritization of risk helps in the decisions regarding risk management on oil tankers, and this is achieved by a good knowledge of an understanding of the acceptability of risk on oil tanker.

Key Concepts

1. Aim of risk management – risk reduction
2. Complex nature of risk management on board
3. Scientific, technical and legal aspects of risk management on board
4. Risk management and law – international, flag State (national) and port State (local)
5. Acceptability of risk
6. Difficult decisions in risk management
7. Zoning of risks

Lecture Suggestions

- Describe the processes for reducing of risk
- Discuss the practical difficulties of risk management on a tanker
- Explain that to a large extent, the control of risk is assisted by legislation
- Discuss the role of oil industry in control of risk on board. Give example of LOT procedures that were developed by the oil industry in the 1960s, the COW also developed by the oil industry in the 1970s, the technical details available at ITOPF on oil hazards and containment of spill. These are just a few of the many examples
- Discuss the limits of acceptance of risk
- Explain the difficult parameters in risk management and discuss that the real acumen of the shipboard management will be tested from time to time in managing the difficult situations where the level of risk involved is very high as well as, the level of safety expected is also very high
- Discuss the limits and limitations of zoning of a risk and reiterate that this acts as a tool for the management of risk on board

Sample Questions

- What does risk management finally entail?
- Why is risk management considered a complex issue on a tanker?
- What are the scientific, technical and legal aspects to be considered in managing risk on board?
- What are the different tiers of rules that help in managing risk on board?

11.5 风险管理实践

1学时

学员应该知道油船上大部分危险都是在日常操作中引起的。例如,在港口和海上油船的风险有明显区别。在该阶段,学员要知道最重要的目标是降低风险。风险的优先顺序有助于针对油船风险管理做出决定,并可以通过理解油船风险的可接受性来实现。

关键概念

1. 风险管理的目标——降低风险
2. 船上风险管理的复杂特性
3. 船上风险管理的科学性、技术性和法律性
4. 风险管理和法律——国际、船旗国(国家)和港口国(地方)
5. 风险的可接受性
6. 风险管理的困难决定
7. 风险分区

教学建议

- 描述降低风险的过程
- 讨论油船风险管理的实际困难
- 解释在很大程度上风险控制需要立法的帮助
- 讨论在控制船上风险过程中石油行业的角色。举例说明石油行业于20世纪60年代发明了LOT程序,又于20世纪70年代提出了原油洗舱,在国际油船污染联合会提出了关于石油危害和溢油控制的可行性技术细节。这些仅是很多实例中的一部分。
- 讨论可接受风险的极限
- 解释风险管理的困难参数,并讨论在管理那些风险等级很高并且要求的安全等级也非常高的艰难处境时,需要对船舶管理进行随时检测。
- 讨论风险分区的极限和局限,重申这可以作为一种船舶风险管理工具。

问题范例

- 风险管理最终需要承担什么?
- 为什么认为油船风险管理是一个复杂的问题?
- 在风险管理中需要考虑哪些科学、技术和法律方面的内容?
- 帮助油船实施风险管理的不同层次的法规有哪些?

- What is the meaning of acceptability of risk?
- How is this factor decided upon?
- What is zoning of risk associated with on an oil tanker?
- Can you define the four risk zones?
- What zone of risk would be considered acceptable in a worst-case scenario?

12 Contingency Planning

Careful planning is an essential preparation for any successful operation, especially an emergency one. Response to accidental spillage of oil is a typical example. Many people may be affected by an oil spill and shipboard personnel on oil tanker have duties to perform apart from the task of physical clean up. The ships therefore carrying oil in bulk have a responsibility to protect the personnel on board and the environment from the adverse effects of marine pollution and to minimize those effects where protection is not possible. The aim of contingency plan is to outline the arrangements for responding to oil spills in the marine environment, with the aim of protecting personnel health and the marine environment from oil pollution or, where this is not possible, to minimize its effects.

It is imperative to understand that the mode of transportation is not important. Transportation of oil is in itself a risk and the presence of risk is indicative of the need of an emergency plan.

This section stresses the point to the trainees that the primary purpose of contingency planning is to be prepared to respond to abnormal events when they occur. The effectiveness of any contingency plan also depends on the personnel regularly exercising their respective roles and responsibilities.

Key Concepts (for the three sub-sections)

1. Risks involved in case of an incidence involving an oil spill
2. Reputation at stake
3. Oil release into the marine environment
4. Fundamentals of effective management of an oil spill
5. Preparation of a contingency plan on board
6. Response teams
7. Communications
8. Oil spill recovery equipment on board
9. Contingency drills

12.1 General

0.5 hour

Every oil tanker can experience a serious incident that can prevent it from continuing normal operations and this can be wide-ranging.

- 风险的可接受性指什么?
- 该因素是如何决定的?
- 油船风险分区是什么?
- 你能确定四个危险区域吗?
- 在最坏的情况下,什么区域的风险是可以接受的?

12 应急计划

认真的计划是成功操作的必要准备,尤其是紧急情况。对事故性溢油的反应是一个典型的例子。很多人都会受到溢油的影响,并且油船上的人员除了参加清理油污工作之外还有其他职责。因此散装油船有责任保护船上人员和海洋环境免受海洋污染的有害影响并且在不可能的情况下将影响降到最低。应急计划的目的是对海上溢油反应安排做一个规划,以保护船上人员健康和海洋环境免受油污染影响,并在不可能的情况下将影响降到最低。

必须理解运输模式并不重要。石油运输本身就是一种风险,而存在的风险暗含了应急计划是需要的。

本节对学员强调的要点是应急计划的主要用途是准备响应发生的异常事件。任何应急计划的有效性也取决于船舶人员是否经常对各自的角色和责任进行练习。

关键概念(三个小节)

1. 万一发生涉及溢油的事件时存在的风险
2. 危机关头的声誉
3. 油排放到海洋环境中
4. 溢油有效管理的基础
5. 船上应急计划的准备
6. 反应小组
7. 通信
8. 船上溢油回收设备
9. 应急演习

12.1 概述

0.5学时

每艘油船都可能经历一个严重事故,以致于使其无法继续运营,并且这种事故范围很广。

The shipboard personnel on oil tanker have a responsibility to recover from any such incidents in the minimum amount of time and with minimum disruption in operations. It requires careful preparation and planning. This section deals with the process of contingency planning in its entirety.

Lecture Suggestions

- Describe the stakes involved in case of an oil spill
- Describe the way oil can enter into the marine environment from an oil tanker – accidental release or, deliberate release (operational release)
- Describe that oil released into the marine environment by way of operations is a far bigger threat than accidental release
- Revise the concept of the toxic load

Sample Questions

- In what way does an oil spill affect the human health, marine environment, coastal amenities, and the reputation of the carrier?
- Do you therefore understand the importance of contingency planning on board?

12.2 Management 0.5 hour

It is vital that the shipboard staff on oil tanker takes the development and maintenance of the contingency plan seriously. It is not one of those tasks that can be left until everyone has time to deal with it. The idea is to sensitize the trainee that a serious incident can affect the ship at any time and this includes the next 24 hours! The contingency plan needs to be managed by a team representing all functional areas of the ship.

This section deals with trainees being well informed that contingency plan on board oil tanker should be established like a formal project, which must have the involvement of the very top management of the ship.

Lecture Suggestions

- Describe the basics of an oil spill contingency plan
- Discuss the concept of oil spill contingency as project management
- Explain the "job description" of everyone involved in the contingency
- Discuss the importance of effective communication
- Explain how tuition and training goes a long way in executing a contingency plan when the need arises
- Discuss the use of equipment
- Reiterate the importance of constant evaluation of the plan

油船人员有责任在最短时间内,以对营运影响最小的方式,从事故中恢复过来。这要求仔细的准备和计划。本节主要讨论应急计划的全部过程。

教学建议

- 描述万一发生溢油事故时的危害
- 描述油类从油船进入海洋环境的途径——事故性泄漏和故意排放(操作性泄漏)。
- 描述操作性溢油给海洋环境带来的威胁比事故性溢油带来的威胁要较大
- 复习毒性负荷的概念

问题范例

- 溢油以何种方式影响了人的健康、海洋环境、沿岸设施和船舶声誉?
- 你由此理解船上应急计划的重要性吗?

12.2 管理 0.5学时

油船船员认真地制订和维护应急计划是至关重要。这不是那些可以等人有时间才去做的事。其理念是要让学员对严重事故可以随时影响船舶变得敏感,包括接下来的24小时!应急计划需要能代表船上各个功能区的小组来管理。

本节需要让学员熟知油船应急计划要像一个规范项目一样建立,必须有船舶高层管理人员的参与。

教学建议

- 描述溢油应急计划的基础
- 讨论溢油应急计划作为项目管理的概念
- 解释每个人在应急计划中的“工作说明”
- 讨论有效通信的重要性
- 解释当出现需求时,教学和培训如何对执行应急计划产生长远影响
- 讨论设备的使用
- 重申经常对计划进行评估的重要性

Sample Questions

- Which are the three fundamentals that make an effective contingency plan?
- What is the purpose of a response team?
- How will you see the contingency plan preparation and practice as project management?
- Apart from technology, what is the role of personnel in effective communication?
- What will constitute a training package on board with regard to contingency planning?
- What are the parameters you will include to have a continuous evaluation of the contingency plan on board?

12.3 Preparation of the contingency plan 1 hour

After the assessment of the types of contingencies on oil tanker, the structure of the plan will need to be established. The plan will contain a range of milestones to move the ship from its disrupted status towards a return to normal operations.

This section highlights the parameters that go into the development of a contingency plan on board oil tanker. It is vital to inform the trainee that the subsequent stages to the development of the contingency plan are testing the plan, personnel training on board and maintain ing the plan.

Lecture Suggestions

- Describe the important sections that form a contingency plan
- Give a description of each of the sections (strategy, action and data) in detail

Sample Questions

- What are the three sections that constitute the contingency plan?
- Do you agree or, you feel that something more should be added?
- How many sub-sections does section 1 have?
- How many sub-sections does section 2 have?
- How many sub-sections does section 3 have?
- What is the importance of going through all the details possible at the time of planning and formulation of the contingency plan?
- Do you agree that a detailed plan helps in dissecting the plan to conduct an evaluation after a drill?

问题范例

- 构成一个有效的应急计划的三个基本原则是什么?
- 应急响应小组的使命是什么?
- 你如何看应急计划作为计划管理的准备和演习?
- 除了技术外,人员在有效通信中扮演了什么角色?
- 是什么构成了油船上应急计划的成套教学素材?
- 对船上应急计划进行连续评估时包括哪些参数?

12.3 应急计划的准备 1学时

在评估了油船上各类紧急事件之后,需要建立应急计划的框架。该计划需要包含一系列的重要节点,能够使船舶从中断状态恢复到正常运营状态。

本节着重强调了制订油船应急计划的决定因素。要告知学员制订应急计划的后期阶段是计划测试、船上人员培训和计划维护,这一点非常重要。

教学建议

- 描述组成应急计划的重要部分
- 对每个部分(策略、行动、数据)给出详细的描述

问题范例

- 组成应急计划的三个部分是什么?
- 你同意,或者你感觉应该有更多东西加进来吗?
- 第一部分有多少小节?
- 第二部分有多少小节?
- 第三部分有多少小节?
- 在应急计划的形成和尽可能详细的规划时间内需要关注的重要事情是什么?
- 你同意一个详细的计划能在演习后实施的评估中有助于对计划进行剖析吗?

13 Assessment and Evaluation 1 hour

(Guidance)

Introduction

Tests are powerful educational tools that serve at least four functions. First, tests help the faculty to evaluate students and assess whether they are learning what they are expected to learn.

Second, well-designed tests serve to motivate and help students structure their academic efforts. Normally it is seen that students study in ways that reflect how they think they will be tested. If they expect an exam focused on facts, they will memorize details, if they expect a test that will require problem solving or integrating knowledge, they will work toward understanding and applying information.

Third, tests can help the faculty to understand how successfully has the material been presented.

Finally, tests can reinforce learning by providing students with indicators of what topics or skills they have not yet mastered and should concentrate on.

Keeping in mind the four points delineated above as well as, the tightness of the schedule of the course, it is suggested that a test containing a mixture of multiple–choice questions as well as one-line answer questions will achieve the objective of assessing the student of the knowledge acquired during the course.

Method of Evaluation

Multiple-choice tests: Multiple-choice items can be used to measure both simple knowledge and complex concepts. Since multiple-choice questions can be answered quickly, the students' mastery of many topics can be assessed in the exam. In addition, the items can be easily and reliably scored.

True-false tests: Because random guessing will produce the correct answer half the time, truefalse tests are less reliable than other types of exams. However, these items are appropriate for occasional use. Therefore, a mixture of multiple–choice and true/false type of questions are suggested for the examination.

Some of the true-false questions could have an added "explain" column in which students write one or two sentences justifying their response.

The following suggestions have therefore been included to enhance the ability of the instructor to design tests that are effective in motivating, measuring, and reinforcing learning.

General Strategies

Spend adequate amounts of time developing the tests. As a test is prepared, the instructor should think carefully about the learning outcomes that are wished to be measured, the type

13 考核和评估　　1学时

(指南)

介绍

测试是强大的教育工具,其提供了至少四个作用。第一,测试有助于教员对学员进行评价并评估他们是否学到了希望他们学习的知识。

第二,精心设计的测试能够激励和帮助学员构建他们的学术成果。一般情况下,显而易见学员的学习方式反映了他们将被测试时的内心想法。如果他们期望考试集中在这些内容上,他们会详细地记忆这些内容;如果他们预期考试注重于问题解答和知识整合,他们会致力于理解和应用知识。

第三,测试有助于教员明白向学员讲授的知识材料哪些是成功的。

最后,测试向学员强调学习的方向标,给学员提供的学习主题或技能他们还没有掌握还需要关注。

熟记上述四点以及紧张的课程时间安排,建议包含多项选择题和简答题的测试能够达到评价学员在课程中的知识掌握程度的目的。

评估方法

多项选择测试:多项选择题可以用来测试简单知识和复杂概念。因为多项选择题可以实现快速回答,因此可以在考试中评价学员对很多知识点的掌握程度。另外,选择题评分也很简单和可靠。

判断正误测试:因为随机猜测都有一半的正确概率,所以判断正误题相对于其他考试而言,可靠性不强。然而,这种题型可以偶尔使用。因此,建议在考试中综合采用选择题和判断正误题。

一些判断正误题可以加上附加解释栏,其中,学员可以用一两句话对其回答进行解释。

因此接下来的建议已经包含了提高教员设计测试题的能力,出一些能够有效激励、衡量和加强学习的测试题。

总体战略

花费足够的时间来设计测试。测试准备好后,教员应该仔细思考希望测试的教学效果、适用

of items best suited to those outcomes, the range of difficulty of items, the choice of answers to each question, the format and layout of the exam, and the scoring procedures.

Match the test to the content that is taught. Ideally, the tests given will measure students' achievement of the set educational goals for the course, which is to have sufficient knowldge to take responsibility of cargo operations on board a tanker. Test items should therefore be based on the content and skills that are most important for the students to learn.

Try to make the tests valid, reliable, and balanced. A test is valid if its results are useful for making decisions about an aspect of students' achievement. Technically, validity refers to the appropriateness of the interpretation of the results and not to the test itself. A practical approach is to focus on content validity, the extent to which the content of the test represents an adequate sampling of the knowledge and skills taught in the course. If the instructor designs the test to cover information in lectures and readings in proportion to their importance in the course, then the interpretations of test scores are likely to have greater validity.

A test is *reliable* if it accurately and consistently evaluates a student's performance. Very short tests are therefore unlikely to be highly reliable. It is suggested that the multiple-choice test should contain between 40 – 60 questions and to be completed in one hour, thus the time spent on each question is between 60 – 90 seconds.

It is also important for a test to be balanced: to cover most of the main ideas and important concepts in proportion to the emphasis they received in class.

Write questions that test skills other than recall. The test administered by the faculty should not rely too heavily on students' recall of information. It is equally important for tests to measure higher learning as well. Here is a suggestive condensation of the methodology to use:

To measure *knowledge* (common terms, facts, principles, procedures). The one-line/ multilechoice questions to include these parameters: Identify, Label, List, Match, Name, Select, State. Example: "*State the particular regulation of, and, the international convention under which it is required to undergo the Advanced TASCO Course.*"

To measure *comprehension* (understanding of facts and principles, interpretation of material). The one-line/multiple-choice questions to include these parameters: Distinguish, Estimate, Explain, Extend, Generalize, and Give examples, Infer, Predict, Summarize. Example: "*Which of the following best summarizes the basic tenets of fire-fighting on an oil tanker?*"

To measure *application* (solving problems, applying concepts and principles to new situations). The one-line/multiple-choice questions to include these parameters: Demonstrate, Operate, Prepare, Relate, and Show, Solve, Use. Example: "*Demonstrate how a flashpoint of a liquid is determined.*"

To measure *analysis* (ability to distinguish between facts and inferences), The one-line/ multiple-choice questions to include these parameters: Differentiate, Distinguish, Illustrate, Infer, Point out, Relate, Select, Separate. Example: "*In the development of a risk management plan, which issues will you consider as based on facts and which as based on assumptions?*"

于这些效果的最佳题型、题目的难度范围、每个问题的答案选项、试卷格式及布局，以及评分步骤。

使考试和教学内容相一致。最理想的是，给予的考试能够衡量学员对课程设定的教学目标所达到的程度，是否具有承担油船上的货物操作的责任所需要的足够的知识。因此考试题型设计应该基于学员需要学习的最重要的内容和技能。

尽量使考试有效、可靠和均衡。如果考试结果对评判学员成绩的某一方面做出决定有帮助，那么测试就是有效的。就技术而言，有效性指的是结果解释的合理性，而不是考试本身。一个实用的方法是专注于内容的有效性，考试内容的拓展代表了对课程教学中的知识和技能的足够取样。如果在教员设计的考试中，教学内容和课外读物的占比与他们在课程中的重要性成比例，那么对考试成绩的解读就更加有效。

如果考试能准确和如实地评价学员的表现，那它就是可靠的。因此，内容简短的考试一般不会很可靠。建议考试中安排40~60个多项选择题，在一个小时内完成。因此每个题花费的时间是60~90秒。

考试内容的均衡性很重要。应该涵盖的主要思想和重要概念要与课上被强调的程度成比例。

笔试题是测试技能而不是记性。由教员主导的考试不应该过于依赖学员对资料的记忆。对于测试那些更深层的学习同样重要。以下是可使用的浓缩的建议方法：

测试知识(一般术语、事实、原理、程序)。简答和多项选择题包含这些因素：识别、标签、列表、匹配、名称、选择、阐述。例如："阐述在哪个特殊的规则和国际公约的要求下需要学习高级TASCO课程？"

测试理解力(理解事实和原理，材料解读)。简答和多项选择题包含这些因素：辨别、估计、解释、扩展、概括、举例、推断、预测、总结。例如："下面哪项最好地总结了油船防火的基本原则？"

测试应用能力(解决问题、针对新情况应用概念和原理)。简答和多项选择题包含这些因素：证明、操作、准备、了解、以及展示、解决、使用。例如："演示如何测定液体的闪点？"

测试分析能力(事实和推断之间的区别)，简答题和多项选择题包含这些因素：区分、识别、图示、推断、指出、了解、选择、分离，例如："在制订风险管理计划时，哪些问题你认为是基于事实，哪些问题你认为是基于假设？"

To measure synthesis (integrate learning from different areas). The one-line/multiple-choice questions to include these parameters: Categorize, Combine, Compile, Devise, Organize, Plan, Rearrange. Example: *"Do you agree with the following categorisation of reactivity hazards of oil cargoes?*

- *With itself*
- *With air*
- *With water*
- *With another cargo*
- *With other materials?"*

To measure evaluation (judging and assessing). The one-line/multiple-choice questions to include these parameters: Appraise, Compare, Conclude, Contrast, Explain, Justify, Interpret, Support. Example: *"Is it true that the context of carriage of oil in bulk by sea, risk management consists of 3 steps: risk assessment (evaluation), emission and exposure control, and risk monitoring?"*

Performance tests on the simulator, in case a simulator is provided as a training tool for this model course. Performance tests may ask students to demonstrate proficiency in executing a series of steps in a reasonable amount of time, following instructions and reacting to simulated situations. Performance tests may be administered individually or in groups. For the simulation exercises:

- Specify the criteria to be used for rating or scoring (for example, the level of accuracy in performing the steps in sequence or completing the task within a specified time limit).

- State the problem so that students know exactly what they are supposed to do (if possible, conditions of a performance test should mirror a real-life situation).

Pass Percentage: 50%

测试综合理解能力(综合学习不同的领域)。简答和多项选择题包含这些因素：分类、联合、汇编、设计、组织、计划、重新安排。例如：“你同意如下货油反应性危害的分类吗？

- 自身反应
- 与空气反应
- 与水反应
- 与另一种货油
- 与其他材料？”

测试评估能力(判断和评估)。简答和多项选择题包含这些因素：评价、比较、结论、差异、解释、证明、翻译、支持。例如：“海上散装石油运输背景下风险管理包括三步：风险评估、排放和辐射控制和风险监控，这种说法对吗？”

假如有模拟器作为课程的训练工具，那么可以做模拟器操作测试。操作测试要求学员熟练地演示：根据指示和模拟的环境的反应在合理的时间内执行一系列的操作步骤。操作测试可能会单独或分组进行。对于模拟练习：

- 规定用来评定和打分的标准(例如，依次完成操作步骤的准确程度或在特定时间限度内任务完成情况)
- 阐述问题要求以便让学员能准确地知道自己应该做什么(如果可能的话，测试环境应该仿照真实环境)。

通过百分比：50%

Appendix 1:

Notes on the Construction, Equipment and Operation of Oil Tankers and Diagrams for Use by the Instructor or Printoffs as Handouts

指导手册附录 (D部分)

附录1:

油船的结构、设备和操作注释以及教员用图表或作为讲义的打印资料

Glossary

The following are frequently used abbreviations.

CBT: Clean Ballast Tanks – Cargo tanks dedicated to carrying ballast. Unlike SBT (see below), CBT do not require separate pipes and pumps for ballast handling.

COW: Crude Oil Washing.

GPI: Glass Pipe Installation – Special equipment for visual inspection of oil content in water and monitoring of water cleaning efficiency.

LFL: Lower Flammable Limit – The limit below which, a mixture of hydrocarbon gas and air cannot ignite and burn owing to insufficient hydrocarbon content.

LOT: Load On Top – Loading of cargo oil on top of cargo residue slops that has been processed according to established LOT procedures.

MARPOL 73/78: International Convention for the Prevention of Pollution from Ships, 1973, and the Protocol of 1978, as amended.

pH: A quantitative measure of the acidic or basic nature of liquid solutions. A solution with a pH of less than 7 is considered acidic and one with a pH of more than 7 alkaline.

PPM: Part per million.

PL: Protective Location (of segregated ballast tanks). These tanks are, in principle, located between the cargo tanks and ship sides/bottom to offer protection in the event of grounding or collision.

RVP: Reid Vapour Pressure.

SBT: Segregated Ballast Tank – Tanks for the carriage of ballast water only. Unlike CBT (see above), SBT require separate pumps and pipes intended for handling ballast water only.

SOLAS 1974: International Convention for the Safety of Life at Sea, 1974, as amended.

术语表

下面是经常用到的缩写

CBT:清洁压载舱。货舱可用于压载。不像SBT(见下面)、CBT不需要单独的泵和管路进行压载操作。

COW:原油洗舱。

GPI:玻璃管装置。用于视觉检查水中油分和监测水清洁效果的专用设备。

LFL:可燃下限。由于烃气成分的不足,低于可燃下限的烃气与空气的混合气不能被点燃和燃烧。

LOT:装于上部。根据已经建立的LOT程序将货油装于货油残渣之上。

MARPOL 73/78:经修订的1973年防止船舶污染的国际公约及其1978年议定书。

pH:液体溶液酸性或基本性质的定量测量。若溶液的pH值小于7,则为酸性;若大于7,则为碱性。

PPM:百万分之一。

PL:保护舱(具有专用压载舱)。原则上,是位于货油舱和船边(或船底)之间在搁浅或碰撞情况下提供保护的舱。

RVP:雷德蒸发压力。

SBT:专用压载舱。仅用于装压载水的舱。不像CBT(见上面),SBT需要独立的泵和管路,仅用于压载水的操作。

SOLAS 1974:经修订的1974年国际海上人命安全公约。

Development of oil tankers

There are three general size categories: large, intermediate and small. Tankers between 100,000 and 540,000 DWT usually carry crude oil from the producers to the refineries, while ships below 100,000 DWT mostly transport refined products, although some are in the crude oil trade. Small ships, less than 20,000 DWT, are typically used in coastal distribution from oil refineries to distribution storage areas.

A brief mention is being made here of the unconventional or, dual–purpose type of a tanker.

Combination carriers

A combination carrier is a tanker designed to carry oil or solid cargoes in bulk and is one of two main types, an Oil/Bulk/Ore (OBO) ship or an Oil/Ore (O/O) ship.

The OBO ship is capable of carrying her full deadweight when trading as an ore carrier with cargoes of heavy ore concentrates. This type of ship is also designed to carry other types of dry bulk cargo, such as grain or coal.

Holds are usually arranged to extend the full breadth of the ship, with upper and lower hopper tanks and double-bottom tanks. In some cases, holds may have wings. Oil or dry bulk cargo is carried in the holds. Oil may also be carried in one or more sets of upper hopper tanks and, if the ship has them, in the wing tanks. Wing tanks for the carriage of oily slops are normally fitted aft of the cargo holds. Segregated ballast may be carried in top and bottom hopper tanks and in double–bottom tanks.

Conventional bulk carrier hatches, normally of the side-rolling type, are fitted with a special sealing arrangement.

Cargo and ballast pipelines are typically installed in a duct keel or in two pipe tunnels located either side of the centreline and separated by a double-bottom tank (Figure 1 and 2).

Holds are constructed to extend approximately one-half of the total breadth of the ship. Conventional wing tanks incorporate the main strengthening sections, allowing smooth sides in the centre holds. Holds are always constructed with double-bottom spaces beneath them.

Future design changes in tankers

A description of the evolution of tankers has been made in the introduction and is therefore not being repeated here. What are discussed, as part of the Appendix, are the types of designs that are, and can be forthcoming in the future.

Discussion on Double Hull Oil Tankers and Equivalents

As a consequence of the EXXON VALDEZ accident in 1989, and the unilateral action by the United States Government in favour of double hull oil tankers, there has been a renewed urgency within the marine industry to find a design of vessel, which offers the most effective protection against oil pollution in the event of a collision or grounding accident. Several authoritative studies have been carried out into the problem and there is almost unanimous

油船的发展

油船一般有三种大小的分类:大、中、小。100 000~540 000 DWT的油船通常用于产地到炼油地的原油运输,而100 000 DWT以下的油船,尽管有些用于原油贸易,但大多数用于运输成品油。20 000 DWT以下的小型油船,通常用于沿岸从炼油厂到各存储地的运输。

这里简要提及新式或双用途型油船。

混装船

混装船是一种用来装载油或散装固体货物的船舶,是两种主要型号中的一种,即:油/散货/矿(OBO)船和油/矿(O/O)船。

OBO船有能力在贸易运输中作为矿物船运输全部净吨位的高密度重矿物。这种类型的船也设计用来运输其他形式的干散装货物,如谷物和煤炭。

带有上、下边舱和双层底的船,通常把货舱扩展布置到船的全宽。某些时候货舱可能有翼舱,油或干散货装在舱内。油可以装在一个或多个上边舱,如果有翼舱,也可以装在翼舱。用于装油渣的翼舱通常设在货舱的后部。专用压载可以装在上、下边舱和双层底舱中。

传统的散货船舱盖,通常是侧边滚动式的,装设专门的密封。

货油和压载管线一般装在龙骨管道中或装在位于被双层底舱分隔的中线两边的两个管隧中(图1和图2)。

建造的货舱宽度可扩展至大约船总宽的一半。传统的翼舱形成船舶主要强度部分,允许中心舱两侧平滑。货舱以下空间总是建造成双层底。

未来油船设计的变化

油船的发展过程已经在前面的介绍部分做了描述,这里将不再重复。作为附则的一部分,这里需要讨论的是在未来可能会出现的设计类型。

有关双壳油船及类似船型的讨论

由于1989年EXXON VALDEZ事故,以及美国政府单方支持使用双壳结构油船,迫使海运行业急需找到一种设计方案,能在船舶碰撞或搁浅后最有效的防止油污染事故。针对这个问题国际上已经进行了几次具有权威性的研究,但是几乎无 例外的表明没有一种可设想的方法能在发

agreement that no one design produces the best results in all the possible grounding or collision scenarios, which can be envisaged. There is also general agreement on the following broad conclusions, namely that:

- Double hull vessels in low energy (typically low velocity) accidents should not pollute
- Vessels that carry cargo in contact with a single skin (with sea on the other side) will cause some pollution in any accident where a cargo tank is penetrated. However, certain design alternatives will minimize the amount of pollution in some specified scenarios
- High-energy accidents nearly always result in pollution. The relative advantages of various design alternatives in reducing pollution from particular scenarios are highly dependent on the assumptions made in the scenarios

There are many design concepts, which have been proposed to reduce the risk of pollution in the event of an accident. International attention is increasingly focused on three main types:

- Double Hull tanker
- Mid-deck tanker
- Coulombi Egg tanker

A typical cross-section for each of these types is shown below, but to date only the double hull tanker type has actually been constructed.

The Double Hull Tanker

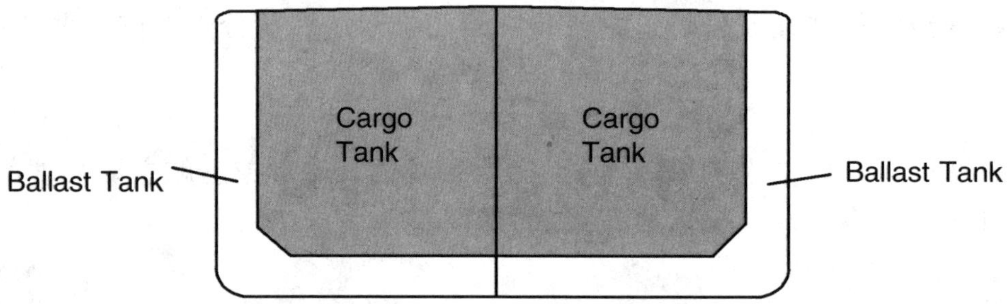

General Layout of Double Hull Tanker

This type of vessel derives its defence against oil spillage, in the event of grounding or collision, by surrounding the entire cargo tank length by a 2 or 3 metre wide void space, which separates the cargo tanks from the outer skin of the vessel. In order for oil spillage to occur the damage has to rupture two skins.

As of now, the double skin does not encase the pump-room. However, as per the latest amendments to MARPOL, likely to come into force by 1st January 2007, the pump-room is to be protected by a double bottom. More protection can be expected in case of double hull tankers in future.

生碰撞或搁浅事故中完全避免漏油。

针对下述结论也达成了一致的协议,即:

- 双壳油船在低能耗(典型的是低速)事故中不应造成污染
- 单层壳(船壳另一侧是海水)载货船舶在事故中发生货舱穿破时,将会引起污染。然而,某些替代设计将会在一些具体情况下使污染量减到最少
- 高能耗事故几乎总能引起污染。各种替代设计在特殊情况下减轻污染的相对优势在很大程度上取决于针对具体情况所做的假设

至今已经提出了很多种设计观念用来在这些事故中降低污染的风险。国际上的注意力逐渐集中在三种设计类型:

- 双壳油船
- 中甲板油船
- Coulombi Egg油船

下面展示了这三种船的横截面,但迄今为止只建造了双层底油船。

双壳油船

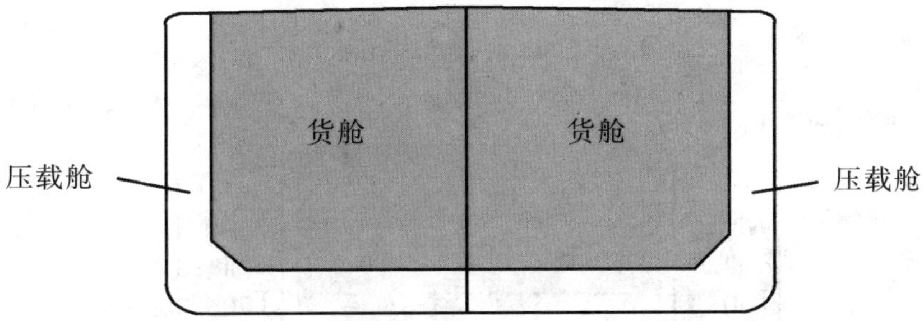

双壳船一般布置图

这种船能在碰撞或搁浅事故中很大程度上防止溢油事故的发生,它是通过环绕整个油船有2~3米的隔离空间,将油舱与船舶外壳分离,事故中只有将两层壳全部穿透才能引发溢油事故。

目前,双壳结构没有对泵舱进行进行保护,根据在2007年1月生效的MARPOL公约修订要求,泵舱也要用双层底结构进行保护。在未来对双壳船如果有要求还会有更多的对泵舱的保护要求。

The Mid-deck Tanker

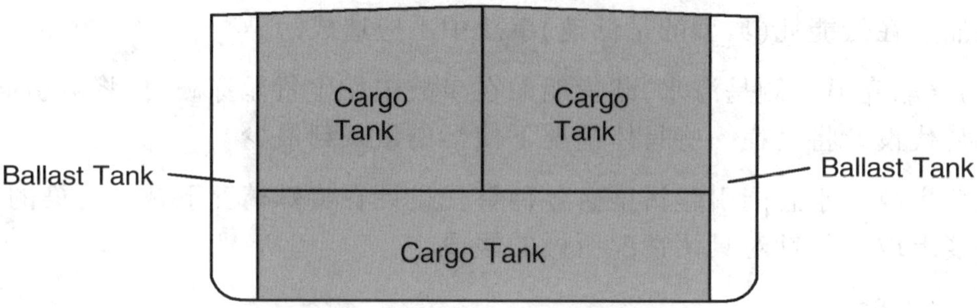

General Layout of Mid Deck Tanker

This type of vessel derives its defence against oil spillage, in the event of collision, by protecting the sides along the entire cargo tank length by a 4 to 5 metres wide void space, which separates the cargo tanks from the outer side skin of the vessel. The underside of the cargo tank region is unprotected and the cargo is in direct contact with the bottom shell. However, an oil-tight deck splits the cargo tanks horizontally. The height of the oil-tight horizontal deck is chosen so that in the event of bottom damage the external water pressure should exceed the head of oil in the lower cargo tanks thus forcing the oil to be retained within the vessel.

The Coulombi Egg Tanker design

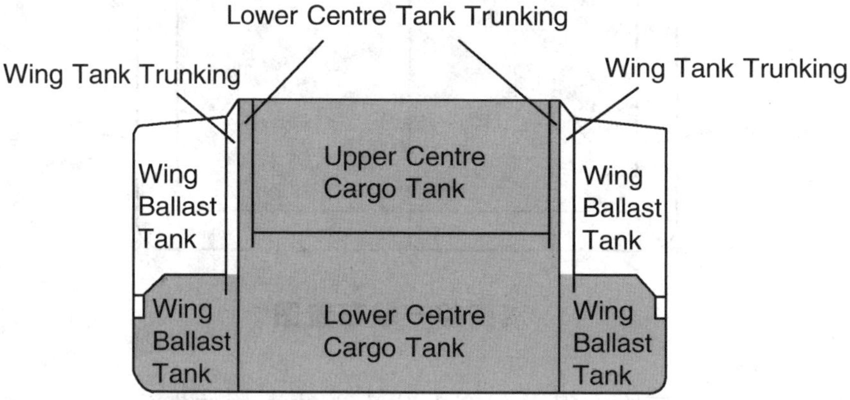

General Layout of Coulombi Egg Tanker

At first sight this configuration appears to be a variant of the mid–deck tanker but it differs in three important respects from that type.

- Firstly the width of the wing tanks is about 50% greater
- Secondly the wing tanks are divided horizontally into upper and lower tanks with the lower wing tanks dedicated to cargo
- Thirdly the upper wing tanks are not only dedicated segregated ballast tanks but also perform the function of "rescue tanks"

中甲板油船

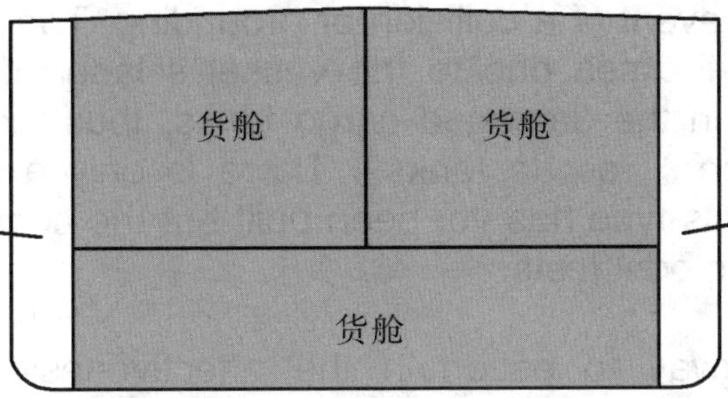

中甲板油船一般布置图

这种船能在碰撞或搁浅事故中防止溢油事故的发生,通过外壳对油舱侧壁的保护,沿全部油舱长度外有4~5米的空间,将油舱侧壁与船外壳分离。但是油舱底部没有保护,直接与船底接触。然而,有一个油封甲板把货油舱水平分开,水平油封甲板的高度之所以这样选择,在于当舱底破损后油封甲板下方的水压会高于上方的油压,从而使油继续留在船内。

Coulombi Egg油船设计

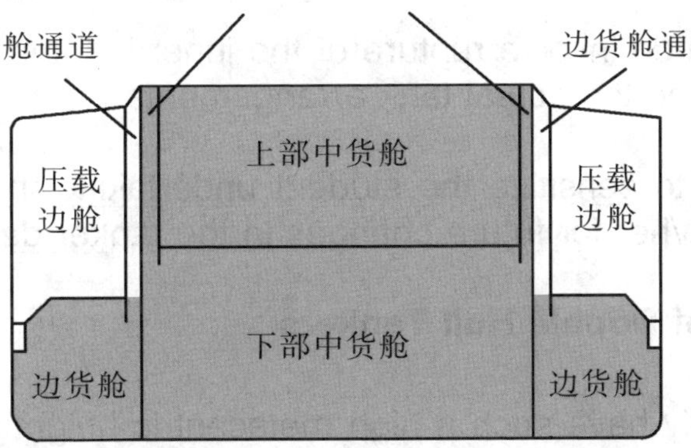

Coulombi Egg 油船的一般布置图

乍一看,这种布置是中甲板型的变形,但是它与中甲板型有三个重要的不同点:

- 首先,边舱的宽度增大50%
- 第二,边舱被专门用来装油的下部边舱水平分成上、下两个货舱
- 第三,边舱的上半部分不仅作为专用压载舱而且也可完成"救生舱"功能

The Coulombi Egg tanker has an emergency cargo transfer system, which allows oil from damaged cargo tanks to be directed into the sound empty upper wing tanks, thus minimising the oil lost to the sea in the event of a collision or grounding. The system utilises the fact that the external pressure from the sea due to the vessel's laden draught will be greater than that due to the head of oil in the damaged cargo tanks, thus the oil in the damaged cargo tanks will be forced into the "rescue tanks". There is only a single skin underneath the pump-room[2]. No vessel of this type has yet been built but the concept of the "rescue tanks" has been shown to work in model tests.

Various studies are underway to ascertain the effectiveness of alternative designs as compared to the double hull tankers. Since the Coulombi Egg design is still being considered, the design has not yet evolved into a comparative study.

However, there are comparative studies, at various levels, into the damage done in case of a collision or grounding, and the behaviour of the two designs. Presented below are the initial findings in a succinct manner:

- In groundings with rupturing of the outer bottom shell plating, no spillage would occur from double hull tankers but some would occur from mid-deck tankers;
- In groundings with rupturing of the outer bottom shell plating as well as the inner bottom shell plating on double hull tankers, the spillage occurring from double hull tankers will be greater than from mid-deck tankers;
- In collisions not resulting in rupture of the inner hull, no spill would occur; and
- In collisions, which do involve rupture of the inner hull the amount of spillage in both types, will depend on the actual tank arrangements.

It is being mentioned here to sensitize the student undertaking the TASCO Modular course 1.02 in order to prepare him/her for future changes in the tanker design.

Stability Considerations of Double Hull Tankers

Single hull oil tankers usually have such a high metacentric height in all conditions of loading and ballasting that they can be considered as being inherently stable. Whilst tanker personnel have always had to take account of longitudinal bending moments and vertical shearforces, the actual stability of the ship has seldom been a prime concern. However the introduction of double hulls into tanker design is likely to change that situation.

The main problem likely to be encountered is the effect on the transverse metacentric height of liquid free surface in the cargo and double bottom tanks.

Depending upon the design, type and number of these tanks, the free surface effect could result in the transverse metacentric height being significantly reduced. The situation will be most severe in the case of wide cargo tanks with no centreline bulkhead and the so-called "U" ballast tanks, which have no centreline bulkhead.

[2] As per the December 2003 amendments, double bottom will be required in cargo pump-room for oil tankers of 5000 tonnes deadweight and above with keel laid on or after 1 January 2007.

Coulombi Egg油船有一套应急货物转运系统，能允许货油从受损的舱直接转到完好的空的上边舱中，从而在发生碰撞或搁浅事故时使货油泄漏到海中的量最少。这个系统应用了这一原理:船舶满载时,来自海水的外部压力要比破损舱室内油的压力大,在水压的作用下,破损舱的油被压入两边的“救生舱”。在泵间[2]下只有一层壳。至今还没有建造这种类型的船,但是这种“救生舱”的概念已经出现在模拟测试中。

各种研究都在对双层底船和其他船型的有效性进行比较，由于Coulombi Egg油船仍在设计中,所以该设计还没有进入对比研究阶段。

然而针对发生搁浅或碰撞时造成的损害有各种不同的研究，以下用简明方式对初始发现予以陈述:

- 因搁浅外底壳板破损,双壳油船没有溢油发生,而有些中甲板油船发生;
- 因搁浅外底壳板以及内底壳板破损,双壳油船发生的溢油比中甲板油船的溢油多;
- 碰撞没有导致内壳破损,没有溢油发生;
- 而碰撞导致内壳破损时,两种形式油船的溢油量将取决于实际的油舱布置。

这里应该提醒学员增强对TASCO示范课程1.02的敏感性，从而为未来油船设计的改变做好准备。

双壳油船的稳性考虑

单层壳油船在所有的装载和压载情况下都有很高的稳心高度，以至于它们被认为具有内在的稳性。油船工作人员总是不得不考虑弯曲力矩和剪切力矩,而很少把实际的稳性当作首要关心的问题。然而油船采用双层船体的设计很可能改变这种情况。

主要可能遇到的问题是货舱内和双层底舱内的自由液面对横向稳心高度的影响。

取决于这些舱的设计、类型和数目,自由液面的影响能导致横向的稳心高度明显下降。在无中央舱壁、宽的货舱和称作“U”型的无中央舱壁的压载舱情况下,影响最严重。

[2] 根据2003年12月的修正案,要求2007年1月1日以后安放龙骨的5000载重吨及以上的油船在货泵舱安装双层底。

The most critical stages of any operation will be whilst filling the double bottom ballast tanks during discharge of cargo, and emptying the tanks during loading of cargo. If sufficient cargo tanks and double bottom tanks are slack simultaneously, the overall free surface effect could well be sufficient to reduce the transverse metacentric height to a point at which the transverse stability of the ship may be threatened. This could result in the ship suddenly developing a severe list. Large free surface area is especially likely to threaten stability at greater soundings with associated high vertical centre of gravity.

It is imperative that tanker and terminal personnel involved in cargo and ballast operations are aware of this potential problem, and that all cargo and ballast operations are conducted strictly in accordance with the ship's loading manual.

Where they are fitted, interlock devices to prevent too much cargo and ballast tanks from being operated simultaneously, thereby causing an excessive free surface effect, should always be maintained in full operational order, and should never be over-ridden.

Revised phase-out schedule for single hull tankers enters into force

In 1992, as a result of the *Exxon Valdez* accident MARPOL was amended to make it mandatory for tankers of 5,000 DWT and more ordered after 6 July 1993 to be fitted with double hulls, or an alternative design approved by IMO. The requirement for double hulls that applies to new tankers has also been applied to existing ships. All tankers have to be converted (or taken out of service) when they reach a certain age if they do not have double hull. This measure is being phased in over a number of years because shipyard capacity is limited and it would not be possible immediately to convert all single hulled tankers to double hulls without causing immense disruption to world trade and industry.

The investigations into the *Erika* incident (off the coast of France in December 1999) carried out by the French Government and the Maltese Maritime Authority concluded that age, corrosion, insufficient maintenance and inadequate surveys were all strong contributing factors to the structural failure of the ship. Following the Erika incident, IMO adopted a revised phaseout schedule for single hull tankers, which set out a stricter timetable for the phasing-out of single-hull tankers and gave the year 2015 as the principal cut-off date for all single-hull tankers. Also, since 1995 all tankers and bulk carriers aged five years and over have been subjected to a specially enhanced inspection programme (ESP) which is intended to ensure that any structural deficiencies such as corrosion, fatigue cracking are detected.

A revised regulation 13G of MARPOL Annex I brings forward the phase-out schedule for existing single hull tankers that was first established in 1992 and was subsequently revised in 2001 following the *Erika* incident. It specifies that tankers of single hull construction should be phased out or converted to a "double hull" according to a schedule based on their year of delivery. The double hull requirements for oil tankers are principally designed to reduce the risk of oil spills from tankers involved in low energy collisions or groundings. Under the phase-out schedule, "Category 1" single hull oil tankers have been prohibited from trading after 5 April 2005 (for ships delivered on or before 5 April 1982) or after their anniversary date in 2005 (for ships delivered after 5 April 1982).

Category 1 oil tankers (commonly known as Pre-MARPOL tankers) include oil tankers of 20,000 tonnes deadweight and above carrying crude oil, fuel oil, heavy diesel oil or lubricating

最关键的操作阶段是卸货期间往双层底舱内装压载水和装货期间排空这些舱的压载水。如果足够多的货舱和双层底舱同时进行操作,所有自由液面的影响能大大地降低横向稳心高度,到达一定程度时船舶横向稳定性将会受到威胁。这能导致船舶突然产生严重的倾斜。油位越高,则垂直方向的重心高,此时较大的自由液面极有可能对船舶稳定性造成威胁。

油船和码头上的与货物和压载操作有关的人员应认识到这种潜在的问题,这是完全必要的,并且,所有的货物和压载操作都应严格按照装载手册进行。

油船应安装连锁装置,防止过多货舱和压载舱同时进行操作,以消除过多自由液面的影响。这些连锁装置应给予很好的维护保养,使其符合操作命令要求,不会发生失效情况。

修订后的单层壳油船淘汰时间表生效

1992年,由于Exxon Valdez号油船事故,MARPOL公约进行了修订,要求在1993年7月6日后建造的5000载重吨及以上的油船全部具有双层船壳或IMO允许的其他结构。双层船壳要求新造船的同时也对旧船提出了要求，所有现存的不具有双壳的船舶在达到一定的船龄时需要进行改造(或退出营运市场)。这个措施要求在几年之内分阶段实行,因为造船厂的容量有限,并且立即改造所有的单壳船势必会对国际贸易和航运业产生大的冲击。

对Erika油船事故(1999年12月在法国近海)的调查由法国政府和马耳他海事机构进行,得出的结论为船龄、腐蚀、保养不良、船检不足等原因共同导致了船结构的失效。针对Erika油船事故,IMO采纳了对单壳油船淘汰时间表的修订案,设定了一个严格的时间表,要求在2015年以前所有的单壳油船全部完成改造。同时在1995年要求船龄在5年及以上的船舶要进行特别加强检验程序(ESP),从而确保能及时发现腐蚀和疲劳裂纹等缺陷。

发生Erika号油船事故以后,MARPOL公约附则Ⅰ中修订的13G提出对于现存的,在1992年及以后建造的单壳船要在2001年完成改造。其明确指出对于单壳船的淘汰或改造时间要求要依据船舶交付使用的时间为准。双壳设计能在低能量碰撞或搁浅事故中降低溢油事故的发生。根据这个“淘汰”时间表,对于“类型1”单壳油船要求在2005年4月5号(1982年4月5日或之前交付使用的船舶)或者2005年年检时期之后(1982年4月5日之后交付使用的船舶)禁止运营。

类型1油船(通常指MARPOL公约前油船)包括20000载重吨或以上,运输原油、重油、重柴油

oil as cargo, and tankers of 30,000 tonnes deadweight and above carrying other oils, which do not comply with the requirements for protectively located segregated ballast tanks.

Category 2 oil tankers, which have some level of protection from protectively located segregated ballast tank requirements will be phased out according to their age up to 2010. The year 2010 is also a final cut off date for Category 3 oil tankers, which are generally smaller oil tankers. Category 2 oil tankers (commonly known as MARPOL tankers) include oil tankers of 20,000 tonnes deadweight and above carrying crude oil, fuel oil, heavy diesel oil or lubricating oil as cargo, and oil tankers of 30,000 tonnes deadweight and above carrying other oils, which comply with the protectively located segregated ballast tank requirements.

Category 3 oil tankers are oil tankers of 5,000 tonnes deadweight and above but less than the tonnage specified for Category 1 and 2 tankers.

Furthermore, Regulation 13H of MARPOL Annex I on the prevention of oil pollution from oil tankers when carrying heavy grade oil (HGO) bans the carriage of HGO in single hull tankers of 5,000 tonnes deadweight (DWT) and above from 5 April 2005, and in single hull oil tankers of 600 DWT and above but less than 5,000 tonnes DWT, not later than the anniversary of their delivery date in 2008.

To make maintenance easy, tar-epoxy coatings are applied to ballast tanks, and glass-fibre reinforced plastic pipes inside the tanks ensure corrosion prevention. The cargo oil and residual oil pipes are made of highly corrosion-resistant chromium-coated cast iron, and inspection accesses including ladders are also provided.

The double hull structure causes a great increase in hull weight, number of structural members, painting area, etc., and accordingly takes a longer building time. However, new structural designs dispense with the conventionally fitted stiffeners on the transverse webs by adopting special apple-shaped slots for the connections between the transverse webs and the longitudinal in the structure in very great numbers (about 20,000 in a double hull VLCC).

Other amendments to Annex I of MARPOL 73/78

Carriage of Heavy Grade Oil

A new MARPOL regulation 13H on the pollution prevention from oil tankers bans the carriage of Heavy Grade Oil (HGO) in single-hull tankers of 5,000 tonnes DWT and above after the date of entry into force of the regulation (16 months after the issued date of changes which is 5 April 2005), and in single-hull oil tankers of 600 tonnes DWT and above but less than 5,000 tonnes DWT, not later than the anniversary of their delivery date in 2008.

The revised definition of HGO means any of the following:

- Crude oils having a density at 15 ℃ higher than 900 kg/m^3;
- Fuel oils having either a density at 15 ℃ higher than 900 kg/m^3 or a kinematic viscosity at 50 ℃ higher than 180 mm^2/s (cSt);
- Bitumen, tar and their emulsions.

或滑油,以及30000载重吨或以上运输其他油类,不满足专用压载舱要求的船舶。

类型2油船会受到专用压载舱要求的保护,该类船会根据船龄在2010年以前被淘汰。2010年也是类型3油船的最后淘汰期限,类型3油船通常是小型船舶。类型2油船(通常认为是MARPOL油船)包括20 000载重吨及以上,运输原油、重油、重柴油或滑油,以及30 000载重吨及以上运输其他油类,满足专用压载舱要求的船舶。

类型3油船是5 000载重吨及以上,但是比类型1和2小的油船。

更进一步,MARPOL公约附则Ⅰ中修订后的13H规定,5000载重吨及以上的单壳船舶禁止在2005年4月5日以后运输重型油(HGO),600载重吨及以上并在5000载重吨以下的单壳船舶在2008年交船周年日之后禁止运输HGO。

为便于维护,将焦油环氧树脂涂层用于压载舱,舱内管系采用玻璃纤维强化塑料管以确保防止腐蚀。货油和残油管材质为高度防腐蚀的镀铬铸铁,并且提供包括梯子在内的检查通道。

双壳结构导致船体重量、构件数量以及涂漆面积等大幅增加,并且会相应地延长建造时间。然而,新型结构设计通过采用大量(VLCC双壳大约需要20 000个)特殊的苹果形卡槽来连接船底横框架与船底纵骨结构来放弃在船底横框架上安装扶强板的传统做法。

MARPOL 73/78附则I的其他修订内容

重油运输

关于油船防污染的一项新MARPOL规定13H自规则生效日起(签署之后16个月,即2005年4月5日),禁止5000载重吨及以上的单壳油船运输重油,对600载重吨及以上但小于5000载重吨的单壳油船,从2008年的交船周年日开始执行该禁令。

对重油定义进行修订后,重油是指:

- 15 ℃时密度高于900 kg/m³的原油;
- 15 ℃时密度高于900 kg/m³或50 ℃时运动黏度高于180 mm²/s (cSt)的燃油;
- 沥青、焦油及其乳浊液。

Operations

The normal cycle of tanker operation comprises loading, cargo voyage, unloading, ballasting, ballast voyage, tank cleaning, de-ballasting and then loading again.

Loading is accomplished by following directions given in the ship's loading orders, which contain an estimate of the quantity of cargo to be loaded, the tanks in which it will be stowed and the tank loading sequence to be followed.

Unloading is accomplished by discharging the cargo (crude oil) directly into a terminal (refinery) tank storage area, or into a tank barge for further transport.

During unloading of a crude oil cargo, the tanker may affect crude oil washing (COW) (dealt with separately in the Instructor Manual).

Ballasting is a process whereby seawater is taken aboard into the cargo tanks or segregated ballast tanks to ensure proper immersion of the propeller and to provide good handling and sea-keeping characteristics. The amount of ballast taken aboard depends upon the anticipated weather conditions, the distance and route of the ballast voyage, and the vessel's light-ship displacement, length-to-depth ratio and other characteristics. The amount of ballast taken aboard generally varies from 20 to 50% of the vessel's total cargo-carrying capacity, but may be greater during periods of severe bad weather.

Ballast put directly into cargo tanks immediately after cargo discharge comes into contact and mingles with the oil that adhered to the tank surfaces and remained below the suction bell–mouths. This oily ballast must be disposed of in some way before arrival at the loading port, unless the loading port has suitable reception facilities. Instead, clean ballast suitable for direct discharge into the harbour at the loading port must be taken aboard. In the absence of segregated ballast tanks, empty cargo tanks must be washed to remove the residue oil (that clings to the sides in the tank) and provide space for the clean ballast.

The number of tanks washed is a function of the particular vessel's proportions; the weather; the route; and the need to clean tanks for internal inspection, for repair at a shipyard or for controlling the build–up of sludge.

Load on top (LOT) procedure

In their teaching instructors should highlight the differences in operations between crude oil and fuel oil tankers and those designed to carry refined (clean/white) oil products.

If all tank washings and dirty ballast were discharged directly into the sea, a considerable quantity of oil (up to 0.5% of the oil carried) would be released, which is unacceptable under international rules. A procedure has been developed which results in most oil being retained on board. The procedure is as follows:

After departure on the ballast voyage, the oily ballast is allowed to settle, resulting in separation of the oil and water. Meanwhile, a number of dirty cargo tanks are being water washed to accept clean ballast for arrival. All tank washings are transferred to the slop-tanks. After ballasting the newly cleaned tanks, the dirty ballast is discharged. The comparatively clean ballast underneath the oily top layer is pumped directly into the sea and the top layer is again

操作

通常油船的操作循环包括装货、载货航行、卸货、压载、压载航行、洗舱、排出压载水然后再装载。

装货是在船舶装货单的指导下实现的，它包括估算载货数量、装舱以及装舱顺序。

卸货是通过直接把货（原油）卸到目的港（炼油厂）存储地或卸到下一步运输的油驳上完成的。

在卸载原油货物期间，油船卸货可能会影响原油洗舱（COW）（在教员手册中单独阐述）。

压载是把海水打进货舱或者专用压载舱的过程，确保螺旋桨适当浸入水中以提供很好的操纵性能和维持船舶上特性。压载的量取决于预期的气象条件、压载航行距离和路线、空船排水量、长深比以及其他特性。压载量一般是船舶总载货量的20%~50%，但在恶劣天气下有可能会更大。

在根据合同卸完货后，加入到油舱的压载水会和黏在舱表面的油以及残留在吸口以下的油混合。这种含油压载水在到达装货港前要用某种方式进行处理，除非装货港有适当的接收设施。否则，卸货时应加入清洁压载水以便在装货港可以直接排出。没有专用压载舱的，空货舱一定要清洁，除去油渣（黏附在舱侧），以便装清洁压载水。

要洗舱的数量取决于特定的船舶比例、天气、航线和为内部检查、船厂修理或控制产生油渣数量而清洗的舱数。

装于上部（LOT）程序

在教学过程中，教员应该强调在原油和燃油油船之间以及和那些设计用来运输精炼油的油船之间在操作上的差别。

如果所有油舱的清洗物和脏污压载水直接排放入海，将会排放大量油类（高达载油量的0.5%），根据国际规则是不允许的。因此，就有了要把这些油留在船上的程序。该程序如下：

在压载航行离港后，含油压载水经过沉淀分离油和水。其间，用水清洗一些脏油舱，干净后进行压载，为到港做好准备。把所有油舱的清洗物排到污液舱。在新清洁过的油舱压载后，要排出污染压载水。在上部油层之下的比较清洁的压载水可直接泵出海，而上部油层再排到污液舱。

transferred to the slop-tank. The contents of the slop-tank are allowed to settle, so that the oil and water separate, known as decanting; heating the slop-tank can assist the process. The position of the interface is then established and the water is discharged into the sea, taking care not to draw the oil/water interface into the pumps by vortex action. This means that the discharge rate must be adjusted and that a certain quantity of water remains in the slop-tank. Upon arrival in the loading port, the clean ballast can be discharged into the harbour and the ship can be loaded. If the next cargo is a similar crude oil or product, it can also be loaded into the slop-tanks on top of the oil and water, which is already there. The whole procedure has become known as the load on top (LOT) procedure. In the case of most products, contamination with slops must be avoided and the contents of the slop-tank must be discharged to shore reception facilities at the loading terminal.

This completes the normal cycle of tanker operations. Before entering a shipyard, however, all tanks must be washed, gas-freed and cleaned to reduce the likelihood of explosion during repair work involving fire and sparks. The tank cleaning entails removing the heavy sludge, which collects at the bottom of tanks.

Disposal of this heavy hydrocarbon sludge is accomplished by a variety of means; the normal procedure is to deliver it to barges (reception facilities) provided by the shipyard.

Basic Properties of Petroleum and its Hazards

Properties of petroleum

General

Petroleum is made up of a range of hydrocarbon molecules, with molecular weights ranging from light to heavy. The structure consists essentially of hydrogen atoms linking in various ways with carbon atoms. Schematic molecular drawings may explain saturated and unsaturated hydrocarbons, cyclical molecular structures and the benzene ring. Mention should also be made of the toxic substances present in crude oil (see also Fig. 3 and 4).

The relationship between light and heavy hydrocarbon molecules can be explained with the following diagram:

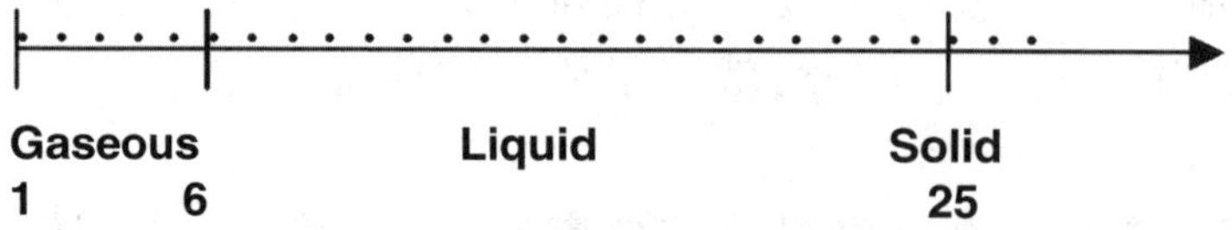

The lightest molecules, methane, are stripped off at the wellhead together with any earthy solids; the remaining petroleum is termed crude oil. The process of refining the crude oil will produce a number of fractions. Each fraction will consist of a range of petroleum molecules, which at atmospheric pressure and temperature will be gaseous, liquid or solid. The refining process does not alter the constituent molecules.

A process whereby molecules are changed, usually breaking up long chains into smaller ones and thereby creating lighter fractions, is called cracking.

让污液舱内的污油沉淀以便油水分离，采取加热措施可以有助于分离过程。而后建立油水分界面,在排水时注意不要由于泵的旋涡作用吸到了油水分界面内的液体。这就意味着必须调节排放速率,并且要有一定量的水留在污液舱内。在到达装货港时,清洁压载水可以排进港里而船可以装货。如果下一次货是相似的原油或成品油,也可以装在污液舱已有的油水上部。整个过程称为装于上部(LOT)程序。在大多数运输成品油的情况下,必须避免污油的污染,所以污液舱中的油污水必须排到装货港的岸上接收设施。

该程序完成了油船操作的基本循环。然而,在进入船厂之前,所有的油舱都必须清洁并且驱除可燃气以减少包括在用火和产生火花的修理过程中发生爆炸的可能性。油舱的清洁需要清除聚集在油舱底部的重质油渣。

处理这些重质碳氢化合物油渣可以用各种方法，通常是驳到由船厂提供的驳船上（接收设施)。

石油的基本特性及其危害

石油的特性

概述

石油是由一系列碳氢化合物分子所组成,随分子重量由轻到重排列。其结构基本上是由以各种形式与碳原子相结合的氢原子组成。分子草图可以解释饱和和不饱和碳氢化合物、环分子结构和苯环。此外在原油中也含有有毒物质(见图3和图4)。

轻、重碳氢化合物分子之间的关系可以用下面的图来解释:

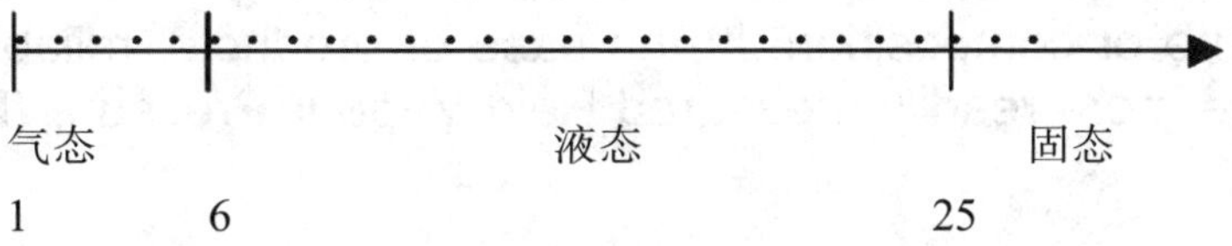

最轻的分子,甲烷,与其他泥状固体聚集在井口;剩下的石油称为原油。原油精炼过程会产生大量成分,每种成分都是包括一系列石油分子。这些石油分子在大气压力和常温下将会是气体、液体或固体状态。该精炼过程不会改变石油的分子成分。

石油分子改变的过程称为裂解,通常是由长链裂解成短链,由此产生了较轻的分子团。

True vapour pressure (TVP)

All crude oils and the usual petroleum products are essentially mixtures of a wide range of hydrocarbon compounds (i.e. chemical compounds of hydrogen and carbon). The boiling points of these compounds range from –162°C (–260°F) (methane) to well in excess of +400°C (+750°F); and the volatility (i.e. the tendency of a crude oil or petroleum product to produce gas) of any particular mixture of compounds depends primarily on the quantities of the more volatile constituents (i.e. those with a lower boiling point).

The vapour pressure characterizes the volatility. When a petroleum mixture is transferred to a gas-free tank or container it begins to vaporize; that is, it liberates gas into the space above it. There is also a tendency for this gas to re-dissolve in the liquid, and an equilibrium is ultimately reached with a certain amount of gas evenly distributed throughout the space. The pressure exerted by this gas is called the equilibrium vapour pressure of the liquid, usually referred to simply as the vapour pressure.

The vapour pressure of a pure compound depends only upon its temperature. The vapour pressure of a mixture depends both upon its temperature and the volume of the gas space into which vaporization occurs; that is, it depends upon temperature and the ratio of gas to liquid by volume.

The TVP or bubble-point vapour pressure is the equilibrium vapour pressure of a mixture when the gas/liquid ratio is effectively zero. It is the highest vapour pressure, which is possible at any specified temperature.

As the temperature of a petroleum mixture increases, its TVP also increases. If the TVP exceeds atmospheric pressure, the liquid commences to boil.

The TVP of a petroleum mixture provides a good indication of its ability to give rise to gas! Unfortunately it is a property, which is extremely difficult to measure, although it can be calculated from a detailed knowledge of the composition of the liquid. For crude oils it can also be estimated from the stabilization conditions, making allowance for any subsequent change, of temperature or composition. In the case of products, reliable correlations exist for deriving TVP from the more readily measured Reid Vapour Pressure (RVP) and temperature.

Flammability

In the process of burning, hydrocarbon gases react with the oxygen in the air to produce carbon dioxide and water. The reaction gives enough heat to form a visible flame, which travels through the mixture of hydrocarbon gas and air. When the gas above a liquid hydrocarbon is ignited, the heat produced is usually enough to generate sufficient fresh gas to maintain the flame, and the liquid is said to burn; in fact, it is the gas which is burning and is being continuously replenished from the liquid.

Flammable limits

A mixture of hydrocarbon gas and air cannot be ignited and burn unless its composition lies within a range of gas-in-air concentrations known as the "flammable range". The lower limit of the range, known as the lower flammable limit (LFL), is that hydrocarbon concentration below which there is insufficient hydrocarbon gas to support and propagate combustion.

绝对蒸发压力

所有原油和一般石油产品基本上是各种碳氢化合物的混合物(即碳氢化合物)。这些化合物的沸点范围从-162 ℃(-260°F)到超过400 ℃(750°F);任何特殊混合物的挥发性(即原油或石油产品产生气体的趋势)基本上取决于易挥发成分的数量(即低沸点成分)。

挥发性由蒸发压力来表征。当石油混合物装到除过烃气的油舱或容器中时,它将开始蒸发;也就是说,释放气体到上部空间。释放的气体也有再溶解进液体的趋势,最终由于一定量的气体平均分配到整个空间而达到平衡。由这个气体产生的压力称为液体的平衡蒸发压力,一般简单地叫作蒸发压力。

纯化合物的蒸发压力只取决于其温度。混合物的蒸发压力取决于其温度和发生蒸发的气体空间体积,也就是说它取决于温度和气体变成液体的体积率。

绝对蒸发压力(TVP)或气泡点蒸发压力是气液转换率确实为零时混合物的平衡蒸发压力。它是在任何特定温度下可能蒸发的最高蒸发压力。

随着石油混合物温度的增加,它的TVP也增加。如果TVP超过大气压力,液体开始沸腾。

石油混合物的TVP很好地表明了其生成气体的能力。不幸的是,尽管它可以根据液体成分的详细资料进行计算,但这一特性极难测量。对于原油,也可以根据稳定条件,考虑不同温度或组分的相应变化进行估算。对于石油产品,由于存在可靠的相关性,可根据更简单的方式测量相对蒸发压力(RVP)和温度得出TVP。

易燃性

在燃烧过程中,烃类气体与氧气在空气中反应生成二氧化碳和水。这个反应产生足够的热量形成可见的火焰,通过烃类气体和空气的混合而蔓延。当点燃液态烃类之上的气体时,产生的热量可以产生足够的新可燃气体以维持火焰,这种情况被称为液体燃烧。事实上,燃烧的是不断从液体中产生的气体。

燃烧极限

除非烃气在空气中的比例在所谓的“可燃范围”内,才能被点燃和燃烧。这个范围的最低值,称为可燃下限(LFL),如果烃类浓度低于可燃下限时,就没有足够的烃类气体支持持续的燃烧。

The upper limit of the range, known as the upper flammable limit (UFL), is that hydrocarbon concentration above which there is insufficient air to support and propagate combustion.

The flammable limits vary somewhat for different pure hydrocarbon gases and for the gas mixtures derived from different petroleum liquids. Very roughly, the gas mixtures from crude oils, motor or aviation gasoline and natural gasoline-type products can be represented respectively by the pure hydrocarbon gases propane, butane and pentane. The following table gives the flammable limits for these three gases:

Flammable Limits (Percentage by Volume of Hydrocarbon in Air)

Gas	Upper limit	Lower limit
Propane	9.5	2.2
Butane	8.5	1.9
Pentane	7.8	1.5

In practice, the lower and upper flammable limits of oil cargoes carried in tankers can, for general purposes, be taken as 1% and 10% by volume respectively.

Test for flammability

Since hydrocarbon gas/air mixtures are flammable within a comparatively narrow range of concentrations of hydrocarbon gas in air, and since the concentration in air depends on vapour pressure, it should in principle be possible to evolve a test for flammability by measuring vapour pressure. In practice, the very wide range of petroleum products and the range of temperature over which they are handled have prevented the development of one simple test for this purpose. This aspect should be well understood by the students.

Flashpoint

In this test, a sample of the liquid is gradually heated in a special pot and a small flame is repeatedly and momentarily applied to the surface of the liquid. The flashpoint is the lowest liquid temperature at which the small flame initiates a flash of flame across the surface of the liquid, thereby indicating the presence of a flammable gas/air mixture above the liquid. The gas/air mixture corresponds closely to the lower flammable limit mixture.

There are many different forms of flashpoint apparatus, but basically they fall into two classes. In one, the surface of the liquid is permanently open to the atmosphere as the liquid is heated and the result of such a test is known as an open-cup (o.c.) flashpoint. In the other class, the space above the liquid is kept closed except for brief moments when the initiating flame is introduced through a small port. The result of this class of test is termed a closed-cup (c.c.) flashpoint.

Because of the greater loss of gas to atmosphere in the open-cup test, the open-cup flashpoint of a petroleum liquid is always a little higher (by about 6 ℃ or 10 °F) than its closed-cup flashpoint. Restricting the loss of gas in the closed-cup apparatus also leads to a much more repeatable result that can be used as a guide in the classification of petroleum. However, figures from open-cup tests may still be found in the legislation of various countries, in classification society rules and in other documents.

这个范围的最高值,被称为可燃上限(UFL),即烃类浓度超过可燃上限,就没有足够的空气维持持续的燃烧。

燃烧极限对不同的纯烃类气体和从不同石油液体中产生的气体混合物来说稍有变化。粗略讲,产生于原油、发动机用油或航空汽油、天然气产品的气体可以分别由烃类气体丙烷、丁烷、戊烷代表。下表给出了这些气体的可燃极限:

可燃极限(碳氢化合物在空气中的体积百分比)

气体	上限	下限
丙烷	9.5	2.2
丁烷	8.5	1.9
戊烷	7.8	1.5

事实上,油船运输的货油,一般来讲,其上、下燃烧极限可以分别采用10%、1%的体积比。

可燃性测试

由于在烃类气体和空气的混合物中烃类气体可燃的浓度范围比较小,并且由于烃类气体在空气中的浓度取决于蒸发压力,因此原理上可通过测量蒸发压力进行可燃性测试。实际上,种类繁多的石油产品及需要考虑的温度范围有碍于这一简单的可燃性测试。学员应该深入理解该问题。

闪点

在该测试中,一种液体的样品在一个专门的容器内逐渐加热,反复地用一个小火焰去点液体表面。闪点就是液体表面被小火焰点着发生闪火的最低液体温度,这也表明液体表面上存在可燃气体和空气的混合物。此时可燃气体和空气的混合物就是所对应的闭口混合物可燃下限。

闪点测试装置有多种类型,但基本上分为两类。一类,液体加热时其液体表面始终开放于大气,这样的测试结果被称为开口闪点。另一类,除了当通过一个小口点火时的短暂时刻外,液体表面的上部空间是封闭的,这样的测试结果称为闭口闪点。

因为在开口闪点测试中有更多的可燃气体流失到大气中,所以石油液体的开口闪点总是比闭口闪点高一点(6 ℃或10 ℉)。在闭口测试装置中限制气体流失也导致了结果更具可重复性,其可以用于石油分类的指导。然而,从开口测试得出的数据仍然可以在各国法规、船级社规定以及其它类似的文件中找到。

Flammability classification of petroleum

There are many schemes for dividing the complete range of petroleum liquids into different flammability classes, based on flashpoint and vapour pressure, and there is a considerable variation in these schemes between countries. Usually the basic principle is to consider whether or not a flammable equilibrium gas/air mixture can be formed in the space above the liquid when the liquid is at ambient temperature.

Generally in this manual it has been sufficient to group petroleum liquids into two categories, entitled ‘non-volatile’ and ‘volatile’, which are defined in terms of flashpoint as follows:

Non-volatile: This is a liquid with a flashpoint of 60 ℃ (140 °F) or above as determined by the closed-cup method of testing. At normal ambient temperature these liquids produce equilibrium gas concentrations below the lower flammable limit. They include residual fuel oils, heavy gas oils and diesel oils.

Volatile. This is a liquid with a flashpoint below 60 ℃ (140 °F) as determined by the closed cup method of testing. Some petroleum liquids in this category are capable of producing an equilibrium gas/air mixture within the flammable range over part of the normal ambient temperature scale, while most of the rest give equilibrium gas/air mixtures above the upper flammable limit at all normal ambient temperatures. Examples of the former are jet fuels and kerosene and the latter are gasoline and most crude oils. In practice, gasoline and crude oils are frequently handled before equilibrium conditions have been attained, and gas/air mixtures in the flammable range may then be present.

The choice of 60 ℃ (140 °F) as the flashpoint criterion for the division between non-volatile and volatile liquids is to some extent arbitrary. Since less stringent precautions are appropriate for non-volatile liquids, it is essential that under no circumstances is a liquid that is capa ble of giving a flammable gas/air mixture, even inadvertently, is included in the non-volatile category. The dividing line must therefore be chosen to make allowance for such factors as the misjudging of the temperature inaccuracy in the flashpoint measurement and the possibility of minor contamination by more volatile materials. The figure of 60 ℃ (140 °F) for a closed-cup flashpoint makes ample allowance for these factors, and is also compatible with the figure adopted internationally by the International Maritime Organization (IMO), as shown in regulation II-2/4.2.1.1 of SOLAS 1974, and by a number of regulatory bodies throughout the world.

Density of hydrocarbon gases

The densities of the gas mixtures evolved from the normal petroleum liquids, when undiluted with air, are all greater than the density of air. Layering effects are therefore encountered in cargo-handling operations and can give rise to hazardous situations.

The following table gives gas densities relative to air for the three pure hydrocarbon gases propane, butane and pentane, which represent roughly the gas mixtures that are produced, respectively, by crude oils, by motor or aviation gasoline and by natural gasoline. These figures are not significantly changed if inert gas is substituted for air.

石油的可燃性分类

基于闪点和蒸发压力,有很多可以把石油液体分成不同可燃等级的方法。这些方法在各国之间有相当大的差别。通常的基本原则认为,当液体在环境温度下,其上部空间是否存在处于平衡态的可燃气体和空气的混合物。

在这本手册中一般把石油液体分成两类已经足够了,定名为“不挥发”和“挥发”,用闪点对其定义如下:

不挥发。由闭口测试方法测定闪点在60 ℃(140 ℉)或以上。在正常环境温度下,这些液体产生平衡态的可燃气体浓度在可燃下限以下。它们包括渣油、重质汽油和柴油。

挥发。由闭口实验方法测定闪点在60 ℃(140 ℉)或以下。这一类中的某些石油液体在正常环境温度下能产生平衡态的可燃气体浓度在可燃范围内。而其他大部分石油液体能在正常环境温度下形成并平衡状态的可燃气体/空气混合物高于可燃上限的。前者的例子是航空燃油和煤油,后者的例子是汽油和大多数原油。事实上,由于汽油和原油经常在获得平衡状态之前就被处理,所以油气混合物可能处于可燃范围内。

选择60 ℃(140 ℉)作为闪点的标准以区分不挥发和挥发液体在某种程度上过于武断。由于可以对不挥发液体采取相对不是很严格的预防措施,在任何情况下,液体都不可以产生油气混合物,即使由于疏忽将其归到不挥发液体类别中,这一点非常重要。因而分界线的选择必须留有余量,考虑到在闪点测量中可能由于温度不准确而产生的判断错误这样的因素,以及被更易挥发物质轻微污染的可能性。60 ℃(140 ℉)闭口闪点数值为这些因素保留了充分的余量,也与国际海事组织(IMO)在SOLAS 1974中的Ⅱ-2/55规则以及世界上许多立法主体所采纳的数值相一致。

烃类气体的密度

从正常石油液体中蒸发的气体混合物的密度在不被空气稀释的情况下,都比空气的密度大。因此,在货物操作过程中就会遇到层积效应并可能形成危险的状况。

下表列出了三种纯烃类气体相对于空气的密度:丙烷、丁烷、戊烷;它们粗略地代表了分别产生于原油、汽车汽油或航空汽油和天然气产品的气体混合物。如果用惰性气体代替空气,这些数字没有很大变化。

Gas	Density relative to air		
	Pure hydrocarbon	*Equal parts of hydrocarbon & air by volume*	*Mixture at lower flammable limit*
Propane	1.55	1.25	1.00
Butane	2.00	1.50	1.00
Pentane	2.50	1.80	1.00

It will be seen that the density of the undiluted gas from a product such as motor gasoline is likely to be about twice that of air and of the gas from a typical crude oil about 1.5 times. These high densities and the layering effects that result from them are only significant while the gas remains concentrated. As it is diluted with air, the density of the gas/air mixture from all three types of cargo approaches that of air, and at the lower flammable limit is indistinguishable from it.

Practical tests

If possible, the behaviour of petroleum and the determination of certain properties of petroleum should be demonstrated by someone knowledgeable; preferably, a video should be shown, as this prevents fire hazards and failures.

Hazards associated with the handling and carriage of petroleum

Toxicity in general

The toxic hazards to which personnel are exposed in tanker operations arise almost entirely from contact with gases of various kinds.

A convenient indicator of the toxicity of gases and the avoidance of health hazards is provided by the Permissible Exposure Limit (PEL) and/or the Threshold Limit Value – Time-Weighted Average (TLV-TWA) (in this guide, all reference to TLV is to time-weighted average TLV). TLV-TWA is kept under regular review and the values quoted in this guide are those adopted at the American Conference of Governmental Industrial Hygienists in 1983. The values are expressed as parts per million (PPM) by volume of gas in air.

Toxicity of petroleum

Liquid petroleum

The risk of swallowing significant quantities of liquid petroleum during normal tanker and terminal operations is very slight. Petroleum has low oral toxicity to man, but when swallowed it causes acute discomfort and nausea. There is then a possibility that liquid petroleum may be drawn into the lungs during vomiting; this can have serious consequences, especially with higher volatility products such as gasoline and kerosene.

气体	相对于空气的密度		
	纯烃类气体	烃类气体和空气的等价部分(体积)	在可燃下限的混合物
丙烷	1.55	1.25	1.00
丁烷	2.00	1.50	1.00
戊烷	2.50	1.80	1.00

从表中看到那些产生于发动机汽油的没有被空气稀释的气体密度大约是空气的两倍，是原油所产生的气体的1.5倍。由它们产生的高密度和层积效应仅在气体浓缩的情况下才有意义。由于被空气稀释,三种石油气体和空气混合物的密度都接近空气密度,在可燃下限与空气没有任何区别。

实际测试

如果可能,应该由知识丰富的人证实石油的表现和确定石油的某些特性;最好通过录像来演示,这样可以防止火灾发生和测试失败。

与石油的运输和装卸有关的危害

一般毒性

在油船操作中人员中毒的危险几乎完全是与各种石油气的接触引起的。

允许辐射极限(PELs)和/或极限值—时间加权平均阈限值(TLV-TWA)(在该指导书中,所有提及的TLV都是时间加权平均阈限值TLV)可以作为一种气体毒性和避免健康危害的方便指标。需要定期对TLV-TWA进行修订,该指导书中引用的值是在1983年美国政府工业卫生学家协会采用的。该值是用空气中气体的百万分体积(PPM)来表示。

石油的毒性

液态石油

在油船正常航行和码头装卸货期间,吸入大量液态石油的风险非常小。石油对人体口部毒性较低,但当吸入体内时会引起极度不适和恶心。然后,呕吐时有可能将液态石油吸进肺里,这可能导致严重后果,特别是像汽油和煤油这样的高挥发性的液体。

Skin contact

Many petroleum products, especially the more volatile ones, cause skin irritation and remove essential oils from the skin, leading to dermatitis. They are also irritating to the eyes. Certain heavier oils can cause serious skin disorders on repeated and prolonged contact.

Direct contact with petroleum should always be avoided by wearing the appropriate protective equipment, especially impervious gloves and goggles.

Petroleum gases

The main effect of petroleum gas on humans is to produce narcosis. The symptoms include headache and eye irritation, with diminished responsibility and dizziness similar to drunkenness. At high concentrations these symptoms are followed by paralysis, insensibility and death.

The toxicity of petroleum gases can vary widely, depending on the major hydrocarbon constituents of the gases. It can be greatly influenced by the presence of some minor components such as aromatic hydrocarbons (e.g. benzene) and hydrogen sulphide. A TLV of 300 PPM, corresponding to about 2% LFL, has been established for gasoline vapours. Such a figure may be used as a general guide for petroleum gases, but must not be taken as applicable to gas mixtures containing benzene or hydrogen sulphide.

Since TLV is an indication of how much of a toxic substance is acceptable during working hours (8) day after day, the human body can tolerate concentrations somewhat greater than the TLV for short periods. The following are typical effects at higher concentrations:

0.1% volume (1,000 PPM)	Irritation of the eyes within 1 hour
0.2% volume (2,000 PPM)	Irritation of the eyes, nose and throat; dizziness and unsteadiness within half an hour
0.7% volume (7,000 PPM)	Symptoms as of drunkenness within 15 minutes
2.0% volume (20,000 PPM)	Paralysis and death occur very rapidly

The smell of petroleum gas mixtures is very variable, and in some cases the gases may fool the sense of smell. The impairment of smell is especially serious if the mixture contains hydrogen sulphide. It must be stressed that *the absence of smell should therefore never be taken to indicate the absence of gas.*

Benzene and other aromatic hydrocarbons

The aromatic hydrocarbons include benzene, toluene and xylene. They are components, in varying proportions, of many typical petroleum cargoes such as gasoline, gasoline blending components, and naphtha and special-boiling-point solvents.

The TLV of aromatic hydrocarbons is generally lower than that of the other hydrocarbons in petroleum gases. In particular, in many countries benzene has a TLV of 0.5 PPM, an expoure level that should not be exceeded. Exposure to benzene vapours in high concentrations leads to chronic disorders of the blood and of the bone marrow. Personnel involved in open loading of the products listed above (i.e. with manual gauging through a

皮肤接触

许多石油产品,特别是易挥发的石油产品,会刺激皮肤和引起皮肤脱脂,最后导致皮炎。他们对眼睛也有刺激。反复和长期接触某些重质油可能引起严重的皮肤病。

为避免与石油直接接触,应该穿戴适当的防护服,特别是不渗透的手套和眼镜。

石油气体

石油气体对人类的主要影响是产生麻醉。其症状包括头痛和眼睛刺激,伴随着象醉酒似的意识减弱和眩晕。在高浓度下,就会出现麻痹、意志丧失等症状,甚至死亡。

根据气体中主要的烃类组分,石油气体的毒性有很大的不同。它很大程度上是受出现的一些像芳香族碳氢化合物(即苯)和硫化氢这样的一些少数组分的影响。汽油气的TLV为300 PPM,相当于2% LFL。这样的数字可以作为石油气体的一般参考,但一定不能取含有苯或硫化氢的气体混合物做参考。

由于TLV值是每日工作(8小时)期间可接受有毒物质总量的指标,因此短时间内可以忍受的浓度会稍微高于TLV值。下面是在高浓度条件下的典型后果:

0.1% 体积(1 000 PPM)	1小时以内眼睛刺激
0.2% 体积(2 000 PPM)	半小时以内眼睛、鼻子、喉咙刺激,眩晕和站立不稳
0.7% 体积(7 000 PPM)	15分钟以内类似醉酒症状
2.0% 体积(20 000 PPM)	很快发生瘫痪和死亡

石油气体混合物的气味多种多样,在某些情况下这些气体会干扰嗅觉。如果油气中含有硫化氢,那么对嗅觉的损害会特别严重。因而必须强调决不应该认为没有气味就是没有油气。

苯和其他芳香族碳氢化合物

芳香族碳氢化合物包括苯、甲苯、二甲苯。它们是许多典型石油产品如汽油、混合汽油、石脑油以及特殊沸点溶剂的成分,只是比例不同。

在石油气中芳香族碳氢化合物的TLV值一般低于其他碳氢化合物种类的TLV值。尤其在许多国家,苯的TLV 值为0.5 PPM,不能超过这个辐射标准。辐射于高浓度的苯气体中将会导致慢性血液疾病和骨髓疾病。那些在露天装载上述石油产品的人员(即通过观察口人工计量),

sighting port), and especially during topping-off, may be exposed to concentrations of benzene vapour above the TLV. Precautions should be taken to avoid harmful exposure during the loading of cargoes containing benzene.

Prior to entry into a tank which has recently carried petroleum products containing benzene, the tank should initially be ventilated to a reading of not more than 1% LFL a combustible gas indicator and then checked using the appropriate instruments to ensure that the concentration of benzene vapours do not exceed Permissible Exposure Limits.

TLV or Permissible Exposure Limit (PEL) for hydrocarbons may vary from one country/flag state to another.

Hydrogen sulphide

Many crude oils leaving the well have a high level of hydrogen sulphide, but a stabilization process usually reduces this before the crude is delivered to the vessel. However, the degree of stabilization carried out may sometimes be temporarily reduced, so that a tanker may receive a cargo of a particular crude with a hydrogen sulphide content that is higher than usual. Some crude oils are never stabilized and always have a high hydrogen sulphide level. Hydrogen sulphide can also be encountered in other cargoes, such as naphtha, bitumen and gas oils.

A crude oil containing appreciable amounts of hydrogen sulphide and/or mercaptans is called sour crude oil.

The TLV of hydrogen sulphide is 10 PPM. The effects of the gas at concentrations in air in excess of the TLV are:

50 – 100 PPM	Irritation of the eyes and respiratory tract after exposure of 1 hour
200 – 300 PPM	Marked irritation of the eyes and respiratory tract after exposure of 1 hour
500 – 700 PPM	Dizziness, headache, nausea, etc., within 15 minutes; loss of consciousness and possible death after 30 to 60 minutes' exposure
1,000 – 2,000 PPM	Instantaneous collapse and cessation of breathing

It is important to distinguish between concentrations of hydrogen sulphide in the atmosphere, expressed in PPM by volume, and concentrations in a crude oil containing 70 PPM by weight. For example, a crude oil containing 70 PPM (by weight) hydrogen sulphide has been shown to produce a concentration of 7,000 PPM (by volume) in the gas stream leaving an ullage port above the cargo tank.

Gasoline containing tetraethyl-lead or tetramethyl-lead

The amounts of tetraethyl-lead (TEL) or tetramethyl-lead (TML) normally added to gasoline are insufficient to render the gases from these products significantly more toxic than those from unleaded gasoline. The effects of the gases from leaded gasoline are therefore similar to those described above for petroleum gases.

特别是在装货结束期间,可能会暴露在苯气浓度超过允许TLV值的环境中。必须采取防护措施避免在装载含苯油类期间的有害辐射。

在进入近期装载过含苯石油产品的油舱之前,这个油舱应先进行通风,然后用可燃气体指示仪测取油舱中可燃气体的含量,其值应不超过1% LFL值,接下来用适当测量仪器进行检查以确保苯气体浓度不超过允许辐射极限。

碳氢化合物的TLV或允许辐射极限可能因国家/船旗国的不同而不同。

硫化氢

许多采出井的原油含有很高的硫化氢,但在这些原油运送到船上之前,一般都经过稳定化过程来减少硫化氢。然而,稳定化过程进行的程度有时候可能会临时性地减低,这就使得某些油船可能接收的原油中,硫化氢含量高于常规值。某些原油没有经过稳定化过程,硫化氢含量总是很高。其他油类中也可能含有硫化氢,像石脑油、沥青和汽油。

含有大量硫化氢或硫醇的原油称为酸性原油。

硫化氢的TLV值是10 PPM。空气中气体浓度超过TLV的后果是:

50~100 PPM	辐射1小时后刺激眼睛和呼吸系统
200~300 PPM	辐射1小时后明显刺激眼睛和呼吸系统
500~700 PPM	辐射15分钟以内出现眩晕、头痛、恶心;辐射30到60分钟后丧失意识并可能导致死亡
1 000~2 000 PPM	瞬间呼吸衰竭和停止

区别空气中硫化氢的浓度(以体积PPM表示的)和原油中重量比为70 PPM的硫化氢浓度是很重要的。例如,含有70 PPM(以重量表示)硫化氢的原油表明会在油舱液面以上空间产生7000 PPM浓度(以体积)的气流。

含有四乙基铅或四甲基铅的汽油

一般加到汽油里四乙基铅(TEL)或四甲基铅(TML)的量是不会引起产生比无铅汽油毒性大的气体。因而有铅汽油产生的气体的影响与上述石油气体是相似的。

Toxicity of inert gas

Cargo tanks filled with an inert atmosphere must be ventilated with air before they are entered, both to increase the oxygen content from less than 5% by volume to 21% by volume and to sufficiently reduce the amounts of carbon monoxide, nitrous gases and sulphur dioxide.

Carbon monoxide (CO) may typically be present in a concentration of about 0.01% by volume in inert gas, corresponding to, 100 PPM. In certain cases it may become significantly higher.

The concentration must be reduced to below the TLV of 25 PPM by dilution or by displacement with air. Carbon monoxide poisoning is caused by carbon monoxide combining with the blood's haemoglobin instead of oxygen, so that the blood loses its ability to take up oxygen in the lungs. This results in internal suffocation, and death occurs when 60 to 70% of the haemoglobin has combined with carbon monoxide. The symptoms are headache and drowsiness, deterioration of consciousness and vomiting. In the treatment of carbon monoxide poisoning it is of the utmost importance to supply oxygen, if necessary in combination with artificial respiration.

Nitrous gases are present as nitrogen monoxide (also known as nitric oxide) (NO) and nitrogen dioxide (NO_2) in concentrations of about 0.02% by volume in inert gas after it has passed through the scrubber, corresponding to 200 PPM. The TLV for nitrogen monoxide is 25 PPM and that for nitrogen dioxide is 3 PPM by volume. Nitrous gases form acids by reaction with the moisture in the air, and may destroy the lung tissue.

The sulphur dioxide content of inert gas will be very low, provided the scrubber is efficient.

Oxygen deficiency

Oxygen deficiency must always be suspected in any enclosed space, which has not been ventilated for some time. It may be caused by vapour emitted from volatile liquids, by the displacement of air by inert gas or by the consumption of the available oxygen in the air by chemical reactions such as rusting or the drying of paint. Air contains 21% oxygen, and spaces should not be entered before establishing that the oxygen content of the atmosphere that is to be entered is in fact 21% by volume throughout.

Flammability and explosiveness

The hazards associated with the flammability of petroleum vapours have been touched upon in section 2.1. It is however important to know that, for an explosion to occur, the elements in all four sides of the tetrahedron must be present; or conversely, that there will be no explosion if one of the sides is removed. Tanker construction, equipment and operations are directed at those different elements.

惰性气体的毒性

在进入充满惰气的货舱之前必须用空气通风,使舱内氧气的体积含量从低于5%增加到21%,同时充分减少一氧化碳、氮气、二氧化硫的含量。

一氧化碳(CO)一般可以在惰性气体中呈现大约0.01%(以容积)的浓度,相当于100 PPM。应该注意在某些情况下可能会更高。

这个浓度一定要用空气稀释或置换,使其可容许浓度减少到25 PPM以下。一氧化碳中毒是由一氧化碳代替氧气与血液中的血红蛋白结合引起的,使血液丧失其在肺中携带氧的能力,这将导致内窒息,当60%到70%的血红蛋白与一氧化碳结合时将会发生人体死亡。一氧化碳中毒的症状是头痛和嗜睡、意识低迷和呕吐。一氧化碳中毒的处理中最重要的是供给氧气,如果有必要,需结合人工呼吸。

含氮的气体是以一氧化氮(也称为氧化氮)(NO)和二氧化氮(NO_2)的形式呈现的,经过洗涤塔后在惰性气体中的体积浓度大约为0.02%,相当于200 PPM。一氧化氮的可容许浓度是25 PPM,二氧化氮的可容许浓度是3 PPM。含氮气体与空气中的水分发生反应形成酸,并可能破坏肺组织。

假如洗涤塔有效的话,惰性气体中二氧化硫的含量非常低。

氧气不足

PPM氧气不足总是让人怀疑是由于封闭空间有时没有进行足够时间通风的结果。它可能是由于挥发性液体产生的气体、惰气置换空气或由于空气中氧气与铁锈或油漆干燥过程中发生化学反应而消耗氧气引起的。空气中含有21%的氧气,在没有使全部空间体积内空气的含氧量事实上达到21%之前,不应该进入封闭空间。

易燃性和易爆性

与石油气体易燃性有关的危害在2.1节中已经提到。然而,重要的是要知道当爆炸发生时,燃烧所需求的四个要素必须同时具备;相反地,如果缺失任何一个要素就不会发生爆炸。油船结构、设备和操作均针对这些不同的要素。

Safety

General precautions

General principles

In order to eliminate the risk of fire and explosion on a tanker, it is necessary to prevent situations in which a source of ignition and a flammable atmosphere are present in the same place at the same time. It is not always possible to exclude both of these factors, and precautions are therefore directed towards excluding or controlling one of them. Flammable gases are to be expected in cargo compartments, pump-rooms and, at times, the tank deck, so that the strict elimination of all possible sources of ignition in these locations is essential.

Cabins, galleys and other areas within the accommodation block inevitably contain ignition sources such as electrical equipment, matches and cigarette lighters. While it is sound practice to minimize such sources of ignition, it is essential to avoid the entry of flammable gas.

In engine-rooms and boiler rooms, it is impossible to avoid ignition sources such as those arising from boiler operations and electrical equipment. It is therefore essential to prevent the entry of flammable gases into such compartments. The contamination of bunker fuel by volatile cargo through bulkhead leaks, pipeline admixture or any other cause will introduce an additional danger. The routine checking of bunker spaces for flammability by tanker and terminal personnel is therefore to be encouraged.

Both flammable gases and ignition sources can be safely controlled in deck workshops, store rooms, forecastles, centre-castles, dry cargo holds, etc., by means of good design and sound operational practice, but the method of control must be rigorously maintained. It should be realized that the contamination of bunker tanks with volatile cargo would increase the danger in such areas.

Although the installation and the correct operation of an inert gas system provides an added margin of safety, it does not preclude the need for close attention to the precautions set out in this chapter.

Smoking

While a tanker is at sea, smoking should be permitted only at times and in places specified by the master. Smoking must be prohibited on the tank deck or any other place where petroleum gas may be encountered. Additional smoking restrictions may be imposed in port.

Matches and cigarette lighters

The use of matches and cigarette lighters outside accommodation spaces should be prohibited except in places where smoking is permitted. Matches and cigarette lighters should not be taken outside these places, nor should they be carried on the tank deck or in any other place where petroleum gas may be present.

The risk involved in carrying matches and, more particularly, cigarette lighters should be impressed upon personnel. Matches used on board should be of the "safety" type.

安全

一般预防措施

一般原则

为了消除油船火灾和爆炸的危险,在同一时间、同一地点有必要防止易燃气体和火源出现。由于不可能总是同时排除这两个因素,因此预防措施就直接指向排除或控制其中一个因素。易燃气体会出现在货油舱、泵舱、有时在油舱甲板,因此在这些地方严格消除所有可能的火源是至关重要的。

房间、厨房及生活区的其他地方不可避免地要有诸如电气设备、火柴、打火机之类的着火源。虽然在实践中理应减少这样的着火源,但是防止易燃气体进入更是至关重要。

在机舱和锅炉间,像锅炉运行和电气设备使用中产生的火源是不可避免的,因此避免可燃气体进入这样的舱室是非常重要的。易挥发的货物通过舱壁漏泄、混用管路或其他原因对加装燃油的污染,将导致额外的危险。因此鼓励油船和岸上的人员对加油船周围空间气体的可燃性进行巡回检查。

通过良好的设计和正确的操作实践,在甲板作业区、储藏间、艏尖舱和舯间舱、干货舱等场所,可燃气体和火源都能得以控制,但控制方式必须得到严格的执行。应该认识到燃油舱受到易挥发货物的污染将增加这些区域的危险性。

虽然安装并正确使用惰性气体系统能提供增加的安全余地,但是也不能排除本章提到的密切注意的预防事项。

吸烟

油船在海上期间,应在船长指定的时间和场所吸烟,在甲板或其他可能遇到油气的地方禁止吸烟。在港口可能还有附加的吸烟限制。

火柴和打火机

除了在允许吸烟的场所外,火柴和打火机应禁止在生活区外使用。火柴和打火机不准携带出这些区域,也不能带到甲板上或其他油气可能存在的地方。

应该使所有人员应认识携带火柴尤其打火机有关的危险性。船用火柴应为“安全”型的。

Naked lights (open flame)

Naked lights must be prohibited on the tank deck and in any other place where there is a risk that petroleum gas may be present.

Notices

Portable and permanent notices prohibiting smoking and the use of naked lights should be conspicuously displayed at the point of access to the vessel and at the exits from the accommodation area. Within the accommodation area, instructions concerning smoking should be conspicuously displayed.

Galley

It is essential that galley personnel be instructed in the safe operation of galley equipment. Unauthorized and inexperienced persons should not be allowed to use such facilities.

A frequent cause of fire is the accumulation of un-burnt fuel or fatty deposits on galley ranges, within flue pipes and filter cowls of galley vents. Such areas require frequent inspection to ensure that they are kept clean. Oil and deep-fat frying mechanisms should be fitted with thermostats to cut off the electrical power and so prevent accidental fires.

Galley staff should be trained in fire-fighting, and the appropriate fire extinguishers and fire blankets should be provided.

Additional restrictions on the use of galleys may be applied while the tanker is in port.

Portable battery-powered equipment

Small battery-powered personal items such as watches, miniature hearing aids and heart pacemakers are not significant ignition sources.

Unless approved for use in a flammable atmosphere, portable radios, tape decks, recorders, electronic calculators, cameras containing batteries, and photographic flash units, portable telephones and radio pagers must not be permitted on the tank deck or in areas where flammable gas may be present.

Synthetic clothing

Experience has shown that clothing made from synthetic material does not give rise to any significant electrostatic hazard under conditions normally encountered on tankers.

However, the tendency for synthetic material to melt and fuse together when exposed to high temperatures creates a concentrated heat source which causes severe damage to body tissue. Clothing of such material is therefore considered unsuitable for persons who may be exposed to flame or hot surfaces in the course of their duties.

裸灯(开放火焰)

在油船甲板上和其他油气可能存在的地方,禁止使用裸灯。

警示牌

禁止吸烟和使用裸灯的便携式和固定式警示牌应明显地悬挂或张贴在船的进出口处和生活区的出口处。在生活区,有关吸烟的说明应张贴在显眼处。

厨房

有必要训练厨房人员安全使用厨房设备。未经授权或无经验的人员应禁止使用这些设备。

在厨房区域内，聚集的没有完全燃烧的燃油和通风管过滤罩上沉积的油脂食品残渣是频繁引起火灾的原因,这些地方应经常检查并确保清洁。油炸箱应配置恒温器,以便切断电源,防止火灾事故。

厨房人员应进行消防训练,应配有适当的灭火器和灭火毯。

油船在港期间,厨房的使用可能有附加限制。

以电池为能源的便携式设备

以电池为能源的私人小型物品,像手表、小型助听器、心脏起博器等不是主要的着火源。

除非准许在油气环境中使用,否则不允许便携式收音机、磁带机、录音机、电子计算器、装有电池的照相机、摄影用的闪光器材、手提电话和传呼机等在货物甲板和可燃气体可能存在的地方使用。

合成布料

实践表明,在油船上,在正常情况下,合成材料制作的衣服不会引起较大的静电危险。

但是,当合成材料暴露在高温热源下有熔化倾向时,可以产生对身体组织有一定损害的集中热源。因此,合成材料制作的衣服不适合供那些在工作过程中可能暴露在火源或热源下人员的穿着。

Power tools and hammering

Before any hammering, chipping or sandblasting is undertaken, or any power tool is used outside the boiler room, engine-room or accommodation space on board a tanker at sea, the responsible officer should satisfy himself that the area will remain gas-free throughout the period during which the tools are being used, and that a hot-work permit has been issued.

Hand tools

Hand tools should be used only for the purpose for which they are designed. The risk of ignition of petroleum gas by frictional sparks produced by metal-to-metal impact in normal use is slight, but care must be taken to prevent incorrect use.

So-called "non-sparking" tools, made of non-ferrous materials, are only marginally less likely to give rise to an incendive[3] spark and because of their comparative softness are not as efficient as their ferrous equivalents; moreover, particles of concrete, sand or other hard rock like substances are likely to become embedded in the working face or edge of such tools and can then cause incendive sparks on impact with ferrous or other hard metals. The use of non-ferrous tools is therefore not recommended.

Repairs

No solvent of any kind should be used when cleaning areas to make them safe for hot work, nor should solvents be present in any such area for the purpose of cleaning equipment.

A work permit should be issued detailing the safety criteria to be observed and the work to be performed. The permit should contain a clear indication as to its maximum period of validity, which in any event, should not exceed a normal working day.

The cargo system should be flushed through with water prior to opening up. Sections should be flushed with water when opened, to clear any petroleum residue. Surfaces should always be cleaned before work is carried out on them.

Hot work on pipelines should be permitted only when the appropriate section has been detached from the system by cold work and the open ends of the system have been sealed off. The section of pipe to be worked on should be gas-freed to hot-work standard.

Hot-work permits should be issued for each intended task. The permit should specify the duration (which should not exceed the responsible officer's working hours), the precautions to be taken, the procedures for fire extinguishing and the means of surveillance and communication.

Approval for hot work

Before approval for hot work is given, the responsible officer should test and examine the area to ensure that the following conditions exist:

3 Incendive sparks are those which release adequate energy to ignite flammable vapours.

动力工具和锤子

油船航行期间,在进行任何锤击、铲或喷沙等工作之前,或在锅炉间、机舱或生活区之外使用动力工具时,主管的高级船员应保证本船在使用这些工具的整个过程中没有可燃气体的存在。并且这些热工作业许可已经得到批准。

手动工具

手动工具只能按它们的设计用途使用。在正确和正常使用手动工具情况下,金属之间摩擦产生的火花点燃油气的危险性很小,但要避免不正确的使用。

所谓的“无火花”工具由无铁质材料制成,仅是将产生点火火花[3]的可能性降至最低限度,并且由于它们相对较软,使用起来不如含铁材料制成的工具有效,另外,混凝土、沙子或其他像石头物质的颗粒容易嵌入这些工具的表面或边缘,当与铁或其硬金属撞击时容易产生点火火花,因此不提倡使用这些无铁质工具。

修理

为安全起见,不能用任何溶剂清洁要进行热工作业的区域。溶剂也不能与用于清洁的设备放在一起。

签发的作业许可要详细标明需要遵守的安全标准以及将要进行的工作。许可证上要标明最长有效期,在任何情况下,不应超过一个正常工作日。

货油系统在打开之前应彻底用水冲洗。打开的区域要用水冲洗,以便清除油渣。要进行作业的表面在作业之前要清理干净。

当通过低温作业将相应的管路与系统隔开,并且系统的敞开端已经密封好时,才允许在管路上进行热工作业。要排尽需要进行热工作业的管系内的油气,以达到热工作业的标准。

每次特定的热工作业都要有许可证。许可证上要标明作业期限(不应超过主管高级船员的工作时间),要采取的预防措施,消防措施,监督和通信方式等。

热工作业的批准

在批准热工作业之前,主管高级船员应试验和检查要进行热工作业的区域,以确保下列状态:

3 点火火花是指能够释放足够能量以点燃可燃气体的火花。

- No flammable or toxic gas is present at the work site, and the oxygen content is 21% by volume
- No oil-impregnated scale or other material, which is likely to generate flammable or toxic gas when heated, is present at the work site
- No flammable material is present at the work site or within an adjacent compartment
- Adjacent compartments have been washed and either gas-freed to a standard safe for hot work or, purged of hydrocarbon gas to less than 1% by volume or, completely filled with ballast water, or brought to the necessary condition through any combination of these
- All interconnecting pipelines have been flushed through with water and drained, vented and isolated from the compartment in which work will be carried out. Cargo lines may then be inerted or completely filled with water if considered necessary
- Vapour lines and inert gas lines to the compartment should also be ventilated and isolated
- All sludge, cargo-impregnated scale, sediment or other material likely to give off vapour, which is flammable, should be removed from an area of at least 10 metres around the area of hot work. Special attention must be given to the reverse sides of frames and bulkheads. Other areas that may be affected by the hot work, such as the area immediately below, should also be cleaned
- The area is well ventilated throughout the work period and periodic testing will be carried out to check that no concentrations of flammable or toxic gases develop
- Adequate fire-extinguishing equipment is ready for immediate use

Spontaneous combustion

If damp or soaked with oil (especially oil of vegetable origin), some materials are liable to ignite without the external application of heat; this results from gradual heating within the material caused by oxidation. The risk of spontaneous combustion is smaller with petroleum oils than with vegetable oils, but it can still occur, particularly if the material is kept warm, for example by proximity to a hot pipe.

Cotton waste, rags, canvas, bedding, jute sacking or any similar absorbent material should therefore not be stowed near oil, paint, etc., and should not be left lying on the jetty, on decks, on equipment, on or around a pipeline, etc. If such materials become damp, they should be dried before being stowed away. If soaked with oil, they should be cleaned or destroyed.

Certain chemicals used for boiler treatment are also oxidizing agents and, though carried in diluted form, are capable of spontaneous combustion if permitted to evaporate.

Precautions concerning corrosion hazards

Some ships' tanks are fitted with metal slabs, known as anodes, to provide cathodic protection against corrosion. Sparks may be caused if an anode or its support is struck or dislodged. Corrosion itself may lead to leakage of oil from tanks and pipes, to malfunctioning of equipment and to lack of oxygen in enclosed spaces.

- 在工作场所,没有可燃气和毒气存在,氧气体积含量达到21%。
- 在工作场所,无被油浸过的物品或其他在加热时能产生可燃气或毒气的材料。
- 在工作场所或邻近的舱室内没有可燃材料。
- 应用水冲洗邻近舱室,并且或对其进行驱气至热工作业安全标准,或将烃类气体体积含量降至低于1%,或充满压载水;或通过联合使用上述方法达到必要的工作条件。
- 相互连接的管路用水彻底冲洗后,进行放残和通风,隔离要进行热工作业的舱室。如果有必要的话,惰化货物管路或货物管路充满水。
- 通往该舱室的蒸汽管路和惰性气体管路也应通风并且隔离。
- 所有油渣、货油浸泡过的东西、沉积物或可能释放可燃气体的其他物质都应被移到距热工作业区域至少10米之外的地方。特别注意舱壁的背面。可能受热工作业影响的其他区域,比如热工作业正下方区域,也应该进行清洁。
- 热工作业区域在整个工作过程中,应保持通风良好,并且要间断性地进行测试,以检查可燃气或毒气的浓度是否增加。
- 准备好充足的消防设备且能立即可用。

自燃

如果油黏或被油浸泡过(尤其植物油),有些材料在没有外部加热的情况下也能够着火。这是由于材料内部氧化逐渐加热引起的。原油浸泡过的比植物油浸泡过的引起自燃的危险性要小,但也可能发生,尤其是如果持续加热该材料时,比如靠近一个热管子。

棉布、抹布、帆布、纤维麻袋或其他任何吸油性的材料不应放在油、油漆等附近,也不应放在码头、甲板、设备、管子上或管子附近,等等。如果这些材料受潮,它们在堆放前应被烘干。如果浸泡过油,应清洁干净或处理掉。

某些用于炉水处理的化学药剂也是氧化剂,虽然浓度不大,但如果允许蒸发,也可自燃。

关于腐蚀危险的预防事项

一些船舶的舱内装有金属厚板,就是所谓的阳极,针对腐蚀提供阴极保护。如果阳极或其支架黏着或移动,可能产生火花。腐蚀本身能导致油舱和管路漏油,导致设备失灵和封闭空间缺氧。

Aluminium

Aluminium equipment should not be dragged or rubbed across steel since it may leave a smear, which if it is on rusty steel and is subsequently struck, can cause an incendive spark. It is therefore recommended that the undersides of aluminium gangways and other heavy portable aluminium structures be protected with a hard plastic or wooden strip.

Entry into enclosed spaces

In view of the possibility of oxygen deficiency and the presence of hydrocarbon or toxic gas in a cargo tank, cofferdam, double-bottom tank or any enclosed space, it is the master's responsibility to identify such spaces and establish procedures for safe entry.

Personnel should consult the responsible officer to determine whether entry into such enclosed spaces is permitted. It is the duty of the responsible officer to check the atmosphere in the compartment, ventilate the space, ensure the appropriate procedures are followed, ensure the safety of the personnel concerned and issue an entry permit.

Pump-rooms

General precautions

By virtue of their location, design and operation, pump-rooms constitute a particular hazard and therefore necessitate special precautions.

Pump-room bilges should be kept clean and dry. Particular care should be taken to prevent the escape of petroleum products or hydrocarbon vapour into the pump-room. All pump seals, valve glands, drain cocks and mud boxes should therefore be maintained in good condition.

In the event of a serious spillage, the application of a layer of fire-extinguishing froth will help to control the generation of hydrocarbon vapour until the situation is brought under control.

Ventilation

The possible presence of hydrocarbon gas within the pump-room necessitates ventilation. Regulations require the mechanical expulsion of mixtures of air and petroleum gas from the bottom of the pump-room (SOLAS Ch 11-2, Reg. 59.3).

A pump-room should be thoroughly ventilated, and its atmosphere checked for petroleum gas, before anyone enters it. Ventilation should be continued until access to the pump–room is no longer required.

The pump-room should be continuously ventilated during all cargo operations.

Special attention should be paid to the space below the lower platform, where petroleum gas is liable to accumulate.

Isolation of the pump-room vent system in the event of fire requires the efficient operation of dampers in the vent trunk. They should therefore be well maintained.

铝

铝材制成的设备不应在钢板上拖动或摩擦,因为这样能造成磨痕,如果该磨痕在生锈的钢板上并受到撞击,可能产生能引起点火的火花。因此,推荐使用硬的塑料或木条保护铝制弦梯或其他较重的便携式铝质构造物的底面。

进入封闭空间

鉴于货舱内、隔离舱内、双层底舱内或者任何封闭空间内有可能缺氧或存在碳氢化合物或有毒气体,船长有责任确认这样的空间并制定安全进入程序。

全体人员应咨询主管高级船员以确定能否进入类似的封闭空间。主管高级船员应负责检查舱室的氧气量,对封闭空间进行通风,保证遵守相应程序,确保有关人员的安全并且签发进入许可证。

泵舱

一般注意事项

由于泵舱的位置、设计和操作,它们存在特殊的危险,因此需要特殊的注意事项。

泵舱的污水井应保持清洁和干燥。应特别注意防止油类产品或碳氢化合物气体进入泵舱。所有泵的轴封、阀的压盖、放残考克和填料箱应保养在良好的状态。

在严重的溢油事故中,在事态被控制之前,泡沫灭火剂的应用将有助于控制碳氢化合物气体的产生。

通风

泵舱内可能存在碳氢化合物的气体,有必要进行通风。法规要求用风机从泵舱的底部排除油气混合物(SOLAS公约11-2章,规则59.3)。

泵舱应彻底通风,在任何人进入之前应进行油气测试。应对泵舱持续通风直至不再要求进入泵间。

货油操作期间,泵舱应保持连续通风。

特别注意低平台下面的空间,在那里油气易于聚积。

发生火灾时隔离泵舱透气系统要求对通风管道中的风门实施有效操作。因此,应该认真维护这些风门。

Pump-room lighting

Care should be taken to ensure that the integrity of the approved lighting system is maintained. If additional lighting is required, only approved equipment should be used.

If there is any reason to doubt the integrity of the pump-room lighting system, it should be switched on only after thorough ventilation of the pump-room. However, new regulations require that pump-room lighting should be interlocked with pump-room ventilation and will come on only after ventilation is put on.

Pump-room entry

No one should enter a pump-room at any time without first obtaining the permission of a responsible officer.

It is the duty of the officer in charge of cargo operations to ensure that adequate ventilation of the pump-room has been accomplished, that the atmosphere within the compartment is suitable for entry and that adequate communication procedures are established and maintained.

Notices should be displayed at the pump-room entrance prohibiting entry without prior permission.

The pump-room lifelines and harness should be rigged ready for immediate use. Where possible, an unobstructed direct lift should be provided.

Pollution Prevention

<u>General</u>

During the past twenty-five years the pollution of the world's oceans has become a matter of increasing international concern. Most of it comes from land–based sources and includes the by-products of industry, runoff from agricultural pesticides and herbicides and effluents discharged from urban areas.

Nevertheless, a very significant amount of pollution is caused by shipping and maritime activities generally. The substances involved vary enormously in quantities transported. The following paragraphs summarize pollution-control situation insofar as the main types of shipping activity are concerned.

<u>Oil</u>

In tonnage terms, the most important pollutant resulting from shipping operations is oil. The National Academy of Sciences (NAS) of the United States estimated in 1980 that as much as 3.54 million tonnes of oil enter the sea every year, some 1.5 million tonnes of which resulted from the transport of oil by sea (the remainder comes from land-based activities and includes industrial wastes, urban runoff and natural seepage).

The best-known cause of oil pollution is *tanker accidents*. Although this may contribute a comparatively small percentage of the total oil entering the sea in a year, the consequence of

泵舱照明

应注意确保认可的照明系统的完整性已得到维护。

如果需要额外的照明,只有经过认可的设备才可使用。

如果有理由怀疑泵舱照明系统的完整性,只有在彻底通风后才可合闸。然而,新规则要求泵舱照明应该与泵舱通风互锁,只有起动通风之后才可以进行照明。

进入泵舱

任何人在任何时候没有得到主管高级船员的许可时,不可进入泵舱。

保证对泵舱进行了适当的通风,使舱室内氧气适合人员的进入,建立并保持适当的通信方式,这些都是负责货油操作的高级船员的职责。

“未经允许,不得进入”的警示牌应张贴在泵舱的入口处。

泵舱的救生索和索具应装配好,能够随时可用。如果可能,应能无阻碍、直接吊起。

预防污染

概述

在过去的二十五年里,世界海洋污染问题不断引发国际关注。大多数污染来自于陆上污染源,包括工业副产品、农业杀虫剂和除臭剂以及城市废弃物等。

然而,海运和海洋活动也逐渐引起大量的污染。运输的货物种类繁多,数量巨大,它们对海洋环境造成很大的潜在危害。根据涉及海运活动的主要类型,以下内容概述了污染控制的情形。

油

从总数量上来讲,来自于海运行业的最主要的污染物是油。美国国家科学院在1980年估计每年有354万吨油进入海洋,其中150甩吨来自于海上油类运输(其余来自于陆地,包括工业产生的废物、城市排泄物以及自然排泄)。

最熟悉的污染原因是油船事故。虽然占每年排放入海总油量的比例很小,但事故后果对事发

an accident can be disastrous to the immediate area, particularly if the ship involved is a large one and the accident occurs close to the coast. The wrecks of the *Torrey Canyon* (1967), the *Amoco Cadiz* (1978), the *Exxon Valdez* (1989) and *Sea Empress* (1996) are examples. The NAS estimates that about 390,000 tonnes of oil a year enters the sea from this source.

A much greater quantity of oil enters the sea as a result of *normal tanker operations*, usually associated with the cleaning of cargo residues (cargo clinging to the tank sides) and the changing of ballast which takes place when the ship is returning from the port of discharge to take on another cargo of oil. The amount of residues normally amounts to about 0.4% of cargo-carrying capacity—about 800 tonnes on a 200,000 DWT crude oil carrier. During ballasting and cleaning, as much as half of this can be lost overboard unless slops are retained on board. In tonnage terms, this is still probably the biggest source of oil pollution from ships—about 700,000 tonnes a year, according to the NAS—but it has declined considerably in recent years.

Other causes of oil pollution include dry-docking (30,000 tonnes); bilge and fuel oil (from dry cargo ships as well as from tankers) (300,000 tonnes); and non-tanker accidents (20,000 tonnes).

Oil affects the marine environment in different ways. It blankets the surface, interfering with the exchange of oxygen between the sea and the atmosphere; its heavier constituents blanket the seafloor, interfering with the growth of marine life; many constituent elements are toxic and get into the food chain; and oil on the beach interferes with recreational uses of that beach. Furthermore, oil may enter seawater distilling inlets and it may be deposited on tidal mudflats, again with detrimental results. In the face of growing oil pollution, international action was taken in the shape of the adoption of the International Convention for the Prevention of Pollution from Ships, 1973. In 1978 a Protocol tightening the provision of the Convention, especially in respect of oil tankers, was adopted. The combined instrument is now known as MARPOL 73/78, with further amendments. Marine pollution is more than oil pollution, and MARPOL 73/78 deals with these different pollution categories. Annex I of the Convention deals with oil pollution.

Annex I of MARPOL 73/78

Annex I deals with pollution caused by accidents occurring to oil tankers and by tanker operation. The prevention of accidents is primarily a safety matter, and is dealt with through safety conventions. Annex I does, however, serve to mitigate the effects of accidents.

With respect to oil tankers, the protection of the marine environment is approached through:

- Construction requirements
- Equipment requirements
- Operational requirements
- Survey and certificate requirements
- Cargo record book

区域而言却是灾难性的。尤其如果事故船舶是一艘大船并且事故地点靠近海岸。Torrey Canyon (1967),Amoco Cadiz (1978), Exxon Valdez (1989) ,Sea Empress (1996) 等船舶的事故,都是这样的例子。NAS 估计每年因此约有39万吨的油进入海里。

由于正常油船操作,每年有更大数量的燃油进入海里,通常与货油的残渣清洁(黏着在舱壁上的货油) 及从卸货港到装油港的途中压载水的更换有关。黏着的货油数量约占船舶载重量的0.4%——对于一艘载重量20万吨的油船,约有800吨。在压载和清洗过程中,一半左右的黏着残油被排到船外,除非污水留在船上。就重量而言,这仍然是来自船舶的最大油污染源——根据NAS的估计,大约每年70万吨——但是在最近几年已有下降的趋势。

其他引起油污染包括坞修(30 000吨),污水和燃油(来自于干货船及油船)(300 000 吨),非油船事故(20 000吨)。

油影响海洋环境的方式有很多。它覆盖海洋的表面,妨碍海洋与大气之间的交换氧气。它的较重成分覆盖海底,影响海生物的生长;许多成分有毒,进入食物链;海边的油污染影响滨海娱乐设施的使用。而且,油可能进入海水蒸馏吸口,并且沉积在滤器中,造成有害的后果。面对不断增长的油污染,国际社会以实施《1973年国际防止船舶造成污染公约》的形式采取了相关行动。在1978年，采纳了加强公约条款的草案，尤其针对油船。合并起来的文件就是所熟悉的《MARPOL73/78公约》,并可以进一步修正。海洋污染不仅是油污染,《MARPOL73/78公约》针对不同种类的污染。公约的附则Ⅰ是有关油的污染。

MARPOL73/78公约附则Ⅰ

附则Ⅰ针对的是发生在油船及油船操作中的事故引起的污染。事故预防主要是安全问题,可以通过安全方面的公约进行解决。然而,附则Ⅰ是用来减轻这类事故的影响的。

关于油船,通过下面的几个方面来实现海洋环境保护:

- 结构要求
- 设备要求
- 操作要求
- 检验和证书要求
- 货物记录簿

- Control procedures
- Penalties

The construction requirements reflect the desire to avoid ballast water coming into contact with cargo oil, thereby restricting the generation of oily water mixtures, and preventing the discharge of oil into the sea. They also reflect the desire to give ships carrying oil a greater survival capability, to protect the oil tanks by means of void spaces, and to limit tank size so that, if an accident does occur, the outflow of oil will also be limited. The equipment requirements reflect the desire to enable a ship to comply with operational requirements. MARPOL 73/78 not only lays down operational requirements but also provides for the means to operate in accordance with those requirements.

A brief outline of the latest amendments has been given earlier. It is therefore not repeated here.

Construction of oil tankers

Segregated ballast tanks (SBT)

New crude oil tankers of more than 20,000 tonnes deadweight and new product tankers of more than 30,000 tonnes deadweight must be provided with segregated ballast tanks of sufficient capacity, so that only in extraordinary circumstances will there be a need to take ballast water in cargo tanks. SBT reduce the need for tank washing and therefore reduce oily water mixtures, but only if they are of adequate capacity. Segregated ballast tanks are defined as tanks which are completely separated from the cargo oil and fuel oil systems and which are permanently allocated to the carriage of ballast. They are served by their own pumps and piping adequate for their purpose. The capacity should be such that, at any time of the voyage:

- The mid-ship's draught is not less than 2.0 + 0.02 *L* metres (*L*–length between perpendiculars)
- The trim by the stern is not more than 0.015 *L*
- The propeller is fully immersed

New tankers, in this context, are those built after 1 January 1980. Ships built before that date are subject to less stringent requirements, in recognition of the fact that retro-fitting segregated ballast systems may be costly and impracticable. Such ships need only be fitted with SBT if they exceed 40,000 tonnes deadweight, but may instead choose to:

- Operate with dedicated clean ballast tanks (CBT), if product tankers
- Be equipped and operate with a crude oil washing (COW) system, if crude oil tankers

Protective location of ballast tanks

In addition to providing sufficient ballast capacity, which results in stipulated mean draught and trim, SBT should also be located so as to offer some degree of protection against stranding and collision. Ideally, this would be a double skin and double bottom against stranding and collision. This is not necessary in practice; instead, the total area of the protected side and

- 控制程序
- 处罚

结构的要求体现在避免压载水与货油接触方面,因此限制油水混合物的产生,防止把油排到海里。结构还应使载货油船具有较强的生存能力,利用空舱保护油舱,并且限制油舱的尺寸,以便一旦发生事故,溢油数量受到限制。设备要求体现在船舶应符合相关操作要求方面。《MARPOL73/78公约》不但规定操作要求,而且制定了符合技能要求程序。

之前已经对最新修订要求作了简要介绍。因此,在此不做赘述。

<u>油船结构</u>

专用压载舱(SBT)

载重量在20 000吨以上的新造原油油船及载重量在30 000吨以上的新造成品油船必须配有专用的有足够大容量的压载舱,以便只有在特殊情况下才能把压载水排到油舱。SBT减少了油舱清洗的需要,因此减少了油水混合物,但只有在舱容足够的情况下才有效。专用压载舱定义为与货油和燃油系统完全分开并且永久地只作压载舱使用。它们具有独立的泵和管系。在航行期间,舱容应该是这样的:

- 船中间的吃水不低于$2.0+0.02L$(L—垂直之间的长度)。
- 艉部吃水差不超过$0.015\ L$。
- 螺旋桨完全浸入水中。

这里所指的新船是那些建造于1980年1月以后的船。考虑到后安装专用压载系统花费大和不现实的事实,对1980年1月之前建造的船,要求要宽松些。这些船舶只有载重量超过40 000吨,才要求安装专用压载舱,但有下面几种替代选择:

- 如果是成品油船,用指定的清洁压载舱作为专用压载舱。
- 如果是原油油船,应配有并操作原油洗舱系统。

有保护作用的压载舱的位置

除了提供足够的压载舱容,可以保证中间吃水深度和吃水差,专用压载舱的布置还应针对搁浅和碰撞提供一定程度的保护作用。理想情况是,具有双壳和双层底,这样对搁浅和碰撞具有保护作用。在实际中没有这个必要,反而是受保护的侧面和底部总面积应符合一定的参数。此外,公

bottom should comply with certain parameters. In addition, the regulations stipulate a minimum width for the wing ballast tanks of 2 metres and a minimum height for the doublebottom ballast tanks of 2 metres or B/15, whichever is the lesser (B = maximum breadth of the ship). There is no requirement for the ratio of the side and bottom protection, as long as the total area complies with Annex I; in practice, this means that in oil tankers the SBT are wing tanks, adjacent to the ship's shell plating.

Limitation for tank size

This requirement concerns the construction of cargo tanks and is applicable to all oil tankers. The provision aims to limit the quantity of oil, which can escape into the marine environment when an oil tanker sustains damage to its cargo tanks. The provision limits the length and width of cargo tanks and, in addition, limits the hypothetical outflow to less than 40,000 cubic metres in the event of assumed damage due to collision or stranding.

Subdivision and stability

Annex I lays down requirements for the subdivision and stability of a vessel in order to ensure a certain survival capability after a collision or stranding. A given extent of longitudinal, transverse and vertical damage is assumed when determining compliance with the requirements. Furthermore, using the ship's length as a parameter, distinctions are made regarding the location of the assumed damage in relation to the ship's length. For tankers above 225 metres in length, the damage is assumed to be anywhere along the length of the ship. For ships of lesser length, neither certain areas, such as machinery spaces and peak tank spaces, nor damage involving a transverse bulkhead are considered in the damage assumption.

Taking the above damage into consideration, the resulting condition of equilibrium of the ship should be such that the waterline, when taking account of the sinkage, heel and trim, should be below the lower edge of any opening through which progressive flooding might take place. In that condition the stability should also comply with certain requirements.

Slop-tanks

Slop-tanks must be of adequate capacity to ensure that tank washings and other oily mixtures can be retained on board for separation of the oil and water and subsequent discharge of the water as part of the LOT procedures; Annex I requires at least one slop-tank for ships of less than 70,000 tonnes deadweight and at least two slop-tanks for larger ships. The capacity of the slop-tank is expressed as a percentage of the cargo-carrying capacity and depends on the tank-washing method used; a larger capacity, and therefore larger tanks, is required for open cycle washing than for washing in the re-circulation mode. SBT and COW tankers and combination carriers may also have smaller slop-tanks. Slop-tank arrangements must be such as to facilitate the separation of oil and water.

Overboard piping

All discharges from cargo and ballast tanks must, in principle, be made above the waterline to ensure that both discharge and water surface may be observed. Since discharge above the waterline may pose hazards in port for persons working on lighters, jetties, passing small

约规定两侧的压载舱最小的宽度为2米,双层底压载舱的最低高度为2米或*B*/15,取两者中较小的数值(*B*为船的最大的宽度)。两侧与底部保护面积比没有要求,只要总面积符合附则Ⅰ的要求。实际上,这意味着在油船上SBT为边舱,靠近船壳。

油舱尺寸的限制

该要求与货舱结构有关,并且适合于所有油船。该规定的目的是限制当油船货舱遭到损坏时,溢入海洋环境中的油量。该规定限制了货舱的长度和宽度,另外,还限制了假设发生了由于碰撞或搁浅而造成损坏,流入海里的货油应少于40 000立方米。

船舶分舱和稳定性

附则Ⅰ对船舶分舱和稳性作了要求,以确保在碰撞或搁浅之后船舶仍具有一定的生存能力。按照要求,对纵向、横向和垂直方向上的损坏应有一定余量。而且,把船长作为一个参数,关于假定损坏的位置相对于船长方向的位置,就可以得到一个的差值。对长度在225米以上的油船,损坏的地方可以假设在沿船长方向的任何地方。对那些长度较短的油船,像机舱和艏尖舱的地方及横向的舱壁都不在假设损坏之列。

考虑到上面的损坏,考虑在船下沉、倾斜和吃水偏差时,船的实际平衡状态应是,吃水线应低于较低的可能大量进水的敞口边缘。在这样的状态下,船舶的稳性应符合一定的要求。

污液舱

污液舱必须具有足够的舱容以确保洗舱污水和其他油水混合物能保存在船上,以便油水分离,并且按照LOT程序排水;附则Ⅰ要求载重吨小于70 000吨的船至少有一个污液舱,对更大的船要求至少两个污液舱。污液舱的舱容表示为载货量的百分比,而且取决于所使用的洗舱方法;开式清洗需要污液舱的舱容比闭式的要大,因此用于更大的油船。SBT和COW油船和混装船需要较小舱容的污液舱。污液舱的设置必须有利于油水分离。

舷外管系

一般而言,所有货油舱和压载舱的出海管都应位于水线以上,保证排放过程和水面都可观察到。在港口,因为高于吃水线的排放可能对在驳船、码头上工作的人员及过往小船等造成危险,所

craft, etc., the discharge of clean and segregated ballast is permitted under the waterline when in port. Pipelines on board reflect these requirements.

On oil tankers of 20,000 tonnes deadweight or more, it should be possible to drain pumps and lines, if necessary by connecting them to a stripping device. A special small-diameter line should be provided to discharge these draining to the shore. A schematic drawing of this arrangement is shown in Fig. 8.

Operational measures in lieu of construction requirements

It is difficult—and may be extremely costly—to modify an existing oil tanker to comply with the SBT requirements; ways had to be found for such oil tankers to be exempted from SBT and at the same time to pose no threat to the marine environment. The Tanker Safety and Pollution Prevention Conference in 1978 investigated this problem.

One method for dealing with the problem is crude oil washing (COW). At the time of the conference, it was not a novel concept, and a number of tanker operators were already practising COW as a matter of routine. Reports indicated that, when carried out effectively, COW could considerably reduce oily residues in cargo tanks so that, in fact, only a water rinse would then be necessary to prepare the cargo tanks for clean ballast. The resulting decrease in oily water mixtures was considered to pose little threat to the marine environment and, as far as existing oil tankers were concerned, COW was accepted as offering protection for the marine environment equivalent to that of SBT. In fact, COW was considered to be so beneficial for the marine environment that the requirement for COW was extended to cover new crude oil tankers as well. COW can only be affected on crude oil tankers, so that other means of protecting the marine environment had to be found for existing product tankers not provided with SBT.

Equivalent protection was provided by the concept of dedicated clean ballast tanks (CBT), whereby a number of cargo tanks are dedicated solely for the carriage of ballast instead of providing the ship with SBT. The main difference is that CBT, by not needing to be served by segregated pumps and piping, allows the cargo system to be used. The capacity and distribution of the ballast tanks are such that the ship meets the requirements for trim and mean draught that are laid down for SBT and is not subject to excessive stress when ballasting.

Crude oil washing (COW)[4]

COW offers the following advantages over washing cargo tanks with water:

- Reduction in pollution potential
- Increased cargo out–turn
- Less dead freight
- Less time required in subsequent tank cleaning

4 COW is discussed in detail in Appendix 4. However, it is being mentioned here to give an idea that COW should not be treated in isolation but is very much a safety aspect of oil tanker operation.

以在港内允许干净的水和专用的压载舱的压载水在吃水线以下排放。船上的管路要体现这些要求。

在20 000载重吨及以上的油船上,如果有必要,应该可以通过连接扫舱装置对泵和管系进行放残。一个小管径的管路用来把这些残物排放到岸上。这种布置的简图如图8所示。

替代结构技能要求措施

为满足SBT的要求来改装现有的油船是很困难的,并且可能花费巨大;必须找到可以替代SBT,同时对海洋环境不会造成危险的方法。1978年的油船安全和防污染会议研究了该问题。

处理这个问题的一个方法是原油清洗(COW)。在那次会议上,原油清洗不是一个新概念,许多油船操作者已经把COW作为一个例行操作。报告表明,有效地进行原油洗舱,就能大量减少货舱内的残渣,这样在实际上,只要用水轻轻冲洗,货舱就可用来装干净的压载水。油水混合物数量的减少,就能减少油水混合物对海洋环境威胁,并且,对于涉及到的现有油轮,原油洗舱被认为相当于SBT一样,对海洋环境提供了一定的保护。实际上,原油洗舱对海洋环境的保护是有利的,所以新造原油油轮也要求有原油洗舱系统。原油洗舱仅对原油油轮有效,对那些没有SBT的现有成品油轮,必须找到保护海洋环境的其他方法。

清洁压载舱(CBT)可作为替代保护措施,其中,一些货舱被指定专门用来装压载水,代替SBT。主要的区别是CBT不需要提供单独的泵和管系,而可以使用货物泵和管系。舱容和压载舱的分配应使船舶符合对SBT制定的吃水差和中间吃水深度的要求,并且压载后不承受过多的应力。

原油洗舱(COW)[4]

相对于水洗货油舱,COW具有以下优势:

- 减少潜在污染
- 增加货油量
- 减少空舱费
- 减少后续的洗舱时间

4 在附件4中详细论述原油洗舱。然而,在此处提及是为给出一个概念:不应该孤立原油洗舱,而应将其视为油船操作中非常重要的一个方面。

- Less time needed to prepare a tank for repairs in dry-dock
- Less corrosion through less contact for the tank with water

The disadvantages of COW are:

- Increased workload on personnel
- Prolonged discharge time
- Costs of COW equipment
- Increased safety risks in port

COW is usually carried out in the port of discharge, although it is also possible to do it on passage between ports, provided there is still a parcel of crude oil in the ship. The source of the oil for COW may be the discharge line, in which case provision must be made to bleed off oil for tank washing. Alternatively, the slop-tank may be used in the re-circulation mode.

When the discharge line is the source of the washing fluid, special measures may be necessary to ensure sufficient pressure in the washing system, especially if the backpressure from the terminal is low. If the slop-tank is used in the re-circulation mode, it may be argued that the sludge being removed from the cargo tanks is being re-injected for further washing. In any case, it is important that sufficient crude oil be available to complete the COW programme.

In order to ensure that COW is effectively protecting the marine environment against oil pollution, the design, operation and control of COW systems are subject to IMO specifications, and only crude oil tankers in which the COW system and its operation are surveyed and found to be in accordance with those specifications will be issued with the IOPP Certificate. Design specifications cover pumps and piping, washing machines and stripping systems. Operations cover washing programmes, pressures, prevention of electrostatic hazards, the dangers of oil leakage and the number of tanks to be washed. Washing programmes cover the different stages and duration of washing. The ship is surveyed on a 'one-off' basis, that is to say that a complete tank-washing programme is performed when the ship is first surveyed for certification. The number of washing machines, washing programmes, duration and pressure are noted and a surveyor examines the effectiveness of cleaning. To do this, the surveyor measures the oil on top of the ballast in a tank, which has been washed with crude oil but not with water. The surveyor will also inspect a number of tanks internally after crude oil washing but before any water washing. Finally, the oil content of any ballast from a tank, which has been washed with both crude oil and water, is determined. In addition to these tests, the whole of the COW system will be inspected.

It is important that, during the subsequent operation of the ship, COW takes place under the same parameters as those used during the tests so that the desired washing results are obtained. Conditions influencing the washing results are:

- The number and location of washing machines
- Nozzle diameter
- Number and size of drain holes
- Effectiveness of the stripping system and the stripping procedure
- Trim of the ship

- 在坞修中,油舱维修的准备时间较少
- 减少因舱与水接触而形成的腐蚀

COW的缺点:

- 增加船员的工作负荷
- 延长卸货时间
- COW设备成本
- 增加港内安全风险

COW通常在卸货港进行,尽管也可以在航行中进行,如果船上仍然有一部分原油。卸货管路可以作为COW的油源,在这种情况下,必须采取措施放出洗舱用原油。或者,在循环模式中采用污液舱。

当卸货管路作为冲洗油源时,必须采取特殊措施以确保冲洗系统中足够的压力,尤其在码头背压较低时。如果在循环模式中使用污液舱时,刚从油舱中清出的油渣又被喷入舱内用来进一步清洗,这种做法存在争议。在任何情况下,为完成COW过程,足够的原油是很重要的。

为确保COW能有效地保护海洋环境,防止油污染,COW系统的设计、操作和控制必须符合IMO规范,只有原油油船的原油洗舱系统及其操作经过检验,符合公约规定后,才可以签发IOPP证书。设计规范包括泵和管、洗舱机和扫舱系统。操作规范包括洗舱程序、压力、静电危险防护、溢油危险和洗舱数目。洗舱程序包括不同的步骤和清洗持续时间。船舶检验是一次性的,也就是说当船舶第一次检验发证时,要进行一个完整的洗舱程序。要记录洗舱机的数目、冲洗程序、持续时间和压力,并且验船师还要检验冲洗效果。为了检验冲洗效果,验船师要测量已用原油清洗但没用水清洗的货舱里的压载水表面的含油量。验船师还将对原油清洗后但用水冲洗前的货舱进行内部检查。最后,测量原油冲洗和水冲洗都完成的舱里的压载水中的含油量。除了这些试验,还要检查整个COW系统 。

在随后的COW操作过程中,要在与试验相同的参数下进行,这样可获得理想的冲洗效果,这一点很重要。影响冲洗效果的因素有:

- 洗舱机的数目和位置
- 喷嘴直径
- 放残孔的数目和大小
- 扫舱系统和扫舱过程的效果
- 船的吃水差

It should be noted that too many machines in use on a branch line could lead to excessive fluid velocity in the line. This causes a pressure drop over the line, impairing the effectiveness of the machines being served. It is therefore important that the correct number of tankwashing machines is used at all times.

In order to ensure that the ship's crew comply with the test parameters, the ship is provided with a COW Operation and Equipment Manual, which not only describes these parameters but also gives examples of typical single and multi-parcel discharges and associated COW operations.

One condition influencing COW results that has not been mentioned so far is the grade, i.e. the source, of the crude oil itself. At one end of the scale there are crude, which lend themselves very well to COW, while at the other end there are crude, which are unsuitable for the purpose owing to their high pour point or viscosity. Such oils may not be carried in crude oil tankers unless they are provided with SBT.

It should be clear that COW is not optional but mandatory for tankers certified for such operations. No ballast water may ever be taken into cargo tanks which have not been crude oil washed. This means cargo tanks ballasted before or shortly after departure (the departure ballast), those ballasted upon or prior to arrival (the arrival ballast), and those, which may need to be ballasted at the discretion of the master. There is a further requirement that cargo tanks not used for ballast should be crude oil washed in rotation for reasons of sludge control. This also applies to new oil tankers provided with both SBT and COW; such vessels must ensure that sufficient cargo tanks are crude oil washed to take additional ballast, if required, and that a quarter of the remaining tanks are crude oil washed to control sludge build-up.

In view of the hazards involved in crude oil washing, this operation may only take place in an inerted tank atmosphere and by specially trained personnel. COW operations should cease if during washing:

- The oxygen level in the tank exceeds 8% by volume, or
- The pressure of the atmosphere in the tanks is no longer positive

Particular attention must be paid to preventing electrostatic hazards caused by the presence of water in the crude oil used for washing. Only "dry crude" may be used. In loaded tanks there is always a risk of water lying underneath the cargo, and water will always be present in the ship tanks if LOT procedures have been executed properly. For safety reasons, cargo tanks that are used as a source of crude for COW must always first be 'de-bottomed', i.e. the bottom 1 metre of cargo, where water is most likely to be present, must always be discharged before using the crude oil for COW. For the same reasons, if a slop-tank is utilized as a supply of crude oil for COW it must first be discharged completely and refilled with dry crude.

Dedicated clean ballast tank (CBT)

Like COW, the use of CBT is aimed at reducing the generation of oil/water mixtures. CBT must be used on oil tankers, which are not provided with SBT, which carry oils other than crude oil, and which, as a consequence, cannot practice COW. In principle, an oil tanker with CBT is the same as an SBT tanker. Since ballast water is carried in tanks designated for that purpose, there is no need to change ballast whilst under way to the loading port. Capacity and distribution should ensure that no additional ballast is needed on most occasions, and

应该注意到许多洗舱机同时用在一个分支管路中会导致管内液体流速过快。这会引起管路压力下降,影响正在使用的洗舱机的效率。因此,整个清洗过程中使用正确数量的洗舱机是非常重要的。

为了保证船员按照实验参数进行操作,船上有一本COW操作和设备手册,不仅描述了这些参数,而且给出了单组和多组排放实例和与COW操作有关的实例。

到目前还没有提到的影响COW操作效果的一个因素是油类等级,即本源,也就是原油本身。处于某种程度的原油非常适合原油洗舱,处于另外一种程度原油由于它们的高倾点和高黏度,不适合原油洗舱。这样的原油不适合用原油船来运输,除非这些船配有SBT。

应该清楚对于持有原油洗舱操作证书的油船,原油洗舱操作不是可选性的,而是强制性的。压载水不许加装到没有进行原油洗舱的货舱内。这指的是离港前或刚离港时的货舱压载(离港压载),到港前或到港时压载(到港压载),以及船长决定的认为有必要的压载。进一步的要求是,为了污油控制的缘故,不用作压载的货舱也应轮流地进行原油洗舱。这也适用于配有SBT和COW的新造油船;这些油船应保证足够的货舱进行原油冲洗,以加装额外的压载水。如果有需要,四分之一的剩余货舱应进行原油洗舱,以控制污油的形成。

鉴于原油洗舱中存在的危险,必须由经过专门训练的人员对已惰化的舱进行该操作。如果洗舱过程中出现如下情况,应停止原油洗舱操作:

- 氧气体积含量超过8%
- 舱内大气压力不再是正值

应特别注意,冲洗原油中含有的水会引起静电危险。只有“干原油”可以使用。在装有货油的油舱里,总会存在货油下方含水的风险,并且如果正确地执行了LOT操作,那么水就总会存在货舱内。为安全起见,为COW提供原油的货舱,必须首先“除油脚”,也就是,在为COW提供原油之前,必须首先排掉货物底部1米下的货物,水最可能积存在这里。同样原因,如果用污液舱为COW提供原油,污液舱必须首先完全排空,再充入干原油。

专用清洁压载舱(CBT)

像COW一样,CBT的使用目的是为了减少产生油水混合物。CBT必须用在不能使用原油洗舱的油船上,这种油船如不装CBT不能用来运输原油。原理上,装有CBT的油船就是SBT油船。因为压载水装在指定用于压载的舱内,所以在驶往装货港途中,没有必要更换压载水。舱容和布置

the location of CBT in the ship's sides, where possible, offers some degree of protection against pollution arising from collision. The measure is a temporary one, only to be used on product tankers of 40,000 tonnes deadweight and above, built before 1980. In practice it has been difficult to allocate cargo tanks in an existing configuration, which would result in compliance with trim and draught requirements. It has often been necessary to utilize peak tanks and cofferdams for ballast to meet the requirements.

In one important respect CBT differs from SBT, and that is in the use of pumps and piping, CBT tankers may have to make use of cargo pumps and piping for ballasting during and after cargo operations, and considerable flushing of pumps and lines may have to take place to avoid contaminating the ballast water. The flushing may not be discharged into the sea and, contrary to practice on non-CBT ships, cannot be transferred to the ballast tanks, since these have been thoroughly cleaned at an earlier stage and must remain clean. Pump and line flushing must therefore be transferred to the slop-tanks and, for that reason; space may have to be left in the slop-tanks even on a loaded voyage. Oil tankers certified as CBT tankers must be provided with a CBT Operation Manual setting out the correct line-flushing procedures for the particular ship.

A number of oil tankers operating with CBT have a dedicated ballast system serving those tanks; for these, operations are very similar to those on SBT tankers. Care must be taken to prevent oil entering the ballast tanks through the cargo piping, and there should be a twovalve separation between cargo and ballast.

Equipment requirements

Oil discharge monitoring and control equipment

The discharge provisions limit both the total quantity of oil that may be discharged into the sea from the cargo–tank area and the instantaneous rate of discharge of oil. Monitoring equipment must be provided to enable oil tankers to comply. The discharge provisions also stipulate that the equipment should be in operation when oil and water mixtures are being discharged into the sea. International specifications for the equipment have been established, and only approved types may be used on board. The equipment must come into operation whenever a discharge takes place. The discharge of segregated and clean ballast (except from CBT tankers) need not be monitored. The equipment must halt the discharge automatically when the permitted quantity of oil or the permitted number of litres of oil per mile has been reached.

The task to be performed requires complicated equipment. Not only must the oil content of the effluent be measured, a difficult enough task, but the discharge rate of the pumps over a wide range of output and the speed of the ship must also be recorded. A computer is needed to transfer input into output, i.e. total quantity of oil and instantaneous rate of discharge (litre of oil per mile). Output must be recorded and the time of discharge must be identified. The principles involved are described briefly below.

An oil discharge monitor and control system consists essentially of four systems:

- An oil content meter that is able to analyse the relative content of oil in the water stream, expressed in parts per million (PPM)

应确保在大多数情况下,不需要额外压载,同时,CBT设在船的两侧,以便对由于碰撞引起的油污染提供一定程度的防护作用。该措施是临时性的,仅适用于1980年前建造、40 000载重吨及以上的成品油船。在实际中,对于现有船体结构,货舱布置很难符合吃水差和吃水深度的要求。经常有必要利用尖舱和隔离舱来压载,以满足这些要求。

CBT与SBT一个重要的不同方面是泵和管系的使用。具有CBT的油船可能不得不在货物操作中或之后,利用货物泵和管系进行压载,泵和管路不得不进行充分冲洗,以避免污染压载水。这些冲洗水不可能排到海里,而且不像无CBT的船,也不能排到压载舱里,因为压载舱已经在较早阶段被彻底净化并必须保持清洁。泵和管路的冲洗水因此必须排到污液舱内。由于这个原因,污液舱即使在载货航行时也必须留有一定的空间。设有CBT的油船,必须提供CBT操作手册,操作手册中应设有为特种油船设置的管路冲洗程序。

许多CBT油船有特定的压载系统供CBT使用,这些操作与在SBT油船上的操作很相似。必须注意防止油从货物管路进入压载舱,在货物和压载水之间应有双向阀隔断。

设备要求

排油监控装置

排放规定限制从货舱区域排放入海的总油量和油的瞬时排放率。为使油船遵守,必须配有检测装置。排放法规还规定当油水混合物排放入海时,这个装置应投入工作。已经建立了该设备的国际规范,只有经过型式认可后才能应用在船上。只要进行排放,该装置就应投入工作。排放专用和清洁压载水(除了从CBT油船)不需要检测。当达到了允许的排油总量或每海里允许的排油量,该装置应立即自动停止排放。

要完成这样的工作需要复杂的设备。不仅必须要测量排出物的含油量,这已经很难了,而且还应该记录泵在大范围输出内的排放速率以及航速。计算机用来把输入转变成输出,也就是,排油总量和油的瞬时排放率(升每海里)。必须记录输出和明确排放时间。包含的原理简述如下。

排油监控系统主要由四部分组成:

- 一个能分析水流中油分相对含量的油分浓度计,以百万分数(PPM)来表示

- A flow meter that is able to measure the flow rate of oily water through the discharge pipe
- A computing unit that is able to calculate the oil discharge rate in litres per nautical mile and total quantity, together with date and time identification
- An overboard valve control system that is able to stop the discharge when the permissible limit has been reached

It is difficult to monitor oil content of water, considering the small concentrations of oil involved and the many disturbing factors (such as widely varying properties of oil, other contaminants in the water and a hostile environment for the equipment).

The most accurate technique for determining the oil content of water is based on analysis of the absorption of infrared light. The absorption of infrared light of a controlled wavelength (about 3.4 μm) is fairly independent of the type of the oil, but the method cannot be used accurately whilst the oil droplets are suspended in water since water also absorbs infrared radiation. The oil is therefore normally extracted in a suitable solvent that is non-soluble in water, such as carbon tetrachloride. This method of oil content measurement cannot easily be adapted to shipboard use because of the need for continuous analysis within a short time.

More practical methods have therefore been adopted for use on board ships. Most are based on optical principles, such as measuring the discolouration or turbidity of the water caused by the oil droplets. The principles employed and other features of these instruments are summarized below.

Ultraviolet fluorescence

This principle was employed in the original ballast monitor. It was based on the phenomenon that molecules of unsaturated hydrocarbons become excited when illuminated with ultraviolet light of a certain wavelength and will then radiate light in the visible spectrum. The method is sensitive to the size of the droplets but is rather insensitive to other impurities in the oil. The main disadvantage, however, is that different oils contain different amounts of unsaturated hydrocarbons, so that the instrument must be calibrated each time for the type of oil being monitored. A considerable number of instruments of this type are installed in tankers, but the model has been discontinued and current production is concentrated on meters working on other principles.

Turbidity meters

If an oil/water mixture with low oil content is heavily agitated so that the oil droplets become very small, the water will turn 'milky' to varying degrees, depending on the amount of oil present; the actual colour of the oil droplets is of no importance. This method can be used for indicating the oil content, provided the conditions for homogenizing the sample are well controlled. If a light beam is projected through a test cell containing sample water with well-homogenized droplets, part of the light passing through the cell will be scattered. The intensity of light picked up by a photocell at the end of a straight path through the cell will be reduced, whereas the intensity of scattered light sensed by a photocell mounted at an angle to the original path will increase. Laser light may be used to obtain a well-defined light beam and possibly a selective light-scattering effect.

- 一个能够测量通过排出管的油水流量的流量表
- 一个能计算每海里排油速率(升每海里)及排油总量的计算单元,同时标明日期和时间
- 当达到允许极限值时一个出海阀控制系统能停止排放

由于水中含油浓度很小并且受到许多干扰因素(比如,油的特性变化很大,水中其他的污染物以及设备所处的恶劣的环境)的影响,检测水中含油量是很难的。

检测水中油分含量的最准确的方法是分析红外线的吸收。吸收一定波长(大约3.4微米)的红外线是油的特性,但是,当油滴悬浮在水中时,这种方法不是很准确,因为水也能吸收红外线。因此,把油萃取到一个适当的、在水中不乳化的溶液中,像四氯化碳。因为需要在短时间连续进行分析,所以这种油分监测方法应用在船上很不容易。

因此,船上应用的方法应该更加实际可行。绝大多数基于光学原理,比如测量油滴中水分引起的色变或浑浊度。这些仪器依据的原理及其特点总结如下。

<u>紫外线萤光法</u>

这种原理应用在最初的压载水检测中。它是基于不饱和碳氢化合物分子在一定波长的紫外线照射下变得活跃,而在可视范围内发光的现象。这种方法对油滴的大小敏感,但对油中其他杂质特别不敏感。然而,主要的缺点是不同的油含有不同数量的不饱和碳氢化合物,因此,针对每次检测的油类型不同,该仪器必须要进行校准。油船上安装了许多这种仪器,但是现在已不再广泛使用这种仪器,而流行的是基于另一种原理的仪器。

<u>浊度计</u>

如果充分搅动油分较低的油水混合物,使油滴变得很小,水将乳化到不同程度,这取决于水中油的数量,实际油滴的颜色并不重要。如果能控制好水样均质化的条件,这种方法可以用来测定油分含量。如果一束照射在装有油滴很均匀的水样的容器上,通过容器的部分光就会散射。装在容器末端的光电单元吸收的直射光强度降低,而由装在与直射光成一定角度的光电单元接收的散射光强度增加。激光可用于获取光束并且可能具有选择性散射效果。

This principle is used in one oil content meter currently available, in which the light beam and the signals picked up by the photocells are transmitted via optical fibres to the electronic part in the engine-room, thereby making the bulkhead penetrations quite small.

A similar instrument, operating with infrared light, is also available.

A third instrument, based on the turbidity principle, operates only on the direct transmitted light through the test cell in which the heavily agitated sample water circulates.

Instruments of this type can measure oils ranging from heavy crude oils to gasoline, but some changes in the calibration are required to cover the extremes of the range. As the instruments measure the number of particles in the water, they are rather sensitive to other contaminants such as rust or air bubbles.

Light absorption and gas measurement

An instrument working on a different principle has also been developed. It is based on a three-step principle:

1. Filtering out the oil in a lipophilic filter tape
2. Determining the discolouration of the tape
3. Determining the amount of gas evaporating from the tape when it is heated

A sample stream of oily water is passed through the tape, which absorbs all of the oil. Solid particles are left on the lower side of the tape. Heavy oils create strong discolouration of the tape but give off a small amount of gas, whereas light oils behave in the opposite way. By adding the signals from the two measuring channels in selected proportions, an output signal is obtained which is relatively insensitive to the type of oil. The instrument is rather more complex mechanically than the others, and has a running cost, as the filter tape is being consumed. However, it is less sensitive to rust and air bubbles than the other types.

The absorption of infrared light by oil can also be measured. As infrared absorption by the background water is also high, an oil-free reference water of relevant quality must be obtained at all times; this is done by purifying a small part of the water in a micro-filter. The infrared absorption by the oily water and by the oil–free water can then be measured. The difference is caused by absorption by the oil and that signal can be calibrated in oil content.

Arrangement of the system

The monitoring and control system must be equipped with a starting interlock arrangement whereby the overboard valves can only be opened when the monitor is in operation. This requirement is waived for small tankers with manual valve operation.

The system information is normally recorded by a digital printer, which does not deliver a continuous record in the true sense. The specifications therefore lay down the minimum requirements for print-out at certain time intervals, at certain changes in the various parameters, when alarm levels are reached, etc.

该原理现在已应用于一种油分浓度计中，光束和光电单元测取的信号在机舱内由光纤维转变成电子信号,因此使隔壁渗透很小。

一种使用红外线的相似仪器也在使用中。

第三种仪器基于浊度原理,其仅直接测取穿过容器的透射光的强度,充分搅动的水样在取样器中循环。

这种类型的仪器从重油到汽油都可使用,但要对刻度进行一些调整以覆盖测量范围的极值。由于该仪器测量的是水中颗粒物的数量,因此对其他诸如灰尘或气泡污染物也很敏感。

光吸收和油气测量

一种利用不同工作原理的仪器已被研制出来。它基于三个步骤:

1. 用亲油性滤纸过滤出油分
2. 确定滤纸的变色的程度
3. 确定当滤纸被加热时从滤纸蒸发出来的气体的数量

含油水样流过滤纸,所有的油被吸收在滤纸上。固体颗粒留在滤纸的下面,重油使滤纸严重变色,但释放的油气少,而轻油正好相反。把从两个测量管路测得的信号加入选择好的比例器,就可得到一个对油的种类相对不太敏感的输出信号。这种仪器在机械方面比其他类型的要复杂得多。因为滤纸被消耗了,所以增加了运行费用。然而,它对灰尘和气泡的敏感度比其他类型的仪器要小。

可以测量到被油吸收的红外线。因为水对红外线的吸收也很强,因此必须一直提供适量无油的水作为参照,参照水可通过在细滤器中过滤一小部分水来获取。这样就可测取被油水混合物及被无油水分别吸收的红外线。两者之差就是被油吸收的红外线,这个信号能量化成含油量。

系统的布置

监控系统必须设置一个起动连锁装置,这样,只有当检测系统投入工作时,出海阀才能打开。对设有手动操作阀的小型油船不作此项要求。

系统信息正常由数字打印机记录,实际中并不连续记录。因此,规范制定了在一定间隔时间内最低打印要求,即在各种参数发生某些变化时以及当达到警报值时打印。

Oil/water interface detector

When decanting slop-tanks, which is an essential operation during LOT procedures, it is necessary to determine the height of the oil/water interface in order to prevent oil from being discharged into the sea. Interface detectors are usually portable, although permanently installed equipment is also used. International specifications have been drawn up, and only equipment that complies with these standards may be used.

The equipment, in this case a portable instrument, consists of a metal tape measure, an ampere meter, a zinc weight and an earthing clamp to connect the equipment to the ship's structure. The principle is that, when the weight is suspended in salt water, galvanic action between the zinc and the steel structure of the ship generates an electric current, which is indicated on the meter. When the zinc weight is suspended in oil, no current is generated. By lowering the zinc weight and registering the height at which the current starts to flow, it is possible to determine the interface. In practice, the weight is first lowered through the oil into the water, to clean the oil from it; it is then raised until the meter shows zero current, indicating the interface.

Matters related to air pollution

Rules to control air pollution from engine exhaust emissions are contained in Annex VI of MARPOL. The loading and ballasting of tanks may cause air pollution from oil tanker operations, as these operations result in inert gas and hydrocarbon gas being vented to the outside atmosphere. Another operation resulting in air pollution is gas freeing. If local regulations limit air pollution, special measures must be taken. These can take two forms, a vapour-return line or gas/vapour displacement. Vapour return entails transferring all gas displaced from cargo tanks to the installation ashore; this requires special provisions that are not normally found on oil tankers.

Gas/vapour displacement is not always possible. If a ship is being discharged and cargo tanks are being ballasted, it is possible to contain the gas/vapour. In this case the venting system is closed to the outside atmosphere and the inert gas will be driven from the tanks being ballasted to those being discharged. The supply of inert gas must be adjusted to keep a slight positive pressure in the tanks.

Enhanced surveys

Since 1995 all tankers aged five years and over have been subject to a specially enhanced inspection programme, which is intended to ensure that any deficiencies such as corrosion or wear and tear resulting from age or neglect are detected. This regulation applies to crude carriers of 20,000 DWT and above and product carriers of 30,000 DWT and above. It applies to inspections during periodical, intermediate and annual surveys. Tankers that are five years old or more will have to carry on board a complete file of survey reports together with a condition evaluation report endorsed by the flag Administration.

Emergency towing arrangements

Amendments to SOLAS 1974 Chapter 11-1 regulation 3-4 require since January 1996 all new tankers of 20,000 DWT and above to be fitted with an emergency towing arrangement fitted

油水分界面的探测器

作为LOT程序中的一项关键操作,当清空污油舱时,有必要检测油水分界面的高度以防止油被排到海里。分界面探测器一般为便携式的,尽管也使用固定式的。国际规范已经规定只有符合这些标准的设备才可使用。

便携式探测器由一个金属卷尺、一个安培表、一块锌块和一个连接这个设备和船体的接地夹子组成。原理是:当锌块悬浮在海水中时,在锌块和船体之间由于原电池作用产生一个电流,这可由安培表显示出来。当锌块悬浮在油中时,没有电流产生。通过放低锌块并且记录开始产生电流的高度,由此可确定油水分界面。实践中,先把锌块从油中降低至水中,洗掉上面的油;然后开始升高锌块的位置,直至安培表显示电流为零,此时即可显示油水分界面。

与空气污染有关的问题

MARPOL公约附则Ⅵ包含了控制发动机排放所造成大气污染的规则。油船操作引起的空气污染可能由装货和压载等操作造成的,因为这些操作导致惰性气体和碳氢化合物气体被排放到大气中。另一个空气污染的操作是除气操作。如果当地法规限制大气污染,则必须采取特殊措施。这些措施有两种形式,采用气体回流管路或油气/气体置换法。气体回流必须把所有的油气从货舱转移到岸上,该项操作需要油船上一般没有的特殊设备。

油气/气体转移并非总是可行,当船正在卸货,而货舱正在压载,可能含有油气/气体。在这种情况下,通风系统对外关闭,惰性气体将从正在压载的舱排到正在卸货的舱中。必须调整惰性气体的供应量,以保证舱内正压。

加强检验

自从1995年起,船龄在5年及以上的油船要进行一次加强检验,目的是要确保检测出任何缺陷像腐蚀、磨损和由于老化或忽略保养造成的裂口。该规定适用于20 000载重吨及以上的原油油船和30 000载重吨及以上的成品油船。它适合于期间检验、中间检验和年度检验。船龄在5年及以上的油船要在船上携带完整的检验报告文件以及船旗国签发的船舶状态评估报告。

应急拖带装备

SOLAS1974修正案中11-1章规则3-4要求自从1996年1月起,所有20 000载重吨及以上的新造

at both ends of the ship. Existing ships must be fitted no later than 1st January 1999. The towing arrangements are to comply with Classification Society rules.

Level gauges

Level gauges have important safety, environmental and commercial effects on oil tanker operations. A description is given here of the different types commonly in use on oil tankers and terminals.

Types of gauge

Mechanically operated float gauges

In this type of gauge, the detecting element is a float. The power to actuate the mechanism comes partly from the movement of the float and partly from the balancing mechanism.

The float is connected to the mechanism by means of a tape or other mechanical or magnetic linkage.

The float is connected to the measuring tape, which runs over a pulley system to enter the gauge head. Inside the gauge head the tape passes over a sprocket wheel driving a counter mechanism, and thence on to a storage drum. A spring, which winds off a storage drum on to a power drum connected to the tape storage drum, keeps the tape under tension without lifting the float clear of the product. As the liquid level in the container rises, the tension applied to the tape by the spring takes up the slack on the tape. On the better types of gauge, the spring tension increases as the liquid level falls, in order to compensate for the additional weight of tape used.

Electrically powered servo-operated gauges

With this type of gauge the detecting element is a surface-sensing device, which follows the variations of level by means of a servo-mechanism. Indication of level can be by various electrical or mechanical methods.

The sensing head is usually designed to sense the liquid surface and to indicate to the control unit the distance from that surface. The control unit endeavours to keep the head at a fixed distance above the product by controlling the driving motor. The tape would actually pass over a sprocket wheel driving a counter mechanism.

Electrical capacitance gauges – comparative types

These gauges measure the liquid level by comparing the electrical capacitance of a partially immersed element with that of a fully immersed, similar element by means of a bridge circuit.

Other types of electrical capacitance gauges

This is a general grouping of all capacitance gauges. They measure the liquid level by means of the differences in dielectric permittivity between the product to be measured and the vapour.

油船应在船首、尾两端安装应急拖带装备,现有的油船必须在1999年1月前安装完毕。拖带装备应符合船级社的规定。

液位计

液位计对油船操作的安全、环境和商业都有重要的影响。在本节中,将介绍在油船和码头上广泛应用的不同类型的液位计。

液位计的类型

机械浮子式液位计

在这种类型的表中,测量元件是一个浮子。带动机械装置的动力部分来自于浮子的运动,部分来自平衡机械装置。

浮子通过线带或其他机械或磁力连接方式连接在机械装置上。

浮子被连接在测量线带上,线带通过一个滑轮系统进入表头。在表头里面,线带通过一个驱动计数器机构的链轮,然后连到储带转筒上。动力转鼓与储带转鼓相连,在弹簧作用下,动力转鼓动作,从而使储带转鼓转动,以便使线带保持绷紧状态,并恰好使浮子不离开油面。随着容器中液位增加,弹簧传递给卷尺的张力逐渐拉起线带松弛的一端。在该类型中比较好的液位计中,弹簧张力随着液位下降而增大以补偿所用线带的附加重量。

电动伺服液位计

在这种仪表中,测量元件是一个表面感应装置,借助一个伺服机构追随液位变化。可用各种电的或机械的方法来显示液位。

一般地,将设计成触头用来感应液体表面以及显示该表面到控制机构之间的距离。控制机构通过控制驱动马达来尽量保持触头在油面以上的某个固定位置。实际上,卷尺将通过一个带动记数器机构的链轮。

电容式液位计——比较型

这种表是通过桥式电路,将一个部分浸入元件的电容与一个全部浸入的相似元件的电容相比较而得出液位。

其他类型的电容式液位计

这是针对所有电容液位计的通用分类,它们是根据要测量的油与气体之间的介电常数的不同来测量液位。

In this case, the sensor usually consists of a wire or single element, the capacitance of which changes according to the amount of product present.

Bubbler gauges

In this type of gauge measuring the backpressure generated by the injection of a gas or vapour derives the head of a liquid of known density. This pressure is normally displayed at the required position on a manometer that is calibrated directly in level units.

It will be noted that the manometer must be compensated for the tank pressure, otherwise level readings will be completely erroneous.

Pneumatic or hydraulic level gauges using a closed cell

In these gauges a pressure-sensitive cell is located near the bottom of the container, and changes in pressure are transmitted by electronic, pneumatic or hydraulic means to a remote location. The capillary system is usually compensated for normal changes in ambient temperature.

Other differential-pressure methods

These methods of level measurement use pressure transducers of various types to measure the hydrostatic pressure at the bottom of the container and at the same time correct the reading for the internal tank pressure, as measured at the top of the container.

Sonic gauges

There are several types of level gauge using this principle. The most commonly available types measure the time difference between a transmitted signal and its reflection from the liquid surface. Gauges can be mounted on the tank top or at the bottom of the tank.

Radioactive methods

In these methods the level is read by measuring the attenuation of radiation by the product. Several methods are employed. Fig. 22 shows three possible arrangements. In (a) a single source and a single detector are used, the attenuation of the radiation being measured to ascertain the liquid level. In (b), indication is in comparatively large steps, each radioactive source being associated with its own detection device. The third method has a single source emitting a fan-shaped beam in the tank. The direct radiation and that attenuated by the product are both measured to determine the liquid level in the tank.

Caution

Radioactive sources can involve a considerable health hazard to operating personnel, and every necessary precaution must be taken.

在这种情况下,传感器通常包含一根导线或单个电极,其电容量随油的数量变化而变化。

气泡式

在这种类型表中,通过测量因喷入油气或气体而产生的背压可以测得已知密度液体的压头。该压力一般会显示在要求的压力计位置上,这个压力计直接把这个压力转换成液位。

应该注意,压力计必须补偿舱内压力,否则,液位读数将完全错误。

使用闭式传感元件的气动或液压式液位计

在这些表中,将一个感压包放置在舱底附近,压力的变化通过电的、气压或液压的方式传递到远处。毛细管系统应因环境温度的变化而应修正。

其他压差方法

这些液位测量方法是使用不同类型的压力转换器来测量舱底部的静压,同时根据舱顶部测得的舱内压力修正这个读数。

声波液位计

有多种液位计利用该原理。最常用的类型是测量从发射器发出信号到接收器收到从液面返回的信号所用的时间。仪表可以装在舱顶部或底部。

放射的方法

在这种方法中,通过测量被油吸收的射线数量来测取液位。这里采用了几种方法。图22显示了三种可能的结构方案。在(a)中,采用单个发射源和单个检测器,测量射线的减少以确定液位高度。在(b)中,步骤相对多一些,每一个发射源对应自己的检测装置。第三种方法有一个单发射源在油舱里发射扇形射线。直接发射的射线和被油吸收的射线都应测量以确定油舱内的液位高度。

注意

放射源对操作人员的身体有一定的损害,必须采取必要的预防措施。

Surface-sensing-type devices

This group covers gauges which cannot be placed under other headings and which depend upon measurable differences in physical properties between the vapour and liquid phases of the product. Measuring elements capable of detecting these differences (e.g. in thermal conductivity, electrical capacitance) are located in the container, thus enabling the liquid level to be determined.

Caution

The user must be careful not to confuse the terms "accuracy" and "repeatability", and cautious about manufacturers' claims of accuracy.

Fundamental measuring accuracy is important, but it is less vital to the user than good repeatability, which is the ability of an instrument to reproduce results under all conditions. An instrument with good repeatability may have a considerable constant error, for which allowance can be made. On the other hand, an instrument with very good statistical accuracy may have poor repeatability; in this case many readings may have to be taken before any reliance can be placed on the results.

Factors affecting accuracy and repeatability

Friction

Friction, the cause of hysteresis in mechanical systems, may increase during the life of a level gauge owing to corrosion, wear, lack of lubrication, etc. The effects of changes in friction will be minimized in a well-designed instrument. One must not forget that some systems also suffer from hysteresis in resolution, although servo-operated gauges are free from this source of error.

Manufacturing tolerances

These are always present in both mechanical and electronic systems; indeed, tolerance variations of 20% are common in electronic components. Mechanical apparatus and electronic circuits should be designed to minimize errors from this source. Where necessary, selected low-tolerance components must be used.

Product density

Changes in product density affect many types of gauge; float gauges will require correction and capacitance gauges will need to be recalibrated unless they are of the comparative type, as will any type using a pressure head. Radioactive gauges are also affected by density.

Product impurities

Small amounts of water and other impurities in the product cause wide changes in readings from capacitance gauges, even comparative types.

表面感应型装置

该类仪表包括了不能归到其他类型中的液位计，这些液位测量装置取决于气态油和液态油之间可测量的物理特性的差别。能检测这些差别(如导热性、电容等)的测量元件被装在舱内,这样能够测量液位。

注意
使用者必须注意不要混淆“准确性”和“重复性”的含义,并且注意制造商对精度的保证。

基本测量精度是很重要的,但是,对使用者来说,良好的重复性更加重要,即在所有的状态下仪器重复结果的能力。重复性好的仪器可能在允许范围内有相当多的恒定误差,即允许产生的误差。另一方面,精度高的仪器重复性可能较差,在这种情况下,许多读数在可信度没确定前不得不进行多次测量。

影响准确性和重复性的因素:

<u>摩擦</u>

摩擦是机械和电气系统中产生滞后的原因,在液位计使用过程中,由于腐蚀、磨损、缺少润滑的原因,可能造成摩擦增加。经过良好设计的仪器会尽量减少摩擦变化的影响。要记住有些系统也会由于摩擦导致动作迟钝,尽管伺服式仪表不会因这种原因造成误差。

<u>制造公差</u>

在机械和电气系统中总存在制造公差。事实上，在电气元件中一般公差为20%左右是常见的。机械装置和电路应该设计成尽量减少由于这种原因造成的误差。必要的场合,必须使用低公差元件。

<u>产品密度</u>

产品密度的变化影响许多类型的仪表,浮子式仪表要求修正,电容式仪表需要重新校准,除非是使用对比型仪表或使用压头型仪表。放射型仪表也受密度的影响。

<u>产品中的杂质</u>

产品中少量的水和其他杂质对电容型仪表,甚至比较型仪表的读数影响较大。

Installation

Installation probably has a greater effect on performance and reliability than any other factor. Most manufacturers suffer from installation being carried out by contractors who employ apparently uninformed personnel. Poor alignment of pulleys, poor lubrication, overlubrication, paint applied where there should be no paint, electronic equipment left exposed to the elements (sometimes for months), bolts over tightened, bolts left loose or even missing, physical damage from accident or sometimes deliberate maltreatment – these are some of the many troubles that can occur.

Cargo calculations

In the above section of this appendix different systems for measuring ullage have been examined. Ullage, in combination with the calibration tables, enables determination of the volume of oil on board. Important though this information may be, it is only one step towards calculating the mass of the cargo, a factor usually of more importance to the ship. Calculations of deadweight, freeboard, trim, stability and stress need information on mass rather than volume, it is therefore essential that volume be converted to mass.

The relationship between the volume and the mass or weight can be expressed by the density at 15 ℃ (vacuum). The density represents the mass per volume unit at 15 ℃, expressed in kg per litre. If a certain volume is observed in a cargo tank with a measured temperature, called the gross observed volume (G.O.V.), this volume is corrected to a volume at 15 ℃ with the aid of the appropriate ASTM table (table 54). The resulting gross standard volume (G.S.V.) is expressed in litres.

The mass or weight in vacuo is calculated by multiplying the G.S.V. with the given density at 15°C (vacuo).

Using the ASTM table 56 the weight in vacuo can be corrected to weight in air as a function of the given density.

The American oil industry uses another scale of mass/volume ratio. This is known as the API scale, which is an arbitrary scale derived from the formula:

$$API = \frac{141.5}{R.D.\ at\ 60\ °F} - 131.5$$

Note that API goes up as the R.D. goes down.

The fact that different units may be used when conveying information on quantities of oil is a possible source of misunderstanding. When exchanging messages, it should be made unequivocally clear which units are being used. With respect to volume and quantity, the following units are in common use:

- Barrels (of 42 US gallons) cubic feet
- Cubic metres
- Imperial and US gallons tonnes of 1,000 kg

安装

安装对仪表的性能和可靠性的影响可能比其他任何因素都大。大多数产品制造商都苦于由于承包商雇佣明显不熟练的人员安装所造成的损坏。滑轮对中不良、润滑差、过度润滑、不该刷油漆的地方刷油漆、电子装置露在元件外面(有时达数月之久)、螺丝上得太紧、螺丝松动或甚至脱落、由于事故或有时人为不正规使用造成的损坏——这些都是可能发生的问题。

货物计算

在本附录的上述内容中,已经了解了测量空挡量的不同方法。空挡量,结合修正表能够确定船上存油体积。尽管这个资料可能很重要,但它只是计算货物重量的一步,货物重量对于船舶来讲通常是一个更加重要的参数。总载重量、空船、吃水差、稳性和应力的计算都需要以质量参数为基准而不是体积,因此把体积转变质量非常重要。

体积和质量或重量间的关系可由15 ℃时的密度(真空)来表示。密度代表在15 ℃时的单位体积的质量,表示为kg/L。如果在测定的温度下测得某一货舱体积,称为测量总体积(G.O.V.),通过参照ASTM表(表54),将该总体积修正为15 ℃时的体积。该标准总体积(G.S.V.)的单位是升。

真空状态下的质量或重量由G.S.V.与给定的15 ℃时(真空)的密度相乘来计算。

利用ASTM表56,在给定密度的作用下,可以把真空中的重量修正为空气中的重量。

美国油工业使用另一种质量/容积比的标度,即大家熟知的API标度,它是由以下公式得到的议定标度:

$$API = \frac{141.5}{R.D.\ at\ 60\ ℉} - 131.5$$

注意:API随R.D.下降而增加。

在传递货物数量资料时,可能用到不同的单位,这很容易造成误解。当交换资料时,应标明所使用的单位。对于体积和质量,通常使用下面的单位:

- 桶(42美国标准加仑)立方英尺
- 立方米
- 英国标准加仑和美国标准加仑,吨(1 000 kg)

- Tonnes of 2240 lbs (avoirdupois)
- Tonnes of 2000 lbs (avoirdupois)

The use of these widely varying units means that books must be available on board for converting one into the other.

Pump theory and characteristics

Pump theory

Strictly speaking, a pump does not draw up a liquid, but rather creates a vacuum on the suction side, allowing atmospheric pressure to push the liquid into the pump. In theory, a pump could therefore draw up a liquid column corresponding to the atmospheric pressure, which equals about 10 metres of water (for which the relative density is 1).

In practice, the situation is different. Theoretical suction height is influenced in a positive way by atmospheric pressure, inert gas pressure and the height of liquid in the tank; it is negatively influenced by the net positive suction head (NPSH) of the pumps, frictional losses in the pipelines, true vapour pressure of the liquid being pumped, and the height of pump and suction piping above the tank bottom. All of these can be expressed in metres liquid column.

The NPSH of a pump is a combination of friction and vacuum losses associated with a particular pump on board. Decreasing fluid velocity through a pump, i.e. by decreasing the flow, can reduce these losses.

Piping friction is caused by the liquid passing through the suction piping, and depends on the length of piping, the number of valves, bends and fluid velocity. Again, decreasing the flow may reduce frictional losses. The height of the liquid column can be improved by trimming the ship.

The order of magnitude of the different factors involved is shown in the table below. Disregarding the column of liquid in the tank, the sum of negative factors will equal or nearly equal 10 metres for a liquid of relative density 1, whatever combination of factors is taken.

Factor	Liquid Column	Remarks
NPSH	4 – m	Single-stage pump
Pipeline friction	1 – 5 m or more	Depending on tank, number of valves and bends
Vapour pressure	5 – 9 m	Gulf area crude
Pump + line above bottom	2 – 2.5 m	Depending on ship type
Trim	0 – 3.5 m	Depending on location of tank and phase of discharge
Liquid level	0 – tank height	Depending on phase of discharge
Atmospheric pressure	Approx. 10 m	Depending on weather and inert gas

- 英吨–2240磅(常衡制)
- 美吨–2000磅(常衡制)

有这么多不同的单位在使用,所以要求船上备有一本这方面的书,以便在换算时使用。

泵理论和特性

泵理论

严格地讲,泵本身并不能吸入液体,只是在吸入口处建立真空,允许大气把液体压入泵内。理论上,泵能够把液体推到相当于一个大气压的液柱高度,即相当于10米水柱(水的相对密度为1)。

在实际中,情况有所不同。理论吸高受到大气压力、惰性气体压力及液体在舱内的高度的正作用方式影响,而受到泵的净正吸入压头(NPSH)、管路中的摩擦阻力损失、要泵送的液体的实际蒸发压力、泵及吸入管系在舱底之上的高度的副作用方式影响。所有这些都可表示为多少米液柱。

对船上特定的泵,泵的NPSH就是摩擦和真空损失之和。通过降低流过泵的液体速度,也就是降低流量,可以降低这些损失。

管路摩擦阻力损失是由液体流经吸入管时引起的,取决于管长、阀和弯头数量及液体流速。摩擦阻力损失可能通过降低流量而减少,液柱高度可以通过调整船的吃水差而改善。

如下表所示为不同参数的大小顺序。忽略液体在舱内的高度,负参数总和等于或近似等于相对密度为1的液体的10米高液柱,也就是所有考虑参数的水头之和。

因素	液柱高度(米)	备注
NPSH	4 – 5 m	单级泵
管路摩擦	1 – 5 m,或更大	取决于油舱、阀和弯头数
蒸发压力	5 – 9 m	海湾区域石油
泵与管系在舱底之上高度	2 – 2.5 m	取决于船的类型
吃水差	0 – 3.5 m	取决于舱位置和排放顺序
液位	0 – 舱的高度	取决于排放顺序
大气压力 大约	大约 10 m	取决于天气和惰性气体

It will be clear that there will be suction when positive factors are larger than the negative ones. If the opposite holds true, there will be cavitation, and suction stops.

P + *H* + *h* > NPSH + LF + TVP	pumping normal
P + *H* + *h* = NPSH + LF + TVP	cavitation begins
P + *H* + *h* < NPSH + LF + TVP	no suction

As the maximum available suction head is approached, bubble pressure is reached and vapour forms throughout the liquid, i.e. the liquid boils. During a short period of time a liquid/vapour mixture of varying relative density is created. The resulting fluctuations in pressure (caused by the liquid column being drawn in) and in pump power can be observed as fluctuations in discharge pressure and in revolutions of the pump.

Cavitation occurs and the rattle of imploding bubbles can be heard distinctly. Since a mixture of liquid and vapour is being pumped, the liquid velocity in the suction piping decreases, line resistance decreases and suction is maintained for a short while. Soon only vapour will be drawn in and the flow will stop, even though a considerable quantity of oil may remain in the tank.

If the pump is to be kept working, both NPSH and line resistance may be influenced by reducing the discharge rate. The lower liquid velocity reduces both line resistance and NPSH, ensuring that the bubble–point pressure is not reached.

Pump characteristics

The characteristics of a given pump can best be seen in a set of curves for a set pump speed; several sets are usually given to cover a range of speeds. Fig. 24 shows such pump characteristics of a centrifugal pump running at 1,800 revolutions per minute.

The vertical axis shows the scales for the various curves, while the horizontal axis shows the discharge rate as a function of head, expressed in metres of liquid column. To every pump speed there is an *Q-H* curve, which gives the relationship between head and discharge rate. If the head is known, it is possible to determine the discharge rate. Head, it should be noted, is not equal to backpressure. To convert backpressure into head, the difference between backpressure and suction pressure should be converted into metres water gauge and divided by the relative density of the liquid being pumped. The design point marked on the curve represents the most economical working condition of the pump. This is also reflected in the efficiency curve (EFF). Other curves to be seen are NPSH and power consumption of the pump in horsepower (HP).

At 1800 rpm, the pump is operating somewhere along the *Q-H* curve. The actual point depends on where the *Q-H* curve crosses the shore curve, which represents the pressure a pump has to work against. The pressure is partially static, depending on the difference in height between liquid levels ashore and on board, and partially dynamic, owing to line resistance. Fig. 25 shows the relationship and the common points between the curves, reflecting the discharge rates for one pump working against shore curve 1 and shore curve 2.

Pumps running in parallel have a common *Q-H* curve, which can be constructed by adding the curves horizontally. It is interesting to note that if the shore curve is steep, i.e. if backpressure is high, the difference in output between one pump and more than one pump is not great, in

非常清楚,当正参数大于负参数时,泵能吸入。如果与实际情况相反,泵将发生气蚀,并且不能吸入。

$P+H+h>$ NPSH+LF+TVP　　泵正常

$P+H+h=$ NPSH+LF+TVP　　气蚀开始

$P+H+h<$ NPSH+LF+TVP　　无吸入

随着吸入压头达到最大值,液体达到汽化压力,液体变成气体,也就是液体汽化。短时间内产生了相对密度变化的气液混合物,最后的压力波动(由吸入液柱引起)和泵的功率波动可以通过排出压力和泵的转速的波动显示出来。

可以明显听到发生气蚀和气泡破碎的声音。由于泵正在输送气液混合物,所以在吸入管内液体速度下降,管路内阻力损失下降,泵在短时间内保持吸入。很快,尽管舱内仍然有大量的油,但此时仅有气体被吸入而液体流动停止。

如果要泵保持工作,NPSH和管路阻力可能会受排放速率降低的影响。降低液体流速能减少NPSH和管路阻力,确保达不到汽化压力。

泵的特性

通过定速下测定的一系列曲线可以清楚地看到给定的泵的特性,在一定的转速范围内测定多条特性曲线。图24显示离心泵在1 800 r/min时的特性。

纵坐标表示不同曲线的标度,横坐标表示排量,即扬程的一个函数,可表示为米液柱。泵在不同转速下都有一个表示扬程与流量的关系的*Q-H*特性曲线。如果已知扬程,则可以算出流量。应该注意到扬程并不相当于背压。为把背压转变成扬程,背压与吸入压力之差应转变成米水柱,再除以输送液体的相对密度。曲线上标注的工况点代表泵的最经济的工作状态。从效率曲线(EFF)上也可以看出这一点。其他的还有NPSH及功率特性曲线,功率单位为马力(HP)。

在1 800 r/min,泵工作于*Q-H*特性曲线上的某一点。实际的工况点取决于*Q-H*特性曲线与接岸管路特性曲线的交点,代表泵要克服的压力。这个压力部分为静压头,它取决于岸上和船上的液位高度差;部分为由于管路阻力引起的动压头。图25表示这种关系,曲线之间的交点反映泵分别工作在管路特性曲线1和曲线2时的流量。

并联运行的泵有共同的特性曲线*Q-H*,可以通过把每个泵的曲线沿水平方向叠加而成。有趣的是,如果管路特性曲线很陡,也就是说背压高,那么,一个泵与一个具有上述特性的泵并联后的

contrast to the situation where the shore curve is more gradually inclined, representing low backpressure.

Emergency Procedures

Emergency plan

All personnel on board oil tankers must know the sound and the character of the different alarms on board and the action they should take if they hear them.

General emergency alarm

Continuous sounding of alarm bells:
Action – all personnel to go immediately to their lifeboat stations.

Seven short blasts followed by one long blast repeated on whistle:
Action – launch of lifeboats, abandon ship.

Fire alarm

Intermittent sounding of alarm bells:
Action – all personnel to go immediately to their fire station.

Carbon dioxide alarm

Continuous sound from typhone:
Action – all personnel to go immediately to their fire stations.

(The alarm is situated in the pump-room, engine-room or other space, which is covered by the CO_2 fire-extinguishing system.)

Other alarms of importance

These include:

- Inert gas alarm
- High-level alarm (liquid level in tank) alarms in engine-room
- Alarms on bridge
- Alarms in accommodation
- Alarms in galley

流量差别并不大。而与背压低的、管路特性曲线平缓的泵并联时则情况相反。

应急程序

应急计划

油船上所有人员必须知道船上警报声及不同警报的特征,并且听到警报声后应立即采取行动。

一般应急警报

连续的警报铃响:
行动——所有人员立刻到相应的救生艇登乘点。

七短声然后是一长声,不断重复:
行动——放救生艇,弃船。

火警

断断续续的铃声:
行动——所有人员立刻到他们相应的消防位置。

二氧化碳警报

从电话中传出连续铃声:
行动——所有人员立刻到他们相应的消防位置。

(警报安放在泵舱、机舱或其他二氧化碳消防系统覆盖的地方)

其他重要的警报

它们包括:

- 惰性气体警报
- 机舱高液位警报(船舱液位)
- 驾驶台警报
- 生活区警报
- 厨房警报

List of Figures

图 录

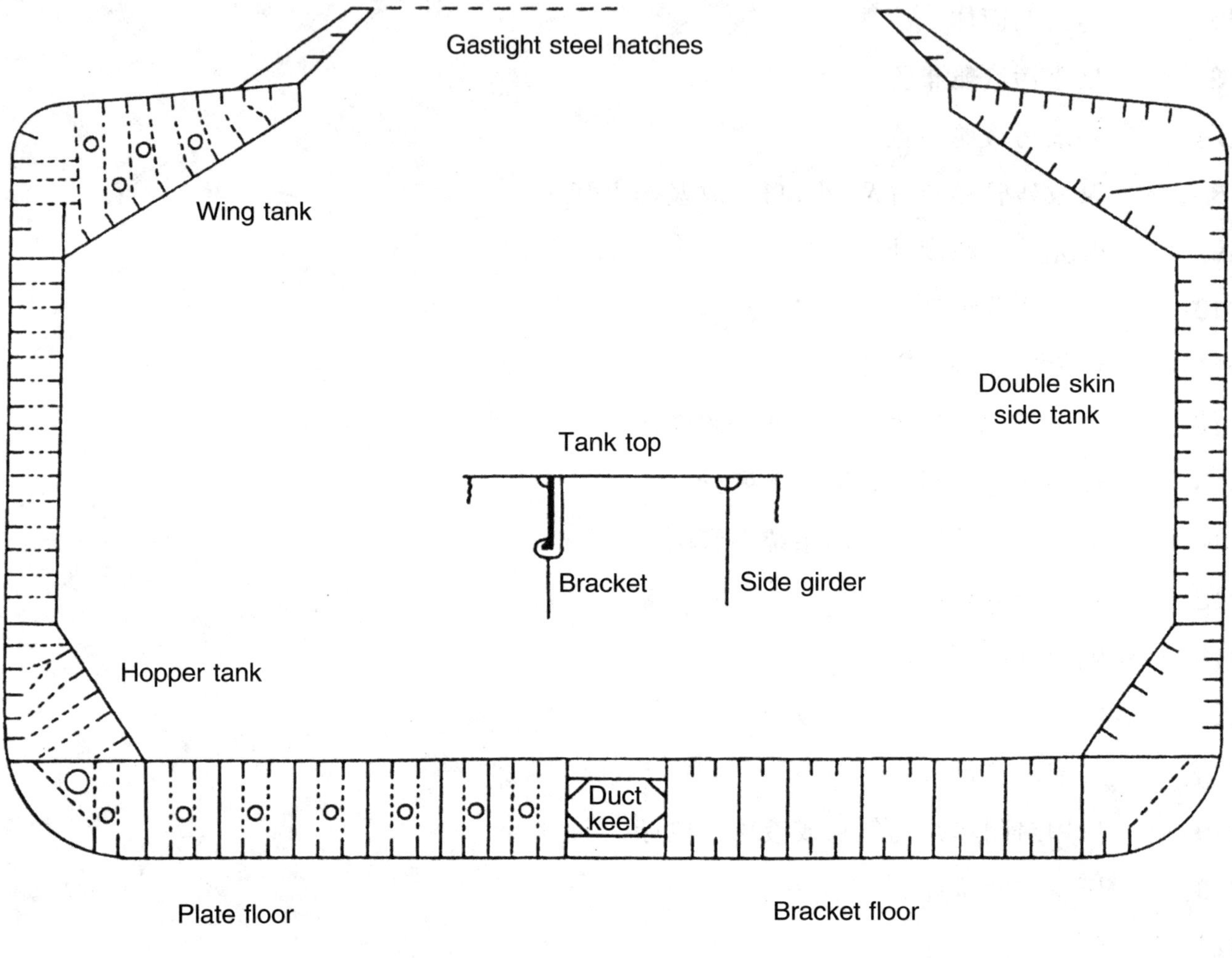

Figure 1: Oil/Bulk/Ore (OBO) ship: cross section

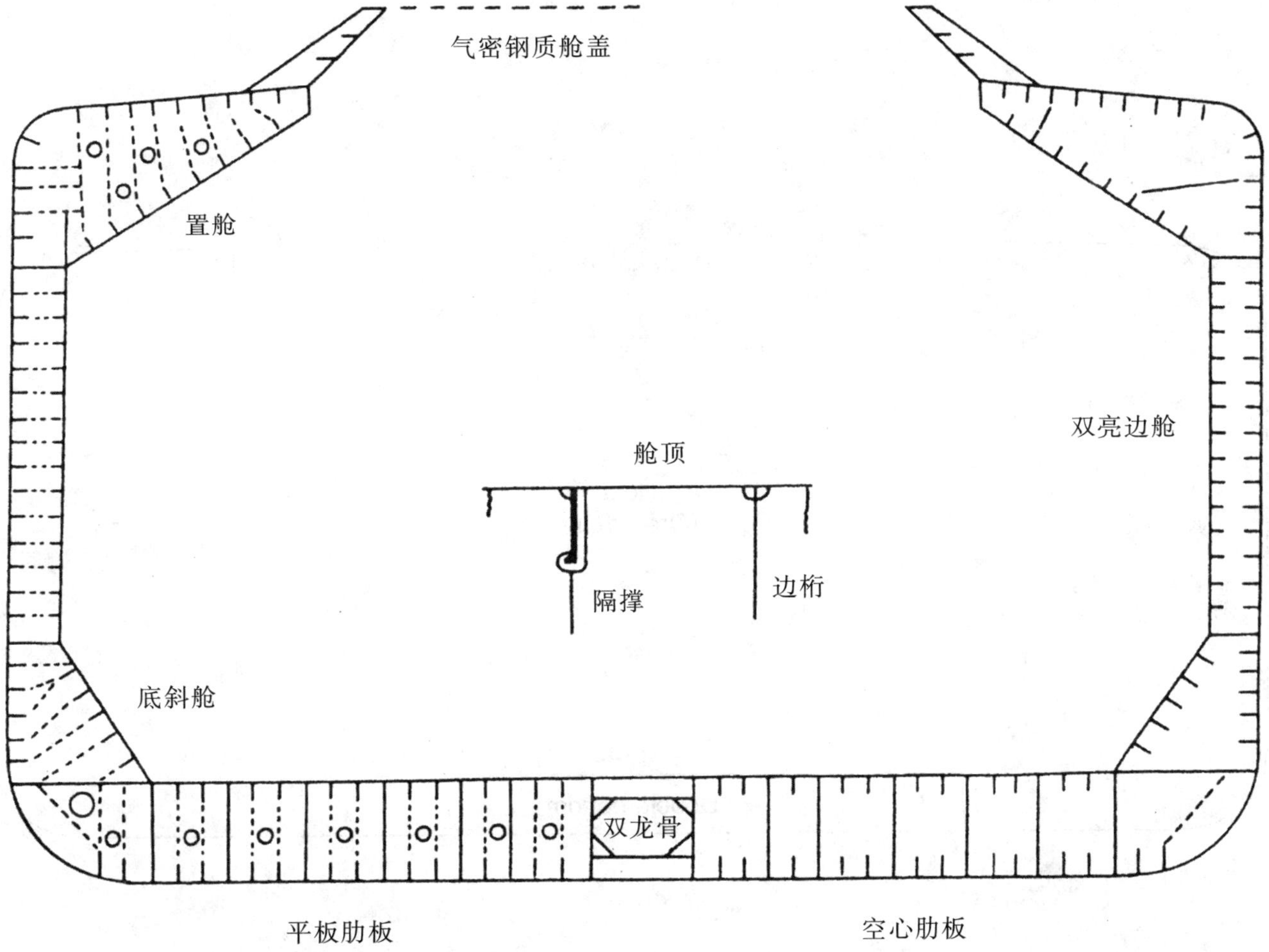

图 1: 油/散货/矿石(OBO)船:横剖图

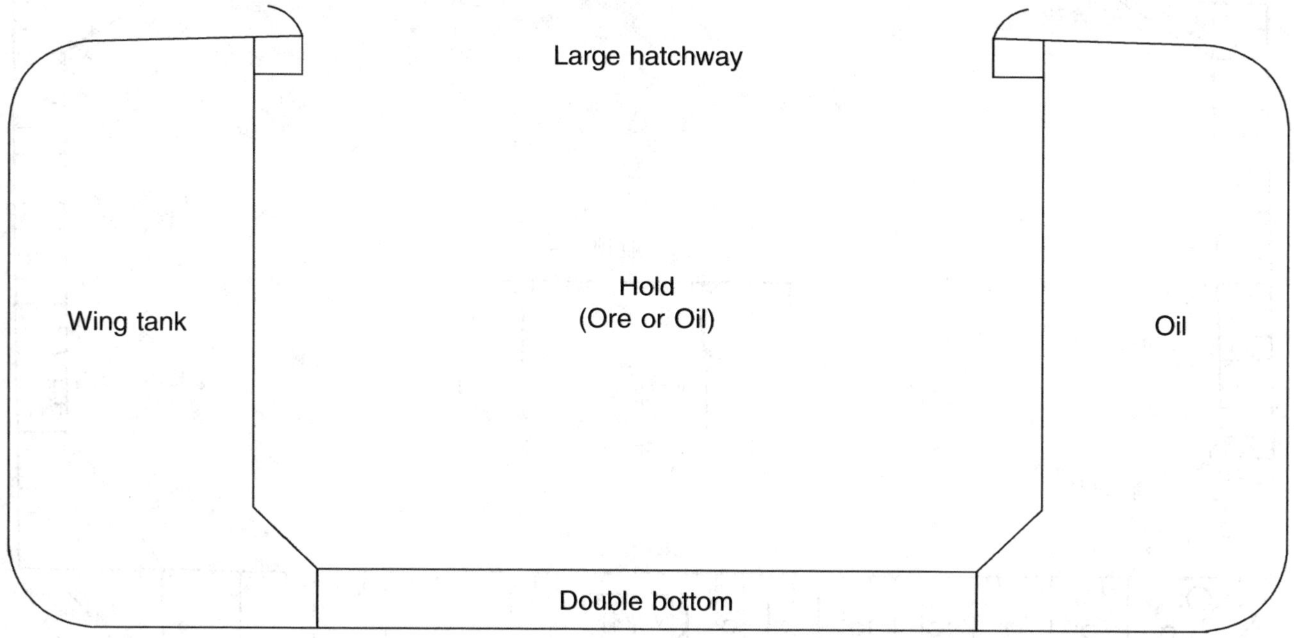

Figure 2: Oil/Ore (O/O) ship: cross section

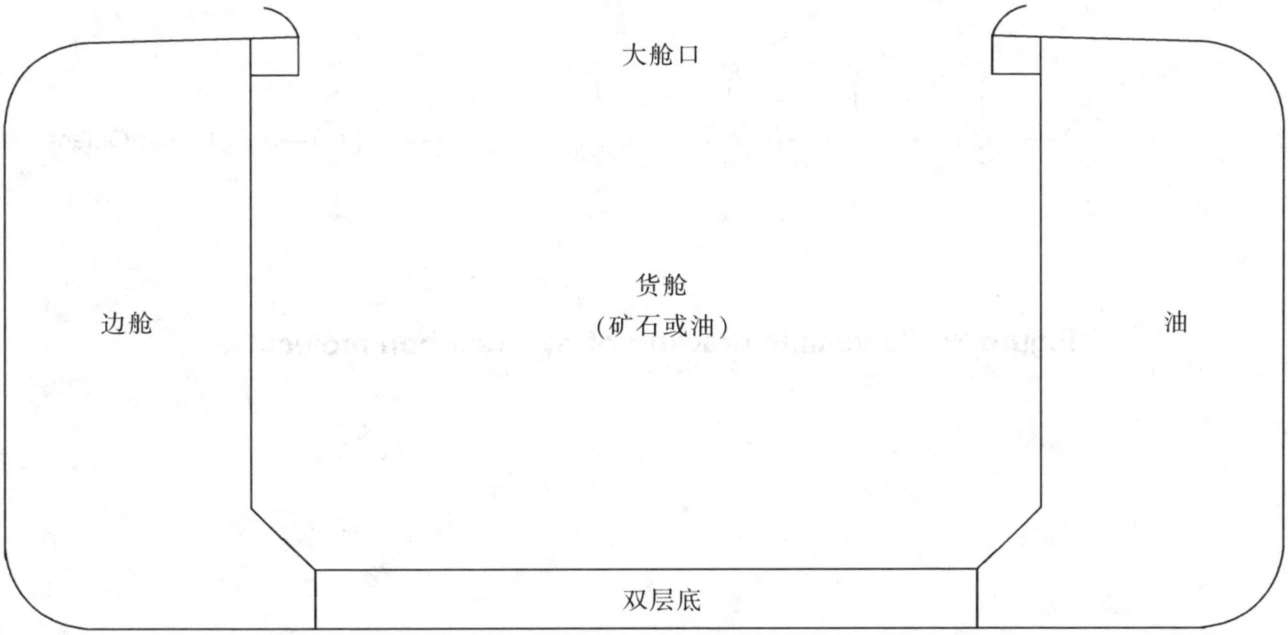

图 2: 油/矿石(O/O)船:横剖图

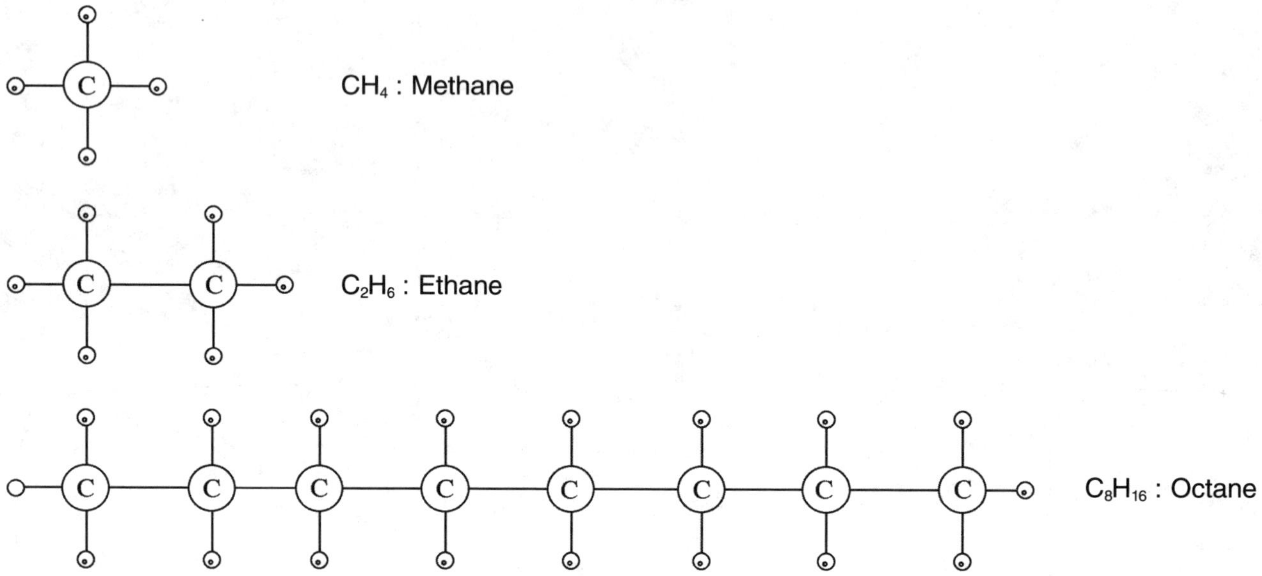

Figure 3: Schematic drawing of hydrocarbon molecules

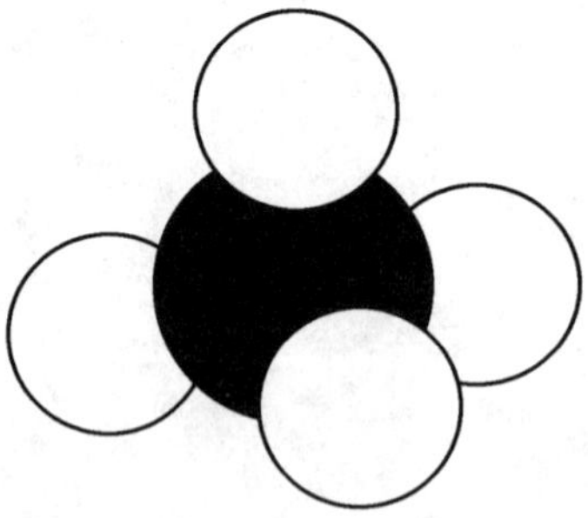

Figure 4: Dimensional drawing of a methane molecule

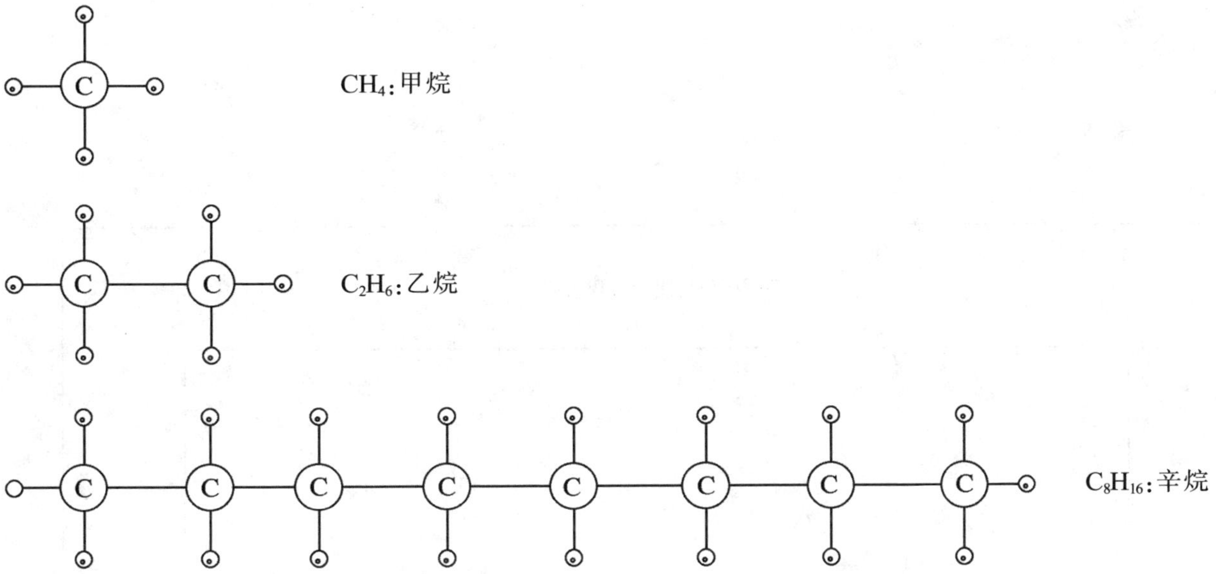

图 3: 烃分子结构图

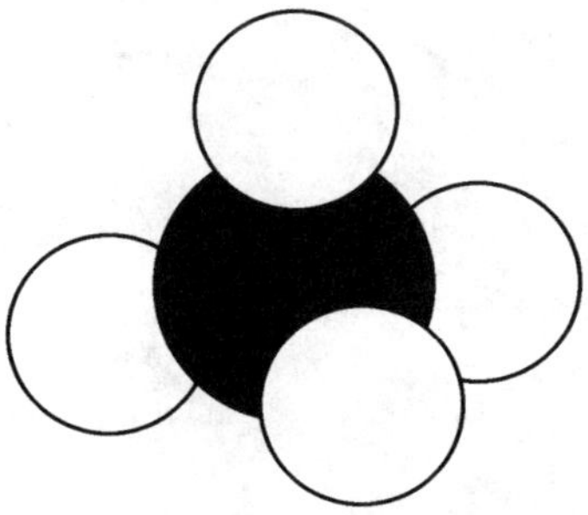

图 4: 甲烷分子三维图

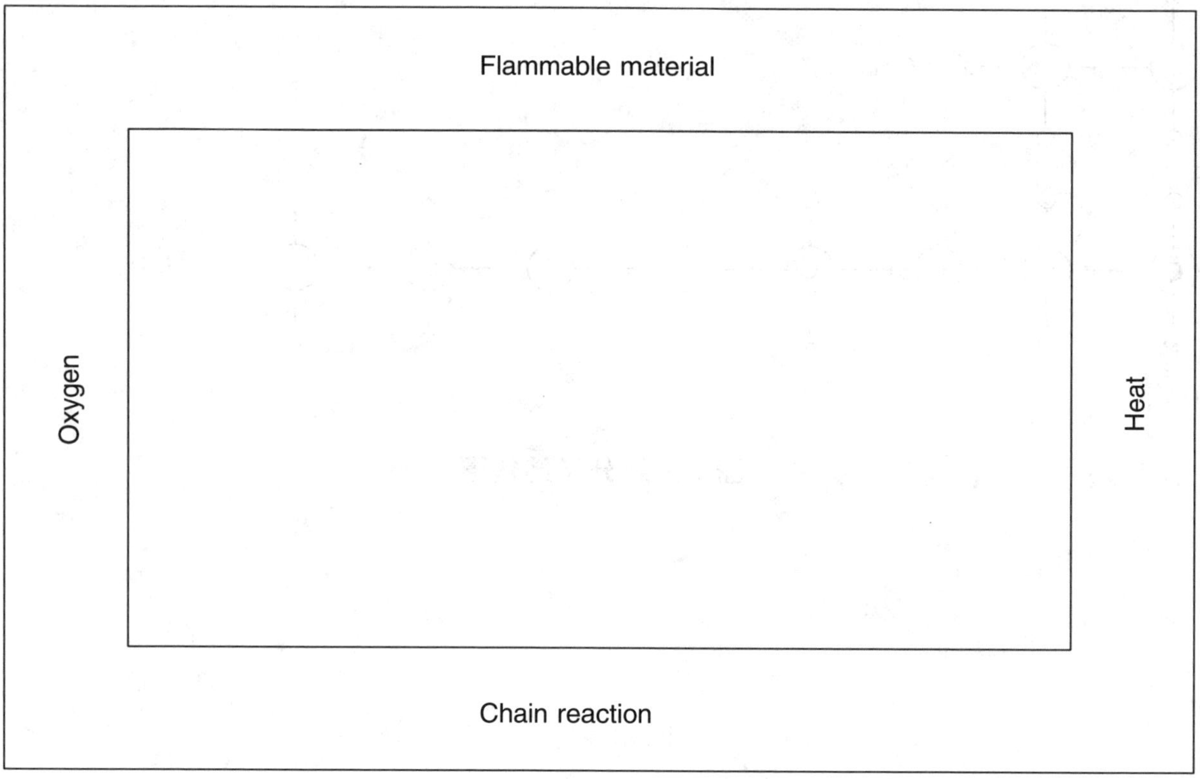

Figure 5: Fire Tetrahedron

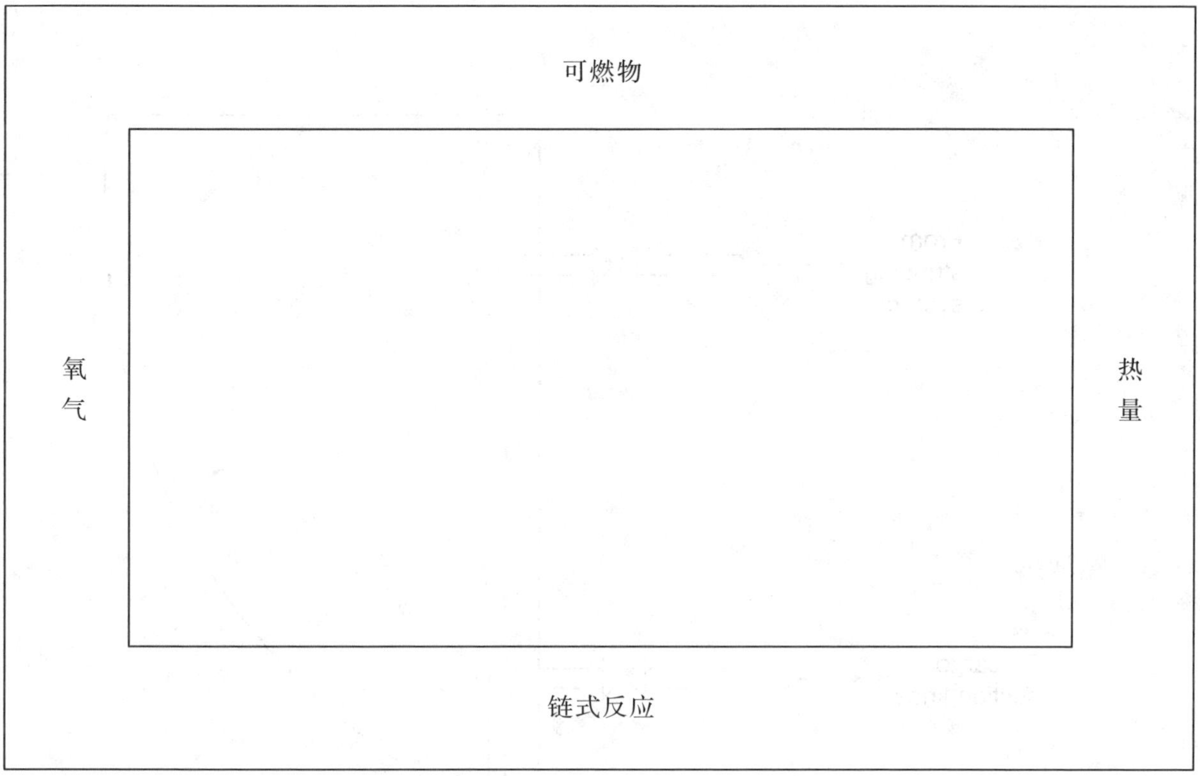

图 5：防火四面体

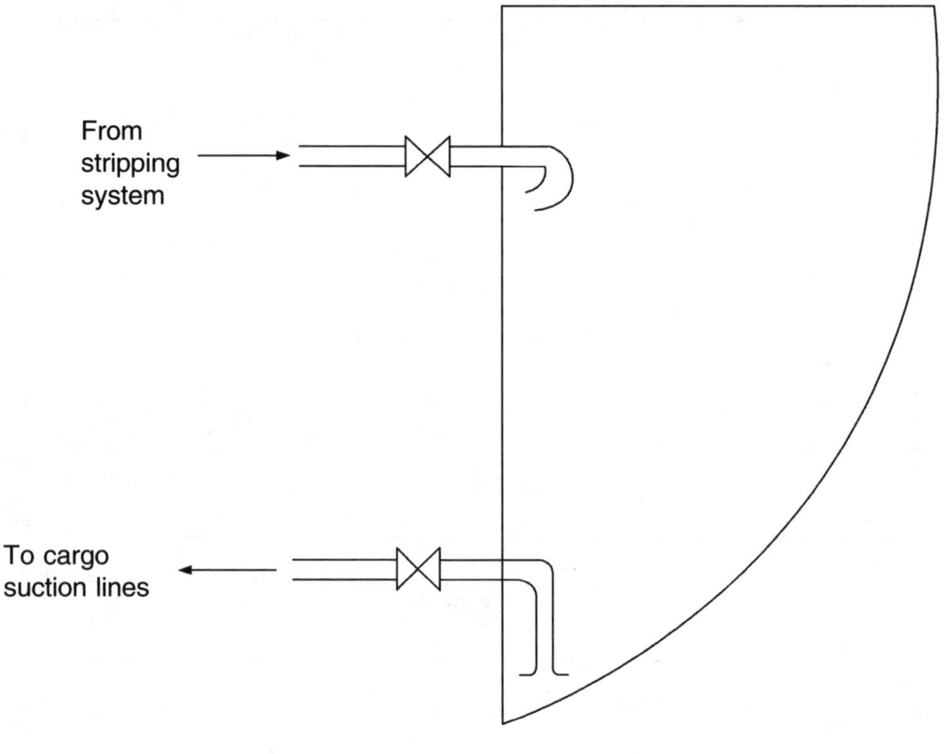

Figure 6: Minimum slop-tank arrangement

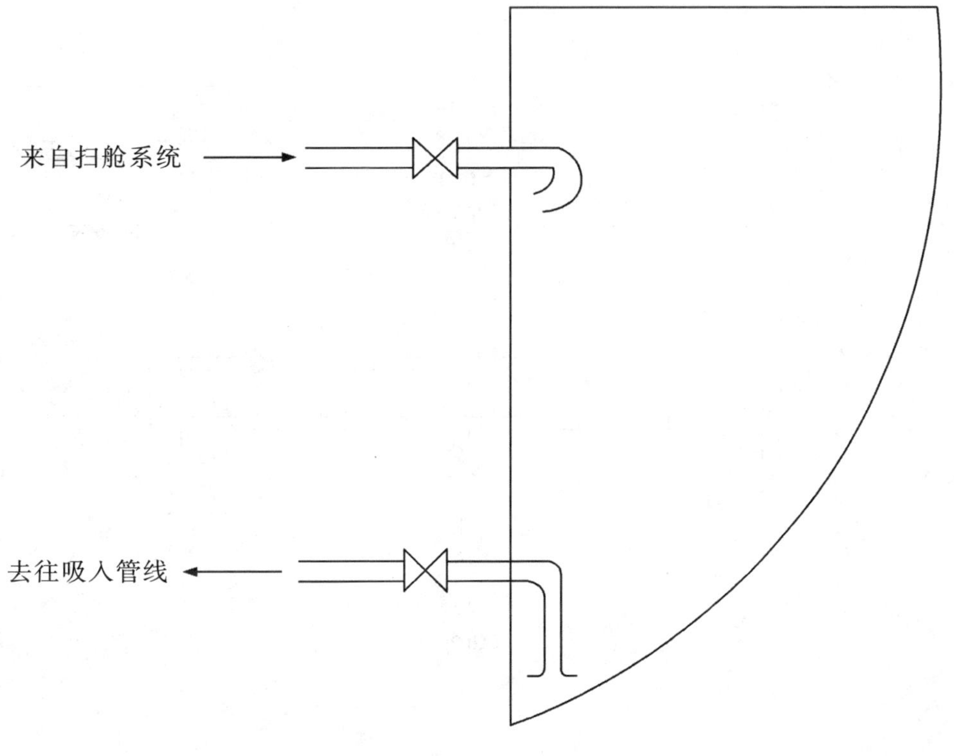

图 6：最小污液舱布置

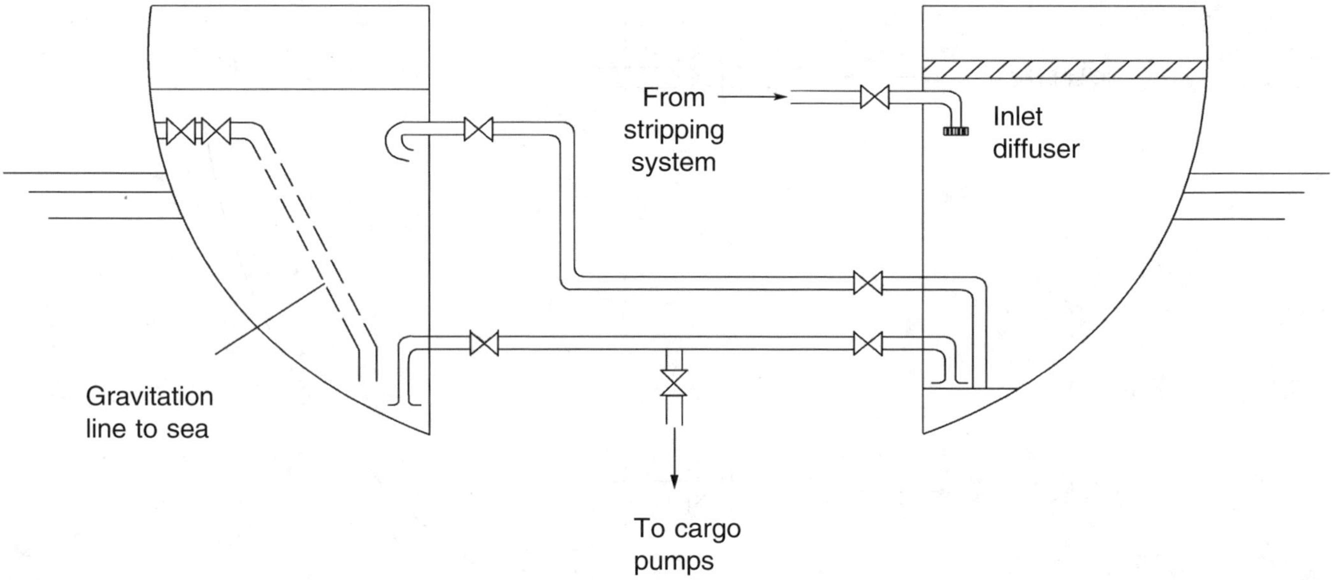

Figure 7:   Efficient slop-tank arrangement

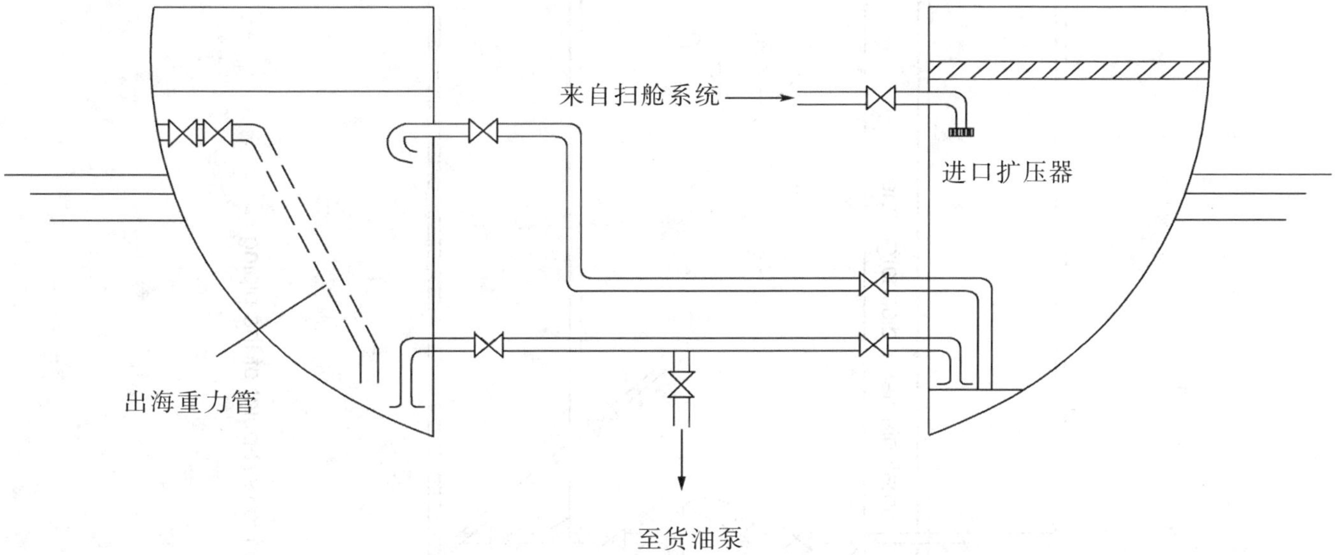

图 7：高效污液舱布置

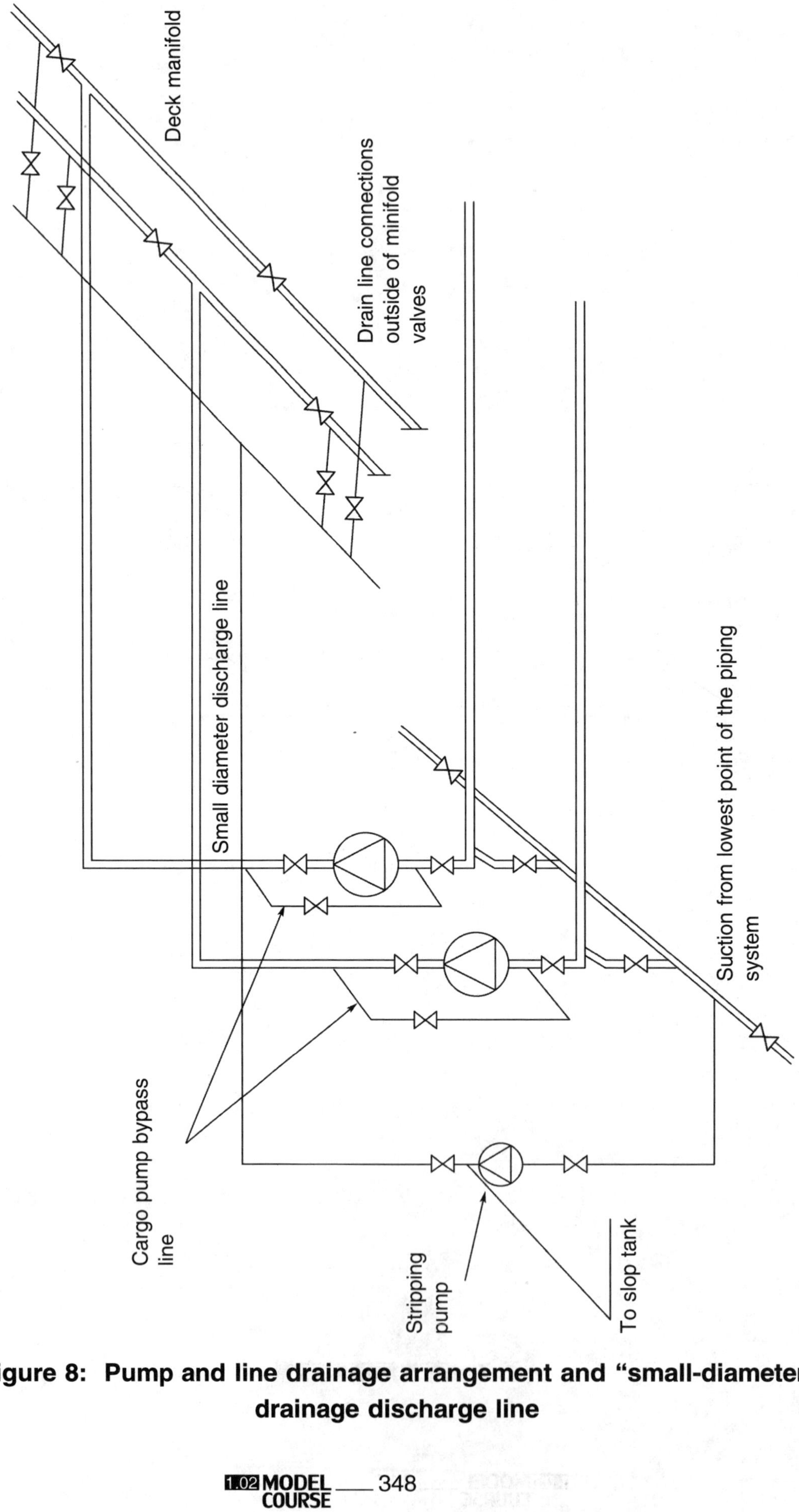

Figure 8: Pump and line drainage arrangement and "small-diameter" drainage discharge line

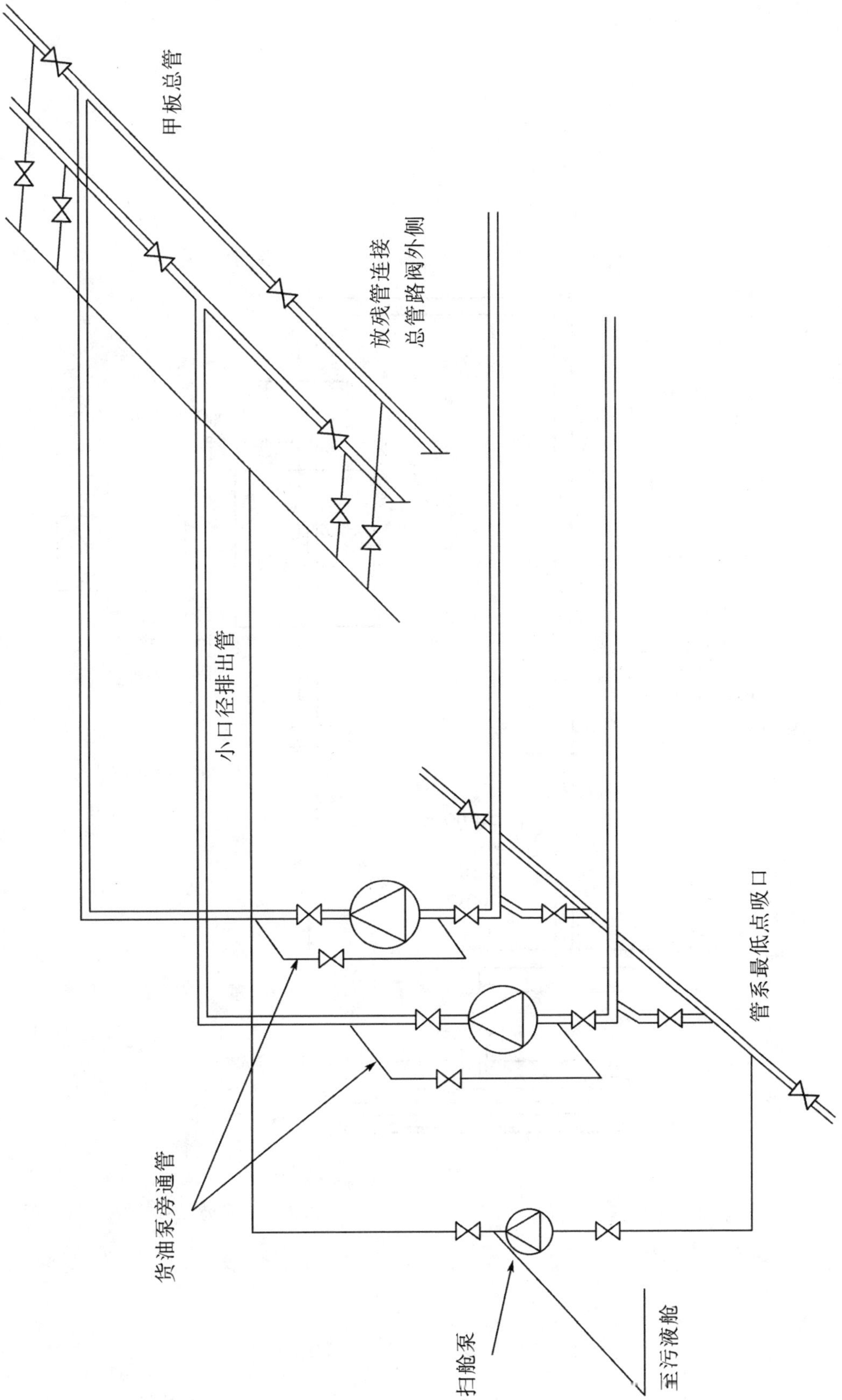

图 8：泵放残管路布置及"小口径"放残排出管

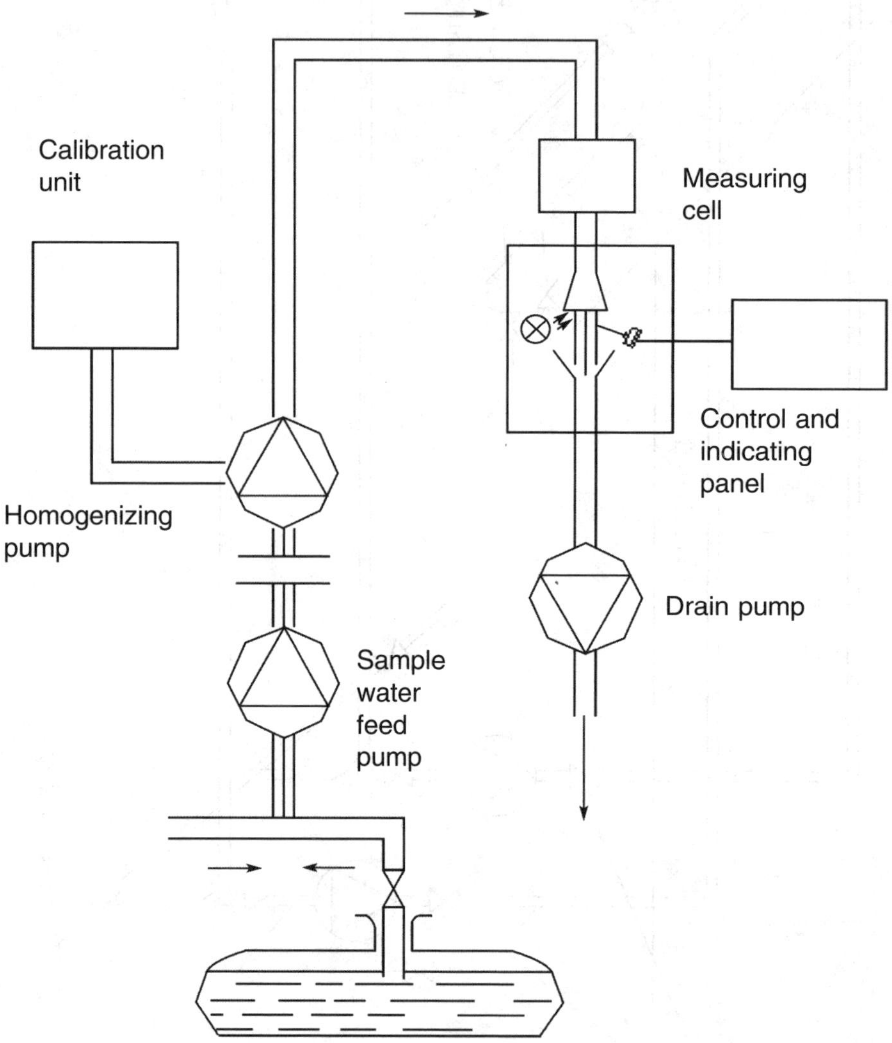

Figure 9: Oil content meter working with fluorescence

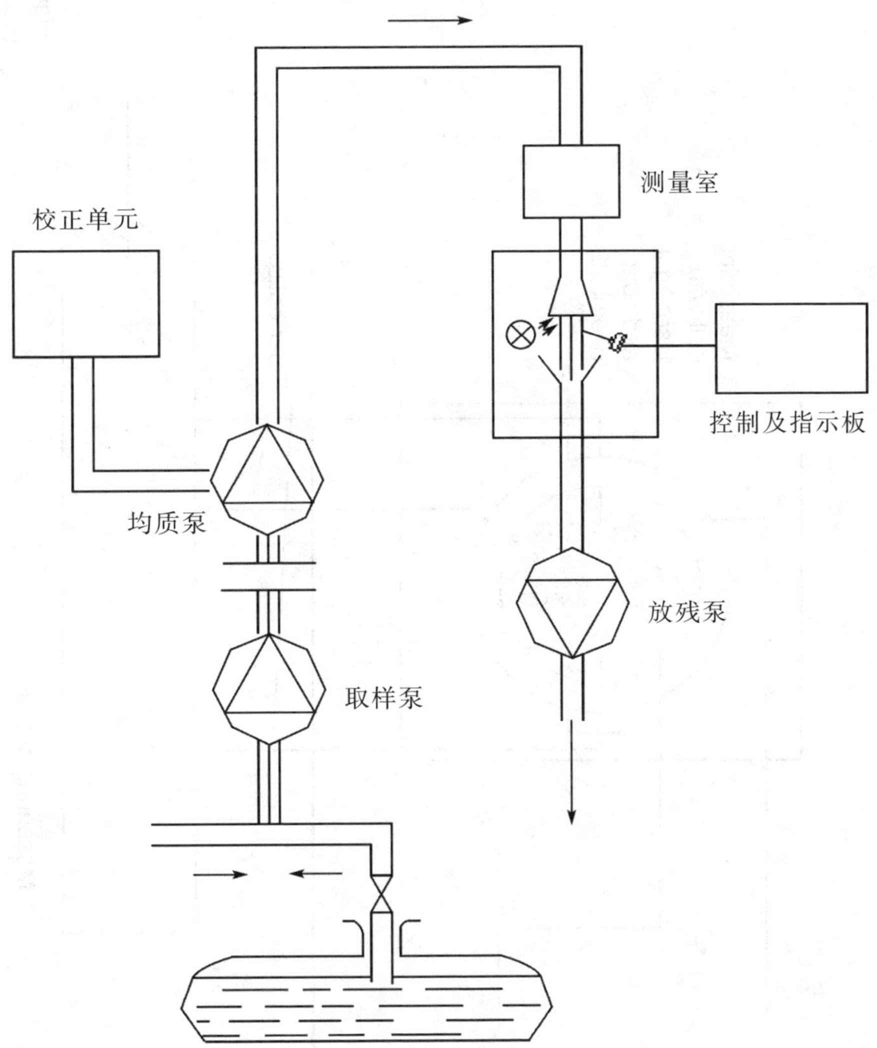

图 9：荧光油分浓度计

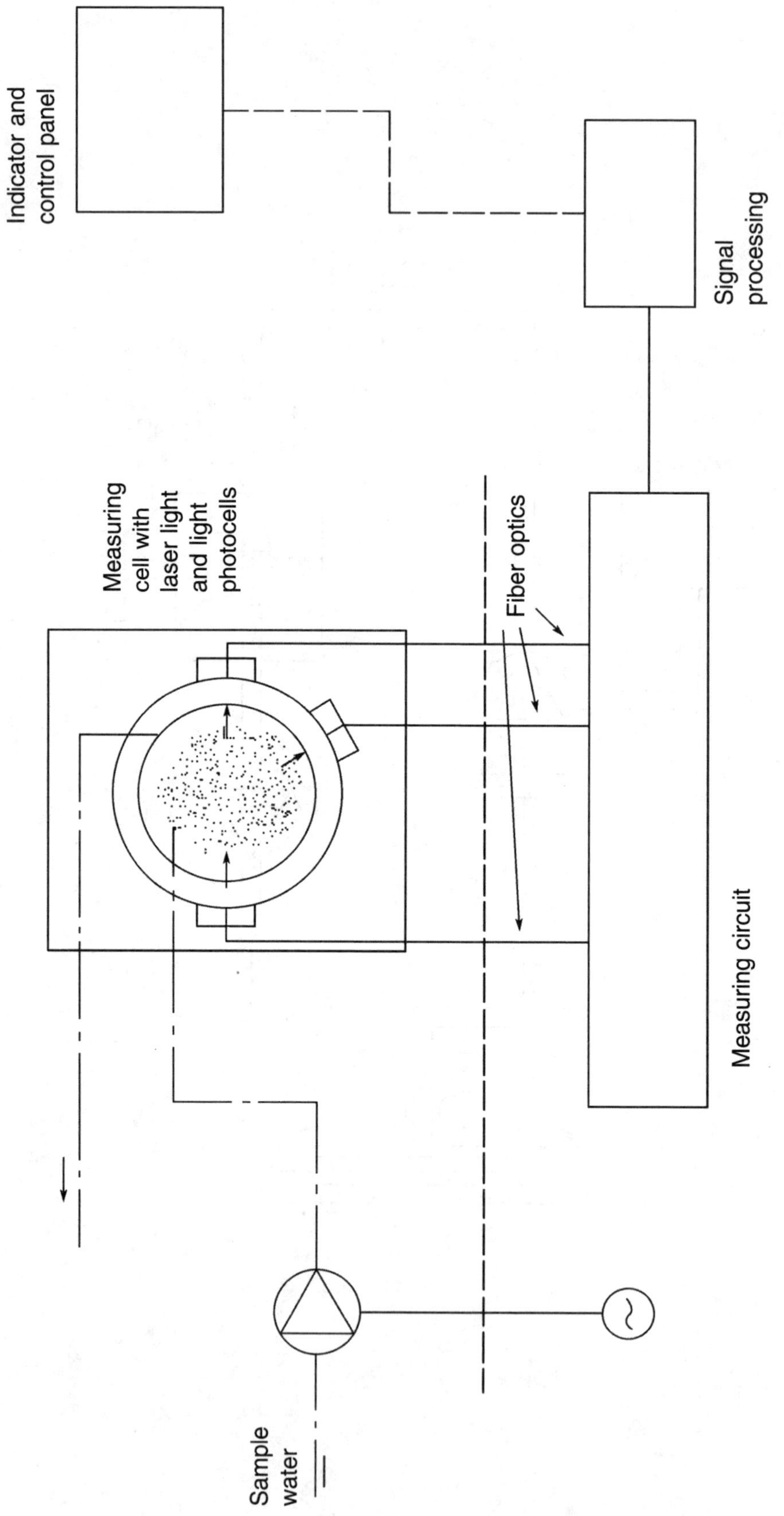

Figure 10: Oil content meter working on light-scattering principle

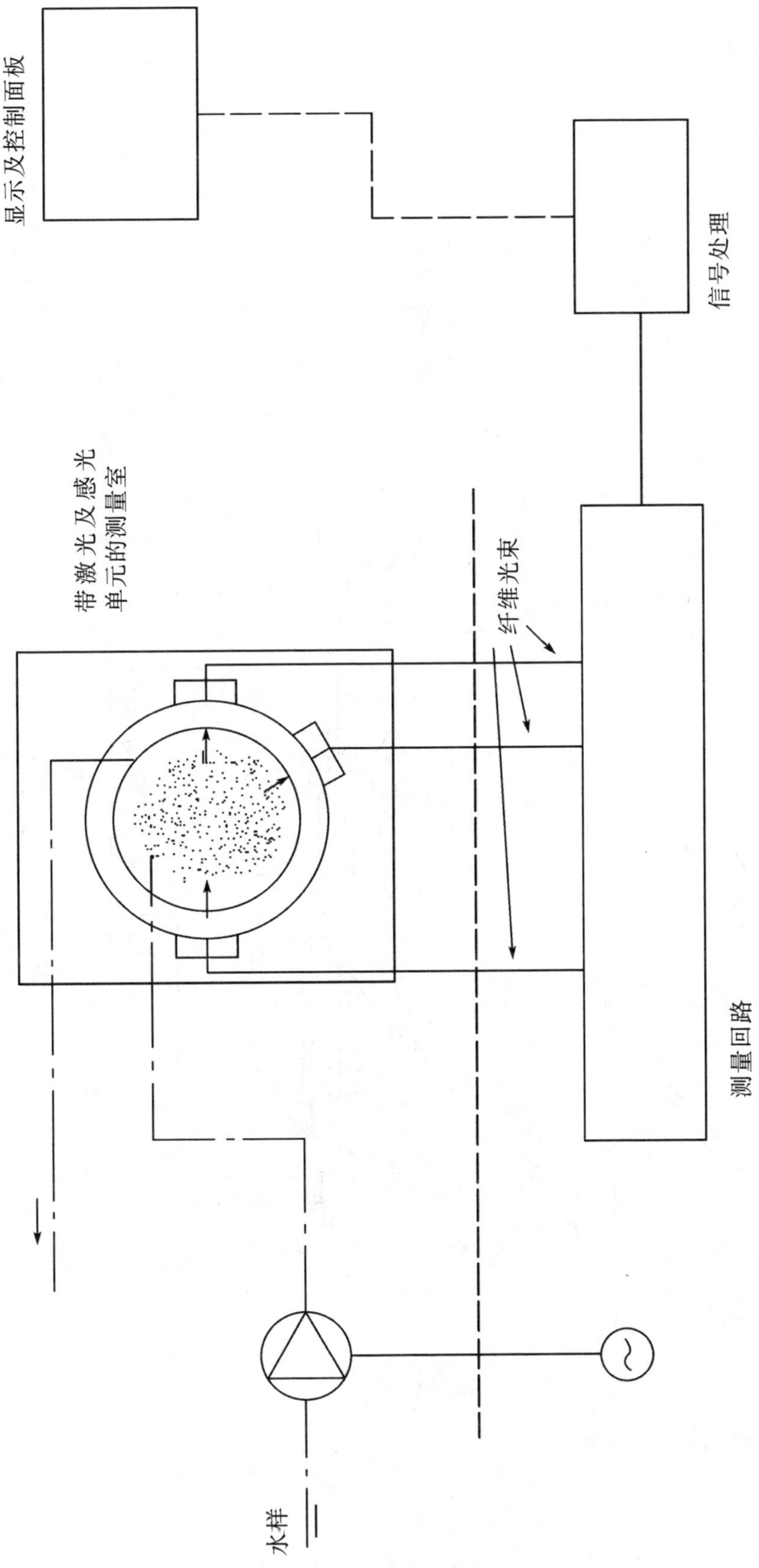

图 10：光散油分浓度计

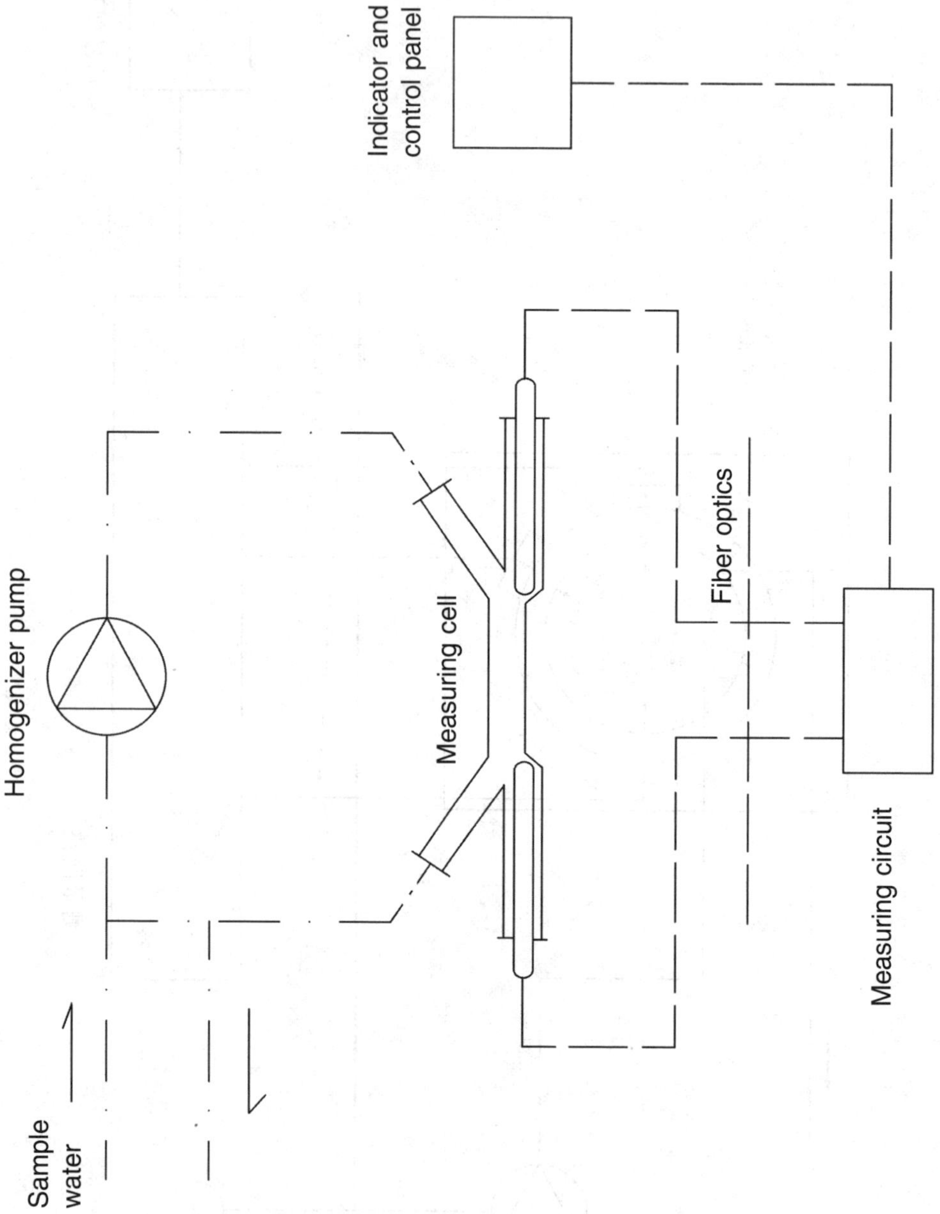

Figure 11: Oil content meter working on turbidity principle

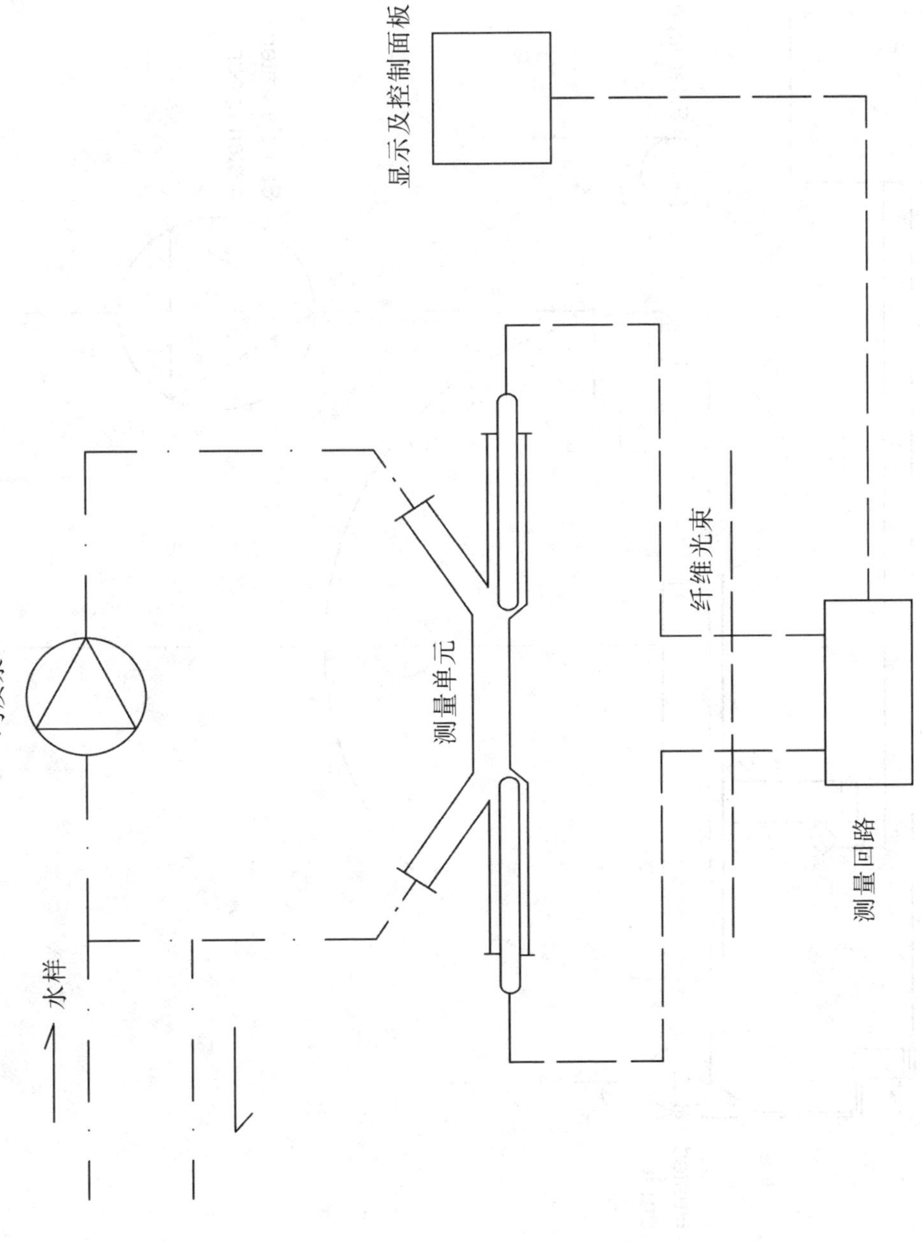

图 11：浊度法油分浓度计

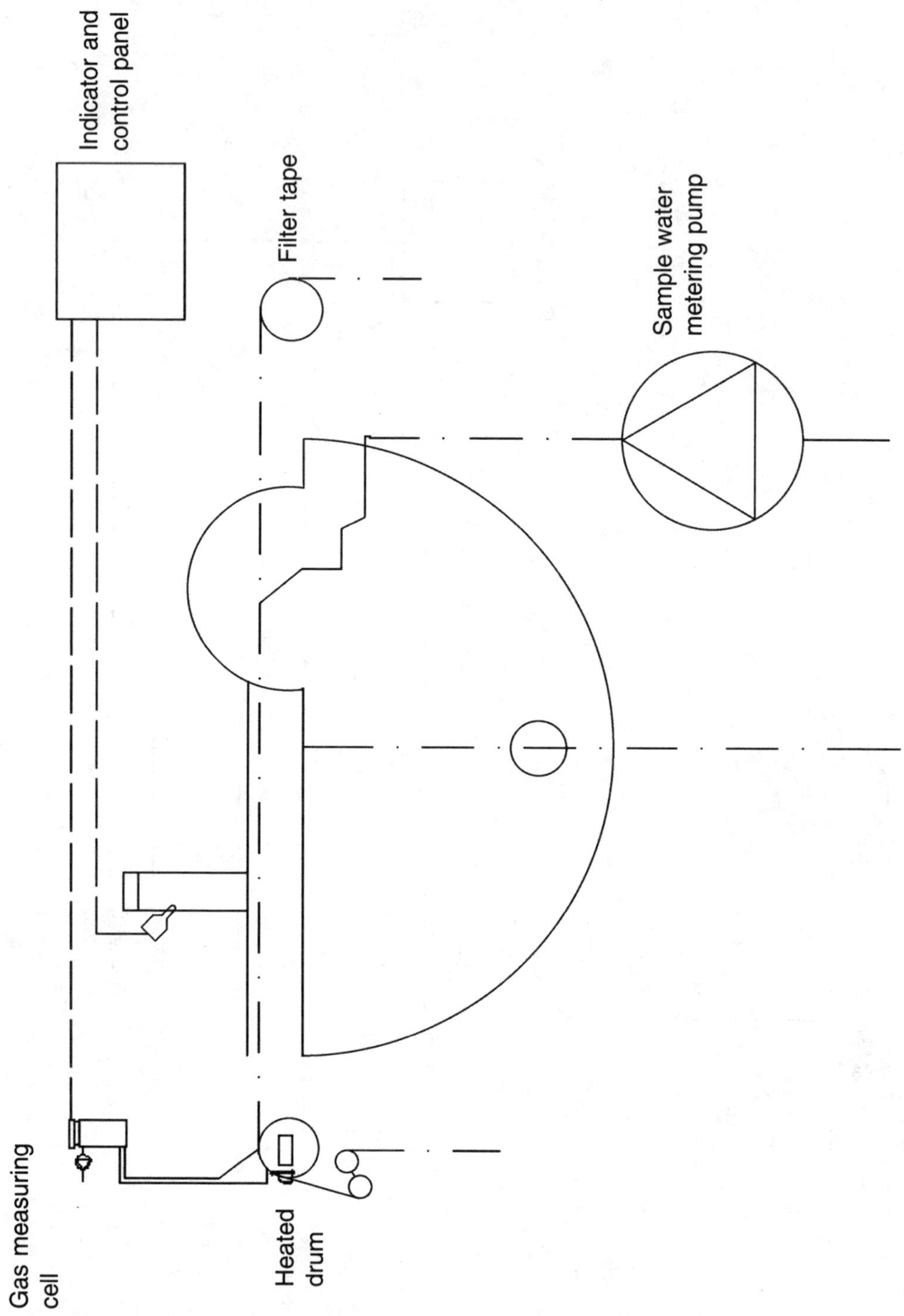

Figure 12: Oil content meter working with discolouration and gas measurements

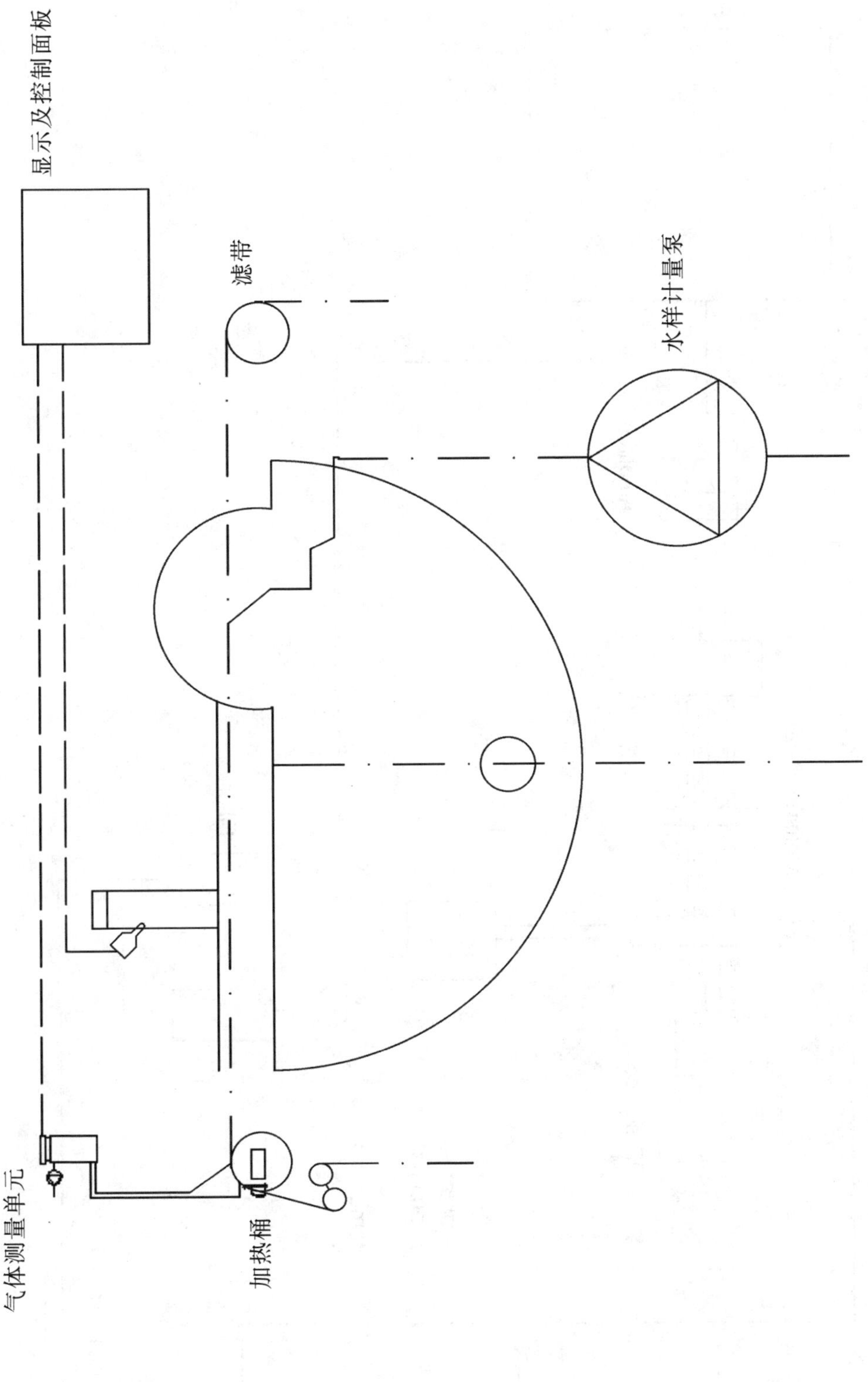

图 12: 基于变色及气体测量的油分浓度计

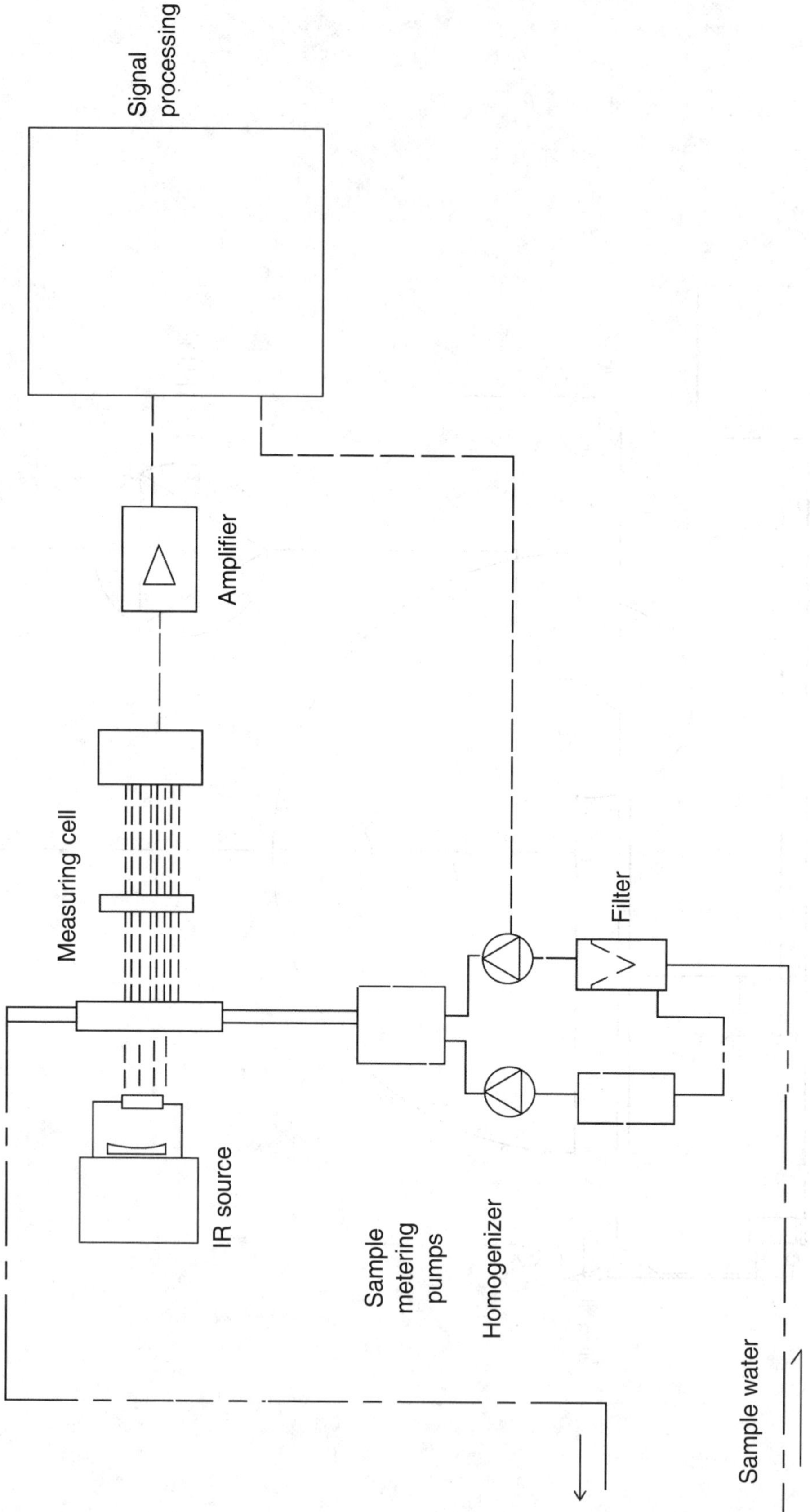

Figure 13: Oil content meter working with direct infrared absorption

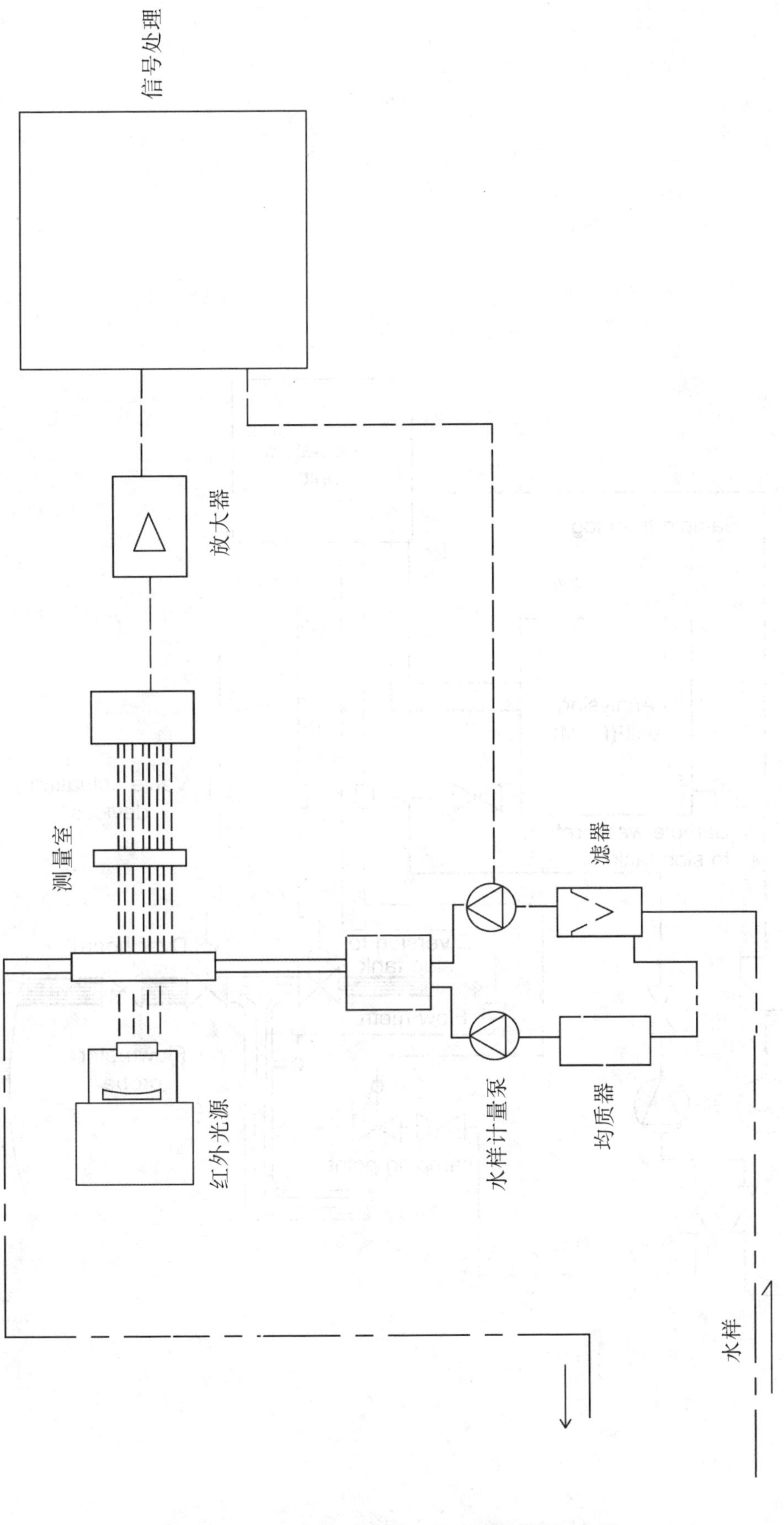

图 13：红外线直接吸收式油分浓度计

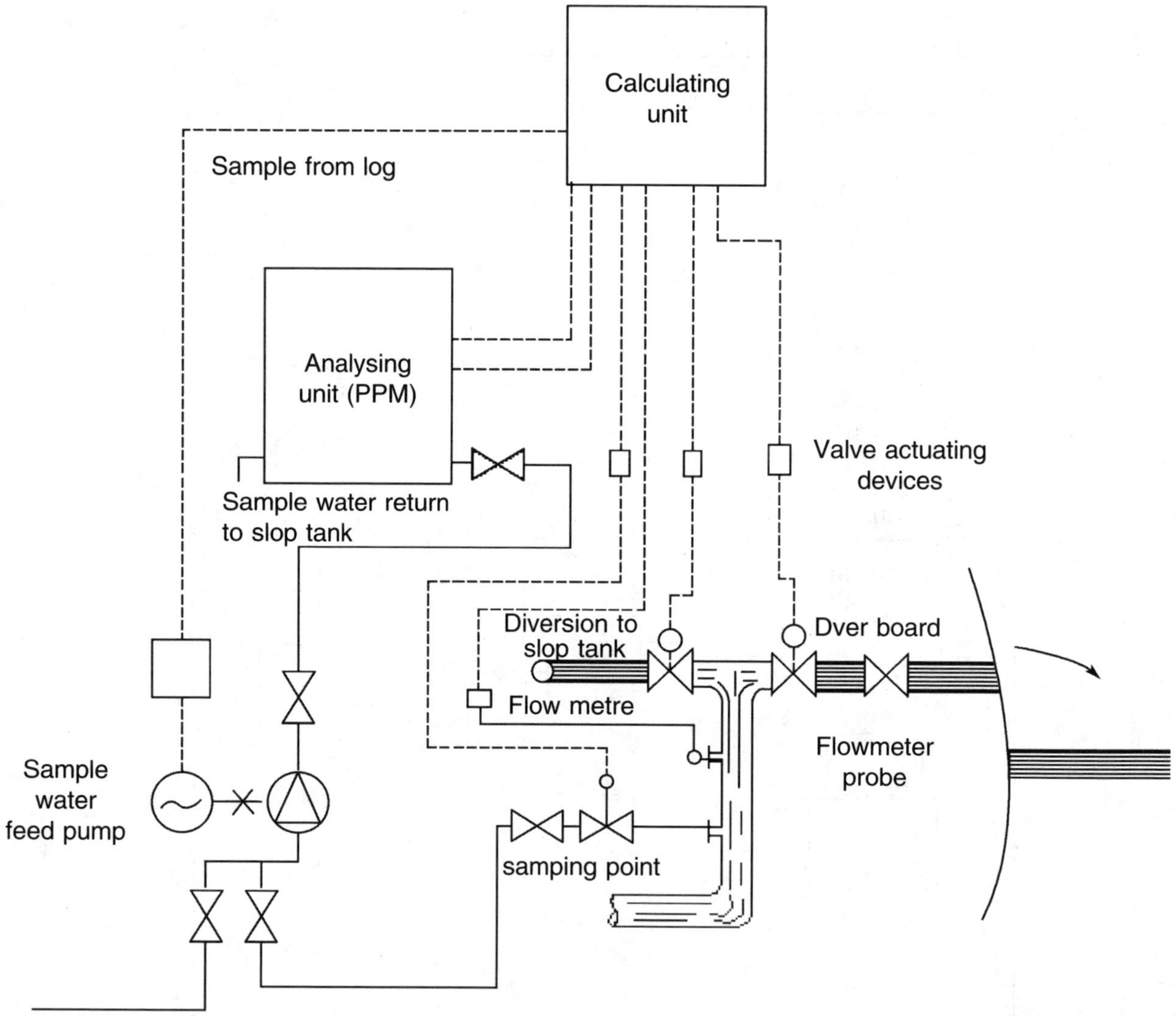

Figure 14: Arrangement of oil-content monitoring and control system

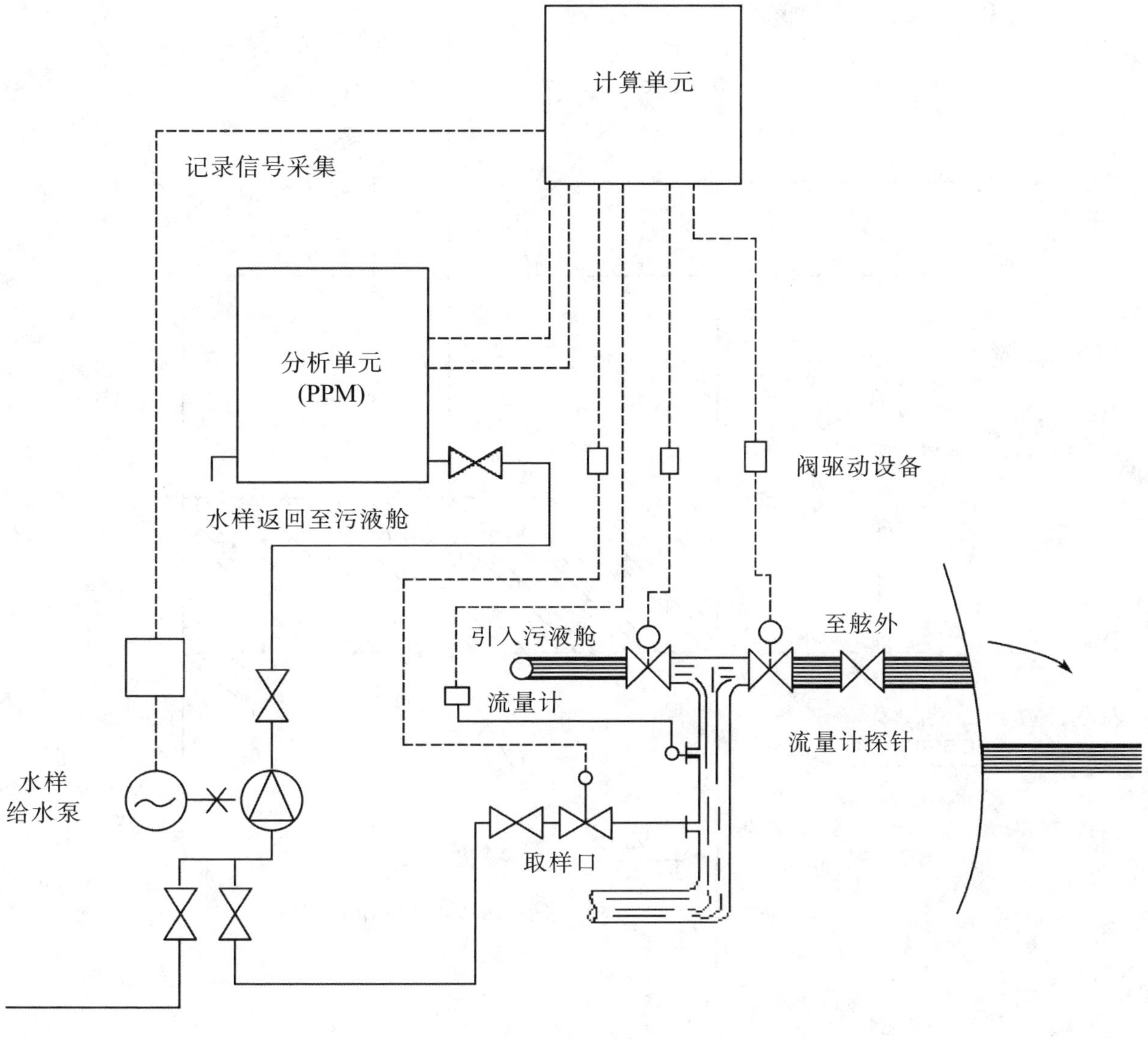

图 14：油分浓度计检测控制系统布置图

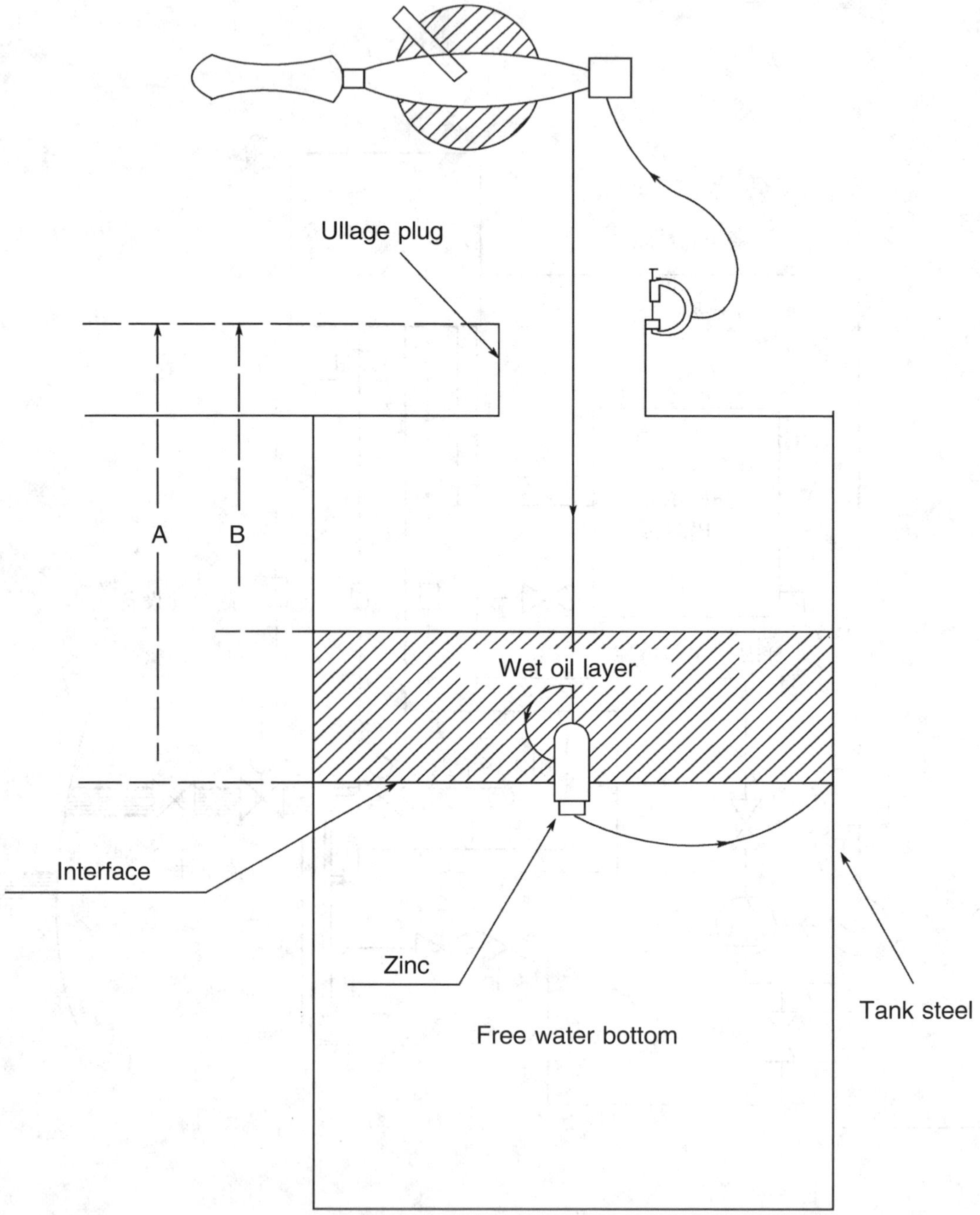

Figure 15: Oil/water interface detector

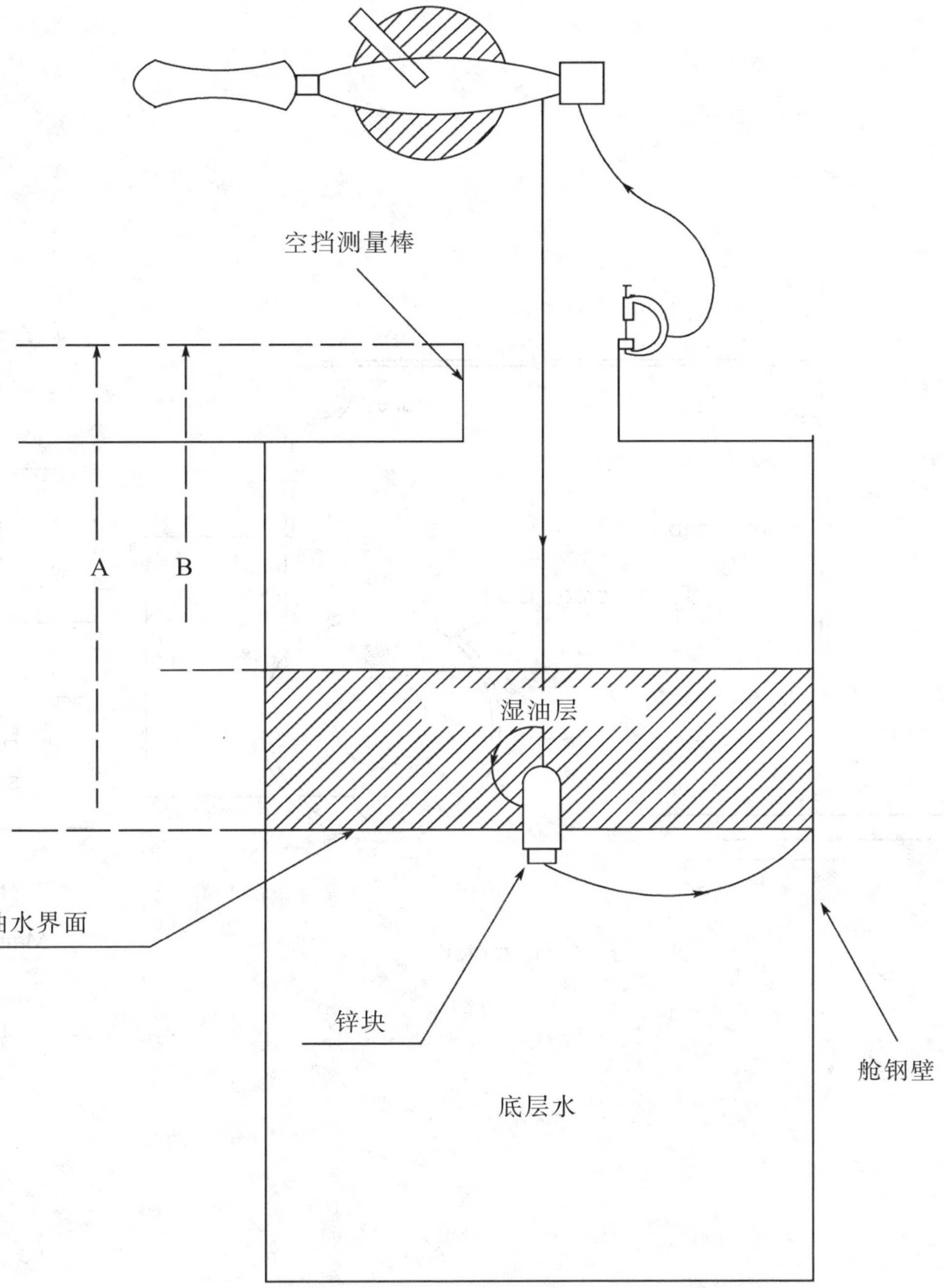

图 15：油水分界面探测器

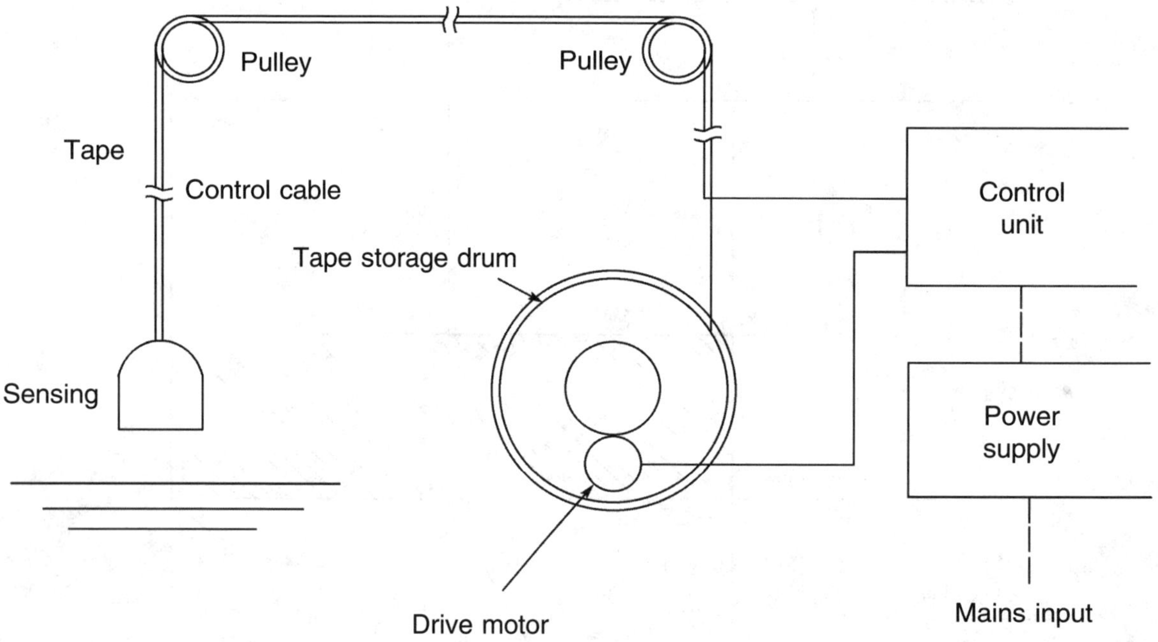

Figure 16: Electrically powered servo-operated gauge

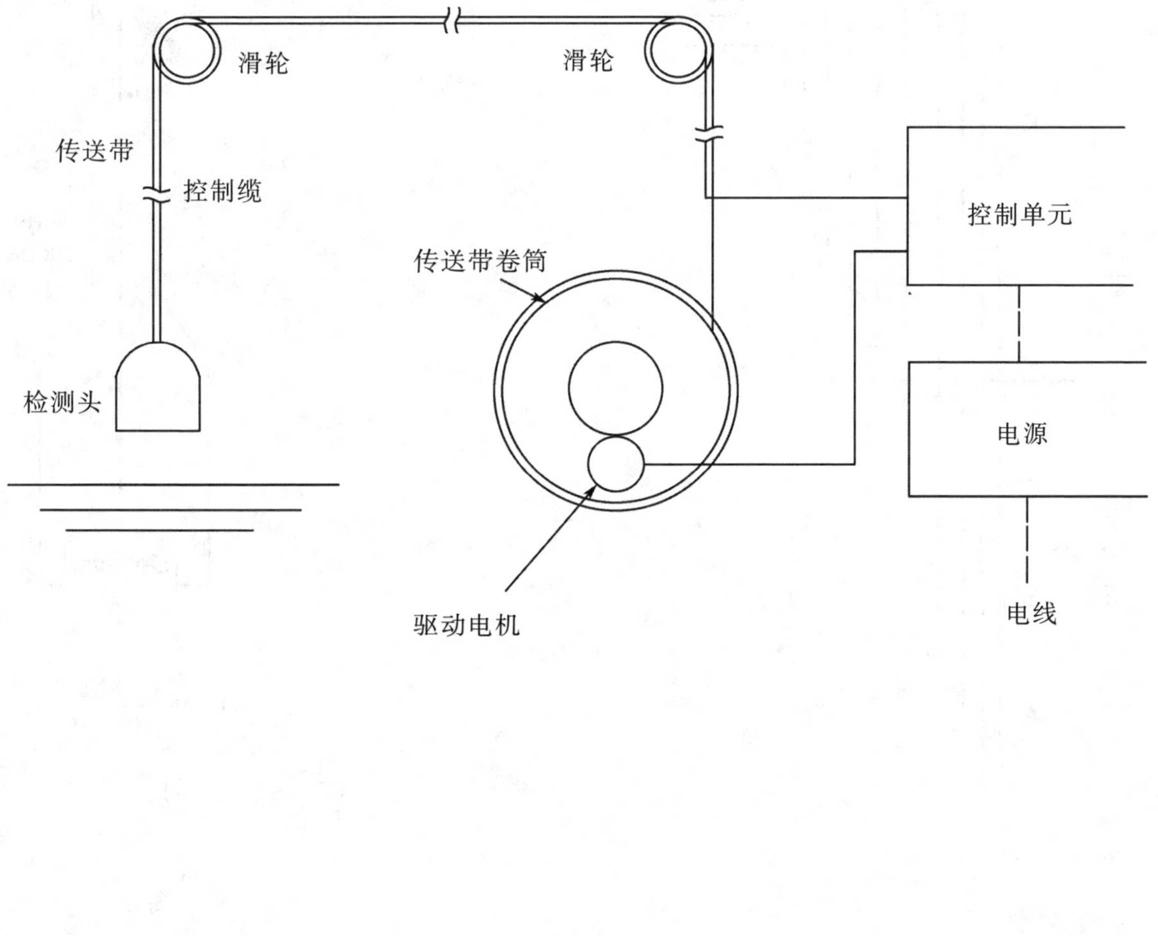

图 16：电力伺服式液位计

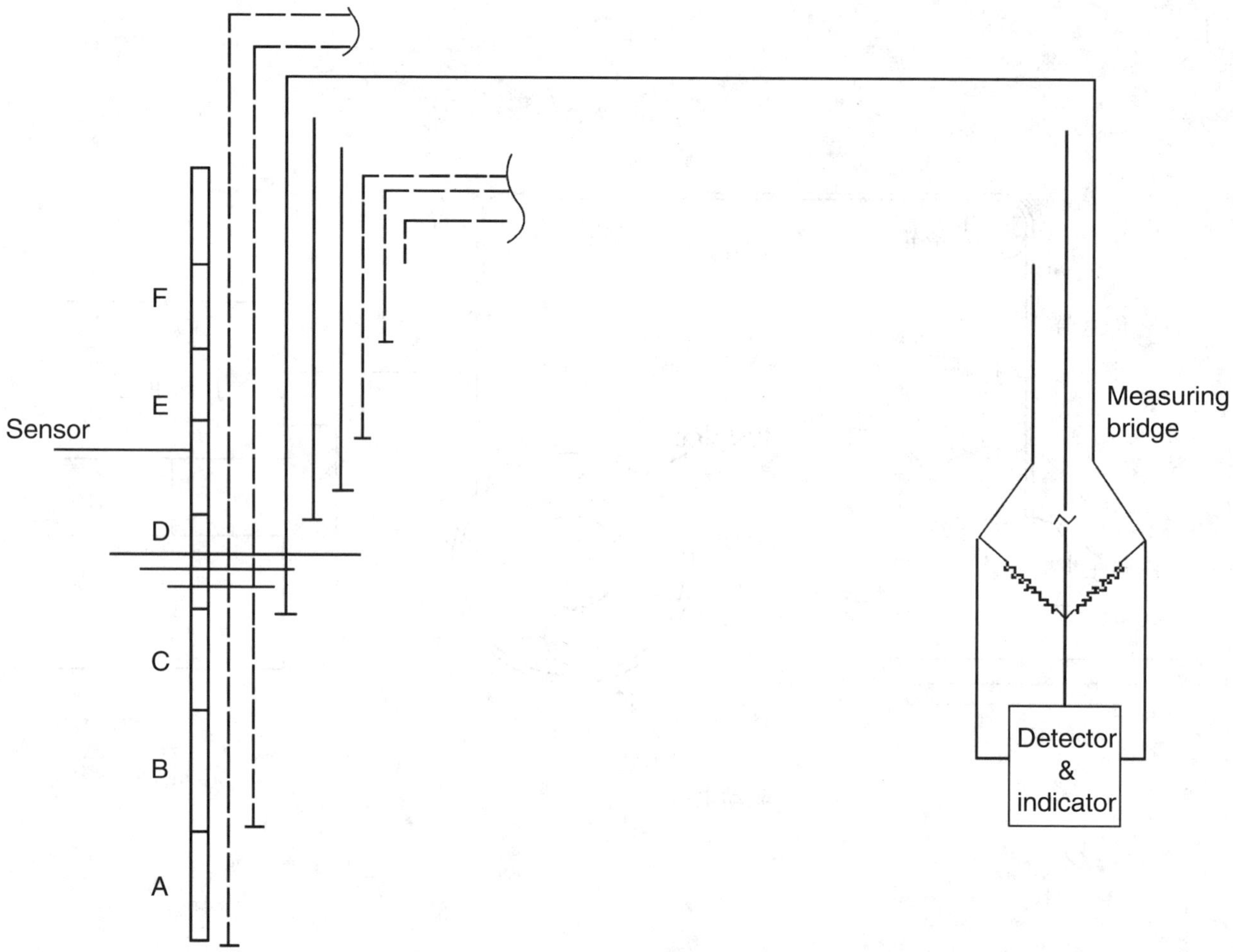

Figure 17: Electrical capacitance gauge – comparative type

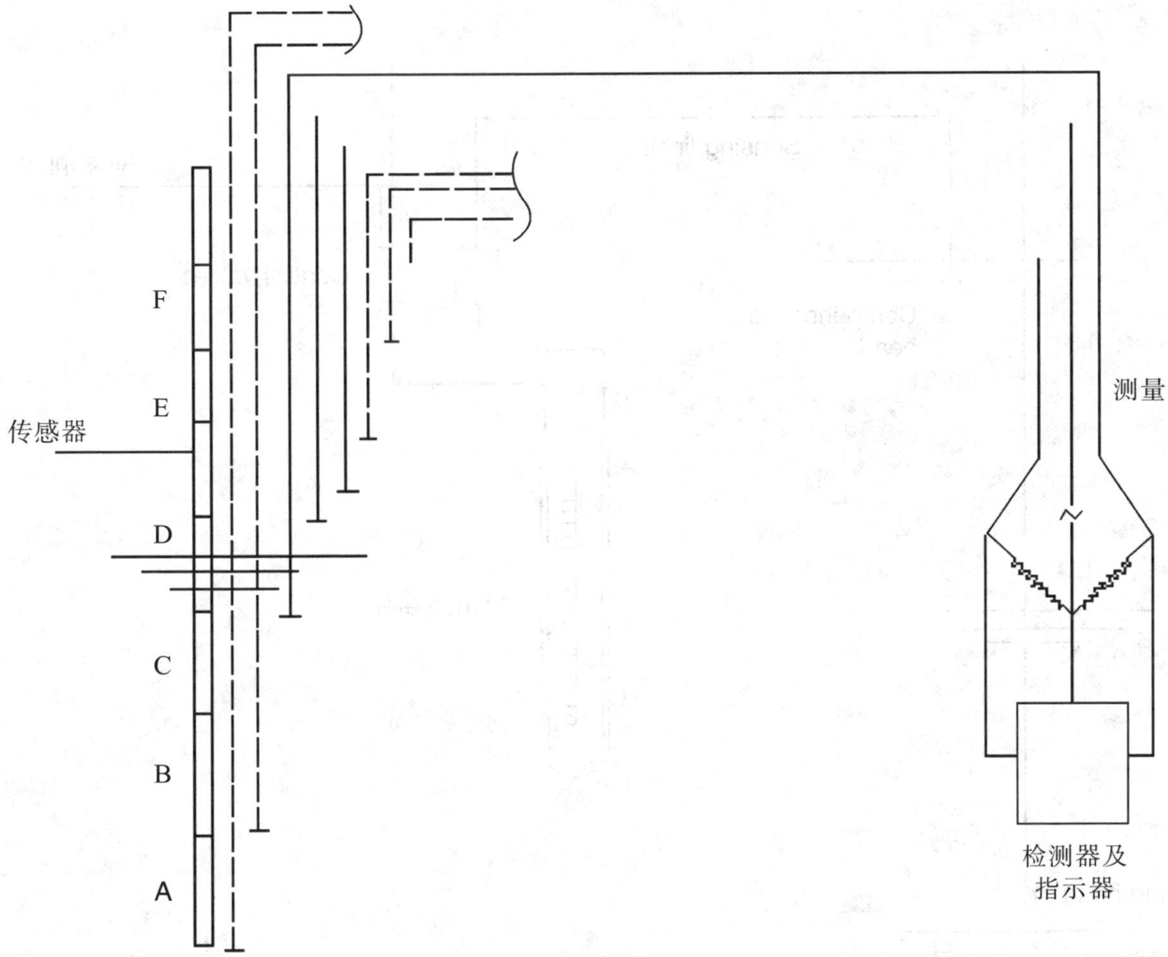

图 17：电容式液位计——比较型

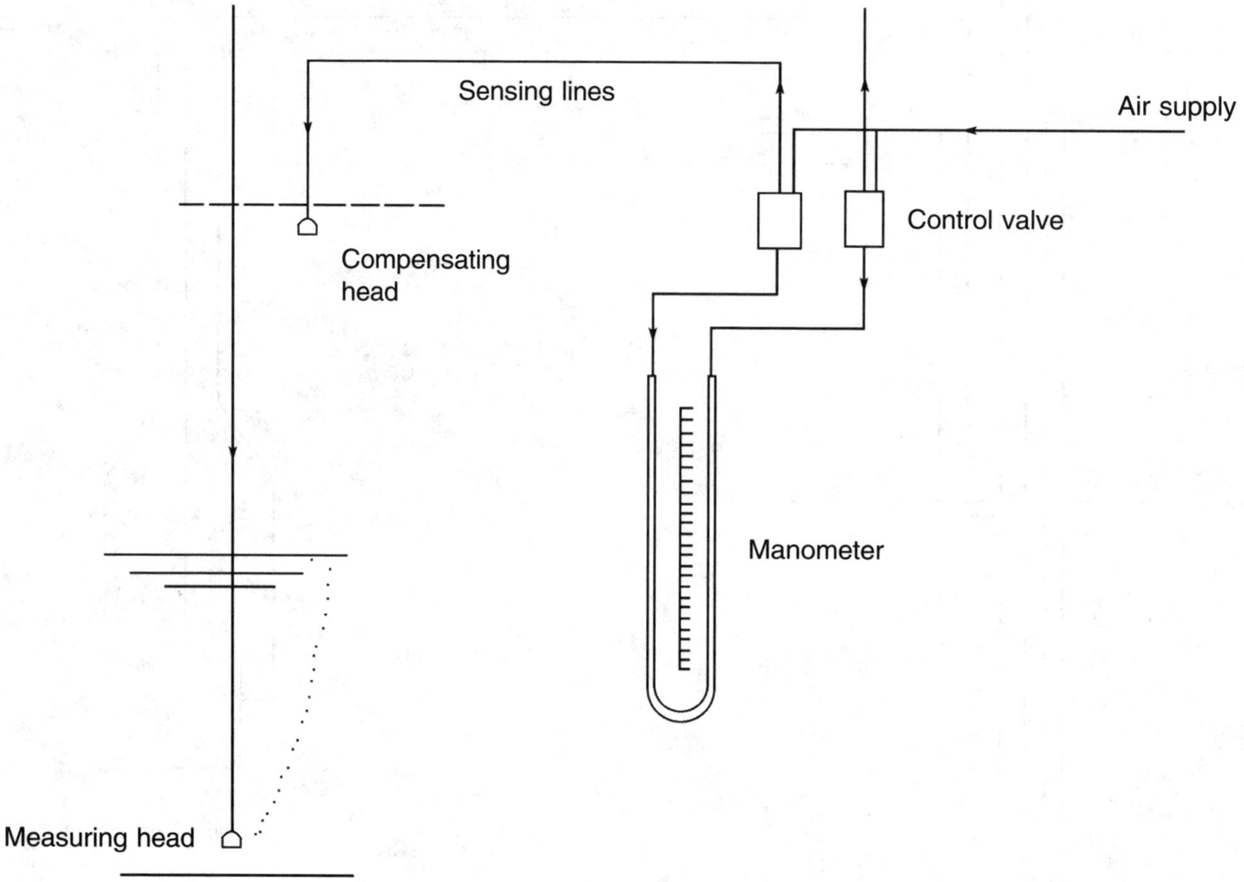

Figure 18: Bubbler gauge

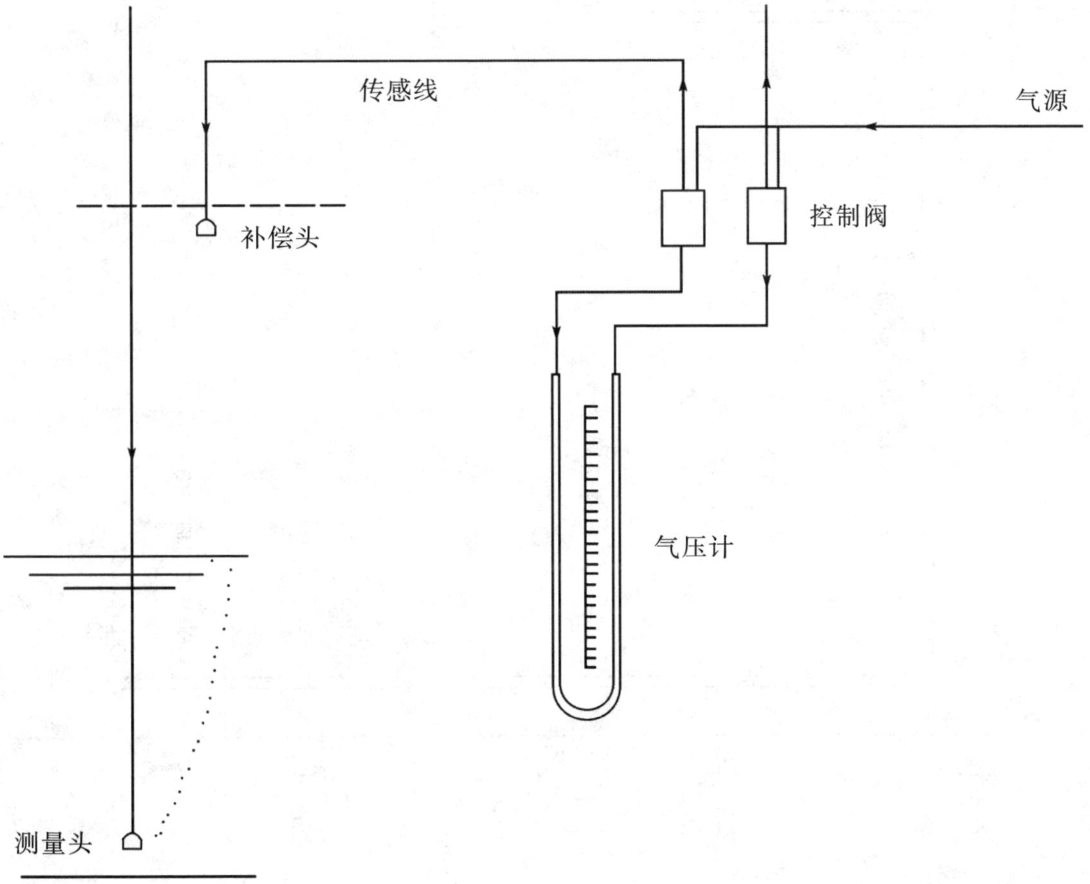

图 18：气泡液位计

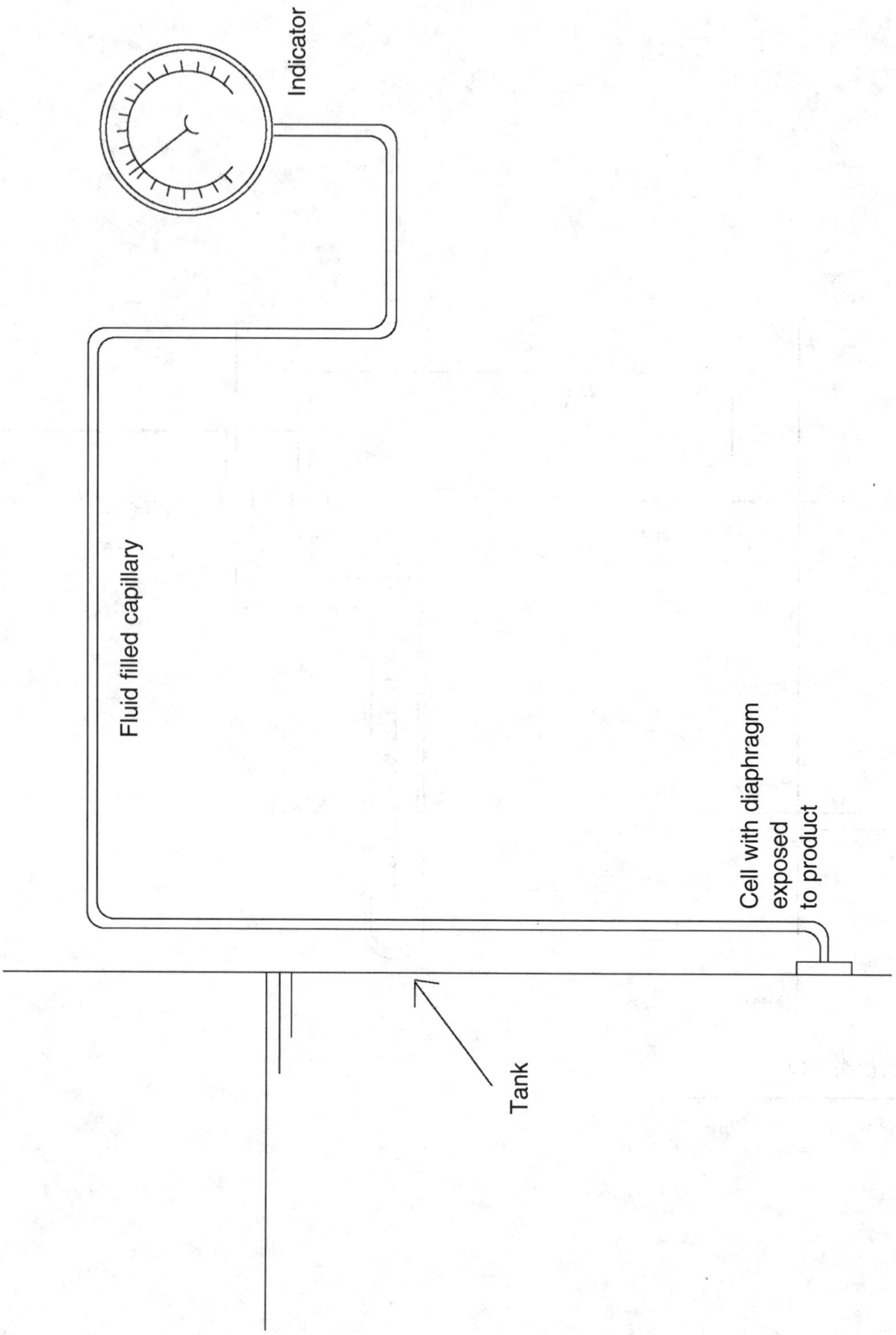

Figure 19: Pneumatic or hydraulic gauges using closed cell

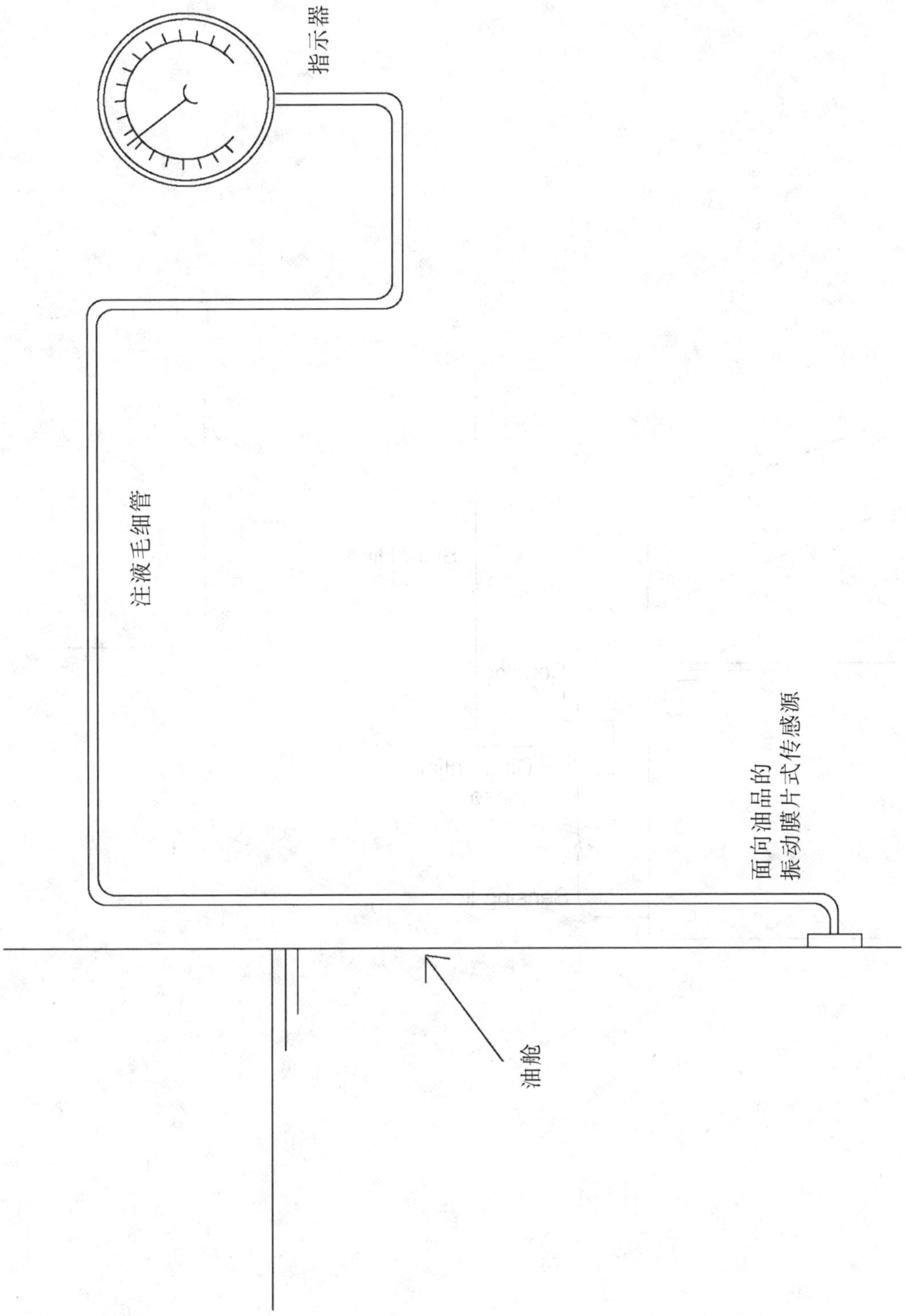

图 19：使用封闭单元的气动或液压液位计

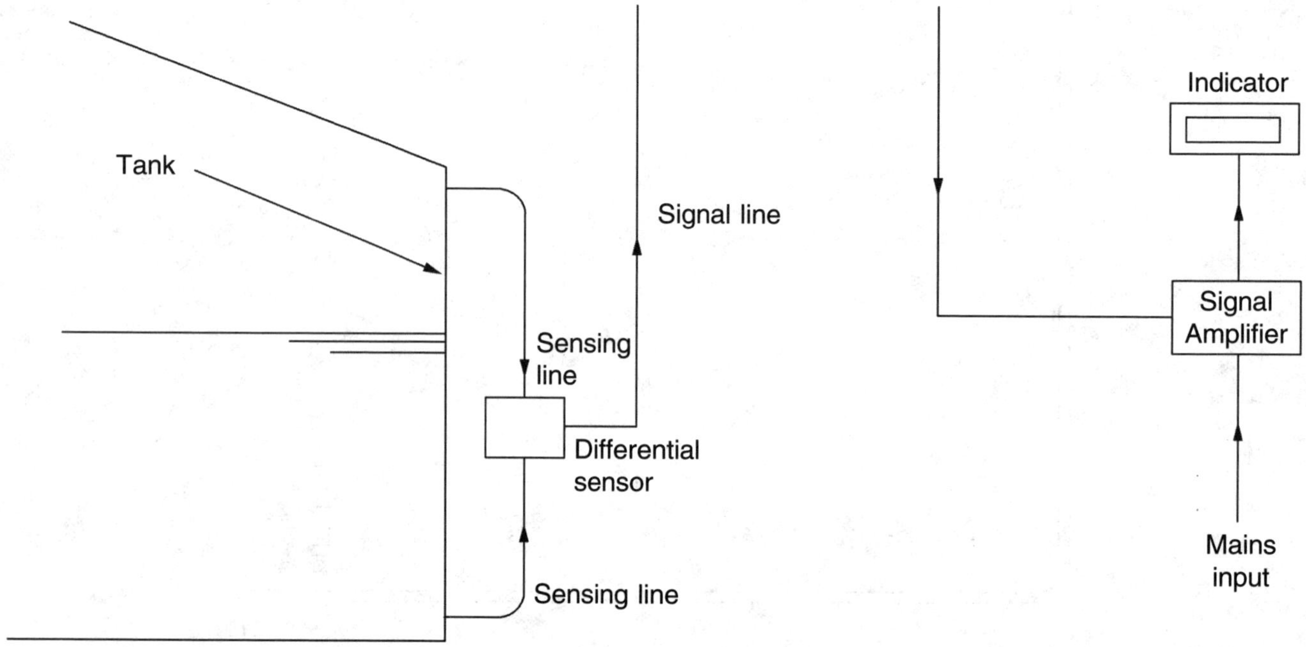

Figure 20: Differential-pressure gauge

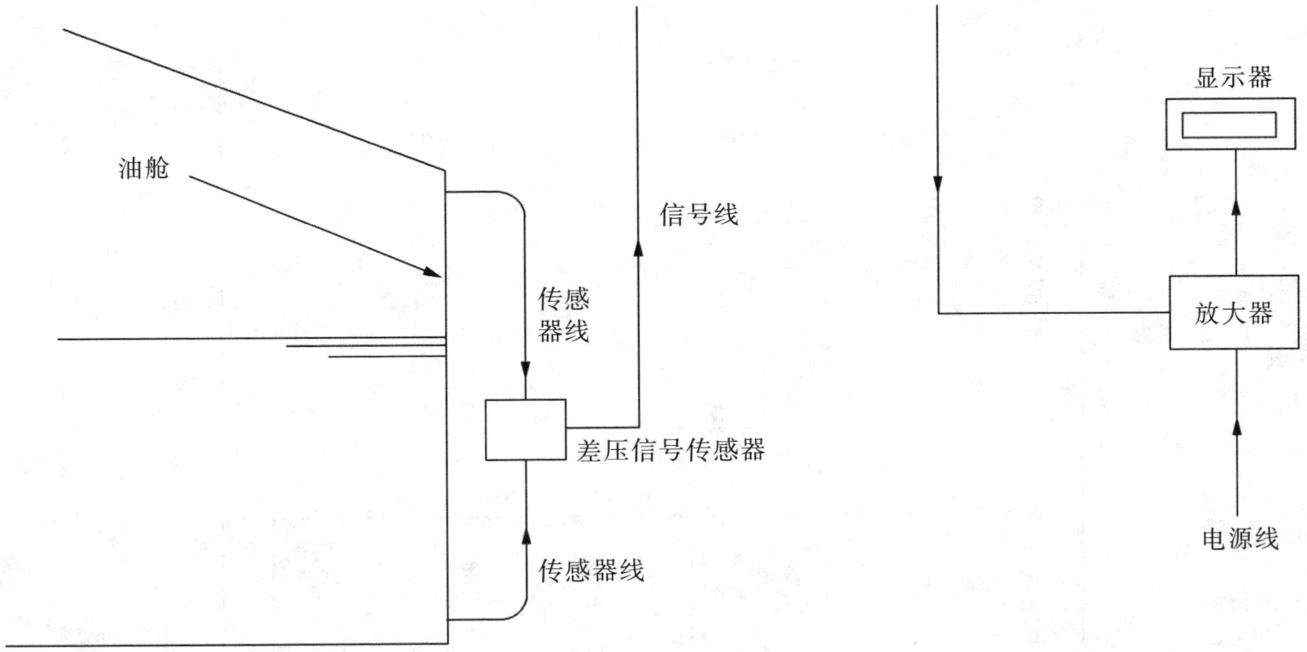

图 20：差压式液位计

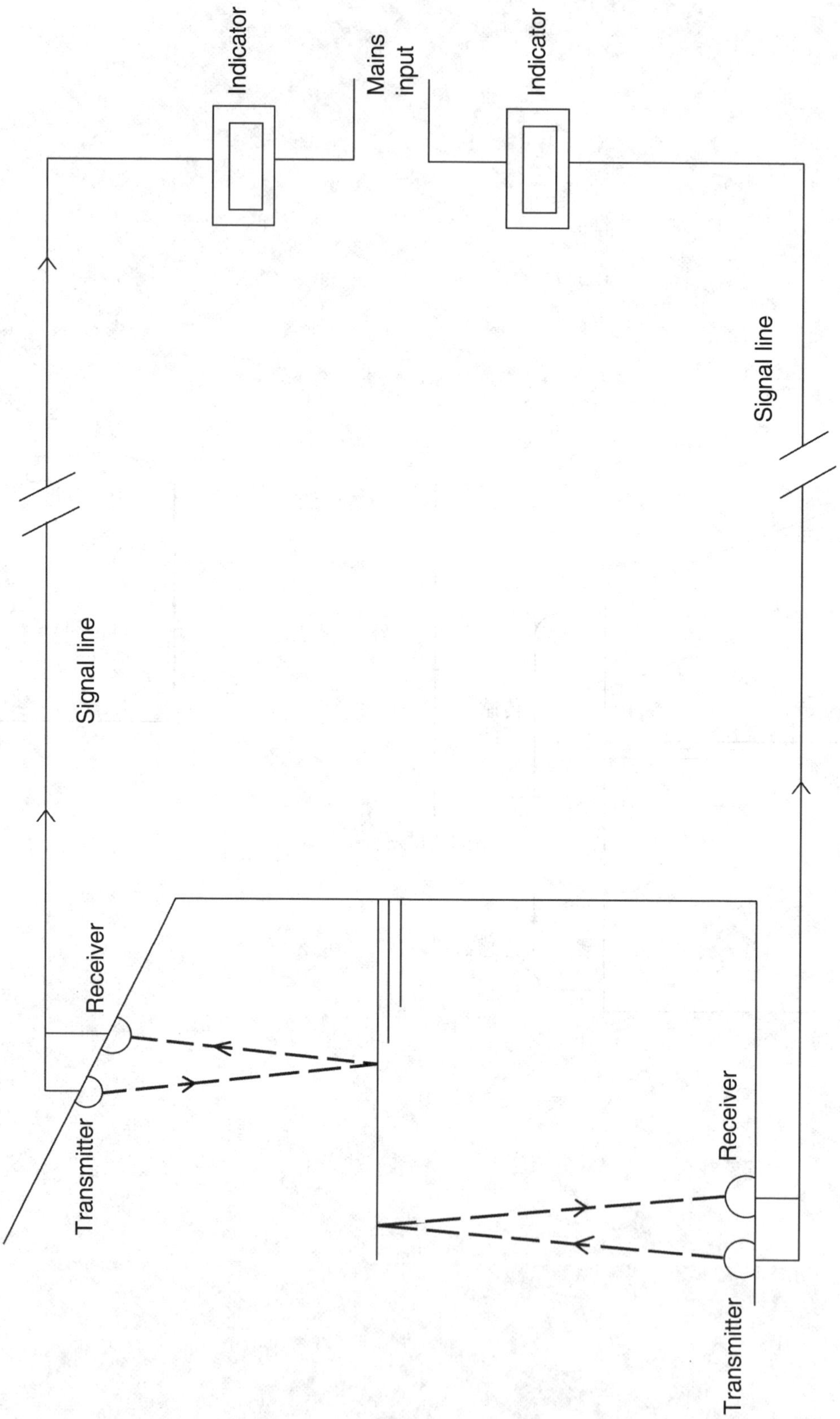

Figure 21: Ultrasonic level gauge

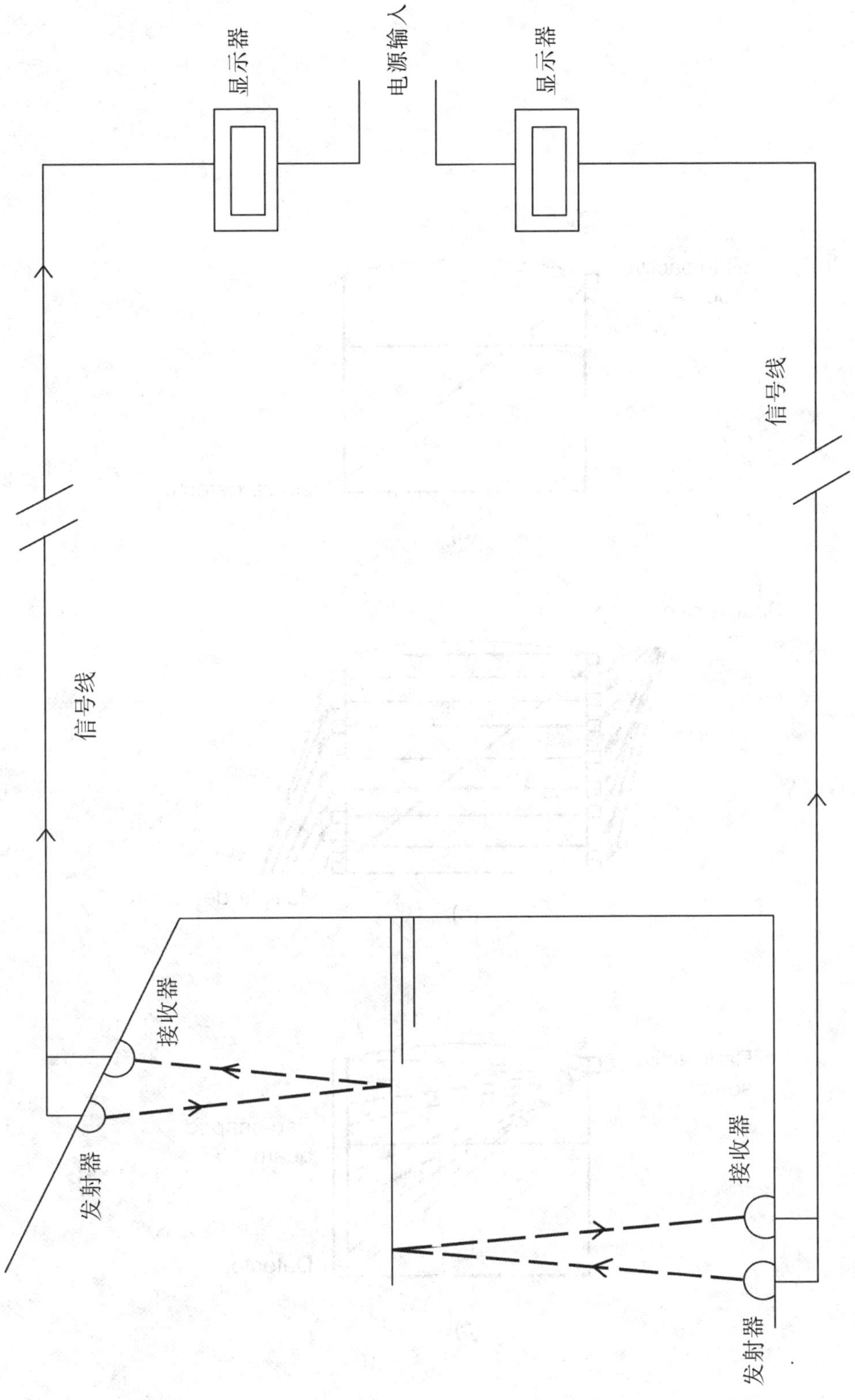

图 21：超声波液位计

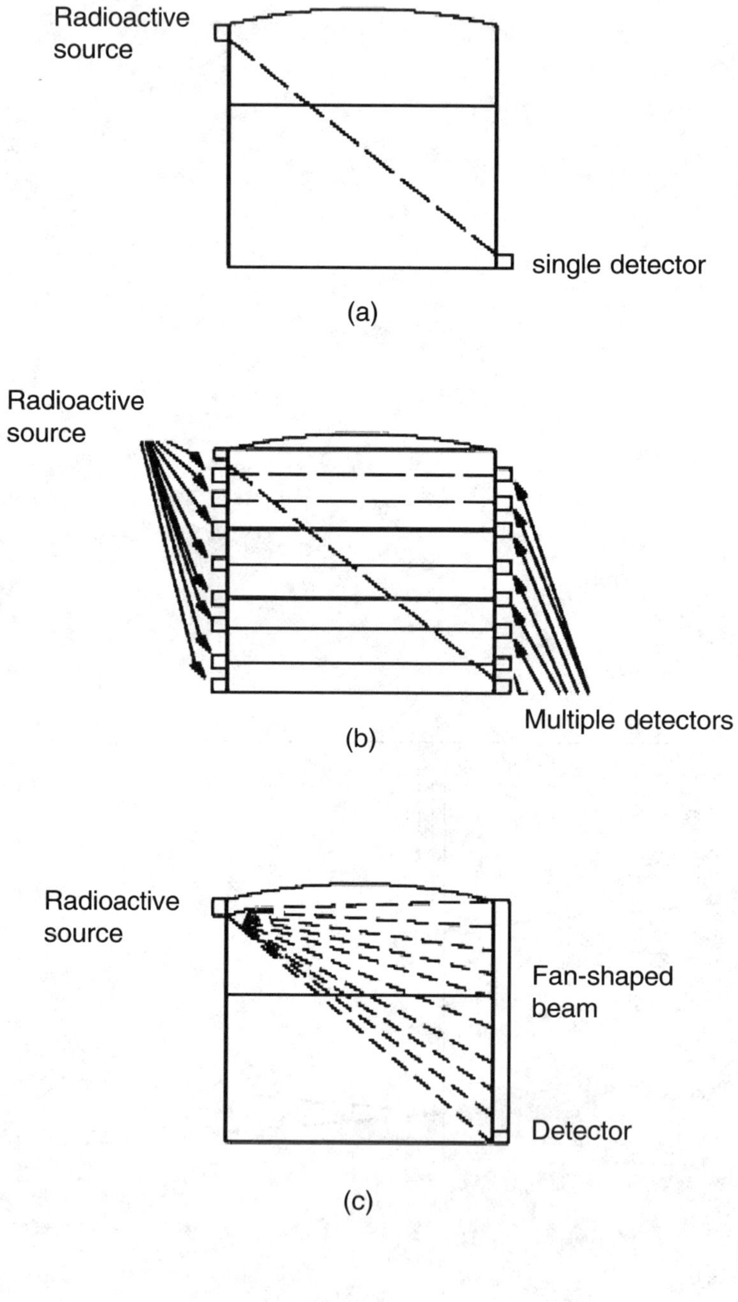

Figure 22: Radioactive level-gauging methods

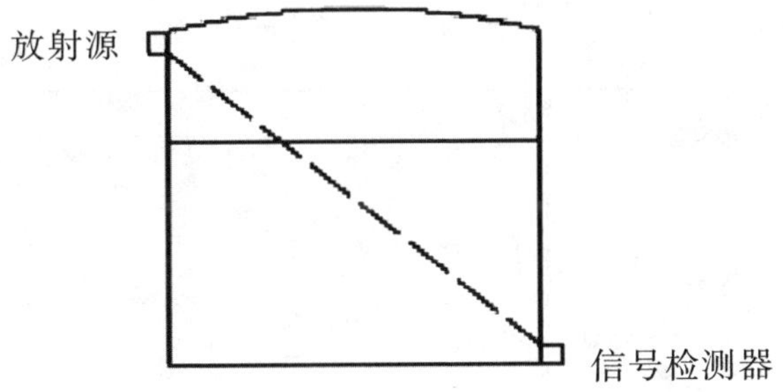

(a)

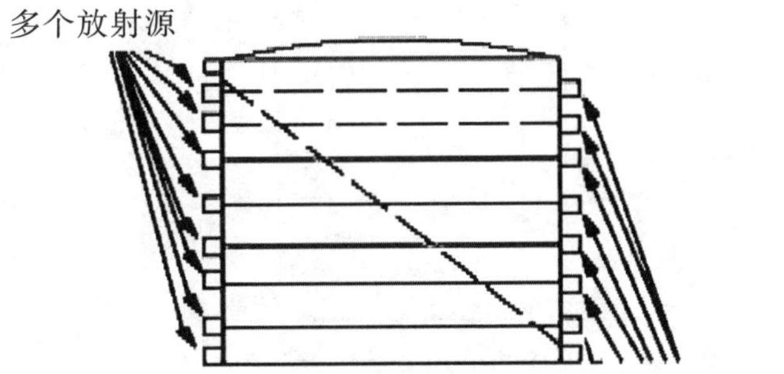

(b)

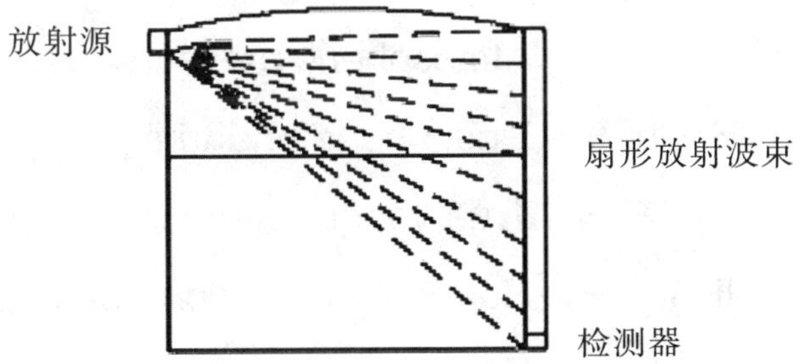

(c)

图 22：基于放射性原理的液位测量方法

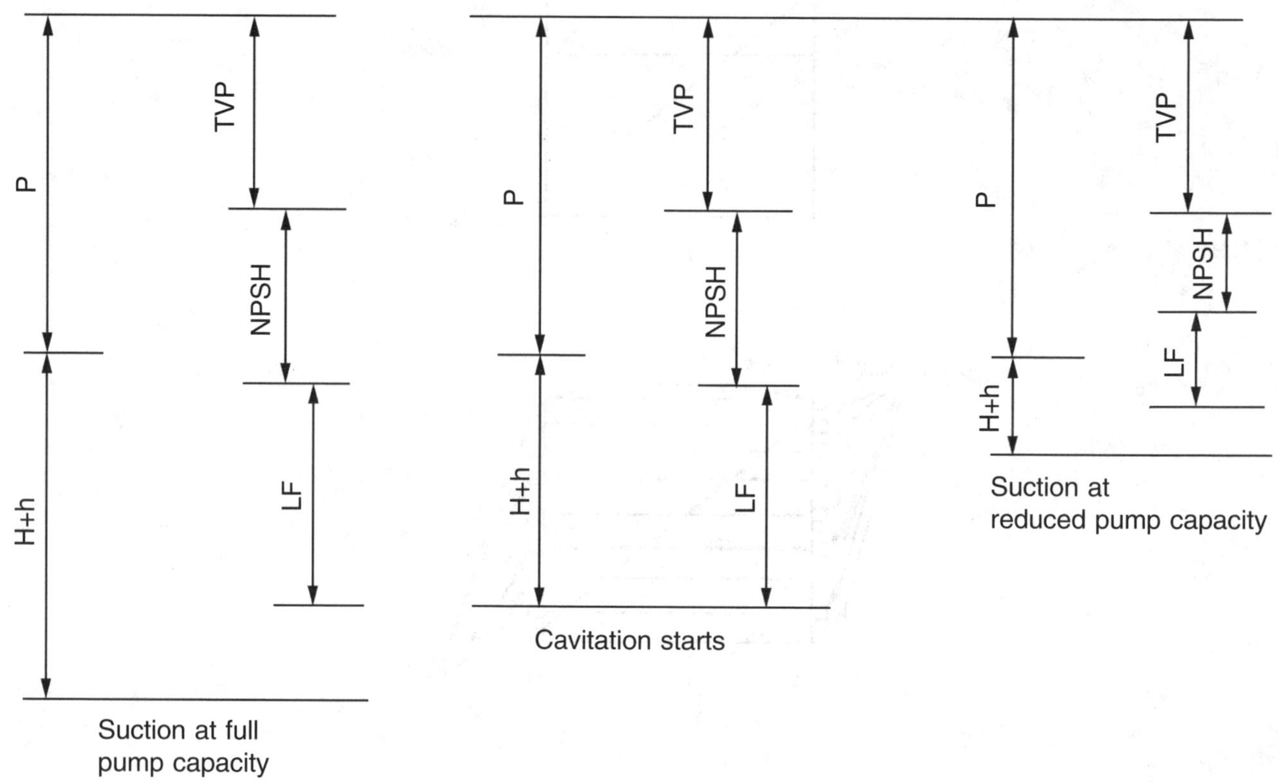

P = Atmospheric pressure

H + h = Liquid head and trim

TVP = True vapour pressure

NPSH = Net positive suction head

LF = Lime friction

Figure 23: Factors influencing suction

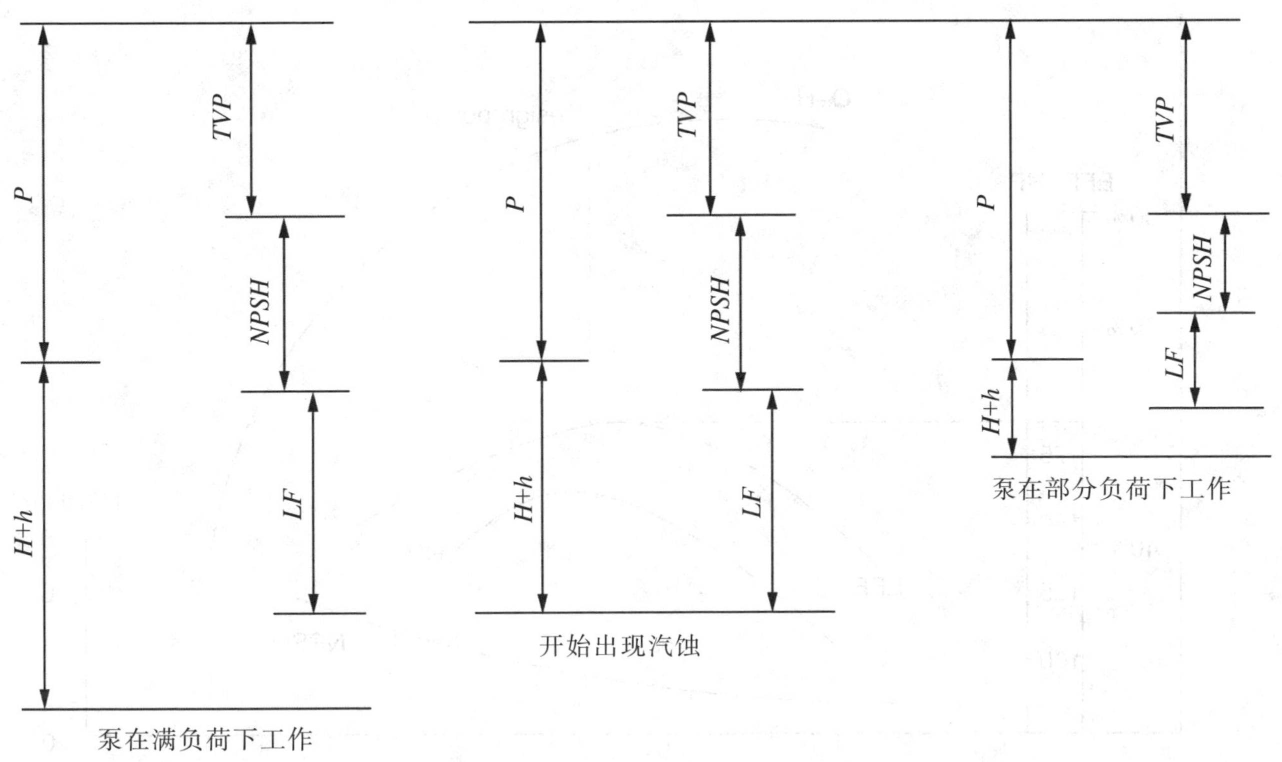

P = 大气压力

$H + h$ = 液柱头及吃水差

TVP = 实际汽化压力

$NPSH$ = 净正吸入压头

LF = 管路阻力

图 23：影响泵吸入的因素

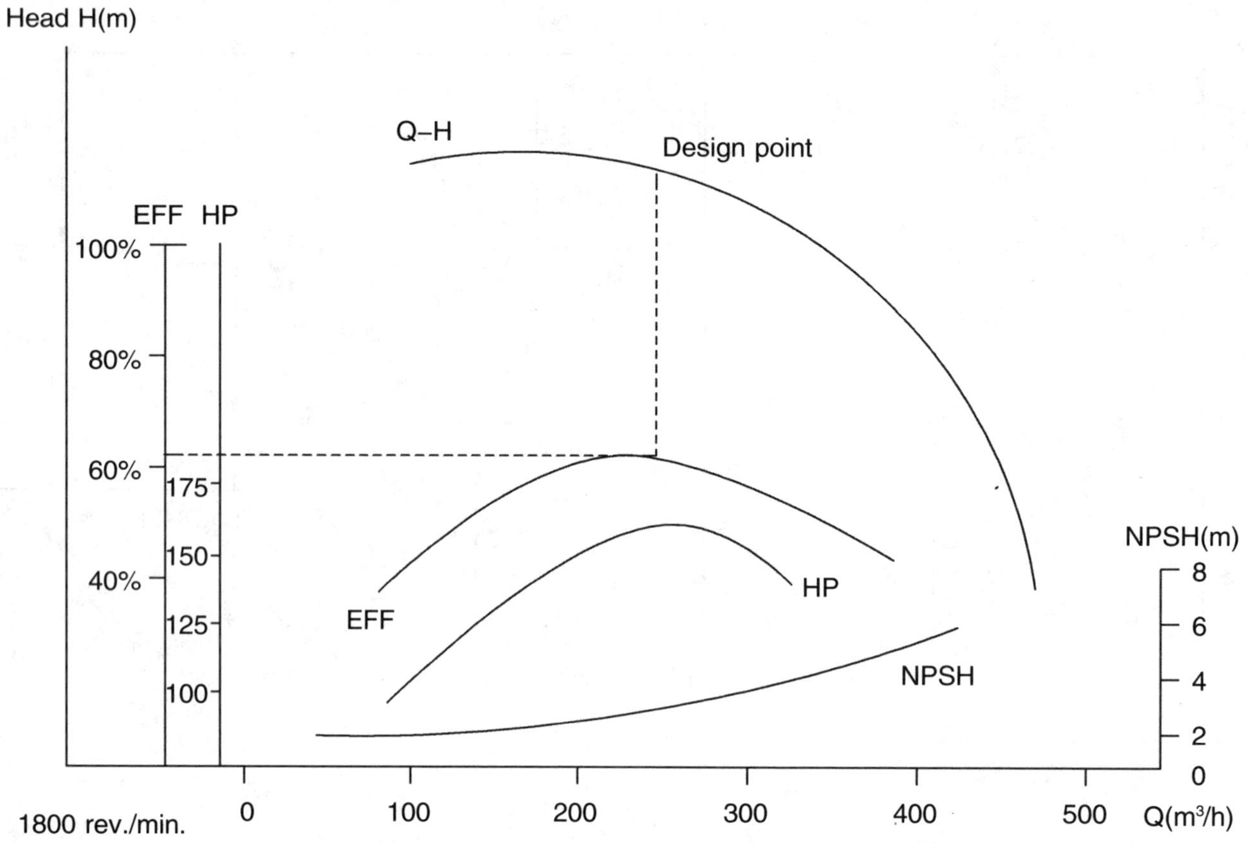

Q = Discharge rate

EFF = Pump efficiency

HP = Power consumption
(R.D of Liquid = 1.0)

NPSH = Net positive suction head

Figure 24: Pump characteristics

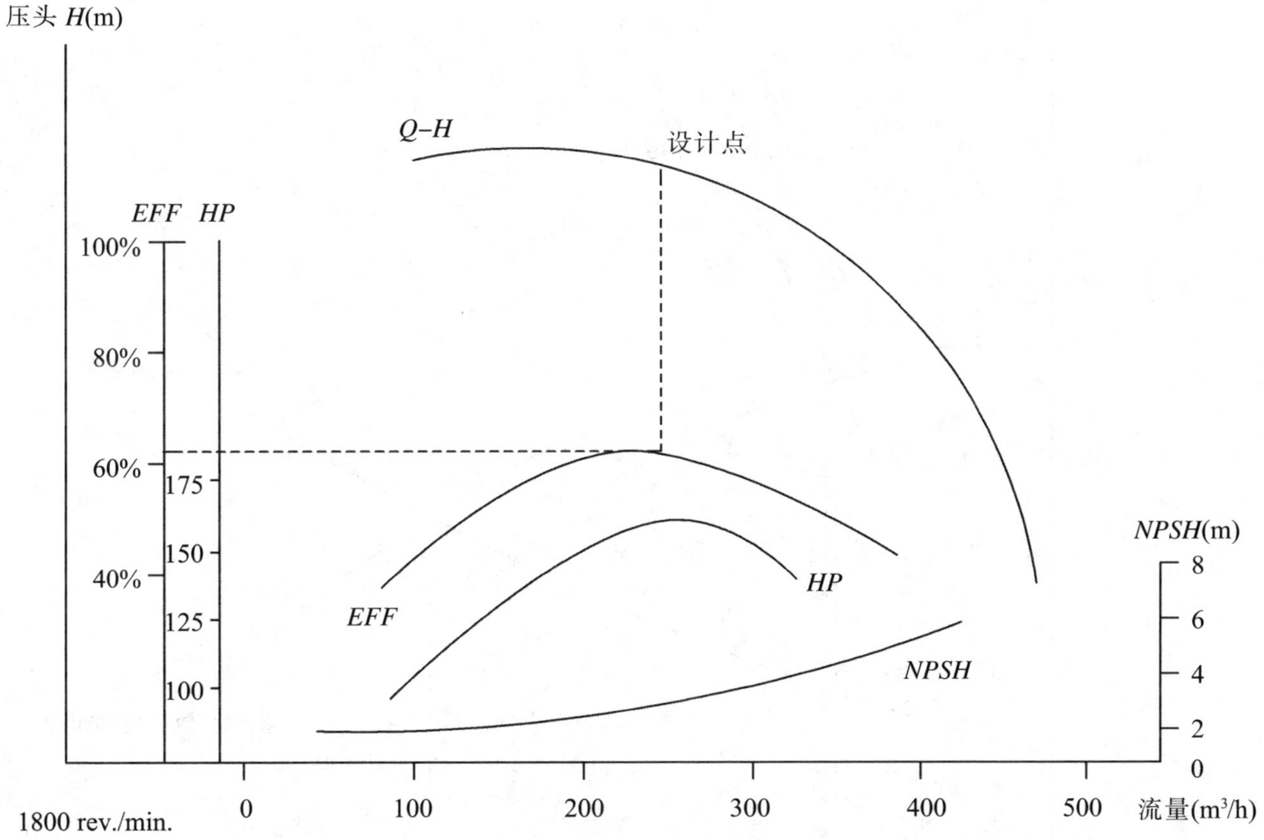

Q = 流量

EFF = 泵的效率

HP = 功耗
(液体的相对密度为1.0)

NPSH = 净正吸入压头

图 24：泵的特性曲线

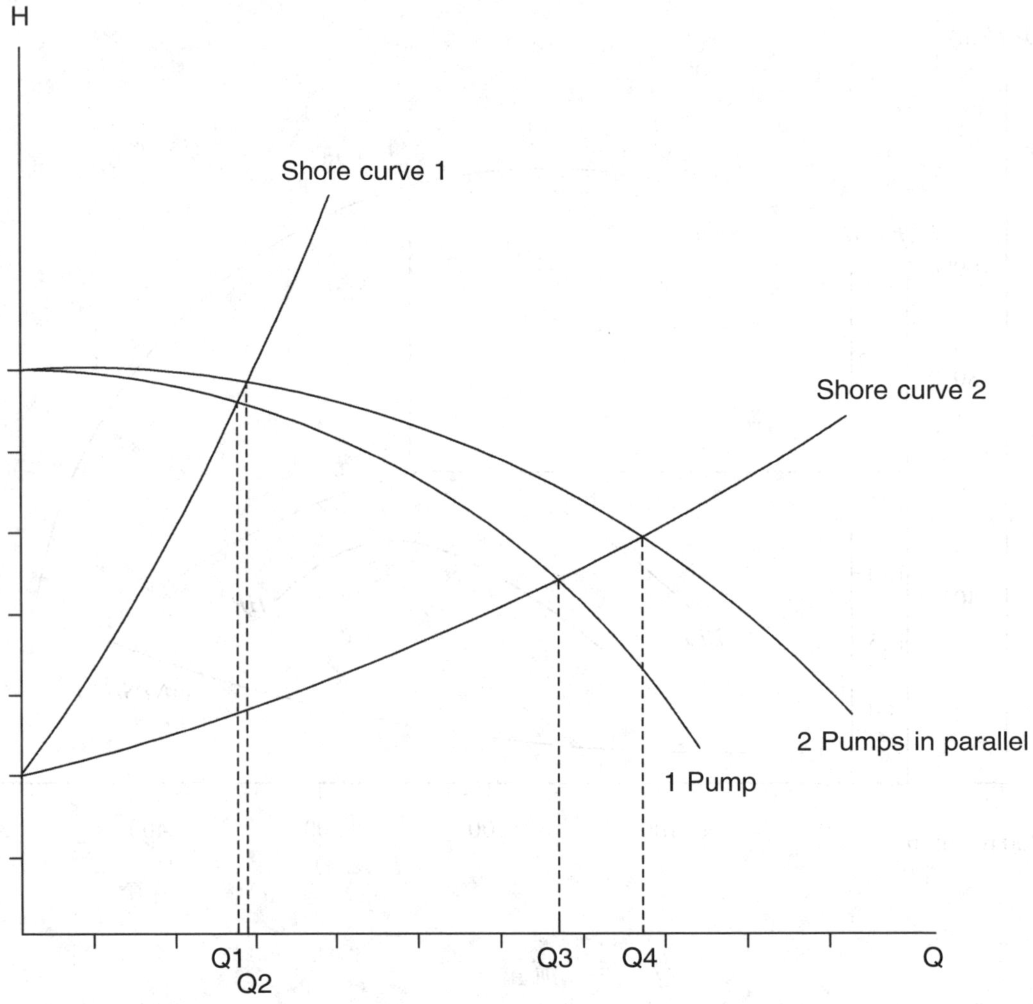

Figure 25: The influence of shore curves on parallel pumps

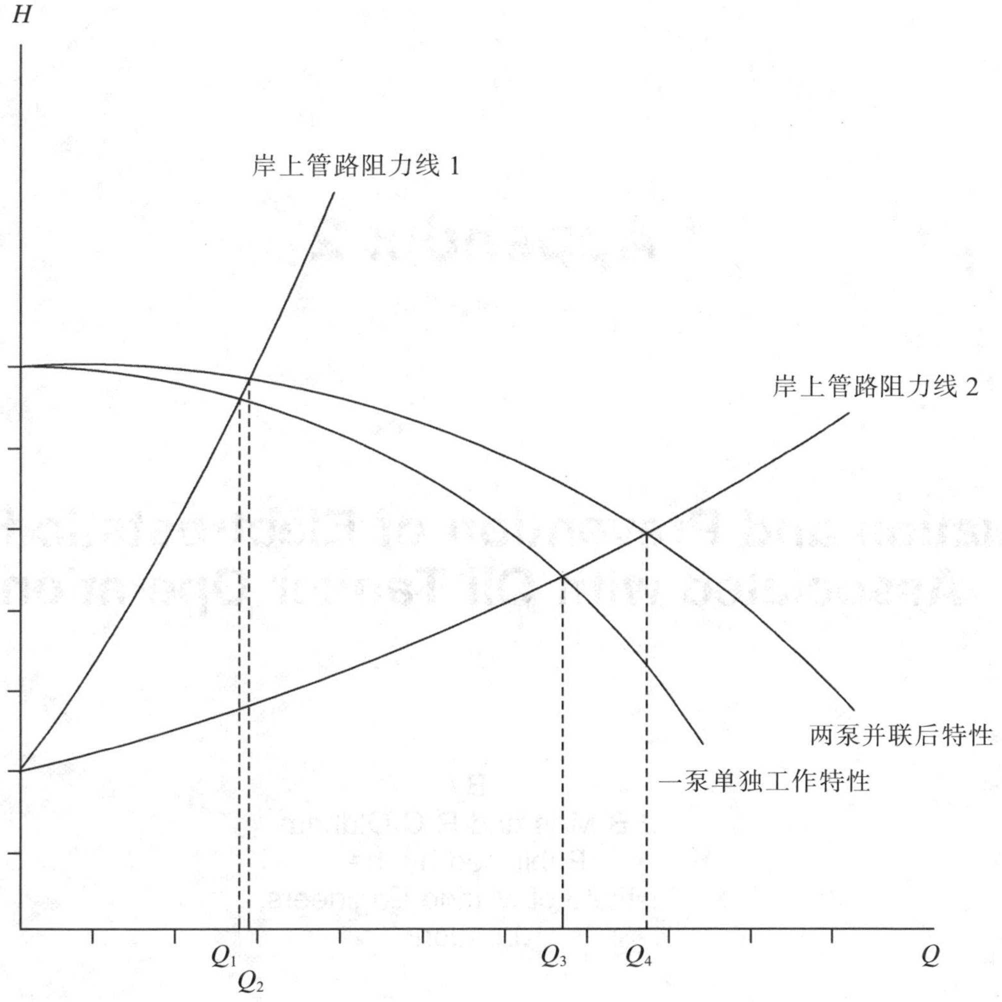

图 25：岸上管路阻力特性对泵并联工作的影响

RETAINED AS IT IS FROM THE EXISTING MODEL COURSE DOCUMENT

Appendix 2:

Evaluation and Prevention of Electrostatic Hazards Associated with Oil Tanker Operations

By
J B Mills and R C Oldham
Published by the
Institute of Marine Engineers,
London

此部分参见现有的示范课程文件

附录 2:

油船作业静电危险的评估和预防

By
J B Mills and R C Oldham
Published by the
Institute of Marine Engineers,
London

RETAINED AS IT IS FROM THE EXISTING MODEL COURSE DOCUMENT

Appendix 3a:

Inert Gas Plants – IGS Theory, Requirements

By
Per O. Hatlen M. Sc.
Chief Research Engineer
The Ship Research Institute of Norway
Oslo, February 1984

此部分参见现有的示范课程文件

附录 3a:

惰性气体系统(IGS)的原理及要求

By
Per O. Hatlen M. Sc.
Chief Research Engineer
The Ship Research Institute of Norway
Oslo, February 1984

RETAINED AS IT IS FROM THE EXISTING MODEL COURSE DOCUMENT

Appendix 3b:

Inert Gas Plants – IGS Operation

By
Per O. Hatlen M. Sc.
Chief Research Engineer
The Ship Research Institute of Norway
Oslo, February 1984

此部分参见现有的示范课程文件

附录 3b:

惰性气体系统(IGS)的操作

By
Per O. Hatlen M. Sc.
Chief Research Engineer
The Ship Research Institute of Norway
Oslo, February 1984

RETAINED AS IT IS FROM THE EXISTING MODEL COURSE DOCUMENT

Appendix 4:

Crude Oil Washing – Implementation and Operating Procedures

By
Captain W. D. J. Barker and T. W. Allsop
Published by
Institute of Marine Engineers
London

此部分参见现有的示范课程文件

附录 4:

原油洗舱的实施和操作程序

By
Captain W. D. J. Barker and T. W. Allsop
Published by
Institute of Marine Engineers
London

Appendix 5:

Case Studies of Oil Tanker Accidents

附录5:

油船事故案例研究

Case Studies

Introduction

In this Appendix, a few case studies on oil tanker accidents have been presented. The objective is to sensitize the students regarding the huge fallout of accidents on board a tanker, in terms of loss of life, property and coastal amenities, and subsequent expenditure of valuable resources in terms of economic cost of a clean up.

Working on board a tanker is very serious business that requires a high degree of professionalism. Majority of incidents that take place on tankers, which in most cases result in a spill, can be avoided by following the basic rules of safety and ensuring that corners are not cut. It does not, after all, pay to behave like a proverbial cowboy and taking unnecessary chances! By doing so, the shipboard personnel, especially the senior management on board, behave in an irresponsible manner. The point of continuous training is to make the student aware of the meaning of responsibility. When the essence of being responsible for one's actions comes from within, rather than being forced upon, it is the first step of safety culture on board.

Each case history is organized as follows:

- A list of headers that summarizes the spill name, location, product, and size of spill
- A brief incident summary including weather conditions and events leading up to the spill
- A description of the behaviour of the oil including movement, evaporation, mousse formation, and dispersion
- A discussion of countermeasures and mitigation
- A description of other special interest issues such as communication problems, unusual hazards encountered, and large losses of organisms, as applicable

The post spill scenario has been delved into in some detail, as compared to the incident summary, in order to make the seafarer aware as to how a small error in judgement on his/her part (be it in terms of navigation or cargo operation) can create a difficult situation for many others ashore.

案例研究

引言

在该附录中,将列举一些油船事故案例研究。目的是让学员们对油船事故所带来的严重后果有所认识,这些严重后果主要体现在生命、财产、港口设施的损失,宝贵资源的浪费,以及事故后进行清理工作所需的巨额费用。

在油船上工作是件非常严肃的事情,这需要高度的职业精神。只要遵守基本安全操作规则并保证没有遗漏任何操作细节,发生在油船上的大多数事故(这些事故通常会引起溢油)都是可以避免的。毕竟,该工作不能采取众所周知的牛仔的工作方式,并进行不必要的冒险尝试!如果这样做,船上人员,尤其是高级管理人员的所作所为就是一种不负责任的行为。持续培训就是为了使学员们认识到责任感的重要性。当学员们能够自主地负起责任,而不需要强制时,就完成了建立船上安全文化的第一步。

各案例是按以下思路进行整理的:

- 通过一系列的标题概括出事故船舶名称、事故发生地点、溢油类型以及溢油量
- 事故摘要包括当时的天气状况及导致溢油的事件
- 对溢油状况的概述,包括其运动、蒸发、形成凝结块以及扩散等
- 关于减轻损失、处理溢油对策的探讨
- 对其他特殊关注问题的描述,如沟通问题、遇到的异常灾害、生物的大量灭亡等

相对于事故摘要,需要对后期溢油现场进行详细研究,以便使船员认识到:在他看来是一个不值一提的小错误(如导航、货物操作上的错误),却可能给岸上的其他人带来巨大的麻烦。

Case Study 1

Name: Al Rawdatain
Spill Date: 29th October 1977
Location: Genoa, Italy
Oil Product: Kuwait crude oil
Tank Vessel: Oil Type
Oil spilled: 7,350 Barrels

Incident Summary

On October 29, 1977, a valve was left open during the offloading of the Al Rawdatain at the Genoa-Multedo dock. Seven thousand three hundred fifty barrels of Kuwait crude oil spilled from the vessel over a period of several hours. The spill was mitigated with chemical dispersants.

Behaviour of Oil

Kuwait crude oil is a medium weight product with an API gravity of 31.2 and a viscosity of 2.53 centistokes. Over-flights on the morning of October 30 revealed a slick extending out 275 yards from the vessel. By October 31, a 7-mile long by 3-mile wide slick extended out to sea. A smaller amount of oil broke off from the large slick and moved west towards Savona. This oil formed a 5-mile long by 3-mile wide slick, which stayed 2 miles off the shore beween Cogoleto and Varazza. No oil contaminated the shoreline.

Countermeasures and Mitigation

The Genoa Port Authority was responsible for cleanup operations. On October 31, dispersants were applied to the offshore slick and in the vicinity of the tanker's mooring by 4 tugboats, which were directed by observers in helicopters. Two tugs were fitted with Warren Springs Laboratory dispersant spraying equipment and storage tanks. The other two tugs used improvised spraying gear. A harbour launch applied dispersants to the smaller slick near Savona on the morning of October 31. Two fire monitoring tugs joined the Savona operations later that day, and sprayed dispersants into the night using search lights. Over-flights revealed that no significant amounts of oil persisted after the dispersants were applied. Operations were considered successful and were completed by November 2 in perfect weather.

案例研究1

船名: A1 Rawdatain
溢油时间: 1977年10月29日
地点: 意大利,热那亚
油品: 科威特原油
油船的类型: 油船
溢油量: 7,350桶

事故摘要

1977年10月29日,A1 Rawdatain船在热那亚穆尔特码头卸货期间,一个阀一直处于打开状态。在几个小时的时间内共溢出7,350桶Kuwait原油。使用化学消油剂后该溢油得到了抑制。

溢油的状况

科威特原油是一种中等原油,其API比重为31.2,其黏度为2.53 cSt。10月30日早上空中观察显示溢油带已扩展至距离该船275码的地方。截止10月31日,一条7英里长、3英里宽的溢油带漂到了外海。少量溢油从巨大的溢油带分离出来向西漂向萨沃纳。这些溢油在科戈莱托和瓦拉兹之间、距离陆地2英里的海上形成了5英里长、3英里宽的溢油带。没有溢油污染海岸线。

溢油的处理措施及减缓

热那亚港口当局负责清理工作。10月31日,对沿海溢油带使用了消油剂,并在事发船舶周围锚泊了4艘拖船,由直升机中的观察员负责指挥。2艘拖船配置有Warren Springs 实验室的消油剂喷洒设备以及储油舱。另外2艘拖船使用临时喷洒装置。10月31日早上,1艘港内船艇向萨沃纳附近较小的溢油带使用了消油剂。当天晚些时候,2艘消防监控拖船也加入到萨沃纳的清理工作中,利用搜寻探照灯在夜间喷洒消油剂。空中观察显示,使用消油剂后,海面上已没有大量溢油。清理工作获得了成功并于11月2日全部结束,当天天气非常好。

Case Study 2

Name: Alvenus
Spill Date: 30th July 1984
Location: Calcasieu River bar channel, 11 miles SE of Cameron, Louisiana
Oil Product: Venezuelan Merey, Pilon Crude
Tank Vessel: Oil type
Oil spilled: 65,000 Barrels

Incident Summary

On July 30, 1984 at 1236 the U.K. Tank Vessel Alvenus grounded in the Calcasieu River Bar Channel 11 miles southeast of Cameron, Louisiana. The vessel suffered a structural failure, which ruptured the hull near the No.2 tanks. The resulting spill of approximately 65,000 barrels of Venezuelan Merey and Pilon crude oil was carried in a westerly direction by wind and currents. Offshore recovery was hampered by rough weather and the magnitude of the spill. The water temperature was 26.5℃ and winds were from the east and northeast 15-20 knots.

The spill moved slowly westward, and into Galveston Bay, Texas between August 2 and August 5. Oil impacts were severe at Rollover Inlet and Crystal Beach, and on August 4 more oil was pushed ashore further south along the Galveston Island coast. The spill affected 90% of Galveston's West Beach, including 80% of the Galveston seawall and the associated rock groins and pilings.

Oil in the seawall area was a concern due to the oil's smothering effect on marine organisms. Organisms in this area were determined to be a minor part of the entire ecosystem and due to their transient nature were able to move to more suitable habitats. Several dead crabs, rays, and fish were recovered along the seawall. Also oiled were marsh grass areas in East Bay (10-20 barrels) and 2 small lagoons. Some oil, which entered Galveston Channel, did affect several small sand islands used as nesting sites for birds. One oiled sea turtle was cleaned and released. Tourism losses were estimated at $1 million per day. Commercial shrimp fishermen filed a suit for $10 million. By October 1 the oiled beaches of Bolivar Peninsula and Galveston Island had been cleaned by the removal of oiled sand.

Behaviour of Oil

Merey crude oil is a medium crude oil with an API gravity of 17.3 and a pour point of −10 degrees F. Pilon crude is a heavy crude oil of API gravity 13.8 with a pour point of −9 degrees F and a viscosity of 1,943 centistokes. The spill formed a heavy, coalescent slick, which was initially predicted to move offshore to the south away from the Texas coast. Changes in wind direction resulted in a westerly trajectory, spreading the oil into a 75-mile long slick with three leading arms. The oil came ashore in the Galveston, Texas area forming as tar balls, sheens, and pancakes floating outside the surf zone. By August 7 an estimated 17,000 – 26,000 bbl (2,500-3,500 tonnes) of oil had accumulated on the shores of Galveston Island and the Bolivar Peninsula. An additional 7400 – 11,100 bbl (1,000–1,500 tonnes) of oil adsorbed onto suspended solid particles (sediment) near-shore and sank in the surf zone where it was trapped among successive sandbars and trenches forming "blankets" to 4 inches in depth. Some of the sub-tidal oil formed cylindrical shaped rolls that moved up and down the beach with wave action. Warm temperatures on the beach (80°F water, 80–100°F air) may have

案例研究2

船名: Alvenus
溢油时间: 1984年7月30日
地点: 美国路易斯安那州卡梅伦县东南方向11英里处的卡尔克苏河道
油品: 委瑞内拉的马瑞、皮隆原油
油船的类型: 油船
溢油量: 65,000桶

事故摘要

1984年7月30日12时36分，英国油船Alvenus在美国路易斯安那州卡梅伦县东南方向11英里处的卡尔克苏河道搁浅。该船结构破损,刺穿No.2舱附近的船体。结果导致溢出了65,000桶委瑞内拉马瑞、皮隆原油,这些溢出的原油被向西的风和涌卷走。岸上的回收装置受到了恶劣天气和溢油量的限制。当时海水温度为26.5℃,东风和东北风的风速为15~20海里/小时。

溢出的油逐渐向西移动，并于8月2日~8月5日进入得克萨斯州加尔维斯顿海湾。溢油对Rollover入口和水晶海岸造成了非常严重的影响,8月4日,更多的原油被冲上沿岸,并沿着加尔维斯顿海岸继续向南扩张。溢油影响了90%的加尔维斯顿西海岸,其中包括80%的加尔维斯顿海堤和相关的岸桩。

溢油对海堤区域的影响备受关注,因为原油的窒息作用会对海洋生物产生巨大影响。该区域的海洋生物只是整个生态系统很小的一部分,毕竟它们还可以迁徙到其他栖息地。在海堤上,遍地都是蟹、鳐鱼等生物的尸体。另外,东海湾的沼泽湿地也被溢油污染了(10~20桶原油),还有2个咸水湖也未能幸免。进入加尔维斯顿海湾的溢油,对几个作为鸟类栖息地的小沙岛同样产生了影响。对一只被原油污染海龟进行清洁后放归大海。旅游产业估计每天损失达100万美元。以捕虾为生的渔民对其起诉,要求获赔1 000万美元。截至10月1日,通过移走油污的沙子,玻利瓦尔半岛和加尔维斯顿岛的海滩已基本清理完毕。

溢油的状况

马瑞原油是一种中等原油,其API比重为17.3,倾点为−10 ℉。皮隆原油是一种重级原油,其API比重为13.8,倾点为−9 ℉,黏度为1 943 cSt。溢油聚结成厚厚的油膜,起初预计这些油膜会从得克萨斯州的海岸移向南部海岸。风向的改变使其变为向西运动,并扩散形成了带有三个突起的75英里油膜。这些原油在得克萨斯州的加尔维斯顿海岸形成了原油球,闪着光泽,在碎波区漂浮着类似薄煎饼的油膜。截至8月7日,估计17 000~26 000 bbI(2 500~3 500 t)的原油积聚在玻利瓦尔半岛和加尔维斯顿海岸。另外,有7 400~11 100 bbI(1 000~1 500 t)原油吸附在近海岸的悬浮固体颗粒(沉淀物)上,并在碎波区沉没，在这里,原油最终被沙洲和海沟捕获,形成了约4英寸厚的“油毯”。 海岸上温暖的气温(海水温度为80℉,空气温度为80~100 ℉)可能会使泄漏的原油保持

contributed to keeping the oil highly fluid and fresh. Unless mixed with sand, the oil was easily dispersed with gentle agitation.

Countermeasures and Mitigation

Oil booms and sea barrier were placed around the vessel on the day following the grounding. Efforts to contain and recover the spilled oil at sea became ineffective due to rough seas, which pushed oil under the barrier, and the refusal of the contracted lightering barge to receive oil recovered from seawater. A second barge and tug were contracted, but delayed due to a line becoming fouled in the screw of the towing vessel. The principal contractor, Clean Gulf Association, an industry cooperative, was not equipped for massive at-sea cleanup and equipment was not immediately available in Cameron, Louisiana. Had the equipment been available, it still may not have been loaned to a non-member company.

Beach cleanup was determined to be best accomplished by using road graders to move newly beached oil above the high tide zone. Graders were most effective when used together in a staggered formation, moving oil up the beach from the inter-tidal area to backshore storage areas. Oiled sand collected in the storage areas was loaded into dump trucks for disposal. This operation involved as many as 50 graders and 100 dump trucks.

Submerged oil in the sub-tidal proved to be the greatest problem because re-oiling necessitated continual re-cleaning of beaches. Removal of the sub-tidal oil was attempted with mesh screening, pumping, and heavy equipment, but none of these techniques proved effective. During beach cleanup, conflict arose between state and private landowners over ownership of the contaminated sand, the state wanting to remove the sand versus the landowners wanting it to remain in place on the beach. Cleaning of the seawall and revetment involved more than 150 workers manually removing oil with sorbent materials, shovels, and rakes. Various "hydro-blasting" methods were tried. Low-pressure (850 psi) warmed seawater left stains on the rocks, a high-pressure "sugar" sand blast was effective on the rocks but not concrete seawall, and dry sand blasting proved too abrasive.

Extensive discussions with experts and representatives of the International Tanker Owners Pollution Federation concerning dispersants concluded that dispersant use on the water was not appropriate due to water depth, proximity of the spill to shore and fisheries resources, and the inability of the dispersant to penetrate thick Venezuelan crude. Since the dispersant would have been only partially effective, the cost benefit of using an ineffective dispersant would have diverted funds from the beach cleanup deemed necessary in either case.

Other Special Interest Issues

Logistics became a problem during the beach cleanup due to the large number of heavy equipment units involved. Traffic constraints at disposal sites resulted in as many as 40 loaded vehicles waiting on the beaches to off-load. Mass balance calculations estimated the volume of the recovered oil at between 63,000 – 78,000 bbl (8700 – 10,700 metric tonnes). This is very high considering that an estimate of the total spill was 65,000 bbl (10,000 metric tonnes)!

液态,因此除非混有沙子,否则原油随着搅动很容易扩散。

溢油的处理措施及减缓

事故发生后,立刻在事故船舶的周围放置了围油栏和水上障碍物,但由于海况非常恶劣,导致为控制和回收海上溢油所作的努力收效甚微,汹涌的海水不仅将原油从围油栏的下面冲出,还阻碍了合同驳船对海上溢油的回收工作。另外,最主要的承包商——海湾清理组织(一个商业合作企业)没有配备针对大型海上溢油事故清理工作的设备,而且在易斯安那州卡梅伦县也不可能及时得到这样的设备。

为了更好地完成海滩的清理工作,使用了平路机来移走潮汐频发地带的油污。这些平路机按一定的顺序交错排列,以便使其以最高效率将污油从潮际地带移至后海岸地带的储油区,储油区的油污沙子最终被装入卡车进行处理。这项工作共动用了50辆平路机和100辆卡车。

浸没在海潮中的原油才是最难处理的,因为反复的油污需要对海滩进行反复的清理。为了清除海潮中的原油,当时使用网筛、泵以及重型机械,但所有的这些设备都无法达到满意的效果。在清理海滩的过程中,政府和私有土地所有人在这些油污染沙子的所有权上产生了冲突:政府想移走这些沙子,而私有土地所有人却想让这些沙子保留在原处。为了清理海堤及护岸上的原油,共有超过150名工人用吸附材料、铁铲、耙子等工具对其进行了人工清除。尝试使用了各种"水力清沙"方法。低压(850 psi)热海水会在岩石上留下污渍,而高压喷砂的方法虽然对岩石很有效,对混凝土的海堤来说却达不到那样的效果,而且干喷砂具有较强的磨损作用。

通过与专家及国际油船船东防污染联合会的代表就消油剂问题进行了大量探讨后, 得出了以下结论:考虑到海水的深度、溢油区离海岸的距离、渔业资源等因素,向海水中投放消油剂并不合适,况且消油剂也无法穿透厚厚的委瑞内拉原油。由于消油剂仅能起到一定的效果,在其他情况下,使用一种无效消油剂实际可能将会分流出海岸清污需要的基金。

其他特别关注的问题

由于在海滩的清理过程中使用了大量的重型机械设备,这使后勤工作成了一大难题。处置场所的交通限制已导致40多辆装有沙子的车辆在海滩上等着倾卸。根据质量平衡计算,估计此次回收的原油有63 000~78 000 bbi(8 700~10 700公吨),考虑到此次溢油总共约有65 000 bbi(10 000公吨),这样的回收率已经非常高了。

Case Study 3

Name:	American Trader
Spill Date:	7th February 1990
Location:	Huntington Beach, California
Oil Product:	Alaskan North Slope Crude Oil
Tank Vessel:	Oil Type
Oil spilled:	9,458 Barrels

Incident Summary

On February 7, 1990 at 1620, the single-hull tank vessel American Trader grounded on one of its anchors while approaching the Golden West Refining Company's offshore mooring. Two holes were punctured in one of the vessel's cargo tanks, releasing 9458 barrels of heavy crude oil into the water approximately 1.3 miles from Huntington Beach, California. The master of the vessel immediately reported the incident to the USCG Marine Safety Office/ Group Los Angeles-Long Beach (MSO/Group LA-LB). The master moved the American Trader into deeper water one mile to the south.

The responsible parties assumed full financial responsibility for the spill and sent representatives to the Long Beach area. Oil began to come ashore on February 8 in light concentrations. By February 9, oil was ashore at Huntington Beach; in some instances, oil in the surf zone here appeared to be in heavier concentrations than observed earlier. Calm seas and fair weather for most of the response period resulted in a rapid and successful cleanup.

The 22,000 barrels of crude remaining in the damaged cargo tank were lightered. By 1200 on February 9, the oil from the damaged tank plus 90,000 barrels from the mid-body tanks had been transferred into barges to decrease the draft of the vessel. Temporary patches were applied to the holes in the hull and the American Trader was moved to an oil transfer facility in Long Beach Harbour to off-load the remaining 470,000 barrels of crude oil. The vessel was moved to San Francisco on February 18 for dry-docking and repair.

Behaviour of Oil

Alaska North Slope Crude Oil is a medium weight oil with an API gravity of 26.5 and a pour point of 0 degrees F. The release of oil from the damaged hull was rapid. Both of the puncture holes were in the No. 1 starboard wing tank. None of the other cargo tanks were damaged. The released oil was driven by the prevailing winds to the NNW of the grounding site. By the morning of the second day, the wind direction had changed and was blowing the oil away from the coastline. Most of the oil was held offshore by winds in a forty square-mile slick for the first five days of the response, which allowed cleanup crews to concentrate on an extensive open-water recovery operation.

Countermeasures and Mitigation

Booming of the sensitive wetlands of the Bolsa Chica National Wildlife Refuge, Newport Bay, and the mouth of the Santa Ana River was completed by 0200 on February 8. Double harbour booms were deployed at Anaheim Bay, Newport Bay, and across the mouth of the Santa Ana River. Small skimmers were stationed behind the first barrier to recover oil, which passed beyond it. Sorbent boom was also deployed between the two hard booms to collect

案例研究3

船名: American Trader
溢油时间: 1990年2月7日
地点: 加利福尼亚州亨廷顿海滩
油品: 阿拉斯加北坡油田原油
油船的类型: 油船
溢油量: 9,458桶

事故摘要

1990年2月7日16点20分，单壳油船American Trader在靠近加州金西炼油公司的近海系泊设施的过程中,压到了该船的一个锚上。一个货油舱立刻被刺破,出现两个洞,9,458桶原油涌入了距加州亨廷顿海滩约1.3英里的水域中。船长立即将该事故向美国海岸警卫队海事安全办公室和洛杉矶长滩集团(MSO/Group LA-LB)报告,并将American Trader转移至向南一英里处的深水水域。

责任方承担了溢油的全部经济责任,并派了代表到长滩(加州西南部港市)。2月8日,开始有少量的的原油被冲到海岸。截至2月9日,溢油抵达了亨廷顿海滩;在某些情况下,此时油的浓度要比之前观察到的浓度更高一些。由于在此期间海面天气状况良好,所以清理工作很顺利。

对破损的货油舱中剩余的22,000桶原油进行了驳运处理。截至2月9日12点,破损油舱中的原油和船中间货油舱里的90,000桶原油都被驳运到驳船上，以便减少船舶的吃水。对American Trader的两个洞进行了临时修补之后,该船驶入长滩港的输油设施中,卸下了余下的470,000桶原油。2月18日,American Trader到旧金山进坞并进行修理。

溢油的状况

阿拉斯加北坡油田原油是一种中等原油,其API比重为26.5,倾点为0 ℉。此次船壳破损后,油的溢流速度非常快。这两个洞都出现在右舷No.1边舱上。而其他舱都没有出破损情况。溢出的原油被西北偏北方向的风由事发地点吹走。第二天清晨,风向发生了改变,并把溢油从海岸线处吹走。在前五天的时间里,大多数的溢油都被风控制在近海区域,且油膜范围也被控制在了40平方英里内,这使得清理溢油的工作人员可以会聚在一个开阔的开放水域对溢油进行回收。

溢油的处理措施及减缓

截至2月8日2点,用围油栏对Bolsa Chica国家野生动物保护区的湿地、纽波特海湾、圣塔安娜河入口进行的围堵工作顺利完成。港内双层围油栏布置在阿纳海姆海湾、纽波特海湾,并横穿圣

oil, which passed the outer barrier. Sorbent boom was placed across the mouths of shallow inland channels in the Bolsa Chica marshlands.

Open-water recovery was done with fifteen skimming vessels and twenty-five support/boom tow vessels.

Other Special Interest Issues

Out of the 1,017 oiled birds taken to the bird rescue centres, 502 birds died as a result of the oiling. Two Pacific white-sided dolphins died from ingesting oil.

The major coastal bird species at risk was the brown pelican, a diving bird that could become completely coated by oil while diving through the surface of the water to feed. The Snowy Plover, a shorebird in the area, could also ingest contaminated organisms at oiled shorelines. One hundred forty one Brown Pelicans, an endangered species, were oiled during the spill; sixty-eight of these died, an estimated 1.5 percent of the population at the time.

塔安那河入海口。首道围油栏后面布置小型撇油器以回收溢过围油栏的溢油。同时吸附性围油栏布置在两个硬质围油栏之间以收集溢过外层围油栏的溢油。吸附性围油栏还布置在波沙奇卡沼泽地区域的浅内陆河的入海口。

由15艘溢油回收船和25艘支持拖船/围油栏拖船在开阔水域完成溢油回收工作。

其他特别关注的问题

在送往鸟类营救中心的1 017只油污鸟类中,有502只死于油污染。2只太平洋斑纹海豚死于吞食石油。

处于危险中的海岸鸟类主要是褐鹈鹕,它是一种潜鸟,当其潜入水中捕食时,身上便沾满油。环颈鸻是该区域的一种岸基鸟类,在油污的海岸线上,这种鸟也在捕食受有污染的有机体。在溢油期间,有141只作为濒危物种的褐鹈鹕受到污染;其中68只已死亡,估计占当时种群总数的1.5%。

Case Study 4

Name: Assimi
Spill Date: 7th January 1983
Location: Oman
Oil Product: Light Iranian Crude Oil
Tank Vessel: Oil Type
Oil spilled: 379000 Barrels

Incident Summary

On January 7, 1983, a fire broke out in the engine room of the tanker Assimi. The crew abandoned ship and the Assimi was taken undertow by the tug Solano. On January 10, an explosion occurred aboard the vessel and it burned fiercely for several days as it was towed into the Arabian Sea. The tanker was towed to a point 200 miles off the coast of Oman where it sank on January 16. A second explosion occurred as the vessel was sinking which ignited the oil on the surface of the water. A slick formed above the area where the vessel sank. There was no coastal pollution resulting from the incident.

Behaviour of Oil

Light Iranian crude oil is a medium weight product with an API gravity of 33.8 and a viscosity of 6.6 centistokes. An over flight on January 19 revealed a slick of silver sheen in the vicinity of the sinking covering 100 square miles and moving towards the northeast. Personnel on an over flight on January 22 found some fresh oil in the slick. The older oil had emulsified, and the total area of the slick was reduced. The northernmost edge of the slick was 180 miles off the coast of Pakistan. An over flight on February 4 showed that most of the oil had dispersed.

Countermeasures and Mitigation

The government of Oman convened a council that included representatives from the Council for Conservation of the Environment and Prevention of Pollution (CCEPP), Sultanate of Oman Navy (SON), Sultanate of Oman Air Force (SOAF), the Royal Oman Police (Marine), the Maritime Affairs Department, the Ministry of Petroleum and Minerals, and the petroleum industry. The council was to form a response strategy in the event of a release of oil. International Transport Company Contractors, the salvers of the Assimi, contracted Smit International to help fight the fire. Equipment and personnel from Smit fought the fire using water and foam from their tug Smit Pioneer. On January 11, the fire was still burning, and the fire-fighters flooded the pump-room in an attempt to keep the fire from spreading from the engine room to the cargo tanks.

The vessel began to sink while undertow by the Solano, and the Oman government ordered the salvers to tow the vessel to a point 200 miles from the coast of Oman and sink it. On January 16, the Assimi was sunk in 3000 meters of water. An explosion occurred as the vessel sank and a slick of burning oil formed on the surface.

The International Maritime Organization (IMO) was contacted to assess the threat to environment and make recommendations to the Oman council. The council also contacted the Regional Organization for the Protection of the Marine Environment (ROPME) to provide

案例研究4

船名: Assimi
溢油时间: 1983年1月7日
地点: 阿曼
油品: 伊朗轻原油
油船的类型: 油船
溢油量: 379,000桶

事故摘要

1983年1月7日,Assimi船的机舱着火。船员弃船,Assimi在拖船Solano的拖拽下逆流而行。在其拖往阿曼海域期间,1月10日,船上发生了第一次爆炸,大火持续了好几天。Assimi被拖船拖拽至离阿曼海岸200英里处,该油船于16日在这里沉没。由于油船下沉时点燃了水面上的原油,因此又发生了第二次爆炸。在油船沉没地点的海面上漂着一层油膜,但该次事故并没有引起沿岸污染。

溢油的状况

伊朗轻原油是一种中等原油,其API比重为33.8,黏度为6.6 cSt。1月19日在空中拍摄的画面显示,Assimi油船沉没地点100平方英里范围内都闪烁着油膜的光泽,且油膜在向东北方向移动。通过1月22日在空中观察发现:在船舶沉没点附近有新油出现,原油已经开始乳化,油膜的总面积在减少,油膜最北面的边缘离巴基斯坦海岸约180英里。2月4日的空中观察发现,大多数的原油都已经分散了。

溢油的处理措施及减缓

事故发生后,阿曼政府立即组建了临时理事会,该理事会主要包括以下单位的代表:环境保护及防污染委员会(CCEPP)、阿曼海军(SON)、阿曼空军(SOAF)、阿曼海警、海事处、石油及矿产部门、石油工业。该理事会旨在提出应对溢油事件的策略。国际运输公司承包商、难船救助者、Smit公司也都来协助灭火。来自Smit公司的工作人员在其拖船“Smit先驱号”上向大火中喷水和泡沫,1月11日,大火仍在燃烧,消防员向泵舱灌水,以防止机舱中的大火蔓延到货油舱。

Assimi油船在拖船Solano的拖拽下逆流而行时,逐渐开始下沉,阿曼政府立即命令Assimi的救助船将其拖至离阿曼海岸200英里处,并使其沉没。截至1月16日,Assimi已沉至水下3 000米处。由于油船下沉时点燃了水面上的原油,因此又发生了第二次爆炸。

该理事会邀请国际海事组织(IMO)就此次溢油事件对环境造成的威胁进行评估,并向该理事会提出建议。另外,该理事会还请保护海洋环境的地区组织(ROPME)提供专业技术指导。负责

expertise. Observers of the sinking suggested that the oil released by the break-up had burned on site. The IMO and ROPME representatives advised further over-flights to determine if the tanker was still leaking oil.

An over-flight on January 19 revealed a slick of silver sheen covering 100 square miles and moving towards the northeast. The government of Pakistan was notified that the slick was heading towards their coast. An over-flight on January 22 found fresh oil on the surface near the sinking. The older oil had emulsified, and the total area of the slick was reduced. The northern most edge of the slick was 180 miles off the coast of Pakistan. An over-flight on February 4 showed that most of the oil had dispersed.

Other Special Interest Issues

The Assimi originally caught fire on January 7, and attempts were made to extinguish the fire. After an explosion on January 10 the fire was burning more fiercely. The salvers of the vessel were refused passage through the Straits of Hormuz. On January 12 the tow had been let go due to fears that the fire could flash back, however, the Solano was able to reconnect the tow and pull the Assimi even further from the coast.

对该船沉没情况进行观察的人员建议在沉没地点将溢油点着。国际海事组织(IMO)和海洋环境保护地区组织(ROPME)的代表们建议继续进行空中观察,以便确定该油船是否还在继续溢油。

1月19日在空中拍摄的画面显示,Assimi油船沉没地点100平方英里范围内,都闪烁着油膜的光泽,且油膜在向东北方向移动。巴基斯坦政府收到通知—油膜正向他们的海岸移动。1月22日的空中观察发现:在船舶沉没点附近有新油出现,原油已经开始乳化,油膜的总面积在减少,油膜最北面的边缘离巴基斯坦海岸有180英里。2月4日的空中观察发现,大多数的原油都已经分散了。

其他特别关注的问题

Assimi最初起火是在2月7日,船员也尝试了灭火,但在1月10日爆炸发生后,火势更加凶猛。救难船本想穿过霍尔木兹海峡,但被拒绝了。1月12日,由于担心火苗会烧过来,本打算让拖船离开,但拖船Solano最终还是将Assimi拖至离海岸更远的地方。

Case Study 5

Name: Betelgeuse
Spill Date: 8th January 1979
Location: Bantry Bay, Ireland Location
Oil Product: Mixed Arabian Crude Oil
Tank Vessel: Oil Type
Oil spilled: 14,720 Barrels

Incident Summary

In the early afternoon of January 8,1979, the tanker Betelgeuse exploded at the offshore pier of the Gulf Oil Terminal at Whiddy Island in Bantry Bay, Ireland. The tanker broke in two and settled in 130 feet of water with 300,000 barrels of oil remaining onboard. The fire burned throughout the day. During the night the fire was extinguished and the stern section sank completely. Approximately 14,720 barrels of oil leaked from the vessel, 3,680 barrels of which impacted the shoreline.

Behaviour of Oil

The Mixed Arabian crude oil contained in the vessel had an API gravity of about 36.5, and a viscosity of 23 centistokes at 20 degrees C. The oil that was released from the tanker burned as it leaked until the fire went out late on January 8. On January 9, a slick began to form, and oil impacted the east shore of Bantry Bay and Reenydonagan Point on Whiddy Island. Inspections revealed that 37 barrels of oil per hour was leaking from the wreck. Oil leaked at this rate for a week. On January 12, the oil impacted the north and south shores of Bantry Bay. By the next day the oil had spread as far west as Castle Townbere on the north shore of the bay, and League Point on the south shore. Bear Island was also impacted.

Countermeasures and Mitigation

The Cork County Council organized cleanup operations. Operations included the manual removal of oil, and the spreading of hay to absorb oil on the shoreline. Suction operations were also conducted on the shore. Booms contained the oil leaking from the tanker. Contained oil was treated with dispersants applied from planes, and was skimmed with a skimmer. Boom was placed across the mouth of the Glengariff Harbour to prevent oil from entering it. Undamaged tanks were lightered using floating hoses running to the shore facilities.

Other Special Interest Issues

Dispersant application began on January 10 off Reenydonagan Point. The Cork County Council and the Department of Fisheries stopped the shoreline applications that morning when it was discovered that the dispersant were being applied incorrectly. Aerial spraying was done thereafter, and only on slicks of fresh oil. A total of about 35 tonnes (approximately 260 barrels) of dispersant was used in a 12-day period. The use of dispersants is believed to have successfully protected the shoreline. The slick prevented fishing in some areas and nets were fouled by sunken oil. The harvesting of shellfish, including periwinkles, scallops and clams were also affected as buyers rejected some catches. Oiled seabirds were also found.

案例研究5

船名: Betelgeuse
溢油时间: 1979年1月8日
地点: 爱尔兰的班特里湾
油品: 阿拉伯混合原油
油船的类型: 油船
溢油量: 14,720桶

事故摘要

1979年1月8日刚到下午,Betelgeuse油船在爱尔兰班特里湾维迪岛的一个油船码头发生爆炸。油船断成了首、尾两段,并沉入水中130英尺,此时在船上还装载着300 000桶原油。大火整整燃烧了一天。到了夜里才将大火扑灭,但船尾的这段船体却完全沉入水中。大约有14 720桶原油溢出,其中的3 680桶原油遍布了整条海岸线。

溢油的状况

当时船上装载的阿拉伯混合原油的API比重为36.5,黏度为23 cSt(在20 ℃下)。原油溢出后被火点燃,继续燃烧,直到1月8日的夜里,大火才被扑灭。1月9日,海面上开始形成油膜,整个班特里湾的东海岸及维迪岛的雷尼当噶都受到溢出原油的影响。据观察发现:每小时大约有37桶原油从船体的残骸中溢出,且原油以此溢油速度持续了一周。到了1月12日,溢油已经覆盖了班特里湾的南海岸和北海岸。截至13日,溢油向西已经扩散到唐波城堡。另外,熊岛也受到了此次溢油的影响。

溢油的处理措施及减缓

溢油发生后,科克郡立即安排了清理工作。清理工作主要包括人工清油,以及把干草扔到海岸线以吸油等。围油栏将从船体中溢出的油包围起来,然后用飞机向溢油中喷洒消油剂,并用撇油器进行撇油操作。在格伦加利福海港的入口处也放置了围油栏,以防止溢油进入。未受损坏的船体中的原油被驳运到了岸上设施中。

其他特别关注的问题

1月10日,在雷尼当噶开始使用消油剂。上午,当科克郡和渔业部门发现相关工作人员使用消油剂的方法不正确时,他们阻止了工作人员继续向海中投放消油剂。随后,工作人员改为以空中喷洒的形式使用消油剂,并且只向油层上喷洒。在12天的时间里,共用了大约35吨的消油剂(约260桶)。使用消油剂被认为成功的保护了海岸线,但实际上沉没的原油堵塞了渔网,这严重影响了渔业。贝壳类海生物(如海螺、扇贝、蛤蚌等)的收益也受到了影响。因为消费者开始拒绝购买这类水产品。另外,还发现了大量的沾满油污的海鸟。

The bow section of the Betelgeuse was salvaged. On February 21, it was towed to sea by a tug. The bow was sunk at 50° 40′ N, 012° 04′ W on February 23. Salvage operations continued throughout the year. Part of the midsection was raised on August 30. The rest of the midsection was raised in December. The stern was raised on July 1,1980. The midsection and the stern were scrapped.

Betelgeuse的船首部分被打捞上来,并于2月21日用拖船拖到海中。船首部分于2月23日在50°40′N,012°04′W沉没。打捞工作持续了一年多,8月30日,部分中间船体被打捞出水面,中间船体其余部分到12月才打捞上来。而船尾部分的船体在1980年的7月1日才被打捞上来,但此时船中、船尾部分的船体都已经报废了。

Case Study 6

Name: Jupiter
Spill Date: 16th September 1990
Location: Saginaw River, Bay City, Michigan
Oil Product: Unleaded gasoline
Tank Vessel: Oil Type
Oil spilled: 20,000 Barrels

Incident Summary

At 0845 on September 16, 1990, the tank vessel Jupiter caught fire and exploded during offloading operations at the Total Oil Company refinery on the Saginaw river near Bay City, Michigan. A wake from a passing bulk carrier apparently caused the parting of the Jupiter's transfer hose, grounding cable, and all but one of its mooring lines. Residual gasoline in the broken transfer hose was believed to have been ignited by a spark on the dock. The Jupiter's stern swung around into the Saginaw River and grounded perpendicular to the direction of the river flow. The grounding resulted in a crack in the vessel's hull from the manifold on the starboard side to 75 feet aft of the manifold on the port side.

Area marinas were evacuated and vessel traffic was halted. The pier fire was extinguished in an attempt to save the last mooring line while the fire onboard the vessel remained out of control. A shore company from Houston, Texas, was contracted to fight the fire due to the lack of locally available trained personnel and equipment. At 1315 on September 17, the shore personnel extinguished the blaze by applying foam. Carbon black accumulations falling from the overhead re-ignited the fire at 2300. This second blaze was cooled with water and extinguished with foam on September 18. The shore personnel also applied foam inside the vessel's cargo tanks to prevent re-ignition of the vessel.

River flow data were obtained to predict the oil movement. Shock waves from the explosion may have contributed to the deaths of several fish that were recovered from around the vessel. Neither pollution nor shoreline contamination was observed during the final survey of the area on October 22.

Behaviour of Oil

Automotive gasoline is a very lightweight, refined product with an API gravity of 60 to 63. No spill of product into the Saginaw River was reported until first light on September 17 when fuel up to three inches thick was observed in the water immediately surrounding the vessel. Some of the spilled product was held against the hull of the vessel by the wind until the starboard side submerged, releasing an additional 100 barrels of the fuel. Since the gasoline was not released rapidly, little environmental damage resulted from the incident.

Countermeasures and Mitigation

On September 16, containment boom was deployed around the vessel as a precaution against further spillage. The boom remained in place until the vessel was re-floated on October 16 and moved to the north side of the river. No product was observed leaking from the vessel as it was relocated. Vacuum trucks were used to recover the gasoline and water mixture. Approximately 262 barrels were recovered by September 28. Small amounts of

案例研究 6

船名: Jupiter
溢油时间: 1990年9月16日
地点: 美国密歇根州海湾城的萨吉诺河
油品: 无铅汽油
油船的类型: 油船
溢油量: 20 000桶

事故摘要

1990年9月16日8点45分,油船Jupiter在美国密歇根州海湾城附近的萨吉诺河上,在向原油精炼厂卸货时发生了着火,并最终发生了爆炸。一条过往的散货船的尾流使Jupiter的输油软管分开了,并因撞到了锚链上而破裂,在破损的输油软管中的汽油最终被岸上的火花点燃了。Jupiter的船尾逐渐沉入到萨吉诺河中,最终船舶发生了搁浅,且船体与水流方向垂直,搁浅导致从右侧折臂到距船尾75英尺处左侧折臂船体出现破裂。

码头立即进行了疏散工作,船舶也禁止通行。码头上的火很快被扑灭了,但是船上的火势却仍然无法得到控制。由于当地没有相应的设备和受过培训的人员,相关部门只好从休斯顿雇佣岸基公司进行灭火。9月17日13点15分,工作人员用泡沫灭火剂将火扑灭,但23点,从高处落下的炭黑物又使其复燃,复燃的大火通过用水冷却、喷洒泡沫,终于在18日被扑灭。另外,工作人员还向货油舱中喷洒了泡沫,以防止其复燃。

为了预测溢油的运动趋势,工作人员搜集了水流的相关数据。爆炸的冲击波可能会导致当时在船舶周围的一些鱼类死亡。在10月22日的最终调查中,没有发现任何海上污染和海岸线污染情况。

溢油的状况

汽车用汽油是一种比重非常轻的油,是经过精炼的产品,其API比重为60~63。此次事故发生后,一直没有关于在萨吉诺河上发生溢油事故的报道,直到9月17日,发生了第一次爆炸,这时才发现在船的周围已有厚度达到3英寸的油层。当右舷沉入水中后,向水中溢出了约100桶油。由于汽油释放的并不快,所以此次事故几乎没有造成任何的环境污染。

溢油的处理措施及减缓

9月16日,为了防止溢油进一步的扩散,工作人员在船舶的周围放置了围油栏。围油栏一直放置到10月16日,船体被打捞上来,并被拖到了萨吉诺河的北部,此后,船体再也没有向外溢油。真空卡车被用来回收溢出的汽油及油水混合物,截至9月28日,一共回收了约262桶。对海岸线上的

carbon residue that impacted the shoreline were manually raked from beaches in the area. On September 19, gasoline odours were reported in the sewers of a residential community near the incident site. Contractors were dispatched to flush and foam the sewers. Sections of boom and a combustible gas detector were set up to monitor the sewer outfall.

On September 27, approximately 770 barrels of product were offloaded from the Jupiter to a lightering barge. Gas freeing operations began on October 5, due to the explosion threat posed by some isolated pockets of product remaining in the #6 starboard cargo tank. Offloaded product was replaced with water to reduce the structural stress to the damaged vessel. Since trace concentrations of benzene, toluene, ethyl benzene, and xylene isomers were found in water samples near the Jupiter, water at a nearby water treatment plant was treated with ozone as a precaution.

Other Special Interest Issues

The fire-fighting foam that was used on the fire was water soluble and moderately toxic. Contaminated water from the fire-fighting operation was collected and brought to a Bay City Wastewater.

少量炭残留物也进行了人工清除。9月19日,有报道称,在事故发生地附近的下水道中有汽油的味道,承包人立即被派遣到当地,对下水道进行冲洗处理,并在下水道的出口处放置了几段围油栏,还安装了可燃气体探测仪。

9月27日,Jupiter上的约770桶汽油被卸到了驳油船上。10月5日,进行了驱气操作,因为右舷No.6货舱仍有爆炸的危险。为了减小破损的船体受到的结构应力,又将卸货后的空间充满了水。鉴于对Jupiter附近水域的水进行采样并检测到了一定浓度的苯、甲苯、乙烷、二甲苯,相关部门对附近的水处理装置用臭氧进行了消毒处理。

其他特别关注的问题

本次事故中,向水中喷洒的是水溶性的、中毒性的泡沫。在灭火过程中被污染的水最终被回收到海湾城的废水处理点。

Case Study 7

Name: Kurdistan
Spill Date: 15th March 1979
Location: Cabot Strait, Newfoundland
Oil Product: Bunker C
Tank Vessel: Oil Type
Oil spilled: 43,900 Barrels

Incident Summary

On March 15, 1979, the British motor tanker Kurdistan, en route from Nova Scotia to Quebec, broke in two sections south of Cabot Strait, Newfoundland. The damage was attributed to a fracture initiated by a weld defect and aggravated by wave impacts on the bow at low temperatures. Although the tanker remained intact for some time after the initial hull plate failure, the bow and stern sections eventually separated and spilled an estimated 43,900 barrels of Bunker C into Cabot Strait. The bow and stern sections drifted towards Canadian waters. Approximately 50,000 barrels of oil remained in the bow section while 115,000 barrels remained in the stern.

A wide band of mobile pack ice initially prevented the spilled oil from reaching the shoreline. The Environmental Protection Service (EPS) immediately initiated the formation of the Regional Environmental Emergencies Team (REET) to provide assistance and advice to the Canadian Coast Guard's (CCG) On-Scene Commander (OSC).

The REET was divided into three sections to deal with the three distinct problems: the bow, the stern, and the oil spill cleanup. Under Lloyds Open Forum, the stern section was towed to Port Hawkesbury, Nova Scotia, to recover remaining oil. The bow section was towed to a deepwater area 200 nautical miles off Nova Scotia and sunk by gunfire from the HMCS Margaree on April 1, 1979. Oil started coming ashore in April and two cleanup control centres were established at Low Point and Mulgrave, Nova Scotia. The oil continued to contaminate shorelines along the eastern coast of Nova Scotia throughout the summer.

Behaviour of Oil

Bunker C fuel oil is a heavy product with an API gravity that ranges from 7 to 14. The oil slick movement was very difficult to track and monitor because the oil appeared to float a meter or two below the surface of the water. Ice-oil mixtures, first seen on March 23, moved to the northwest during the following two days at a mean rate of 8 to 10 miles per day. Oil first came ashore on March 28, although the majority of oil did not come ashore until mid-April, after shore-fast ice was gone. Oil on the beaches was not in the form of mousse as expected, rather, it consisted of “toffee-like” particles ranging in diameter from millimetres to several meters.

The Cape Breton shoreline and the mainland coast of Nova Scotia were most severely contaminated. Oil washed ashore in varying amounts from St. Ann's Bay in north Cape Breton to as far south as Canso in Guysborough County, Nova Scotia. By April 14, Scatarie Island off the eastern extremity of Cape Breton Island and 25 miles to the southeast of Sydney was heavily oiled. Reports of oil on Fox Island were received on April 18. Oil was discovered on

案例研究 7

船名: Kurdistan
溢油时间: 1979年3月15日
地点: 卡伯特海峡(纽芬兰)
油品: C类燃油
油船的类型: 油船
溢油量: 43 900桶

事故摘要

1979年3月15日,英国内燃机油船"Kurdistan"号,从加拿大的新斯科舍省驶向魁北克的途中,经过纽芬兰的卡伯特海峡南部时断裂成两部分。破损开始于一处焊接缺陷的断裂,在低温海浪对船头的不断冲击下,使其不断加重。虽然在破损发生后船体在一段时间内保持了完整,但最终断裂成首、尾两部分,并将大约43 900桶C类燃油溢入了卡伯特海峡。断裂的船首和船尾部分随波逐流至加拿大海域。大约有50 000桶燃油留在船首部分,115 000桶留在了船尾部分。

一条较宽的移动冰带在事故开始之初阻止了溢油流向海岸线。环境保护服务部(EPS)立即组成区域环境问题应急小组(REET)以便于向加拿大海岸警卫队的(CCG)现场指挥官(OSC)提供帮助和建议。

REET分成了三组用于处理不同的三部分问题:船首部分、船尾部分以及溢油的清理。根据劳氏开放论坛的处理规范,船尾部分被拖至新斯科舍省的霍克斯伯里港对剩余燃油进行回收。1979年4月1日,船首部分被拖至距新斯科舍省200海里的深水区,在加拿大皇家海军舰艇玛格丽特号的炮火轰鸣中被击沉。溢油于四月份开始登岸。两个清理控制中心分别建立在新斯科舍省的罗恩波特和马尔格雷夫。整个夏天这些溢油持续污染着新斯科舍省的东部海岸线。

溢油的状况

C类燃油是API燃油比重范围为7~14的重油产品。因为其溢油悬浮于水下一至两米处,所以这些浮油运动状况很难被跟踪和监控。在3月23日第一次发现冰油混合物,在接下来的两天以8~10英里/天的速度向西北漂去。溢油在3月28日第一次登岸,而大部分的溢油直到4月中旬才开始登岸,登岸后冰迅速地消失。溢油在沙滩上并没有如预期中的形成乳状物,相反,它由直径从几毫到几米不等的"太妃糖状"颗粒组成。

布雷敦角海岸线和新斯科舍省大陆海岸线均遭受了严重的污染。从布雷敦角北部的摩根安的湾一直往南到新斯科舍省盖斯伯勒县的坎索均遭到了不同程度的溢油污染侵袭。到4月14日,布雷敦角最东端的,距悉尼最南边25英里处的斯卡塔里岛遭到溢油的严重污染。4月18日收到了

the Lingan sandbar on April 21. On gravel/cobble beaches, the oil often mixed with thick bands of accumulated kelp along the upper foreshore.

Oil continued to come ashore with little warning throughout the summer of 1979 along 700 miles of eastern Nova Scotia and southern Newfoundland shoreline. Cleanup operations lasted six months due to continual re-oiling of beaches by tidal action.

Countermeasures and Mitigation

In an attempt to clean the oil from the ice before it reached the shoreline, the CCG fitted a barge with backhose, booms, and sorbent material. The barge attempted to scoop the oil from the water with little success. Rakes, shovels, and pitchforks were the main shoreline cleanup tools. The oil was very viscous by the time it reached the beach and was easily placed in sturdy plastic bags and 45–gallon drums. Ordinary rakes and garden hoses were carefully used in marsh areas to protect the root systems for future growth. The CCG flew cleanup crews onto uninhabited Scatarie Island. Manual cleaning methods using hand tools, 45-gallon drums, and heavy plastic bags were employed. Over 1,000 barrels and 4,000 bags of oil and oil soaked debris were collected on the island within several days.

A temporary on-site incinerator was constructed to dispose of the oily waste. Driftwood placed in the firebox was used to fuel the kiln. During peak operations, the kiln processed 350 bags of beach material an hour. The incinerator proved to be a cost-effective oil pollution countermeasure technique. A total of approximately one million bags and 1,500 barrels of oily debris were collected over the 550 miles of shoreline that were accessible. Much of the oily waste was disposed of at municipal landfills and strip mines on Cape Breton Island. With increasing concerns over the amount of debris, new disposal sites were developed at Hadleyville, Forchu, and St. Peter's on Cape Breton Island.

Other Special Interest Issues

Over 2,600 birds, primarily gulls and ducks, are known to have died as a result of oiling from this spill. The actual number of birds affected by this oil spill was much higher due to three primary factors. First, the slick was essentially hidden from view from March 16 to April 9. It is suspected that many oiled birds died during this period and sank. Second, little attempt was made during cleanup to separate, count and identify dead birds from among the other oiled debris. Third, much of the Cape Breton and Guysborough County shoreline was inaccessible, so dead birds on these beaches were not counted. Considering all factors, the bird mortality count from this incident is estimated at between 12,000 and 25,000.

福克斯岛的溢油污染报告。4月21日琳安沙洲发现溢油。在砾石/鹅卵石海滩,溢油往往搀杂着厚厚的海藻积聚在海滩的上边。

整个1979年的夏天伴随着微弱的警示，溢油污染持续侵袭着纽芬兰南部和加拿大新斯科舍省东部的超过700千米长的海岸。因为在清理过程中海岸不断反复地遭受到溢油的侵袭,所以清理工作一直持续了6个月。

溢油的处理措施及减缓

CCG在驳船上安装了后软管、围油栏、吸附材料尝试着在溢油登岸前清除附着在冰上的油。驳船尝试着从海水里将油分离出来,但收效甚微。在岸上耙子、铲子、叉子等是主要的清理工具。溢油在抵达海岸时具有很大的黏性,所以很容易清理并将其放进朔料袋和容量为45加仑的桶中。在湿地区域,为了保护植物的根系以便于其来年的生长,普通的耙子和花园软管被谨慎的使用。CCG飞行清理组用于清理无人居住的斯卡塔里岛。人工清理用的是手动工具,以及提供的45加仑容量的桶和厚重的塑料袋。几天内岛上清理出了超过1 000桶的溢油和4 000包浸油残渣。

在现场,修建了一座临时焚烧炉用于处理油污垃圾。废木料置于燃烧室内作为焚烧炉的焚烧材料。在最高峰时,焚烧炉每小时处理350包清理出的溢油残渣。焚烧炉被证明是经济有效的污油处理手段。在人类可进入的超过550英里的海岸线，清理出了大约有100万袋和1500桶的污油残渣。在布雷敦角岛,大部分的油污垃圾通过就地掩埋和置于露天矿场的方式进行了处理。出于对越来越多的污油残渣进行处理的考虑,在布雷敦角岛的海德里维尔、佛楚及皮特街建立了新的污油处理场所。

其他特别关注的问题

有超过2 600只鸟,主要是海鸥和鸭子因为这次溢油事故死去。主要有三个因素导致了鸟类受到溢油影响的实际数量远超想象。第一,从3月16日到4月9日这个时间段内,溢油悬浮隐藏于水中,在海水表面很难被发现。怀疑很多鸟类在这段时间里遭受溢油污染导致溺死于水中。第二,在清理过程中,只稍稍的尝试着进行了从污油残渣中分离、清点、识别死鸟的工作。第三,布雷敦角和盖斯伯勒县的很多区域是人类不能进入的,所以不能清点在那些海岸上的死鸟数量。考虑全部的因素,由于这次溢油事故导致死亡的鸟类的数量在12 000~25 000只之间。

Case Study 8

(Although it is a non-tank vessel, the case study is mentioned here because it is a double-hull accident)

Name: Sanko Harvest
Spill Date: 13th February 1991
Location: Esperance, Western Australia
Oil Product: Fuel Oil
Tank Vessel: Non-Tank Vessel
Oil spilled: 4,400 Barrels 4,400 Source

Incident Summary

On the night of February 13, 1991, the Panamanian bulk cargo carrier Sanko Harvest grounded on a submerged rock pinnacle 23 miles south of Esperance, Western Australia. The vessel, out of the shipping lane at the time of the incident, was loaded with 30,000 metric tonnes of fertilizer, di-ammonium phosphate, and triple superphosphate. The double hull of the vessel was ripped open in the grounding and the freighter began leaking its fuel oil. On February 18, the ship broke in two in a storm and sank with its entire cargo and bunker fuel. Approximately 3,500 barrels of fuel oil were spilled during the incident. The remaining 900 barrels of oil sank with the ship.

Behaviour of Oil

The spilled oil initially created a slick approximately 2 miles long and 1000 feet wide. As the slick grew to 9 miles long, it began to threaten nearby islands. Approximately 2,100 barrels of the fuel oil came ashore along 17 miles of the northeast islands and the mainland of Australia. The worst of the oiling was on beaches to the west of Esperance, particularly Hellfire Bay, Thistle Bay, Lucky Bay, and Rossiter Bay. Oil sank into these coarse-grained beaches to a depth of approximately one-half inch. The incident occurred approximately six miles from Cape Le Grand, which is east of Esperance, and the beach at Cape Le Grand National Park also received heavy oiling. On the beaches with fine-grained sand, the oil did not penetrate the tightly compacted beach sand, and was deposited on top.

Countermeasures and Mitigation

The Department of Marine and Harbours (DMH) deployed nearly 1,700 feet of containment boom around the ship in two rows. The sea and wind conditions at the time were very rough. More than two–thirds of the boom was damaged at sea and lost. Less than one-fifth of the deployed boom was recovered and cleaned enough to be reused. The primary response tool was chemical dispersant spraying. Dispersants were used in limited amounts to lessen environmental effects. Twenty-two 200-liter drums of dispersant were sprayed on parts of the slick from helicopters and tugboats. The spraying reportedly dispersed approximately 700 barrels of the spilled oil.

Sorbents were used to clean the beaches, which were reportedly only moderately oiled. Mechanical cleanup was performed on the heavily impacted beaches. This included the use of graders and front-end loaders to remove the oiled debris. Lightly oiled beaches were rapidly cleaned naturally along the high–energy coastal environment. Many of the oiled sites

案例研究 8

(虽然这不是一艘油船,但是仍然作为案例在此对其研究,这是因为该船具有双层船壳)

船名: Sanko Harvest
溢油时间: 1991年2月13日
地点: 埃斯佩兰斯(澳大利亚西部)
油品: 燃油
油船的类型: 非油船
溢油量: 4 400桶 4 400处

事故摘要

1991年2月13日晚,在澳大利亚西部的埃斯佩兰斯南23英里处,"Sanko Harvest"号,一艘巴拿马型散货船因为一块水下的岩石导致搁浅。发生事故时,船舶满载着30 000吨化肥、磷酸铵和三重过磷酸钙偏离了航线。在搁浅事故中船舶的双重船壳被撕开,并开始漏油。2月18日,船舶在暴风雨中被一分为二,整条船和其燃油随即沉没。此事故中大约泄漏了3 500桶燃油。剩余的900桶燃油也随船沉没。

溢油的状况

溢油首先形成了一条大约两英里长、1 000英尺宽的溢油带。当溢油带增长至9英里长时,开始对附近的小岛构成了威胁。大约2 100桶燃油在澳大利亚本土及最北部的岛屿登岸,形成了17英里长的污染带。油污最严重的地方发生在埃斯佩兰斯西部的海岸,特别是地狱火湾、蓟色湾、幸运湾、水钒钙石湾。石油陷入这些粗粒沙海滩大约半英寸深。这一事故发生在距埃斯佩兰斯东部勒格兰角大约6英里的地方,勒格兰角国家公园的海滩也遭到这些重油的污染。在细沙海滩上,这些油不能渗透进紧实的细沙而堆积在它们的表面。

溢油的处理措施及减缓

港口和海事部门(DMH)在船的周围部署了两条近1 700英尺的围油栏。当时的海洋和海风状况很糟糕,有近三分之二的围油栏摧毁并丢失了。不到五分之一的围油栏足够清洁可重新使用。主要的应急措施是化学喷雾消油剂。限量使用消油剂来减轻溢油对环境的污染。22桶两百公升的消油剂被直升机和拖船喷洒在溢油带上。据报道,这些消油剂大约分解了700桶溢油。

吸附剂被用来清理海滩,据说其只能稍稍缓解溢油污染。机械清理用于遭受严重污染的海岸。包括各种级别的前置式铲车用于清除溢油残余。溢油污染较轻的海滩被具有巨大能量的沿海环境迅速地清理干净。

were difficult for cleanup personnel and equipment to reach. Contractors and volunteers manually cleaned the very fine sand beaches by scraping off the oiled sand, since the oil did not penetrate deeply into the beach in these areas. A substantial amount of oiled sand was placed in a gravel pit near Lucky Bay. The oil penetrated into the coarser sand beaches. Tar balls of stranded oil were reported on the beaches.

Other Special Interest Issues

An unknown number of birds were killed as a result of the spill. The oil also impacted Hood Island and Seal Rock, which were important breeding grounds for New Zealand fur seals.

清理人员及设备很难进入一些油污地点。合同商和志愿者通过铲除油污沙子来手动清洁细沙海滩,因为在这些地方油污不会进入沙滩深层。大量油污沙子放在幸运湾附近的一个采砾坑中。油污深入粗粒沙滩中。据报道,沙滩有很多溢油污染物。

其他特别关注的问题

有不计其数的鸟类因溢油而死亡。溢油还影响了作为新西兰海豹重要繁殖地的艾斯潘诺拉岛和锡尔罗克。

Case Study 9

Name:	Sansinena
Spill Date:	17th December 1976
Location:	Los Angeles Harbour, California
Oil Product:	Bunker C
Tank Vessel:	Tank Vessel
Oil spilled:	30,000 Barrels

Incident Summary

At 1938 on December 17, 1976, the Sansinena exploded, caught fire, and sank during re-fuelling at the Union Oil Terminal, Berth 46, in Los Angeles Harbour, California. The vessel was loaded with 22,000 barrels of Bunker C at the time of the incident. The apparent cause was a still-air situation that developed between the mid-ship house and the afterdeck house. Vapours emitting from the cargo tank vents created a vapour cloud during ballasting. These were ignited in the amidships house and flashed back through the vent piping system. The largest explosion took place in the number 10 centre cargo tank. The force of the explosion propelled the main deck over the cargo tanks into the air. When the deck landed, it severed a 36-inch cargo line on top of the inshore isolation valve. This severed line fed fuel to the fire until response personnel discovered and capped it on December 21. Nine lives were lost as a result of the explosion. Debris and oil scattered in all directions. Approximately 400 boats in the vicinity were damaged by the fine mist of airborne oil, resulting in millions of dollars in property damage. An estimated 30,000 barrels of oil were released into Los Angeles harbour from the ship and the severed pipeline.

A U.S. Coast Guard boat and a Los Angeles City Fire Department boat arrived on-scene within five minutes of the explosion to assist in fire-fighting and rescue operations. Pollution surveys were conducted after the fire was under control. Initial reports concluded that much of the oil had burned off, but on December 19, underwater divers discovered a large quantity of oil on the bottom of the harbour. Boom deployment began within two hours of the explosion. Boom and other containment gear were utilized for the next 120 days, while mechanical removal of oil from the bottom of the harbour continued for 16 months. Total oil removal costs exceeded three million dollars.

Behaviour of Oil

Bunker C fuel oil is a heavy product with an API gravity that ranges from 7 to 14. The lighter, more toxic fractions of oil burned on the surface of the water following the explosion. The remaining thick residue sank to the bottom of the harbour in approximately 50 feet of water. Large pools of oil were found on the harbour floor and in the lower portions of the cargo tanks resting on the bottom. The pools of oil, up to nine feet deep, had settled into hard, clay packed pockets and crevices along the bottom. By January 17, 1977, the amount of grease and oil on the surface of the water had increased and was greatest in the slip area and shallow beach area to the northwest and west of the spill site. In July 1977, grease and oil levels in the water column rose slightly while levels in the sediments decreased. The total amount of retrieved oil from the surface and the bottom of the harbour was 33,000 barrels, partly as an oil/water emulsion.

案例研究9

船名: Sansinena
溢油时间: 1976年12月17日
地点: 洛杉矶港(美国加利福尼亚州)
油品: C类燃油
油船的类型: 油船
溢油量: 30 000桶

事故摘要

1976年12月17日19点38分,在美国加利福尼亚州洛杉矶港46号泊位,在联合加油站的加油过程中“Sansinena”号发生爆炸导致起火并沉没。事故发生时,船上装载了22 000桶C类燃油。明显的事故原因是由后甲板建筑和船中建筑间隙形成的油汽引起的。在压载过程中通过油舱通风口出来的油气形成了油气云。船舶中部的建筑点燃了这些油气并通过通风系统回火至油舱。最大的爆炸发生在十号中央油舱。巨大的力量将油舱上的主甲板掀至空中。当甲板落地时切断了海边隔离阀上的一条36英寸粗的货油管线。切断的管线持续向大火供油直到12月21日相关应急人员发现才将其关闭。爆炸导致9人丧生。碎片和燃油向四面八方散落。附近的近400艘船舶受到空气中落下的细小油雾的损害,导致了数百万美元的财产损失。据估计通过船舶和输油管路大约30000桶燃油被释放进洛杉矶港。

一艘美国海岸警卫队的船舶和一艘洛杉矶消防局的船舶在爆炸后的五分钟之内赶到了事故现场协助灭火和救护工作。火灾得到控制后进行了污染调查。最初的报告推断出大部分的油已经烧掉,但是在12月19日,潜水员在港口底部发现了大量的油。在爆炸两小时内围油栏的部署工作就已经开始进行。在接下来的120天围油栏和其他控制设备被用来处理溢油,而通过机械手段清理港口底部的燃油则持续了16个月。总的溢油清理费用超过了三百万美元。

溢油的状况

C类燃油是API燃油比重范围在7~14的重油产品。较轻、具有毒性的溢油部分在水的表面随着爆炸被燃烧掉。剩下厚厚的残油沉入港口底部近50英尺的水下。在油船底部较低的部分和港池底部形成了很多巨大的油池。这些深达9英尺的油池位于坚硬的泥土块上以及水底的缝隙中。1977年1月17日,水表面积聚的溢油和滑油的数量不断的增多,最严重的地方是溢油地点西北部和西部的溢油带区域和浅滩地区。1977年7月,水体中的燃油和滑油数量缓慢上升,而沉积物中的油量在下降。从水面和港口底部回收的溢油总量达到了33 000桶,其中部分是油水混合乳液。

Countermeasures and Mitigation

The first boom deployed consisted of 2,000 feet of 8-inch skirted harbour boom in a reverse "J" configuration from the bow of the vessel to 1,000 feet off her port beam. The boom contained a large portion of the floating oil while still allowing emergency and fire-fighting access to the area.

After emergency vessels cleared the area, a second set of boom was deployed to enclose the Sansinena. The final set of boom was deployed along the breakwater and the beach area. These placements were selected to isolate the heaviest concentrations of oil along the sides of the outer harbour to enable easier removal of the oil. Beach areas were cleaned by manual removal of oil-soaked sand. This phase of cleanup was completed by December 20. By December 24, all collectable surface crude and diesel oil had been removed with two self–contained skimming devices and sorbent pads. The oil was pumped from the bottom and transferred via a three-inch hose to an oil collection tank mounted on the salvage barge. This oil was then transferred to an on-shore settling tank for disposal. As removal operations continued and pumping became more difficult due to smaller crevices, the suction head had to be re-designed into a configuration with three smaller satellite heads. In sixty days, 10,000 barrels of oil had been removed from the harbour bottom.

Other Special Interest Issues

This was the first known Bunker C spill where both pre and post spill biological and water quality data had been collected. Studies revealed that most marine environmental damage was in the inter-tidal zone of the beach and the breakwater and pilings. Phytoplankton was most heavily impacted during the first month of the spill, while copepod numbers significantly increased in the spill area between January and April. Although small benthic organisms were heavily impacted about 3–4 months after the spill, the community returned to normal 9 to 11 months after the incident when the residual oil had lost its toxicity.

溢油的处理措施及减缓

从船头到距左舷1 000英尺处部署首条呈倒J字型的、2 000英尺长8英寸厚的港口围油栏。围油栏容纳了大部分的浮油,尽管允许应急和消防出入此区域。

当应急船舶清理完该区域后,用第二条围油栏围住"Sansinena"号。最后一条围油栏沿着防浪堤和海滩进行部署。选取这样的布置是为了沿着港口外边缘隔离溢油集中区,以便于清除溢油。海滩上被油浸染的沙子是通过人工清理的。这一阶段的清理工作在12月20日完成。截12月24日,用两套撇油装备和吸油垫清除了可收集的水面原油和柴油。通过三英寸粗的软管,将港池底部的溢油泵送至装在海上救助驳船上的溢油收集箱。这些油被送往岸上的沉淀柜进行处理。随着清除操作的进行,细小裂缝中的油污越来越难被清理,吸头被重新设计成三个小卫星头的形式。在60天中,港口底部清理出了10 000桶的溢油。

其他特别关注的问题

这是所知的第一次对C类燃油溢油发生前后生物与水质数据进行收集。研究发现大部分海洋环境破坏发生在海岸、防浪堤和金属桩的潮汐区。浮游植物在溢油事故发生的第一个月中受到严重影响,而溢油区域桡足动物的数量在一月至四月间显著增长。虽然小的海底栖生物有机体在溢油发生后3~4个月受到严重影响,但是当残留溢油失去其毒性后,这些生态群落在事故发生后的9~11个月得到恢复。

Appendix 6:

Contingency Planning

附录6：

应急计划

Contingency Planning

The issue

An oil spill – almost more than any other single issue – can seriously damage the industry as well as, the owner/operator's reputation. While the initial focus must be on prevention, the industry also gives the highest priority to developing comprehensive and well-rehearsed contingency plans that will ensure a prompt response to minimize the impact of an oil spill. In practice, this involves the Master working closely with people on board, the Company and the local authorities.

The threat

Between 1983 and 2002, world sea-borne trade rose from around 12 billion tonne miles to some 23 billion tonne miles, an increase of over 90%. The carriage of oil and petroleum products accounts for a significant part of this increase, rising to approximately 76% from 5.6 billion tonne miles to 9.9 billion tonne miles during the same period. In tonnage terms, the amount of oil transported by sea increased from 1.21 billion tonnes in 1983 to almost 2 billion tonnes in 2002. (*Source: Fearnleys Review*)

The oil can enter the marine environment as a result of accidental or deliberate releases. Accidental releases can occur as a result of natural disasters, human error or due to technical and mechanical faults in oil transfer and storage equipment. Intentional releases could include dumping oily wastes, acts of war, terrorism or sabotage. Incidents involving vessel groundings, collisions, fire, explosion, cargo reaction etc. could also cause oil spills from vessels involved.

With an awareness of the aforementioned threat, it therefore becomes imperative that the shipboard personnel be well trained in terms of handling contingencies should an incident so warrant, in order to minimize the damage.

Aim of the plan

Careful planning is essential for any successful operation, especially an emergency one. Response to accidental spillage of oil is a typical example. Many people may be affected by an oil spill and many organizations have duties to perform apart from the task of physical clean up. For example, an incident involving an oil tanker may entail search and rescue, lightering of cargo and salvage activities, all of which may impinge upon any spill response. For all of these operations, the vessel has to work in collusion with the shore authorities.

There is often concern for the effects on the environment, fisheries, industry and recreation as well as considerations for public health and safety. There will inevitably be conflicting interests and the news media are always quick to expose any indecision, weakness or disagreement. Such situations are easier to resolve when a well-prepared and tested contingency plan is available.

The ships therefore carrying oil in bulk have a responsibility to protect the personnel on board and the environment from the adverse effects of marine pollution and to minimize those effects where protection is not possible. The aim of emergency/contingency plan is to

应急计划

事件

溢油事故的严重性远超其他任何事故，它的发生将严重损害该行业及船东/经营者的名誉。首先重点在于预防,行业也对制定综合并经过精心准备的应急计划给予了最高优先权,以确保以最快的速度将溢油事件的影响缩减至最小。在实践中,该计划需要船长与船上人员、公司以及地方当局密切合作。

威胁

1983至2002年间,世界海上贸易从120亿公吨英里升至230亿公吨英里,涨幅超过了90%。石油及石油产品的运输在增长中占很大比例，在该时期其贸易量由56亿公吨英里升至99亿公吨英里,涨幅大约为76%。以吨位定义,石油的海上运输总量由1983年的12.1亿吨升至2002年的接近20亿吨。(来源:Fearnleys Review)

石油是通过事故性排放和故意性排放这两种方式进入海洋环境的。其中事故性排放是由于自然灾害、人员操作失误或原油的传输储存设备出现的机械技术故障导致的。故意性排放包括倾倒燃油废物,战争行动,恐怖活动或蓄意破坏等。其他的船舶事故,像搁浅、碰撞、火灾、爆炸、货物反应等也可能导致船舶溢油事故的发生。

通过对上述船舶事故威胁的认识了解,船上的所有人员都必须经过严格的应急操作训练,以确保将其损害降至最低。

计划目标

任何可行的操作都离不开细致的计划,特别是针对应急操作。对事故性漏油事故的应急反应是一个典型案例。溢油事故会影响很多人,同时很多组织需要对漏油的物理清理工作负责。例如,一起油船事故可能会包括搜寻救助、货物驳运和打捞行动等,所有这些都是溢油应急的内容。对于以上行动,必须与岸上有关当局进行有效沟通。

我们通常关心的是事件对环境、渔业、工业和娱乐的影响,也为公共健康和安全考虑。那就不可避免的会产生利益冲突,而新闻媒体也总会迅速地揭露出其中的优柔寡断、虚弱和分歧。但是通过做好充分准备和测试的应急计划可以很轻易的解决这个问题。

因此,油船有责任在船舶污染的不利情况下,保护好船上所有人员和海洋环境,并且在无法阻止船舶污染的情况下,应尽量减少其不良影响。应急计划的目的在于当船舶在海洋环境下发生

outline the arrangements for responding to oil spills in the marine environment, with the aim of protecting personnel health and the marine environment from oil pollution or, where this is not possible, to minimize its effects.

It is imperative to understand that the mode of transportation is not important in case of oil. Transportation of oil is in itself a risk and the presence of risk is indicative of the need of an emergency plan. Contingency plan should therefore include the following:

- Risk identification i.e. physical and chemical properties like specific gravity, solubility in water, vapour pressure and density, fire and explosion hazardous data, health hazard data
- Risk evaluation like ship safety data, environmental effects data, containment action, abatement action, warning and evacuation
- Risk control and
- Risk communication

Scope of the plan

The emergency plan on board relates primarily to incidents involving releases and spills from ships' bulk oil cargoes and as a result of the loss of oil overboard at sea.

Contingency plans are best divided into two distinct parts. The first should be a descriptive policy document outlining the overall strategy of the plan, while the second should form the operational plan concerned with procedures to be followed when a spill occurs. The strategy segment of the plan should define the policy, responsibilities and rationale for the operational plan, which is essentially an action checklist with pointers to information sources. A plan should be reasonably complete in itself and should not entail reference to a number of other publications, which causes delay. A loose–leaf format facilitates regular updating and there should be provision for listing and dating amendments.

Legislation

Contingency planning is essential for addressing to any kind of emergency. In case of oil spill, an oil contingency plan is required to be in place before hand where, the primary effort is to contain spill, recovery and cleaning the area of hydrocarbon. As mentioned in the introduction, today this is an IMO requirement. The plans will contain specific details of the vessel, evacuation details e.g. emergency response and fire-fighting equipment, floor plans, emergency/evacuation assembly etc.

Contingency planning

It should be reiterated at the onset that apart from formulating the plan, the effectiveness depends on the personnel regularly exercising their respective roles and responsibilities.

Operational plan

Plans for tanker operations are prepared in accordance with operational orders, company procedures, the ISM Code, international and national codes, conventions and regulatory requirements.

溢油事故时对应有安排的快速反应进行描述，以确保在船舶污染不可避免时确保船上人员的健康并尽可能将不良影响减至最小。

我们必须要明白的是在发生油类事故的时候,油的运输形式是不重要的。油的运输本身就具备一定的风险,这种风险的存在也证实了应急计划的必要性。因此,应急计划应包括以下几个方面:

- 风险识别,即一些理化特性,例如:比重、水溶性、蒸气压力、密度、火灾及爆炸危险指数、健康危害指数等
- 风险评估,例如:船舶安全指数、环境影响指数、遏制行动、减排行动、警告及撤离等
- 风险控制
- 风险沟通

应急计划范围

船上的应急计划主要与船舶货油泄漏及溢油事故相关,并且这些事故会导致原油入海。

应急计划最好分为明显不同的两个部分。第一部分应在整体上对应急计划的政策方针进行概括描述。第二部分应对在发生溢油事故时所遵循的操作规程进行阐述。计划的战略部分应对可操作性计划的方针、职责、基本原理进行定义,以形成具备信息资源指向功能的行动列表,此列表不可或缺。该计划应确保相对完整而又不必参考其他引起延误的大量资料。通过活页的方式有助于计划的定期更新,也便于对列表与日期进行修改。

法规

应急计划必须针对于解决任何紧急情况。例如发生溢油事故时,原油应急计划应随手可用,其主要作用是限定溢油范围,回收并清洁溢油区域的碳氢化合物。今天这是国际海事组织(IMO)的要求,在简介说明中已有提及。计划应包括船舶的具体细节和疏散细节,例如:应急反应、消防设备、各层甲板平面布置图、应急/逃生设备等。

应急计划

应该反复强调,除了制定应急计划具体内容,其有效性还取决于相关人员定期演练其各自所承担的任务与责任。

操作计划

油船操作计划应依照操作指令、公司流程、国际安全管理(ISM)规则、国内外规则、公约及其规定的要求进行准备。

The operational procedure can be divided into six main parts, generally following the chronological order of occurrence during a spill: Notification, Evaluation, Response, Clean up, Communication, and Termination.

The information required to allow an accurate evaluation of an incident should be detailed i.e. date, time, position, source, cause, amount and type of oil etc. A programme for alerting response personnel and the relevant authorities should be included.

The plan should allow the consideration of various response options according to the situation. Procedures for placing manpower and equipment on standby prior to mobilisation should be included. The following points need to be adhered to, and kept ready at all times, in order to avoid confusion at the time of emergency:

- Contact directory of response personnel – out of office contact details should be included where appropriate
- Contact directory of third parties – parties likely to have an interest in an incident e.g. police, parties of likely impact and other authorities (P & I Club representative)
- Primary response equipment

Topics to be included in a ship-oriented contingency plan while a vessel is en route to, from or at the terminal or transhipment site should deal with:

- Emergency responses to incidents involving the uncontrolled release of cargo(es) during cargo transfer operations
- Fire and explosions
- Operations monitoring systems
- Inspection, testing, and preventative maintenance procedures
- Cargo handling precautions
- Neutralizing electrical hazards
- Detection and alarm systems
- Emergency shut-down of cargo transfer operations
- Countermeasures which ameliorate, contain or neutralize the harmful effects of cargo released into the marine environment
- Outline of personnel emergency equipment and the evacuation procedure for personnel
- Security at the ship's berth
- Terminal-ship communications and chain-of-command

The instructions delineated in the emergency plan should be explicit, succinct, unequivocal, and communicated in a loud and clear manner. When in port, it will be acting in a proactive manner when the Master apprises himself of the terminal-ship chain of command.

A few questions for assessing the adequacy of a contingency plan

1. Is the plan compatible with international regulations and company's policy?

一般而言,按照溢油期间进行各项工作的时间顺序,操作程序可以分为6个主要部分:通报、评估、响应、清理、沟通以及结束。

应详细列出对事故进行准确评估的信息,包括日期、时间、船位、油源、起因、油的数量及类别等。还应该包括警报应急响应人员和相关当局的计划。

该计划应该考虑各种情形下的应急响应选项。还应该包括在采取行动之前布置备用人力和设备。为了避免在应急期间的混乱,需要遵守以下几点,并时刻做好准备。

- 应急响应人员联系名录——如果适用,应包括办公室之外的联系信息
- 第三方联系名录——与该事故存在利益关系的相关方,比如警察、可能受影响的相关方以及其他主管机关(保赔协会代表)
- 基本应急设备

当船舶驶向、驶离或在码头或转船点期间,面向船舶的应急计划的内容应该包括:

- 针对货物移驳期间货油泄漏失控事故的应急响应
- 火灾和爆炸
- 作业监控系统
- 检查、测试以及预防性维护程序
- 货物操作预防措施
- 消除用电危害
- 检测和报警系统
- 货物转运操作的应急停止
- 减轻、限制、消除货物泄入海洋环境中的有害影响的对策
- 概述人员应急设备以及人员应急逃生程序
- 船舶系泊时的安保
- 船岸沟通以及指令链

应急计划中的指令描述应该明确、简明、不含糊,并且沟通过程中应声音响亮、口齿清晰。在港内期间,船长应该以积极的姿态评价其在船岸指令链中的作用。

评估应急计划完整性的几个问题

1. 该计划是否符合国际规则和公司方针?

2. Has there been a realistic assessment of the nature and size of the possible threat (spill), and what is likely to be at risk?
3. Have priorities for protection been agreed on board, taking into account the viability of the various protection and clean-up options?
4. Has a strategy for co-operation with shore authorities, with regard to protecting and cleaning the various areas been agreed and clearly explained on board?
5. Has the necessary organization been outlined and the responsibilities of all those involved been clearly stated with no 'grey areas'? Will all who have a task to perform aware of what is expected of them?
6. Are the levels of equipment, materials and manpower sufficient to deal with the anticipated size of spill? If not, have back-up resources been identified and the company informed?
7. Have temporary storage sites on board and, the final disposal mechanism for collected debris been identified?
8. Are the alerting and initial evaluation procedures fully explained as well as arrangements for continual review of the progress and effectiveness of the clean–up operation?
9. Have the arrangements for ensuring effective communication between shore, sea and air been described?
10. Are actions taken during an emergency drill, with regard to machinery or equipment failure or emergency, to secure the machinery and the tanker and maintain the safety of the tanker and persons involved as per shipboard emergency and contingency plans?
11. Is the emergency shutdown of oil cargo operations initiated upon identification of a defined emergency situation in accordance with the tanker's ISM Safety Management Plan, international and national codes, conventions and regulatory requirements and company procedures?
12. Are the escape equipment, breathing apparatus, personal protective clothing and equipment, correctly used in emergency situations in accordance with manufacturer's instructions, regulatory requirements and company procedures?
13. Is proper medical first aid applied in relation to oil cargo accidents in accordance with established first aid practice and company procedures?
14. Have all aspects of the plan been regularly reviewed and nothing significant found lacking?

The contingency plan can be broken into small parts for easy application. These small parts take the form of checklists. Checklists can be used for dual purposes in a way that they originate from the main plan on one hand and, can be used to update the larger plan on the other.

Presented below are a few of the checklists, with a basic content, to give an idea of the larger picture. The idea is to follow a logical sequence of actions in an emergency. That is what contingency planning should be able to achieve because it is part of human nature for the judgement to be clouded in an emergency and, using the dictum of human nature as an alibi

2. 是否对可能存在的威胁(溢油)的性质和大小有一个真实的评估？可能会有什么风险？
3. 考虑各种保护和清理选项后,保护措施的优先级在船上是否达成一致意见？
4. 针对保护和清理各种区域与岸基主管机关开展的合作，船上是否形成了一致意见并对其进行清晰地解释？
5. 是否对相关组织及其非灰色区域的职责进行过概括描述？是否所有有任务需要执行的人都明白自己要做什么？
6. 是否设备、材料、人力的水平足以应对预期中溢油的规模？如果不能,是否确认了后备资源及通知相关公司？
7. 在船上是否有明确的临时储存站和用于收集残油的最终处理机制？
8. 对于报警和初始评估程序和对连续修订工作程序的安排以及清理操作的效果是否有清晰的阐述？
9. 是否对用于确保岸上与海空之间进行有效沟通的安排进行了阐述？
10. 在机械设备故障和应对紧急事故的应急训练中，根据船舶应急计划为了保护机械与油船,维护船舶和人员安全,应采取哪些行动？
11. 根据油船ISM安全管理计划、国内外规则、公约及其规定的要求、公司相关程序,在确认紧急情况后是否进行了货油操作紧急停止操作？
12. 在紧急情况下,是否根据厂商说明书、法规规定和公司程序正确使用逃生设备、呼吸设备、个人防护衣物与设备等？
13. 油船相关事故中是否采用了适当的符合已制订的急救操作和公司程序的医疗急救？
14. 计划的各个方面是否进行了定期检验以确保没有重大缺陷？

应急计划可以分成很多细小的部分以便于实施。这些细小的部分可以通过表格列出。通过列表可以达到双重用途,一方面可以对主要计划方便进行追本溯源,另一方面可以对较大的计划进行更新。

下面的几个包含基本内容的检查列表对整个计划给出了一个概框图。这个概框是遵循紧急行动的逻辑顺序。这是应急计划应该实现的目标,因为在紧急情况下,需要隐藏人性主观的判断,

for complacency is absolutely unacceptable on a tanker where life, property and environment are at stake. This is where contingency planning and practice comes in.

The following are examples of checklists to be used in various types of emergencies on oil tankers.

A

LOGICAL SEQUENCE OF ACTIONS IN EMERGENCY		
SHIPBOARD OIL POLLUTION EMERGENCY PLAN ***CARGO OVERFLOW/OIL PIPELINE LEAKAGE***		
Action to be considered	**Action taken**	**Responsibility**
IMMEDIATE ACTION		
Sounding Emergency Alarm	Yes/No	Person discovering incident
Initiate vessel emergency response procedure	Yes/No	Officer on duty
INITIAL RESPONSE		
Cease all cargo operation	Yes/No	Chief Officer & Officer on duty
All crew to stand-by position	Yes/No	All
Close manifold valves	Yes/No	Chief Officer & Officer on duty
Inform terminal/loading master	Yes/No	Master/Officer on duty–Terminal
SECONDARY RESPONSE		
Consider stopping air intake into accommodation/engine room	Yes/No	Chief Engineer
Locate source of leakage	Yes/No	Ch. Officer & Officer on duty
Stop or reduce flow of cargo	Yes/No	Chief Officer
Assess fire risk from release of flammable substances, or health hazards from toxic substances	Yes/No	Master
Man fire station on deck if necessary	Yes/No	Duty Officer
Drain affected section of pipeline/hose into an empty tank	Yes/No	Chief Officer
Contain spill with seals or absorbent materials	Yes/No	Duty Deckhands
Check scupper plugs for tightness	Yes/No	Duty Officer/Duty hands
Prepare portable pumps where it is possible to transfer spill into an empty or slack tank	Yes/No	Chief Officer
If required, change vessel's trim	Yes/No	Chief Officer
Consider relief of pressure from relevant sections of pipelines	Yes/No	Chief Officer/Ch. Eng.
Consider notification of authorities	Yes/No	Master
FURTHER RESPONSE		
Clean-up as required by using material from provided contingency unit	Yes/No	Chief Officer & Officer on duty
Transfer deck washing into empty tank	Yes/No	Chief Officer
Ensure that any residues collected in the clean-up operation are stored carefully prior to disposal	Yes/No	Chief Officer
Comply with reporting procedures	Yes/No	Master
If required, obtain permission from local authorities and/or the terminal to continue normal operation	Yes/No	Master

当油船上的生命、财产及环境受到威胁的时候,绝对不允许通过主观的臆想进行解决。这就是应急计划的落脚点与实际操作的出处。

以下相关检查列表的例子可以用于油船各种应急事件。

A

紧急行动的逻辑顺序		
船舶油类污染应急计划 货油溢出和燃油管路泄漏		
可考虑的行动	**是否采取**	**责任**
立即行动		
拉响应急警报	是 / 否	事故发现人
启动船舶应急反应程序	是 / 否	值班驾驶员
初级响应		
停止所有货油操作	是 / 否	大副 & 值班驾驶员
所有船员到准备位置	是 / 否	所有人
关闭总阀门	是 / 否	大副 & 值班驾驶员
通知码头 / 装载负责人	是 / 否	船长 / 值班驾驶员——码头
二级响应		
考虑切断机舱 / 生活区通风	是 / 否	轮机长
泄漏源定位	是 / 否	大副 & 值班驾驶员
停止或减少货油的流动	是 / 否	大副
根据泄漏的易燃物质,评估是否存在火灾风险,或根据有毒物质,评估是否存在健康威胁	是 / 否	船长
如有必要,甲板消防站就位	是 / 否	值班驾驶员
将受影响的管路 / 软管放残至空舱	是 / 否	大副
用密封或吸附材料限制溢油	是 / 否	值班水手
检查排水塞的紧密性	是 / 否	值班驾驶员 / 值班水手
准备便携式泵,在条件允许情况下把溢油驳入空舱或缓冲舱	是 / 否	大副
如有需要调整船舶吃水差	是 / 否	大副
考虑对部分相关管路减压	是 / 否	大副 / 轮机长
考虑通知有关当局	是 / 否	船长
进一步的响应		
要求使用应急计划体系提供的材料进行清洗	是 / 否	大副及值班驾驶员
将甲板清洗水转移至空舱	是 / 否	大副
确保清理出的残余物质在被处理前进行妥善保存	是 / 否	大副
遵守报告程序	是 / 否	船长
如果需求的话,获得地方当局或码头方允许才可继续正常操作	是 / 否	船长

B

LOGICAL SEQUENCE OF ACTIONS IN EMERGENCY		
SHIPBOARD OIL POLLUTION EMERGENCY PLAN ***HULL LEAKAGE***		
Action to be considered	**Action taken**	**Responsibility**
IMMEDIATE ACTION		
Sounding Emergency Alarm	Yes/No	Person discovering incident
Initiate vessel emergency response procedure	Yes/No	Officer on duty
INITIAL RESPONSE		
Cease all cargo operation	Yes/No	Chief Officer & Officer on duty
All crew to stand-by position	Yes/No	All
Close manifold valves	Yes/No	Chief Officer & Officer on duty
Inform terminal/loading master	Yes/No	Master/Officer on duty–Terminal
SECONDARY RESPONSE		
Use the Pollution prevention team in an attempt to locate the source of leakage	Yes/No	Chief Officer
Consider stopping air intake into accommodation/engine room	Yes/No	Chief Engineer
Assess fire risk from release of flammable substances, or health hazards from toxic substances	Yes/No	Master
Reduce the tank level by dropping cargo into an empty tank	Yes/No	Chief Officer
Prepare pumps for transfer of cargo to shore/barge, if necessary	Yes/No	Chief Officer
Man fire station on deck if necessary	Yes/No	Chief Engineer
Notification of authorities	Yes/No	Master
FURTHER RESPONSE		
If the leakage is located below the waterline, call in divers for further investigation	Yes/No	Master-PORT
If it is not possible to identify the leaking tank, reduce level in the tank	Yes/No	Chief Officer
Consider the effect on hull stress and stability of the vessel	Yes/No	Master/Chief Officer
Consider clean-up actions	Yes/No	Master/Deck Duty Officer/
Port/Coast Guards assists in clean up actions		Chief Engineer
Comply with reporting procedures	Yes/No	Master/Port-Coast Guards
If required, obtain permission from local authorities and/or the terminal to continue normal operation	Yes/No	Master/Port

B

紧急行动的逻辑顺序		
船舶油类污染应急计划 船体泄漏		
可考虑的行动	**是否采取**	**责任**
立即行动		
拉响应急警报	是 / 否	事故发现人
启动船舶应急反应程序	是 / 否	值班驾驶员
初级响应		
停止所有货油操作	是 / 否	大副和值班驾驶员
所有船员到准备位置	是 / 否	所有人
关闭总阀门	是 / 否	大副和值班驾驶员
通知码头 / 装载负责人	是 / 否	船长 / 值班驾驶员——码头
二级响应		
通过防污染小组尝试定位泄漏源	是 / 否	大副
考虑切断机舱 / 生活区通风	是 / 否	轮机长
根据泄漏的易燃物质,评估是否存在火灾风险,或根据有毒物质,评估是否存在健康威胁	是 / 否	船长
通过将油转移至空舱来降低漏油舱液位	是 / 否	大副
如有必要,准备油泵以将油移至岸上 / 驳船	是 / 否	大副
如有必有,甲板消防站就位	是 / 否	轮机长
通知有关当局	是 / 否	船长
进一步的响应		
如果泄漏位于水线以下,派潜水员做进一步检查	是 / 否	港口负责人
如果不能确定泄漏舱应降低油舱液位	是 / 否	大副
考虑对船舶船体应力及稳定性的影响	是 / 否	船长 / 大副
考虑清理行动	是 / 否	船长 / 甲板值班驾驶员
港口 / 海岸警卫协助清理工作		轮机长
遵守报告程序	是 / 否	船长 / 港口—海岸警卫
如果需求的话,获得地方当局或码头方允许才可继续正常操作	是 / 否	船长 / 港口

C

LOGICAL SEQUENCE OF ACTIONS IN EMERGENCY		
SHIPBOARD OIL POLLUTION EMERGENCY PLAN ***COLLISION/GROUNDING***		
Action to be considered	**Action taken**	**Responsibility**
IMMEDIATE ACTION		
Sounding Emergency Alarm	Yes/No	Duty officer on bridge
Initiate vessel emergency response procedure	Yes/No	Master
INITIAL RESPONSE		
Ascertain stability of vessel	Yes/No	Chief Officer
All crew to stand-by position	Yes/No	All
Assess fire risk from release of flammable substances, or health hazards from toxic substances and man fire station	Yes/No	Chief Engineer
Assess hull damage	Yes/No	Officer/Engineer on duty
Inform closest port	Yes/No	Master
Inform operators	Yes/No	Master
SECONDARY RESPONSE		
Use the Pollution prevention team in an attempt to locate the leakage, if any	Yes/No	Chief Officer/2nd Engineer
Consider stopping air intake into accommodation/engine room	Yes/No	Chief Engineer
Prepare pumps for transfer of cargo to reduce the tank level by dropping cargo into an empty tank, if possible	Yes/No	Chief Officer
FURTHER RESPONSE		
If the leakage is located below the waterline, call shore assistance immediately	Yes/No	Master-PORT
If it is not possible to identify the leaking tank, reduce level in the tank, if possible	Yes/No	Chief Officer
Consider the effect on hull stress and stability of the vessel	Yes/No	Chief Officer
Consider clean-up actions	Yes/No	Deck Duty Officer/Chief Engineer
Port/Coast Guards assists in clean up actions	Yes/No	Master/Port-Coast Guards
If required, obtain permission from local authorities to proceed to port of refuge	Yes/No	Master/Port

C

紧急行动的逻辑顺序		
船舶油类污染应急计划 碰撞/搁浅		
可考虑的行动	**是否采取**	**责任**
立即行动		
拉响应急警报	是 / 否	驾驶室值班驾驶员
启动船舶应急反应程序	是 / 否	船长
初级响应		
确定船舶稳定性	是 / 否	大副
所有船员到准备位置	是 / 否	所有人
通过易燃或有毒物质的排放,评估是否存在火灾风险或健康威胁,同时消防站就位	是 / 否	轮机长
评估船体损坏状况	是 / 否	值班驾驶员 / 轮机员
通知最近港口	是 / 否	船长
通知经营者	是 / 否	船长
二级响应		
如有泄漏,通过防污染小组尝试定位泄漏源	是 / 否	大副 / 大管轮
考虑切断机舱 / 生活区通风	是 / 否	轮机长
如果可能,通过将油转移至空舱来降低漏油舱液位	是 / 否	大副
进一步的响应		
如果泄漏位于水线以下,立即通知岸上寻求帮助	是 / 否	港口负责人
如果可能的话,在不能确定泄漏舱时应降低油舱液位	是 / 否	大副
考虑对船舶船体应力及稳定性的影响	是 / 否	大副
考虑清理行动	是 / 否	甲板值班驾驶员 / 轮机长
港口 / 海岸警卫协助清理工作	是 / 否	船长 / 港口—海岸警卫
如有需要取得地方当局的许可以进入避难港	是 / 否	船长 / 港口

D

LOGICAL SEQUENCE OF ACTIONS IN EMERGENCY		
CHECKLIST FOR USE IN EMERGENCY		
SHIPBOARD OIL POLLUTION EMERGENCY *FIRE*		
Action to be considered	**Action taken**	**Responsibility**
IMMEDIATE ACTION		
Sounding Emergency Alarm	Yes/No	Person discovering incident
Initiate vessel emergency response procedure	Yes/No	Officer/Engineer on duty
INITIAL RESPONSE		
Stop vessel/Cease all cargo operation	Yes/No	Master/Chief Engineer/ Chief Officer
All crew to stand-by position	Yes/No	Officer on duty
Man fire station	Yes/No	Chief Engineer
Inform terminal/loading master (in port)	Yes/No	Master
If fire out of hand, seek shore assistance (port)/abandon vessel	Yes/No	Master
SECONDARY RESPONSE		
Consider stopping air intake into accommodation/engine room	Yes/No	Chief Engineer
Check stability of vessel	Yes/No	Chief Officer
Assess risk of release of flammable substances, or health hazards from toxic substances	Yes/No	Chief Officer
Assess damage to hull and/or equipment	Yes/No	Chief Officer/2nd Engineer
Contain spill, if any, with seals or absorbent materials	Yes/No	Duty Officer
Prepare portable pumps where it is possible to transfer spill into an empty or slack tank	Yes/No	Chief Officer
If required, change vessel's trim	Yes/No	Duty Deckhands
Consider relief of pressure from relevant tanks	Yes/No	Duty Officer/Duty hands
Consider notification of authorities	Yes/No	Master
FURTHER RESPONSE		
Clean-up as required by using material from provided contingency unit	Yes/No	Chief Officer & Officer on duty
Transfer deck washing into empty tank	Yes/No	Chief Officer
Ensure that any residues collected in the clean-up operation are stored carefully prior to disposal	Yes/No	Chief Officer
Comply with reporting procedures	Yes/No	Master
Confirm the status of the vessel to resume her voyage	Yes/No	Master

D

紧急行动的逻辑顺序		
紧急处理列表		
船舶油类污染应急计划 火灾		
可考虑的行动	**是否采取**	**责任**
立即行动		
拉响应急警报	是 / 否	事故发现人
启动船舶应急反应程序	是 / 否	值班驾驶员 / 轮机员
初级响应		
停船 / 停止所有货油操作	是 / 否	船长 / 轮机长 / 大副
所有船员到准备位置	是 / 否	值班驾驶员
消防站就位	是 / 否	轮机长
通知码头 / 装载负责人(港内)	是 / 否	船长
如果火势失去控制,寻求岸上帮助(港口)/ 弃船	是 / 否	船长
二级响应		
考虑切断机舱 / 生活区通风	是 / 否	轮机长
检查船舶稳定性	是 / 否	大副
通过易燃或有毒物质的排放,评估是否存在火灾风险或健康威胁	是 / 否	大副
评定船体 / 设备损坏程度	是 / 否	大副 / 大管轮
用密封或吸附材料限制溢油,如有溢油	是 / 否	值班驾驶员
准备便携式泵,在条件允许情况下把溢油驳入空舱或缓冲舱	是 / 否	大副
如有需要,改变船舶吃水差	是 / 否	值班水手
考虑相关舱室进行减压	是 / 否	值班驾驶员 / 值班水手
考虑通知有关当局	是 / 否	船长
进一步的响应		
要求使用应急计划体系提供的材料进行清洗	是 / 否	大副和值班驾驶员
将甲板清洗水转移至空舱	是 / 否	大副
确保清理出的残余物质在被处理前进行妥善保存	是 / 否	大副
遵守报告程序	是 / 否	船长
确定船舶状态以重新开始航行	是 / 否	船长

Appendix 7:

Sample Exercise Scenarios for Liquid Cargo Handling Simulator (Oil)

The exercises mentioned here are to be used as a guideline in case a simulator is being used for training as part of the model course

附录7:

液货模拟器操作(油类)练习场景范例

如果模拟器训练作为示范课程的一部分,则将此处述及的练习作为指南

Example of simulator training, where provided

Introduction

Simulator-based training and assessment is not a mandatory requirement for this oil tanker training programme. However, it is widely recognized that well-designed lessons and exercises can improve the effectiveness of training.

In case a simulator is being used as an additional tool for the conduct of this model course then it is suggested that the instructor will use his/her professional judgement to decide as to which part of the course syllabus can be covered by the simulator training. S/he can then adjust the classroom training accordingly in order to follow the objective of the model course, as well as the time frame given.

As a guidance tool, a brief description of a suitable simulator, and the subsequent training, is highlighted below:

This simulator will be used to demonstrate the following STCW 95 competencies:

STCW-95 Reference	Competence
Table A-II/1.9 Table A-II/3.6	Monitor the loading, stowage, securing and unloading of cargoes and their care during the voyage
Table A-II/1.11 Table A-II/3.8 Table A-III/1.11	Maintain seaworthiness of the ship
Table A-II/2.11	Plan and ensure safe loading, stowage, securing, care during voyage and unloading of cargoes
Table A-II/2.12	Carriage of dangerous cargoes
Table A-II/2.13 Table A-III/2.12	Control Trim, Stability and Stress
Table A-II/2.14 Table A-III/2.13	Monitor and control compliance with legislative requirements and measures to ensure safety of life at sea and protection of the marine environment
Section A-V/1.12	Ship operations (oil tanker)
Section A-V/1.14	Emergency operations (oil tanker)

The choice of a simulator should take into consideration the following international standards:

- International Convention on Standards for Training, Certification and Watchkeeping, 1978, with 1995 amendments
- IMO Resolution A.830 (19) – Code on Alarms and Indicators
- IMO Model Course 1.02 – Specialized Training Programme for Oil Tankers
- ICS/OCIMF/IAPH International Safety Guide for Oil Tankers and Terminals

模拟器训练范例(如果提供的话)

介绍

基于模拟器的培训及评估并不是该油船培训课程的强制要求。然而,精心设计的教学及练习可以提高培训效果已经得到了广泛认可。

如果模拟器作为推进该示范课程的一项附加工具,则建议教员根据其职业判断能力决定课程教学大纲的哪些内容可以利用模拟器进行培训。然后教员相应地调整课堂教学内容,以便能够符合示范课程的教学目标以及规定的时间框架要求。

作为一项指导工具,对适当模拟器及其后续培训的简要说明应重点强调:

该模拟器将用于证明满足下述《STCW95公约》的适任能力要求:

STCW-95	适任能力
表 A-Ⅱ/1.9 表 A-Ⅱ/3.6	监督装货、配载、系固和卸货以及航行期间的管理
表 A-Ⅱ/1.11 表 A-Ⅱ/3.8 表 A-Ⅲ/1.11	维护船舶适航性
表 A-Ⅱ/2.11	计划并确保安全装载、配载、系固、航行期间管理以及卸货
表 A-Ⅱ/2.12	运输危险货物
表 A-Ⅱ/2.13 表 A-Ⅲ/2.12	控制吃水、稳性以及应力
表 A-Ⅱ/2.14 表 A-Ⅲ/2.13	监控符合法律要求和规定以确保海上人命安全和海洋环境保护
表 A-Ⅴ/1.12	船舶操作(油船)
表 A-Ⅴ/1.14	应急操作(油船)

模拟器的选择应该考虑以下国际标准:

- STCW78/95公约及修正案
- IMO A.830(19)决议——报警及显示规则
- IMO 示范课程1.02——油船特殊培训
- ICS/OCIMF/IAPH油船及码头国际安全指南

The inclusion of simulation may be utilised to enhance the training of the model course and can be used as a tool to achieve the following:

- Training for tanker staff at all levels for obtaining the statutory Dangerous Cargo Endorsements
- Trai ning for experienced staff before increasing their level of responsibility e.g. promotion from operation level to management level

The simulator may fulfil the following requirements:

Physical realism

- Can simulate a typical cargo handling system found on an oil tanker based on real operational vessels
- Equipment is arranged in a ship-like manner
- The simulator includes the following components and sub-systems:
  - Cargo Control system
  - Ballast Control system
  - Tank Cleaning system
  - Overboard discharge monitoring systems
  - Tank content Monitoring Systems
  - Inert/Venting Control system including loading/discharging, gas freeing, purging and aerating
  - Tank atmosphere control system
  - Alarm system
  - Communication system
  - Cargo pumping system (hydraulic, electric or steam dependant on vessel type)
  - The simulator includes a system for communicating with the 'outside world'
  - The simulator includes a stability and stress calculator

Behavioural realism

The simulation model should be able to replicate the dynamic behaviour of the cargo handling system and its parameters. Furthermore, the simulation model should be able to simulate the components, their processes and control systems. It should also be possible to introduce failures, breakdowns and wear to all equipment simulated.

Operating Environment

The simulator should be able to simulate restrictions and failures in the cargo transfer for instance, introduced by the simulated shore terminal. Alarms may be announced by flashing alarm lamps and sound in the 'Cargo Control Room'.

模拟器可用来强化示范课程的培训效果,并且可以作为一项工具,以实现以下各项:

- 为油船上各种水平的人员开展培训,以获取法定危险货物签证
- 为有资历的人员在提升其责任之前开展培训,比如从操作级提升为管理级

该模拟器可能需要具备如下要求:

物理层面

- 能够模拟真实营运油船上的典型货物操作系统
- 设备布置符合实船情况
- 该模拟器包括以下组成部分以及子系统:
  - 货物控制系统
  - 压载控制系统
  - 货舱清洁系统
  - 舷外排放监测系统
  - 货舱成分监测系统
  - 惰化/除气控制系统,包括装卸货、除气、驱气以及通大气
  - 货舱气体控制系统
  - 报警系统
  - 通信系统
  - 货物泵送系统(液压、电气或蒸气,取决于船舶类型)
  - 该模拟器包括与“外界”进行通信的系统
  - 该模拟器包括稳性和应力计算器

行为层面

模拟器模型应该能够复制货物操作系统及其各参数的动态过程。而且,该模拟器模型应该能够模拟各组成部分、它们的过程以及控制系统。还应该引入所模拟全部设备的故障、大修以及磨损。

操作环境

该模拟器应该能够模拟货物操作过程中的局限以及故障,比如由模拟的岸基码头引入。报警可能会在“货物控制室”以声光报警的形式得到激发。

An example of what the ship model may contain?

Oil Tanker

- This model is based on a 105,000 Mt DWT Crude Oil carrier. The main components of the model include:
  - Six pairs of cargo tanks and 1 pair of slop-tanks
  - Segregated Ballast System with 6 pairs of ballast tanks and peak tanks
  - Inert Gas Generation (Flue Gas) and Distribution & Control Systems
  - Fixed Gas Detection System
  - Portable Gas Detection System
  - Tank Cleaning system with programmable & non-programmable machines
  - Oil Discharge Monitoring & Control System
  - UTI Gauging System
  - Alarm & Monitoring System
  - Cargo tanks are connected to the cargo unloading system through main and stripping suction lines. Additionally drop lines provide a direct connection from manifolds to cargo tanks thus bypassing the pump-room during loading operations
  - The cargo system is designed to enable the carriage of three segregated cargoes. All systems can be interconnected as required for loading, discharging or inerting purposes. Three manifolds are provided on either side, one for each cargo "system"
  - Level indications together with high level, low level and overfill alarms/shutoff are provided on each cargo tank using a "Radar" type of level monitoring system. The tanks are also fitted with temperature monitoring facilities at three levels together with pressure monitoring enabling the accurate determination of cargo contents and temperature distribution during all stages of operation
- Cargo Oil Pumps: Main Cargo pumps are horizontal centrifugal type located in the pump-room and driven by steam turbines located in the engine room. Total 3 cargo pumps are provided. Rated capacity of the cargo pumps is 2800 m^3/hr at 130 mlc. Pumps are suitable for pumping oil & SW. Rated capacity refers to 1310 rpm (±3%)
- Cargo Oil Stripping Pump: Steam driven vertical reciprocating pump of rated capacity 300 m^3/hr at 130m total head
- Cargo Eductor: Suction capacity ~ 430 m^3/hr, Drive pressure at rated capacity ~ 10 bars, Drive liquid consumption at rated capacity ~ 1,200 m^3/hr
- Ballast Eductor: Suction capacity ~ 400 m^3/hr, Drive pressure at rated capacity ~ 3.4 bars, Drive liquid consumption at rated capacity ~ 1,500 m^3/hr
- Stripping pump suction and discharge pressure indication
- Stripping pump strokemeter

在一个船舶模型实例中应包含哪些内容?

油船

- 该模型是基于105 000载重吨的原油油船。该模型的主要组成部分包括:
  - 6对货油舱和1对污液舱
  - 专用压载系统中含有6对压载舱和一个艏尖舱
  - 惰性气体发生装置(烟道气)及其分布和控制系统
  - 固定式气体检测装置
  - 便携式气体检测装置
  - 带有可编程和不可编程洗舱机的油舱清洁系统
  - 排油监控系统
  - 油水界面测量系统
  - 报警及监测系统
  - 货舱通过主管路和扫舱吸入管连接到卸货系统中。另外,下降管路在装货期间通过在泵舱旁通将货舱直接与总管相连接。
  - 设计的货物系统能够运输三种独立的货物。所有的系统能够按照要求为了实现装卸货和惰化而进行内部连接。船舶两侧各有三套总管,分别对应各自的货物系统。
  - 每个货舱配置雷达式液位监测系统,以显示高液位、低液位以及溢油报警及停止。货舱在三个液位高度上设置有温度监测装置,并同时监测压力,以便在货物操作的各个环节准确界定货物成分及其温度分布。
- 货油泵:主货油泵是水平离心式泵,位于泵舱,由机舱的蒸汽透平驱动。共有3台主货油泵。货油泵的额定排量是2800 m^3/h(130mlc)。该泵适用于泵送油及海水。额定排量时的转速为1 310 r/min(±0.3%)
- 货油扫舱泵:蒸汽驱动立式往复泵,额定排量为300 m^3/h,总扬程为130 m。
- 货物喷射泵:吸入能力大约为430 m^3/h,额定排量时的驱动压力为10 bars,额定排量时动力液体的消耗量大约为1 200 m^3/h。
- 压载喷射泵:吸入能力大约为400 m^3/h,额定排量时的驱动压力为3.4 bars,额定排量时动力液体的消耗量大约为1 500 m^3/h。
- 扫舱泵吸、排压力指示
- 扫舱泵(活塞)行程表

- Cargo Eductor suction, drive and discharge pressure indication
- Cargo Pump separator tank level
- Following controls are provided:
  - Valves operation – COP discharge valves are remotely operated butterfly valves with position control
  - COP RPM control knob
  - Stripping Pump strokes control knob
  - Non-return valves on COP
  - Vacuum pump start/stop
  - Auto/Manual control buttons for vacuum pumps
  - Auto/Manual control buttons for COP discharge valves
  - Auto-Unloading System: The system is installed to complete the unloading work with Cargo Oil Pump (COP) alone. The main purpose of installing this system is to perform stripping operation efficiently, while preventing the entry of vapour into COP, and achieving minimum oil residue in cargo tanks
- Fixed gas Detection system consists of a monitoring and control panel in the CCR with all its associated monitoring and control systems. The system draws vapour samples sequentially from all monitored spaces at intervals not exceeding 30 minutes. The spaces being monitored are – Ballast tanks, Engine Room air uptakes, Pump-Room Top & Bottom and areas in the accommodation. The sampled gas is passed through the analyser and an alarm is indicated if the vapour concentration in the sample exceeds the alarm limit set by the user. Maximum permissible alarm limit is 30% LEL.

Product tanker

- This model is based on a 46,000 Mt DWT Product carrier. The main components of the model include:
  - Seven pairs of cargo tanks and 1 pair of slop-tanks
  - Segregated Ballast system with 8 pairs of Ballast tanks and peak tanks
  - Inert gas generation (Flue Gas) and distribution & Control systems
  - Fixed Gas Detection system
  - Portable gas detection system
  - Tank Cleaning system with programmable & non-programmable machines
  - Oil Discharge Monitoring & Control System
  - UTI Gauging System
  - Alarm & Monitoring system
- Cargo tanks are connected to the cargo unloading system through main and stripping suction lines. Additionally drop lines provide a direct connection from manifolds to cargo tanks thus bypassing the pump-room during loading operations

- 货物喷射泵吸压、驱动压力以及排压指示
- 货物泵分离舱液位
- 提供以下控制:
  - 阀操作—货油泵排放阀是在控制站进行遥控操作的蝶阀
  - 货油泵转速控制手柄
  - 扫舱泵冲程控制手柄
  - 货油泵上的止回阀
  - 真空泵的起/停
  - 真空泵的自动/手动控制按钮
  - 货油泵排放阀的自动/手动控制按钮
  - 自动卸货系统:安装该系统后,仅需货油泵即可完成卸货工作。安装该系统的主要目的是提高扫舱效率,同时防止蒸汽进入货油泵并减少货舱内的货油残留量。
- 固定式气体检测系统包括货物控制室内的监控面板及其所有相关的监控系统。该系统从所有受监控空间以不超过30分钟的时间间隔顺序提取气体样本。受监控空间是压载舱、机舱烟道、泵舱上部和底部以及生活区。气体样本通过分析器,如果样本蒸气浓度超过了用户设定的报警上限值就会显示报警。最大允许报警限值为30% LEL。

成品油船

- 该模型是基于一艘46 000载重吨的成品油船。该模型的主要组成部分包括:
  - 7对货油舱和1对污液舱
  - 专用压载系统中含有8对压载舱和一个艏尖舱
  - 惰性气体发生装置(烟道气)及其分布和控制系统
  - 固定式气体检测装置
  - 便携式气体检测装置
  - 带有可编程和不可编程洗舱机的油舱清洁系统
  - 排油监控系统
  - 油水界面测量系统
  - 报警及监测系统
- 货舱通过主管路和扫舱吸入管连接到卸货系统中。另外,下降管路在装货期间通过在泵舱旁通将货舱直接与总管相连接

- The cargo system is designed to enable the carriage of four segregated cargoes. All systems can be interconnected as required for loading, discharging or inerting purposes. Four manifolds are provided on either side, one for each cargo 'system'
- Level indications together with high level, low level and overfill alarms/shutoff are provided on each cargo tank using a 'Radar' type of level monitoring system. The tanks are also fitted with temperature monitoring facilities at three levels together with pressure monitoring enabling the accurate determination of cargo contents and temperature distribution during all stages of operation
- Cargo Oil Pumps: Main Cargo pumps are horizontal centrifugal type located in the pump–room and driven by electric motors located in the engine room. Total 4 are provided. Rated Capacity:
  - No.1 And No.4 – Variable RPM (500–1750), Max. Capacity–1200 m^3/H
  - No.2 And No.3 – Two Speed (800 RPM and 1200 RPM), Max. Capacity –800 m^3/H at 1200 RPM and 400 m^3 at 800 RPM
- Cargo Stripping Pump; Number And Type: 1, Positive Displacement, Steam Driven, Variable Rpm (0-37 Strokes); Location: Cargo Pump–Room. Rated Capacity: 150 m^3/Hr At Max. RPM
- Cargo Stripping Eductor Capacity: 400 M^3/Hr
- Ballast Pump; Number And Type: 1, Centrifugal, Electric Driven; Location: Cargo Pump-Room; Rated Capacity: Fixed RPM, Max. Capacity –1500 m^3/H
- Inert Gas System; Number And Type: 1 Unit, Purity: 98 Vol. %; Capacity: 2500 × 2 M^3/Hr; Pressure: 7.5 To 8.5 Kg/cm^2
- Vapour Control System; P-V Valve Settings: High Pressure-Lifts At 1400 mm Aq, Closes At 900 mm Aq; Vacuum-Lifts At –350 mm Aq, Closes At –330 mm Aq; P-V Breaker Settings: High Pressure-Lifts At 1890 mm Aq, Vacuum; Lifts At –630 mm Aq
- Ballast Pump; Number And Type: 1, Centrifugal, Electric Driven; Location: Ballast Pump-Room; Rated Capacity: Fixed RPM, Max. Capacity –300 m^3/Hr × 25 mlc
- Two hydraulic driven ventilation fans of capacity 200 m^3/hr × 6 kPa, with heater, are pro ided – one each in mid-ship fan room and ballast pump-room. Dry air from gas free fan can be supplied to cargo tanks through 150 A liquid loading line

An example of what the student station may contain?

As an example, each student station may be active singly and independently. If this is the case, then in such a mode it may be possible to have any number of stations using the same or any number of different exercises e.g. one or more stations may be engaged in operational level training while other student stations can be involved in management level training – each with its own exercise if necessary.

Two or more stations can be linked together and engaged in a joint exercise. A "Role playing" mode can be extremely useful for training a group of mariners of different ranks and experience levels who may be required to work together as a team in the future. If such a mode is provided, then in this mode it may be possible to control access levels in a way that

- 设计的货物系统能够运输四种独立的货物。所有的系统能够按照要求为了实现装卸货和惰化而进行内部连接。船舶两侧各有四套总管,分别对应各自的货物系统
- 每个货舱配置雷达式液位监测系统,以显示高液位、低液位以及溢流报警及停止。货舱在三个液位高度上设置有温度监测装置,并同时监测压力,以便在货物操作的各个环节准确界定货物成分及其温度分布
- 货油泵:主货油泵是水平离心式泵,位于泵舱,由机舱的电机驱动。共有4台主货油泵。额定排量为:
  - 1号泵和4号泵—可变转速(500~1 750),最大排量为1 200 m^3/h
  - 2号泵和3号泵—两个转速 (800和1 200), 最大排量为1 200 r/min时800 m^3/h,800 r/min时为400 m^3/h
- 货油扫舱泵;数量及型号:1台,容积式泵,蒸汽驱动,可变转速(0–37冲程);地点:货泵舱。额定排量:最高转速时150 m^3/h
- 货物扫舱喷射泵:排量为400 m^3/h
- 压载泵;数量及型号:1台,离心式泵,电力驱动;地点:货泵舱;额定排量:固定转速,最大排量为1 500 m^3/h
- 惰气系统; 数量及型号:1套, 纯度:98%体积含量; 排量:2 500×2 m^3/h; 压力:7.5~8.5 kg/cm^2
- 蒸汽控制系统;PV阀设置值:1 400 mm水柱时高压抬起,900 mm水柱时关闭;真空–350 mm水柱抬起,–330 mm水柱关闭;P-V破坏阀设定值:1 890 mm高压水柱抬起,真空– 630 mm水柱抬起
- 压载泵;数量及型号:1台,离心式泵,电力驱动;地点:压载泵舱;额定排量:固定转速,最大排量为300 m^3/h × 25 mlc
- 两台液压驱动风机,排量为200 m^3/h × 6 kPa,带有加热器。船中风机间和压载泵舱各一台。风机产生的不含油气的干空气经过150A液货装载管线通往货舱

在一个学员操作台实例中应包含哪些内容?

作为实例,每个学员操作台应该是独立和单独进行。如果情况是这样,那么就可能会有一种模式,在该模式下,多个操作台可以使用同一个或多个练习,比如一个或多个操作台在进行操作级培训的同时,其他学员操作台则在进行管理级培训。如果有必要,每个操作台都有自己的练习项目。

两个及以上的操作台可以连接到一起完成联合练习。“分角色”模式对于培训一群具有不同级别和资历、将来可能作为一个团队一起工作的海员而言,将会非常有用。如果采用这种模式,那

every trainee has access to information and controls, which is limited to his/her sphere of responsibility within that exercise.

An example of what the instructor station may contain?

The instructor console is to act as the heart of a simulator. It may provide the instructor with a series of panels covering the entire range of operations depicted with total control over every aspect of the simulation session.

么在该模式下可以在某种程度上控制访问权限，即每个学员只能访问其练习中规定职能范围内的信息和控制权内容。

在一个教员操作台实例中应包含哪些内容?

教员操作台是模拟器的核心。可以提供给教员一系列的面板,覆盖了控制整个模拟器各个方面的操作。

Sample Exercise Scenarios

Exercise No. 1: Cargo Handling Simulator Layout

Exercise No. 2: Inerting Cargo tanks

Exercise No. 3: Loading full cargo

Exercise No. 4: Purge and ventilate cargo tanks for entry

Exercise No. 5: Discharging, Crude Oil washing (COW) and ballasting

Exercise No. 6: Cleaning/washing cargo tanks

Exercise No. 7: Settling and decanting of slop-tanks

Please note that the exercises mentioned here are as a guidance tool in cases where a simulator is provided.

实例练习场景

练习1：　货油操作模拟器概述

练习2：　货油舱惰化

练习3：　满舱装载

练习4　进入货油舱之前的驱气与通风

练习5：　卸货、原油洗舱和压载

练习6：　清洁/清洗货油舱

练习7：　污液舱的沉淀和转驳

请注意如果有模拟器的话,此处述及的练习可以作为操作指南。

Exercise No. 1: Cargo Handling Simulator Layout

Introduction to the simulator to be given prior commencing the exercises on the simulator

Objectives: Understanding of the sub-systems and their overall interactivity in the cargo handling simulator and the operations involved. Becoming familiar with terminology used in liquid cargo transport and operations.

Prerequisites: The trainees should know the theoretical aspects of the various kinds of liquid cargo transport. Basic Naval architecture related to tankers will have been studied prior to simulator exercises. Basic stability, strength and stress theory will have to be known by the trainees.

Training materials: OHP, Pipeline diagram of the vessel modelled in the liquid cargo simulator.

Simulator condition: Not applicable.

Briefing: Explanation of the ship type modelled.

Explanation of the various sub-systems and how they connect in real life.

Expla nation of the following LOADICATOR functions: trim, draft, and heel indicators in the simulator.

Student action: Attend lecture.

Repeat various theories learned on cargo systems, naval

architecture, stability and stress.

Instructor action: Apart from system mimics emphasize overall connection of the systems in the vessel.

Explain symbols used in mimics.

Explain LOADICATOR.

Debriefing: Check if all systems understood and interconnection of systems in simulator.

Discuss if relationships with previous theory are properly understood.

Evaluation: By means of one or more diagrams, have trainees show understanding of sub-systems and symbols by describing system and/or indicating various symbols etc.

练习1:货物操作模拟器概述

在模拟器上进行练习之前简要介绍该模拟器

目标: 理解货油操作模拟器的子系统、整体内部关联及其相关操作。熟悉液货运输和操作所使用的术语。

预备知识: 学员应知道各种液货运输理论方面的知识。模拟器训练前应学习关于油船的船舶基本结构。学员应事先了解基本的稳型、强度和应力理论。

培训资料: 投影仪、液货模拟器的模型船管系布置图。

模拟条件: 不适用。

简要介绍: 模型船介绍。

说明各种子系统以及在实际中他们之间的联系。

随后的配载仪功能介绍:模拟器中吃水差、吃水、横倾指示器。

学员任务: 听课。

事先复习所学的货油系统、船舶结构、稳性和应力的理论知识。

教员任务: 除了Mimic系统外,详细说明船舶系统间整体关联。

解释Mimic系统中所用的符号意义。

解释配载仪。

总结: 检查模拟器中所有系统及系统间的内部联系是否均被理解。

讨论与之前所学的理论知识之间的关系是否得到正确理解。

评估: 通过学员对一个或多个子系统图中系统的描述或者不同符号的说明等方式评价其对教学内容的理解程度。

Exercise No. 2: Inerting cargo tanks

Duration: 2 hours

Objectives: Understanding the principles, operations and safety precautions involved with inerting of cargo and slop-tanks.

Prerequisites: Introductory exercises will have been completed such as No. 1. Theory of UEL, LEL and explosive mixtures will have been covered as well as explosion triangles.

Training materials: OHP, diagram of the IG distribution line and inerting mimics of the cargo tanks.

Simulator Condition: Cargo tanks empty, filled with air and normal ballast condition.

Briefing: Composition of the tank atmosphere to be checked and students explained levels of safe inerting.

Student action: After checking tank atmospheres, choices to be made for which tanks to start inerting.

Start up IG plant.

Continuous monitoring of IG system and O_2 content in the tanks.

Instructor action: Check choice of tanks, system used and route chosen to tanks, which are to be inerted.

Debriefing: The instructor should ascertain that the tank atmospheres are at the required level of O_2. Check that the students have understood the principles of inerting and explosion levels and limits.

Evaluation: By question and answer confirm that students have understood the principles of, and reasons for, the inerting of cargo and slop-tanks. Based on the achieved levels of IG and O_2 in the tanks the trainees' understanding and skills in inerting can be evaluated.

练习2:货油舱惰化

时间: 2小时

目标: 理解关于货舱及污液舱惰化的原理、操作及安全注意事项。

预备知识: 已完成如练习1所示的初级练习。已掌握爆炸上限(UEL)、爆炸下限(LEL)和爆炸混合物等爆炸三要素基本理论。

培训材料: 投影仪、惰气分配管系图和货舱惰化模拟图。

模拟条件: 填充空气的空货油舱,正常的压载状态。

简要介绍: 检查舱室气体成分,向学员讲清惰化安全标准。

学员任务: 在检查舱室气体后,开始选择进行惰化操作的舱室。

启动惰气(IG)装置。

持续监测惰气(IG)系统和舱室内的氧气含量。

教员任务: 检查舱室的选择、系统的使用和惰化舱室的选择路径。

总结: 教员应确认舱室的气体环境处于要求的氧浓度等级。确保学员已经理解了惰化原理、爆炸等级和极限。

评估: 通过提问及回答,确认学员理解了货油舱及污液舱的惰化原理及为什么要惰化的原因。基于达到的舱室惰气和氧气水平,可对学员的理解和惰化操作技能进行评价。

Exercise No. 3: Loading full cargo

Duration: 3.5 hours

Objectives: By loading a full cargo into the vessel, appreciating efficient cargo planning, stability and stress criteria and maximum allowable draft and trim.

Prerequisites: The trainees will have performed familiarization exercises on the simulator and they will have knowledge of loading zones, stability, shear forces and bending moments.

Training materials: OHP, diagram of the vessel cargo system, LOADICATOR and Loading zone chart.

Simulator Condition: Cargo tanks empty, tanks inerted and normal ballast condition. Shore connection for 1 grade and 1 temperature of cargo in all tanks.

Briefing: Trainees should be told that all tanks are empty and segregated ballast tanks full for normal ballast condition.

Tanks have to be filled to 98%.

Shear forces and bending moments to be kept within limits; preliminary check can be done by off-line LOADICATOR. Whenloading, tank gas to be vented to shore (or vent riser on vessel or from individual high velocity PV valves according to instructor choice).

Student action: Trainees can perform preliminary stress check with the LOADICATOR.

Connection of shore manifold to be made and tank filling to commence simultaneously or in order according to stress limitations.

When loading tanks, levels to be monitored as well as tank atmosphere and shear forces and bending moments.

Ballast to be pumped out in accordance with the loading sequence.

Instructor action: Check preliminary stress calculations.

Check tanks loaded in planned sequence in order to keep stresses within limits.

Check tank levels after filling and topping off.

Check ballast pumping operation in synchronization with loading sequence.

练习3:满舱装载

时间: 3.5小时

目标: 通过向船舶装满货油,理解有效的货物计划、稳性和应力标准及最大允许吃水和吃水差。

预备知识: 学员事先熟悉了模拟器的练习操作,并且掌握了载重区、稳性、剪切力和弯曲力矩等知识。

培训材料: 投影仪、船舶货油系统图、配载仪以及装货区图纸。

模拟条件: 船舶货油舱空、已惰化以及正常压载条件。通岸接头满足全部1级和1级温度等级的货油的要求。

简要介绍: 学员应被告知这次练习所有货油舱均为空舱并且在正常压载条件下所有专用压载舱为满舱。

舱室要装载至98%的舱容。

剪切力和弯曲力矩要保持在限制范围内,初始检查可通过离线配载仪进行。

装油时油气排至岸上(根据教员的选择,或排至船舶上空或经过单个高速PV阀)。

学员任务: 学员可以使用配载仪进行初步的应力检查。

连接通岸管路,货油舱同时加注或根据应力极限按顺序进行。

在装载过程中,检测液位、舱室气体、剪切力和弯曲力矩。

根据装载顺序排放压载水。

教员任务: 核对计算的初始应力。

核对是否按计划顺序装载,以确保应力在允许范围内。

在注油和平舱完成后检查货舱液位。

检查与装载顺序同步的排放压载水操作。

If the exercise of filling all tanks takes too long in real time, a start can be made and then continued fast time until a further stage whereby topping off of tanks is again a useful learning experience.

Alternatively, fast speed simulation can be skipped and replaced by another scenario where cargo tanks are at or near topping off level and exercise commenced from that condition.

Debriefing:

Trainees should understand possibilities and limitations of a full cargo being loaded.

Stability and stresses to be monitored and final draft, heel, tank ullages and atmospheres to be checked.

Evaluation:

By means of observation of final condition assessing if trainees have reached required condition and that all values of levels, volumes, trim and list, shear forces and bending moments are within the determined limits.

如果实际装满所有油舱的练习占用了太长的时间,系统重新起动,快速加油又达到下一个平舱阶段,也是一个有用的学习过程。

作为一种选择,用另一个场景替代的方法可略过快速模拟,在该场景下,已达到或接近平舱环节,并从此处开始进行练习。

总结: 学员应该理解满舱装载的可能性和局限性。

监测稳性和应力以及检查最终的吃水、横倾、货舱空挡及其大气含量。

评估: 通过查看最终状态,评估学员是否达到了要求的状态,以及所有液位、容积、吃水差、剪力以及弯矩的数值是否在规定的范围内。

Exercise No. 4: Purge and ventilate cargo tanks for entry

Duration: 1 hour

Objectives: Preparing cargo tanks for entry after containing hydrocarbon cargo.

The trainee will learn how to purge cargo tanks with inert gas to safe level before starting to ventilate with air.

Prerequisites: Familiarization exercise No. 1.

Inerting exercise No. 2.

Theory of explosion limits – LEL and UEL.

Threshold limit values (TLV).

Training materials: OHP, diagram of the vessel IG system.

Simulator Condition: Vessel ballasted to normal seagoing condition.

All cargo tanks empty.

Tank atmosphere – Empty and under HC vapour.

Briefing: The different status of tanks to be explained to trainees.

HC and O_2 differences to be pointed out.

Use of IG system, P/V valves and venting system.

Objective is to maintain proper tank atmosphere composition during whole operation.

Student action: Start purging selected cargo tanks with inert gas to safe HC concentration before starting to ventilate with air.

Make one or two tanks gas free for entry.

Tank atmosphere to be constantly monitored.

Instructor action: Check proper operation of IG plant.

Check that trainees observe tank atmosphere and that selected tanks are at safe HC-level before starting to ventilate with air.

Debriefing: Ensure the trainees have understood the correct use of tank atmosphere diagrams.

The importance of purging with IG down to safe HC concentration before ventilating with air is to be stressed.

Evaluation: By means of tank atmosphere screens, the oxygen and hydrocarbon contents in the vented tanks can be monitored.

练习4:进入货油舱之前的驱气与通风

时间: 1小时

目标: 为进入装载过碳氢化合物的油舱做准备。

学员学习开始通风前如何使用惰气对货油舱进行驱气操作。

预备知识: 熟悉练习1。

惰化练习2。

爆炸极限的理论——爆炸下限(LEL)和爆炸上限(UEL)。

阈限值(TLV)。

培训材料: 投影仪、船舶惰气系统图。

模拟条件: 船舶压载到正常的航行状态。

所有货油舱为空舱。

舱室气体环境—空舱以及烃类气体。

简要介绍: 向学员讲明舱室的各种状态。

指出碳氢化合物(HC)和氧气(O_2)的差异。

惰气系统、压力真空(P/V)阀和透气系统的使用。

目的是在整个操作过程中保持合适的舱室气体组成。

学员任务: 在开始通风前,先对所选舱室用惰气驱气,最终使碳氢化合物浓度处于安全范围。

使得一个或两个舱室内的气体环境能够允许人员自由进入。

持续监测舱室气体环境。

教员任务: 检查惰气装置的合理使用。

确保学员遵守舱室的气体环境要求，并且在通风前所选的舱室碳氢化合物浓度处于安全等级。

总结: 确保学员已经正确的理解了舱室气体环境分析图的使用方法。

强调在通风前正确使用惰气驱气至安全的HC 浓度的重要性。

评估: 通过舱室气体环境监测屏，透气操作的舱室内的氧气和碳氢化合物的浓度能够被监测。

Exercise No. 5: Discharging, Crude Oil washing (COW) and ballasting

Duration: 5 hours

Objectives: By means of this exercise the relationship between the various sub-systems is supposed to be demonstrated and the overall understanding of simultaneously discharging, ballasting and COW to be demonstrated and realized.

Prerequisites:

Familiarization exercises.

Discharging exercise.

Washing/cleaning exercise.

Ballasting exercise.

IG usage exercise.

Theoretical knowledge of shear force, stress, trim, heel is required.

Pollution prevention rules and procedures have been discussed.

Training materials: OHP, diagram of the vessel cargo, IG and tank cleaning systems.

Simulator Condition:

Cargo tanks loaded with crude oil.

Slop-tanks 50% full.

Tanks inerted, IG system standby.

No ballast.

Briefing:

The trainees should be convinced of the complexity of the exercise, which should be built up step by step.

Discharging and inerting is to be started first.

Stress, trim and heel to be monitored.

Discharging, COW operation and ballasting according to preprepared plan.

Student action:

The trainees will start with preparing a discharging and COW plan, which will keep stress, trim and heel within the acceptable limits.

Discharging, inerting, COW operation and ballasting and stripping will take place simultaneously.

In this order operations will continue until all tanks empty, COW operation and ballasted according to IMO requirements.

Instructor action: The instructor should ascertain that the choice of discharging order takes stress, trim and heel into consideration.

练习5:卸货、原油洗舱和压载

时间: 5小时

目标: 通过这个练习,应掌握各个子系统之间的关系,并对同时进行地卸载、压载和原油洗舱(COW)等过程有一个整体性的理解。

预备知识: 熟悉练习。

卸载练习。

清洗/清洁练习。

压载练习。

惰气使用练习。

剪切力、应力、纵倾、横倾的相关理论知识。

对防污染规则和程序进行了讨论交流。

培训材料: 投影仪、船舶货物布置图,惰气及货舱清洁系统。

模拟条件: 货油舱装载原油。

污液舱液位为50%。

舱室已惰化,惰气系统已备好。

无压载。

简要介绍: 学员应当一步一步地开展练习,从而确信其过程的复杂性。

先开始做卸载和惰化。

监测应力、纵倾和横倾。

按预定计划进行卸载、原油洗舱和压载。

学员任务: 学员首先准备一个卸载和原油洗舱的计划,这个计划要求保证船舶的应力、纵倾和横倾在接受的限度内。

卸载、惰化、原油洗舱、压载以及扫舱将同时进行。

按此顺序进行,直至所有舱室都按国际海事组织(IMO)的要求完成清空、原油洗舱及压载。

教员任务: 教员应确保在选择卸载顺序时考虑了应力、纵倾和横倾这几个因素。

During discharging the tank atmospheres are monitored and inert gas supplied.

That COW commences at the right tank level and ballasting commences in time for vessel's trim, heel and stresses to be maintained within limits.

As this exercise includes several aspects and comprises a full cargo, breakdown in separate sessions is possible or alternatively the instructor can run routine parts in fast time if the trainees have started up the sub-processes properly.

Debriefing: By means of discussion bring up problems in operations and problems due to complexity.

Check which order tanks have been handled and in which order ballast has been loaded.

Check that inerting has taken place during discharging as well as during COW.

Evaluation: By means of question and answer determine understanding of operations.

Time needed to complete operations will be a measure of efficient conduct of operations.

All cargo should be discharged, tanks COW operation and inerted.

Pump performance during discharging (including, rpm racing, overheat and tank residue) is an indicator of correct use of AUS and pump operating procedures.

After completion of discharging operations, vessel should be in correct trim, heel and within acceptable limits of stresses and stability.

在卸载过程中监测舱室气体环境及向舱内供应惰气。

原油洗舱应在正确的液位条件下开始,同时在船舶的纵倾、横倾和应力维持在要求的限度内开始进行压载。

由于该练习包括好几个部分并且包含满载的情况，可以分解为几个独立环节进行,或者如果学员们已经很好地启动了相应的子过程,教员可以将常规部分快进。

总结: 通过讨论找出操作过程中的问题及由于过程复杂而产生的疑问。

检查油舱的卸载顺序以及压载顺序。

检查在卸载和原油洗舱过程中进行的惰化操作。

评估: 通过问答判断学员对各个操作的理解。

完成操作所用的时间是评判操作是否高效的一个考量因素。

应将所有货油全部卸载,并对所有舱室进行原油洗舱和惰化。

在卸货中泵的性能(包括每分钟转速、过热度和舱内残渣)可指示出AUS的使用及泵的操作程序是否正确。

在完成卸货操作后,船舶应保持适当的艏艉吃水差、侧倾值,并保证其处于允许的应力与稳性极限内。

Exercise No. 6: Cleaning/washing cargo tanks

Duration: 2 hours

Objectives: The trainees will be able to perform tank cleaning operations. The trainees will appreciate the use of inert gas during the washing operations. The trainees will be able to properly process any washing water and slops in order to prevent marine pollution.

Prerequisites: Familiarization exercises.

Cargo discharging exercise.

IG usage exercise.

Theory of tank washing: principles, equipment, dangers, limitations, slop processing.

Training materials: OHP, diagram of the vessel cargo, IG and tank cleaning systems.

Simulator Condition: Cargo tanks empty and inerted.

Vessel ballasted to normal seagoing condition.

Briefing: Trainees to be explained which tanks to be washed and in which sequence.

Differences between water washing and crude oil washing to be explained.

Washing cycle system (open and closed cycle) to be explained.

Student action: Trainees should start choosing which tanks to wash, in which order.

Tank cleaning pumps, deck lines and machines to be indicated and lined up.

Washing water to be directed to slop-tanks to settle.

Instructor action: Ascertain that tanks, routes and pumps are properly lined up.

During washing trainees should use IG and monitor tank atmospheres.

No washing water should be discharged overboard, but all to slop-tanks (closed cycle).

Debriefing: By means of question and answer trainees to be checked on understanding of washing methods and principles.

Pollution prevention by retaining slops on board is also to be discussed. Dangers associated with washing to be understood by trainees.

练习6:清洁/清洗货油舱

时间: 2小时

目标: 学员能够针对不同种类的货油进行油舱清洁操作。在洗舱过程中体会到惰气的用途。学员能够正确处理各种洗舱水和污油以防止造成海洋污染。

预备知识: 已进行熟悉练习。

已进行货油卸载练习。

已进行惰化练习。

洗舱理论知识,包括原理、设备、危险、限制和污油的处理。

培训材料: 投影仪、船舶货物布置图、惰气及洗舱系统图。

模拟条件: 货油舱为空并已惰化。船舶为正常航行压载状态。

简要介绍: 向学员解释哪些舱需要清洗和清洗顺序。

解释用水洗舱和用原油洗舱的区别。

解释清洗循环系统(开式和闭式)。

学员任务: 学员需选择清洗哪些货油舱以及清洗的顺序。

指明相应的洗舱泵、甲板管系和机器并建立系统连接。

洗舱水直接送入污液舱进行沉淀。

教员任务: 确保货油舱、使用的管路和泵都正确连接。

在洗舱过程中,学员应使用惰气并监视舱内气体环境。

禁止任何洗舱水排出舷外,都应排放到污液舱(闭式循环)。

总结: 通过问答方式,检查学员对于洗舱方法和原理的理解。

讨论将污油保留在船上的方法来防止造成污染。学员理解了洗舱伴随的危险。

Evaluation:

Tank atmospheres to be checked for explosion danger.

Slop-tank content should contain washing water and/or washing oil.

Levels of water and oil to be determined by using MMC tape.

评估: 检查舱内气体环境是否有爆炸危险。

污液舱中的成分应包含洗舱水和/或洗舱油。

水和油的液位通过使用MMC色带来确定。

Exercise No. 7: Settling and decanting of slop-tanks

Duration: 2 hours

Objectives:
Proper uses of double tank slop system.
Understanding of separation and settling of specific different liquids.

Prerequisites:
Tank cleaning exercises.
Loading exercise.
Ballasting exercise.
Theory of tank loading alternatives.
Theory of oil/water separation.

Training materials: OHP, diagram of the vessel cargo systems.

Simulator Condition:
Cargo tanks empty and inerted.
Vessel ballasted to normal seagoing condition.
Slop-tanks full with oil/water mixture.

Briefing:
Trainees to be explained system of double slop-tanks – primary and secondary.
First settling to take place in primary tank, water then decanting to secondary tank and here further settling.
Separated water then via ODME overboard if vessel underway (outside special areas).

Student action:
Trainees will first observe levels and content of slop-tanks (by use of MMC tape).
Additional slops to be produced from tank washing and pumped to primary tank.
After settling, decanting of water to secondary tank.
After further settling, pumping slops overboard direct via ODME.
Set up and operate ODME to pump out slops overboard.

Instructor action:
Check that trainees understand layout of slop-tanks, decanting system, pumps, slop discharge line etc.
Check that proper monitoring of oil/water interface takes place before pumping slops to other tank or overboard.
Check that ODME is correctly operated.

练习7:污液舱的沉淀和转驳

时间: 2小时

目标: 正确使用双污液舱系统。

理解特定的不同液体的分离和沉淀。

预备知识: 已进行洗舱练习。

已进行装油练习。

已进行压载练习。

另外的油舱装载理论知识。

油/水分离理论知识。

培训材料: 投影仪、船舶货物系统布置图。

模拟条件: 货油舱空舱和惰化。

船舶为正常航行压载状态。

污液舱充满油/水混合物。

简要介绍: 向学员说明双污液舱系统——一级和二级。

首先在一级污液舱沉淀,之后将污水转驳至二级污液舱,进行进一步沉淀。

如果船舶正在航行(特殊区域以外),分离出的水经排油监控装置(ODM)检测后排出舷外。

学员任务: 学员首先需观察污液舱的水位和成分(通过使用MMC色带)。

将洗舱产生的额外污油泵送到一级污液舱。

在沉淀之后,将污水转驳至二级污液舱。

在进一步沉淀之后,直接将污水通过排油监控装置排出舷外。

建立并运行排油监控装置将污水排至舷外。

教员任务: 检查学员对于污液舱、转驳系统、清洗泵、污油排放管系等设施布局的理解。

检查在污水排到另一舱柜或排出舷外之前, 是否对油水分界面进行了正确的监测。

检查排油监控装置是否正常运转。

Debriefing:

Discuss slop-tank system and what difficulties encountered by trainees when pumping slops.

Check knowledge of trainees in processing slops.

Evaluation:

Slop-tank contents to be monitored.

Oil/water interface is a measure of how much water has been pumped away and how well settling has taken place.

Correct operation of ODME.

总结: 讨论污液舱系统和泵送污油时学员所遇到的困难。

检查学员关于污油处理的知识。

评估: 监测污液舱的成分。

油/水分界面是判断泵出多少污水和沉淀效果如何的度量标准。

正确操作排油监控装置。

Appendix 8:

Sample Screen Shots of Liquid Cargo Handling Simulator (Oil)

The snap shots are mentioned only to be used as a guideline tool as to what parameters should go into a liquid cargo handling simulator (oil) in case a simulator is being used for training as part of the model course

附录8:

液货船模拟器(油类)操作截屏样例

万一模拟器被用来做为行为规范课的一部分,参数变量要结合液货操作模拟器才有意义,故提及的截屏图仅作为示范工具。

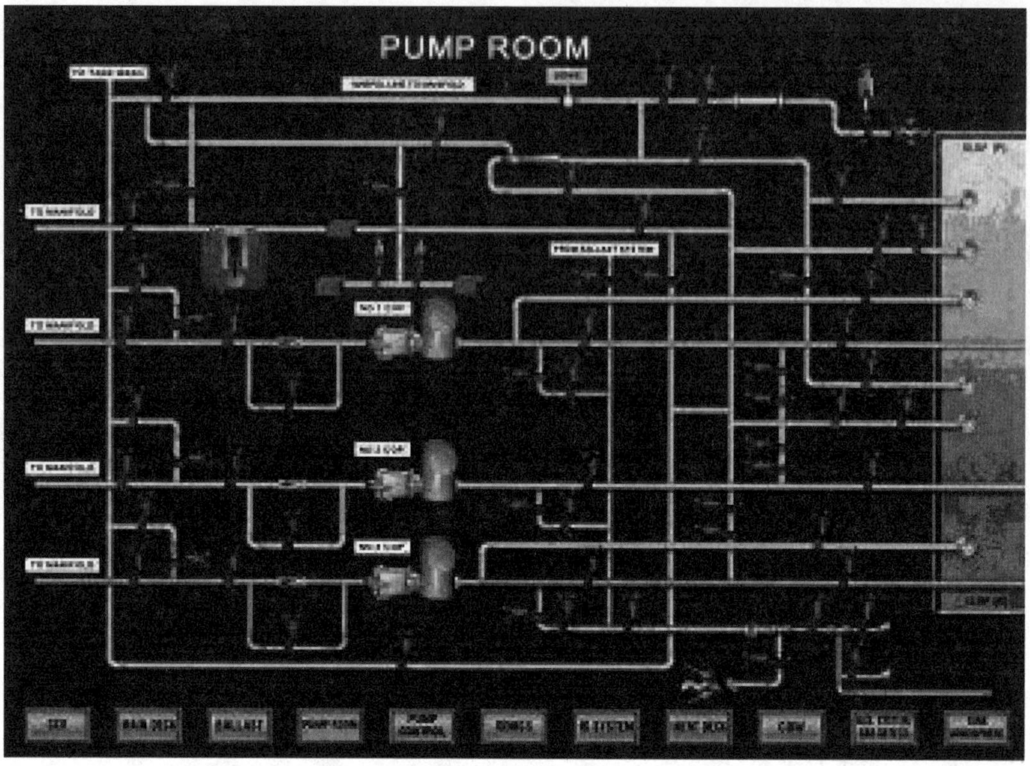

Oil tanker pump-room layout

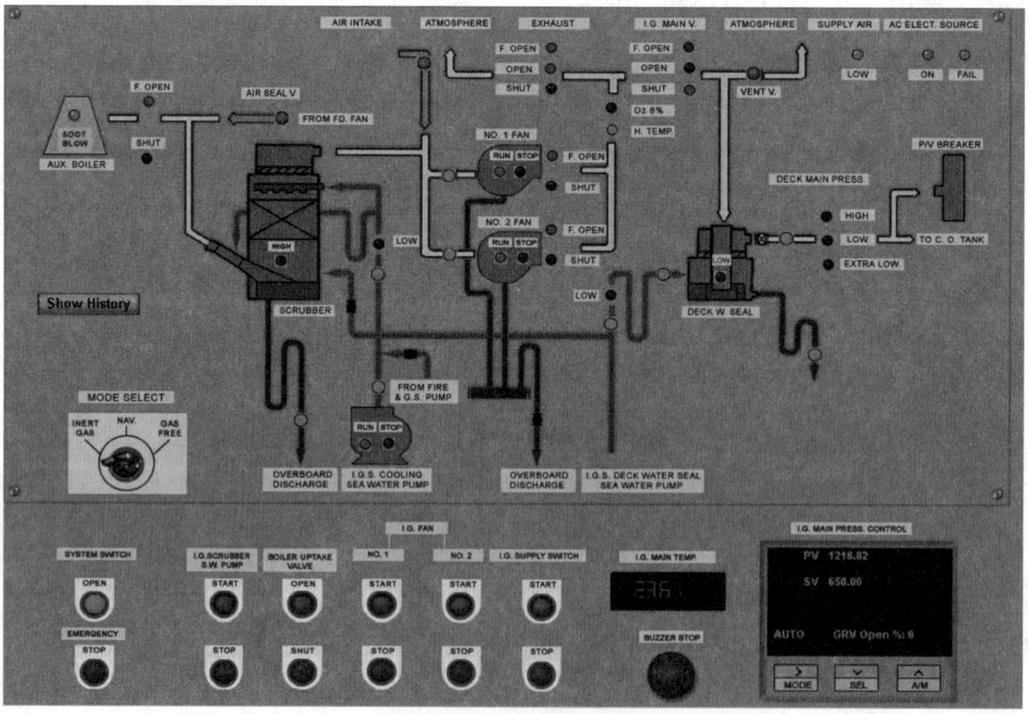

Inert Gas panel

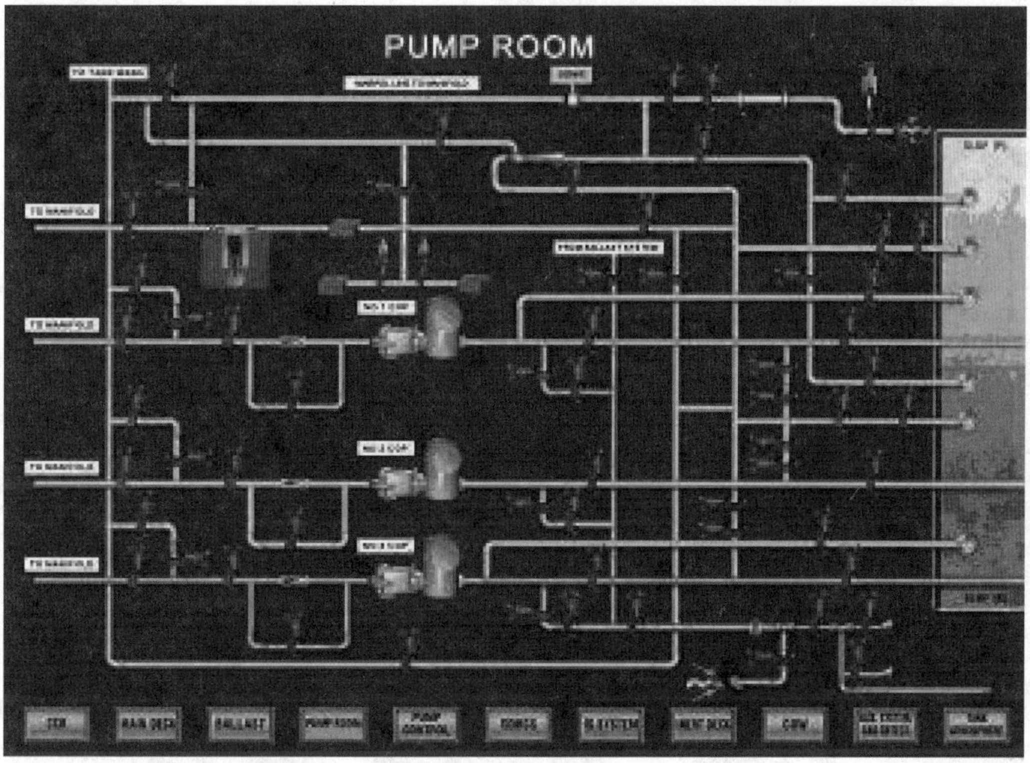

油船泵舱布置图

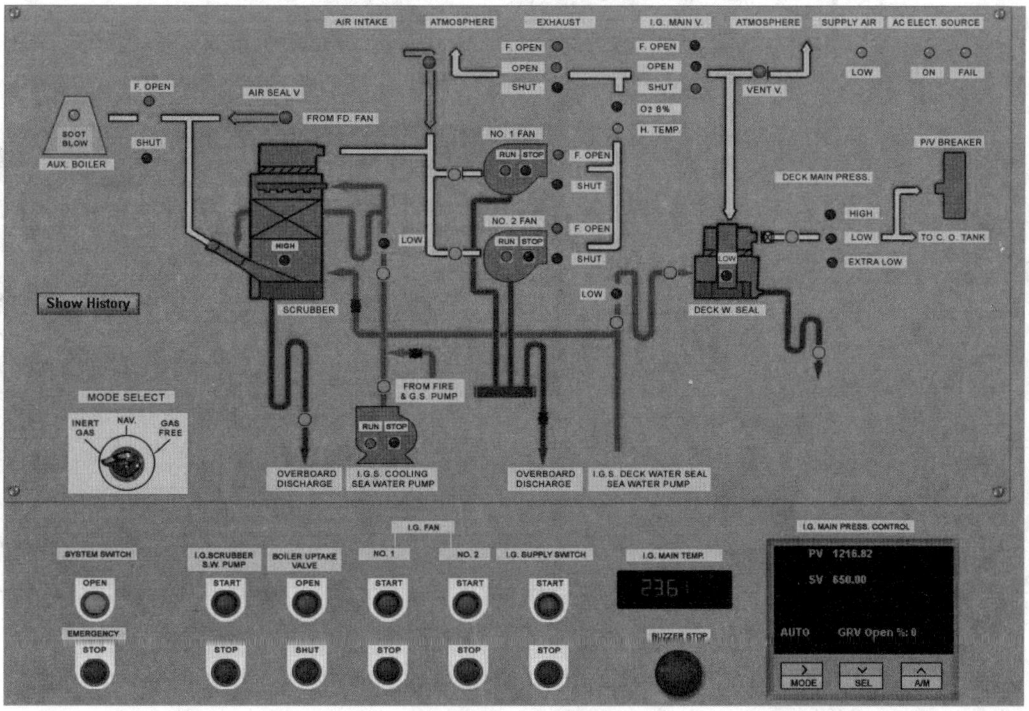

惰性气体控制板

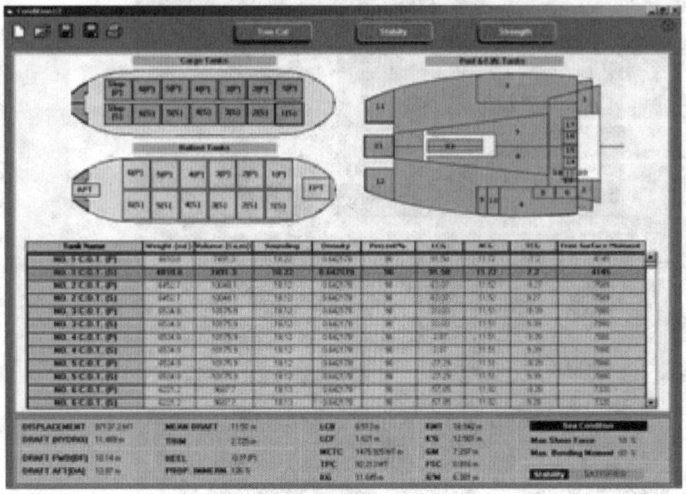

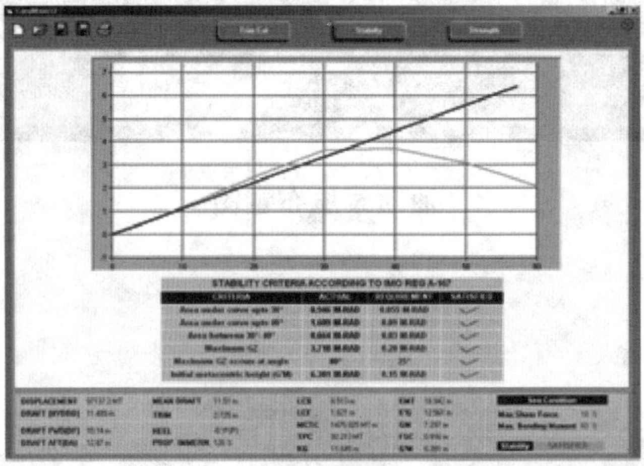

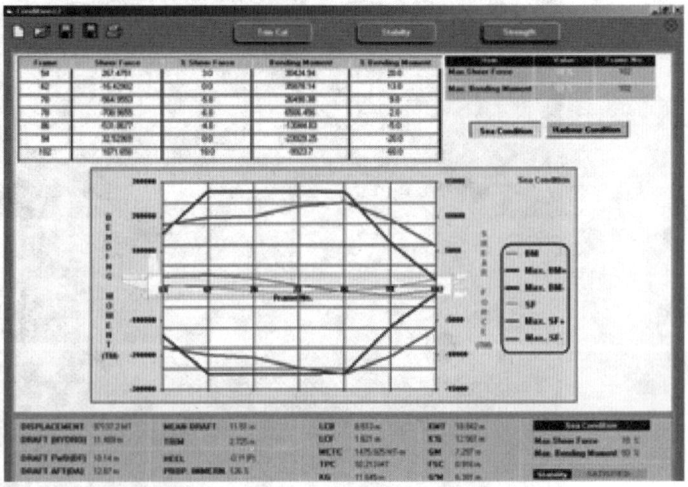

LOADICATOR

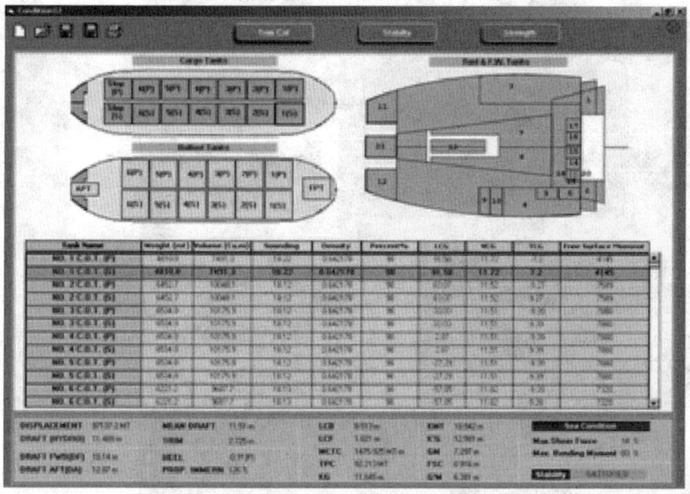

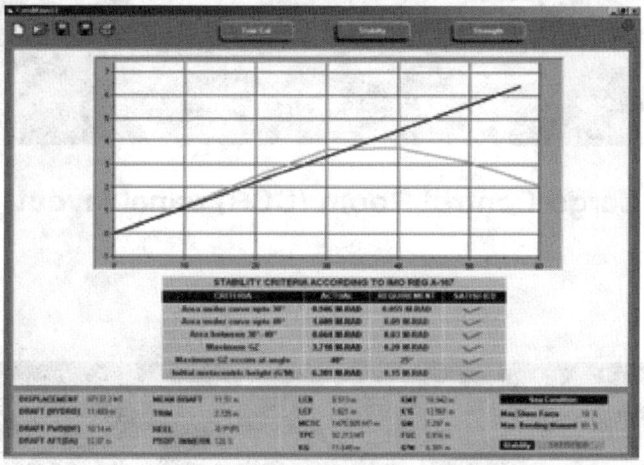

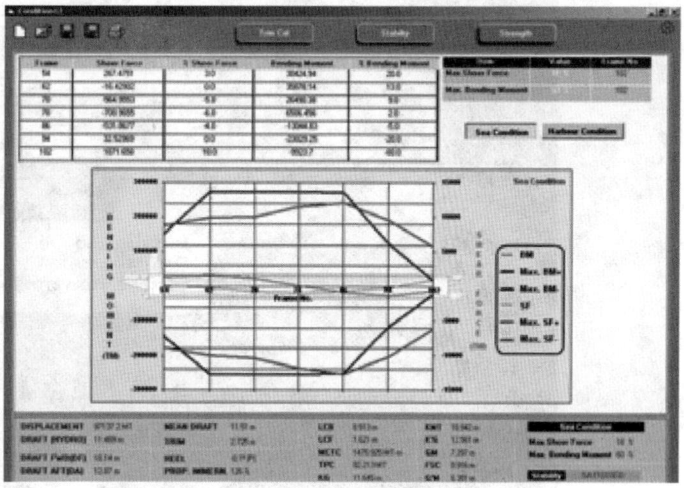

配载仪

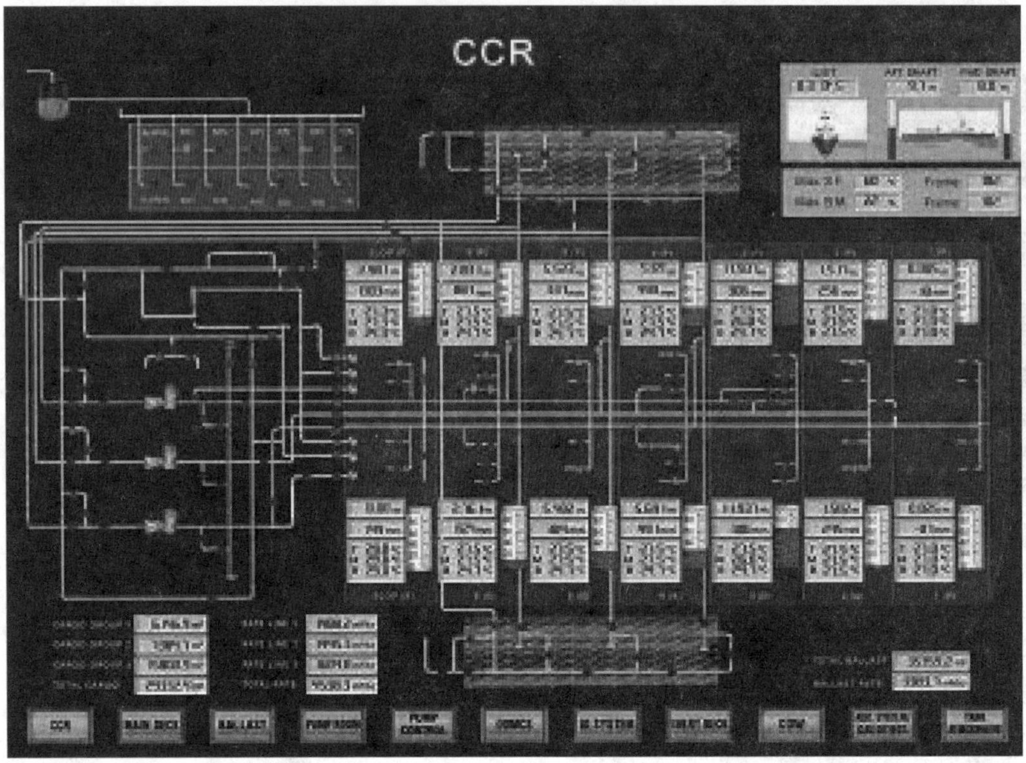

Cargo Control Room (CCR) panel layout

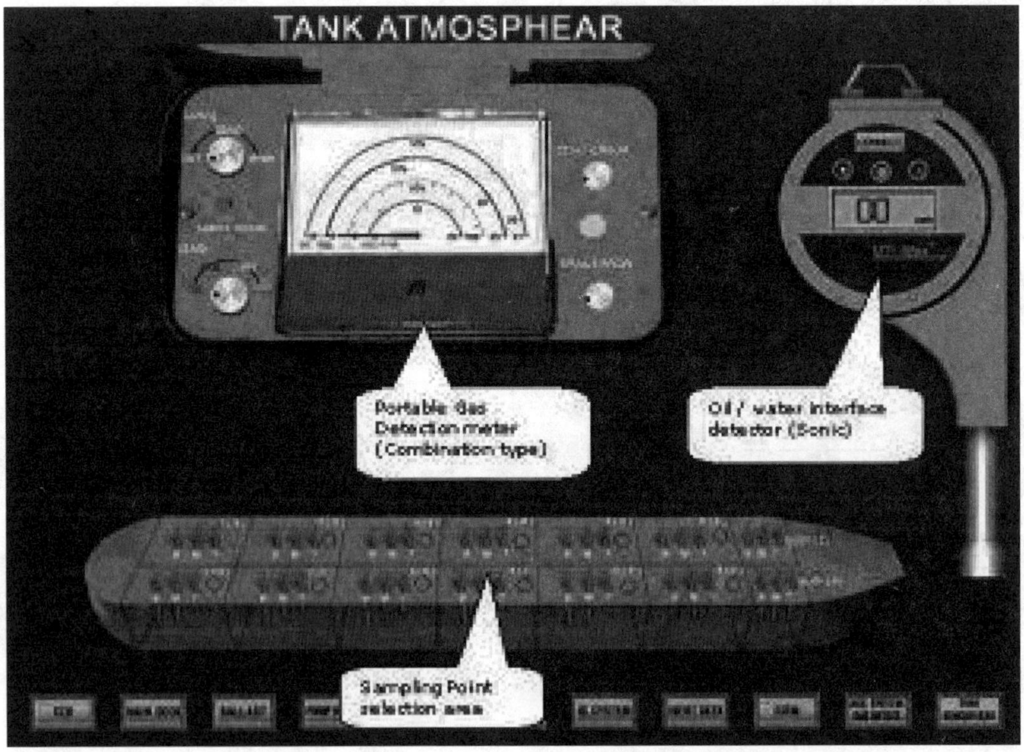

Measurement of tank atmosphere layout

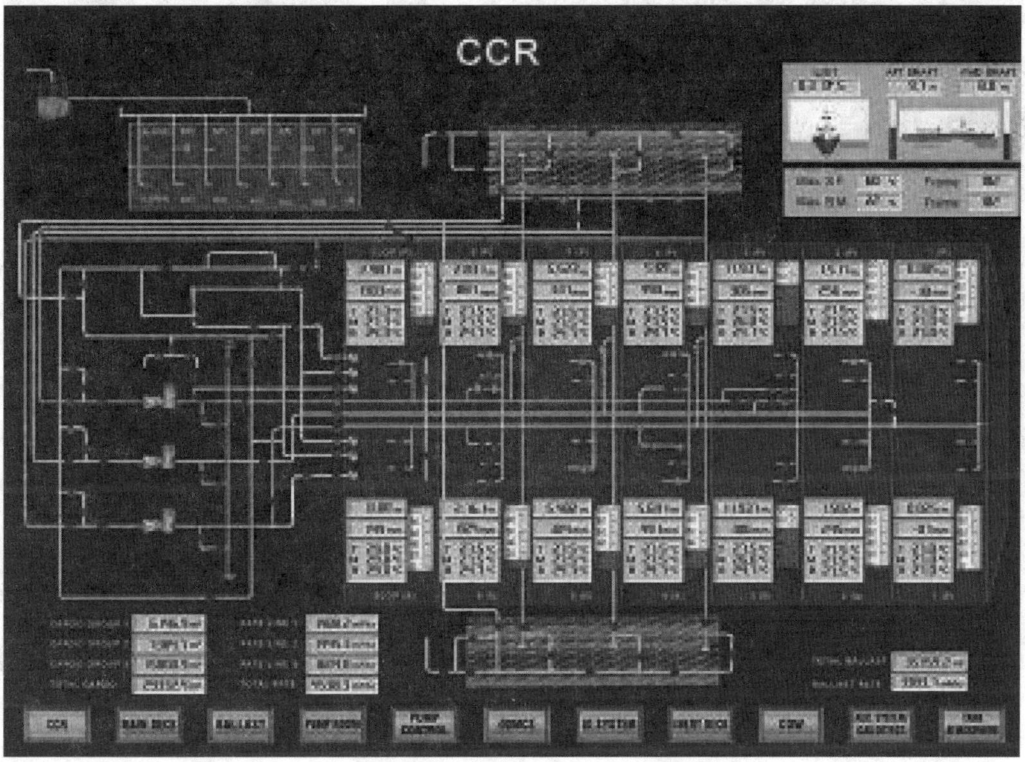

货控室 (CCR) 面板布置图

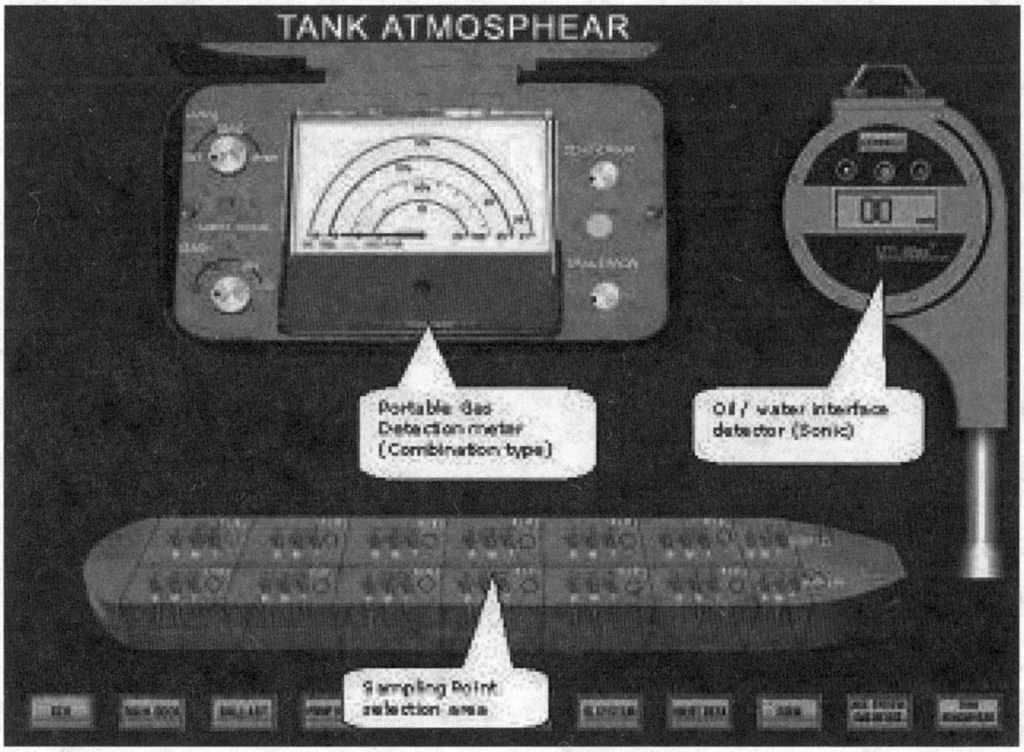

大舱气体测量布置图

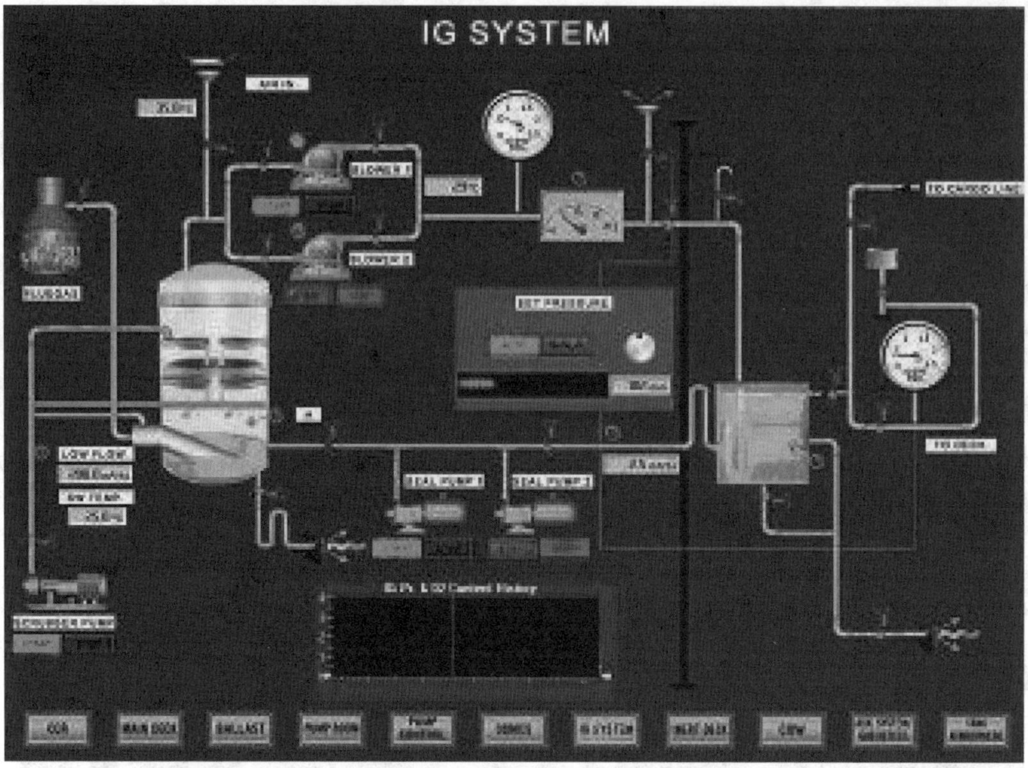

Inert Gas System panel layout

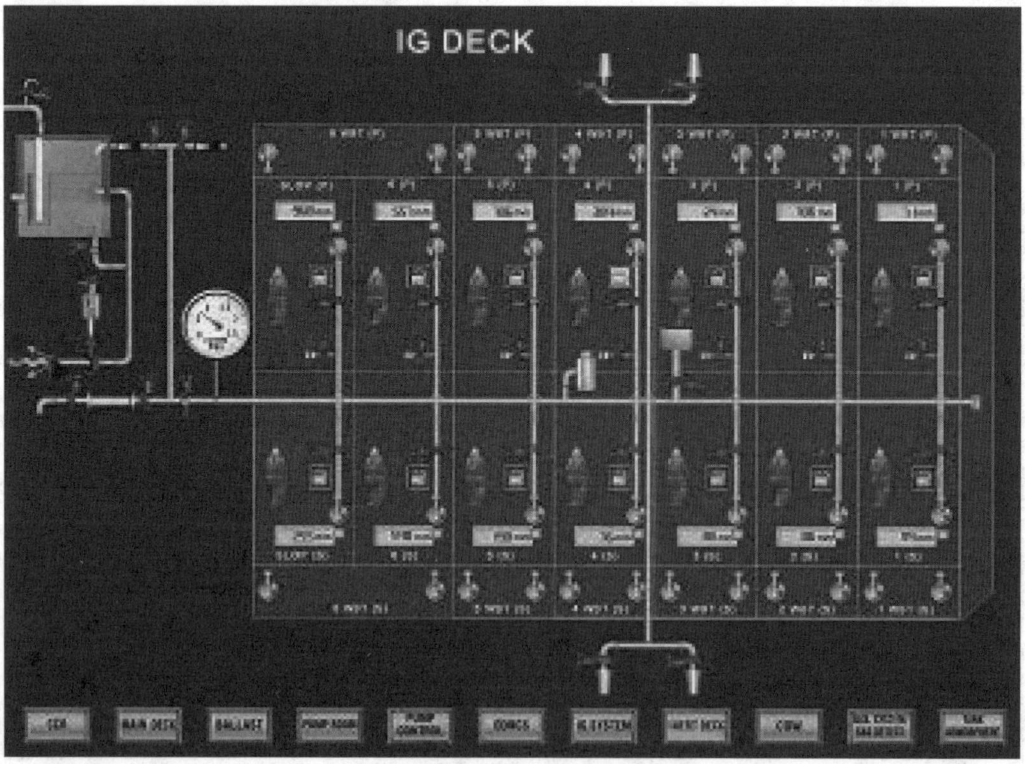

Layout of Inert Gas panel (For deck)

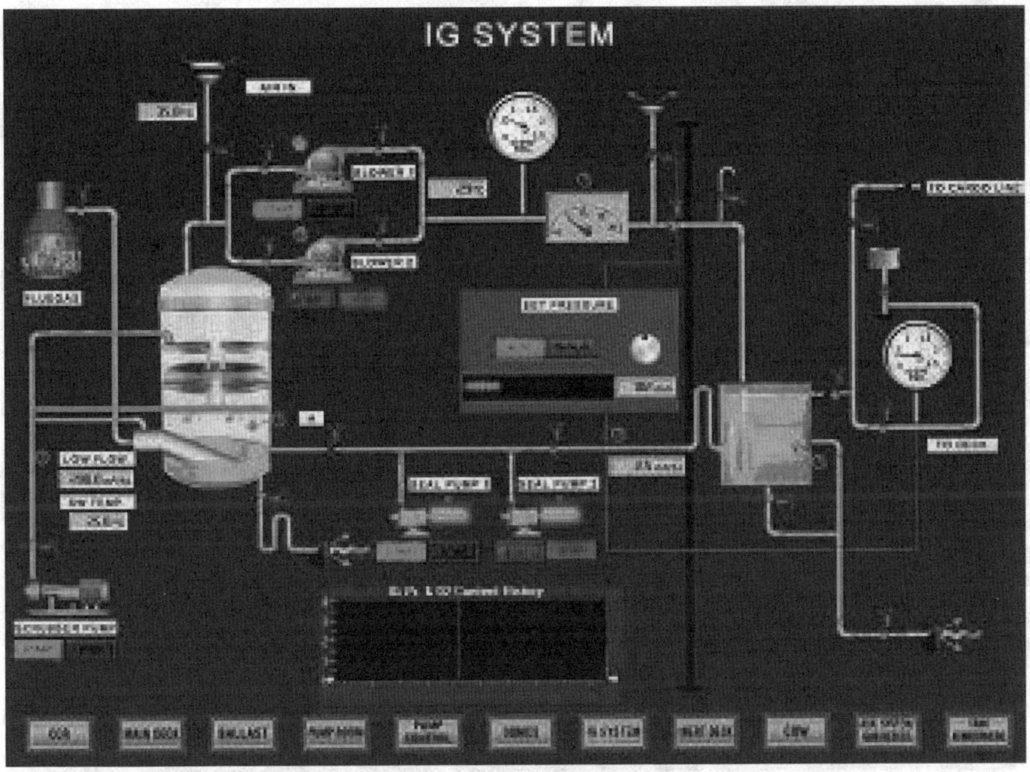

惰性气体面板布置图

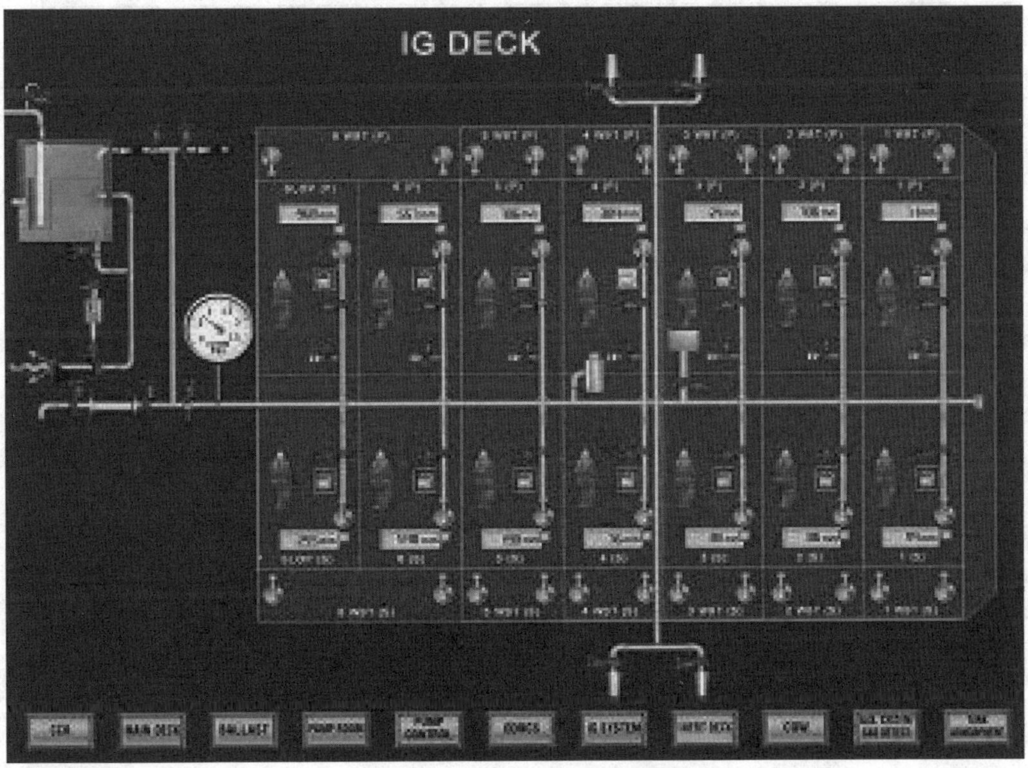

惰性气体面板布置图 (甲板部)

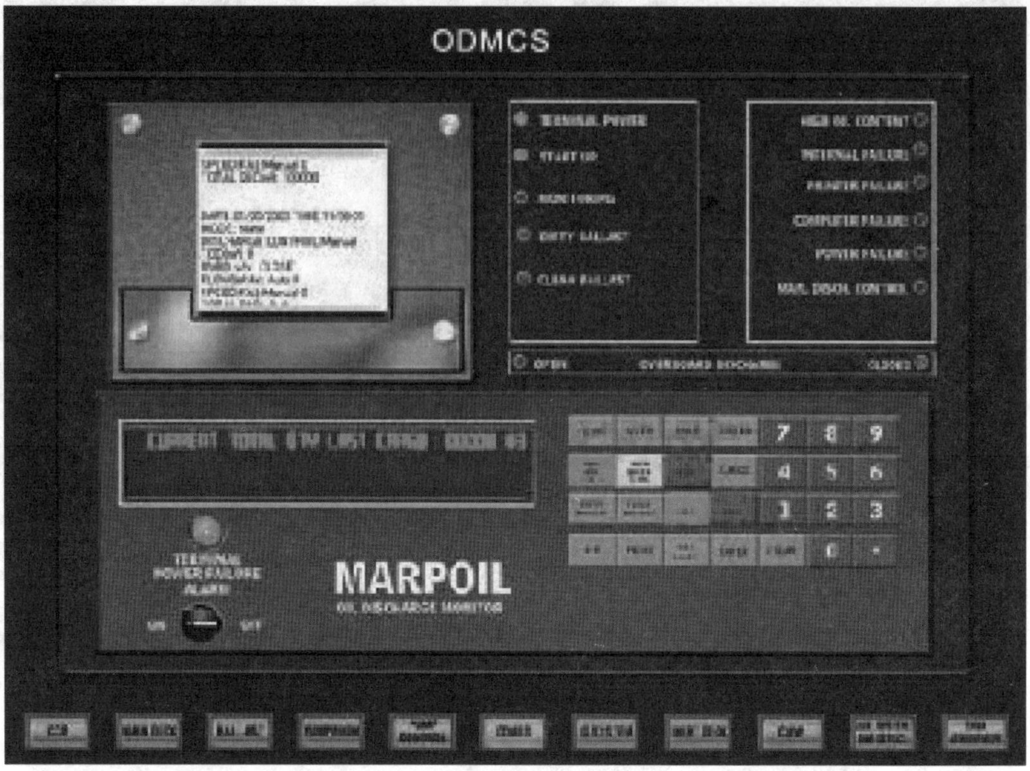

Oil Data Monitoring and Control System (ODMCS) panel layout

Ballast panel control layout

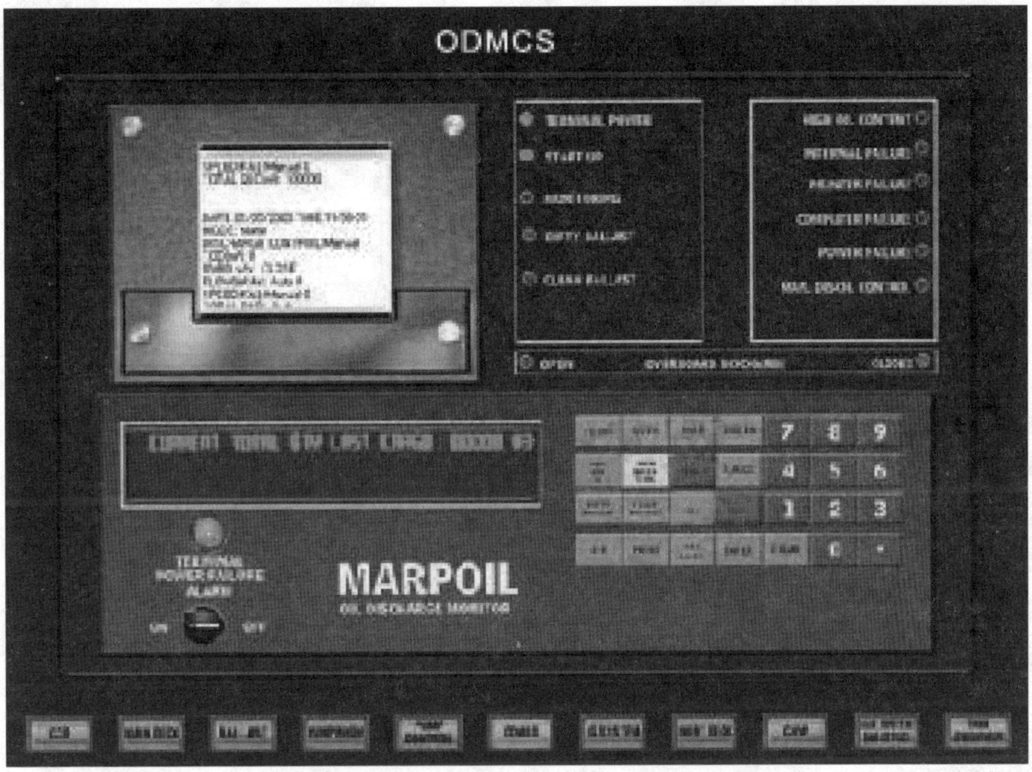

排油监控控制系统 (ODMCS)面板布置图

压载控制面板布置图

Appendix 9:

Definitions

附录9:

定义

Definitions

Anti-static additive

A substance added to petroleum product to raise its electrical conductivity above 100 pico Siemens/meter (pS/m) to prevent accumulation of static electricity.

Approved equipment

Equipment of a design that has been tested and approved by an appropriate authority such as a government department or classification society. The authority should have certified the equipment as safe in a specified hazardous atmosphere.

Cathodic protection

The prevention of corrosion by electrochemical techniques. On tankers it may be applied either externally to the hull or internally to the surface of tanks. At terminals, it is frequently applied to steel pipes and fender panels.

Clingage

Oil remaining on the walls of a pipe or on the internal surfaces of tanks after the bulk of the oil has been removed.

Cold work

Work which cannot create a source of ignition.

Combination carrier

A ship which is designed to carry either petroleum cargoes or dry bulk cargoes.

Combustible (also referred to as "Flammable")

Capable of being ignited and of burning. For the purposes of this guide the terms "combustible" and "flammable" are synonymous.

Combustible gas detector

An instrument for measuring the composition of hydrocarbon gas/air mixtures, usually giving the result as a percentage of the lower flammable limit (LFL).

Dangerous area

An area on a tanker, which for the purposes of the installation and use of electrical equipment is regarded as dangerous.

定义

防静电添加剂

加到石油产品中的一种物质,使其导电率达到100 pS/M以上,以防止静电的积聚。

认可的设备

经过有关权威机构如政府部门或船级社测试和认可的一种设备。此机构需颁发该设备在特定危险环境下安全运行的相关证书。

阴极保护

运用电化学技术防止腐蚀。油船上用于船壳外部或油舱内表面的防腐。在码头,则经常用于铁管及护板的防腐。

油垢

在大部分油被清除后仍残留在管壁和舱内表面的油。

冷工作业

不能引起着火源的作业。

混装船

被设计成即能装载石油也能装载干散货物的船。

可燃(有时也称为“易燃”)

能被点燃并燃烧的。在这里“可燃”和“易燃”是等同的。

可燃气体检测仪

用于测量烃气与空气的混合物的一种仪器,通常显示占可燃下限的百分比这一结果。

危险区域

在油船上用于安装和使用危险电气设备的区域。

Earthing (also referred to as "Grounding")

The electrical connection of equipment to the main body of the earth to ensure that it is at earth potential. On board ship, the connection is made to the main metallic structure of the ship, which is at earth potential because of the conductivity of the sea.

Entry permit

A document issued by a responsible person permitting entry to a space or compartment during a specific time interval.

Explosion-proof ("Flame-proof")

Electrical equipment is defined and certified as explosion-(flame-) proof when it is enclosed in a case, which is capable of withstanding the explosion within it of a hydrocarbon gas/air mixture or other specified flammable gas mixture. It must also prevent the ignition of such a mixture outside the case either by spark or flame from the internal explosion or as a result of the temperature rise of the case following the internal explosion. The equipment must oper te at such an external temperature that a surrounding flammable atmosphere will not be ignited.

Explosive range

See "Flammable range".

Flame screen

A portable or fitted device incorporating one or more corrosion resistant wire woven fabrics of very small mesh which is used for preventing sparks from entering a tank or vent opening or, for a short time, preventing the passage of flame. (Not to be confused with flame arrester.)

Flammable (also referred to as "Combustible")

Capable of being ignited and of burning. For the purposes of this guide the terms 'flammable' and 'combustible' are synonymous.

Flammable range (also referred to as "Explosive range")

The range of hydrocarbon gas concentrations in air between the lower and upper flammable (explosive) limits. Mixtures within this range are capable of being ignited and of burning.

Flashlight (also referred to as "Torch")

A battery operated hand lamp. An approved flashlight is one, which is approved by a competent authority for use in a flammable atmosphere.

接地(也称“触底”)

通过设备和大地的导电连接,以确保设备的接地保护。在船上是利用海水的导电性通过设备与船舶主要金属结构的连接,作为接地保护。

进入许可

在特殊的一段时间间隔内,由负责人签发的允许进入某一空间或舱室的文件。

防爆(“防燃”)

电气设备应经过防爆认证,其在密闭空间内有能力抵挡烃气与空气的混合气体或其他可燃气体混合物引起的爆炸。它必须也能防止因其内部爆炸导致的火花、火焰或温度上升而点燃密闭空间外部的混合气体。该设备需工作在外部温度不能将周围可燃性气体点燃的环境下。

爆炸范围

见“可燃范围”。

防火网

一种便携式或固定式装置,由一根或以上防腐蚀金属线编织而成的小网眼网状物,可用来防止火花进入舱室或通风口,或者在短时间内防止火焰的通过。(不要与阻火器混淆)

易燃(也称为“可燃”)

能被点燃并燃烧的。在这里“易燃”和“可燃”是等同的。

燃烧范围(有时也称为“爆炸范围”)

空气中烃气浓度在可燃上下限之间的范围。在这个范围内的混合气体能被点燃并燃烧。

手电筒(也称“火炬”)

以电池为能量的手提式照明设备。被权威机构认可的,可以用在可燃气环境的电筒。

Flashpoint

The lowest temperature at which a liquid gives off sufficient gas to form a flammable gas mixture near the surface of the liquid. It is measured in a laboratory in standard apparatus using a prescribed procedure.

Foam (also referred to as "Froth")

An aerated solution, which is used for fire prevention and fire-fighting.

Free fall

The unrestricted fall of a liquid into a tank.

Froth

See "Foam".

Gas free

A tank, compartment or container is gas free when sufficient fresh air has been introduced into it to lower the level of any flammable, toxic, or inert gas to that required for a specific purpose, e.g. hot work, entry, etc.

Gas free certificate

A certificate issued by an authorised responsible person confirming that, at the time of testing, a tank, compartment or container was gas free for a specific purpose.

Halon

A halogenated hydrocarbon used in fire-fighting which inhibits flame propagation by virtue of breaking the chain reaction. Please note that the use of Halon is now prohibited under the Montreal Protocol of the Vienna Convention on Depletion of ozone layer, 1985.

Hazardous area

An area on shore which for the purposes of the installation and use of electrical equipment is regarded as dangerous. Such hazardous areas are graded into hazardous zones depending upon the probability of the presence of a flammable gas mixture.

Hot work

Work involving sources of ignition or temperatures sufficiently high to cause the ignition of a flammable gas mixture. This includes any work requiring the use of welding, burning or soldering equipment, blow torches, some power driven tools, portable electrical equipment which is not intrinsically safe or contained within an approved explosion-proof housing, and internal combustion engines.

闪点

使液体在其表面挥发出足够的气体以形成可燃混合气体的最低温度。在实验室内通过标准设备用规定的程序测得。

灭火泡沫(有时也称为“泡沫”)

一种用来防火和救火的暴露在空气中的溶液。

自由下落

进入舱内液体没有限制地下落。

泡沫

见“防火泡沫”。

除气

把充足的空气引入舱内、房间或容器内使可燃气、毒气或惰气降低到为完成某种特殊的目的(如热工作业,进入等)所需要的水平,这个过程叫除气。

除气证书

在测试期间,由被授权责任人所签发的能确认舱、房间或容器因为某种特殊目已经除气完毕的证书。

卤化烃

通过破坏燃烧反应链来灭火的卤素碳氢化合物。请注意根据1985年维也纳破坏臭氧层公约中的蒙特利尔议定书,目前已经禁止使用卤化烃。

危险区域

认为安装和使用电器设备的岸基区域具有危险性。根据出现可燃气体混合物的可能性,将这些危险区域分为多个危险等级。

热工作业

涉及火源或者可引起可燃气体燃烧的高温的工作。其中包括需要使用焊接、燃烧、钎焊设备,使用喷灯、动力驱动工具和便携式电气设备等并不是绝对安全的工作,或者在认可的防爆壳体内或内燃机内的工作。

Hydrocarbon gas

A gas composed entirely of hydrocarbons.

Inert condition

A condition in which the oxygen content throughout the atmosphere of a tank has been reduced to 8% or less by volume by the addition of inert gas.

Inert Gas Plant

All equipment fitted to supply, cool, clean, pressurise, monitor and control the delivery of inert gas to the cargo tank systems.

Inert Gas System (IGS)

An inert gas plant and inert gas distribution system together with means for preventing backflow or cargo gases to the machinery spaces, fixed and portable measuring instruments and control devices.

Inerting

The introduction of inert gas into a tank with the object of attaining the inert condition.

Insulating flange

A flanged joint incorporating an insulating gasket, sleeves and washers to prevent electrical continuity between pipelines, hose strings or loading arms.

Interface detector

An electrical instrument for detecting the boundary between oil and water.

Intrinsically safe

An electrical circuit or part of a circuit is intrinsically safe if any spark or thermal effect produced normally (i.e., by breaking or closing the circuit) or accidentally (e. g. by short circuit or earth fault) is incapable, under prescribed test conditions, of igniting a prescribed gas mixture.

Loading overall

The loading of cargo or ballast 'over the top' through an open ended pipe or by means of an open ended hose entering a tank through a hatch or other deck opening, resulting in the free fall of liquid.

Naked lights

Open flames or fires, lighted cigarettes, cigars, pipes, or similar smoking materials, any other unconfined sources of ignition, electrical and other equipment liable to cause sparking while in use, and unprotected light bulbs.

烃气

一种完全由烃组成的气体。

惰化状态

通过向舱内加入惰气,使舱内的气体中氧气的含量下降到体积比为8%或以下的状态。

惰气设备

包括提供惰气、冷却清洁惰气、给惰气加压和对舱内输送惰气进行监控的全部设备。

惰气系统(IGS)

这个系统包括惰气设备、防止烃气倒流和烃气进入机舱的惰气分配系统、固定的和便携式测量仪以及控制设备。

惰化

通过将惰气输入舱内来达到惰气状态的过程。

绝缘法兰

为防止管线、软管绳索或装卸臂之间的电气连接而在中间添加绝缘垫片、衬套和填料的一种法兰。

界面检测器

用来检测油水界面的电气仪器。

绝对安全

绝对安全指的是电路或部分电路在规定的测试状态下正常 (开关电路)或偶然(短路或接地不良) 情况下产生的火花或高温不能点燃规定气体混合物的状态。

装货溢流

通过经舱盖或甲板上的开口而伸入的末端开口管路或末端开口软管对货物与压载水进行装载造成的"过顶"现象,导致液体自由下落的情况。

明火

无遮挡的火焰或者点燃的香烟、雪茄、烟斗或者类似的冒烟的材料、其他不确定的火源、使用时能产生火花的电气和其他设备以及没有保护的灯泡。

OBO, OIL/ORE

See "Combination Carrier".

Oxygen analyser/meter

An instrument for determining the percentage of oxygen in a sample of the atmosphere drawn from a tank, pipe or compartment.

Petroleum

Crude oil and liquid hydrocarbon products derived from it.

Petroleum gas

A gas evolved from petroleum. The main constituents of petroleum gases are hydrocarbons, but they may also contain other substances, such as hydrogen sulphide or lead alkyls, as minor constituents.

Pour point

The lowest temperature at which a petroleum oil will remain fluid.

Pressure surge

A sudden increase in the pressure of the liquid in a pipeline brought about by an abrupt change in flow velocity.

Pressure/vacuum relief valve (P/V valve)

A device which provides for the flow of the small volumes of vapour, air or inert gas mixtures caused by thermal variations in a cargo tank.

Purging

The introduction of inert gas into a tank already in the inert condition with the object of:

(1) Further reducing the existing oxygen content; and/or

(2) Reducing the existing hydrocarbon gas content to a level below which combustion cannot be supported if air is subsequently introduced into the tank.

Reid vapour pressure (RVP)

The vapour pressure of a liquid determined in a standard manner in the Reid apparatus at a temperature of 37.8 ℃ and with a ratio of gas to liquid volume of 4:1. Used for comparison purposes only. See "True Vapour Pressure".

油/散货/矿石,油/矿石

见“混装船”。

氧气分析仪

为了检测从舱内、管路或房间内提取的气体样品中氧气百分含量的仪器。

石油

从中提取原油以及液体碳化氢产品。

石油气

从石油中产生的气体。石油气的主要成分是烃气,但可能还包含少量的其他物质如硫化氢或含铅烃基。

倾点

石油保持液态的最低温度。

压力冲击

由于管路内液体流速的突然变化引起的压力突然升高。

压力/真空释放阀

一种因舱内温度变化引起的能使烃气、空气或惰气少量流入和流出舱内的装置。

驱气

为了下列目的把惰气引入已经处在惰化状态下的舱内:

(1) 进一步减少氧气含量。

(2) 减少烃气含量,达到即使在后来空气继续进入舱内也不能支持燃烧的状态。

相对蒸气压力RVP

用标准方法得到的,在液体处于37.8 ℃时气体和液体的体积比为4∶1的情况下蒸气压力的相对值。仅用于对比。见“绝对蒸气压力”。

Responsible officer (or person)

A person appointed by the employer or the master of the ship and empowered to take all decisions relating to a specific task, having the necessary knowledge and experience for that purposes.

Resuscitator (resuscitation equipment)

Equipment to assist or restore the breathing of personnel overcome by gas or lack of oxygen.

Static accumulator oil

Oil with an electrical conductivity less than 50 pico Siemens/meter (pS/m), so that it is capable of retaining a significant electrostatic charge.

Stripping

The final operation in pumping bulk liquid from a tank or pipeline.

Tanker

A ship designed to carry liquid petroleum cargo in bulk, including a combination carrier when being used for this purpose.

Tank cleaning

The process of removing hydrocarbon vapours, liquid or residue. Usually carried out so that tanks can be entered for inspection or hot work.

Threshold limit value (TLV)

The time-weighted average concentration of a substance to which workers may be repeatedly exposed, for a normal 8-hour workday or 40-hour workweek, day after day, without adverse effect.

Topping up

The introduction of inert gas into a tank, which is already in the inert condition with the object of raising the tank pressure to prevent any ingress of air.

Torch

See "Flashlight".

Toxic

Poisonous to human life.

负责的船员(人员)

由船东或船长指定的,授予可以做出与某种特殊任务相关的各种决定的,并且必须具有相关知识和经验的人。

呼吸器(生命复苏设备)

克服因为烃气或缺少氧气能帮助或恢复人员呼吸的设备。

静电积聚性油

一种导电率在50 pS/m以下能够积聚大量静电电荷的油。

扫舱

从舱内和管路内泵卸散装液体的最后的操作过程。

油船

油船是指设计运载散装液体石油的船,包括以装载石油为目的的混装船。

洗舱

除掉烃气、液体或油渣的过程。通常是为了进入内部检查或热工作业而进行的。

阈限值(TLV)

工人重复接触下的一定物质积聚平均时间一负重值, 正常每天工作8小时或每周40小时,日复一日,没有不利影响的情况。

完舱

把惰气引入已经处在惰化状态的舱内提高舱内的压力防止空气的吸入。

手电筒

见“手电筒”。

有毒的

对人身生命有毒害作用。

True vapour pressure (TVP)

The true vapour pressure of a liquid is the absolute pressure exerted by the gas produced by evaporation from a liquid when gas and liquid are in equilibrium at the prevailing temperature and the gas/liquid ratio is effectively zero.

Ullage

The depth of the space above the liquid in a tank.

Upper flammable limit (UFL)

The concentration of a hydrocarbon gas in air above which there is insufficient oxygen to support and propagate combustion. Sometimes referred to as upper explosive limit (UEL).

Vapour

A gas below its critical temperature.

Vapour lock system

Equipment fitted to a tank to enable the measuring and sampling of cargoes without release of vapour/inert gas pressure.

Volatile petroleum

Petroleum, having a flashpoint below 60℃ as determined by the closed cup method of testing.

Water fog

A suspension in the atmosphere of very fine droplets of water usually delivered at a high pressure through a fog nozzle for use in fire-fighting.

Water spray

A suspension in the atmosphere of water divided into coarse drops by delivery through a special nozzle for use in fire-fighting.

Work permit

A document issued by a responsible person permitting specific work to be done during a specific period in a defined area.

绝对蒸气压力(TVP)

绝对蒸气压力是指在某一温度下气体和液体达到平衡状态并且气/液比率达到零有效时,由液体产生的气体形成的绝对压力。

空挡

舱内液面上部空间的深度。

可燃上限(UFL)

在空气中烃气的浓度再高就没有足够氧气支持燃烧和蔓延的最大浓度。有时可以作为爆炸上限。

蒸气

在临界温度以下的气体。

蒸气锁定系统

安装在舱上的能在不释放蒸气/惰气的情况下对货物进行测量和取样的设备。

挥发性石油

由闭口杯法测试的闪点在低于60 ℃以下的石油。

水雾

水在高压下通过消防用雾化喷嘴产生的悬浮在空气中很小的小水滴。

喷雾

水通过消防用特殊喷嘴形成的悬浮在空气中较大的水滴。

工作许可

由相关责任人签发的在特定时间、指定区域内进行特殊工作的证明。

Attachment:

Guidance on the Implementation of IMO Model Courses

附件:

IMO示范课程实施指南

Contents

目 录

Part 1 Preparation

1 Introduction

1.1 The success of any enterprise depends heavily on sound and effective preparations.

1.2 Although the IMO model course "package" has been made as comprehensive as possible, it is nonetheless vital that sufficient time and resources are devoted to preparation. Preparation not only involves matters concerning administration or organization, but also includes the preparation of any course notes, drawings, sketches, overhead transparencies, etc., which may be necessary.

2 General considerations

2.1 The course "package" should be studied carefully; in particular, the course syllabus and associated material must be attentively and thoroughly studied. This is vital if a clear understanding is to be obtained of what is required, in terms of resources necessary to successfully implement the course.

2.2 A "checklist", such as that set out in annex A1, should be used throughout all stages of preparation to ensure that all necessary actions and activities are being carried out in good time and in an effective manner. The checklist allows the status of the preparation procedures to be monitored, and helps in identifying the remedial actions necessary to meet deadlines. It will be necessary to hold meetings of all those concerned in presenting the course from time to time in order to assess the status of the preparation and "trouble-shoot" any difficulties.

2.3 The course syllabus should be discussed with the teaching staff who are to present the course, and their views received on the particular parts they are to present. A study of the syllabus will determine whether the incoming trainees need preparatory work to meet the entry standard. The detailed teaching syllabus is constructed in "training outcome" format. Each specific outcome states precisely what the trainee must do to show that the outcome has been achieved. An example of a model course syllabus is given in annex A2. Part 3 deals with curriculum development and explains how a syllabus is constructed and used.

2.4 The teaching staff who are to present the course should construct notes or lesson plans to achieve these outcomes. A sample lesson plan for one of the areas of the sample syllabus is provided in annex A3.

2.5 It is important that the staff who present the course convey, to the person in charge of the course, their assessment of the course as it progresses.

3 Specific considerations

3.1 Scope of course

In reviewing the scope of the course, the instructor should determine whether it needs any adjustment in order to meet additional local or national requirements (see Part 3).

第1部分　备课

1　介绍

1.1　任何事业的成功很大程度上都依赖于周全和有效的准备。

1.2　尽管IMO的示范课程的制作已经尽可能全面,但用充分的时间和资料进行备课还是十分重要的。备课不仅涉及管理或组织方面的事务,还包括准备任何可能需要的课程注释、图纸、草图和投影胶片等。

2　总体设想

2.1　应仔细研究整套课程,特别是对教学大纲和相关资料必须专注和透彻地研究。从成功实施本课程所需要的资源这一角度清楚地理解所需要的内容,是十分重要的。

2.2　在备课的所有阶段应当使用如附录A1中所示的那种"检查表",以确保尽早、有效地进行所有必要的行动和活动。检查表能使备课程序的状态受到监控,并且有助于确认满足期限所必需的纠正措施。为评估备课的状况并"诊断"任何困难,有必要经常召集与授课有关的所有人员开会。

2.3　应当与要讲授该课程的教学人员讨论该教学大纲,而且应当接纳他们针对要讲授的特定部分的观点。对大纲进行的研究将决定入学的学员是否需要准备工作以便满足入学标准。教学大纲细则是以"培训效果"的格式制定的。每一个特定的效果准确地阐述了学员必须做什么来表明已经达到了该效果。在附录A2中给出了示范课程大纲的示例。第3部分涉及课程的制定并解释了如何编制和使用大纲。

2.4　将要讲授本课程的教学人员应当编写讲课注释或教案来达到这些效果。在附录A3中提供了大纲示例中某个科目的教案示例。

2.5　讲授本课程的人员随课程的进展向该课程负责人转达他们对课程的评估,这是很重要的。

3　具体设想

3.1　**课程范围**

在审查课程范围时,教员应当决定是否需要做出任何调整以便满足额外的地方或本国的要求(见第3部分)。

3.2 Course objective

3.2.1 The course objective, as stated in the course material, should be very carefully considered so that its meaning is fully understood. Does the course objective require expansion to encompass any additional task that national or local requirements will impose upon those who successfully complete the course? Conversely, are there elements included which are not validated by national industry requirements?

3.2.2 It is important that any subsequent assessment made of the course should include a review of the course objectives.

3.3 Entry standards

3.3.1 If the entry standard will not be met by your intended trainee intake, those entering the course should first be required to complete an upgrading course to raise them to the stated entry level. Alternatively, those parts of the course affected could be augmented by inserting course material which will cover the knowledge required.

3.3.2 If the entry standard will be exceeded by your planned trainee intake, you may wish to abridge or omit those parts of the course the teaching of which would be unnecessary, or which could be dealt with as revision.

3.3.3 Study the course material with the above questions in mind and with a view to assessing whether or not it will be necessary for the trainees to carry out preparatory work prior to joining the course. Preparatory material for the trainees can range from refresher notes, selected topics from textbooks and reading of selected technical papers, through to formal courses of instruction. It may be necessary to use a combination of preparatory work and the model course material in modified form. It must be emphasized that where the model course material involves an international requirement, such as a regulation of the International Convention on Standards of Training, Certification and Watchkeeping (STCW) 1978, as amended, the standard must not be relaxed; in many instances, the intention of the Convention is to require review, revision or increased depth of knowledge by candidates undergoing training for higher certificates.

3.4 Course certificate, diploma or document

Where a certificate, diploma or document is to be issued to trainees who successfully complete the course, ensure that this is available and properly worded and that the industry and all authorities concerned are fully aware of its purpose and intent.

3.5 Course intake limitations

3.5.1 The course designers have recommended limitations regarding the numbers of trainees who may participate in the course. As far as possible, these limitations should not be exceeded; otherwise, the quality of the course will be diluted.

3.5.2 It may be necessary to make arrangements for accommodating the trainees and providing facilities for food and transportation. These aspects must be considered at an early stage of the preparations.

3.2 课程目标

3.2.1 课程材料中所阐述的课程目标应当非常仔细地予以斟酌,以便完全理解其含义。为涵盖本国或地方性规定对成功完成本课程的学员要求的其他任务,课程目标是否需要做一步扩充?反过来,未经本国行业要求确认的要素是否包括在内?

3.2.2 对课程所做的任何后续评估应当包括对课程目标的审查,这一点很重要。

3.3 入学标准

3.3.1 如果计划入学的学员不能满足入学标准,则应当首先要求入学的学员完成一个提高班,使其提升到规定的入学水平。或者,通过插入会覆盖所需知识的课程材料使受影响的课程部分能够得到扩充。

3.3.2 如果计划入学的学员超出入学标准,你不妨删节或省略不需要教授的或可以用修订的方式来处理的课程部分。

3.3.3 带着上述问题来研究课程材料,并且着眼于评估在参加课程之前学员是否需要进行准备工作。学员准备材料的范围可以是复习笔记、从教科书中选择的题目、技术论文选读,直至讲授的正式课程。将准备工作和修改形式的示范课程材料结合起来使用可能是必要的。必须强调,在示范课程涉及国际要求,例如经修正的《1978年海员培训、发证和值班标准国际公约》(STCW)的条款时,不得降低标准;在很多情况下,该公约的意图就是要求为获得高一级证书而接受培训的申请人对其知识进行复习、更新或深化。

3.4 课程证书、文凭或文件

如果要给顺利完成本课程的学员发放证书、文凭或文件,则要保证能够签发这类证明并且措辞恰当以及本行业和所有相关机关完全知晓其目的和意图。

3.5 课程人数限制

3.5.1 本课程设计人已对可能参加课程的学员人数的限制提出了建议。尽可能地不要突破该限制,否则课程的质量就会降低。

3.5.2 可能需要就学员的住宿、就餐和交通设施做出安排。这些方面必须在早期准备时就予以考虑。

3.6 Staff requirements

3.6.1 It is important that an experienced person, preferably someone with experience in course and curriculum development, is given the responsibility of implementing the course.

3.6.2 Such a person is often termed a "course co-ordinator" or "course director". Other staff, such as lecturers, instructors, laboratory technicians, workshop instructors, etc., will be needed to implement the course effectively. Staff involved in presenting the course will need to be properly briefed about the course work they will be dealing with, and a system must be set up for checking the material they may be required to prepare. To do this, it will be essential to make a thorough study of the syllabus and apportion the parts of the course work according to the abilities of the staff called upon to present the work.

3.6.3 The person responsible for implementing the course should consider monitoring the quality of teaching in such areas as variety and form of approach, relationship with trainees, and communicative and interactive skills; where necessary, this person should also provide appropriate counselling and support.

3.7 Teaching facilities and equipment

Rooms and other services

3.7.1 It is important to make reservations as soon as is practicable for the use of lecture rooms, laboratories, workshops and other spaces.

Equipment

3.7.2 Arrangements must be made at an early stage for the use of equipment needed in the spaces mentioned in 3.7.1 to support and carry through the work of the course. For example:

.1 blackboards and writing materials;
.2 apparatus in laboratories for any associated demonstrations and experiments;
.3 machinery and related equipment in workshops;
.4 equipment and materials in other spaces (e.g. for demonstrating fire fighting, personal survival, etc.).

3.8 Teaching aids

Any training aids specified as being essential to the course should be constructed, or checked for availability and working order.

3.9 Audio-visual aids

Audio-visual aids (AVA) may be recommended in order to reinforce the learning process in some parts of the course. Such recommendations will be identified in Part A of the model course. The following points should be borne in mind:

3.9.1 Overhead projectors

Check through any illustrations provided in the course for producing overhead projector (OHP) transparencies, and arrange them in order of presentation. To produce transparencies, a supply of transparency sheets is required; the illustrations can be transferred to these via photocopying. Alternatively, transparencies can be produced by writing or drawing on the sheet. Coloured pens are useful for emphasizing salient points. Ensure that spare projector lamps (bulbs) are available.

3.6 教员要求

3.6.1 由富有经验的人,最好是有编制教程及整套课程经验的人,负责实施本课程,这一点很重要。

3.6.2 这样一个人经常被称作“课程协调人”或“课程指导人”。为有效实施本课程,还需要其他的人员,例如讲师、教员、实验室技师、车间教员等。需要向从事授课的人员适当地简要说明其将要处理的课程工作,而且必须建立制度来核查可能要求他们准备的材料。为做到这一点,关键是要彻底地研究大纲并且根据被召来授课的人员的能力分配课程工作的内容。

3.6.3 负责实施课程的人应当考虑在下列方面监控教学的质量,如实施的种类和形式、与学员的关系以及交流和互动的技巧;必要时,还应当提供适当的咨询和支持。

3.7 教学设施和设备

场所及其他服务

3.7.1 对使用的教室、实验室、车间和其他场所尽量实际可行地提早预定,这是很重要的。

设备

3.7.2 对在3.7.1中提到的场所中所需设备的使用,必须及早做出安排以便支持和进行课程的工作。例如:

.1 黑板和书写材料;

.2 用于任何相关演示和试验的实验室器材;

.3 车间内的机械和相关设备;

.4 其他场所中的设备和材料(例如用于演示灭火、个人求生等)。

3.8 教具

应当制作被列为对课程至关重要的任何培训教具或检查其可用性以及工作状况。

3.9 视听教具

为加强课程某些部分的学习过程,建议使用视听教具。这类建议将在示范课程第1部分中予以确认。应当牢记以下要点:

3.9.1 投影仪

查看本课程中提供的用于制作投影片的任何插图,并按授课的顺序排好。为制作投影片,需要提供透明胶片。插图可以通过复印转到透明胶片上。或者,可以通过在透明胶片上书写或画图的方式制作投影片。强调重点时,彩色的笔十分有用。应确保有备用的投影仪灯泡。

3.9.2 Slide projectors

If you order slides indicated in the course framework, check through them and arrange them in order of presentation. Slides are usually produced from photographic negatives. If further slides are considered necessary and cannot be produced locally, OHP transparencies should be resorted to.

3.9.3 Cine projector

If films are to be used, check their compatibility with the projector (i.e. 16 mm, 35 mm, sound, etc.). The films must be test-run to ensure there are no breakages.

3.9.4 Video equipment

It is essential to check the type of video tape to be used. The two types commonly used are VHS and Betamax. Although special machines exist which can play either format, the majority of machines play only one or the other type. Note that VHS and Betamax are not compatible; the correct machine type is required to match the tape. Check also that the TV raster format used in the tapes (i.e. number of lines, frames/second, scanning order, etc.) is appropriate to the TV equipment available. (Specialist advice may have to be sought on this aspect.) All video tapes should be test-run prior to their use on the course.

3.9.5 Computer equipment

If computer-based aids are used, check their compatibility with the projector and the available software.

3.9.6 General note

The electricity supply must be checked for voltage and whether it is AC or DC, and every precaution must be taken to ensure that the equipment operates properly and safely. It is important to use a proper screen which is correctly positioned; it may be necessary to exclude daylight in some cases. A check must be made to ensure that appropriate screens or blinds are available. All material to be presented should be test-run to eliminate any possible troubles, arranged in the correct sequence in which it is to be shown, and properly identified and cross-referenced in the course timetable and lesson plans.

3.10 IMO references

The content of the course, and therefore its standard, reflects the requirements of all the relevant IMO international conventions and the provisions of other instruments as indicated in the model course. The relevant publications can be obtained from the Publication Service of IMO, and should be available, at least to those involved in presenting the course, if the indicated extracts are not included in a compendium supplied with the course.

3.11 Textbooks

The detailed syllabus may refer to a particular textbook or textbooks. It is essential that these books are available to each student taking the course. If supplies of textbooks are limited, a copy should be loaned to each student, who will return it at the end of the course. Again, some courses are provided with a compendium which includes all or part of the training material required to support the course.

3.9.2　幻灯机

如果你要排列课程框架中注明的幻灯片,则需对其核对并按授课的顺序排好。幻灯片通常用照片的负片制作。如果需要更多的幻灯片但当地不能制作,则应当使用投影仪。

3.9.3　电影放映机

如果要使用电影片,则检查其与放映机(即16 mm、35 mm、声响等)的兼容性。必须对电影片进行试播以保证没有断点。

3.9.4　视频设备

检查所用录像带的类别是十分重要的。通常使用的两种是VHS和Betamax。尽管存在能够播放任一种磁带的特殊机器,但大多数机器只能放映其中一种。注意,VHS和Betamax不兼容;要求用正确的机型来与磁带相配。另外,检查磁带中使用的电视光栅(即线数、帧/秒、扫描顺序等)是否适合所用的电视设备(这方面可能需要寻求专家的意见)。在课程使用之前应当对所有录像带进行试播。

3.9.5　计算机设备

如果使用基于计算机的教具,则检查其与放映机和可用软件的兼容性。

3.9.6　总体提示

必须检查电源的电压以及是交流电还是直流电,而且必须采取每一项预防措施以保证设备稳定、安全地运行。使用正确设置的适当幕布是重要的;在有些情况下,可能需要遮挡日光。必须进行检查以保证有适当的纱窗或百叶窗。所有要讲授的材料应当予以试用以便清除任何可能的故障并要按播放的正确顺序放好,并且在课程时间表和教案中进行适当的确认和对照。

3.10　IMO参考书目

本课程的内容及其标准反映了所有相关IMO国际公约的要求以及示范课程中注明的其他文件的规定。相关出版物可以从IMO出版服务处获得,如果其注明的摘录没有包含在随课程提供的提纲内,则至少应当向参与讲授本课程的人员提供这些出版物。

3.11　教科书

大纲细则可以引用一本或多本教科书。参加课程的每一名学生能够得到这些教科书是十分重要的。如果教科书的供给有限,则可以将这些教材的复印本借给学生用,在课程结束时再归还。一些课程还配有一个摘要,该摘要包括所有或部分支持本课程所需要的培训材料。

3.12 Bibliography

Any useful supplementary source material is identified by the course designers and listed in the model course. This list should be supplied to the participants so that they are aware where additional information can be obtained, and at least two copies of each book or publication should be available for reference in the training institute library.

3.13 Timetable

If a timetable is provided in a model course, it is for guidance only. It may only take one or two presentations of the course to achieve an optimal timetable. However, even then it must be borne in mind that any timetable is subject to variation, depending on the general needs of the trainees in any one class and the availability of instructors and equipment.

3.12 参考文献

任何有用的补充性原始材料由课程设计人确认并列入示范课程中。应当向学员提供该目录,以便使其知道可以获得额外资料的来源,而且在培训机构图书馆中,每一本书或出版物应当有至少两本供参阅。

3.13 时间表

示范课程中提供的时间表,仅供指导。可能只需一到两次授课就能确定一个最优化的时间表。但是,即使在此时也必须牢记,依据任一班级中学员的一般要求以及教员和设备的可使用情况,任何时间表都有待于变更。

Part 2 Notes on Teaching Technique

1 Preparation

1.1 Identify the section of the syllabus which is to be dealt with.

1.2 Read and study thoroughly all the syllabus elements.

1.3 Obtain the necessary textbooks or reference papers which cover the training area to be presented.

1.4 Identify the equipment which will be needed, together with support staff necessary for its operation.

1.5 It is essential to use a "lesson plan", which can provide a simplified format for co-ordinating lecture notes and supporting activities. The lesson plan breaks the material down into identifiable steps, making use of brief statements, possibly with keywords added, and indicating suitable allocations of time for each step. The use of audio-visual material should be indexed at the correct point in the lecture with an appropriate allowance of time. The audio-visual material should be test-run prior to its being used in the lecture. An example of a lesson plan is shown in annex A3.

1.6 The syllabus is structured in training outcome format and it is thereby relatively straightforward to assess each trainee's grasp of the subject matter presented during the lecture. Such assessment may take the form of further discussion, oral questions, written tests or selection-type tests, such as multiple-choice questions, based on the objectives used in the syllabus. Selection-type tests and short-answer tests can provide an objective assessment independent of any bias on the part of the assessor. For certification purposes, assessors should be appropriately qualified for the particular type of training or assessment.

REMEMBER–POOR PREPARATION IS A SURE WAY TO LOSE THE INTEREST OF A GROUP

1.7 Check the rooms to be used before the lecture is delivered. Make sure that all the equipment and apparatus are ready for use and that any support staff are also prepared and ready. In particular, check that all blackboards are clean and that a supply of writing and cleaning materials is readily available.

2 Delivery

2.1 Always face the people you are talking to; never talk with your back to the group.

2.2 Talk clearly and sufficiently loudly to reach everyone.

2.3 Maintain eye contact with the whole group as a way of securing their interest and maintaining it (i.e. do not look continuously at one particular person, nor at a point in space).

第2部分　教学技巧注释

1　备课

1.1　确认要涉及的那部分大纲。

1.2　充分阅读和研究所有大纲要素。

1.3　获得与要讲授的培训科目相关的必要教科书和参考论文。

1.4　确认所需的设备及其运转所需的辅助人员。

1.5　使用"教案"十分关键,教案能够为协调讲稿和辅助活动提供简化的格式。教案将材料细分成可识别的步骤,使用可能加入关键词的简要陈述并注明为每一步骤分配的适当时间。应当在讲稿中的正确节点做好使用视听材料的索引并留出适当的时间。视听材料应当在授课使用前试运行。在附录A3中给出了一个教案示例。

1.6　大纲由培训效果的格式构成,因此它相对直接地评估了每名学员对授课期间所讲主题的掌握。这类评估可以基于大纲中使用的目标,采用进一步讨论、口答、笔试或诸如多项选择题的选择型测试的形式。选择型测试和简答测试能够提供独立于评估员任何偏见的客观评估。为了发证的目的,评估员应当具有特定培训和评估的相应资格。

记住——准备不足是使一个团体丧失兴趣的必由之路

1.7　在讲课之前检查要使用的房间。确保所有设备和器材备好待用,辅助人员也准备就绪。要特别检查黑板是否清洁,书写和擦拭材料是否立即可用。

2　授课

2.1　要始终面对听课的人;千万不要背对着班级。

2.2　说话声音要清晰、洪亮,让每一个人都能听到。

2.3　与整个班级保持目光接触作为吸引并保持其兴趣的方法(既不要持续地盯着某一个人,也不要盯着场所中的某一点)。

2.4 People are all different, and they behave and react in different ways. An important function of a lecturer is to maintain interest and interaction between members of a group.

2.5 Some points or statements are more important than others and should therefore be emphasized. To ensure that such points or statements are remembered, they must be restated a number of times, preferably in different words.

2.6 If a blackboard is to be used, any writing on it must be clear and large enough for everyone to see. Use colour to emphasize important points, particularly in sketches.

2.7 It is only possible to maintain a high level of interest for a relatively short period of time; therefore, break the lecture up into different periods of activity to keep interest at its highest level. Speaking, writing, sketching, use of audio-visual material, questions, and discussions can all be used to accomplish this. When a group is writing or sketching, walk amongst the group, looking at their work, and provide comment or advice to individual members of the group when necessary.

2.8 When holding a discussion, do not allow individual members of the group to monopolize the activity, but ensure that all members have a chance to express opinions or ideas.

2.9 If addressing questions to a group, do not ask them collectively; otherwise, the same person may reply each time. Instead, address the questions to individuals in turn, so that everyone is invited to participate.

2.10 It is important to be guided by the syllabus content and not to be tempted to introduce material which may be too advanced, or may contribute little to the course objective. There is often competition between instructors to achieve a level which is too advanced. Also, instructors often strongly resist attempts to reduce the level to that required by a syllabus.

2.11 Finally, effective preparation makes a major contribution to the success of a lecture. Things often go wrong; preparedness and good planning will contribute to putting things right. Poor teaching cannot be improved by good accommodation or advanced equipment, but good teaching can overcome any disadvantages that poor accommodation and lack of equipment can present.

2.4 人各不相同,其行为和反应也各不相同。讲师的一个重要作用就是保持学员的兴趣及班级学员之间的互动。

2.5 某些要点或阐述比另一些更重要,因此应当加以强调。为保证能记住这些要点或阐述,必须对其重复说明几次,最好使用不同的措辞。

2.6 如果要使用黑板,其上的任何书写必须清晰并且足够大,让每个人都能看清。使用彩色来强调重点,特别是在草图中。

2.7 在较短时间内保持高水准的兴趣的可能性较低;因此,可将讲课分成不同段的活动,将兴趣保持在最高水准。为达到这一目的,可以使用说、写、画、视听材料、提问和讨论。当班级在写或画时,在他们中间走动、看他们的作业,必要时对个别学员提出评论和建议。

2.8 在主持讨论时,不允许班级的个别学员垄断这一活动,而要保证所有学员都有表达其意见或观点的机会。

2.9 当向班级提问时,不要向全班发问,否则就可能每一次由同一个人回答。相反地,应轮流向每一个人提问,这样每个人都会被邀请参与。

2.10 接受大纲内容的指导而不是受引诱去采用可能太过于深奥或对课程目的作用不大的材料,这一点很重要。教员之间经常存在欲达到太过深奥水平的竞争。另外,教员经常极力抗拒将水准降至大纲要求的水平。

2.11 最后,有效的备课对成功授课起到了主要作用。失误在所难免,但精心的准备和良好的计划将有助于改正错误。拙劣的教学不能用良好的设施和先进设备来改进,但是,优良的教学能够克服不良设施和缺少设备带来的不利影响。

Part 3 Curriculum Development

1 Curriculum

The dictionary defines curriculum as a "regular course of study", while syllabus is defined as " a concise statement of the subjects forming a course of study". Thus, in general terms, a curriculum is simply a course, while a syllabus can be thought of as a list (traditionally, a "list of things to be taught").

2 Course content

The subjects which are needed to form a training course, and the precise skills and depth of knowledge required in the various subjects, can only be determined through an in-depth assessment of the job functions which the course participants are to be trained to perform (job analysis). This analysis determines the training needs, thence the purpose of the course (course objective). After ascertaining this, it is possible to define the scope of the course.

(NOTE: Determination of whether or not the course objective has been achieved may quite possibly entail assessment, over a period of time, of the "on-the-job performance" of those completing the course. However, the detailed learning objectives are quite specific and immediately assessable.)

3 Job analysis

A job analysis can only be properly carried out by a group whose members are representative of the organizations and bodies involved in the area of work to be covered by the course. The validation of results, via review with persons currently employed in the job concerned, is essential if undertraining and overtraining are to be avoided.

4 Course plan

Following definition of the course objective and scope, a course plan or outline can be drawn up. The potential students for the course (the trainee target group) must then be identified, the entry standard to the course decided and the prerequisites defined.

5 Syllabus

The final step in the process is the preparation of the detailed syllabus with associated time scales; the identification of those parts of textbooks and technical papers which cover the training areas to a sufficient degree to meet, but not exceed, each learning objective; and the drawing up of a bibliography of additional material for supplementary reading.

6 Syllabus content

The material contained in a syllabus is not static; technology is continuously undergoing change and there must therefore be a means for reviewing course material in order to eliminate what is redundant and introduce new material reflecting

第3部分 课程开发

1 课程

字典将“课程”定义为一个“常规的学习过程”,同时“大纲”被定义为“对组成学习过程的科目的简明陈述”。因此,通常而言,课程就只是一个教程,而大纲可以被认为是一个目录(传统上,一个“要教授的内容的目录”)。

2 课程内容

组成培训课程所必要的科目及不同科目所要求的精确技能和知识深度,只能通过对课程参加者接受培训并履行的工作职能的深入评估来确定(工作分析)。这一分析确定了培训需求,继而得出课程目的(课程目标)。对此确认之后,才可能界定课程的范围。

(注:确定是否达到课程的目标很可能需要在一段时间内对完成课程人员的“在职表现”进行评估。但是,细化的学习目标很具体而且可以立即评估。)

3 工作分析

工作分析只能通过一个群体来适当实施,这个群体的成员能够代表与本课程所覆盖工作领域有关的组织和团体。如果要避免培训不足和培训过度,通过当时就职相关工作的人员的审查来确认其结果是十分重要的。

4 课程计划

在界定课程目标和范围之后,就可以起草课程计划或概要。然后必须确认本课程的潜在学员(学员目标群),决定本课程的入学标准以及界定先决条件。

5 大纲

这一过程的最后一步就是准备教学大纲细则和相关的时间尺度;确认教科书和技术论文中涉及培训范围的部分,这种涉及要达到足够的程度以便满足但不突破每一项学习目标;以及起草用于补充性阅读的额外材料的参考文献。

6 大纲内容

大纲中所载的材料不是静态的;技术在不断地变化,必须存在审查课程资料的手段以便剔除多余的内容并引入反映当代实践的新材料。如上述所界定的,大纲可以被认为是 个目

current practice. As defined above, a syllabus can be thought of as a list and, traditionally, there have always been an "examination syllabus" and a "teaching syllabus"; these indicate, respectively, the subject matter contained in an examination paper, and the subject matter a teacher is to use in preparing lessons or lectures.

7 Training outcomes

7.1 The prime communication difficulty presented by any syllabus is how to convey the "depth" of knowledge required. A syllabus is usually constructed as a series of "training outcomes" to help resolve this difficulty.

7.2 Thus, curriculum development makes use of training outcomes to ensure that a common minimum level and breadth of attainment is achieved by all the trainees following the same course, irrespective of the training institution (i.e. teaching/lecturing staff).

7.3 Training outcomes are trainee-oriented, in that they describe an end result which is to be achieved by the trainee as a result of a learning process.

7.4 In many cases, the learning process is linked to a skill or work activity and, to demonstrate properly the attainment of the objective, the trainee response may have to be based on practical application or use, or on work experience.

7.5 The training outcome, although aimed principally at the trainee to ensure achievement of a specific learning step, also provides a framework for the teacher or lecturer upon which lessons or lectures can be constructed.

7.6 A training outcome is specific and describes precisely what a trainee must do to demonstrate his knowledge, understanding or skill as an end product of a learning process.

7.7 The learning process is the "knowledge acquisition" or "skill development" that takes place during a course. The outcome of the process is an acquired "knowledge", "understanding", "skill"; but these terms alone are not sufficiently precise for describing a training outcome.

7.8 Verbs, such as "calculates", "defines", "explains", "lists", "solves" and "states", must be used when constructing a specific training outcome, so as to define precisely what the trainee will be enabled to do.

7.9 In the IMO model course project, the aim is to provide a series of model courses to assist instructors in developing countries to enhance or update the maritime training they provide, and to allow a common minimum standard to be achieved throughout the world. The use of training outcomes is a tangible way of achieving this desired aim.

7.10 As an example, a syllabus in training-outcome format for the subject of ship construction appears in annex A2. This is a standard way of structuring this kind of syllabus. Although, in this case, an outcome for each area has been identified–and could be used in an assessment procedure–this stage is often dropped to obtain a more compact syllabus structure.

录,而且,传统上存在着“考试大纲”和“教学大纲”,分别表明试卷中含有的主题以及教师在备课或讲课时要使用的主题。

7 培训效果

7.1 任何大纲中所呈现出的主要交流困难就是如何传达所要求知识的“深度”。大纲通常作为一系列的“培训效果”来编写,以便有助于化解这一困难。

7.2 如此一来,课程的制定利用培训效果来保证学习同一课程的所有学员获得共同的最低水准和广度的成绩,而不论培训机构(即教学/讲课人员)如何。

7.3 培训效果是面向学员的,即这些效果描述了学员要达到的最终结果,并以此作为学习过程的结果。

7.4 在很多情况下,学习过程与技能或工作活动相联系,而且为了适当表明达到了目标,学员的反应可能需要基于实际实施和运用或者基于工作经验。

7.5 培训效果,尽管主要着眼于学员,以保证其达到特定的学习步骤的成果,但也向讲师或教员提供了可以基于编写功课或讲稿的框架。

7.6 培训效果是具体的,并精确描述了学员必须做的事情来表明其作为学习过程最终产品的知识、理解或技能。

7.7 学习过程就是在课程期间发生的“知识获得”或“技能发展”。这一过程的效果就是获得的“知识”、“理解”、“技能”;但仅有这些术语尚不足以精确地描述培训的效果。

7.8 编制具体培训效果时,必须使用诸如“计算”、“界定”、“解释”、“列出”、“解决”和“阐述”等动词,以便精确界定学员有能力做的事情。

7.9 IMO的示范课程计划,目的是提供一系列的示范课程以协助发展中国家的教员提高或更新其提供的海事培训,并使得全世界达到共同的最低标准。培训效果的使用就是达到这一预期目的的可行方法。

7.10 作为一例子,在附录A2中,以培训效果的格式列出了船舶构造科目的大纲。这是编写这类大纲结构的标准方法。尽管在这种情况下,每个科目的效果已经得到了确认——而且可以用于评估程序——但这一阶段往往被降格成要获取一个更加精简的大纲结构。

8 Assessment

Training outcomes describe an outcome which is to be achieved by the trainee. Of equal importance is the fact that such an achievement can be measured OBJECTIVELY through an evaluation which will not be influenced by the personal opinions and judgements of the examiner. Objective testing or evaluation provides a sound base on which to make reliable judgements concerning the levels of understanding and knowledge achieved, thus allowing an effective evaluation to be made of the progress of trainees in a course.

8 评估

培训效果描述了学员要达到的效果。同样重要的事实是,通过不受考官个人意见和判断影响的评价可以客观地衡量这一成绩。客观的测试和评价提供了对学员所达到的理解和知识水准做出可靠判断的牢固基础,这就能对学员的学习过程进行有效的评价。

Annex A1 Preparation checklist

Ref.	Component	Identified	Reserved	Electricity supply	Purchases	Tested	Accepted	Started	Finished	Status OK
1	Course plan									
2	Timetable									
3	Syllabus									
4	Scope									
5	Objective									
6	Entry standard									
7	Preparatory course									
8	Course certificate									
9	Participant numbers									
10	Staffing									
	Co-ordinator									
	Lecturers									
	Instructors									
	Technicians									
	Other									

附录 A1　备课检查表

参考	构成	已确认	预定	电源	购买	已测试	已接受	已启动	已结束	状态OK
1	课程计划									
2	时间表									
3	大纲									
4	范围									
5	目标									
6	入学标准									
7	预备课程									
8	课程证书									
9	参训人数									
10	人员配置									

协调员 ________

讲师 ________

教员 ________

技师 ________

其他 ________

Annex A1 Preparation checklist *(continued)*

Ref.	Component	Identified	Reserved	Electricity supply	Purchases	Tested	Accepted	Started	Finished	Status OK
11	Facilities									
(a)	Rooms									
	Lab									
	Workshop									
	Other									
	Class									
(b)	Equipment									
	Lab									
	Workshop									
	Other									
12	AVA Equipment and materials									
	OHP									
	Slide									
	Cine									
	Video									
13	IMO reference									
14	Textbooks									
15	Bibliography									

附录 A1　备课检查表(续表)

参考	构成	已确认	预定	电源	购买	已测试	已接受	已启动	已结束	状态 OK
11	设施									
	(a) 教室									
	实验室									
	车间									
	其他									
	班级									
	(b) 设备									
	实验室									
	车间									
	其他									
12	视听教具和材料									
	投影仪									
	幻灯机									
	电影放映机									
	录像机									
13	IMO 参考书目									
14	教科书									
15	参考文献									

Annex A2 Example of a Model Course syllabus in a subject area

Subject area:	Ship construction
Prerequisite:	Have a broad understanding of shipyard practice
General aims:	Have knowledge of materials used in shipbuilding, specification of shipbuilding steel and process of approval
Textbooks:	No specific textbook has been used to construct the syllabus, but the instructor would be assisted in preparation of lecture notes by referring to suitable books on ship construction, such as *Ship Construction* by Eyres (T12) and *Merchant Ship Construction* by Taylor (T58)

附录A2　某一科目示范课程教学大纲的示例

科　　目：船舶构造

先决条件：对船厂实践有广泛的理解

总体目的：了解造船所用材料、造船用钢的规格和认可程序

教 科 书：在编制该大纲时没有使用特定的教科书，但参考关于船舶建造的合适书籍会有助于教员准备讲稿，例如Eyres的《船舶构造》(T12)以及Taylor的《商船构造》(T58)

COURSE OUTLINE

Knowledge, understanding and proficiency		Total hours for each topic	Total hours for each subject area of required performance
Competence:			
3.1 CONTROL TRIM, STABILITY and STRESS			
3.1.1 FUNDAMENTAL PRINCIPLES OF SHIP CONSTRUCTION, TRIM AND STABILITY			
.1	Shipbuilding materials	3	
.2	Welding	3	
.3	Bulkheads	4	
.4	Watertight and weathertight doors	3	
.5	Corrosion and its prevention	4	
.6	Surveys and dry-docking	2	
.7	Stability	83	102

课程概要

知识、理解和熟练	每一标题的总学时	技能要求中每一科目的总学时
适任:		
3.1 控制吃水差、稳性和应力		
3.1.1 船舶构造、吃水差和稳性的基本原理		
.1 造船材料	3	
.2 焊接	3	
.3 舱壁	4	
.4 水密和风雨密门	3	
.5 腐蚀及其预防	4	
.6 检验和进坞	2	
.7 稳性	83	102

Part C3: Detailed Teaching Syllabus

Introduction

The detailed teaching syllabus is presented as a series of learning objectives. The objective, therefore, describes what the trainee must do to demonstrate that the specified knowledge or skill has been transferred.

Thus each training outcome is supported by a number of related performance elements in which the trainee is required to be proficient. The teaching syllabus shows the *Required performance* expected of the trainee in the tables that follow.

In order to assist the instructor, references are shown to indicate IMO references and publications, textbooks and teaching aids that instructors may wish to use in preparing and presenting their lessons.

The material listed in the course framework has been used to structure the detailed teaching syllabus; in particular,

Teaching aids (indicated by A)
IMO references (indicated by R) and
Textbooks (indicated by T)

will provide valuable information to instructors.

Explanation of information contained in the syllabus tables

The information on each table is systematically organized in the following way. The line at the head of the table describes the FUNCTION with which the training is concerned. A function means a group of tasks, duties and responsibilities as specified in the STCW Code. It describes related activities which make up a professional discipline or traditional departmental responsibility on board.

The header of the first column denotes the **COMPETENCE** concerned. Each function comprises a number of competences. For example, the Function 3, Controlling the Operation of the Ship and Care for Persons on board at the Management Level, comprises a number of COMPETENCES. Each competence is uniquely and consistently numbered in this model course.

In this function the competence is **Control trim, stability and stress.** It is numbered 3.1, that is the first competence in Function 3. The term "competence" should be understood as the application of knowledge, understanding, proficiency, skills, experience for an individual to perform a task, duty or responsibility on board in a safe, efficient and timely manner.

Shown next is the required TRAINING OUTCOME. The training outcomes are the areas of knowledge, understanding and proficiency in which the trainee must be able to demonstrate knowledge and understanding. Each COMPETENCE comprises a number of training outcomes. For example, the above competence comprises three training

C3部分: 教学大纲细则

介绍

教学大纲细则是以一系列学习目标呈现的。因此,该目标描述了学员必须做的事情来表明他已经获得了规定的知识或技能。

因此,每一项培训效果都由一些有关的表现要素来支持,要求学员熟练掌握。教学大纲显示了下述表格中对学员期望的“技能要求”。

为了帮助教员, 列出了参考书目来注明教员在备课和授课中可能希望使用的IMO参考书目和出版物、教科书和教具。

课程框架中列举的材料已用于拟定教学大纲细则;尤其是,

教具(由A表示)
IMO参考书目(由R表示)以及
教科书(由T表示)

将向教员提供有价值的信息。

大纲表格里的信息说明

每个表格里的信息均以下述方式进行了系统的组织。表格抬头一行描述了与培训相关的职能。职能是指STCW规则中规定的一组任务、职责和责任。它描述了组成船上职业素养或传统部门责任的相关活动。

第1栏的标题概述了有关的适任。每一项职能包含了多项适任。例如,职能3“管理级船舶作业管理和船上人员管理”包括了多项适任。在本示范课程中,对每一项适任都做了唯一且一致的编号。

本职能中的适任就是控制吃水差、稳性和应力。其编号为3.1,即职能3中的第1项适任。术语“适任”应当理解为个人运用知识、理解、熟练、技能、经验以安全、有效和及时的方式履行船上的一项任务、职责或责任。

下一项表明的是要求的培训效果。培训效果是学员必须有能力表明了解和理解的知识、理解和熟练的范围。每一项适任包括多项培训效果。例如,上述适任包括了三项培训效果。

outcomes. The first is concerned with the FUNDAMENTAL PRINCIPLES OF SHIP CONSTRUCTION, TRIM AND STABILITY. Each training outcome is uniquely and consistently numbered in this model course. That concerned with fundamental principles of Ship Construction, Trim And Stability is uniquely numbered 3.1.1. For clarity, training outcomes are printed in black type on grey, for example TRAINING OUTCOME.

Finally, each training outcome embodies a variable number of required performances—as evidence of competence. The instruction, training and learning should lead to the trainee meeting the specified required performance. For the training outcome concerned with fundamental principles of ship construction, trim and stability there are three areas of performance. These are:

3.1.1.1 Shipbuilding materials
3.1.1.2 Welding
3.1.1.3 Bulkheads

Following each numbered area of required performance there is a list of activities that the trainee should complete and which collectively specify the standard of competence that the trainee must meet. These are for the guidance of teachers and instructors in designing lessons, lectures, tests and exercises for use in the teaching process. For example, under the topic 3.1.1.1, to meet the required performance, the trainee should be able to:

—state that steels are alloys of iron, with properties dependent upon the type and amounts of alloying materials used
—state that the specifications of shipbuilding steels are laid down by classification societies
—state that shipbuilding steel is tested and graded by classification society surveyors who stamp it with approval marks

and so on.

IMO references (Rx) are listed in the column to the right-hand side. Teaching aids (Ax), videos (Vx) and textbooks (Tx) relevant to the training outcome and required performances are placed immediately following the TRAINING OUTCOME title.

It is not intended that lessons are organized to follow the sequence of required performances listed in the Tables. The Syllabus Tables are organized to match with the competence in the STCW Code Table A-Ⅱ/2. Lessons and teaching should follow college practices. It is not necessary, for example, for ship building materials to be studied before stability. What is necessary is that all of the material is covered and that teaching is effective to allow trainees to meet the standard of the required performance.

第一项是有关船舶构造、吃水差和稳性的基本原理。在本示范课程中,对每一项培训效果都做了唯一且一致的编号。与船舶构造、吃水差和稳性的基本原理有关的培训效果被唯一编为3.1.1。为清楚起见,培训效果被印成灰底黑体,例如培训效果。

最后,每一项培训效果体现了不定数目的技能要求——作为适任的证据。授课、培训和学习应当使学员满足规定的技能要求。对于船舶构造、吃水差和稳性的基本原理,有三个科目技能要求。它们是:

3.1.1.1 造船材料
3.1.1.2 焊接
3.1.1.3 舱壁

在技能要求的每一项编号科目之后,有一个学员应当完成的活动清单,这些活动共同规定了学员必须满足的适任标准。它们用于指导教师和教员设计在教学过程中使用的功课、讲课、测验和练习。例如,在标题3.1.1.1之下,为满足技能要求,学员应当能够:

—阐述钢是铁的合金,其特性依赖于所使用合金材料的种类和数量
—阐述船级社制定了造船用钢的规格
—阐述船级社验船师对造船用钢进行测试和定级并对其加盖认可标志

等等。

IMO参考书目(Rx)列在右侧一栏中。与培训效果和技能要求相关的教具(Ax)、录像(Vx)和教科书(Tx)紧跟在培训效果标题之后。

并不打算按表中所列技能要求的次序来组织功课。大纲表格的组织是与STCW规则表A-Ⅱ/2中的适任相匹配的。课程与教学应遵循大学中的实践情况。例如,没有必要在学习稳性之前先学习建造材料。必要的是,所有这些材料要全部涉及而且教学要有效以便使学员达到技能要求的标准。

FUNCTION 3: CONTROLLING THE OPERATION OF THE SHIP AND CARE FOR PERSONS ON BOARD AT THE MANAGEMENT LEVEL

COMPETENCE 3.1 Control trim, stability and stress **IMO reference**

3.1.1 FUNDAMENTAL PRINCIPLES OF SHIP CONSTRUCTION, TRIM AND STABILITY

Textbooks: T11, T12, T35, T58, T69

Teaching aids: A1, A4, V5, V6, V7

Required performance:

1.1 Shipbuilding materials (3 hours) R1

–states that steels are alloys of iron, with properties dependent upon the type and amounts of alloying materials used
–states that the specifications of shipbuilding steels are laid down by classification societies
–states that shipbuilding steel is tested and graded by classification society surveyors, who stamp it with approval marks
–explains that mild steel, graded A to E, is used for most parts of the ship
–states why higher tensile steel may be used in areas of high stress, such as the sheer strake
–explains that the use of higher tensile steel in place of mild steel results in a saving of weight for the same strength
–explains what is meant by:
- tensile strength
- ductility
- hardness
- toughness

–defines strain as extension divided by original length
–sketches a stress-strain curve for mild steel
–explains:
- yield point
- ultimate tensile stress
- modulus of elasticity

–explains that toughness is related to the tendency to brittle fracture
–explains that stress fracture may be initiated by a small crack or notch in a plate
–states that cold conditions increase the chances of brittle fracture
–states why mild steel is unsuitable for the very low temperatures involved in the containment of liquefied gases
–lists examples where castings or forgings are used in ship construction
–explains the advantages of the use of aluminium alloys in the construction of superstructures
–states that aluminium alloys are tested and graded by classification society surveyors
–explains how strength is preserved in aluminium superstructures in the event of fire
–describes the special precautions against corrosion that are needed where aluminium alloy is connected to steelwork

职能3:管理级船舶作业管理和船上人员管理

适任3.1	控制吃水差、稳性和应力	IMO参考书目

3.1.1 船舶构造、吃水差和稳性的基本原理

教 科 书:T11,T12,T35,T58,T69

教 具:A1,A4,V5,V6,V7

技能要求:

1.1 造船材料 (3 小时) R1

—阐述钢是铁的合金,其特性依赖于所使用合金材料的种类和数量

—阐述船级社制定了造船用钢的规格

—阐述船级社验船师对造船用钢进行测试和定级并对其加盖认可标志

—解释A到E级的低碳钢用于船舶的大部分构件

—阐述为什么较高强度的钢可以用于高应力的区域,例如舷顶列板

—解释在相同强度条件下用高强度钢代替低碳钢可减轻重量

—解释下列术语的含义:

- 抗拉强度
- 延展性
- 硬度
- 韧性

—界定应变就是以原长度除以延长

—画出低碳钢应力—应变曲线图

—解释:

- 屈服点
- 极限抗拉应力
- 弹性模数

—解释韧性与脆性断裂的趋势有关

—解释应力破裂可能由钢板上的小裂缝或槽引起

—阐述冰冷条件加大了脆性断裂的机会

—阐述为什么低碳钢不适宜于装运液化气所涉及的超低温

—列出在船舶建造中使用铸件或锻件的实例

—解释上层建筑建造中使用铝合金的优点

—阐述铝合金是由船级社验船师进行测试和定级

—解释在发生火灾时铝制上层建筑是如何保持强度的

—描述在铝合金与钢制件连接处所需要的防腐特别预防措施

Annex A3 Example of a lesson plan for annex A2

Subject area: 3.1 Control trim, stability and stress **Lesson number: 1** **Duration: 3 hours**

Training Area: 3.1.1 Fundamental principles of ship construction, trim and stability

Main element Specific training outcome in teaching sequence, with memory keys	Teaching method	Textbook	IMO reference	A/V aid	Instructor guidelines	Lecture notes	Time (minutes)
1.1 Shipbuilding materials (3 hours)							
States that steels are alloys of iron, with properties dependent upon the type and amounts of alloying materials used	Lecture	T12,T58	STCW II/2, A-II/2	V5 to V7	A1	Compiled by the lecturer	10
States that the specifications of shipbuilding steels are laid down by classification societies	Lecture	T12,T58	STCW II/2, A-II/2	V5 to V7	A1	Compiled by the lecturer	20
Explains that mild steel, graded A to E, is used for most parts of the ship	Lecture	T12,T58	STCW II/2, A-II/2	V5 to V7	A1	Compiled by the lecturer	15
States why higher tensile steel may be used in areas of high stress, such as the sheer strake	Lecture	T12,T58	STCW II/2, A-II/2	V5 to V7	A1	Compiled by the lecturer	10
Explains that use of higher tensile steel in place of mild steel results in a saving of weight for the same strength	Lecture	T12,T58	STCW II/2, A-II/2	V5 to V7	A1	Compiled by the lecturer	15

附录 A3　附录A2教案的示例

科目: 3.1 控制吃水差、稳性和应力　　**课程编号:1**　　**学时:3小时**

培训范围: 3.1.1船舶结构、吃水差和稳性的基本原理

要素 按教学次序列出的具体培训效果,附记忆要点	教学方法	教科书	IMO 参考书目	视听教具	教员指南	讲稿	时间 (分钟)
1.1 造船材料(3小时)							
阐述钢是铁的合金，其特性依赖于所使用合金材料的种类和数量	讲课	T12,T58	STCW Ⅱ/2, A-Ⅱ/2	V5 至 V7	A1	讲师自编	10
阐述船级社制定了造船用钢的规格	讲课	T12,T58	STCW Ⅱ/2, A-Ⅱ/2	V5至V7	A1	讲师自编	20
解释A到E级的低碳钢用于船舶的大部分构件	讲课	T12,T58	STCW Ⅱ/2, A-Ⅱ/2	V5至V7	A1	讲师自编	15
阐述为什么高强度的钢可以用于高应力的区域，例如舷顶列板	讲课	T12,T58	STCW Ⅱ/2, A-Ⅱ/2	V5至V7	A1	讲师自编	10
解释在相同强度条件下用高强度钢代替低碳钢可减轻重量	讲课	T12,T58	STCW Ⅱ/2, A-Ⅱ/2	V5至V7	A1	讲师自编	15